# A WORLD OF NATIONS

## THE INTERNATIONAL ORDER SINCE 1945

WILLIAM R. KEYLOR

*Boston University*

NEW YORK    OXFORD
OXFORD UNIVERSITY PRESS
2003

Oxford University Press

Oxford   New York
Auckland   Bangkok   Buenos Aires   Cape Town
Chennai   Dar es Salaam   Delhi   Hong Kong   Istanbul   Karachi
Kolkata   Kuala Lumpur   Madrid   Melbourne   Mexico City   Mumbai
Nairobi   São Paulo   Shanghai   Taipei   Tokyo   Toronto

Copyright © 2003 by Oxford University Press, Inc.

Published by Oxford University Press, Inc.
198 Madison Avenue, New York, New York, 10016
http://www.oup-usa.org

Oxford is a registered trademark of Oxford University Press

**Library of Congress Cataloging-in-Publication Data**

Keylor, William R., 1944-
    A world of nations : the international order since 1945 / by William R. Keylor.
        p. cm.
    Includes bibliographical references and index.
    ISBN 0-19-510601-6 (cloth : alk. paper)—ISBN 0-19-510602-4 (pbk. : alk. paper)
        1. World politics—1945- 2. International relations. 3. War—History—20th century.
        4. Protracted conflicts (Military science) I. Title.

D840 .K42 2003
327'.09'045—dc21                                                                      2002025239

9 8 7 6 5 4 3 2 1

Printed in the United States of America
on acid-free paper

*For Rheta*

# CONTENTS

# MAPS

# PREFACE

At the end of World War II, the survivors of this most lethal and destructive conflict in human history faced an uncertain future. Few imagined that what lay ahead could be anything worse than what had just transpired: For the second time in less than thirty years the international order had degenerated into an anarchic state of global conflict. The consequences of World War II were felt much more widely and deeply than those of what had been previously been known as The Great War. For the first time in history, owing to technological innovations in ballistics and weaponry, civilians on the "home front" were just as vulnerable to the terrible effects of war as soldiers at the battle front. The invention and prompt use of nuclear weapons by the United States against Japan represented a quantum leap in the destructiveness of military power. The advent of the nuclear age rendered obsolete the hallowed maxim of Prussian strategist Karl von Clausewitz that war was simply an extension of politics, the tool of last resort for a state intent on enhancing its power and influence in the world. For the first time in history, war could result in the extinction of the victor as well as the vanquished.

For a brief moment at the end of World War II, the victorious powers entertained high hopes of forging a new world order based on cooperation rather than conflict. The newly established United Nations, which replaced the defunct League of Nations that had been set up after World War I, was expected initially to serve as an effective instrument for the peaceful resolution of international disputes. But the two states whose armies had played the most important role in defeating Nazi Germany and that emerged at the end of the war as the world's only two "superpowers" promptly fell into a bitter rivalry that dashed those illusory hopes for postwar international cooperation. The twists and turns of that competitive relationship between the United States and the Soviet Union, which touched the lives of millions of people across the globe for the next four and a half decades, is a salient topic in the pages that follow.

Among the many important consequences of the end of that "Cold War" and the breakup of the Soviet Union in the early 1990s was the availability of historical records from the former Communist states that had long been off-limits to scholars.

The accessibility of these materials has prompted a full-scale reassessment of the history of those tension-filled years. Previous studies had to rely almost exclusively on records from U. S. (and, to a certain extent, British) archives. The result was an incomplete (and, in my view, distorted) understanding of the subject. In recent years historians have been able to transcend what one critic has aptly called "the view from Washington" to consider the view from Moscow and other Communist capitals. The expanding body of historical research based on these newly available records, as well as the publication of some of the original documents themselves, enables us for the first time to study the Cold War from the perspective of international history in the broadest sense of that term.

It rapidly will become evident to the reader of this book, however, that what follows is much more than an account of the origins, evolution, and consequences of the Cold War. As important as that overarching theme is to this narrative, the relations between the two superpowers form only part of the story of the history of international relations since World War II. Throughout this turbulent period, other powers often pursued goals within their particular region that were not related directly to the global rivalry between the United States and the Soviet Union. In the course of writing this book I have been at pains to address these regional developments on their own terms instead of condescendingly treating them as mere sideshows of the main event. When the main event came to an abrupt and entirely unexpected end in 1989–1990, some observers prematurely predicted the "end of history" and the emergence of a new world order of peace and stability. Instead, the last decade of the twentieth century and the early years of the twenty-first have been buffeted by a bewildering array of regional conflicts—ethnic, religious, cultural, commercial, and military—that prompted some sardonic observers to apply the label "new world disorder" to the post–Cold War era. This book strives to accord these regional tensions the attention they deserve. It also retraces their roots to the early period after World War II, when the attention of the world (and of most historians) was so riveted on policy-making in Washington and Moscow that it neglected these chickens on the periphery of world power that have since come home to roost.

Anyone with the effrontery to attempt a history of the entire world since 1945 is condemned to a heavy dependence on the scholarship of others. In composing this book I have had to consult an enormous and constantly expanding body of historical research produced by specialists in the various topics addressed herein. The sheer magnitude of this secondary literature poses a daunting challenge to the author of a synthetic text such as this one. In addition to my reliance on the written works listed in the Select Bibliography, I have incurred many debts to individual scholars who have enriched immeasurably my understanding of the history of international relations. It is a genuine privilege and pleasure to have regular access to an extraordinarily talented group of colleagues in the departments of history, international relations, and political science in the College of Arts and Sciences and in the Social Science Division of the College of General Studies at Boston University, whose interdisciplinary interests intersect with my own and from whom I have learned more than I can acknowledge here. The following list of people whose written work and conversation have made me a better historian undoubtedly is marred by inadvertent omissions, for which I apologize: Betty Anderson, Andrew Bacevich, Houchang

Chehabi, Walter Clemens, Walter Connor, Jay Corrin, David Fromkin, Irene Gendzier, William Grimes, Erik Goldstein, Fred Leventhal, Igor Lukes, David Mayers, H. Joaquim Maitre, Cathal Nolan, Richard Norton, Dietrich Orlow, D. Scott Palmer, Randall Poole, Uri Ra'anan, Vivien Schmidt, William Tilchin, and Henry Wend. In addition to these individual colleagues, two institutions at Boston University deserve special mention: The Center for International Relations and the International History Institute have sponsored or cosponsored a number of conferences, speeches, and presentations that have fortified my understanding of many issues addressed in this book. Both organizations have enjoyed the strong and steady support of the longtime dean of the College of Arts and Sciences and provost, Dr. Dennis Berkey.

I also have profited from the wisdom of several scholars outside Boston University. Paul Kennedy has graciously hosted me at the annual conferences on "Recent Work in International History" sponsored by the International Security Studies program at Yale University, where presentations of works-in-progress by advanced graduate students from a wide range of universities, followed by commentaries by senior scholars, have helped me to clarify many issues over which I had long puzzled. Vojtech Mastny has kept me abreast of developments in his intriguing Parallel History Project, which has begun to locate and publish on line important documents from former Warsaw Pact states and current members of NATO. Charles Cogan has enriched significantly my understanding of French foreign policy. Jolyon Howorth generously has shared with me his formidable knowledge about the development of European security cooperation in recent years. Stimulating conversations with John Gaddis and Marc Trachtenberg have given me a greater appreciation of what we now (provisionally) know about the origins and evolution of the Cold War. William Lee displayed warm hospitality to me as I peppered him with questions in his living room and over dinner about the nuclear arms race in general and national missile defense in particular. Although he will not agree with every conclusion in this book, he will recognize how much I learned from him and how seriously I took his arguments as I grappled with the sharply conflicting claims of the historical literature. I have been an avid consumer of the periodic bulletins issued by the Cold War International History Project at the Woodrow Wilson International Center for Scholars in Washington, which presents declassified documentary material from the former Communist bloc that is invaluable to historians of the Cold War. I have also found *Strategic Survey,* the annual publication of the International Institute of Strategic Studies, an indispensable resource. My students Chad Keller and Michael Peacock were very helpful in the preparation of the Select Bibliography as well as in many other matters. Notwithstanding all that I have learned from these and other scholars, I bear sole responsibility for whatever factual errors or untenable interpretations that may have crept into the pages that follow. Peter Coveney, Robert Tempio, Lisa Grzan, and Linda Harris of Oxford University Press have been superb editors, promptly responding to my various queries and shepherding this manuscript through the production process with aplomb.

Finally, it would not have been possible to complete this book without the continuing encouragement, forbearance, intellectual stimulation, and love of my wife, Dr. Rheta Grenoble Keylor; the manifold joys that my son Daniel and daughter Justine have brought me; and the fraternal love and friendship that my brother Jim and I have shared during the era that is covered by this book.

# ONE

# The Ideological Partition of Europe

"With the defeat of the Reich," Adolf Hitler lamented to a subordinate shortly before his suicide on April 30, 1945, "there will remain in the world only two Great Powers capable of confronting each other—the United States and Soviet Russia. The laws of both history and geography will compel these two powers to a trial of strength, either military or in the fields of economics and ideology." Five days before Hitler took his own life, the military forces of the United States and the Soviet Union converged at the Elbe River in the center of Germany. With the formal German surrender on May 8, Hitler's "Thousand-Year Reich" expired after only twelve years of coercive diplomacy, destructive warfare, and unprecedented brutality. It left behind a desolate continent whose political future was uncertain, despite the provisional plans for the postwar world that had been cobbled together by the leaders of the Grand Alliance against Hitler during their wartime conferences.

In the meantime the disappearance of the Nazi military and administrative apparatus in the spring of 1945 left an enormous vacuum of power throughout that part of the European continent that had been occupied or controlled by Germany. That vacuum was filled temporarily by the ad hoc authority of the liberating armies that converged from west and east to compel the German capitulation. But the long-term question of which indigenous political forces in Europe would grasp the reins of power relinquished by the defeated conqueror remained unresolved at the end of the war. So too did such critical questions as how the borders of liberated Europe would be recast, how and how much defeated Germany would be required to pay to repair the damage it had wrought, and how the victors of 1945 could ensure that Germany would never again disturb the tranquillity of the European continent.

It was assumed widely that these and other complicated issues would be resolved in face-to-face negotiations at a peace conference, as they had been after the last war. As it turned out, however, there would be no Versailles settlement after World War II. The fate of Europe after 1945 would depend not on statesmen and diplomats bargaining at the conference table, but rather on generals and soldiers advancing on the battlefield. Each half of the continent would eventually adopt the political, social, and economic institutions of the victorious power whose military forces had liberated it from Nazi oppression. That portion of Europe that fell within the jurisdiction

*Winston Churchill, Harry S. Truman, and Joseph Stalin at a break during the Potsdam Conference, July 1945. This turned out to be the last meeting between Soviet and Western leaders until the Geneva Conference ten years later. (National Archives)*

West - capitalist
East - Communist

of the Anglo-American armies advancing from their hard-won continental beach-heads in northern France would establish or reestablish democratic political institutions and capitalist economic systems. The states on the eastern half of the continent, despite their prewar record of hostility to the Soviet Union and the presence of popular non-Communist political parties in their midst, would adopt the political and economic institutions imposed by their Soviet liberators.

## The Formation of the Soviet Satellite Empire

The ideological fault line separating the two halves of Europe did not appear immediately after the Anglo-American and Soviet military forces converging in the center of Germany brought an end to the Nazi imperium. In the countries of Eastern Europe that were liberated by the Red Army, non-Communist political parties were permitted to operate and their leaders to participate in coalition governments at the end of the war. The available evidence from the Soviet archives reveals no master plan by Josef Stalin to ensure Moscow's total control of all of the countries of Eastern Europe through a massive crackdown on ideological enemies. The strongman in the Kremlin appears to have insisted on achieving undisputed primacy in only three countries in that strategically vital region beyond Russia's western frontier—Poland, Romania, and Bulgaria. Even in those three countries Stalin seemed prepared to settle for the gradual elimination of non-Communist political organizations and their transformation into one-party states.

The political future of Poland had become the most troublesome bone of contention between the Anglo-Americans and the Russians as the war in Europe drew to a close. For the two Western allies, the case of Poland was rooted much more in sentiment than in strategic or economic interest. England had gone to war in September 1939 in response to Hitler's unprovoked invasion of that geographically cursed country sandwiched between Germany and Russia. For the rest of the war, British Prime Minister Winston Churchill and many of his compatriots retained an emotional attachment to—and perhaps a lingering feeling of guilt toward—the Polish officials who had fled Warsaw and then Paris to set up a government-in-exile in London. This determined band of patriots preserved the heroic illusion of Polish sovereignty while their hapless country was being oppressed by its Nazi overlords. After the United States entered the war, President Franklin D. Roosevelt was attentive to the plaintive pleas of six million Polish Americans, not only for the liberation of their country of origin but also for its right to self-determination and national independence after the war.

For Josef Stalin, by contrast, the question of Poland's future hinged on cold-hearted calculations of national interest. These were rooted in the unrelenting animosity between Russia and the new state of Poland that had been resurrected at the end of World War I. As the fledgling Bolshevik regime in Moscow fought for its life against a group of counterrevolutionary armies arrayed against it on all fronts during the Russian Civil War of 1918–1921, the military forces of the new Polish state drove as far east as Kiev in a bid to seize as much Russian territory as possible. Although the Red Army eventually repulsed the Polish assault, the Treaty of Riga that terminated the Russo-Polish War in 1921 left the new Polish state in possession of a large portion of former Russian territory that was inhabited by Ukrainians and Belorussians. Poland's seizure of this former Russian land, together with the presence of resolutely anti-Communist governments in Warsaw throughout the interwar period, guaranteed perpetual hostility between the two countries. Hitler's invasion of Poland on September 1, 1939, had been preceded by the infamous Nazi-Soviet Pact of August 23, which sealed that country's fate. One of its secret provisions authorized the Soviet Union to regain the territory lost to Poland at Riga in 1921 and Germany to regain the territory lost to Poland at Versailles in 1919. By the end of September 1939 the German army that had overrun Poland from the west and the Soviet army that had attacked it from the east partitioned the country according to plan.

Following the German invasion of the Soviet Union in June 1941, the Kremlin developed correct if not cordial relations with the Polish exile government in London on the basis of the hallowed principle that "the enemy of my enemy is my friend." But that relationship was disrupted in April 1943 when the German government

announced the discovery of a mass grave in the Katyn Forest near the city of
Smolensk that contained the bodies of more than ten thousand Polish army officers
who had been shot. The site of this gruesome deed was located within the section of
Poland that had been occupied by the Soviet army from September 1939 to June
1941. The Polish government-in-exile in London promptly asked the International
Red Cross to investigate the German allegations. Stalin responded by angrily denouncing the London Poles for giving credence to what he labeled scurrilous Nazi
propaganda designed to slander the Soviet Union. Within a few days he had broken
off all relations with them. We now know, thanks to revelations from the Soviet
archives in 1990, that Stalin personally had ordered the execution of these Polish officers. His reason for doing so is not difficult to fathom: The upper echelon of the
Polish army was noted for its anti-Communist inclinations and would therefore pose
a serious threat to Stalin's postwar plans for Eastern Europe, which included the
creation of a Polish state that was "friendly" to the Soviet Union.

Having severed all ties to the Polish government-in-exile in London, Stalin
promptly formed a rival Polish political organization in Moscow that was controlled
by members of the Polish Communist Party who had fled to the Soviet Union at the
beginning of the war. As the Red Army drove across Polish territory in the summer
of 1944, it was accompanied by officials of this Polish Communist organization, who
assumed political authority in the cities and towns that were liberated from the German occupation. Once in office these Communist functionaries announced their allegiance to a Polish Committee of National Liberation that Stalin had set up on July 22
in the liberated city of Lublin. The anti-Communist exile government in London was
unable to influence political developments in Poland because its underground military apparatus in Warsaw (the so-called Home Army) had been wiped out when it
rose against the German occupation authorities on August 1, 1944. Soviet troops that
were approaching the city declined to intervene in support of the Warsaw rising,
while Stalin rebuffed pleas from his two Western allies for permission to use Soviet
airfields for bombing raids against German positions in the city. At the beginning of
1945 the two rival Polish "governments"—one in Lublin and the other in London—
jockeyed for position as the Allied armies closed in on the Germans from west and
east. The anti-Communist Polish leaders in London enjoyed the patronage of the
United States and Great Britain, while the Communist Poles in Lublin continued to
receive the backing of the Soviet Union. If possession is nine points of the law, as the
old saying goes, then the outcome of this rivalry was foreordained. The Red Army
was the agent of Poland's liberation from German occupation, and its Polish Communist protégés were on the spot to press their political advantage against their anti-
communist rivals.

When Roosevelt, Churchill, and Stalin held their last wartime meeting at Yalta on
Russia's Crimean Peninsula in February 1945, the issue of the political future of
Poland occupied a prominent place on the agenda. In response to pressure from his
two Western interlocutors, Stalin reluctantly agreed to enlarge the Communist ad-
ministration that was establishing control of the country to include members of the
London group. He also issued a vague pledge that free elections would be conducted
once the war was over to enable the Polish people to determine their political future.
At the Potsdam Conference in July 1945 Washington and London extended formal

recognition to the Communist-dominated coalition regime in Warsaw, but on the condition that the free elections promised at the Yalta conference would be held in Poland within a year.

There was never the slightest possibility that Stalin would tolerate nationwide elections in Poland that might bring to power an anti-Communist government hostile to the Soviet Union. The Communist-dominated government in Warsaw accordingly postponed the elections that had been scheduled, in accordance with the deadline established at Potsdam, for the summer of 1946. In the meantime it staged a rigged referendum that endorsed decrees nationalizing heavy industries and large landholdings. When the deferred national elections were finally held in January 1947, they were marred by repressive tactics and electoral fraud on a grand scale. This electoral chicanery hastened the demise of the Peasant Party, which represented the only viable alternative to the Communists. In the autumn Stanislas Mikolajczyk, the Peasant Party leader who had served in the governing coalition as deputy prime minister, fled to London for what turned out to be permanent exile. Those of his followers who remained soon lost their posts in a massive political purge. By early 1948 the last vestiges of a multiparty system in Poland vanished when the Communist Party absorbed the Socialist Party while the purged Peasant Party joined the governing "coalition" in what had in fact become a one-party state.

Like Poland, prewar Romania shared a hotly contested border with the Soviet Union as a result of its annexation of Russian territory at the end of World War I. As with the case of Poland Stalin had secured Hitler's approval of the reannexation of this disputed territory, which was known as Bessarabia. Unlike Poland, Romania had allied with Germany during the war and participated in the German invasion of the Soviet Union. After recovering Bessarabia, Stalin took steps to ensure that postwar Romania would be governed by a political elite that was well disposed toward the Soviet Union. Although Romania capitulated to the Red Army in August 1944, it took several months for a stable political authority to be established there. During that transitional period Romania enjoyed the paradoxical status of a monarchy occupied by the Red Army and governed by a Communist-controlled organization known as the National Democratic Front. In March 1945 King Michael asked Petra Groza, the leader of the left-wing Plowman's Front, to form a government. The coalition that Groza assembled was entirely dominated by the National Democratic Front until Anglo-American complaints led to the enlargement of the governing coalition to include representatives of non-Communist parties.

Romania's first postwar elections in November 1946 were stage-managed by the ruling Communist-controlled electoral alliance to ensure a comfortable government majority. In the summer of 1947 the National Peasant Party was suppressed and its leader, Julius Maniu, was sentenced to life imprisonment. All other parties were dissolved except the Social Democratic Party, which in November 1947 was merged with the Communist Party to form the United Workers' Party as the only legal political entity in the country. King Michael, the last monarch permitted to reign behind the Iron Curtain, was driven to abdication and exile in December 1947. In 1948–1949 Romania was fully transformed into a Soviet satellite, while the government in Bucharest proceeded to complete the nationalization of industry and the collectivization of agriculture that had begun at the end of the war.

Unlike Poland and Romania, Bulgaria did not share a common border with the Soviet Union. But it lay astride that country's path to the Turkish Straits connecting the Black Sea to the Mediterranean, and therefore its political reliability became a prime concern of Stalin's at the end of the war. During the war Bulgaria had joined Romania as an ally of Nazi Germany. As the Red Army drove the German forces from Soviet territory in September 1944, Moscow declared war on Bulgaria in September 1944 and compelled it to sign an armistice. The Russian occupation forces that took control of the country permitted the establishment in the autumn of 1944 of a broad-based coalition government that contained only a few members of its indigenous Communist Party. But by the summer of 1945 the powerful Agrarian Union and the Socialist Party, under intense pressure from the Romanian Communists backed by the Red Army, resigned from the government. Over the next two years the Communists gradually consolidated their hold on power at the expense of their political rivals. In the summer of 1947 the leader of the Agrarian Union, Nikola Petkov, was arrested and later executed for treason as his party was dissolved. The last remaining opposition group, the Socialist Party, was purged of its ideologically suspect personnel and then merged with the Communist Party. When Soviet military forces evacuated Bulgaria at the end of 1947 they left behind a one-party state under the leadership of the veteran Communist militant Georgi Dimitrov, who had returned to his homeland from Moscow to assume control.

In contrast to the tightening of the Communist grip on Poland, Romania, and Bulgaria, the other countries of Eastern Europe enjoyed considerable latitude to conduct their own political affairs in the years after World War II. In Hungary Moscow seemed content to settle for predominant influence rather than tight control after Foreign Minister Vjacheslav Molotov got Churchill to revise the "percentages agreement" that he and Stalin had reached in October 1944 from a fifty-fifty split to a three-quarters' Soviet advantage there. The government installed in Budapest in April 1945 was a genuine coalition that included non-Communist parties in positions of power. In the autumn of 1945 the Soviet military commander in the Hungarian capital, Marshal Kliment Voroshilov, permitted free national elections in which the Smallholders Party, which represented the farmers who dominated the economic system of this largely agrarian country, won with 57 percent of the vote against 7 percent for the Communists. The Smallholders' leader, Ferenc Nagy, became prime minister of a coalition government in which the Communists held subordinate positions. At the time the Communist Party leader, Mátyás Rákosi, was content to compete with the non-Communist parties at the ballot box and refused to contemplate the use of extralegal means to achieve power.

By the middle of 1946, however, the political tensions between Washington and Moscow had escalated to the point where the Kremlin decided that drastic steps were required to ensure a friendly government in Budapest. The Soviet authorities there began to muscle the Smallholder leaders out of government positions and replace them with compliant Communist functionaries. In May 1947 Nagy himself was obliged to resign his post while on vacation in Switzerland. In the next several years pro-Communist members of the Smallholders' party joined with the Communists in governing coalitions until May 1949, when a rigged election gave total victory to the Communist-controlled National Independence Front.

## Czechoslovakia between East and West

Czechoslovakia represented a striking anomaly in the early stages of the emerging political division of Europe. It served as a unique bridge between East and West, as Communists and non-Communists shared political power with a remarkable spirit of cooperation. Edvard Beneš, the country's prewar president who returned from his London exile in the spring of 1945 to resume his post, had maintained cordial relations with the Soviet Union since the mid-1930s. During the war Beneš concluded an informal agreement with Stalin that presaged a postwar relationship between their two countries similar to the one between the Soviet Union and Finland: Czechoslovakia would refrain from opposing Soviet foreign policy goals while enjoying wide latitude in the conduct of its internal political and economic affairs. In December 1945 all Soviet military forces withdrew from the country, leaving behind a coalition government that operated under impeccably democratic political procedures. In May 1946 the Czechoslovak Communist Party obtained 38 percent of the popular vote in a free and fair election after conducting a relatively restrained and moderate campaign. Much of the party's support came from peasants who had benefited from land reform measures that the Communists had proposed. Many voters optimistically expected that the friendly relations with Czechoslovakia's powerful neighbor to the east would continue and regarded the Communist Party as a useful tool for perpetuating that cooperation. Communist political organizers in the country energetically prepared to campaign for a parliamentary majority in the next elections scheduled for 1948.

But as East-West tensions heated up elsewhere, Stalin's spokespersons berated the Czechoslovak party leaders for having squandered the opportunity to seize power in Prague and eliminate their political opponents. By meekly adhering to the country's Western-style electoral procedures, they risked being excluded from the governing coalition as their French and Italian counterparts had been in the spring of 1947 (see page 26). In the face of this Soviet criticism the Czechoslovak party boss and prime minister, Klement Gottwald, executed an abrupt about-face and abandoned the "electoral" road to total power. He began to insinuate party operatives into the country's internal security apparatus with a view to gaining control of the state through other means. The non-Communist parties had earlier criticized the Prague government's decision to bow to Soviet pressure and boycott the Paris conference on the Marshall Plan in the summer of 1947 (see page 22). They now loudly complained about Gottwald's blatant scheme to pack the police with Communist agents.

In response to this mounting discontent within Czechoslovakia, the Kremlin pressed Gottwald to take decisive action, hinting that Soviet military assistance would be available if required. The Czechoslovak party boss declined the offer, confident that his party was capable of managing the political situation without the aid of Soviet arms. His optimism proved entirely warranted: When the non-Communist members of the governing coalition provoked a cabinet crisis by resigning their posts on February 20, 1948, Gottwald intimidated Beneš into appointing a new government in which the Communists alone were authorized to choose its few non-Communist members. Two weeks later the sole surviving non-Communist member of the cabinet, Foreign Minister Jan Masaryk, jumped (or was pushed) to his death from his office window. After Beneš resigned the presidency in June, Gottwald succeeded him as head of state. Thus ended the transformation of Czechoslovakia from a promising model of Communist–non-Communist cooperation into a one-party state.

## The Anomaly of Yugoslavia

By the end of World War II Yugoslavia had fallen under the complete control of the leader of that country's principal resistance movement, Josip Broz, who had adopted the pseudonym Tito. Tito was a dedicated Communist who had fought valiantly against the German occupation and therefore enjoyed widespread popular support among his compatriots. The new master of Belgrade occupied a singular status among the Eastern European Communist rulers at the end of the war in two important respects. First, his Yugoslav partisans had filled the vacuum of political power left by the departing Germans without significant assistance from the Soviet Union. (Although the Red Army did enter Yugoslavia during the German retreat, it played a minor role in the liberation and soon withdrew from the country.) This circumstance endowed Tito and his associates with a much greater sense of independence and self-reliance than was evident in the servile Communist functionaries who had been installed in power elsewhere in Eastern Europe by the advancing Red Army. Second, Tito harbored regional ambitions that extended far beyond the historic borders of Yugoslavia and were rooted less in orthodox Communist orthodoxy than in traditional *Realpolitik*. He had developed plans for a vast federation encompassing the entire Balkan peninsula under Yugoslav hegemony: This bloc would include the neighboring states of Albania and Bulgaria, where Communist regimes had recently been installed, as well as the northern province of Greece, whose pro-British royalist regime faced a Communist insurrection actively supported by Belgrade (see page 17).

In the early postwar years Stalin winked at Tito's pursuit of an independent, aggressive foreign policy on behalf of Yugoslavia's regional ambitions, recognizing that country's predominance in the Balkans and tacitly tolerating its bid to topple the British-backed government in Greece. In return the Yugoslav leader remained a staunch supporter of Moscow in its mounting conflict with Washington. As late as the summer of 1947, when the Communist parties of Poland, Czechoslovakia, France, Italy, and Finland flirted with the idea of endorsing the Marshall Plan (see page 26), Tito loyally echoed the Kremlin's denunciation of the U.S. aid program to Europe. But the Soviet dictator began to develop second thoughts about the increasingly assertive and independent Communist regime in Belgrade. During the winter of 1947–1948 Stalin denounced a proposed bilateral treaty of friendship between Yugoslavia and Bulgaria that the leaders of these two Communist Balkan states had proposed the previous August. He criticized the Greek Communist insurgency that Tito had been supporting so avidly. His spokesman Andrei Zhdanov berated the Yugoslav leader for attempting to replace Soviet advisers with his own henchmen. On June 19 at a meeting in Bucharest of the Communist Information Bureau, which Stalin had recently created to facilitate his control of the European Communist parties (see page 27), the delegates denounced Yugoslavia for challenging Moscow's authority and expelled it from the organization.

During the Soviet-Yugoslav struggle, Stalin had boasted that he could "move his little finger and there will be no Tito." But his attempts to make good on that boast were embarrassingly unsuccessful, from a botched conspiracy with two Yugoslav military officers in August 1948 to an economic boycott of the renegade Communist country by the entire Eastern bloc launched in 1949. By that time Tito, although remaining an orthodox Communist in his domestic policies, had turned to the West for economic assistance. The Truman administration was only to happy to oblige. Perhaps the most significant consequence of Yugoslavia's defection from the Soviet bloc was the increase in Stalin's obsessive anxiety about political opposition to his authority within the bloc. From the moment of Yugoslavia's defection right up to his death in 1953, the Soviet dictator waged a pitiless campaign throughout the Soviet Union's satellite empire in Eastern Europe against suspected "Titos" who might dare to pursue an independent road to socialism (see page 53).

## Early Western Concerns about Soviet Expansionism

By the middle of 1948 Stalin had succeeded in forging a protective chain of docile client states from the Black Sea to the Baltic, astride the broad invasion route that had brought marauding German armies to the heart of Russia twice within his own lifetime. But what appeared to the Soviet leader and his associates as a prudent strategy of erecting a defensive barrier against a revived Germany was viewed by officials in Washington in a very different light. The communization of Eastern Europe during the first three years after the end of World War II precipitated a fundamental reassessment of American foreign policy toward the Soviet-Union. What the Kremlin may have regarded as a legitimate attempt to secure Russia's vulnerable western frontier with a *cordon sanitaire* of compliant buffer states—a policy that both Roosevelt and Churchill had approved tacitly during their wartime meetings with the Soviet leader—the new Truman administration began to interpret as the first stage of a Russian campaign to acquire control of the entire continent of Europe.

Had Stalin remained content with the forcible installation of "friendly regimes" throughout Eastern Europe, it is entirely possible that Washington and Moscow would have worked out a modus vivendi in the postwar world. It was only when officials in Washington came to believe that the Soviet leader intended to project his country's power beyond the informal line separating the spheres of influence of the two victors after the war that the U.S. government decided to take remedial action. The first hint of this more aggressive Soviet policy came on February 9, 1946, in a well-publicized election speech that Stalin delivered to voters in Moscow. Omitting all of the customary references to the wartime alliance with the United States and Great Britain, the Soviet leader ominously announced that the world was now divided into two hostile camps—communist and capitalist—that were destined to come to blows. He warned the Soviet people of the economic hardships that lay ahead as the country geared up to confront its new adversary now that Nazi Germany had been defeated. A week later the Kremlin seemed to confirm the belligerent turn in Soviet foreign policy by announcing its refusal to join the International Monetary Fund and the World Bank, the new international financial organizations that had been established at Bretton Woods Conference in the summer of 1944 (see page 24). What Washington viewed as indispensable instruments of international monetary stability Moscow regarded as tools of American economic imperialism that had to be resisted at all costs.

These provocative messages emanating from Moscow prompted the State Department to solicit assessments of recent Soviet behavior from its recognized experts on the subject. Among the respondents to this request was George Frost Kennan, a professional diplomat who had spent most of his professional career in the American embassy in Moscow since its reopening in 1933 when Franklin Roosevelt finally accorded diplomatic recognition to the U.S.S.R. On February 22, 1946, this hitherto obscure foreign service officer dispatched an eight-thousand-word cable to his superiors in Washington that purported to explain the sources of the Soviet Union's increasingly belligerent posture toward the West as reflected in Stalin's incendiary electoral rhetoric. Despite its forbidding length, Kennan's analysis of Soviet foreign policy was a model of lucidity and simplicity: The rulers of Russia, whether tsars or commissars, depended on a "hostile international environment" to preserve their iron grip on the enormous country's disparate population. Russia's traditional enemies at the two ends of the Eurasian land mass, Germany and Japan, had been vanquished. Its only two remaining rivals, Great Britain and the United States, now had to be converted from wartime allies to dangerous enemies to justify the regime's internal repression. This institutionalized paranoia, which Kennan believed was endemic to the Russian political system, ruled out the type of diplomatic bargaining that Roosevelt and Churchill eagerly had engaged had in with Stalin at the wartime conferences. Although the junior foreign service officer who composed this mordant message in the Moscow embassy did not propose an alternative to negotiation as a means of dealing with the Russians, his cable unmistakably implied the need for a radical reevaluation of U.S. policy toward the Soviet Union.

The contents of what came to be known as the "Long Telegram" had an electric effect on the Truman administration in Washington. It was promptly circulated throughout the highest echelons of the State Department, the War Department, and the White House, where it received an enthusiastic reception from officials who had been searching for a conceptual framework to explain the breakdown of Soviet-American cooperation since the end of the war. Those who read and pondered Kennan's elegantly phrased assessment of Soviet intentions instantly acquired an intellectual rationale for the new policy of toughness toward Moscow that they had instinctively come to favor.

Kennan's alarming evaluation of Soviet motivations remained a carefully guarded secret as administration officials feverishly debated its implications for American foreign policy. But two weeks later some of the salient themes that had been adumbrated in the "Long Telegram" and privately discussed by officials in Washington and London were aired in public for the first time in a stinging denunciation of recent Soviet actions by a renowned world statesman. Winston Churchill, leader of the Conservative opposition in the British House of Commons since his electoral defeat at the end of the war, had accepted an invitation to receive an honorary degree at Westminster College in Truman's home state of Missouri on March 5. The eloquent British orator used the occasion of his acceptance speech, which was widely publicized in advance, to review the record of the Soviet Union's aggressive behavior in Europe since the German surrender. "From Stettin in the Baltic to Trieste in the Adriatic," he declared, "an iron curtain has descended across the Continent. Behind that line lie all the capitals of the ancient states of Central and Eastern Europe. Warsaw, Berlin, Prague, Vienna, Budapest, Belgrade, Bucharest, and Sofia; all these famous cities and the populations around them lie in what I must call the Soviet sphere. . . . [T]his is certainly not the Liberated Europe we fought to build up. Nor is it one which contains the essentials of permanent peace." Churchill followed with a stirring call for an Anglo-American alliance against the Soviet Union to halt that country's expansionist policy in its tracks.

Although out of office and therefore not speaking for the government in London, Churchill's prestige as Britain's wartime leader lent an air of authority to his provocative assessment of Soviet policy. Stalin immediately denounced Churchill's "Iron Curtain" speech as a provocation from a longtime adversary whose hostility to the Soviet Union dated from the Bolshevik Revolution. The U.S. government remained publicly neutral in the escalating war of words between the two wartime leaders who had sparred at the conference table in Teheran and Yalta. Truman had not yet uttered a word of public criticism of Soviet foreign policy. But his conspicuous presence on the speaker's platform in his home state of Missouri, grinning and nodding as the British leader inveighed against the Soviet menace, left little doubt where his sympathies lay.

In fact tensions between Moscow and Washington had deteriorated markedly before Churchill publicly exposed the fault line between the Communist and non-Communist world. The first direct confrontations between the Soviet Union and the United States after World War II took place not in Europe but in southwest Asia. The neighboring countries of Iran and Turkey, which blocked Russian access to the Mediterranean and Persian Gulf, respectively, had been objects of Russian interest since tsarist times. At the end of World War II Stalin decided, for a set of complex reasons presently to be discussed, to pursue what he regarded as Russia's traditional security interests at the expense of those two countries. That pursuit would elicit a sharp response from Washington, further fraying the relationship between the two former wartime allies.

## Confrontation at the Periphery: Iran, Turkey, Greece

In the latter part of the nineteenth century and the early part of the twentieth, a major foreign policy objective of Great Britain had been to prevent the projection of Russian power and influence southward across the line of communications to Britain's imperial possessions in Asia. These two historic rivals came into direct conflict in Persia, or Iran (the new name that it would adopt in 1935). The Anglo-Russian rivalry in Persia was temporarily resolved in 1907 when the two powers divided the country into spheres of interest. After the Bolshevik Revolution in 1917 Russia's position in Persia was temporarily weakened, while the British used the country as a base from which to intervene militarily against the Bolsheviks in the Russian Civil War. An ambitious officer of the Persian Cossack Brigade named Reza Khan staged a coup in 1921 with British support and proceeded to dominate the military junta that

## A World of Nations

ruled in the capital city of Teheran under the titular authority of the Qajar monarchy. Reza Khan promptly concluded a treaty of friendship with the newly established Soviet Union. He did so to use Russia as a counterweight to Great Britain's economic predominance in his country, which stemmed from the lucrative oil concessions that the Anglo-Persian Oil Company (later renamed British Petroleum) had acquired before the war. In 1925 Reza Khan deposed the figurehead Qajar ruler and had himself proclaimed monarch as Reza Shah Pahlavi. Inspired by the impressive policy of modernization undertaken by Turkey's Kemal Atatürk, Reza Shah launched a nationwide program of economic development that included road-building and the construction of a railway connecting the Caspian Sea and the Persian Gulf.

Always striving to preserve a balance between the European powers with interests in Iran in order to maximize his country's freedom of maneuver, Reza Shah cultivated cordial relations with Nazi Germany in the 1930s as a counterweight to Great Britain and Russia. By the beginning of World War II more than 40 percent of Iran's foreign trade was with Germany, while the two governments discussed ambitious plans for industrial development in Iran. Reza Shah's rapprochement with Hitler's regime brought some six hundred German technicians to Iran during the early years of World War II, while Great Britain was diverted by its conflict with Hitler's forces in Europe. Then the cooperative relationship between Teheran and Berlin presented the anti-German coalition with a serious logistical challenge after the German invasion of the Soviet Union in June 1941. The Iranian highlands suddenly became the most convenient transit point for the delivery of Lend-Lease aid that President Roosevelt had undertaken to provide to the U.S.S.R. Since neutral Turkey had closed the Straits to belligerents, the only alternative supply routes were through the ports of Murmansk on the Arctic Sea and Vladivostok on the Pacific. But neither could handle the huge volume of equipment the United States offered.

When the Iranian government rejected urgent requests from Moscow and London to expel all German agents from the country and to allow the transit of supplies from the mouth of the Persian Gulf to the Soviet border, Soviet and British troops invaded Iran on August 25, 1941. By prior arrangement the two armies divided the country into occupation zones. The Russians obtained control of the five northern provinces, the British moved into the rest of the country, and the capital of Teheran became a neutral enclave. In September agents of the two wartime allies forced the pro-German Reza Shah to abdicate in favor of his twenty-two-year-old son, Mohammed Reza. Britain and Russia eventually concluded a Tripartite Treaty of Alliance with the new pro-Ally government in Teheran on January 29, 1942. The pact guaranteed transit rights across Iran, reaffirmed its political independence, and stipulated the withdrawal of all foreign troops within six months of the end of the war. On January 1, 1943, a contingent of thirty thousand American noncombatant troops arrived in the British zone to supervise the Lend-Lease deliveries, while Washington also pledged to evacuate its forces according to the timetable specified in the Tripartite Treaty.

The main preoccupation of the British and Soviet officials in Iran during the war was the construction of an efficient supply line (in the form of a rail and road system) between the Gulf and the Soviet frontier. Although each occupying power remained aloof from political developments within its zone, tensions within the Soviet zone caught the attention of the Kremlin. The area was inhabited by a set of linguistic and ethnic minorities that had long sought to protect their cultural identity against encroachments by the Persian-speaking majority in Iran. The largest of these minority peoples were the Azeris, who shared a common language and cultural identity with the citizens of the Azerbaijani Soviet Socialist Republic across the border. After the Red Army began its occupation of northern Iran, Stalin dispatched the Communist party boss of Soviet Azerbaijan to promote Soviet interests there. The agent soon recognized a great opportunity both to expand Soviet influence and to help his kinsmen residing in what he began to call "Southern Azerbaijan" preserve their linguistic and cultural rights. With ample financing from Moscow, a team of Soviet Azeris established schools and newspapers in the local language while winning popular support by providing a broad range of services.

During World War II Stalin became acutely aware of the critical importance of oil to national security and took note of the immense reserves of that resource that lay beneath the arid deserts of neighboring Iran. Soon after the Red Army moved into its occupation sector in the north, Soviet engineers and geologists arrived to evaluate the extent of the petroleum resources there. When American oil companies began to explore the possibility of securing a drilling concession similar to the existing British one in September 1944, Soviet officials turned up in Teheran with a request for their own concession but were rebuffed by the Iranian government. Moscow promptly mobilized the Iranian Communist movement, the Tudeh (Masses) party, to organize protests against the government's refusal to grant the Russians the same advantages that Britain and the America had received. When the Tudeh failed to generate much support for its campaign, Stalin reverted to an alternative scheme proposed by the Communist Party leader in Soviet Azerbaijan: the creation in Iranian Azerbaijan of a separatist political party controlled from Baku, the capital of Soviet Azerbaijan, that would demand greater autonomy and closer links with the "other Azerbaijan" across the border. The new Azerbaijani Democratic Party (ADP) that was formed in September 1945 agitated for self-determination and language rights in northern Iran under the protection of the Soviet occupation forces. By the end of the year a separate parliament controlled by the ADP was functioning in the provincial capital of Tabriz. An Azerbaijani National Conference sent a resolution to the central government in Teheran proclaiming the province's autonomy, while ADP partisans gathered arms in anticipation of a showdown with the military forces of the young Shah.

A few days after the German surrender in May 1945, the Iranian government formally requested the withdrawal of the three occupation forces from the country. The following September the Soviet Union, Great Britain, and the United States confirmed their commitment to remove their troops by March 2, 1946—six months to the day after the Japanese surrender—as specified in the wartime agreement of January 1942. But as the Iranian army attempted to advance into Azerbaijan to suppress the separatist movement there, the Soviet occupation forces in the province barred the way. The March 2 deadline passed with Soviet units still in place after the Americans and British had departed on schedule. The Iranian government proceeded to file a formal protest against these Soviet machinations in Azerbaijan at the opening session of the newly established United Nations, which was meeting in London. The American and British delegates vigorously supported the Iranian complaint and denounced the Kremlin for violating its pledge to withdraw. As Soviet tanks approached the Iranian border in early March 1946, U.S. Secretary of State James Byrnes fired off a harshly worded message demanding the immediate evacuation of northern Iran. Truman privately remarked that the time had come to find out whether the Russians were "bent on world conquest."

Amid this atmosphere of crisis, Soviet and Iranian officials patched together a negotiated settlement on April 5. Fearing the secession of Azerbaijan (and possibly its merger with the Soviet Socialist Republic of Azerbaijan to the north), Iranian prime minister Ahmad Qavam made two crucial concessions to Moscow: The first was a promise to grant a substantial degree of autonomy to the northern province on the condition that it reaffirm its acceptance of Iran's sovereignty. The second was a formal authorization for a Soviet-Iranian oil company to exploit the petroleum resources in the northern part of the country for fifty years (the same duration as the Anglo-Iranian petroleum concession granted in 1933). In exchange, Stalin terminated his support of the separatist movement in Azerbaijan and ordered the evacuation of the Soviet occupation force from the province, which was completed by May 9. On June 13 the separatist government in Tabriz dutifully converted itself into a provincial assembly, formally acknowledging the authority of the central government in Teheran while retaining military control of the province.

But what seemed to be a mutually advantageous solution to a potentially explosive situation soon unraveled, resulting in a severe diplomatic setback for the Soviet Union. The central government in Teheran reneged on its promise of greater autonomy for Azerbaijan. In December 1946 Iranian military units entered the northern province to suppress the separatist movement in violation of the June 13 agreement, killing hundreds of its partisans and forcing its leaders into embittered exile across the Soviet border. After interminable delays the Iranian parliament (Majlis), emboldened by the strong diplomatic support the country had received from Washington, defiantly voted on October 22, 1947, to repudiate the oil agreement that the Iranian prime minister had negotiated with the Soviet Union.

Recent studies of the relevant archives indicates that Stalin's policy in Iran during the 1945–1946 crisis represented a cautious probe of Western resolve to oppose the extension of Soviet influence that was abandoned promptly as soon as it encountered resistance. Stalin and his advisers originally viewed the separatist ferment in northern Iran as a tempting opportunity for the Soviet Union to secure political influence and economic advantage (through the proposed oil concession) in an adjacent state, at a time when the counterveiling power of Russia's traditional rival in the region, Great Britain, was receding rapidly. It also provided the occasion to enhance the credibility of Soviet Communism as the instrument of historical progress by supporting an indigenous national liberation movement, a policy that Stalin and his successors would continue to pursue.

The vociferous reaction in Washington to the Iranian crisis in 1946 had less to do with the complex ethnic and political tensions in that country than with the deteriorating relations between the two superpowers in Europe. Assessing the Iranian conflict in the context of recent events in Eastern Europe, apprehensive American officials incorrectly interpreted the Kremlin's intrusive policy in Azerbaijan as an aggressive drive for hegemony in southwest Asia (which would mean control of

Iran's oil resources and access its ports on the Persian Gulf). The Truman adminis- *Reza* tration therefore decided to reinforce its diplomatic support of Iran with military *Shah* muscle. In October 1947 Washington concluded an agreement with Teheran for the *US* provision of American military assistance and the assignment of a U.S. military *forced* advisory mission to the country. By the end of the 1940s the regime of Shah *a* Mohammed Reza Pahlavi had forged a strong security relationship with the United *relationship* States that would remain in force for the next three decades. The Soviet Union would *to keep* be completely excluded from this traditional Russian sphere of influence, while the *Russia* United States replaced Great Britain as the hegemonic power in Iran. *out*

Moscow's humiliating retreat in the Iranian crisis of 1945–1946 was followed by another disappointment as it sought to obtain strategic advantages at the expense of Turkey. The historic rivalry between Russia and Turkey, which had periodically degenerated into armed conflict in the era of the Romanov tsars and the Ottoman sultans, was attenuated following the establishment of the Soviet Union and the Turkish Republic after World War I. The two regimes signed a treaty of friendship in 1925, which included reciprocal pledges of nonaggression and ushered in a remarkable period of political and economic cooperation between these two historic adversaries. But the Russo-Turkish rapprochement came to an end on March 19, 1945, when the Soviet Union informed Turkey of its decision to denounce the 1925 nonaggression pact. On June 7 Soviet Foreign Minister Molotov unveiled the new terms that Moscow would insist on in a modified treaty between the two states: The first of these was the cession of the provinces of Kars and Ardahan in the Caucasus region, which had been conquered by Russia in 1878 and retaken by Turkey after the Bolshevik Revolution. The second and the most controversial Soviet condition required the revision of the Montreux Convention of 1936 governing access rights to the Turkish Straits (the interconnected waterways of the Dardanelles, the Sea of Marmara, and the Bosporus that linked the Black Sea to the Mediterranean).

In the course of the next year and a half the Kremlin spelled out in a series of diplomatic dispatches to the Turkish government the amendments it sought to the Montreux Convention. The most important was the demand for the establishment of a new security system for the Straits under the joint control of the Black Seas powers, which in effect meant the presence of Soviet military forces on Turkish territory. When the government in Ankara indignantly rejected this overt threat to its sovereignty, Stalin unleashed a violent press and radio campaign to bring the Turks to heel. He also deployed twenty-five Soviet divisions on the two countries' frontier in the Caucasus Mountains as an instrument of intimidation.

The Kremlin's bid to obtain control of the strategically important Turkish Straits was nothing new. The tsars had energetically pursued that objective right up to the end of the Romanov regime: Just before he was swept from power in March 1917 Nicholas II had secured from his British and French allies a secret pledge to support Russia's claim to control the vital link between Russian ports on the Black Sea and the Mediterranean. During the period of Russo-Turkish friendship between the wars, the new Bolshevik regime temporarily abandoned this historic Russian goal. But it resurfaced during World War II. Stalin discussed the postwar status of the Straits with Churchill at their summit meeting in Moscow in October 1944 and with Roosevelt at Yalta in February 1945. In both cases the Soviet leader received from his Western allies expressions of sympathetic understanding of Russia's strategic interest in the waterway.

Soviet concern about the Turkish Straits represented the defensive reflex of a country that had suffered the terrible consequences of German military aggression. In World War II the Turkish Republic had clung to a precarious neutrality despite British and Soviet efforts to secure its support. Like Sweden, Switzerland, and other neutrals Turkey maintained a lucrative trading relationship with Nazi Germany, exporting chrome and other strategic raw materials required by Hitler's war machine. Turkey also proved incapable of preventing German submarines from sneaking through the Straits into the Black Sea, where they attacked Russian shipping. From Stalin's perspective the Turkish Straits were as vital to Soviet security as the Panama and Suez Canals were to American and British security, respectively. But what may have seemed to Moscow a precautionary move to protect Russia's vital interests by controlling the approaches to the Black Sea was viewed in Washington as a Soviet drive for open access to the Mediterranean, which would threaten Western Europe's access to the Middle East and Asia. To Truman administration officials, the prevention of such a geostrategic breakthrough called for the same type of vigorous response that had thwarted Stalin's alleged designs on northern Iran. As in Iran, the decline of British influence in Turkey left the United States as the only foreign power capable of stepping into the breach.

For these reasons Washington decided to support the beleaguered Turkish regime in its diplomatic tug-of-war with Moscow. In response to a harshly worded Soviet note of August 7, 1946, reiterating the Russian demand for joint control of the Straits, Truman dispatched the most powerful aircraft carrier in the American fleet to the eastern Mediterranean and reinforced an existing American naval task force in the area. This gunboat diplomacy emboldened the Turkish government to withstand the Soviet pressure for a settlement of the Straits dispute, just as Washington's strong support for Iran had enabled it to repudiate the petroleum agreement it had signed with the Soviet Union. The war of words between Moscow and Ankara continued, but Turkey did not budge in its determination to retain sole control of the Straits.

Amid the crises in Iran and Turkey an unsettling development across the Aegean in Greece presented Washington with what it viewed as another instance of Russia's southward expansionism. As German occupation forces withdrew from Greece in October 1944, British troops arrived to police the liberated country's major cities. But the anti-German resistance movement in the country, which was dominated by the Communist Greek People's Liberation Army (ELAS) and its political wing, the National Liberation Front (EAM), controlled the countryside. When it became evident that the British authorities were preparing to restore the exiled Greek royal government to power in Athens, ELAS and EAM staged an insurrection against the British military forces and their conservative royalist allies in the country. When British troops intervened to suppress the rebellion in the winter of 1944–1945, the Greek Communists' pleas for Soviet support fell on deaf ears in Moscow. Stalin scrupulously honored the agreement he had reached with Churchill in October 1944 to consider Greece within the British sphere of interest.

The two warring factions in Greece concluded a cease-fire in February 1945, and plans were promptly drawn up for a referendum on the question of the restoration of the constitutional monarchy and an internationally supervised election to determine the political future of the country. Recognizing that they had no chance of winning more than a quarter of the vote, the leftist coalition boycotted the general election that was held on March 31, 1946. The abstention of the left enabled the royalist Popular Party—which had received the active support of British diplomatic and military agents in the country—to assume power and assure the conservative, pro-British orientation of the regime. This trend was confirmed in September, when 69 percent of the voters in a national referendum supported the restoration of the monarchy.

In the meantime the Communist forces, which had boycotted both the election and the referendum as they reassembled in the rural areas of the north, took up arms against the right-wing government in Athens. In the spring of 1946 the Greek Communists began to receive military aid and political support from the neighboring Communist states of Yugoslavia, Bulgaria, and Albania. As we have seen, Yugoslavia's Marshal Tito operated independently of the Kremlin and harbored regional ambitions of his own that had nothing to do with Moscow's objectives: He privately spoke of incorporating Albania (which at the time was a Yugoslav client state) and Bulgaria in a vast Balkan Communist confederation under Yugoslav domination. Tito also backed the Communist insurgency in Greece in the hope of annexing its northern province of Macedonia, whose predominantly Slavic population was playing a prominent role in the insurrection against the Athens regime.

From evidence uncovered in the Soviet archives it appears that Stalin's attitude toward the Greek Civil War was painfully ambivalent. On the one hand he permitted Bulgaria, which was ruled by orthodox Stalinists obsequiously subservient to Moscow, to join Yugoslavia and its satellite Albania in providing material support to the Greek rebels. On the other hand he refused to recognize the rebel EAM "government" in northern Greece and provided no significant Soviet aid to the insurgents operating there. This cautious policy toward the Greek Civil War was apparently dictated by two overriding considerations. The first was the Soviet dictator's realistic assessment of the Communist-led insurgency's prospects for success. He correctly anticipated that the United States and Great Britain would never permit an unfriendly regime to be established in such a strategically situated country in the eastern Mediterranean. He also recognized that British and, if need be, American military power could easily be brought to bear against the rebels in Greece, whereas that country was beyond the reach of Soviet power. Furthermore, even a rebel victory against the royalist regime in Athens would have been a mixed blessing for the Soviet Union. As he was demonstrating in his ambivalent attitude toward the Chinese Civil War that was raging at the same time, Stalin instinctively distrusted Communist revolutions that he could not directly control.

## The British Withdrawal, the Truman Doctrine, and "Containment"

The subtleties and ambiguities of Soviet policy toward the Greek Civil War were lost on officials in the Truman administration. They saw the Greek insurgency as yet another instance of Soviet meddling that had already been witnessed in Iran and

Turkey. What rendered the Greek Civil War particularly ominous for the West was that Great Britain, the historic protector of Greek independence, was at the time mired in a severe economic crisis that would prevent it from fulfilling its traditional role. Britain had financed its war effort by selling a large proportion of its gold and foreign exchange reserves before American credit was forthcoming under the Lend-Lease Act of 1941. The abrupt termination of Lend-Lease at the end of the war precipitated a severe financial crisis in Washington's wartime ally. Truman had to use all of his powers of persuasion to induce a tight-fisted Congress to approve in 1946 an emergency loan of $3.75 billion to tide that country over while it struggled to restore its foreign trade. But the funds thus obtained were spent promptly to import desperately needed food and fuel rather than invested in productive enterprises that would revive the country's flagging export trade. The British economy continued its downward slide, which was hastened in the winter of 1946–1947 by the coldest period in the country's history. The national transportation system come to a virtual standstill while shortages of coal, gas, and electricity caused more than half of Britain's factories to shut down.

Great Britain's grave economic crisis in 1946–1947 rendered that country incapable of furnishing the financial assistance and military aid that was urgently requested by the Greek government in order to stabilize the deteriorating economic situation and suppress the Communist-led insurgency in the north. Recognizing that British funds would not be forthcoming, the royalist regime in Athens frantically turned to Washington for emergency assistance. The Truman administration furnished as much as it could under existing legislative authority, but by early 1947 the Greek economy appeared to be on the verge of total collapse while the costly and destructive civil war continued to rage. The likelihood that the U.S. Congress would approve a large American financial aid package to bail out the fragile government in Athens was slim. The Republican Party, which had gained control of both houses in the midterm elections of 1946, showed no inclination to support expensive foreign aid programs proposed by the Democratic president.

Suddenly, on February 21, 1947, the British Foreign Office officially notified the U.S. State Department that the dire economic conditions at home would oblige Great Britain to terminate all financial assistance to Greece and Turkey. It also announced that all of the forty thousand British troops that had been stationed in Greece since the end of the war to help the government suppress the Communist-led insurgency would be evacuated by the end of March. Noting that both Greece and Turkey would continue to require financial assistance to prevent their economic collapse and military aid to bolster their armed forces, London appealed to Washington to step into the breach.

British Foreign Secretary Ernest Bevin feared that his decision to abandon Greece and Turkey might lead the American public to conclude that Great Britain was a declining imperial power that was itself no longer worth supporting. The legislative debate during the British request for the emergency loan in 1945–1946 had revealed a virulent strain of Anglophobia in Congress that was graphically captured by the oft-repeated metaphor about how tired Americans were of "pulling British chestnuts out of the fire." But the foreign policy elite in Washington did not share this uncharitable view of America's old wartime ally. On the contrary, Truman administration officials had reached a consensus in favor of a positive response to the British request for assistance. But they recognized the need to frame the issue in language designed to rally bipartisan support in the Congress: Aid to Greece and Turkey could not be sold to parsimonious legislators as a means of bailing out the British as they disengaged from their dwindling imperial commitments. Rather, it had to be represented as an essential component of a new foreign policy initiative that was necessary to protect the vital interests of the United States itself. This argument proved persuasive when it was privately tested on the Republican foreign policy spokesman in the Senate, Arthur Vandenberg of Michigan, who pledged his full support if the president would lay the facts before the Congress and the public in a dramatic call to arms.

Truman obliged by delivering a historic speech before a special joint session of Congress on March 12, 1947. The stirring phraseology of the address revealed that the request for emergency aid for the two countries that were thought to be in imminent danger was merely the opening salvo in a much more far-reaching, ambitious campaign. The meaning of Truman's bold declaration that the United States must be prepared to "support free peoples who are resisting subjugation by armed minorities or by outside pressures" was plain: The essence of what would soon be known as the "Truman Doctrine" was the unconditional pledge of American assistance to countries anywhere in the world that were threatened either by external aggression from the Soviet Union or an indigenous Communist insurgency backed by Moscow.

The U.S. Congress promptly responded to this emergency situation by appropriating $250 million for Greece and $150 million for Turkey. The Greco-Turkish assistance law that went into effect on May 22, 1947, set a precedent for what would later become a multibillion-dollar foreign assistance program to countries that were deemed vulnerable to Soviet intimidation or indigenous Communist insurrection. The concrete results of this assertive new foreign policy, which was reinforced by the dispatch of U.S. military advisers to help the two recipient governments reorganize their armed forces, were soon apparent. Soviet diplomatic pressure on Turkey ceased and the topic of joint control of the Straits vanished from the diplomatic communications between Moscow and Ankara. By 1948 Stalin was warning Tito's emissary Milovan Djilas that the Greek insurrection was doomed and "must be stopped, and as quickly as possible." Throughout that year the Royal Greek Army, bolstered by American advisers and military equipment, overran all of the rebel strongholds in the northern mountains and drove the Communist partisans across the border into exile in Bulgaria and Albania. Their chief source of military supplies, Tito, had sealed their fate by closing his frontier and cutting off all Yugoslav aid in July 1948 after his dramatic break with the Soviet Union the previous month (see page 8).

Throughout the early months of 1947 officials at the State Department and the newly established Department of Defense had been hard at work fashioning an intellectual justification for a new strategy of coping with the perceived Soviet threat across the globe. They were now able to tap the expertise and analytical acumen of George Kennan, author of the famous "Long Telegram," who had been recalled from the Moscow embassy to head the State Department's newly established in-house "think tank" called the Policy Planning Staff. Kennan promptly prepared a succinct summary of his top secret analysis of Soviet foreign policy for presentation to the American public.

The fruit of his labors was an article entitled "The Sources of Soviet Conduct," published under the mysterious pseudonym "Mr. X" in the July 1947 issue of the influential journal *Foreign Affairs*. The underlying theme of the brief article was crystal clear: Historic Russia's age-old sense of insecurity, combined with the messianic ideology of Marxism-Leninism, drove the Soviet Union to probe the weak spots all along its periphery in a compulsive campaign to expand its power at the expense of weak and vulnerable neighbors to establish absolute security against real or imagined enemies. Moscow would seek to achieve these expansionist goals by the direct annexation of territory if possible, or by the creation of subservient satellites if necessary, wherever and whenever the opportunity presented itself. The great powers that had served historically as counterweights to this inherently expansionist empire— Germany in Europe, Japan in Asia, and Great Britain in the Eastern Mediterranean and the Persian Gulf—were no longer in a position to fulfill that role. The United States was alone capable of imposing limits on the expansion of Russian power. It must do so not overtly and directly through the application of military force, but discreetly and indirectly by promoting the prosperity, stability, and security of those countries in danger. Confronted with a ring of economically robust, politically stable, militarily powerful states along its periphery, Kennan believed, the Soviet Union would be obliged to accept the geographical limits to its power that had been informally agreed to at Yalta.

This new doctrine of "containment," as it would soon come to be known, was rooted in the assumption that a major objective of Soviet foreign policy was the achievement of hegemony over the non-Communist western half of Europe. This region (including the three western occupation zones of Germany) comprised the highest concentration of industrial potential in the Eastern Hemisphere. Control of Western Europe's vast economic resources would immeasurably strengthen the Soviet Union in its emerging rivalry with the United States. The prospects for success in such a venture had never been greater because of the dire economic straits of the countries located there, whose efforts to recover from the massive destruction of their industrial plant and equipment and the depletion of their capital had been unsuccessful in the early postwar years. To make matters worse, the powerful Communist parties in France and Italy, together with the nationwide labor organizations they controlled, were increasingly viewed by apprehensive officials in Washington as subversive "fifth columns" that might exploit the widespread economic distress in those strategically located countries to undermine the stability of their pro-Western democratic governments. In short, Kennan and his expanding circle of supporters in the Truman administration had come to view Western Europe as the most important test case for the embryonic doctrine of containment. They had also come to regard the restoration of that region's economic viability as the key to the success of the new strategy.

## The European Recovery Program

Truman's new secretary of state, George C. Marshall, had returned from the Moscow Conference of Foreign Ministers that broke up in acrimony on April 24, 1947, filled with apprehension about the future. In his tense private conversations with Stalin, he had been subjected to the Soviet dictator's blunt and belligerent predictions that the capitalist economic system in Western Europe was about to collapse. As he digested these ominous forecasts, Marshall was receiving reports from the American embassies in Paris and Rome that the French and Italian Communist parties had gained so much political support because of the deteriorating economic conditions in those countries that they even stood a chance of assuming power through democratic means within a year.

On returning to Washington Marshall and Secretary of Defense James Forrestal agreed over lunch that the most effective means of preventing such a calamity would be a massive infusion of American financial aid to rescue the faltering economies of Europe. Marshall assigned the task of drafting specific plans for such a program to Kennan and his fellow intellectuals on the Policy Planning Staff. The final version of the proposal was composed by several State Department officials and received the endorsement of the president. But Truman overruled suggestions that he lend his own name to the project (whose official title was the European Recovery Program) because of his spreading unpopularity in the Republican-controlled Congress that would have to appropriate the funds. Since his new secretary of state enjoyed bipartisan respect because of his distinguished military career, Truman suggested that the measure that would become the economic component of the containment policy be designated as the Marshall Plan.

The secretary of state took advantage of an invitation to receive an honorary degree at the Harvard University graduation ceremonies on June 5 to unveil the proposal to the world. Recounting the sad tale of economic distress that continued to afflict Europe two years after the end of the war, Marshall traced the inability of the European countries to recover economically to the shortage of capital required to purchase essential raw materials, commodities, and machinery. To remedy this deficiency, he proposed that Washington provide financial assistance to the countries of Europe to cover the costs of essential imports during a transitional period until their export trade had revived. The one critical condition that the U.S. government appended to the offer of assistance was that it be distributed on a multilateral rather than a bilateral basis: The individual European countries would have to devise procedures for coordinating their requests for the American financial assistance that was being offered.

Marshall's historic speech contained not a word about the perceived Soviet threat to Western Europe, nor a single hint that the American offer was in any way connected with the strategy of containment enunciated in Kennan's Mr. X article that was in press as Marshall spoke. Indeed, the secretary of state's failure to restrict the American offer to the democratic capitalist countries of Western Europe implied that the Communist countries of Eastern Europe, as well as the Soviet Union itself, were welcome to apply. The American initiative elicited an immediate response in London and Paris. British Foreign Secretary Ernest Bevin and French Foreign Minister Georges Bidault promptly convened a conference in Paris to discuss the preparation of a comprehensive list of reconstruction requirements for submission to Washington. Invitations were issued to representatives of seventeen European nations on both sides of the Iron Curtain.

The invitation to the Paris conference precipitated a heated debate within the Kremlin concerning the wisdom of associating with the West European governments in this American-inspired undertaking. On the one hand, the Soviet economy was in desperate shape and in dire need of foreign financial assistance. Indeed, Soviet representatives had quietly angled for a large American reconstruction loan ever since the idea of such financial aid was first broached by the U.S. Treasury Department in January 1945. On the other hand, Stalin loudly had been predicting the imminent demise of the capitalist order, most recently in his remarks to Marshall at the Moscow Foreign Ministers' Conference in April. It would be embarrassing to solicit financial assistance from an economic system that was supposedly on the verge of extinction. In the end Stalin decided to sound out the American government's intentions. Soviet Foreign Minister Molotov arrived in Paris with nearly a hundred technical advisers in tow on June 26 to evaluate the American initiative and devise an appropriate response to it.

In issuing the blanket invitation to all European states, Marshall had gambled that two of the conditions attached to the aid program would prove unacceptable to the Soviet Union. The first was the provision for a jointly formulated and executed program of economic recovery that would treat all of Europe, including Germany, as a single economic entity. Rejecting this all-European strategy, Molotov insisted in the Paris talks that each recipient country be permitted to prepare its own estimate of its national requirements and submit them directly to Washington. The second was the requirement that each recipient open its economy to American trade and its budget to American inspection, a proviso that predictably elicited sharp criticism from the Soviet delegation. After several days of fruitless haggling Molotov abandoned the conference on July 1, denouncing the American recovery plan as a conspiracy to wrest control of the European economies and an unwarranted intrusion into the domestic affairs of sovereign states.

The British and French governments proceeded to invite all European countries except the Soviet Union and Spain (which had been excluded as punishment for its pro-Axis sympathies during World War II) to attend a follow-up conference that would draft a coordinated response to the Marshall proposal. Through an oversight the Kremlin had neglected to instruct the governments of Poland and Czechoslovakia (both of which had expressed avid interest in the American aid plan) to decline the invitation, so Warsaw and Prague were obliged to withdraw their letters of acceptance. Thus the six Eastern European Communist states, together with Czechoslovakia (still ruled by a coalition government with Communist participation) and Finland (bowing to pressure from its powerful neighbor to the east), would join the Soviet Union in boycotting what would become a Western European, non-Communist recovery program financed by the United States.

Delegates from the remaining European states, joined by the Allied military governors of the three Western occupation zones of Germany, met in Paris on July 12 and formed a committee to prepare a joint response to the American proposal. Western Europe and the United States breathed a collective sigh of relief at the Communist bloc's self-exclusion from the Marshall Plan. The amount of financial aid required to restore Eastern as well as Western Europe would have far exceeded the spending limits Congress was expected to impose. In any case it was inconceivable, amid the mounting anti-Communist sentiment in the United States, that legislators would appropriate American taxpayers' money to promote the economic recovery of the Soviet Union and its Communist satellites.

The supreme irony in this dispute was the fact that the Soviet counterproposal, which rejected any form of Europe-wide cooperation, came very close to what the Western European governments themselves actually favored at this stage. Moscow's complaints that unrestricted American government access to the budgetary procedures of the recipient states represented an intolerable infringement on national sovereignty echoed concerns that had been aired quietly in London and Paris, but which those governments did not dare express openly for fear of antagonizing the Americans whose dollars they desperately needed. Moreover, Moscow's strenuous objections to the requirement that most of the Marshall aid be spent on American products tapped into a suspicious strain in European political thinking—on both sides of the Iron Curtain—that detected an ulterior motive behind the altruistic rhetoric of the Marshall offer. Communist commentators evaluated the Marshall Plan through an updated version of Lenin's old definition of imperialism as the final stage of a dying capitalist order: American industrial firms, threatened by a drop in profits when the demand for war-related goods declined, sought an outlet for their surplus production in Europe and pressured their government to finance these desperately needed exports. Some non-Communist critics in Western Europe shared this cynical view that the U.S. aid program was designed to subordinate their economies to American export interests. The credibility of this interpretation was unintentionally bolstered by the public statements of Truman administration officials, who sold the European aid program to a penny-pinching Congress with the effective argument that an increase in Europe's purchasing power through the provision of U.S. government credits would produce profits for American firms engaged in the export trade and jobs for the workers they employed.

In the early postwar years the United States, blessed with an enormous internal market for its industrial output and an abundant and easily accessible supply of most critical raw materials and foodstuffs, was much less dependent on foreign trade for its economic prosperity than were other industrialized countries. But the Truman administration's decision to dramatize the domestic economic benefits of the Marshall Plan was a supremely successful political strategy, designed to secure public support for a policy whose underlying purpose was not to promote American trade but to bolster the capacity of Western Europe to resist the threat of Communism. The Republican-controlled Congress, the press, and the public were converted to the cause of internationalism despite the absence of domestic economic incentives to do so.

On September 22 a committee of Western European officials meeting in Paris submitted to Washington a combined request for $33 billion over a four-year period. Truman reduced the total to $17 billion before sending the massive aid legislation to Capitol Hill. After trimming the final bill to $13 billion, Congress approved the European Recovery Program (ERP) on April 3, 1948. Two weeks later the sixteen recipient nations established the Organization for European Economic Cooperation (OEEC) to distribute the funds and promote the coordination of their national economic policies. Between 1948 and 1952 the ERP supplied loans and grants totaling slightly over $12 billion. The largest amounts went to Great Britain and its dependencies ($3.2 billion), France ($2.7 billion), Italy ($1.5 billion), and what was in 1949 to become the Federal Republic of Germany ($1.4 billion). From the depths of economic despair in the years immediately after World War II the major countries of

Western Europe embarked on a period of sustained growth in the early 1950s that continued for more than two decades. Most economic historians agree that they would have recovered eventually from the devastation of World War II on their own, without the infusion of American financial aid. But the Marshall Plan undeniably hastened that postwar reconstruction through the provision of dollar credits at a critical juncture of European history. By including the non-Communist part of Germany in the program, Washington also contributed to the integration of that new state into the Western European economic system.

## The Emergence of the Postwar International Economic Order

The impressive postwar recovery of the industrialized countries of the Western world was facilitated by the relatively efficient operation of the new international monetary system that had been established at a meeting of treasury officials from forty-four allied nations at the Bretton Woods resort in the White Mountains of New Hampshire during the first three weeks of July 1944. The main achievement of this conference was a program to restore stability to the system of international financial transactions, which had disintegrated during the Great Depression when most countries abandoned the gold standard, allowed the value of their currencies to float, and resorted to *ad hoc* expedients such as exchange controls and competitive devaluations. The wildly fluctuating exchange rates of the world's major currencies discouraged international trade, lending, and investment, since export firms and financial institutions were understandably reluctant to convert their funds into a foreign currency whose exchange value was highly unpredictable. Since the United States possessed over half of the world's gold supply, the Roosevelt administration decided to rely on that precious metal as the basis for establishing a modified system of fixed exchange rates: The dollar was declared to be freely convertible into gold at the fixed rate of $35 per ounce. Other countries agreed to peg their currencies to the dollar at the rates in effect at the opening of the conference. The participating governments pledged to maintain their currency's exchange rate within a narrow band around the fixed one by intervening in foreign exchange markets (that is, by buying and selling currencies) as necessary. Since the American dollar was officially convertible into gold at a fixed price, it became the world's reserve currency and was widely used as payment for international transactions by foreign governments and firms. The reliability of the dollar and the stability of its value facilitated the growth of world trade after World War II by providing liquidity to an international monetary system that had been clogged since the 1930s. The Bretton Woods system of fixed exchange rates based on the dollar's convertibility into gold enabled exporters, importers, lenders, and borrowers to conduct their international transactions without concern about fluctuating currency values.

Another landmark innovation of the Bretton Woods Conference of 1944 was the establishment of two international lending agencies that would play an increasingly important role in the postwar international economic order: the International Monetary Fund (IMF) and the International Bank for Reconstruction and Development (commonly known as the World Bank). The IMF was created to provide short-term loans to enable countries experiencing a current account deficit in their balance of payments to settle their international accounts without resorting to the customary expedient of currency devaluation. Devaluation was declared to be a last resort and would be permitted by the IMF only if the deficit was deemed too large to be corrected by a temporary loan from the international agency. The Fund's financial resources consisted of a pool of currencies contributed by the member states, with the United States originally supplying over 30 percent of the total. IMF lending was to be accompanied by stringent conditions that were designed to erase the borrowing country's deficit, such as cuts in government spending, an increase in taxes, and a reduction of the money supply. These deflationary measures would increase unemployment and reduce inflation, which would in turn promote exports, discourage imports, and eventually restore the country's balance of payments surplus. The World Bank was set up to provide long-term loans for economic development. It was eventually provided by the member states with $10 billion in capital and was authorized to borrow additional funds in world money markets. After a slow start, the World Bank became a major source of development loans by the end of the 1950s.

One of the principal goals of the Bretton Woods system of fixed exchange rates and a multilateral payments mechanism was the expansion of world trade. But international monetary instability was not the only legacy of the Great Depression that inhibited the revival of exports and imports after the war. The other was the policy of "beggar-thy-neighbor" protectionism that all major nations had adopted in the 1930s. The United States had been one of the first countries to abandon free trade with the Hawley-Smoot Tariff of 1930. But Roosevelt's secretary of state, Cordell Hull, campaigned vigorously throughout his long term in office from 1933 to 1944 for the restoration of a free and open trading system as a panacea for all the world's ills. At the end of the war the Truman administration took the lead in pressuring other nations to dismantle the Depression-era trade barriers that blocked access to foreign markets. The original American plan had foreseen the establishment of an International Trade Organization (ITO), which would sponsor multilateral negotiations for the removal of trade barriers. But after protectionist sentiment in the U.S. Congress torpedoed the ITO project, Truman reverted to what he thought would be a temporary expedient until the project for a global trade organization could be revived. On October 30, 1947, representatives of twenty-three nations signed the General Agreement on Tariffs and Trade (GATT). In subsequent years GATT served as a forum for periodic negotiations between trading partners aimed at reducing the complicated set of trade restrictions that had accumulated over the years. The GATT agreement stipulated that all parties negotiating under its auspices adhere to the nondiscriminatory "most favored nation" principle, which meant that trade concessions on specific products negotiated with one trading partner would automatically be extended to all others.

The reduction of tariffs, import quotas, and other barriers to the free exchange of goods and services during a succession of GATT bargaining sessions, or "rounds," promoted an unprecedented expansion of world trade, which grew at an annual rate of almost 7 percent in real terms between 1948 and 1970. When it became evident that the more grandiose plan for the ITO was dead in the water, GATT was eventually converted from a temporary agreement to a permanent agency with a secretariat based in Geneva. GATT, the IMF, and the World Bank thus became the three pillars of the Bretton Woods system of postwar international economic relations, which was dedicated (at least in theory) to the principle of free trade, the convertibility of currencies, and the gold standard linked to the American dollar. The dominant participants in this system were the industrial capitalist countries of North America, Western Europe, and Japan. Although Stalin had sent a delegation to the Bretton Woods conference in the summer of 1944, it soon became evident that Communist economic practices were entirely incompatible with the free market principles underlying the proposed postwar international economic order. The Communist bloc would thereafter operate outside the Bretton Woods system, cut off from the global network of trade, investment, and lending that linked the industrialized countries of the non-Communist world.

## The Political Consequences of the Marshall Plan

As the non-Communist parties were being marginalized in Eastern Europe, a parallel development was unfolding in two countries in Western Europe whose national Communist parties had been participating in coalition governments since the liberation. At the end of the war the Communist parties in France and Italy, which had won widespread public sympathy for their active role in the resistance to fascism, accepted subordinate positions in governing coalitions dominated by non-Communist parties. But in May 1947 the Communist parties of these two countries were excluded from power. The French Communists were dismissed by the Socialist prime minister after they opposed a government-imposed wage freeze in solidarity with workers in the recently nationalized Renault automobile company who had gone on strike for higher pay. The ruling Christian Democrats in Italy evicted the powerful Italian Communist Party from the governing coalition at the end of the month, in the anticipation that Washington would be more likely to grant financial assistance to a government without Communist members.

The French and Italian Communist parties had originally accepted their exclusion from political power as a temporary setback. They continued to pursue moderate policies in the hopes of rejoining a governing coalition in alliance with other parties of the left. The Italian Communist Party even expressed support for its government's participation in the Marshall Plan. But Stalin had come to view the American aid program as a serious threat to Soviet interests in Europe and resolved to employ the Western European Communist parties to sabotage it. In September 1947 representatives of the principal European Communist parties were summoned to a conference in the Polish resort town of Szklarska Poremba that had been organized by Soviet officials Andrei Zhdanov and Georgi Malenkov. The Italian and French party leaders were chided for their conciliatory behavior and sent home with instructions to wage all-out war against their "bourgeois" governments and the American financial aid program that they had recently endorsed.

To manage this campaign against the Marshall Plan, the Kremlin needed a supranational vehicle to transmit the appropriate instructions to the national Communist parties of Western Europe. Stalin had abolished the Communist International (or Comintern) in 1943 to please his American and British allies, who had strenuously objected to the organization's overt advocacy of revolution and covert sponsorship of subversion abroad. As a replacement for the defunct Comintern, Zhdanov and Malenkov established at the Szklarska Poremba conference a Communist Information Bureau (or Cominform). Ostensibly designed to coordinate the political activities of European Communist parties, the Cominform in fact became the instrument of the Kremlin's campaign to sabotage the Marshall Plan.

The rapidity with which the West European Communist parties adapted to the new Kremlin line revealed the extent of their subservience to Moscow. In France the Communist-controlled General Labor Confederation (CGT) issued an impassioned call for a general strike in November, which brought three million workers into the streets and resulted in the occupation of several factories and bloody clashes with French security forces. Labor unrest in Italy was somewhat more restrained, probably due to the presence of British and American troops (which did not depart until the end of 1947). But the Truman administration worried that the French and Italian Communist parties would use their predominant influence in the unions to exploit the severe economic difficulties in those two countries and seize control of the state.

Washington strove to prevent such an outcome by resorting to the type of covert action that would become a mainstay of U.S. strategy during this new era of East-West conflict, which received its label from a book published in 1947 by the journalist Walter Lippmann: the Cold War. American labor organizations, later replaced by the Central Intelligence Agency (CIA), surreptitiously financed a renegade French union movement that competed with the Communist-controlled CGT. Worried that the leftist coalition of Communists and Socialists would win the 1948 elections in Italy, the CIA covertly financed a wide range of anti-Communist organizations and publications in that country. The collapse of the strike movement in France, followed by the electoral triumph of the pro-American Christian Democratic Party in Italy, demonstrated the efficacy of this U.S. policy. From 1945 to 1948 the Soviet Union and its indigenous Communist allies in Eastern Europe had removed the non-Communist political opposition through intimidation backed by the implicit threat of intervention by the Red Army. The United States and its indigenous non-Communist allies tamed the Communist opposition in Western Europe through the much less intrusive but equally effective combination of covert political action and overt economic incentives.

## The Division of Germany

As the European continent split into Communist and non-Communist halves in the first three years after World War II, the most important issue on the European political scene was the political future of Germany. The wartime allies had decided at the Yalta Conference of February 1945 to subject the enemy to an inter-Allied military occupation after its defeat. In the original plan Germany was to be divided into three military occupation zones under American, British, and Soviet jurisdiction. But when Churchill heard Roosevelt's prediction at Yalta that all American military forces would be removed from Europe within a few years (as they had been after World War I), the British Prime Minister insisted that an occupation zone also be assigned to France so that Great Britain would not be left facing the Soviet Union alone after the anticipated American withdrawal. Stalin grudgingly acquiesced in this modified arrangement, on the condition that the territory assigned to France be carved out of the American zone.

The decision for a temporary military occupation left open the question of the defeated country's permanent political status. In the heat of war the Allied leaders had entertained various vengeful schemes to ensure that Germany would never rise again. In offhand comments both Churchill and Stalin proposed dismemberment as a permanent solution to the "German problem" that had plagued Europe since Bismarck unified the country in 1871. Roosevelt initially endorsed a plan proposed by Secretary of the Treasury Henry Morgenthau in September 1944 for the "de-industrialization" of Germany and its transformation into a peaceful society of farmers and small tradesmen. But in the three months between the Yalta Conference and Germany's surrender in May 1945, the victorious allies began to have second thoughts about these vindictive projects. The American and British governments came to the conclusion that a revived Germany, purged of its Nazi institutions and personnel, was essential to the recovery of Europe as a whole. Stalin too gave up his wartime fantasies of dismembering Russia's historic adversary. He flirted with the idea of unilaterally creating a united Communist Germany under tight Soviet control, but proved unwilling to risk the showdown with his Western allies that such a maneuver would entail. In the end he settled for the imposition of stringent controls over the Soviet occupation zone in eastern Germany as the surest guarantee against a German revival.

The occupation would be administered by a Four-Power Allied Control Council located in Berlin, the former capital of Hitler's Reich that lay 110 miles within the Soviet occupation zone. The city was in turn divided into four occupation sectors for the purposes of convenience, although (like the defeated country as a whole) it was to be administered as a single political unit. The Allied Control Council operated under guidelines formulated at the summit conference held in the Berlin suburb of Potsdam in July 1945. Truman, Stalin, and Churchill (who was replaced midconference by Clement Attlee after the British Labour Party defeated the Conservatives in a general election) labored to reach agreement on postwar policy toward Germany. But the discussions rapidly degenerated into an testy dispute between the Anglo-Americans and the Russians over how to deal with the economic crisis that was causing severe hardship to the German population.

Roosevelt, Churchill, and Stalin had agreed at Yalta that Germany would be required to pay reparations to those countries that had suffered at the hands of Hitler's armies and that the Soviet Union, as the most damaged victim, would receive half of those funds. But at Potsdam the U.S. and British delegations began to worry about the consequences of huge reparation demands on defeated Germany. The two Western powers feared that a starving, impoverished German population would become an intolerable drain on their financial resources. While Washington and (to a lesser extent) London provided food, clothing, and shelter to the destitute inhabitants of occupied Germany, Moscow was planning to extract from that country whatever economic assets it could as recompense for the devastation that Hitler's armies had caused during Operation Barbarossa. In such a situation U.S. taxpayers would in effect be financing the postwar reconstruction of the Soviet Union. Truman therefore insisted at Potsdam that the first charge on German production cover the cost of importing enough food and raw materials to provide the German people with a minimum standard of living so they would not have to depend indefinitely on American benevolence.

The Russians reluctantly agreed to this U.S. proposal, but were greatly displeased with another American policy that threatened to reduce the total amount of the reparation payments they would receive: Moscow expected to extract a minimum of $8 billion worth of reparation payments from Germany, at least a quarter of which would have to come from the center of German industrial productivity in the western part of the country, particularly in the Ruhr Valley. But the Ruhr was located in the British occupation zone, and London was reluctant to allow the Russians to strip Germany's most productive industrial region of its economic assets while British taxpayers continued to foot the bill for the provision of food and other essential goods to the German population in the British zone.

While the diplomats haggled about the rules for reparation payments, the Soviet occupation authorities were already removing industrial equipment from their own occupation zone in such haste and with such total disregard for accountability that it was impossible to assign an accurate value to the material already collected. To break the impasse at Potsdam over how to calculate the value of reparation deliveries, U.S. Secretary of State James Byrnes devised a simple, straightforward solution to a complex problem: Each occupying power would be authorized to obtain such reparation it was entitled to, but only from its own zone. This seemed to the Americans an eminently fair concession to what they regarded as the Soviet Union's legitimate financial claims against Germany. The United States and Great Britain had no intention of collecting reparations for themselves from their zones and had taken no steps to do so. On the contrary, they were spending an increasing amount to support the meager living standards of the impoverished German populations in their charge. The Russians would thereby be able to obtain from the part of Germany they controlled the reparation payments they had been promised at Yalta.

Blocked in his bid to secure equal access to the centers of industrial productivity in the western zones of Germany, Stalin retreated to a second line of defense. He demanded the right to at least some reparation payments from the western zones to supplement the requisitions from the Soviet zone. To meet the Soviet position halfway, Byrnes patched together a complicated compromise: The three Western allies agreed that 10 percent of the industrial equipment dismantled in their zones would be sent east as reparations to the Soviet Union; another 15 percent would be exchanged with the Soviets for an equivalent value of food and raw materials, which were abundantly available in the largely agricultural Soviet zone and desperately needed by the malnourished inhabitants of the three western zones. This compromise arrangement was obviously meaningless until the occupying powers had settled on the total amount of reparations to which these percentages referred. But a final figure could not be set until they agreed on the level of production that Germany would be permitted to attain in order to yield such payments.

The Potsdam agreements included a provision for the eventual establishment in Berlin of all-German administrative bodies, in keeping with the policy of treating the defeated power as a single political unit. But the plan to preserve German unity was

*Germany Between East and West*

disrupted by the French government of Charles de Gaulle, whose foreign policy was inspired by the old maxim of Cardinal Richelieu that German unity and French security were incompatible. In the autumn of 1945 France called for the separation from Germany of that country's three most productive industrial regions, the Saar, the Ruhr, and the Rhineland. When that French initiative met with fierce opposition from the United States and Great Britain, Paris became a source of obstructionism in the Allied Control Council (and remained so even after the resignation of de Gaulle in January 1946). The French delegate vetoed all proposals designed to fulfill the Potsdam promise to set up German administrative organizations. In the meantime the French occupation authorities administered their zone with such a heavy hand that it reminded some observers of the harsh occupation policy in the Soviet zone. The United States was thoroughly disgusted with what it viewed as French vindictiveness and intransigence, but avoided a public row with the government in Paris for fear of undermining the shaky political coalition to the benefit of the then powerful French Communist party. The Soviet leaders doubtless were grateful to the French for pursuing obstructionist policies that they themselves favored despite their public endorsement of German political and economic unity.

In line with the Potsdam principle of "zonal reparations," the Soviet authorities methodically stripped their occupation zone of most of its portable economic assets. In addition to collecting enormous quantities of coal and other raw materials, they dismantled entire factories, power plants, and railway tracks, which were cut into numbered sections and shipped east to the Soviet Union. The Russians also reneged on their Potsdam pledge to ship foodstuffs and raw materials from their own predominantly agricultural zone to the three Western zones in exchange for the industrial equipment they were receiving from the Ruhr and other industrial centers in the west. That policy provoked the ire of the U.S. representative on the Four-Power Allied Control Council in Berlin, who complained that the Soviet Union was looting its own zone and collecting reparation deliveries from the Western zones while the U.S. government was feeding and housing the German populations in the west. In short, American taxpayers were indirectly financing German reparations to the Soviet Union, precisely the predicament that Byrnes's policy of zonal reparations had been designed to prevent.

The occupying powers finally reached agreement in March 1946 on the maximum level of industrial production that Germany would be permitted to attain: roughly half the level of 1938. This understanding should have set the stage for the orderly selection of plants in all four zones to be dismantled for shipment to the various claimants to German reparations and for the development of an export-import program for the entire country to alleviate its economic plight. But progress was slow on the first policy and nonexistent on the second. Convinced that Germany's recovery was vital to the economic rehabilitation of Europe as a whole, the U.S. delegates to the Allied Control Council tried in vain to persuade their Soviet counterparts to treat reparations as part of a comprehensive plan for the management of the entire German economy. In May the United States suspended all reparation deliveries from its zone to the Soviet zone in an effort to pressure the Russians to halt their unilateral requisitions of German machinery and resources and to resume four-power cooperation. In the meantime, the Russians had introduced measures of economic reform in their own zone—such as the nationalization of heavy industry and the confiscation and redistribution of large landholdings—that violated American economic principles as well as the Potsdam decision to treat all of Germany as a single economic entity. The British and American governments were beginning to fear the consequences of Soviet pressure on Germany as much as they feared the consequences of a German national recovery.

The year 1946 was enlivened by the intensifying rivalry between the two super-powers for the allegiance of the German people. At the Paris meeting of Allied foreign ministers in July, Molotov abruptly jettisoned Stalin's hard-line policy toward Germany in favor of a much more conciliatory position. He accused the United States of implementing an updated version of the Morgenthau Plan for the destruction of Germany's industrial potential by imposing restrictions on Germany's coal and steel production. He called for the creation of a single German government and castigated France for demanding the detachment of the Ruhr from the rest of the country. In the meantime Soviet occupation authorities pandered to German nationalist sentiment by permitting the Communist Party in their zone to raise incendiary questions about Germany's postwar border with Poland at the Oder and Western Neisse rivers, which had deprived Germany of about a third of its prewar territory in the east. That border had been unilaterally imposed by the Russians in the spring of 1945 to compensate Poland for the seventy thousand square miles of its own territory that the Soviet Union had annexed. It was evident that the Kremlin was earnestly seeking to win the support of the German people by depicting the Western occupying powers as their oppressors and Moscow as their friend.

U.S. Secretary of State James Byrnes responded on September 5 to Molotov's public relations campaign in a historic speech before an audience of fourteen hundred German dignitaries in Stuttgart that enunciated a new American occupation policy. He called for the economic rehabilitation of Germany to help the Germans win back "an honorable place among the free and peace-loving nations." He buried once and for all the French proposal for the detachment of the Ruhr. He urged the prompt formation of a provisional government for the entire country that would pave the way for German self-rule. He promised that the American army would remain in Germany as long as the Red Army did, thereby scotching rumors that the popular GIs would depart and leave the inhabitants of the western zones at the mercy of the detested Russians. He refused to recognize the frontier between Germany and Poland, widely known as the Oder-Neisse Line, that Stalin had peremptorily redrawn to Poland's benefit. By endorsing the German nationalists' protest against the territorial losses in the east, Washington forced Moscow to choose between its Communist satellite in Poland and the German people whom it had begun to woo. The Soviet leader opted to support the country he already controlled. By doing so he alienated public opinion in the three Western zones of Germany, forfeiting whatever opportunity that may have existed to bring about the Western powers' ultimate nightmare: a revived, reunited Germany aligned with and subservient to Moscow.

At the Council of Foreign Ministers' meeting in Paris in July 1946, British Foreign Secretary Bevin pressed hard to achieve inter-Allied agreement on the policy of all-German economic recovery. He demanded the full implementation of the Potsdam program of economic unity, which would have subordinated reparation payments to the elimination of the German trade deficit that was being financed exclusively by the American and British treasuries. He threatened that if no such agreement were reached, Great Britain would reorganize its occupation policies in such a way as to spare the British taxpayer the burden of financing German recovery. Molotov defiantly retorted that the Soviet Union would continue to collect reparations from current production and would refuse to deliver food and raw materials from its zone to the three western zones. Realizing that the goal of a united Germany was no longer feasible in light of inter-Allied squabbling, U.S. Secretary of State Byrnes finally decided that the only feasible alternative was to unite the three western zones into a viable political and economic entity that could sustain its population without foreign support. When Byrnes offered to merge the American zone with any of the others, the British responded favorably in late July. For the rest of 1946 the two English-speaking occupying powers laid the groundwork for the amalgamation of their two zones, which formally took place on January 1, 1947.

The four occupying powers made one last attempt to reach an all-German settlement at the Council of Foreign Ministers' conference in Moscow in March 1947. But the negotiations promptly foundered on the question of how central agencies should be set up and who should run them. As the Moscow conference broke up in disagreement over the details of managing the occupation, it had become evident that only the three western zones could become a viable vehicle for promoting the economic and political rehabilitation of Germany. It also would have been very difficult to incorporate the Soviet zone into the three western zones, since it already possessed a Communist economic system through the nationalization of industry and the confiscation of private landholdings. In the following May the British and Americans established an economic advisory committee in their merged zones consisting of fifty-two delegates of the regional (Land) assemblies that had been democratically elected. In July the United States agreed to extend Marshall Plan aid to the three Western occupation zones, confirming what in fact was becoming the fait accompli of an economic partition of Germany.

For obvious historical reasons France had consistently and vigorously opposed all policies promoting the political or economic integration of the three western occupation zones in Germany. But the prospect of financial assistance through the Marshall Plan rendered Germany's historic adversary much more amenable to the American point of view on the occupation. By the summer of 1947 French representatives had began to participate in discussions on a "trizonal" economic policy. To allay French anxieties about the consequences of Germany's rehabilitation, the British and Americans agreed to the establishment of an International Authority for the Ruhr (IAR) to oversee Germany's most productive industrial region once it had become evident that the Soviet Union would not be involved. Soon the rudiments of a coordinated plan for economic recovery emerged in the three western zones of Germany in the form of a newly created organization called the Supreme Economic Council. Moscow predictably refused to permit its occupation zone to participate in this venture, which was based on free market economic principles that were entirely incompatible with the Communist economic institutions that had been established there.

The Council of Foreign Ministers' conference in London in November–December 1947 ended in deadlock over the issue of German reparations: The Soviet Union refused to agree, in advance of a general settlement, that the amount of reparations already removed from Germany would be counted in the final bill. The three Western powers thereupon decided that further cooperation with Moscow on German affairs was impossible and resolved to proceed separately with a common policy for their three zones. During the early months of 1948 one last initiative was launched within the Four-Power framework, when the American and British delegates on the Allied

Control Council in Berlin (with the tacit support of their French colleague) sought agreement on a plan to replace the occupation currencies with a new German currency that would become legal tender and circulate freely in all four zones. When this project encountered stiff Soviet resistance, the three Western powers proceeded on March 1 to establish a central bank that would issue a single German currency for use in the three Western zones. The Soviet delegate thereupon walked out of the Allied Control Council in March 20, never to return. The final obstacle to the economic unification of the three Western zones of Germany fell on June 18, when France formally agreed to fuse its zone with the already unified Anglo-American zone.

On the same day the three Western powers introduced in their merged zones a new currency, the deutsche mark, in an effort to eradicate the hyperinflation and black market activities that had hampered German economic recovery. The Soviet Union proceeded to establish its own mark in the Soviet zone on June 23. In the meantime a conference of the three Western powers in London authorized the convocation of an assembly of German delegates to draft a constitution for what would presumably become some form of a German political entity in the three merged western zones. This flurry of activity in the spring and early summer of 1948 signified the total breakdown of inter-Allied cooperation in the occupation of Germany. The Western powers had since concluded that the economic recovery of the defeated enemy was essential for the economic rehabilitation of Europe as a whole. They now recognized that the Soviet Union would never permit its occupation zone to be part of an all-German economic revival. The only alternative was to convert the American, British, and French zones into a unified political and economic unit that could survive on its own.

The three Western zones of Germany contained 75 percent of that country's population as well as the most productive industrial region of prewar Europe in the Ruhr, the Rhineland, and Westphalia. The prospect of an economically advanced West German state, flush with American funds from the Marshall Plan and closely linked economically and politically to the United States, generated acute anxiety in Moscow for two reasons: First, this embryonic political entity threatened to exert a powerful attraction on German citizens of the Soviet zone. Second, in light of the simultaneous request by Truman for the restoration of conscription in the United States and the formation of a rudimentary Western European security system (see page 40), the emerging West German state might become the spearhead of an American-backed coalition of capitalist powers in Western Europe directed against the Soviet Union and its client states in Eastern Europe.

Stalin decided on one last-ditch effort to frustrate the Western allies' bid to forge a West German state out of their three occupation zones by applying pressure on the West's most vulnerable position in Germany: the American, British, and French sectors of Berlin, whose highway and railroad links to the three Western occupation zones passed through Soviet-occupied territory. The immediate occasion for Soviet action was an arcane dispute concerning the two new German currencies issued by the Western powers and the Soviets in their respective zones. The question arose as to which one would circulate as legal tender in the city of Berlin—the Soviet zone mark, the Soviet zone mark but issued under Four-Power supervision, or both the Soviet and Western zone marks. The three Western powers agreed to permit the Soviet zone mark to circulate throughout the city (which was, after all, located within the Soviet occupation zone). But they adamantly insisted that the new currency be printed under Four-Power supervision because they feared that if the Russians were granted sole authority to manage the money supply of Berlin, they would flood the city with a currency that would rapidly lose its value and impoverish the citizens of the three western sectors. The Soviet occupation authorities just as adamantly rejected Four-Power supervision of Berlin's money supply and unilaterally began to distribute the Soviet zone mark throughout the entire city. The Western allies responded by introducing in their three sectors the newly minted deutsche mark, which was bound to find its way into the Soviet sector and destroy the weak Soviet currency. On June 24, 1948, the authorities in the Soviet zone retaliated by severing all road and rail links between the three Western zones and Berlin. From Moscow came a proclamation that the Four-Power government in the city had come to an end.

The Soviet leader's real objective in blockading the three Western sectors of Berlin was only tangentially related to the currency reform. It was in fact a last desperate bid to pressure the Western powers into revoking their plans to convoke a constituent assembly in their merged zones preparatory to the creation of a West German state. The blockade immediately threatened the 2.5 million inhabitants of the city's three western sectors with starvation, since they possessed food supplies for only five weeks. The American high commissioner in Germany, General Lucius Clay, was convinced that the Soviets were bluffing. He therefore proposed that a convey of trucks escorted by Allied armored and infantry units force its way into the beleaguered city to supply its inhabitants. But Washington and London were unwilling to run the risk of the first armed confrontation in the Cold War. Instead, they improvised an airlift of food, fuel, and medicine as a temporary expedient to buy time, although no one believed that 2.5 million people could be indefinitely supplied by air. In the meantime the Soviet Union repudiated the democratically elected municipal government of Berlin and set up a separate administration for its sector of the city. Henceforth, Berlin would be divided into two political entities.

Supplies to what henceforth would be called West Berlin dropped to a very dangerous level in December 1948 as poor visibility caused by fog restricted the number of daily flights. But with the advent of good weather in January 1949 the supplies returned to an adequate level. The improvised operation, which utilized three air corridors connecting Hamburg, Hanover, and Frankfurt to the three airfields in the Western sectors of the city, lasted a total of 324 days. At its height C-47 transport planes landed in the city at a rate of one every three minutes carrying a daily cargo of thirteen thousand tons of supplies. Stalin finally called off the blockade on May 12, 1949, when the Western allies agreed to another Four-Power meeting on Germany later in the month. This gathering produced no agreement of any significance, since the two sides had already begun to lay the groundwork for the establishment of two separate German states. President Truman persevered with the Berlin airlift because he knew that the Soviet leader would not dare risk war by shooting down American and British aircraft. The United States enjoyed a monopoly on nuclear weapons, and had a fleet of B-29 bombers capable of carrying them to Soviet targets. In the summer of 1948 the British government had asked the United States to transfer the B-29s to the United Kingdom as a deterrent to Soviet aggression in Western Europe. The Truman administration honored this request, but the sixty bombers that were dispatched to the

British isles during the Berlin blockade did not include those that had been converted to carry atomic bombs. Nevertheless, a major consequence of the Berlin blockade was the establishment in Britain of the first forward base for American nuclear weapons in Western Europe.

In the latter stages of the blockade the occupying powers proceeded with their plans for the partition of Germany. The British, French, and Americans permitted the promulgation of the Basic Law of the German Federal Republic on May 8, the fourth anniversary of Nazi Germany's surrender. The new West German state was formally established on May 23, with its capital in the sleepy city of Bonn on the Rhine. The first elections for a national parliament on August 14 produced a plurality for the conservative, pro-Western Christian Democratic Union. Its seventy-three-year-old leader, a former mayor of Cologne named Konrad Adenauer, became chancellor of the new Federal Republic of Germany. He would occupy that position for the new nation's first fourteen years. Resolutely anti-Communist, profoundly suspicious of Soviet intentions, and firmly committed to the free market policies pursued by his minister of economics, Ludwig Erhard, this shrewd Catholic politician from the Rhineland was determined to guide his fledgling state toward closer cooperation with the United States and support for its policy of containment and economic recovery in the non-Communist half of Europe.

Although still legally an occupied country, the Federal Republic ceased to be treated as a former enemy from the very day of its birth. Restrictions on industrial production were relaxed and the dismantling of German industries ceased. The trials of Nazi leaders for war crimes came to an end on the very day that Adenauer assumed the chancellorship, while the process of de-Nazification in the middle and lower echelons of German society gradually faded away. From a despised former enemy West Germany rapidly became a staunch supporter of the United States in the Cold War as well as a valuable trading partner of its former enemies in Western Europe. The influx of American economic aid through the Marshall Plan, together with Erhard's strategy of encouraging savings, investment, and the revival of industrial production and exports, began to cure the economic paralysis of this bombed-out, shell-shocked country of displaced persons. By November 1949 West Germany had already surpassed its the prewar level of production. In the early 1950s the Federal Republic embarked on a remarkable period of economic growth that would restore it to the front ranks of the world's industrial powers by the end of the decade.

As the three western occupation zones of Germany were transformed into the Federal Republic, a constituent assembly in the Soviet zone approved a draft constitution on March 19, 1949, for a separate German state in the east. The official proclamation of the German Democratic Republic with its capital in the Berlin suburb of Pankow on October 7 marked the end of a four-year period of uncertainty in the aftermath of World War II about the political future of defeated Germany. It was to be divided into Communist and non-Communist states, each adopting the political and economic institutions of its respective superpower patron. The agreement at Potsdam to treat defeated Germany as a single political and economic unit was derailed by the advent of the bitter rivalry between the United States and the Soviet Union. The partition of Germany along ideological lines was a microcosm of Europe's division into Communist and non-Communist halves. Despite periodic proposals for political reunification, Germany would remain divided for the next four decades—until the political division of Europe as a whole and the Cold War that gave rise to it came to an end.

## The Creation of an Atlantic Security System

As the non-Communist states of Western Europe began to receive American financial aid under the Marshall Plan, their political elites expressed concern that the program of economic reconstruction that was about to begin would be jeopardized seriously by what they had come to view as the security threat from the east. The formation of the Cominform and the outbreak of Communist-inspired labor agitation in France and Italy during the second half of 1947 seemed to herald a new Soviet policy of relying on the compliant Communist parties of Western Europe to destabilize that region's democratic political systems and disrupt its plans for economic recovery (see page 27). These apprehensions were aggravated in February 1948 when the Communist Party of Czechoslovakia, which had previously accepted the rules of parliamentary democracy and participated with non-Communist parties in a governing coalition, staged a coup d'État that transformed that once proudly democratic country into a one-party state subservient to Moscow (see page 7). For anxious Western European leaders the coup in Prague set an ominous precedent that the Communist parties in Western Europe might be inclined to follow. The temptation for Moscow to fish in troubled waters west of the Iron Curtain might be too great to resist.

The European statesman who worried most about the vulnerability of Western Europe to Communist intimidation was the one whose own country had the least to fear from a Communist threat from within. Pondering the consequences of Prime Minister Neville Chamberlain's discredited policy of appeasement in the 1930s, British Foreign Secretary Ernest Bevin and his colleagues in the ruling Labour Party abandoned the traditional British posture of aloofness from the European continent. In March 1947 Britain and France had concluded the Treaty of Dunkirk, a mutual defense pact that obliged each country to defend the other against aggression. But this unprecedented British security arrangement on the European continent was insufficient to calm Bevin's mounting concerns. The Treaty of Dunkirk involved only two countries and was directed specifically at the menace of German aggression, which neither signatory had much reason to fear. Between December 1947 and January 1948 the British foreign secretary campaigned tirelessly to transform the treaty's bilateral concept of mutual defense into a multilateral security system embracing other countries in Western Europe. He also emphasized that the threat to be concerned about emanated not from Germany but from the Soviet Union.

When the British Foreign Office solicited Washington's approval of this embryonic project for collective European defense, the State Department responded favorably. Fortified by this American endorsement, Bevin induced the three countries that had recently formed the Benelux customs union (Belgium, the Netherlands, and Luxembourg) to open discussions with the two Treaty of Dunkirk powers (Great Britain and France). On March 17 representatives of these five countries signed the Brussels Treaty, which committed its signatories to repel an armed attack in

Europe against any one of them. Although ostensibly serving as an insurance policy against a revival of German aggression, it was evident to all of the contracting parties that the real danger lay further to the east. It was also obvious that these five countries were incapable of defending themselves against the Soviet Union and its Eastern European satellites without the active support of Washington. Accordingly, on April 23 London initiated top secret negotiations with the United States—in which Canada was invited to participate—concerning the possibility of joining the five Brussels Treaty powers in some type of transatlantic security system directed against the Soviet bloc.

Before the Truman administration could respond favorably to this European initiative, it had to find a way of making U.S. participation in a mutual defense system covering a particular geographical area compatible with the principle of collective security enshrined in the Charter of the United Nations. As it turned out, a ready solution to this apparent difficulty was at hand in the form of Article 51 of the UN Charter, which authorized member states to enter into regional defense arrangements outside the world organization. It was this loophole in the UN's commitment to global security that had enabled the United States to join its neighbors in the Western Hemisphere in the regional security arrangements incorporated in the Rio Treaty (see page 98). Armed with this precedent, administration officials prepared to seek the requisite consent of the U.S. Senate to join America's transatlantic friends in an expanded version of the Brussels Treaty.

Like Woodrow Wilson thirty years earlier, Harry Truman faced a hostile Republican majority in the Senate that had traditionally opposed American involvement in European affairs in peacetime. But an increasing number of Republicans in the upper house were beginning to repudiate their party's isolationist tradition, which had thwarted Wilson's plans for American participation in the new international order at the end of the last war. One of these former isolationists was Senator Arthur Vandenberg of Michigan, who had helped in the drafting of Article 51 at the UN's founding conference in the spring of 1945. When the Republicans gained control of the Senate after their victory in the midterm elections of 1946, Vandenberg became chairman of the Foreign Relations Committee. Administration officials assiduously courted him in an effort to persuade the Republican legislative leader to head a bipartisan coalition in the Senate in support of the new internationalist foreign policy toward Europe. In the spring of 1948 Senator Vandenberg cooperated with Under-Secretary of State Robert Lovett in the preparation of a resolution authorizing the United States to join regional security systems across the globe in order to circumvent the Soviet veto in the UN Security Council. Introduced in the Senate on May 19, the so-called Vandenberg Resolution was adopted by a lopsided vote on June 11, 1948. The stage was set for the United States to affiliate with the European security arrangement that had recently been established in Brussels.

The second major stumbling block to U.S. participation in the emerging Atlantic security system was the lack of sufficient military manpower and weaponry to support the extensive foreign commitments implicitly envisioned by the Vandenberg Resolution. As soon as the fighting in the Pacific had come to an end, American public opinion insistently demanded the prompt demobilization of the victorious U.S. army, just as it had at the end of the last war. Within two months of Japan's defeat most American military units had lost more than half of their combat value. The draft was promptly abolished as the country reverted to its traditional preference for a small volunteer army in peacetime. The formidable American defense industry that had churned out the tanks, aircraft, ships, and artillery pieces required to defeat the Axis was rapidly reconverted to peacetime production. The Western allies sold their stock of weapons and equipment to scrap dealers in Europe. By the end of 1947 American military manpower had dwindled from 12 million to 1.4 million. All that remained of the victorious U.S. army on the continent were two lightly armed infantry divisions on occupation duty in Germany and Austria.

The formidable military power of the United States melted away so soon after World War II because there did not seem to be any reason to retain a large, well-equipped army in peacetime. The bombing of Hiroshima and Nagasaki had demonstrated that the United States was capable of subjecting any potential aggressor to utter devastation with the powerful new weapon that it alone possessed. In fact, this conception of American omnipotence was illusory because the atomic arsenal of the United States was nonexistent at the end of World War II. Japan's prompt surrender after the nuclear devastation of its two cities eliminated the necessity to construct the additional atomic bomb that was to be used against a third target had the war continued. The United States tested two more atomic bombs in 1946. By the spring of 1947, when the Truman administration began to worry about Soviet aggressiveness in Europe, the American strategic stockpile consisted of only fourteen unwieldy and unassembled nuclear weapons. But it was America's unique capability of producing these weapons of mass destruction on short notice, not the size or condition of the existing stockpile, that gave Truman and his advisers the supreme confidence that no foreign power would dare risk atomic attack by directly threatening the United States. This novel strategy of what would later be called nuclear deterrence seemed to afford a greater degree of protection for the American homeland than the Atlantic Ocean ever had in the prenuclear era.

America's monopoly of nuclear weapons, and the status of strategic invulnerability that that advantage was thought to confer, initially reinforced the country's tradition of isolationism that had been so abruptly interrupted at Pearl Harbor. To be sure, a growing number of officials in the Truman administration privately complained about the brutal manner in which the Soviet Union was consolidating its control of Eastern Europe. The new president did not hesitate to express privately his displeasure at the tightening of the Soviet grip on Eastern Europe, beginning with the tongue lashing he reportedly administered to Soviet Foreign Minister Molotov on April 23 as he passed through Washington on his way to San Francisco for the conference to establish the United Nations. But Truman fully appreciated two aspects of the Soviet Union's acquisition of hegemony in Eastern Europe that dissuaded him from venturing beyond the realm of harsh rhetoric. The first was that there was little that the United States could do to prevent it, short of waging nuclear war. The second was that Soviet domination of Eastern Europe did not threaten the vital interests of the United States and therefore did not justify the unsheathing of the nuclear sword.

But the deterioration of the relationship between the Communist and non-Communist halves of Europe in the early months of 1948 caused American officials to have second thoughts about the policy of postwar demobilization, retrenchment, and reconversion. The Communist takeover of Czechoslovakia in February played an important role in spurring the Truman administration into action to reverse this trend. On March 17, the very day the Brussels Treaty was signed in Europe, the president submitted to Congress an urgent request for the reinstatement of conscription to enhance American preparedness. While the bill was under consideration on Capitol Hill in the spring and summer of 1948, the Soviet delegate walked out of the Allied Control Council in Germany for good and Stalin imposed the blockade on Berlin (see page 34). The prospect of a military confrontation in Europe bolstered the administration's case for the peacetime draft. On June 24, 1948, Congress approved the Selective Service Act, which subjected all able-bodied males from nineteen to thirty-five years of age to compulsory military service of twenty-one months.

Armed with the Vandenberg resolution and the legislative authorization for a large conscript army, Under-Secretary of State Lovett began a series of discussions with representatives of the five Brussels Treaty powers and Canada on July 5. The objective of these talks was to draft an agreement for American participation in the embryonic European mutual defense system. By the end of the year five other West European countries—Italy, Norway, Denmark, Iceland, and Portugal—had been brought into the negotiations. After months of intensive discussions representatives of these twelve nations convened in Washington on April 4, 1949, to sign the North Atlantic Treaty. It was to be a regional defense pact whose signatories pledged to provide mutual assistance to one another against military aggression under the auspices of an entity to be called the North Atlantic Treaty Organization (NATO). With the full support of Senator Vandenberg and most of his fellow Republicans, the treaty sailed through the Senate by a vote of 82 to 13 and was signed into law by President Truman on July 25.

By joining NATO the Truman administration had repudiated two long-cherished and interrelated traditions of American foreign policy. The first was the belief that America had no business becoming entangled in European quarrels unless and until its own vital interests were directly at stake, as in 1917 and 1941. Membership in NATO entailed a solemn undertaking in peacetime to defend countries three thousand miles across a vast ocean in the event that *their* vital interests were threatened. The second historic tradition that NATO violated was the principle of pan-Americanism, which emphasized the common interests of the independent republics of the Western Hemisphere and regarded Europe as an alien civilization and a potential threat. In 1949 the United States affirmed for the first time that, along with Canada and the NATO allies in Western Europe, it belonged to an "Atlantic Community" of nations sharing a common cultural heritage that had to be defended. The new ideology of Atlanticism supplanted the traditional conception of the Atlantic Ocean as a vast moat protecting the new world from the destructive wars and noxious political ideologies of the old. The Atlantic had become instead a unifying symbol of the common principles shared by peoples of European heritage on both sides of the ocean.

# TWO

# THE MILITARIZATION
# OF CONTAINMENT

## · Nuclear Anxieties and the Shadow of NSC-68

In spite of all of its precedent-shattering elements, American membership in the Atlantic alliance fell far short of an iron-clad commitment by the United States to defend Western Europe against Soviet aggression. The NATO treaty contained a number. of loopholes through which the American government could easily slip should it determine that a military intervention in Europe was not in the national interest. Article 5 obliged each signatory only to take "such action as it deemed necessary" in response to an armed attack on another ally; this provision reserved for each member the prerogative of determining that only token action, or even no action, was called for. Article 11, which had been inserted at the behest of congressional critics of untrammeled presidential power, stipulated that the treaty's provisions be carried out in accordance with each signatory's "constitutional processes." In the American case, this meant that any use of military force under the treaty would have to be approved by Congress, which retained the sole authority to declare war. In the lexicon of diplomacy the North Atlantic Treaty lacked a provision for "automaticity," that is, an explicit pledge of prompt military intervention in response to a specified infraction such as the violation of a national frontier. In short, it constituted little more than a declaration of intent qualified by various escape clauses, hardly an iron-clad commitment on which America's European allies could rely with confidence.

The credibility of the American commitment to NATO was further eroded by the universally held assumption in the West that the Soviet Union enjoyed overwhelming military superiority in Europe. As U.S. military manpower declined drastically after the war, Soviet armed forces also dropped significantly, from 12 million in a 500-division wartime force to less than 3 million in a 175-division peacetime army. But the full extent of the Soviet demobilization was not appreciated by Western intelligence analysts at the time, who continued to believe erroneously that the Soviet Union had retained four million combat troops under arms, including 2.5 million in

*Europe in the Cold War*

a 175-division active army and 140 reserve divisions.* Even if the American president had instantaneously agreed to commit American combat forces to a war in
Europe and obtained the prompt approval of Congress to do so, it would take several

---

*Western intelligence analysts assumed that the average number of on-duty draftees was much
higher that was actually the case. Khrushchev revealed in January 1960 that Soviet military
forces in 1948 had included only 2,870,000 men rather than the four million consistently cited
by Western analysts.

months for an expeditionary force to be mobilized, trained, and transported across the Atlantic. Based on the Red Army's record during World War II, U.S. intelligence estimated that 50 of the 175 active divisions could be committed to battle thirty days after mobilization and 50 of the 140 reserve divisions within sixty days.

U.S. intelligence also noted that the Russians had retained plenty of tanks, artillery, and military aircraft from the war and had embarked on a major arms production program as well. In short, by the time an American expeditionary force returned to the continent for the third time in the twentieth century, the Russian army would probably be at the Rhine River if not at the English Channel. Although the Truman administration had persuaded Congress to reinstate the draft to help rectify NATO's perceived manpower shortage, it stopped short of requesting a substantial increase in military spending to arm and equip the Western army that was forming in Europe. The defense budget was kept at a very low level throughout the second half of the 1940s in deference to congressional pressures for lower taxes and balanced budgets. Nor did the administration dare to suggest placing American GIs in harm's way through the deployment of prepositioned American military forces across the Atlantic to bolster the outgunned, outmanned, dispersed forces of the European allies.

To compensate for NATO's inferiority in conventional forces the Truman administration chose to rely on the American nuclear monopoly, which it confidently expected to last for the foreseeable future. By threatening the prompt use of nuclear weapons against the Soviet homeland, the United States could effectively deter a Communist attack against Western Europe. But the credibility of that deterrence was undermined on August 29, 1949, when the Soviet Union conducted its first successful test of an atomic bomb, a feat that was detected by American air sampling techniques and announced by President Truman on September 22. The end of the U.S. atomic monopoly set off a wave of anxiety in Washington about the future effectiveness of the American nuclear deterrent to protect Western Europe from invasion. Truman soon learned about the possibility of fabricating a much more powerful type of weapon through the process of nuclear fusion rather than fission. He recognized that the Soviet scientists who had recently developed the fission bomb would be perfectly capable of producing the "super," as American physicists originally called the new weapon. The president therefore announced on January 30, 1950, five months after the Soviet atomic test, that the United States would begin work to construct what eventually came to be known in popular parlance as the "hydrogen bomb."

Truman subsequently instructed the National Security Council to prepare a comprehensive assessment of American security requirements in light of the Soviet nuclear test. Drafted in utmost secrecy during February and March 1950, a top secret document known as National Security Council Memorandum 68 (NSC-68) landed on the president's desk on April 7. Its authors were at pains to persuade Truman, and eventually the members of Congress and the public at large, of the urgent necessity for a full-scale program of national rearmament to cope with the Soviet threat across the globe. The memorandum painted an alarming portrait of an expansionist, messianic power that had already engulfed Eastern Europe and China (see page 177) and could conquer the rest of the Eurasian land mass unless extraordinary steps were taken by the United States. Although lacking an intercontinental delivery system that could expose American territory itself to their new weapon of mass destruction, the Soviets were expected to achieve one within five years. In the meantime Moscow could brandish the nuclear sword to browbeat America's nonnuclear allies in Europe and Asia into accepting Soviet domination. The authors of NSC-68 concluded that the shopworn containment policy devised by Kennan was insufficient to halt the inexorable advance of Communism in the world. The memorandum proposed a number of measures to meet the Communist threat in the next five years: These included a crash program to develop the hydrogen bomb to preserve America's nuclear advantage over the Soviet Union, which was expected to possess an arsenal of atomic weapons by the mid-1950s; a substantial increase in U.S. ground, air, and naval forces; and the expansion of American defense industries to produce the weapons and equipment required for this military buildup. To finance such a massive program of remilitarization, NSC-68 proposed a stunning 300 percent increase in the defense budget from $13 billion to $50 billion a year.

After examining this incendiary document and pondering the fundamental transformation of American defense policy that it implied, Truman referred NSC-68 to the appropriate specialists for an assessment of its budgetary implications. The policy recommendations contained in the memorandum sparked an intense debate within the administration throughout the spring of 1950. Secretary of State Dean Acheson became the most avid advocate of the tough new approach, contending that it was essential to counteract what he viewed as the threat of Soviet expansionism. The opponents of NSC-68, which surprisingly included Secretary of Defense Louis Johnson, retorted that the drastic increase in military spending required for the projected rearmament program would damage the country's economy and therefore compromise its long-range defense capabilities. The State Department's two most knowledgeable experts on Soviet affairs, George Kennan and Charles Bohlen, strenuously opposed the scheme on the grounds that it reflected a gross exaggeration of Moscow's geopolitical ambitions beyond the Soviet bloc and that it risked imposing an excessively rigid set of guidelines on American foreign policy. The budget-conscious Secretary of Defense and the two sober Kremlinologists found themselves in a minority within the small circle of administration officials who participated in the internal debate over NSC-68. But its proponents discovered that the president, although impressed by the force of the arguments in favor of the emergency military buildup, was reluctant to go public with the ambitious scheme for fear of generating congressional opposition because of the enormous costs that it would entail.

As the Truman administration engaged in this fundamental reassessment of national defense policy, a succession of sensational events during the winter and spring of 1950 generated widespread public anxiety in the United States about the Communist menace not in some far-off country but at home: A former State Department official and longtime friend of Secretary Acheson's named Alger Hiss was convicted of perjury for denying allegations that he had delivered top secret diplomatic documents to a fellow member of the American Communist underground. The British government announced that a German scientist named Klaus Fuchs, who had immigrated to Great Britain and then worked at the Los Alamos atomic bomb project during the war, had confessed to passing atomic secrets to the Kremlin that may have significantly assisted the Soviet nuclear program.* Six days after the Fuchs bomb-shell an obscure Republican Senator from Wisconsin named Joseph R. McCarthy claimed in a spellbinding speech in Wheeling, West Virginia, to possess irrefutable evidence that the State Department was infested with a vast network of Communist spies. It was no mere coincidence, McCarthy hinted darkly in subsequent inflamma-tory remarks, that Eastern Europe and China had succumbed to Communism and the Soviet Union acquired the atomic bomb while the Democratic Party controlled the executive branch of government. McCarthy's partisan attacks on the Truman admin-istration for being "soft" on Communism ironically occurred at precisely the mo-ment that Acheson and his allies were secretly imploring the president to adopt the "hard line" toward the Soviet Union that had been spelled out in NSC-68. But de-spite the internal advice from his closest advisers and the external pressure from the Republican opposition to "get tough" on Communism, Truman hesitated to issue a public appeal for American citizens to endure the painful economic sacrifices re-quired for a massive program of rearmament in a time of peace and prosperity.

## From Cold War to Hot War

Amid this intense bureaucratic infighting and heated political rhetoric, the Cold War was transformed into a hot war on June 25, 1950, when the Communist state of North Korea invaded the non-Communist state of South Korea (see page 185). After the United States intervened militarily on the Korean peninsula and expanded its commitments to other non-Communist states in Asia, the Truman administration took the opportunity afforded by the initial public support for the war in Korea to se-cure congressional authorization for many of the ambitious defense policies that had been envisioned by NSC-68. Most importantly, the State and Defense departments developed an elaborate plan to increase the military effectiveness of, and expand America's contribution to, NATO's strategy for the defense of Western Europe. As we have seen, the North Atlantic Treaty did not envision the deployment of U.S. mil-itary forces in Western Europe. During the congressional debate over the treaty in the spring of 1949, Secretary of State Acheson had solemnly assured nervous Senators that no GIs would be dispatched across the Atlantic in advance of a declaration of war. The U.S. role in the alliance would be to furnish technical support for the West European forces and to deter Soviet aggression through the implicit threat of nuclear retaliation. The large American conscript army that was being trained after the restoration of the draft in 1948 would be held in reserve, three thousand miles from the anticipated theater of operations across the Atlantic.

In September 1950, at the height of the Korean emergency, Truman modified this policy by making the decision to send four combat divisions to Europe to bol-ster NATO forces there. This brought the total troop commitment on the conti-nent, including the two divisions on occupation duty in West Germany, to six. This

---

*It was later discovered that a second Soviet spy at Los Alamos, a young Harvard physicist named Theodore Hall, independently supplied the plans of the first atomic bomb to Soviet intelligence in New York City. The first Soviet bomb tested in 1949 was a carbon copy of the one that was exploded in New Mexico four years earlier.

prepositioning of U.S. ground forces in Europe represented tangible proof of America's willingness to participate in the defense of Western Europe rather than simply to support it from afar. In December the NATO foreign ministers approved the transformation of the alliance's military organization from a loose-knit collection of national forces into a tightly integrated force under a central command that could deter the Soviet bloc and, if deterrence failed, defeat it on the battlefield. On December 19 Truman appointed as the first supreme allied commander General Dwight D. Eisenhower, the preeminent symbol of America's commitment to defend Europe. It was henceforth understood that that office would always be occupied by an American general. After a lengthy debate the U.S. Senate endorsed the entire package—the integrated command, the nomination of Eisenhower, and the transfer of the four American divisions to Europe—on April 4, 1951, the second anniversary of the signing of the North Atlantic Treaty.

The Truman administration proceeded to engineer a massive buildup of U.S. nuclear and conventional forces. In early 1951 the president submitted to Congress a defense budget more than three times as large as the previous one, and expanded the size of the standing army by half to 3.5 million men. In the same year Congress approved the Mutual Security Act, which merged the government's various foreign aid programs and adapted them to the requirements of Western rearmament. In 1952 the president requested a 20 percent increase in defense spending to $60 billion, most of which was earmarked for NATO to supply the U.S. troops recently deployed in Europe. The new supreme Allied commander in Europe presided over the renovated alliance system's elaborate new infrastructure that had been established at the Lisbon Conference of the Atlantic Council in February 1952, which took the form of an elaborate administrative apparatus dispersed throughout the Paris metropolitan region. At Lisbon the Allied representatives also approved an ambitious project to increase the number of NATO divisions from 14 to 50 (with an ultimate goal of 96) to counter the 175 smaller Soviet divisions, to upgrade the combat readiness of existing forces, and to complete the centralization of the command structure and the integration of the member states national forces.

Steps were also taken to develop new base facilities to accommodate the expanded military forces of the alliance. In the summer of 1952 the Truman administration opened negotiations with Spain, which up to that time had been treated as an international pariah. The European members of NATO detested the regime of General Francisco Franco, which had come to power with the assistance of Hitler and Mussolini and cooperated with the Axis during World War II. But the U.S. coveted access to Spanish territory as part of its strategy of forward defense in Europe and was willing to let bygones be bygones. In September 1953 Washington and Madrid concluded a bilateral agreement authorizing the United States to construct military bases in Spain in exchange for American economic and military aid to Franco's government. In the meantime Greece and Turkey had been admitted to NATO in 1952 because of their strategic location in the Eastern Mediterranean. Their admission revealed how far American foreign policy in the Cold War had evolved in the five years since the Truman Doctrine had been promulgated for the purpose of protecting those same two countries from the Communist menace. The original strategy of containing Soviet expansionism indirectly through the provision of economic assistance and political support to countries thought to be in jeopardy had been transformed into the direct application of American military power for that purpose. By assuming direct command of a tightly integrated military alliance and deploying its own combat forces in forward positions on the European continent, the United States had explicitly accepted the responsibility of guaranteeing the security of the non-Communist half of Europe.

The American ground forces were to be stationed along the border separating West and East Germany for two purposes that were represented to the public in metaphorical terms. First, they would serve as a "trip wire" that would trigger American retaliation with nuclear weapons (at the time borne by the long-range bombers based in the United States) in response to Soviet military aggression against Western Europe. In this sense the American troops deployed along what came to be known as the "central front" enhanced the credibility of the American nuclear deterrent, since no American president could be expected to refrain from unleashing a nuclear strike against the Soviet Union if American GIs were dying in West Germany during a conventional attack from the east. Second, the American and West European ground troops were regarded as a "shield" to delay the Communist offensive until the Strategic Air Command could unsheath and wield its nuclear "sword" against the Soviet Union.

This "shield and sword" strategy for forward defense in Western Europe was impressive in theory. But American officials had long recognized that the "shield" in the metaphor was not sturdy enough to delay a Soviet attack for long because of the acute manpower shortages that plagued the Allied armies. The Western European nations had drastically reduced their defense spending after World War II in order to concentrate on economic reconstruction. France, Great Britain, and the Netherlands had to deplete their troop strength in Europe to conduct counterinsurgency operations in their Southeast Asian possesssions (see pages 215, 251). As a result NATO's ground forces, even with the arrival of the four new American divisions, remained numerically inferior to those of the Soviet Union and its satellite armies. It was evident that drastic measures would have to be taken to bridge the manpower gap if the Western alliance's strategy of deterrence was to retain its credibility.

## The French Scheme for Western European Military Integration

The State Department had identified a solution to the problem of NATO's manpower deficit in the form of the vast, untapped reservoir of potential conscripts in the newly created state of West Germany. To American officials it seemed ludicrous to pursue a strategy of forward defense along the intra-German border while the West Germans, whose territory would inevitably serve as the battleground for any future war in Europe, were prohibited from contributing to their own security. The first overt American move in this direction had come in April 1950, when the Joint Chiefs of Staff endorsed a plan calling for West German rearmament. Secretary of State Dean Acheson refrained from raising the issue at the NATO Council meeting in May for fear of upsetting the European allies, especially the touchy French, who were expected to oppose the military revival of their historic adversary across the Rhine.

But the outbreak of the Korean War a month later spurred the U.S. secretary of state into action. At the NATO Council meeting in New York City on September 12, Acheson formally proposed the addition of ten West German divisions to NATO to shore up the alliance's defenses while American troops were tied down fighting Communist forces in Korea. The Truman administration faced a major challenge in persuading its European allies only five years after the Nazi defeat that West Germany could be trusted to bear arms. The West German people themselves were not at all enthusiastic about rearming and joining NATO. By throwing in its lot with the anti-Communist alliance system in the west, the Federal Republic would have to abandon all hope of reunification with the Communist German state in the east. But West German Chancellor Konrad Adenauer recognized the issue of rearmament as a useful bargaining chip in his bid to secure the restoration of full sovereignty for the Federal Republic: If it were to become an active participant in the defense of non-Communist Europe, West Germany's American, British, and French allies would no longer be justified in treating it as an occupied country. As early as August 1950 Adenauer had called for the formation of a West German paramilitary police force to counter the one already deployed in East Germany, and gingerly broached the sensitive subject of a German military contribution to NATO. The government in Paris refused even to consider the prospect of German rearmament, resisting Acheson's pressure at the NATO meeting in September with all the resources it could muster. But Washington bluntly warned Paris that the U.S. commitment to NATO, which the French eagerly sought, was contingent on the addition of West German units to a European force.

Faced with this U.S. campaign on behalf of German rearmament, France mounted a diplomatic counteroffensive on two fronts in the fall of 1950. First of all, it bargained hard for, and eventually secured, the deployment of U.S. military forces in Europe as insurance not only against the immediate threat from Russia but also against a future threat from Germany. (This dual concern prompted the wry comment by NATO Secretary General Lord Ismay that the purpose of the alliance from the West European perspective was "to keep the Russians out, the Americans in, and the Germans down"). Second, French policymakers had reluctantly concluded that some form of West German participation in European defense would be preferable to a Federal Republic cast adrift from its Western neighbors and susceptible to a siren song from the Eastern bloc promising reunification with East Germany. The challenge was how to enable West Germany to rearm and forge military links with her western neighbors without posing a future threat to their security.

To achieve this goal French Prime Minister René Pleven proposed on October 24, 1950, a bold scheme to break the deadlock. The Pleven Plan, which had actually been drafted by the director of the French Planning Commission, Jean Monnet, called for the creation of an all-European military force within which the national contingents of the member states would be integrated at the lowest possible level. While not permitted to have a national army of its own, West Germany would be allowed to contribute military units to this multinational force, which would be coordinated with but separate from NATO. The original proposal envisioned small German units of about one thousand men each, but after intense bargaining the French finally accepted German contingents of divisional (twelve-thousand-person) strength in the interests of efficiency. The Pleven Plan had the virtue of bolstering

*U.S. Secretary of State Dean Acheson, tireless campaigner for a North Atlantic security system that would include West Germany and deter a Soviet attack in Europe. (LBJ Library Photo by Yoichi Okamoto)*

European defense with West German manpower without creating what the other European members of the alliance were not prepared to accept: an independent German army, officer corps, and general staff. The proposed German units would be dispersed thinly throughout the ranks of a supranational army. They would receive orders from a European rather than a German commander, who would in turn report to a European minister of defense. Since the German soldiers' sense of national identity would be diluted within this supranational military organization, the prospect of a resurgence of German militarism virtually would be eliminated.

France's two principal NATO allies were initially cool to Pleven's daring proposal. The Truman administration viewed the French project as little more than a diversionary tactic to deflect U.S. pressure for German rearmament within NATO. British Foreign Minister Anthony Eden flatly refused to participate in the preliminary discussions of the initiative. But by the end of the year Washington had come to appreciate the advantages of the Pleven Plan for a European army. U.S. officials began to hail it as a brilliant means of integrating West Germany into the common European defense effort without alarming the other member countries. With the abstention of Great Britain, Pleven's proposition was taken up only by the six continental states of France, Italy, West Germany, and Benelux (Belgium, the Netherlands, and Luxembourg)—"inner Europe," as the group came to be known. A conference in November 1951 drafted the outlines of the proposed military organization, which was to be formally designated as the European Defense Community (EDC): It would comprise fourteen French, twelve West German, twelve Italian, and five Benelux divisions with an integrated supranational command only at the corps and army level.

West Germany predictably demanded an end to the inter-allied occupation controls as the price for its projected manpower contribution to the embryonic military organization. As an insurance policy against a renewal of German aggression in the future, France extracted from the United States and Great Britain a joint declaration that a threat to any member of the community would be considered a threat to their own security. With great fanfare the EDC treaty was signed in Paris on May 27, 1952, by representatives of the six member states. A day earlier American, British, and French representatives had concluded an agreement with Adenauer's government in Bonn terminating the occupation regime in the three former Western zones. West Germany would regain full sovereignty when the EDC pact entered into force after ratification by the parliaments of the six member states.

## The French Scheme for Western European Economic Integration

The French plan for a European army including West German contingents reflected a historic transformation in Franco-German relations. These two ancient antagonists had decided to bury the hatchet and join forces in the defense of Western Europe against the Soviet bloc. This *military* rapprochement between Paris and Bonn was complemented by a simultaneous bid for an *economic* partnership that the French government had launched five months before the Pleven Plan for the EDC was unveiled. On May 9, 1950, French Foreign Minister Robert Schuman issued an intriguing proposal that had been drafted by Jean Monnet, the same official who would a few months later become the ghostwriter of the Pleven Plan. Schuman suggested to Adenauer that the coal and steel production of France and West Germany be pooled and administered by a supranational authority and that all other interested European countries be invited to participate in this joint venture.

   The French authors of what came to be known as the Schuman Plan appreciated two fundamental truths about the economic situation of Western Europe. The first was that the metallurgical industries of France and Germany were complementary: West Germany possessed an abundance of high-grade coking coal while France was blessed with substantial reserves of iron ore. It therefore made perfect economic sense for the two countries to combine their resources and cooperate rather than protect their domestic steel industries and compete with one another. The second was that a prosperous and productive Western Europe was inconceivable without the full participation of West Germany. Just as the Pleven Plan for a European army had been conceived as a means of tapping Germany's vast reserves of manpower for the cause of European defense, the Schuman Plan was designed to harness Germany's potential economic productivity to the cause of European economic growth. In both of these supranational entities that crafty French planners had devised, Germany would be so enmeshed in a network of linkages with its military allies and economic partners that the former enemy's recovery would benefit rather than threaten its neighbors.

   On May 27 Great Britain turned down the invitation to participate in the preliminary discussions of the Schuman project. London was not prepared to become entangled in supranational undertakings on the continent for fear of jeopardizing both its privileged political and security relationship with the United States and its special economic ties to the remnants of its overseas empire. But Adenauer responded favorably to Schuman's proposal, which provided the Federal Republic with a creative solution to a vexing problem stemming from the allied occupation statutes: One of the concessions that France had obtained for its acquiescence in the merger of the three Western occupation zones into a West German state was the creation of the International Authority for the Ruhr (IAR), an organization dominated by the three occupying powers plus Benelux that controlled the distribution of the region's coal, coke, and steel (see page 33). By offering West Germany equal status in the newly proposed supranational authority, the Schuman Plan represented for Bonn an attractive alternative to the IAR (in which it occupied a subordinate position).

A conference attended by representatives of the same six states that planned to join the European Defense Community—France, West Germany, Italy, and Benelux—opened on June 20, 1950, and remained in session for nine months. On April 18, 1951, the six signed a treaty in Paris pledging to merge their coal, iron, and steel industries under a supranational entity called the European Coal and Steel Community (ECSC). The signatories agreed to work for the elimination of all duties on coal and steel products within the community and the establishment of a free labor market for the industries concerned. With its ratification by the six national parliaments the ECSC formally began operation on July 25, 1952, under the supervision of a nine-member High Authority headed by Jean Monnet, the French technocrat who had fed the idea to Schuman in the first place. This daring initiative in the direction of "Europeanism" did not transcend the deep-rooted traditions of national sovereignty. A parallel body known as the Special Council of Ministers that was selected from the national governments severely restricted the supranational features of the High Authority, which was hampered from the outset by petty bureaucratic infighting among the member states. When the Germans refused to accept French as the lingua franca of the community, it had to operate with four official languages. Bitter disputes over the location of its headquarters resulted in the compromise choice of Luxembourg, a temporary expedient that would eventually become permanent.

The commitment to eliminate all national barriers to the free exchange of coal and steel products among the six member states of the ECSC had strategic as well as economic implications that had been fully anticipated by its French architect. As an attentive witness to both world wars, Monnet recognized the centrality of steel production to military power. If the output of the blast furnaces in the Ruhr, the Rhineland, and Westphalia could be combined with the steel products of France, Italy, and Benelux under supranational supervision, the Federal Republic's incentive and as well as its ability to wage war against its Western European neighbors would diminish. Germany's prosperity would be inextricably linked to that of its partners in the ECSC and would therefore contribute to Europe-wide peace and security.

By opting for closer military and economic integration with Western Europe through the EDC and the ECSC, Konrad Adenauer knew that he had sacrificed the cherished goal of German reunification that was enshrined in the Federal Republic's constitutional laws: The Soviet Union would never permit its East German client state to merge with a West German entity so closely tied to the West. But three months before the EDC treaty was signed and sealed, Josef Stalin unexpectedly launched one final attempt to woo West Germany from its Western suitors. On March 10, 1952, the

Kremlin dispatched a note to the other three occupying powers proposing free elections throughout all of Germany to select a government for a reunified, rearmed, neutral state. The Soviet note was designed to block the Federal Republic's entry into the EDC by dangling before the West Germans the bait of reunification if they would accept neutrality in the Cold War. It was also directed at public opinion in the West, which might welcome a simple, straightforward solution to the German problem that lay at the heart of the Cold War in Europe. A variation of Stalin's proposal for a reunited, neutral Germany had been floated three years earlier by none other than George Kennan, the original architect of the U.S. doctrine of containment, who had concluded during the Berlin blockade that the division of Germany was a source of perpetual friction that could and should be removed in the interests of European stability.

The Western powers reacted to the Soviet note with unalloyed skepticism. While Acheson toyed with the idea of reunification and was willing to consider negotiations with the Russians to probe their intentions, France and Great Britain bristled at the prospect of a rearmed, reunited Germany cut loose from its Western moorings. After carefully considering the Soviet overture, Adenauer turned it down flat. He recognized that a reunited, neutral Germany, in light of its Soviet neighbor's preponderance of military power, would eventually fall under the sway of a regime whose political ideology he despised. In any case the West German chancellor had always regarded German reunification as a subsidiary goal. His top priority was the economic integration of West Germany into Western Europe and the development of a strong security tie to the United States. From such a position of strength the Federal Republic could eventually pursue the ultimate goal of reunification. In the long run Adenauer's policy of patience paid off, although the forty years it took was much longer than he had anticipated. Adenauer's rejection of Stalin's note was the coup de grâce for the aging Soviet dictator's belated attempt to solve the German problem through diplomacy. Throughout the spring of 1952 the three Western powers exchanged a number of notes with the Kremlin in a maneuver to buy time until the EDC treaty entered into force with West German participation. Reading the handwriting on the wall, Stalin promptly buried his proposal for good (no doubt eliciting a sigh of relief from East German Communist Party boss Walter Ulbricht and his anxious comrades). Thereafter the Soviet Union would concentrate on defending and strengthening "its Germany," discounting the other German state as a lost cause.

# THREE

# EAST–WEST GLOBAL RIVALRIES
# IN THE EISENHOWER YEARS

In early 1953 the two principal players in the first stage of the Cold War left the world scene. In January General Dwight D. Eisenhower, who had returned from his NATO command to receive the Republican nomination for president, succeeded Harry S. Truman in the White House after the presidential election held the previous November. Six weeks later, before the new administration in Washington had a chance to formulate its foreign policy, Josef Stalin died of a stroke in Moscow. Toward the end of his life the Soviet dictator appears to have suffered a severe decline in his mental faculties. He had become obsessed with imagined threats to his position from within the ruling elites of the Soviet Union and from Communist officials abroad. In 1951 he was overheard to remark, "I'm finished. I trust no one, not even myself."

What seems to have been a form of clinical paranoia prompted Stalin to dust off the old repressive methods employed during the purge trials of the 1930s to cleanse the Communist parties of the Eastern European satellites of putative critics of Soviet hegemony. The conviction of Hungarian foreign minister László Rajk of conspiracy in the summer of 1949 set the stage for a sweeping campaign against party members suspected of disloyalty to the Kremlin. The deputy prime minister of Bulgaria, Traicho Kostov, was executed along with ten associates at the end of the year. After a two-year hiatus the Soviet dictator initiated a new round of witch hunts in 1952. This time the principal victims were mostly Jews, reflecting Stalin's increasingly pathological anti-Semitism after he had reversed his earlier support for the establishment of the state of Israel and began to denounce Zionism with the same vehemence that he had customarily directed at capitalism (see page 149). In the autumn of 1952 fourteen Jewish members of the Communist elite in Czechoslovakia (including Vice Prime Minister Rudolf Slansky and Foreign Minister Vladimir Clementis) were convicted of "Titoism" and "Trotskyism." Three (including Slansky) were executed and the rest were sentenced to life imprisonment. Then in January 1953 Stalin ordered the arrest of nine Soviet physicians, six of whom were Jews, for conspiring with unnamed foreign powers to hasten the deaths of government and party leaders. There is no evidence that the Soviet dictator succumbed two months later from other than natural causes (although there are some unverified reports that his associates hastened his demise by the leisurely pace with which they summoned medical assistance when he was found unconscious).

In the immediate aftermath of Stalin's death on March 5, 1953, the Communist bloc was rife with uncertainty about the future. The purges of the Eastern European governmental and party leadership had left the satellites in the hands of timorous, subservient yes-men who owed their positions to the dead dictator, while those independent-minded officials who had escaped the executioner languished in prison. Stalin's heir-apparent in the Kremlin, Georgi Malenkov, immediately assumed control of both the government as prime minister and the party as its first secretary. But a week later his two powerful rivals within the ruling elite—the world-famous Foreign Minister Vjacheslav Molotov and the feared head of the secret police Lavrenti Beria—forced him to relinquish the top party post to an obscure operative whose modest credentials and apparent lack of ambition rendered him acceptable to all three: Nikita Khrushchev. For the next two years Prime Minister Malenkov, First Secretary of the Communist Party Khrushchev, and their colleagues were obliged to govern by the unfamiliar process of consensus—or "collective leadership" in the Communist lexicon—rather than by the customary *Diktat* of a single chief.

The almost simultaneous departure of Harry Truman and Josef Stalin from the leadership of the two superpowers in early 1953 marked the end of the critical transition from World War to Cold War. An assessment of the Soviet leader's foreign policy record in those eight years must acknowledge the extraordinary expansion of his country's power and influence at both ends of the Eurasian land mass despite the U.S. effort to prevent it. This achievement was all the more remarkable because it occurred during a period when the Soviet Union suffered two acute strategic disadvantages vis-à-vis the United States. The first was America's exclusive possession of the weapons of mass destruction that would set the standard of military power in the postwar world. While the Soviets broke the American atomic monopoly in 1949, they did not have a single atomic bomb operationally deployed at the end of the Stalin-Truman period. By that time the United States had stockpiled sixteen hundred such weapons and possessed the means—in the form of long-range bombers—of delivering them to Soviet targets without fear of reprisal. Second, the expansion of American naval power had left the United States in a position of absolute dominance on the high seas, while the diminutive Soviet navy was relegated to coastal defense. Yet despite this egregious strategic inferiority, Stalin was able to annex territory beyond his country's prewar western frontier and set up a ring of client states in Eastern Europe that were ruled by Communist political operatives slavishly subservient to Moscow. In Asia he installed a Communist client state in North Korea, assisted the Communist-controlled Vietminh in its increasingly effective guerrilla war against the French in Indochina, and had the satisfaction of witnessing the establishment of what at the time seemed a loyal Communist regime in China. All in all, it was an impressive legacy.

The United States had also vastly expanded its power and influence throughout the world in the eight years of the Truman presidency. As part of the new policy of containment it shored up the non-Communist countries of Western Europe through the provision of economic aid and military protection, which enabled them to recover from their wartime devastation and organize their regional defense. In the

Middle East Washington blocked Moscow's probes in Iran and Turkey and proceeded to develop extensive security ties with those two countries bordering on the Soviet Union. In East Asia it employed military force to prevent Communist North Korea from absorbing non-Communist South Korea, deployed its navy to prevent the new Chinese Communist regime from seizing the Nationalist Chinese redoubt on the island of Taiwan, and forged an intimate bilateral security relationship with Japan (see pages 194, 202).

In short, the two victorious nations in the war against Nazi Germany had become—in the two dominant slogans of the new age—the only two superpowers in a bipolar international system. With the crushing defeat of Germany and Japan and the decline of the British and French empires, the United States and the Soviet Union remained the only countries in the world capable of pursuing global rather than regional ambitions. Their duopoly of nuclear weapons confirmed that exalted status in the hierarchy of nations. What remained to be seen, after the disappearance of the leaders in Washington and Moscow who had presided over the creation of this bipolar world from 1945 to 1953, was whether their successors would resume the bellicose policies of the Cold War or discover means of settling their differences through diplomacy rather than confrontation.

## The Evolution of American Military Strategy

The U.S. presidential campaign of 1952 in part became a referendum on the Truman administration's foreign policy toward the Communist world. The Democratic candidate, Governor Adlai E. Stevenson of Illinois, staunchly defended the strategy of containment as an appropriate response to the Soviet threat. The Republican candidate, General Dwight D. Eisenhower, represented the new "internationalist" wing of the Republican Party that favored an active role for the United States in the world and supported many of the Truman administration's foreign policy initiatives, such as NATO and the Marshall Plan. But a vocal minority within the Republican ranks, headed by Senator Joseph R. McCarthy of Wisconsin, loudly denounced Truman and his associates for allowing Eastern Europe to fall under Soviet domination, for "losing" China to the Communists, and for pursuing a "no-win" strategy in the seemingly endless war that continued to rage on the Korean peninsula. Under pressure from McCarthy and his allies, the Republican convention of 1952 adopted a platform that condemned the policy of containment as cowardly and immoral because it abandoned millions of human beings to servitude under Communist rule. In the course of the campaign, Republican foreign policy spokespersons such as vice presidential candidate Richard M. Nixon and Wall Street attorney John Foster Dulles issued shrill demands for the "liberation" of Eastern Europe's "captive nations" through a campaign to "roll back" the Iron Curtain.

After his electoral victory Eisenhower selected Dulles as his secretary of state and delegated a substantial amount of authority to this experienced diplomat, who boasted a distinguished record of foreign policymaking from participation in the Versailles Conference of 1919 to the negotiation of the peace treaty between the United States and Japan that was signed in 1951. Dulles combined two contradictory personality traits in his approach to foreign affairs. His privately tendered advice to

Eisenhower was usually cautious and restrained, reflecting the shrewdness of the lawyer seeking an out-of-court settlement between two parties to a dispute. In public he often took rigid positions on international issues that seemed to leave no room for compromise. A strict Calvinist and stern moralist, Dulles publicly portrayed the Cold War not as a rivalry between two great powers seeking to pursue their interests in the world but rather as a Manichean struggle between the forces of good and evil, pitting the freedom-loving nations of the West against the godless despotism in the East. Judging from Dulles's fervid rhetoric, the defeat and elimination rather than the containment of Communism were to be the overriding foreign policy objectives of the new administration in Washington.

The conduct of such aggressive diplomacy obviously required the maintenance of substantial military forces to sustain it. American defense spending had already increased fourfold in the last three years of the Truman administration, as the United States fought a costly war in Korea while building up the strength of its ground forces in Europe. But the Soviet Union was able to expand the size of its conventional forces from a low of 2.8 million in 1948 to a peak of 5.7 million by 1953. It was evident that the United States would not even be able to prevent the Communist armies from overrunning Western Europe, let alone mount a campaign to "roll back" the Iron Curtain in Eastern Europe, without a substantial increase in the size of the American ground forces on the continent to reduce the Eastern bloc's overwhelming conventional superiority there. But such a military buildup would require a massive increase in the defense budget at a time when the Eisenhower administration was committed to the traditional Republican goals of reduced government spending, lower taxes, and a balanced budget. Borrowing a term from Parisian fashion magazines, the White House unveiled in 1954 what it called the "New Look" in American defense policy: It would perform the formidable feat of expanding America's military capabilities while limiting defense spending to less than 10 percent of gross national product. The plan adopted by NATO at the Lisbon Conference of 1952 to field fifty divisions in Europe was quietly abandoned because of the prohibitive cost of such a drastic increase in military manpower. Instead, the alliance would rely on U.S. superiority in nuclear weapons to dissuade the Soviet Union from waging a conventional war in Europe. The new strategy, Dulles insisted, would provide "more basic security at less cost." Secretary of Defense Charles Wilson put it more bluntly: It would yield "more bang for the buck."

The Eisenhower strategy of nuclear deterrence was not only an effective means of reducing military expenditures. It also represented a very effective means of preventing Soviet aggression in Europe: While American bombers based at home and in allied countries were capable of delivering nuclear weapons to Soviet targets, the Russians lacked a comparable means of retaliation. The Soviet Union had tested its first atomic bomb in 1949 and its first hydrogen bomb in 1953. (see page 43). But it had accumulated no stockpiles of nuclear weapons until the middle of the 1950s. Even if it had, Moscow possessed neither long-range bombers capable of reaching American targets nor bases for its air force in the Western Hemisphere. This capability of the United States to threaten the Soviet Union with nuclear devastation without fear of retaliation against its own territory reassured West European governments that the American pledge of extended deterrence would be honored.

## The Demise of EDC and the Rearmament
## of West Germany

The new American strategy for the defense of Western Europe also depended on the successful completion of the project for West German rearmament within a new European army, which would compensate for the absence of the large U.S. combat force on the continent that Washington was unwilling to deploy. Signed by representatives the six member states of the European Coal and Steel Community on May 22, 1952, the treaty establishing the European Defense Community was ratified by West Germany and the Benelux countries by the beginning of 1954. Italy prudently preferred to await the treaty's fate in the French National Assembly, where the project that had been initially proposed by the French government ran into a crossfire of criticism from both ends of the political spectrum. Followers of retired General Charles de Gaulle and other nationalist spokespeople on the right denounced the proposed European army as a smokescreen for the rearmament and revival of Germany, an intolerable infringement of French sovereignty, and a threat to the very existence of the French army. On the left the Communist Party and its allies condemned the EDC as an instrument of American hegemony in Europe that was aimed at the Soviet Union and its fraternal Socialist partners in Eastern Europe. The following summer Soviet Premier Malenkov launched an energetic campaign against the EDC, imploring France and the other West European powers to reject membership in an anti-Communist military organization that would permanently divide the continent into two hostile camps. He did not hesitate to indulge in some subtle intimidation by reminding them of the Soviet Union's recent acquisition of the hydrogen bomb. (What he did not dare admit was that the Russians did not possess a stockpile of fusion bombs, which they would not accumulate until the end of the 1950s).

Dulles applied intense pressure on the French to withstand the combination of inducements and threats emanating from the Kremlin and to acquiesce in the proposed scheme for a European army with West German participation. He warned that the U.S. Congress might refuse to continue financing American military forces on the continent if the Europeans themselves proved unwilling to bear their rightful share of the burden by supporting this regional defense organization. He heated up the rhetoric on December 14, 1953, bluntly informing a press conference in Paris that a French rejection of EDC would compel the Eisenhower administration to engage in an "agonizing reappraisal" of its European security commitments. When it later became evident that the treaty was in deep trouble in the French parliament, the American secretary of state threatened to consult with Great Britain and the countries that had ratified EDC to explore means of facilitating German rearmament without French participation.

But this pressure from Washington was to no avail. The French National Assembly buried the EDC on August 30, 1954, by a vote of 319 to 264 against a procedural motion to open debate on the ratification of the treaty. Apart from the familiar objections from the Gaullist right and the Communist left, many French legislators had been troubled by the adamant refusal of Great Britain to participate in the scheme for a European army beyond the token commitment of a single armored division to the continent: French officials feared that without full British participation in the

projected European army, France would fall under the sway of a rearmed, economically superior West Germany. But perhaps the most important cause of the EDC's
demise was the reduction of Cold War tensions in Europe following the death of
Stalin and the end of the Korean War the previous year. As the likelihood of military
conflict with the Communist bloc faded amid the improvement in East-West relations, so did the sense of urgency that had originally spawned the revolutionary idea
of fusing the national armies of Western Europe into a supranational military entity.

France's rejection of the EDC in the summer of 1954 was greeted with elation in
the Kremlin and momentarily shattered the hopes of several interested parties: Washington's hope for the prompt rearmament of West Germany so that it could share the
burden of European defense; Bonn's hope for the restoration of full West German
sovereignty as a reward for its services to the common defense of Western Europe;
and the hope of the dedicated band of European federalists within all of the prospective EDC countries that a common army, combined with the supranational management of coal and steel production already undertaken by the ECSC, would bolster
their campaign to promote the unification of Europe.

In the wake of the EDC fiasco, officials from the six signatory states joined representatives of the United States and Great Britain in the autumn of 1954 to seek an
alternative means of ensuring European defense. Dulles was inclined to revert to
Acheson's original proposal to convene the member states of NATO and simply
invite a rearmed West Germany to join, the very plan that had prompted Paris to propose the alternative of a European army in the first place. But British Foreign Secretary Anthony Eden came up with a more complicated scheme to secure West German
participation in European defense without antagonizing the French and risking a
full-blown crisis in the Atlantic Alliance. Eden proposed that the Brussels Treaty
Organization of 1948, the embryonic European security system comprising Great
Britain, France, and the Benelux countries that had been rendered irrelevant by the
formation of NATO a year later, be revived and expanded to include the two former
enemy countries West Germany and Italy. By joining the Brussels Treaty Organization, which was renamed the Western European Union (WEU), West Germany
would become a member of and contribute twelve combat divisions to NATO.

In a frenetic round of negotiations several amendments were added to Eden's
original proposal to prevent the Germans from dominating the alliance they were
about to join. As a member of the WEU Great Britain pledged to retain its own military forces on the continent, a commitment France valued as a means of offsetting
West German military power. The Federal Republic was obliged to accept a number
of restrictions on its sovereignty in military matters: No separate West German
army would be permitted to operate independently of the NATO command (in
contrast to France, for example, whose armies had fought a long war in Indochina
and were currently embroiled in a bloody conflict in Algeria); West Germany also
formally pledged never to produce the so-called ABC (atomic, biological, or chemical) weapons on its territory and to refrain from building long-range missiles, heavy
bombers, large warships, or submarines without the consent of a two-thirds majority
of the WEU.

In exchange for these restrictions on its sovereignty (which mollified the French)
and its military contribution to NATO (which pleased the Americans), the Federal

Republic obtained what Adenauer had eagerly sought since assuming power in Bonn: the end of the inter-allied occupation regime in his country and the restoration of its sovereignty. On October 23, 1954, representatives of the Brussels Treaty nations plus the United States, Canada, West Germany, and Italy convened in Paris to sign a series of agreements incorporating the aforementioned provisions. This hastily crafted alternative to the EDC smoothed the path for the termination of the occupied status of the Federal Republic and its rearmament and entry into NATO on May 9, 1955. Ten years to the day after Nazi Germany's surrender, West Germany reemerged as an ally of the United States against the other victor of World War II. The WEU would remain little more than a paper organization until it was reactivated in the 1980s by French president François Mitterrand to serve as a vehicle for European defense cooperation amid concerns about a possible reduction in U.S. forces in NATO. In the meantime, however, France's rejection of the EDC had ironically produced the result that Pleven's proposal for a European army had been designed to thwart: the emergence of a separate West German military force at the heart of the Atlantic alliance.

The Soviet Union sought to cope with the challenge of West Germany's rearmament and entry into NATO by summoning representatives of the seven Communist satellites of Eastern Europe to Warsaw for an emergency meeting. In mid-May they signed a twenty-year mutual security treaty creating a multilateral alliance that superceded the ad hoc collection of bilateral agreements that Stalin had concluded with each Communist regime. Ostensibly the Eastern bloc's counterpart to NATO, the so-called Warsaw Pact Organization would operate in the future less as a military alliance directed against the United States and its allies in Western Europe than as a mechanism for enforcing Moscow's dominance in Eastern Europe.

The rearmament of West Germany in the mid-1950s significantly strengthened NATO's conventional military capabilities for the remainder of the decade. But it did not reduce the alliance's dependence on a nuclear-based defense policy for Europe. America's intercontinental bomber force under the Strategic Air Command remained perpetually poised to deliver nuclear weapons to Soviet targets in response to a Soviet attack along the European central front. Moreover, NATO had begun in 1954 to deploy tactical (that is, short-range) nuclear weapons for battlefield use in order to compensate for the alliance's numerical inferiority in ground troops and conventional weapons. In December of the same year the alliance formally authorized its commanders to predicate their planning on the prompt use of nuclear weapons in response to a conventional offensive from the east. As Dulles put it in a pithy phrase, America had developed a capacity "to retaliate instantly by means and at places of our own choosing." This new strategy of "massive retaliation," as it came to be known, required that the United States be prepared to threaten nuclear war in order to prevent it. (The ironic motto of the Strategic Air Command, whose long-range bombers would be the instrument of such retaliation, was "Peace Is Our Profession.") The essence of deterrence was credibility. The United States, in Dulles's memorable phrase, must be willing "to get to the verge without getting into war." Although he had used the word "verge" rather than "brink," the term "brinkmanship" promptly became the reigning metaphor for his policy toward the Communist bloc.

As the Eisenhower administration moved toward a greater reliance on nuclear weapons at the expense of conventional forces, a similar trend was occurring in the Soviet Union. After consolidating his power in the mid-1950s, Nikita Khrushchev also undertook to reduce conventional military spending in favor of a buildup of Soviet nuclear capabilities that did not get into high gear until 1958 (see page 76). During the second half of the 1950s Soviet armed personnel dwindled from 5.7 million to less than 3 million as Moscow concentrated on expanding its strategic nuclear force. As the threat of a conventional attack by the Warsaw Pact in Europe receded and the U.S. army's deployment of tactical nuclear weapons in Europe permitted reductions in manpower, America's European allies hastened to reduce the size of their own conventional forces as well. In 1954 France began withdrawing divisions (ultimately four) for use in suppressing the rebellion in Algeria. West Germany reduced its manpower goals from half a million to 350,000 in 1956. Great Britain withdrew two divisions from the continent in 1957 and abolished the draft in 1959. These manpower reductions left only eighteen combat-ready NATO divisions for use on the central front, compared to the twenty-five that were envisaged after the original goal of fifty set at the Lisbon Conference of 1952 had been scrapped as unrealistic. Those that remained depended heavily on the early use of nuclear weapons in response to an attack from the east. Even the West German Bundeswehr began to deploy nuclear weapons in 1958, although the supreme commander of NATO (always an American) retained control of their warheads. By the end of the Eisenhower years war in Europe seemed unlikely, since it would immediately escalate into the full-fledged nuclear exchange that neither side was willing to risk.

### The Tortuous Path to European Economic Cooperation

The collapse of the elaborate scheme for a multinational European army was a bitter disappointment to those who had pinned their hopes on the EDC as the engine of European unification. They had assumed that since a European army would be directed by a European administrative authority and would operate in pursuit of a common European foreign and defense policy, military integration contained the seeds of political integration in the form of a federation of European states. The six signatories of the EDC pact had even gone so far as to develop a draft treaty for a European Political Community (EPC), which included such customary trappings of sovereignty as an Executive Council, a Council of National Ministers, a Court of Justice, and a popularly elected European Parliament. All of these daring ideas went down the drain with the EDC in 1954 and would be deferred for an indefinite period.

Yet the failure of the premature project for European military integration did not sound the death knell for the federalist cause. The devotées of European union promptly shifted their attention to the much more successful (although much less audacious) experiment in economic integration represented by the European Coal and Steel Community (ECSC). Jean Monnet, the visionary chairman of the French Planning Commissariat who had inspired both the Schuman Plan for the ECSC and the Pleven Plan for the EDC in 1950, resigned as head of the Coal and Steel Community's High Authority in 1955 to found an Action Committee for the United States of Europe as a means of keeping alive the federalist ideal in the wake of the EDC's demise.

Monnet had long preferred the so-called functional approach to European integration: The trick was to forge links between individual economic sectors of those nations willing to participate in a modest experiment of supranational union. Successful integration in a single sector would demonstrate the advantages of integration and produce a "spillover" effect, whereby other sectors of the economic system would be pushed toward greater integration as well. Although the economic record of the ECSC was a mixed one during the first half of the fifties, steel production had increased twice as fast within the Community as in Great Britain (which had opted to remain outside it), demonstrating the advantages of a larger market. The ever cautious, methodical Monnet floated the idea of extending sectoral integration from coal and steel to nuclear power, which he assumed would replace fossil fuels as the premier source of energy in the future and would therefore become an important catalyst of closer integration throughout the economies of the Six. In the meantime Belgian Foreign Minister Paul-Henri Spaak, supported by his colleagues from the Netherlands and Luxembourg, proposed that this gradualist approach of sectoral integration be replaced by a comprehensive attempt, first suggested by the Dutch government in 1952, to set in motion procedures for economic integration in *all* sectors of the national economies of the six ECSC member states.

In the summer of 1955 the foreign ministers of the Six met in Messina, Italy, to discuss the Benelux proposal as well as similar plans advanced by West Germany and Italy, both of which had been converted to the comprehensive (as opposed to the functionalist) approach to European integration. On June 3 the group formally endorsed the goal of creating a customs union as the first step toward a common market in goods and services and the free circulation of capital and labor within a proposed economic community. They formed an intergovernmental committee under the leadership of the indefatigable Spaak that was instructed to prepare recommendations for the implementation of these goals. In deference to the French, shell-shocked by the recent struggle over EDC and wary of comprehensive approaches to European integration, the foreign ministers forbade the Spaak Committee to recommend actual treaties and instructed it to give equal consideration to Monnet's more modest scheme for an atomic energy community modeled on the existing one for coal and steel. In the course of almost two years of arduous negotiations, most of which were conducted at the Château of Val-Duchesse outside Brussels, the Intergovernmental Committee and its various working groups systematically tackled and eventually surmounted the principal obstacles to an agreement.

The main holdout was France, which demanded special consideration for its particular social and economic institutions: To ensure that France's advanced social welfare and labor legislation would not handicap French producers obliged to compete with Community firms with lower wage and benefit costs, the other five members pledged to improve their own social legislation in order to achieve harmonization of such costs within the proposed community. Second, France obtained agreement to establish a minimum set of commodity prices that would protect its large and politically powerful farmers from cheap imports of agricultural products and to convene an interministerial conference in the future to develop a "common agricultural policy" for the Six. Third, France (backed by Belgium) persuaded the other four states that lacked or had lost their overseas empires to support a system of preferential trade links between the emerging European economic entity and the French and Belgian colonies. The two colonial powers also won acceptance of a "development fund" to finance economic projects in these overseas territories.

The proposal for preferential commercial arrangements with French colonies irritated German export and import interests, which resented having to reorient their foreign trade in order to preserve French economic dominance in Africa. German taxpayers and banking firms also balked at the proposed "development fund" for the overseas territories as a wasteful and unproductive commitment of investment capital in an unstable, risky part of the world. But in the end the Germans sacrificed their particular commercial and financial interests to the larger goal of European political integration. With these agreements in place the foreign ministers of the six ECSC countries signed the Treaty of Rome on March 25, 1957, which established the European Economic Community (EEC) and the European Atomic Energy Community (EURATOM).

EURATOM rapidly faded into insignificance and ceased to represent the agent of sectoral integration that Monnet had foreseen, as the member states insisted on according priority to their national programs of nuclear power and refused to provide adequate funds for its operation. The most significant legacy of the Treaty of Rome, which entered into effect on January 1, 1958, after the parliaments of all six signatories had ratified it, was the EEC. Its governing structure, based largely on the ECSC model, consisted of a quasi-executive commission of nine members appointed by the member governments that was charged with initiating regulations, submitting them to a Council of Ministers for adoption, and implementing those agreed to; a Council of Ministers, comprising one representative from each state and based on a complicated system of weighted voting that ensured effective control by the three largest member states (France, West Germany, and Italy), which would function as the organ of the six national governments; a Parliamentary Assembly (later renamed the European Parliament) with 142 seats (a number that later increased with the addition of new members), whose powers were purely advisory and which fell far short of the supranational legislature of which devout federalists dreamed; and a Court of Justice composed of seven judges (one from each member state plus one appointed by the Council of Ministers) that was empowered to adjudicate disputes within the three constituent communities (EEC, EURATOM, and ECSC) and interpret the provisions of the Treaty of Rome.

The purpose of the EEC was twofold. The first goal was the gradual elimination of all discriminatory restrictions such as tariffs and import quotas that hampered trade among the six member states. In addition to promoting the free movement of goods and services within the Community, the signatories of the Treaty of Rome also envisioned the eventual removal of politically imposed obstacles to the free circulation of capital (such as exchange controls) and labor (such as immigration restrictions). The second objective was to establish a coordinated trading policy toward the rest of the world. That would be achieved through a common external tariff that would shield producers within the Community from destructive competition from imports originating outside it. Both the common market and the common external tariff were to be phased in within twelve to fifteen years (although as it turned out, the latter was achieved after slightly more than ten).

Great Britain had conspicuously abstained from the lengthy and complex process that created the EEC, just as it had remained aloof from the negotiations that had produced the ECSC in the early 1950s. London's refusal to "join Europe" was prompted by two powerful motivations. First of all, it was not prepared to jeopardize what it continued to regard as its "special relationship" with the United States, which conferred upon the island kingdom a degree of prestige and influence far greater than its economic and military strength warranted. Second, even as Great Britain adapted to the inevitable loss of its far-flung empire, it was unwilling to sacrifice the preferential trade arrangements that it enjoyed with the Commonwealth. This was particularly true of the advantageous connections with those three of its member states—Canada, Australia, and New Zealand—that were populated by a European majority and from which the mother country was able to import food and raw materials at artificially low prices.

Nevertheless, the British government was taken aback by the stunning speed with which the ECSC was transformed into the much more ambitious EEC from the Messina Conference of 1955 to the Treaty of Rome in 1957. British Prime Minister Anthony Eden and his successor, Harold Macmillan, were concerned that their country would suffer adverse consequences from the emerging continental economic bloc of the Six, with whom Britain had long-standing trade relations. From the mid-1950s on British leaders had expressed open and vigorous opposition to a common market confined to the six members of "inner Europe." They advocated instead a much broader free trade area that would include all of Western Europe. Other European countries outside the Six were also concerned about the implications of the emerging economic entity and welcomed the British initiative. Such mutterings of discontent aroused suspicions among the members of the Community of a plot to derail the movement toward European economic integration. After the signing of the Treaty of Rome, the British government turned for support to the Organization of European Economic Cooperation (OEEC), the group of sixteen recipient countries under the Marshall Plan that had been formed to work cooperatively for economic recovery. In October 1957 the OEEC established a committee under the leadership of the British statesman Reginald Maudling to review the British proposal for an alternative to the emerging continental bloc.

The British government found an ally in West German Finance Minister Ludwig Erhard, who was attracted to the concept of a wider free trade area both because of his ingrained liberal economic principles and because of Germany's extensive trade relations with non-EEC European countries. But devout Europeanists among the Six began to worry that the British scheme would sidetrack the Community's progress toward full economic integration. The plan was finally killed in December 1958 by the determined opposition of the new French president, Charles de Gaulle, whose skepticism about the integrationist features of the Common Market was outweighed by his hostility to a wider free trade area in which Britain would play an important role and France's power would be diluted. De Gaulle secured German Chancellor Konrad Adenauer's support for closing down the Maudling Committee's inquiry in exchange for France's strong support for West Germany during the Soviet Union's pressure on Berlin in November 1958 (see page 80).

The demise of its project for an all-encompassing free trade zone including the six member states of the EEC prompted London to revert to the alternative of a separate organization comprising seven European countries outside the Community (Austria, Denmark, Norway, Portugal, Sweden, and Switzerland). By the end of 1959 representatives of these countries signed the Stockholm Convention, the "outer seven"'s answer to the "inner six"'s Treaty of Rome, which led in May 1960 to the establishment of the European Free Trade Association (EFTA). The latter was a much more loosely organized entity than the EEC, lacking its elaborate set of political institutions. The EFTA was also much more geographically diffuse (with members from the Iberian peninsula, Scandinavia, and Central Europe) and politically diverse (with four NATO members and three neutrals). It also had much less ambitious goals. The seven members of the EFTA simply aspired to the reduction of tariffs among themselves and showed no interest in pursuing the ambitious objectives of the Six (such as a common agricultural policy, the harmonization of social policies, a common external tariff, or closer political union). By the end of the 1950s, therefore, non-Communist Europe had been split into two separate and competitive economic blocs. This incipient rivalry complicated and even threatened the movement toward European economic cooperation that had made such headway since the beginning of the decade.

## The "Thaw" in East–West Relations after the Death of Stalin

The "collective leadership" that assumed power in the Kremlin after Stalin's death in March 1953 promptly began to implement a set of political reforms at home that commentators linked metaphorically to the improvement in weather conditions from the harsh Russian winter to the long-awaited spring. The title of a novel by the Russian writer Ilya Ehrenberg captured the essence of this evolution and provided the watchword for the new era: *The Thaw.* The new masters in the Kremlin granted amnesty to political prisoners, released the physicians who had been jailed by the paranoid Stalin shortly before his death, and restricted the power of the secret police. A flurry of economic reforms addressed the concerns of interest groups within Soviet society. These included the reduction of mandatory deliveries from the collective farms, an increase in the prices paid to individual farmers, and a decrease in retail food prices paid by urban consumers. The domestic innovations introduced by the post-Stalinist leadership were accompanied by conciliatory gestures in foreign affairs, particularly with regard to the two wars raging in Asia. The two-year-long logjam in the Korean armistice talks at Panmunjom was broken when the North Koreans and Chinese (with some prodding from Moscow) dropped their demand for the compulsory repatriation of their prisoners of war, which paved the way for the signing of an armistice agreement in July (see page 179). A year later the Vietminh were pressured by their Soviet and Chinese patrons in July 1954 to swallow a compromise settlement at Geneva that denied them the fruits of their recent military successes against the French colonial army in Vietnam (see page 223).

The pace of this trend toward greater flexibility in Soviet foreign policy increased dramatically after Party First Secretary Nikita Khrushchev finally completed his patient bid for primacy in the Kremlin on February 8, 1955, when his rival Georgi Malenkov was forced to resign as prime minister in favor of the amiable nonentity

Nikolai Bulganin. The first important foreign policy initiative undertaken by the new undisputed leader in Moscow concerned the long-deferred question of the political fate of Austria, which had been severed from Germany at the end of the war and was subjected to a Four-Power military occupation regime on the German model. Austria's unique postwar experience demonstrated that a joint occupation by Communist and non-Communist powers need not result, as it had in Germany, in the partition of the country along ideological lines. The four occupying powers in Austria had permitted free nationwide elections to be conducted in November 1945. The Austrian Communist Party received a paltry 5 percent of the popular vote and had to settle for a minor post in the coalition government that was formed. But the emergence of a freely elected government in Vienna with jurisdiction over the four occupation zones did not immediately lead to independence and the end of foreign military occupation, because Moscow insisted on linking Austria's political future to progress on the much more important and contentious issue of Germany. But once the German question was settled to the detriment of the Communist bloc at the end of 1954 with the rearmament of the Federal Republic and its incorporation into NATO, the Soviet leaders decided to liquidate the Austrian affair once and for all. The Austrian State Treaty that was signed on May 15, 1955, provided for the evacuation of all four occupation forces from the country, which would regain its political sovereignty on the condition that it remain perpetually neutral. The withdrawal of the Soviet troops from their occupation zone in eastern Austria marked the first such pull-back since the evacuation of northern Iran in 1946. Thereafter neutral, independent Austria would represent a remarkable anomaly at the center of Europe next to a Germany that had been divided along ideological lines and whose two halves had aligned with one of the two superpowers in the Cold War.

In addition to evacuating its occupation zone in eastern Austria, the new Kremlin leadership took other steps in 1955 that seemed to confirm its new taste for disengagement and détente. On May 14 the Soviet Union relinquished its lease of the naval base at Port Arthur (Lüshun) and the right to use the commercial port at Dairen (Dalny) on the Liaotung Peninsula of Manchuria, in accordance with an agreement reached in the previous year with the People's Republic of China. On September 19 Moscow signed a treaty with Finland restoring to that country the Porkkala naval base, which Stalin had obtained on a fifty-year lease in 1947. In an act of contrition designed to heal the rift with Marshal Tito and normalize relations with the renegade Communist regime of Yugoslavia, Khrushchev and Bulganin had flown to Belgrade in May. This symbolically potent pilgrimage encouraged reform-minded Communist Party notables throughout the rest of Eastern Europe, many of whom had been purged and imprisoned on charges of "Titoism" in the last years of Stalin, to envision the possibility greater freedom from Moscow's control.

This new Soviet posture of accommodation in foreign policy was related to the intense struggle for succession in the four years after Stalin's death. Khrushchev shrewdly outmaneuvered his political rivals by playing one off against the other. He initially allied with Molotov (a staunch defender of Stalin's legacy) to topple Malenkov from the premiership, then turned on Molotov later in 1955 to remove the old Stalinist hard-liner from the center of power (while retaining him as foreign minister). The wily Khrushchev finally acquired total political primacy in 1957 (although he did not add the title of prime minister to his portfolio until March 1958). He achieved his final triumph by fending off a campaign mounted by the so-called Anti-Party Group to depose him, engineering the expulsion of his three principal rivals (Malenkov, Molotov, and Kaganovich) from the Presidium and the Party Central Committee.

While the post-Stalin leadership in the Soviet Union was laboring to develop a foreign policy aimed at reducing global tensions, a renowned leader in the West was moving in the same direction. British Prime Minister Winston Churchill, who had returned to power in 1951 after six years in political opposition, became a staunch advocate of détente with the Soviet Union because of his mounting anxiety about the threat of nuclear war. Churchill had been a staunch supporter of nuclear weapons at a time when the United States alone possessed them. During the war he adamantly had opposed sharing nuclear secrets with the Soviet Union and encouraged Truman to use the atomic bomb against Japan. As leader of the opposition during the early years of the Cold War, the author of the virulently anti-Communist "Iron Curtain" speech urged that Stalin be threatened with nuclear attack unless he halted his aggressive policies in Europe. But the USSR's acquisition of the atomic bomb in 1949 filled Churchill with dread about the prospects of an atomic Armageddon that would wipe out civilization. Once in power he concluded that the most effective means of averting a nuclear holocaust were periodic face-to-face contacts between the leaders of East and West. Stalin's death and the emergence of more flexible successors prompted Churchill to take action in pursuit of that goal. On May 11, 1953, this seasoned veteran of the wartime meetings of the Big Three publicly proposed the convocation of the first summit conference since the meeting at Potsdam eight years earlier. It was evident that the eminent British statesman hoped to crown his long career with a personal encounter with the new Soviet leadership to test its willingness to resolve the outstanding disagreements inherited from the Stalin era and perhaps even bring the Cold War to an end.

To convert the new Soviet leadership to the idea of a summit meeting, Churchill addressed the one problem that stood in the way of East-West détente in Europe by privately refloating Stalin's moribund scheme for a reunited, neutral Germany. Churchill's proposal prompted a sharp split in the Kremlin as the pretenders to Stalin's throne jockeyed for position. On May 27 the powerful chief of the secret police, Lavrenti Beria, dropped a bombshell by calling for the reunification of Germany and the abandonment of Moscow's puppet state in East Germany, arguing that a neutral, unified Germany would pose no threat to the Soviet Union. Arrayed against him in an intense political struggle over Soviet policy toward Germany was the powerful troika of Molotov, Khrushchev, and Malenkov. In early June the dispute within the Politburo resulted in a compromise: No action would be taken on Beria's proposal for reunification; but the East German party leaders were ordered to abandon their recently announced policies of rapid socialization of industry and collectivization of agriculture, in the hopes that such a policy reversal would stem the East German public's growing dissatisfaction with its government. East German party boss Walter Ulbricht dutifully announced the abrupt about-face on June 10, but committed a fateful blunder by failing to rescind a recent decree requiring a 10 percent increase in work norms (which in effect meant a cut in wages). The retention of this unpopular policy poured cold water on the rising expectations among the East German population that had been stimulated by the suspension of Ulbricht's harsh measures of socialization. Enraged workers in East Berlin staged massive strikes on June 16–17 to protest the oppressive new working conditions. This labor unrest spread to several other cities and rapidly escalated into provocative political demands for free elections and German reunification, posing the first serious challenge to Moscow's authority in Eastern Europe since the end of the war.

The East German riots of June 1953 confronted the new Eisenhower administration in Washington with a painful dilemma: This unprecedented outbreak of unrest behind the Iron Curtain seemed to provide an ideal opportunity to convert the aggressive Republican rhetoric of "rollback" and "liberation" into an effective policy. Since the three Western allies enjoyed the right to unimpeded movement throughout the entire city of Berlin, the unrest in the Soviet sector unfolded in full view of American, British, and French occupation officials as well as news media from the non-Communist world. Emotionally charged reports of the Berlin uprising were transmitted to the rest of East Germany by Radio Free Europe, an ostensibly private (but covertly CIA-financed) anti-Communist broadcasting station operating in Munich. As the insurrection spread to several other East German cities, Soviet troops were called in to restore order. But the Western response was confined to the aggressive use of radio propaganda to embarrass the Soviet Union and its East German clients. The CIA station chief in Berlin was denied permission to furnish weapons to the rioters, while American, British, and French occupation forces in the city looked on as Soviet troops crushed the revolt with tanks and infantry.

The East German party boss, Walter Ulbricht, was initially blamed for the unrest and was edged out as party secretary. But on June 26 Khrushchev, Malenkov, and Molotov exploited the crisis in East Germany to make their move against Beria, whose provocative proposal for German reunification they blamed for the explosion of political unrest in the GDR. This conspirational trio persuaded the Presidium to order the arrest of the feared police chief on trumped up charges of treason. Profiting from Beria's sudden fall from power, Ulbricht skillfully engineered his own rehabilitation by denouncing his domestic opponents as accomplices of the disgraced Soviet police chief, who was promptly convicted and executed. In time the ruthless East German strongman purged his rivals and consolidated his grip on power with the full support of the Soviet leadership. Meanwhile, the Central Committee Plenum that had been convened in Moscow in July to approve Beria's arrest also denounced his proposal for German reunification. Khrushchev angrily charged that it would sacrifice the East Germans to Western domination, and warned that a united Germany, even if established as a neutral state, was bound to threaten the Soviet Union in the future. Stalin's successors had finally resisted the alluring prospect of a reunited, neutral Germany under indirect Soviet influence, preferring half of Germany under direct Soviet control.

In the meantime Churchill's own attempt to revive the cause of German reunification as a means of ending the Cold War failed to obtain the support of his cabinet for the opposite reason: The British worried that a unified, disarmed Germany with no ties to the West would inevitably fall under the control of the superpower to the East. If permitted to rearm, a neutral Germany could revert to its traditional policy of playing off East against West or, worse, align itself with the Soviet Union. In short, both sides had come to appreciate the danger of allowing Germany to reunite while Europe was divided into two armed camps because the newly united country would be free to lean to one side or the other and thereby radically upset the continental balance of power. A divided Germany was a safer alternative for both blocs, although Western statesmen continued to pay lip service to the cause of reunification for fear of offending the West German public that still believed in it.

Although abandoning his scheme for German reunification, Churchill continued to press for a summit conference to sort out the set of unresolved issues related to the political status of Germany. Eisenhower had continually fended off Churchill's insistent pleas from the early days of his presidency for a high-level meeting. But in November 1954 the American president reduced his preconditions to a satisfactory settlement of the Austrian question, which was finally achieved with the signature of the Austrian State Treaty on May 15, 1955 (see page 65). The day before the signing ceremony, Molotov had informally agreed to a summit meeting in July. Eisenhower was finally persuaded that such a face-to-face meeting might be useful, if for no other reason than to get a sense of who was in charge in the Kremlin after Malenkov's replacement by Nikolai Bulganin as prime minister earlier in the year.

For the first time since the Potsdam Conference ten years earlier, the leaders of the major powers met at the former headquarters of the League of Nations in Geneva on July 18–24 1955. The "Big Four" gathering included Eisenhower, Bulganin (accompanied by the Communist Party First Secretary, Nikita Khrushchev), and Prime Ministers Anthony Eden of Great Britain and Edgar Faure of France. Eden had finally succeeded Churchill the previous April, depriving the old war-horse of his long-cherished hope of one final meeting with the Soviet leadership before fading from the world scene. Nothing of significance resulted from the private conversations of the four leaders in Geneva. The heads of government issued impassioned pleas for a political settlement in Europe and a halt to the nuclear arms race, but offered no practical proposals for how to achieve those ambitious goals. They agreed to an innocuous endorsement of German reunification on the basis of free elections. But they failed to address the insuperable obstacle to a political settlement for Germany—the fundamental question of how those elections should be organized— and Bulganin and Khrushchev stopped off in East Berlin on their return to Moscow to reassure East German party leader Walter Ulbricht that his regime's interests would not be compromised. Bulganin's stirring call for the total abolition of nuclear weapons was disingenuous, since it ignored the single most important roadblock to such an agreement: As we shall see, the United States had consistently demanded on-site inspection to verify compliance as a condition for any arms control agreement, while the Soviet Union had just as consistently rejected such inspection as a violation of its national sovereignty (see page 115).

The only dramatic moment at the Geneva summit occurred when Eisenhower strove to break the deadlock on arms control with his so-called Open Skies proposal: To overcome the Kremlin's objections to intrusive on-site inspection of its nuclear facilities, the American chief of state proposed that the two superpowers permit aerial photography of each other's sites. When Bulganin, the ostensible head of the

Soviet delegation, surprised everyone by expressing interest in this imaginative solution to the deadlock on arms control, Communist Party chief Khrushchev revealed who was really in charge in the Kremlin by buttonholing Eisenhower to denounce the scheme as a cover for American espionage and reject it out of hand. The abortive Open Skies proposal represented a last-minute effort by Eisenhower to secure Soviet agreement on a mutual reconnaissance arrangement before the United States proceeded unilaterally to implement such a program of its own. In November 1954 he had ordered the development of a high-altitude aircraft called the U-2 that would be capable of conducting aerial photography beyond the range of Soviet surface-to-air missiles and fighter aircraft. The U-2 flew its first missions over Moscow and Leningrad in July 1956, a year after Khrushchev had turned down Eisenhower's Open Skies offer at Geneva.

Despite the absence of agreement on Germany or arms control, the Geneva Conference represented a symbolically important breakthrough in the Cold War. Newspaper photographs of Soviet and Western leaders chatting amiably on the lawn of the conference center provided a vivid contrast to the confrontational style of the previous ten years, when they communicated only by harshly worded memoranda and press releases. The world press hailed the "spirit of Geneva" for ushering in a new era of East-West cordiality. It soon became evident that the conciliatory gestures emanating from Moscow in the mid-1950s reflected more than just a crafty public relations ploy. They seemed to herald a genuine effort on the part of the new leaders in the Kremlin to inaugurate a fundamental transformation of both the foreign and domestic policies of the Soviet Union.

The apotheosis of this new orientation came in February 1956, when Khrushchev convened the Twentieth Congress of the Communist Party of the Soviet Union, the first such gathering since Stalin's death three years earlier. In a well-publicized speech the Soviet leader formally abandoned the Leninist doctrine that war was inevitable between the capitalist and Communist world and explicitly defended a new policy of "peaceful coexistence" with the West. Then, in the late evening of February 24, Khrushchev abruptly summoned the delegates to a special session from which all outsiders were excluded. Around midnight he began a rambling, four-hour harangue against the "crimes" of Josef Stalin: the imprisonment and murder of innocent people in all walks of life; the "cult of personality" that had enervated the leadership of both government and party; the insistence on absolute and unquestioned subordination by foreign Communist leaders that had led to the break with Yugoslavia's Tito. The stunned delegates left the conference with copies of the remarkable speech with instructions to discreetly reveal its contents to party officials at closed meetings throughout the country. Soon thereafter Khrushchev took a number of other steps to reaffirm his commitment to relax the Soviet grip on the Eastern European satellites. In April he dissolved the Communist Information Bureau (or Cominform), which Stalin had created in 1947 to ensure Soviet control of the European Communist parties. In June he removed the unreconstructed Stalinist Molotov as foreign minister. Later that month he accorded a lavish welcome to Marshal Tito, who visited Moscow for the first time since the Soviet-Yugoslav break in 1948 and delivered a stern lecture to his hosts about the need to grant greater freedom to the Communist regimes in Eastern Europe.

## The Consequences of De-Stalinization in the Satellites

Khrushchev had launched this campaign of "de-Stalinization" in the hope of promoting an orderly transformation of the relations between the Soviet Union and its
satellites on the basis of the principle of "separate roads to socialism." This shift
from a coercive to a more consensual relationship was intended to alleviate the smol-
dering resentments in the Eastern European countries against Soviet domination,
which threatened the cohesion of the Communist bloc. The first country to test the
Kremlin's new conciliatory policy was Poland. Throughout the spring of 1956 ambitious reformers in Warsaw seized the opportunity afforded by the recent death of the
hard-line Communist Party leader Boleslaw Bierut to purge a number of orthodox
Stalinists in high places and to release some twenty-eight thousand political prisoners.
To justify these liberal measures to hard-liners in the ruling elite, Polish officials
began to circulate copies of Khrushchev's "secret speech." One of these was obtained
by U.S. intelligence and leaked to the *New York Times,* which published it on June 4.
By the end of the month thousands of factory workers in the city of Poznan were on
strike to protest the deterioration of their living standards, which had been caused in
part by Soviet pressure on the Polish government to shift resources to heavy industry
at the expense of consumer goods. As the strike degenerated into a bloody clash with
police, the labor unrest began to acquire ominous political overtones: Demonstrators
began to chant anti-Russian slogans and to demand government reforms, such as an
end to collectivization in agriculture and the establishment of workers' councils in
industry on the Yugoslav model of "self-management." When the army and police
refused to fire on the demonstrators, the government promptly caved in to many of
their demands for better working conditions in the hopes of defusing a potentially
explosive political situation.

   Amid this growing turmoil the political leadership in Warsaw turned to the only
man deemed capable of steering a middle course between an anti-Communist insurrection and a Soviet military intervention: Wladyslaw Gomulka, an openly anti-
Stalinist party leader who had been jailed from 1951 to 1954 for "Titoist" activities.
On October 19, as the Polish Communist Party prepared to elect Gomulka party secretary, a high-level Soviet delegation headed by Khrushchev himself suddenly flew
uninvited to Warsaw and demanded entry to the party meeting. To the astonishment
of the Soviet visitors the Polish Communist Party plenum refused them admission,
elected Gomulka party secretary, and warned that if the Soviet army intervened in
Poland the new reformist government in Warsaw would arm the Polish workers and
resist the invaders. In the face of ominous troop movements beyond Poland's border
with the Soviet Union, Gomulka reassured the agitated Russian officials of Poland's
loyalty, declaring that he and his reformist colleagues were merely following the
lead of the de-Stalinization campaign that Khrushchev himself had launched the
previous February. Satisfied with these reassurances, Khrushchev announced his
support for Gomulka and abruptly returned to Moscow. For the first time since the
establishment of the Soviet satellite empire in Eastern Europe, a national Communist leader had successfully negotiated a compromise agreement with the Kremlin
bosses rather than simply capitulate to their demands or (in the case of Tito) leave
the fold.

The Gomulka government proceeded to develop plans for the de-collectivization of agriculture and the de-emphasis on heavy industry, two quintessentially anti-Stalinist policies. It formed a working relationship with the influential Catholic church after releasing from prison Stefan Cardinal Wyszynski, who had been interned by the previous Stalinist government. On the other hand Gomulka prudently reaffirmed Poland's membership in the Warsaw Pact, announced full support for Soviet foreign policy goals, retained the Communist Party's monopoly on political power, and kept a tight lid on the Polish press to prevent criticism of the regime and its Soviet backers. By steering this middle course, the shrewd advocate of "national communism" in Warsaw was able to preserve a substantial margin of maneuver without provoking overt Soviet interference in Poland's domestic affairs.

In the meantime the political unrest in Poland had spilled over into Hungary, where two competing factions within the Communist Party had been struggling for supremacy for the past three years. In July 1953 the reform-minded Hungarian Communist leader Imre Nagy had replaced Matthias Rakosi after the latter's orthodox Stalinist economic policies had generated widespread popular discontent. Rakosi's campaign to promote heavy industry at the expense of consumer goods led to a notable decline in living standards and alienated the urban worker class. His compulsory collectivization of agriculture generated food shortages and antagonized the farmers. Once in power, the reformer Nagy acquired widespread popularity by shifting resources from heavy to light industry, suspending the collectivization campaign, and tolerating a considerable degree of intellectual freedom. But when Nagy's Soviet patron Malenkov fell from power in February 1955, Rakosi regained the premiership in Budapest and tried to revive his hard-line political and economic policies. Amid this bitter struggle in Hungary between orthodox Stalinists and reformers, Khrushchev's denunciation of Stalin and then Poland's successful defiance of the Kremlin played into the hands of Rákosi's domestic critics. Khrushchev's decision to replace the unpopular Rákosi with the hard-liner Ernö Gerö enraged the reformers, who clamored for the return of Nagy. When Hungarian police fired into a crowd of demonstrators praising the Polish reforms on October 23, events in Budapest began to career out of control. With members of the police and army defecting to the rebels, Prime Minister Gerö appealed for Soviet military assistance to suppress the spreading insurrection.

Workers' and students' councils spontaneously sprouted throughout the country, demanding free elections, the withdrawal of all Soviet troops, and the end to government repression. The alarmed Kremlin leaders hesitated to resort to military force and turned in desperation to the reformer Nagy, whom they hoped would emulate Gomulka by co-opting the insurrectionary movement with conciliatory gestures without threatening Soviet hegemony in the country. But popular rage at the Soviet Union and its political stooges in Budapest had reached such a height of intensity that a Gomulka-type policy of co-optation was no longer possible in Hungary. As Soviet military units began to evacuate the capital on October 28, Nagy formed a coalition government including the non-Communist Smallholders Party, which had been outlawed since the advent of the Cold War. To placate his aroused domestic constituency, the new prime minister thereupon took an additional step that was guaranteed to provoke a sharp reaction in the Kremlin. He announced plans for nationwide elections in which all political parties would be permitted to participate, a policy that carried the direct threat that the unpopular Communist Party would be voted out of power. In the meantime the Soviet military units pulling out of Budapest interrupted their departure and began to regroup near the airport, while others began to enter the country from Romania. In a panic over these ominous troop movements, Nagy announced on October 1 Hungary's withdrawal from the Warsaw Pact and its intention to join its neighbor Austria in absolute neutrality. Anticipating the hostile reaction that was certain to emanate from Moscow, the Hungarian prime minister issued a frantic appeal to the United Nations for protection.

Suddenly the reformist trends in the Communist bloc that had begun under Malenkov in the immediate aftermath of Stalin's death and accelerated by Khrushchev's secret speech three years later had reached a crossroads. The process of de-Stalinization had opened a Pandora's box in Eastern Europe. A non-Communist, neutral Hungary would set a dangerous precedent that could undermine Soviet dominance in a region that Moscow deemed essential to its security. Khrushchev therefore resolved to nip the Hungarian insurrection in the bud. On November 4, the 250,000-man Soviet army accompanied by five thousand tanks reversed its withdrawal from Budapest and reentered the Hungarian capital. In three days of pitched battles the invasion force killed over twenty thousand Hungarian citizens, removed Prime Minister Nagy from office, and replaced him with the new secretary of the Communist Party, János Kádár, (who had fled to the Soviet Union during the crisis and requested Soviet military intervention to "rescue" Hungary from the reactionary counterrevolution).*

The brutal suppression of the Hungarian Revolution in the autumn of 1956 revealed the limits of Khrushchev's reformist impulses and provided the West with a powerful weapon in its propaganda war with the Soviet Union. The images of unarmed freedom fighters in Budapest facing Soviet tanks inflamed public opinion throughout the non-Communist world. It prompted an exodus of intellectuals from the Communist parties of Western Europe and a flurry of recriminations from disillusioned supporters of Khrushchev's de-Stalinization campaign. But while the Kremlin suffered acute embarrassment in the West, the consequences of the Hungarian affair were negligible within the Communist bloc. Khrushchev had sought and obtained the prior approval of Poland's Gomulka and even Yugoslavia's Tito for the intervention in Budapest. From Beijing Communist Party leader Mao Zedong conveyed a message of support. They all agreed that the Hungarian Revolution had gotten out of hand and had to be liquidated.

Nor did the Kremlin have anything to fear from the governments in the West. The Eisenhower administration had been caught completely unawares by the events in Hungary and remained entirely disengaged as the crisis moved toward its bloody dénoument. The NATO countries had no common border with Hungary and therefore could not easily have sent military assistance to the revolutionaries in Budapest even if they had wanted to. Eisenhower vetoed proposals for airdrops of small arms to the

---

*After seeking asylum in the Yugoslav embassy, Nagy departed with a guarantee of safe passage from the new regime. On leaving the embassy he was seized, imprisoned, and eventually executed in June 1958.

rebels. The West's support for the Hungarian insurgents was confined to verbal encouragement on the airwaves of Radio Free Europe and Voice of America. Some of
the Hungarian rebels erroneously interpreted these propaganda broadcasts as hints
that NATO was prepared to intervene if the Soviet Union resorted to military force to
suppress the revolt. In fact, the U.S. government was distracted by the forthcoming
presidential elections, and a unified Western response to the Hungarian drama was
precluded by the bitter dispute between the United States and its British and French
allies during the Suez crisis (see page 157).

## The Extension of the Cold War to the "Third World"

By the middle of the 1950s the political situation in Europe had stabilized after a
decade of tension. The Soviet Union had acquiesced in the rearmament of West
Germany and its inclusion in the Atlantic Alliance. The United States had signaled
its acceptance of Soviet hegemony in Eastern Europe by its refusal to interfere with
Moscow's suppression of the Hungarian Revolution. During this period of stability
in Europe, the Soviet leadership began to direct its ideological appeals abroad to
curry favor with peoples inhabiting the "Third World," a new term referring to the
region that had recently achieved, or was about to achieve, emancipation from
European colonial domination. Khrushchev's accession marked the triumph of the
leadership faction that rejected the traditional Stalinist strategy, doggedly defended
by Molotov until his fall from power in 1955, of according top priority to Europe in
the formulation of Soviet foreign policy. The new number one in the Kremlin had
come to view the anticolonial struggle by the nonwhite peoples of the earth as a
golden opportunity for the Soviet Union: By courting the anti-imperialist movements of Africa and Asia, Moscow could circumvent the obstacles to the expansion
of Soviet influence that the West had erected in Europe. The means to this end would
be words rather than bullets, propaganda rather than armed force.

The Soviet Union was well positioned to pose as the champion of self-determination on behalf of the victims of European colonial exploitation. While in exile before
the Bolshevik Revolution, Lenin had written an eloquent denunciation of European
imperialism: He depicted it as an inevitable outgrowth of industrial capitalism in its
advanced stage of development, as the great powers lunged for overseas sources of
cheap raw materials as well as markets for their surplus products and capital. Once in
power in Russia Lenin established in the spring of 1919 the Communist International
(or Comintern) to promote the cause of revolution across the globe. The Comintern
was particularly active in the colonial world, where its agents combined the old
rhetoric of social revolution with the new language of national liberation in an effort
to win the sympathy of the indigenous peoples. This campaign against imperialism
had proved uniformly unproductive and was later abandoned by Stalin, who preferred to deal with foreign leaders rather than foreign revolutionaries and concentrated on building up the economic and military strength of his own country. But the
haunting strains of the Communist anthem, the *Internationale,* continued to herald
this historic link between Marxism-Leninism and anti-imperialism: "Arise, ye prisoners of starvation, arise, ye wretched of the earth. Let justice thunder condemnation, a
better world is in the birth."

In November 1955 Khrushchev and Bulganin revived the long-dormant cause of anti-imperialism with a whirlwind tour of South Asia, which included public speeches before large and appreciative audiences in India, Burma, and Afghanistan. This tour by the two top Soviet leaders was not merely ceremonial. It resulted in concrete pledges of economic assistance to the three host countries, a development that marked a new phase of the rivalry between Moscow and Washington. Thereafter the two superpowers would compete for the favor of developing nations through the mechanism of what came to be known as "foreign aid." Its autocratic political system and the command economy gave Moscow an initial advantage in this rivalry, since it could mobilize and channel economic resources into politically prescribed directions without regard to the dictates of the market or the complaints of taxpayers. The Soviet Union was too economically undeveloped to dispense its largess without requiring something in return. Since the ruble was inconvertible, the typical medium of exchange was the primitive practice of barter: Developing countries would pay for Soviet manufactured goods with commodities or raw materials. The level of Soviet foreign aid paled beside that of the much wealthier United States, while the disappointing record of Soviet agricultural production prevented Moscow from dispensing the one product that was in great demand in the Third World: food. But this strategy of competing with the capitalist West in the world beyond Europe reflected Khrushchev's serene confidence in the future: He was convinced of the ultimate superiority of the Soviet system of central economic planning, whose success in the USSR would serve as a model for the developing countries as they faced the challenge of economic development.

The Soviet economy actually achieved an impressive record of growth in the 1950s, largely by concentrating on production in heavy industry at the expense of the consumer sector. This success attracted the attention of the new ruling elites in a few non-Communist countries of the Third World such as India and Egypt, which saw Soviet-style state planning as an efficient way to overcome centuries of economic backwardness through a crash program of modernization. Yet despite Moscow's energetic campaign to woo them, none of the newly independent states—with the notable exception of North Vietnam—embraced the Communist ideology or aligned with the Soviet Union in the Cold War. Instead, some were drawn into anti-Communist alliances with the United States and its European allies, while others clung to the policy of nonalignment in the East-West struggle.

The Eisenhower administration had undertaken a vigorous campaign to enlist Third World countries to join regional security systems that were designed to block the expansion of Soviet or Chinese power across the globe. The first of these was formed as France prepared to evacuate Indochina after the Geneva Conference of 1954 (see page 224). Concerned that the French withdrawal from Southeast Asia would leave a dangerous power vacuum that might be filled by the Communist regimes in China and North Vietnam, American Secretary of State Dulles convened a conference of pro-American states in Manila in September 1954 to meet the challenge. The product of these deliberations was the Southeast Asia Collective Defense Treaty, whose signatories included the United States, the former European colonial powers Great Britain and France, and two countries in the region with governing elites of European origin—Australia and New Zealand. Although all non-Communist countries in the area had been invited to sign the pact, only three of them that were heavily dependent on American aid—Pakistan, the Philippines, and Thailand—accepted. To implement the provisions of the treaty, the eight signatories established in 1955 the South East Asia Treaty Organization (SEATO), which would be administered by a council of permanent representatives and a secretariat located in Bangkok, Thailand. Although advertised by Dulles as an Asian counterpart to NATO designed to contain Communism in the region, SEATO was much more loosely organized than the American-dominated alliance in Europe: It had no integrated military command structure, its member states were committed only to mutual consultation in the event of aggression, and there was no formal connection to the American nuclear deterrent.

To bridge the geographical gap between NATO in the West and SEATO in the East, Dulles encouraged the pro-Western states in the Middle East to form a regional security organization as well. Two of them, Turkey and Iraq, had signed a bilateral defense treaty known as the Baghdad Pact in February 1955. By the end of the year they were joined by Pakistan, Iran, and Great Britain (which remained a power in the region by virtue of its continuing naval presence in the Persian Gulf). Although all of the Arab states in the Middle East were invited to join, none of them followed the lead of the pro-British regime in Iraq. Although the United States did not formally accede to the Baghdad Pact, it acquired observer status in the new regional organization's governing council, furnished military assistance to its member states, and later signed bilateral agreements with Turkey, Iran, and Pakistan pledging to defend them against Communist aggression.

The United States and its European allies had thus succeeded by the mid-1950s in forging a network of alliances spanning the southern rim of Eurasia that were collectively committed to block the southward expansion of Soviet or Chinese power. But this chain of containment states suffered from a number of weak links. The conspicuous absence of India, the most populous country in Asia apart from Communist China, damaged the credibility of SEATO. The Baghdad Pact (later renamed CENTO) was hamstrung by its failure to attract a single Arab state save Iraq, which withdrew a few years after it had joined (see page 161). Great Britain's membership in and U.S. support for the organization facilitated Moscow's propaganda campaign in the Arab world to portray the Baghdad Pact as a neocolonialist plot to perpetuate Western presence in the region.

## The Contest for Strategic Superiority

In the course of the 1950s the United States and the Soviet Union engaged in a costly and dangerous nuclear arms race that would persist for the remainder of the Cold War. After the Russians had tested the atomic bomb in 1949, President Truman authorized the development of the hydrogen (or thermonuclear) bomb on January 31, 1950. The first successful laboratory test of the destructive new nuclear device, originally dubbed "the super" by its proponents, was conducted on the Pacific atoll of Eniwetok on November 1, 1952. It had taken the Russians four years to break the American monopoly on atomic weapons. It took them only nine months to catch up with their rivals in the race for this new weapon with the detonation of a hydrogen bomb at the Soviet testing site in Kazhakstan on August 12, 1953. The United States conducted the first test of a deliverable thermonuclear weapon on March 1, 1954, at Bikini atoll in the Marshall Islands in the Pacific. The race for nuclear superiority was on.

U.S. officials were persuaded by the results of the hydrogen bomb test (code-named BRAVO) at Bikini that nuclear weapons could destroy the entire planet. At the Geneva Conference of July 1955, Eisenhower lectured Khrushchev and Bulganin about the devastating consequences of nuclear war for human life. Khrushchev also fully appreciated the ominous implications of the nuclear arms race, as revealed in his repudiation of Lenin's doctrine of the inevitability of war between the Communist and capitalist world at the Twentieth Party Congress in February 1956. His new policy of "peaceful coexistence" seemed the only suitable alternative to a conflict that would leave both capitalist and Communist societies in ruins. Nevertheless, the two superpowers resumed their energetic rivalry in nuclear weapons production throughout the 1950s. As we have seen, the so-called New Look in American defense strategy was in part prompted by economic considerations: Reliance on nuclear deterrence was more cost-effective than building up sufficiently large conventional forces to match those of the Communist bloc (see page 56). But Eisenhower had also come to believe that the most effective way of preventing the outbreak of a major war—conventional or nuclear—was to build up American nuclear forces and express an unmistakable willingness to use them in retaliation against a Soviet strike. Khrushchev shared both of Eisenhower's assumptions about the value of nuclear weapons. The Soviet leader fully appreciated the savings that could be achieved by cutting conventional forces while increasing spending on strategic forces. He also embraced his U.S. counterpart's seemingly Orwellian conviction that the key to avoiding nuclear war was the ability and willingness to wage it. The key difference between the two leaders' position was that while the American president envisioned nuclear weapons as the keystone of a strategy of deterrence, the Soviet first secretary seemed willing to contemplate their use to wage and win a nuclear war. In line with this thinking, Khrushchev initiated sharp cuts in conventional Soviet forces and diverted resources to his country's nuclear program. The two problems that the Soviet nuclear weapons program faced were the following: First, it took the Russians much longer than it did the Americans to move from the successful test of a new weapon (such as the atomic and hydrogen bomb) to series production of the device. That was a problem that Khrushchev addressed but was never able to solve during his tenure. In the meantime, he set out to rectify another serious defect in the Soviet force structure that had severely undermined the credibility of its nuclear deterrent: the absence of a delivery system that could carry nuclear weapons from Soviet bases to their intended targets in North America.

By the middle of the 1950s the Russians had finally deployed a long-range bomber, the M-4 "Bison," that was capable of making the round-trip flight to American territory. But they chose not to produce sufficient numbers of this airplane to counterbalance the formidable arsenal of American B-52s, an aircraft that was first deployed by the Strategic Air Command in June 1955. To overcome this inferiority in intercontinental bombers, the Soviet Union began to engage in what historian

John Lewis Gaddis has called "strategic Potemkinism,"* constructing an impressive showcase of nuclear hardware to foster the illusion that much more lay behind the facade of military power. The Russians successfully bamboozled U.S. observers at the Moscow air show of July 1955 by flying the few Bison bombers they possessed over the reviewing stand several times to convey the impression of a formidable nuclear delivery system. This shrewd little act of legerdemain prompted vastly exaggerated estimates of Soviet air power by U.S. intelligence, at a time when the United States possessed five times as many long-range aircraft. The resulting perception of American inferiority fueled fears in Washington of a "bomber gap" that seriously threatened the country's national security.

The major challenge to the Soviet Union's intercontinental delivery system was the exceedingly effective American radar system, which could detect incoming aircraft and direct fighter planes to intercept and destroy them, and the NIKE anti-aircraft missile batteries that were deployed around the country's major cities. To overcome this obstacle, Soviet scientists labored to develop an alternative intercontinental delivery system that would be much more difficult to intercept: the intercontinental ballistic missile (ICBM). The Germans had employed a short-range rocket armed with conventional warheads called the "V-2" against the British Isles toward the end of World War II. The United States government had recruited many of the German rocket scientists after the war to work on a project to develop long-range missiles capable of delivering atomic warheads to Soviet targets. But it was the Russians who successfully tested the world's first ICBM on August 21, 1957. Launched at the huge Soviet testing site in Kazakhstan, its dummy warhead reached an imaginary target in the Pacific Ocean some four thousand miles away. After a second successful test on September 7, the third launch on October 4 projected a small metal ball into orbit around the earth that became the first man-made space satellite. On November 3 the Soviets sent up a second satellite, or Sputnik, containing the first passenger in a space flight: a dog that survived for several days. The United States quickly followed suit by successfully testing a five-thousand-mile range Atlas ICBM in December 1957 and then by launching its own space satellite, the Explorer, in February 1958. But the damage to American prestige caused by the Sputnik flights had been immense. The Russians had won the first round in the space race. More ominously, it was evident that the Soviet Union had acquired a delivery system capable of exposing American territory to nuclear attack against which—unlike manned bombers—there was no defense. For the first time in its history, the United States faced the prospect of instantaneous and massive devastation by a foreign power.

As it turned out, the United States recovered rapidly from the spectacular Soviet breakthrough in the technology of nuclear delivery systems. By the end of the Eisenhower administration it had begun to deploy a formidable ICBM system and expand both the quantity and quality of its already superior long-range bomber force. In the meantime the long-range missiles that the Soviet Union tested in the fall of 1957 had

---

*The "Potemkin village" in Russian history was a model village lavishly endowed by the authorities to impress foreign visitors with the country's economic achievements, concealing the reality of economic backwardness.

proved so expensive and unwieldy that Khrushchev canceled production and ordered the development of new prototypes. As a result, the USSR possessed by 1960 a grand total of four ICBMs capable of reaching targets in the United States. To compensate for this gross inferiority in strategic missiles, the Russians concentrated on developing intermediate-range and medium-range ballistic missiles (IRBMs and MRBMs) that were targeted on Western Europe and American bases all along the periphery of the Soviet Union. By the early 1960s more than seven hundred such nuclear-tipped missiles were lined up like artillery pieces against U.S. military bases in Europe and Asia.

Khrushchev knew that while the Russian cities were exposed to a massive U.S. ICBM strike, the languishing strategic missile program of the Soviet Union posed no immediate threat to American territory. The Soviet leader therefore successfully launched a second campaign of "Potemkinism" similar to the one that had sparked American anxiety about the fictitious "bomber gap" in the mid-1950s. Khrushchev's inflated claims about the Soviet ICBM force ignited a full-blown controversy over a "missile gap" in the United States that was successfully exploited by Democratic candidate John F. Kennedy during the presidential campaign of 1960. The strategic situation that Kennedy inherited after his election in November 1960 could indeed be accurately described as a "missile gap": But it was the United States rather than the Soviet Union that enjoyed the overwhelming advantage in missiles capable of attacking the other's homeland. America's land-based "Minutemen" ICBMs protected in their hardened underground silos, together with the newly deployed Polaris submarine armed with submarine launched ballistic missiles (SLBMs) that lurked in the ocean depths, constituted a virtually invulnerable nuclear deterrent at a time that the Soviet Union had failed to capitalize on its earlier achievement in the technology of rocketry symbolized by Sputnik. Candidate Kennedy had apparently spoken with total sincerity when he warned that the Soviet Union enjoyed a numerical superiority in ICBMs. But on September 21, 1961, the new president received the first National Estimate of Soviet strategic capability based on the new photographic information provided by satellites orbiting the earth. It revealed that Khrushchev's boasts about Soviet ICBM production were in fact statements about IRBMs and MRBMs, that is, missiles that could not reach U.S. territory. The Russians had managed to deploy no more than twenty operational ICBMs through the first year of the Kennedy administration.

Nevertheless, the incontestable reality remained that the United States had lost the immunity from nuclear attack that it had enjoyed since the advent of the atomic age. In time some of America's European allies drew a somber conclusion from this perception of American vulnerability to massive death and destruction. This was the mounting suspicion that the president of the United States would hesitate to endanger millions of his country's citizens by retaliating with nuclear weapons against a conventional (that is, nonnuclear) Soviet attack on the continent. European skeptics began to question the reliability of the American nuclear "umbrella" under which the NATO allies had huddled with a sense of security for a decade. Would any American chief executive in his right mind be willing to sacrifice New York for Paris, Boston for Bonn? These growing doubts about the credibility of the American nuclear deterrent eventually led some NATO leaders to worry about the "decoupling" of Western Europe from the United States. Concerned about such an Allied reaction to the recent round of Soviet nuclear tests, Kennedy arranged for Deputy Secretary of Defense Roswell Gilpatric to expose the Kremlin's deception in a low-key speech to business executives in Hot Springs, Virginia, on October 21, 1961. Gilpatric revealed for the first time that the United States possessed such decisive superiority in ICBMs that its second-strike capability was more than sufficient to deter a Soviet nuclear attack. The exposure of the Soviet Union's striking inferiority in both the quality and quantity of its ICBM force caused a serious loss of credibility and prestige in Moscow. As we have seen, Khrushchev had sought to bridge that missile gap in the late 1950s by ordering the development of second generation of ICBMs to replace the unsatisfactory Sputnik-era series. At the same time the Soviet Union undertook its first large-scale production program of SLBMs. Khrushchev would later attempt to devise a temporary substitute for Soviet Union's insufficient ICBM and SLBM force by installing MRBMs and IRBMs on the island of Cuba in 1962 (see page 109).

## Berlin: The Bone in Khrushchev's Throat

The controversies that beset NATO in the wake of Suez and Sputnik afforded Khrushchev the opportunity to probe the West at its most vulnerable point. This was the three Western occupation sectors of Berlin, which remained an anomalous relic of the wartime alliance despite the partition of Germany into two sovereign states and the termination of the occupation regime for which the political arrangements in Berlin had originally been devised. Ever since the blockade of 1948–1949, the city had been administratively divided into two distinct municipal entities. The three western sectors, united under the authority of an elected mayor, came to be known as "West Berlin." The Soviet sector, run by a local Communist administration, became "East Berlin." The inhabitants of the politically divided city assimilated into their respective German states—one democratic, capitalist, and pro-American; the other a one-party Communist dictatorship loyal to the Soviet Union. But all Berliners were free to circulate throughout the entire city, which remained legally subject to the joint supervisory authority of the four occupying powers.

Since the divided city was situated 110 miles inside what had originally been the Soviet occupation zone, the three Western powers enjoyed the right to unrestricted overland access to their sectors in Berlin through the territory of what in 1949 became East Germany. That right of access was guaranteed by a complex set of agreements that had been originally approved by the four occupying powers and were reaffirmed after the failure of the Berlin blockade in 1949. When the Soviet Union finally granted full political independence to East Germany in 1955, this awkward arrangement became a source of acute embarrassment for the Kremlin in its relations with the East German state. The latter suffered the acute indignity of having to allow the diplomatic, military, and intelligence personnel of three hostile foreign powers to travel unimpeded across its territory and to circulate freely throughout its capital city.

Worse, in the course of the fifties the West German government had regularly provided the city of West Berlin with lavish financial subsidies that had transformed it into a glittering showcase of Western consumer capitalism. The citizens of East Berlin, entitled to travel at will to the western part of the city, could readily compare this seductive symbol of capitalist prosperity to the drab living conditions in their own neighborhoods. To add insult to injury, neither the three Western occupying powers nor West Germany recognized the sovereignty of East Germany, considering it an illegitimate Soviet puppet state kept in power by Russian bayonets. It is scarcely surprising, therefore, that the ruling elite in East Germany became almost pathologically insecure about that country's status. East German Communist Party Secretary Walter Ulbricht periodically complained to the Soviet government about this unsatisfactory situation, focusing particularly on the need to secure international recognition of his government as well as to reach a settlement of the irritating problem of Berlin.

On November 27, 1958, Khrushchev finally bowed to the wishes of his anxious East German protégé. The Soviet ambassador in Bonn informed the West German government of Moscow's intention to terminate the juridical arrangement that governed the inter-Allied occupation of Berlin. That démarche was followed by a Soviet note to the three Western occupying powers proposing the end of the Allied presence in Berlin and the transformation of the western half of the former German capital into a demilitarized "free city" whose access to both West and East Germany would be guaranteed by the four occupying powers. Moscow set a deadline of six months for the conclusion of a quadripartite agreement. If none were reached, Khrushchev threatened to sign a separate bilateral peace treaty with East Germany and peremptorily transfer to that government all of the Soviet Union's powers under the occupation statute (including control of the access routes from West Germany to West Berlin). Such a unilateral Soviet move would have placed the West Berliners' fates in the hands of the East Germany government. Ulbricht's regime would most certainly have proceeded to close down the Western access routes across its territory and then absorb the isolated outpost of capitalism in the western half of its capital city.

Khrushchev reopened the "Berlin question" that had lain dormant for a decade after Truman's airlift foiled Stalin's blockade in 1948–1949 because of the Soviet leadership's deep-seated concern about the expanding military power and diplomatic influence of the West German state. At the end of the Berlin blockade the fledgling Federal Republic had no army to defend itself and the United States had no military forces in Europe to protect it. But after West Germany joined NATO and began to rearm in 1955, the Bundeswehr soon developed into Western Europe's most effective fighting force alongside the U.S. contingent that was deployed in forward positions along the intra-German border. It was obvious, however, that a West German army, no matter how formidable, would be incapable of defending its national territory without access to nuclear weapons. This was to become one of the most contentious issues of the Cold War.

In December 1957 the NATO heads of government endorsed the U.S. offer to create a NATO atomic stockpile in Europe, an initiative that was intended to reassure America's allies in the wake of the recent Soviet ICBM tests that they would retain nuclear weapons on their own territory for use in response to a Warsaw Pact attack. By the end of Eisenhower's term in office about five hundred of them had become operational in Allied countries. The United States eventually deployed intermediate-range ballistic missiles (IRBMs) across the Atlantic (Thor missiles in Great Britain, Jupiter missiles in Italy and Turkey). Control of these nuclear weapons, which were capable of reaching targets deep within the Soviet Union, was in theory shared by the United States and the host country in a so-called dual-key system. However, as historian Marc Trachtenberg has shown, these joint custody arrangements constituted an elaborate subterfuge that transpired with the tacit approval of the Eisenhower administration. The president had long chafed under the legislative restrictions of the McMahon Act, which forbade the sharing of nuclear weapons with America's alliance partners. The dual-key system was so weak and ineffectual that it enabled the NATO allies to acquire de facto control of U.S. nuclear weapons in Europe, while the White House could assure Congress that is was complying with the law. Although the Thor-Jupiter offer was not extended to the Federal Republic, the possibility that that state might gain access to the arsenal of nuclear weapons that the Americans had begun to supply to its other European allies rekindled old fears in the Kremlin of an aggressive Germany armed with the ultimate weapon.

These Soviet anxieties were fed by the assertive diplomacy of the resolutely anti-Communist Adenauer, which gnawed away at the edifice of Soviet power in Eastern and Central Europe. The grizzled old Rhinelander periodically reiterated the ultimate goal of German reunification that was codified in his country's constitution. The West German government not only refused to recognize the existence of the East German state or conduct any business with it. With the promulgation of the Hallstein Doctrine in 1955, Bonn also severed diplomatic relations with the all of the Communist states (except the Soviet Union, which it prudently exempted from the doctrine) that recognized the East German regime. Moreover, West Germany insistently refused to acknowledge the territorial gains that Poland and Czechoslovakia had forcibly obtained from Germany at the end of World War II. Millions of ethnic Germans who had been expelled from western Poland and the Sudetenland in Czechoslovakia after World War II had resettled in West Germany. There they formed a powerful interest group in the Federal Republic that continually pressured the Adenauer government to demand the convocation of a conference that would adjudicate the contested border in the East. Few of these expelees wished to return to their former homes in Poland or Czechoslovakia. They had fully integrated into West German society and enjoyed a much higher standard of living than would be possible in the land they had left. What most of them sought was financial compensation from the Polish and Czechoslovak governments for their loss of property and wealth. But by refusing to affirm the sanctity of the postwar frontiers in the east, the West German government evoked bitter memories in Prague and Warsaw of an earlier German regime that had acquired Czechoslovak territory by diplomatic intimidation at Munich in 1938 and Polish territory by military force in 1939.

In addition to the notable increase in West Germany's military power and diplomatic assertiveness during the second half of the 1950s, the spectacular growth of its economy provoked intense anxiety within the Communist bloc. In contrast to the industrial stagnation and deteriorating living conditions in Eastern Europe, the West German "economic miracle" raised the citizens of the Federal Republic to a level of prosperity unimaginable in the immediate postwar years. This model of economic success in the heart of Europe represented not only an embarrassment but also a potential threat to the neighboring Communist regimes, whose citizens had become attentive listeners to Western radio broadcasts touting the achievements of West German capitalism. The effects of this boom were particularly ominous for the government of East Germany because of the eccentric political status of Berlin. Throughout the 1950s the prospect of freedom and wealth lured to the Federal Republic millions of East Germans, who simply traveled to East Berlin, crossed to West Berlin, and flew to West Germany in pursuit of a better life. Doctors, lawyers, engineers, and other highly skilled professionals continued to pour through this one remaining hole in the Iron Curtain, depriving East Germany of the educated elite that would otherwise have contributed to its own economic development.

Khrushchev's ultimatum on Berlin in the autumn of 1958 was designed not only to halt this "brain drain" by transferring to East Germany de facto control of the entire capital city. It was intended to achieve other objectives as well. The eventual absorption of West Berlin by the East German state would remove once and for all the irritating presence deep within its borders of the bustling enclave of capitalist prosperity. The departure of the token Allied garrisons from West Berlin and the transfer to the East German government of control over the West's access to the city would signify the tacit acknowledgment of the legitimacy of Ulbricht's regime. Such a change in the city's status would doubtless shake West Germany's confidence in Washington's commitment to look after its interest and might therefore tempt Bonn to seek an accommodation with Moscow. But these various scenarios became moot when the three Western occupying powers unanimously rejected the Soviet ultimatum in a note issued on December 31, 1958. While agreeing to participate in Four-Power negotiations on the political status of Berlin, the United States, Great Britain, and France refused to be bound by the six-month deadline set by Moscow. They also defiantly reaffirmed their access rights to and occupation rights within the divided city that had been stipulated in the Potsdam agreement. Khrushchev avoided a show-down on these issues by hinting that he was prepared to postpone the deadline for the transfer of the Western access routes to East German control and tacitly to tolerate Allied occupation rights in the city pending a permanent settlement.

The Four-Power foreign ministers held several meetings on the Berlin issue in Geneva from May 11 to August 5, 1959. While the foreign ministers deliberated, Khrushchev's six-month deadline expired on May 27 without incident. The three Western delegates at Geneva offered to reduce the size of their Berlin garrisons and to refrain from deploying nuclear weapons there if the Soviet Union would agree to guarantee Western access to the city. But when the discussions bogged down over technical details, Eisenhower tried to break the logjam with a dramatic gesture. In the run-up to the conference Khrushchev had dropped several hints of his strong desire to visit the United States. The president decided to issue an invitation in the hope that the two leaders could achieve progress on Berlin in a few days of face-to-face exchanges. The Soviet leader promptly accepted and then, to Eisenhower's dismay, announced plans to arrive in September for a twelve-day tour of the entire country.

On September 15, 1959, Nikita Khrushchev became the first Russian leader in history to set foot on American soil. He spent the first ten days of his visit in a remarkable cross-country excursion that brought him into contact with a wide range of Americana, from a corn farm in Iowa to a movie set in Hollywood. On his return to Washington the Soviet visitor huddled with Eisenhower for intensive talks at Camp David, the presidential retreat in Maryland's Catocin Mountains. While no dramatic breakthroughs resulted from these discussions, Eisenhower persuaded his guest to cancel his Berlin ultimatum and to attend a Four-Power summit meeting the follow-

*Dwight Eisenhower and Nikita Khrushchev outside Aspen Lodge at Camp David, the presidential retreat in Maryland, during the Soviet leader's unprecedented visit to the United States in September 1959. (Courtesy Dwight D. Eisenhower Library)*

ing year to negotiate a definitive settlement of the nettlesome issue. Amid the air of cordiality Eisenhower accepted Khrushchev's invitation for a return visit to the Soviet Union after the forthcoming summit.

The Eisenhower-Khrushchev conversations at Camp David represented a public relations bonanza for the Soviet leader. He had dealt with the U.S. head of state on equal terms, dramatically boosting his own prestige at home. He had come across to the American public not as the bloodthirsty tyrant depicted in Cold War propaganda but as an eccentric, amiable grandfather with whom it should be possible to make a deal over Berlin and the other Cold War disputes. Shortly after his return to Moscow Khrushchev announced a unilateral reduction of the Soviet army by one-third. The Soviet press waxed lyrical about the "spirit of Camp David," while Western media speculated about the prospects of reducing East-West tensions at the summit conference scheduled for the following spring. In addition to Berlin, another item added to its agenda was the nuclear test ban agreement on which the three nuclear powers (the United States, the Soviet Union, and Great Britain) had made substantial progress in recent months. (see pp. 116). From the brink of confrontation over Berlin in 1958, the two contending blocs seemed poised for a major breakthrough that promised a dramatic improvement in East-West relations.

## The Summit That Never Was

The high-level conclave that was to lay the groundwork for a settlement of the Berlin issue and conclusion of a nuclear test ban agreement was set to convene in Paris in mid-May 1960. It was generally expected that this gathering of the leaders of the United States, the Soviet Union, Great Britain, and France would inaugurate a regular series of Big Four discussions that would address the most dangerous conflicts of the Cold War. But on May 5, eleven days before the opening of the first summit conference since the one at Geneva five years earlier, the Kremlin cast a pall over the forthcoming proceedings with an announcement that a high-altitude U-2 American spy plane had been shot down thirteen hundred miles within Soviet territory on the first of the month.

As the nuclear arms race between the superpowers began to escalate in the mid-1950s, American defense officials had worked hard to develop effective methods for monitoring Soviet defense capabilities. In the absence of a reliable intelligence network within the Soviet Union, the U-2 aircraft proved a godsend. The detailed photographs of Soviet military installations that it was able to produce yielded information that was impossible to obtain by conventional espionage. Soviet radar had managed to detect many of these reconnaissance flights that the CIA had conducted, each with the express authorization of the president, since the summer of 1956. The Kremlin indignantly protested a number of these egregious violations of Soviet air space. But the complaints always arrived through secret channels, presumably because the Soviet leadership wished to avoid the humiliation of having to concede to the world (and to its own citizens) the inability to control its own skies. In any case there was nothing that could be done about these flights because the high-altitude planes flew beyond the range of Russian fighters and surface-to-air missiles (SAMs), until improvements in Soviet anti-aircraft capabilities finally brought down the first U-2 over the city of Sverdlovsk on May Day 1960.

The American president had been assured by his intelligence officials that the flimsy aircraft would disintegrate on impact and that all of its equipment would be destroyed beyond recognition. He also assumed that the CIA pilot, Francis Gary Powers, would follow his instructions to commit suicide with the cyanide-tipped pen in his possession to ensure that the purpose of his flight would not be disclosed under interrogation. The State Department therefore concocted a cover story that the plane had been conducting meteorological observations in Turkey and had unintentionally flown off course. Khrushchev thereupon produced both the plane (with its intelligence-gathering equipment intact) and the pilot (who not only survived but confirmed the true nature of his mission). The red-faced American president promptly reversed himself, sheepishly confessing on May 11 that he had personally authorized the intelligence-gathering flight and that his government had not told the truth in its previous announcement.

Eisenhower did not stop with this unprecedented admission of espionage and deception. He went on to defend such aerial reconnaissance on the grounds that it was essential to protect the United States against a surprise attack in light of the veil of secrecy that the Soviet Union had drawn around its nuclear facilities. He also suggested that the over-flights might have to continue until less intrusive means of gathering crucial intelligence were developed. Khrushchev decided not to permit these last two portions of Eisenhower's public statement to pass unchallenged as he arrived in Paris for the summit meeting. In his opening statement at the Paris summit meeting, the Soviet leader angrily demanded a public apology from Eisenhower for the violation of Soviet airspace, the punishment of those responsible, and formal assurances that the flights would be terminated.

When the American chief executive rejected these humiliating demands, Khrushchev insisted that the summit conference that had just opened be postponed for eight months—by which time Eisenhower would be out of office—and then announced that he was returning to Moscow immediately. To pour salt on the wound, the Soviet leader revoked his earlier invitation to Eisenhower to visit the Soviet Union in June. Eisenhower was left to commiserate with British Prime Minister Harold Macmillan and French President Charles de Gaulle about the aborted conclave. Khrushchev's decision to sabotage the Paris summit revealed that the Kremlin had lost all interest in dealing with America's lame-duck president. It preferred to await the installation of his successor before tackling the unresolved issues of the Cold War.

The dramatic public posturing of both leaders as the Paris summit collapsed was replete with ironies. Eisenhower could hardly have issued an abject apology to the Russians during an election year in the United States, nor could he have disciplined subordinates for carrying out his own orders. But he could have acceded to the Soviet demand for an end to the over-flights without jeopardizing American intelligence objectives, since he knew that the U-2 was about to be superceded by satellite technology. The Discoverer satellites, the first of which was placed into orbit only three months after the U-2 affair on August 18, 1960, eventually yielded much more valuable photographic evidence of Soviet military capabilities without the stigma of violating Soviet air space or the risk of being shot down. Khrushchev could certainly have turned a blind eye to a U.S. intelligence operation he had been aware of for four years and which he knew would soon be rendered obsolete by spy satellites orbiting the earth.

Why did the Soviet leader seize on this relatively trivial incident as a convenient pretext to cancel the Paris summit conference and revoke Eisenhower's invitation to visit the Soviet Union, both of which he had originally regarded as important components of his policy of peaceful coexistence with the West? The principal reason for Khrushchev's abrupt reversal seems to have been a compensatory reaction to the vigorous opposition to his policy of East-West détente that emanated from two sources within the Communist world. One was a growing faction within his own government that opposed negotiations with the West on Berlin and other issues for fear that the resulting concessions might threaten Soviet domination of Eastern Europe. The other was Mao Zedong's regime in China, which had begun to criticize Khrushchev's policy of peaceful coexistence with the capitalist West as a betrayal of the Communist mission of world revolution (see page 213).

## The Superpowers and Africa through the Early 1960s

The Cold War had begun in Europe during the second half of the 1940s and spread to Asia in the form of military conflicts in Indochina and Korea during the 1950s (see pages 190, 219). A region of the world that had remained totally exempt from the rivalry between the two superpowers in the first fifteen years after World War II was the continent of Africa. This was true largely because, with the single exception of Liberia,* Africa had fallen under the control of European imperial powers and remained their special preserve well into the 1950s. The disintegration of European colonial authority in Africa began in the 1950s in the northern part of the continent. The Italian colony of Libya that had been conquered by British forces during World War II was granted its independence in 1951. The year 1956 saw other outposts of empire in North Africa disappear: France left Morocco and Tunisia. Great Britain evacuated the Suez Canal Zone, the last vestige of its imperial position in Egypt, and withdrew from Sudan. All of these instances of decolonization had transpired with a minimum of bloodshed. The one notable exception to that rule was Algeria, an arid land in North Africa that had been conquered by the French between 1830 and 1848.

If India was the "crown jewel" of the British Empire, Algeria was even more central to the imperial pretensions of France. In contrast to the rest of the French colonial empire in Africa and Asia (which, like British India, had been run by a small contingent of political administrators and military forces), Algeria had attracted a large European settler population. Legally, Algeria was regarded not as a colony or protectorate but as an overseas department of France. The "French Algerians," some of whose ancestors had arrived in the early nineteenth century, considered the country their home as much as the indigenous Arab population did. They dominated the commercial life of the coastal cities, owned most of the arable land, and monopolized political power through a complex electoral system that in theory accorded legal equality to all citizens but in practice disenfranchised the Arab Muslim majority. These privileged white European settlers, who numbered about a million in this country of ten million, adamantly refused any concessions to the increasingly resentful indigenous population. The costs of that determination would be high for all concerned. On November 1, 1954, a coalition of radical Arab nationalist groups known as the National Liberation Front (FLN) launched a nationwide rebellion against French authority in forty-five Algerian cities. In the course of the next seven years France dispatched some 750,000 troops across the Mediterranean in a desperate, foredoomed bid to retain control of its Algerian possession. After his return to power in 1958, it took President Charles de Gaulle four years to reach an agreement with the FLN that finally brought independence for Algeria in 1962 (see page 124).

What was noteworthy about this first stage of African decolonization during the 1950s was the absence of the two superpowers from the process. Neither the United States nor the Soviet Union had any significant economic or strategic interests in

---

*The Republic of Liberia was established in 1822 as a colony for freed American slaves. It gradually evolved into a de facto protectorate of the United States, a privileged status that shielded it from encroachments by the British and French imperial forces in control of the rest of West Africa.

Africa or a history of involvement in the continent's affairs. In a rare example of agreement between the Washington and Moscow, both openly criticized colonialism and supported the efforts of the nonaligned members of the United Nations to hasten the end of European rule. The United States found itself in an awkward position because the principal colonial powers in Africa—Great Britain, France, Belgium, and Portugal—were also its allies in NATO against the Communist bloc. The Eisenhower administration was therefore reluctant to apply more than gentle diplomatic pressure on the colonial powers to divest themselves of their overseas possessions. But the Soviet Union had no need for such reticence, since the imperial powers in Africa were its adversaries in Europe. In the mid-1950s, as we have seen, Khrushchev reactivated the original anti-imperialist rhetoric of Leninism, which had been de-emphasized by Stalin during his tenure in the Kremlin, as part of an energetic campaign to court nationalist movements in the Third World (see page 00). But this Soviet bid to curry favor with the newly independent states in Africa produced very meager results during the second half of the 1950s. The former European possessions in North Africa either pursued a resolutely independent, nonaligned course (as in the case of Egypt and Tunisia) or gravitated toward the West (as in the case of Libya and Morocco).

The most promising prospect for the extension of Soviet influence in Africa during the late 1950s was the former British colony of the Gold Coast. Renamed Ghana after an ancient African kingdom from the tenth century, it became in 1957 the first sub-Saharan country to obtain its independence. The new country's first prime minister, Kwame Nkrumah, became the preeminent champion of African independence and the most vociferous critic of European colonial rule. In December 1958 Nkrumah hosted an All-Africa People's Conference, to which anticolonial militants flocked from one end of the continent to another. Khrushchev observed with mounting satisfaction the simmering anticolonial discontent on the continent, which he saw as an opportunity to be exploited in the interests of the Communist cause. In 1959 he established in Moscow an Africa Institute and a year later a People's Friendship University to promote links between the Soviet Union and the emerging liberation movements there.

One of the delegates to Nkrumah's All-Africa Peoples' Congress in Ghana was a young postal worker from the Belgian Congo named Patrice Lumumba. He returned home to assume control of the Congolese National Movement, the more radical of the colony's two major organizations that were agitating for an end to Belgian rule. The rival movement, the Alliance des Bakongo (ABAKO), was led by a former teacher and civil servant named Joseph Kasavubu. In January 1960 the Belgian government summoned representatives of the various political factions in the Congo to Brussels and abruptly informed its astonished guests that total independence for the country would be granted on June 30. The Belgian colonial administration in the Congolese capital of Leopoldville selected Kasavubu to become president and Lumumba to become prime minister of the new state. The two designated leaders of an independent Congo were expected to permit Belgian political and military authorities to retain predominant influence in the government and armed forces of the new state as well as to allow Belgian copper-mining firms to resume their lucrative operations in the country.

Within a few days of independence in June 1960, however, the Belgian government's plans for a smooth political transition in the Congo were derailed. Congolese members of the military police mutinied against their Belgian officers. Angry mobs attacked Belgian nationals and seized their property, causing a mass exodus from the country. Belgian troops returned to protect the Europeans who remained, as the political authority of the central government began to unravel. On July 11 Moise Tshombe, the regional leader of the southern province of Katanga where most of the Belgian copper-mining operations were located, declared his province's independence from the central government with the covert support of the copper companies and the former colonial power. The newly independent country seemed on the verge of total chaos.

Faced with the twin threats of Katanga's secession and the restoration of Belgian colonial authority, Prime Minister Lumumba issued frantic appeals to the United States, the Soviet Union, and the United Nations for assistance to preserve the Congo's national unity and independence. Suddenly this resource-rich country in the heart of Africa became a tempting target for the intervention of the superpowers, as Washington and Moscow watched the deteriorating situation with growing interest. To prevent the extension of Cold War rivalries to the continent, the United Nations preemptively intervened. After calling for the withdrawal of Belgian military units from the country, the UN offered to send a peacekeeping force to restore order in the country. Worried that Moscow might exploit the degenerating political situation in the Congo to gain a foothold in Central Africa, the Eisenhower administration threw its support behind the UN mission. But UN Secretary General Dag Hammarskjøld, who played a commanding role in organizing the intervention, refused to order the peacekeeping force to crush the secessionist movement in Katanga mounted by Lumumba's rival Tshombe. In desperation Lumumba turned to the Moscow for assistance. Soon Soviet-made trucks and airplanes accompanied by Russian crews and maintenance personnel were pouring into the country.

Lumumba's appeal for Soviet support sealed his fate in the eyes of the Eisenhower administration. The CIA station chief in the capital city of Leopoldville hastily recruited the staunchly anti-Communist commander of the Congolese army, Colonel Joseph-Désiré Mobutu, to take action against what Washington increasingly regarded as the pro-Communist prime minister. Under intense pressure from Mobutu and his fellow officers, President Kasavubu dismissed Lumumba on September 5 and was shortly thereafter induced to designate Mobutu as his successor. While attempting to escape Lumumba was captured by Mobutu's soldiers and eventually handed over to the authorities in Katanga, where he was murdered (with probable CIA connivance) on January 17, 1961. In the meantime a pro-Soviet renegade government had been established in the Congolese city of Stanleyville (Kisangani) in October 1960. But when a small Russian expeditionary force was deployed there to bolster the breakaway regime, it antagonized the local residents and had to withdraw. Within a few years the central government was able to suppress both the pro-Soviet regime in Stanleyville and the Belgian-backed breakaway government of Katanga. In November 1965 Mobutu deposed Kasavubu in a bloodless coup, assumed total control of the government apparatus, and instituted a repressive system of one-man rule. Renaming the country Zaire and himself Mobutu Sésé Sékó (ostensibly as part of a campaign to shed the symbols of the country's European colonial heritage), the anti-Communist strongman in the renamed capital of Kinshasa became a staunch supporter of the West in the Cold War (see page 290).

The Soviet Union had thus failed miserably in its first modest attempt to extend its influence to Africa. But Khrushchev tried as best he could to exploit the Congo crisis for propaganda purposes. He renamed Moscow's People's Friendship University in honor of the martyred Lumumba. The school was soon attracting radical nationalists from all over the Third World who sought Moscow's guidance and assistance in their anti-imperialist struggles. In a fiery speech before the UN General Assembly on September 24, 1960, the Soviet leader assailed Western colonialism before a body that included sixteen newly emancipated African states. Accusing Hammarskjöld of secretly supporting the colonial interests in the Congo crisis, Khrushchev demanded that the office of secretary general be abolished and replaced by a tripartite executive consisting of one delegate from the Western bloc, one from the Eastern bloc, and one from the nonaligned nations. Although this Soviet proposal for a "troika" directorate was turned aside by the United Nations, the tenor of the debate on the issue reflected the new political realities in the world body. In the first fifteen years of its operation the membership of the world organization had doubled, transforming it from an exclusive club dominated by the powerful white nations of the West to one in which the newly independent nations of the Third World, if they joined with the nations of the Communist bloc, would wield the balance of power.

## The Resolution of the Berlin Problem

Moscow's failure in 1960–1961 to expand its influence in Central Africa and to reorganize the United Nations was soon overshadowed by a revival of the Berlin question, which had lain dormant since the collapse of the Paris summit in 1960. For Khrushchev the unresolved status of West Berlin represented both an opportunity and a curse. It was an opportunity because the government in Bonn had come to regard Berlin as the litmus test of Washington's willingness to protect West Germany's interests in Europe. Moscow could therefore exploit the geographically vulnerable West Berlin at will in order to promote tension between the United States and its West German protégé. The non-Communist half of the divided city became a pressure point to be squeezed, or, in Khrushchev's more earthy metaphor, "the testicles of the West."

At the same time, however, West Berlin also represented a potential source of dissension between the Soviet Union and *its* German client state. To East Germany, West Berlin represented a "cancer" that had to be removed if that regime were ever to feel secure about its future. The Western garrisons in the city, together with the access agreements that permitted the Western powers extraterritorial transit rights through East Germany territory, continued to mock the Communist state's claim to sovereignty. A more concrete threat was represented by the open border between the Western and Eastern sectors of the divided city. Since the creation of the two German states in 1949 more than 2.5 million East Germans, a sixth of the country's population, had fled to West Germany through the escape hatch in Berlin. The annual outflow reached 200,000 in 1960 and continued to increase in the first six months of

1961. Recognizing the grave threat that the hemorrhaging of professionals and skilled workers posed to the viability of his state, East German Communist leader Walter Ulbricht began to increase the pressure on Khrushchev to do something about the brain drain. Ulbricht was even prepared to play the "China card" to increase his leverage on the Kremlin: In January 1961 he dispatched an East German delegation to Beijing to seek an improvement in relations with Moscow's openly declared rival for primacy in the Communist world.

Khrushchev finally acceded to East Germany's urgent pleas for remedial action after the advent of the Kennedy administration in Washington. The new occupant of the White House had immediately proposed a Soviet-American summit conference to address the outstanding issues between the two superpowers that he had inherited from Eisenhower. Moscow waited for the most auspicious moment to respond to the American overture. It arrived in May when Kennedy suffered the humiliating setback in his first foreign policy venture at the Bay of Pigs (see page 107). Khrushchev promptly endorsed the American suggestion for a summit conference, and the two leaders met for the first (and, as it turned out, the last) time in Vienna on June 3–4, 1961. At the top of their agenda was the unresolved issue of Berlin. During his talks with Kennedy in the Austrian capital, Khrushchev dusted off his earlier proposal for a Berlin settlement that Eisenhower had rejected in 1958: a Four-Power peace treaty that would rid Berlin of all foreign troops, formally recognize East Germany's sovereignty, and leave West Berlin to its own devices as a demilitarized "free city." He also reissued the earlier threat that if such a quadripartite arrangement were not reached within six months, Moscow would sign a separate bilateral pact with East Germany and transfer to it control of the access routes to the city.

Kennedy conceded the Soviet Union's right to conclude a separate agreement with East Germany, but denied East Germany's right to alter the political status of West Berlin or to interfere with the Western allies' access to the city. The assertive Soviet leader exploited the recent American fiasco at the Bay of Pigs to browbeat his untested young interlocutor: How could a president who was incapable of dislodging a Communist regime ninety miles from his own country hope to defend a city thousands of miles away that was surrounded by Communist forces? Khrushchev speculated about the terrible consequences of nuclear war. He reminded Kennedy that the Soviet Union had lost twenty million people in World War II compared to America's 350,000, implying that the Russians were capable of enduring formidable sacrifices to get their way. As he departed the conference Kennedy observed wryly to his aides that he anticipated "a cold winter." After returning to their respective capitals the two leaders took steps to give the appearance of national strength and determination. On July 8 Khrushchev rescinded the plan he had announced in 1960 to eliminate 1.2 million men from the Soviet armed services and announced a one-third increase in the defense budget. Kennedy responded on July 25 with requests for congressional authorization to triple draft calls, summon reserves to active service, and launch a civil defense program to construct a vast network of fallout shelters across the United States to reduce the number of civilian casualties in a nuclear war.

As the two superpowers postured in this provocative manner, the flow of East Germans through the Berlin gap became a torrent, as a thousand citizens lined up at refugee centers in West Berlin each day to flee west. At a meeting of the Warsaw Pact

Organization in late July and early August, Ulbricht renewed his impassioned plea that something be done to end the situation that was draining his country of critical skills and condemning it to economic disaster. Since the refugees could leave West Berlin only by air, the East German party boss urged Moscow to halt the exodus by closing the air corridors to West Germany. But such an act would constitute a blatant violation of the access agreements that was sure to provoke a dangerous showdown with the Western powers, so Khrushchev turned thumbs down. In the meantime signals emanating from Washington suggested a novel and imaginative method of defusing the crisis that would solve Ulbricht's "brain drain" problem without violating Western occupation rights in and access rights to West Berlin. Senator J. William Fulbright, the influential chairman of the Senate Foreign Relations Committee who was known to have close ties to the White House, publicly wondered why East Germany did not simply close its sectoral border in Berlin to stem the flow of refugees to the West.

Khrushchev finally authorized the East German government to test Kennedy's reaction to a variation of the Fulbright suggestion that would not infringe on Allied rights. In the early morning of August 13, East German police halted all traffic between the two sectors of the city and proceeded to string barbed wire along the sectoral border. The absence of an immediate response from the White House revealed that while the Americans were prepared to fight if the Western allies were denied access to West Berlin, they would not risk war to preserve the undivided status of the city. Three days later East German construction crews began to replace the temporary barbed wire barrier with a permanent concrete wall that blocked all access between the city's two sectors except through a few closely guarded checkpoints.

After a long delay, the White House responded to the erection of what would come to be known as the Berlin Wall with a public display of toughness that camouflaged a policy of caution and restraint. In September Kennedy appointed General Lucius Clay—the renowned organizer of the Berlin airlift of 1948–1949—to assume command of U.S. forces in Berlin as a symbolic gesture to reassure the West Berliners. Clay arrived amid a smokescreen of bluster and bravado. He insisted on reasserting the right of Allied military personnel to enter East Berlin and circulate freely within it. This demand precipitated on October 27 what became the first (and, as it turned out, the last) direct confrontation between the two superpowers' military forces, when Soviet and American tank units faced each other at "Checkpoint Charlie," which connected the American and Soviet sectors of the divided city. This ominous standoff was defused when the Soviet Union backed down and tolerated symbolic forays by Western military units into East Berlin to show the flag and reaffirm the intercity access agreements. But the Berlin Wall remained and would admirably serve the purpose for which it was constructed. The torrent of East Germans escaping to the West dwindled to a trickle. No more than a few thousand a year were able to sneak over, under, or through the formidable barrier. Those left behind were deterred from attempting a breakout by the East German police's "shoot to kill" policy, which was implemented with brutal efficiency on several notorious occasions.

The Berlin Wall became a public relations disaster for the government that had built it. Ulbricht was reduced to offering the ludicrous explanation that the barrier had been erected to keep Western espionage agents from infiltrating the German

Democratic Republic. But in a more important sense the wall was a godsend to him: It guaranteed the viability of the East German state, which had been very problematic as long as emigration remained an option for its most economically productive and best-educated citizens. Those who were caught behind the wall were obliged to make their peace with the regime and apply their skills to its economic development. Although East Germany would continue to lag far behind West Germany in productivity, it would become the most economically advanced of the Soviet satellites in Eastern Europe.

But while Ulbricht got his wall, he did not get the peace treaty he craved as the formal acknowledgment of his country's sovereignty. When Four-Power discussions on Berlin resumed in the fall of 1961, it rapidly became evident that while Kennedy had accepted the division of the city he was not prepared to sign a treaty recognizing East Germany. So on October 17 Khrushchev was again obliged to cancel his December deadline for the treaty of recognition, to the dismay of the East German party boss. In the meantime Washington's acquiescence in the construction of the wall had antagonized the West German government, which bitterly resented the abandonment of the East Berliners to their tragic fate. In part because of his disappointment over the American failure to prevent the construction of the wall, Adenauer would later respond with alacrity to overtures from French president Charles de Gaulle for a Franco-German entente to supplement and perhaps even some day replace Bonn's close ties to Washington (see page 128). The Social Democratic mayor of West Berlin, Willy Brandt, also concluded that the Americans could not be relied on to look after West Germany's interests. He thereafter began to develop his plans (to be implemented once he became West German chancellor eight years later) to seek an accommodation with the Eastern bloc (see page 130).

The resolution of the Berlin crisis of 1958–1961 emancipated the two superpowers from their paradoxical dependence on their respective German protégés. During the 1950s the ultimate nightmare of a united Germany aligned with the other side in the Cold War enabled each German state to exercise considerable leverage over its superpower protector. Adenauer had acquired a powerful influence over American policy toward Berlin, while Ulbricht's insistent complaints about the anomalous political status of the city were taken very seriously in Moscow. Kennedy's acceptance of the Berlin Wall and Khrushchev's cancellation for the second time of his ultimatum for a German peace treaty revealed that, in the last analysis, the two superpowers did not consider Berlin worth a war. They both were prepared to seek a mutually acceptable accommodation over the heads and at the expense of their respective German clients. On June 12, 1964, the Soviet Union finally concluded a bilateral treaty of friendship, mutual aid, and cooperation with East Germany that fell far short of the multilateral peace treaty that Ulbricht had desperately craved for so long. It left in place the three irritating constraints on East German sovereignty: the privileged, protected status of the capitalist enclave of West Berlin, the presence of the token Allied garrisons in the city, and the Western powers' access rights across East Germany. But the contentious issues of the political status of West Berlin and East Germany, which had poisoned East-West relations in Europe since the formation of the two German states, would recede in importance until the crisis of the Communist bloc in 1989–1990.

# FOUR

# FROM CHAPULTEPEC TO CASTRO: THE UNITED STATES AND LATIN AMERICA, 1945–1962

## The Formation of the Inter-American System

Throughout the first three decades of the twentieth century the United States achieved a position of military, political, and economic hegemony in the Western Hemisphere. U.S. export firms and banking institutions edged out their British and German competitors to dominate the foreign trade and financial markets of Latin America. Until 1933 Washington exercised an informal police power in Central America and the Caribbean, intervening militarily in that region to curb political instability and social unrest and imposing financial supervision over several Latin American countries to ensure the timely payment of their foreign debts. With the advent of Franklin Roosevelt's "Good Neighbor Policy," direct U.S. military intervention gave way to an indirect method of dominance, whereby Washington relied on a cooperative relationship with pro-American political, economic, and military elites in the region. The result of Roosevelt's conciliatory approach was a substantial improvement in relations between the United States and its neighbors. Old Latin American fears about heavy-handed interference in their affairs by the Colossus of the North dissipated as the more ominous threat posed by Nazi Germany and the million German immigrants residing in Latin America drew the countries of the Western Hemisphere together in a common cause.

After the Japanese attack on Pearl Harbor, the Roosevelt administration promoted an unprecedented degree of military, economic, and political cooperation between the United States and its neighbors to the south. In sharp contrast to World War I, when many Latin American countries successfully resisted Washington's pressure to join the United States in declaring war against Germany, all of the republics of Latin America had done so by the time of the German surrender in May 1945. The two closest allies of the United States during the war were Brazil and Mexico, the only Latin American states to sent combat forces abroad.* Brazil's authoritarian president Getulio Vargas allowed the U.S. Army Air Corps to establish a base at Natal at the tip

---

*Brazil sent a twenty-five-thousand-person infantry division to Italy in the summer of 1944, where it fought alongside the U.S. fifth army as it drove German military forces from the peninsula; a Mexican air squadron flew fifty-nine missions in support of U.S. ground forces in the Philippines in the spring of 1945.

*The United States and Latin America*

of the Brazilian bulge into the south Atlantic. Natal became the busiest American air base in the world during the war, accommodating tens of thousands of U.S. fighters, bombers, and cargo planes that were being transferred to the European theater. In exchange Brazil received U.S. financing for its steel industry, which eventually became the largest in Latin America. Moreover, the rubber trees of Brazil's Amazon basin provided the United States with latex, an essential commodity for war industries, after Japanese forces had seized the rubber-producing colonies of Britain, France, and the Netherlands in Southeast Asia.

In contrast to its stormy relations with the United States during World War I, Mexico also became a staunch ally of the United States after Pearl Harbor. After declaring war on Germany in May 1942, Mexican farms and mines produced a wide range of strategic raw materials for the American-led campaign against the Axis. Three hundred thousand Mexican laborers worked in farms and factories as replacements for Americans sent overseas to fight Germany and Japan. The Mexican government cracked down on German spies who had been operating with impunity in the country and permitted the establishment of U.S. air bases in the country.

Ecuador and several Caribbean islands also granted base facilities to U.S. military forces, while all of the Latin American countries furnished strategic raw materials to the U.S. war machine. Reinforcing this intensive hemispheric military cooperation was a tightening of economic ties between the United States and its neighbors during the war: The Latin American trade of the two prewar economic competitors of the United States in the region, Germany and Great Britain, had been ruined during the war by submarine attacks in the Atlantic. At the end of the war neither country was in a position to recapture its prewar markets for manufactured products and capital investment in Latin America that had been taken over by U.S. industrial firms and financial institutions. U.S. exports to, direct foreign investment in, and military cooperation with Latin America had reached unprecedented levels by 1945. The hoary myth of Pan-Americanism, which emphasized the ideological unity of the twenty-one republics of the Western Hemisphere in contrast to the autocratic powers of the old world, reigned supreme as Europe lay in ruins and the United States basked in its military triumph and economic prosperity.

The lone obstacle to this wartime trend toward greater hemispheric cooperation was Argentina, a country that had long resisted Washington's efforts to employ the ideology of Pan-Americanism to mobilize Latin American support for U.S. foreign policy goals. Argentina had a number of special characteristics that account for this defiant posture. First, its large immigrant population from Germany and Italy identified more closely with Europe than with the United States. Second, its economic system was competitive rather than complementary with that of the United States: Unlike other Latin American countries, which exported subsoil minerals or tropical fruits to the American market in exchange for manufactured goods, Argentina's principal exports—wheat and beef—went to Europe in competition with the products of American farms and ranches.

These transatlantic commercial links reinforced Argentina's political and cultural ties to the old continent and rendered it much more independent of U.S. economic pressure. During World War II the officer corps of the German-trained Argentine army expressed admiration for the authoritarian regimes of Benito Mussolini in Italy and Francisco Franco in Spain. Sensitive to the ethnic pride of the country's large Italian and German immigrant population, the group of Germanophile military officers that seized power in 1943 resisted U.S. pressure to break relations with the Axis. When a new general assumed the office of president in 1944, the U.S. State Department expressed its displeasure with Argentina's insistence on neutrality by withholding recognition of the new government in Buenos Aires. When high-ranking Argentine officers led by Colonel Juan Péron defended their country's sovereign prerogatives and opposed any compromise with the United States, relations between Washington and Buenos Aires approached the breaking point.

Anxious about this growing breach, the Mexican government invited the foreign ministers of the American states that had declared war on the Axis powers (that is, all but Argentina) to Mexico City for an emergency conference to resolve the Argentine crisis and reaffirm the principle of hemispheric solidarity. The issue of Argentine neutrality was expeditiously resolved at the high-level conclave, which met at Chapultepec Palace in the Mexican capital from February 21 to March 8, 1945. The foreign ministers sharply criticized Buenos Aires for its hesitation to join the rest of the American republics in declaring war against the Axis. This diplomatic pressure from its neighbors in the hemisphere, reinforced by the expectation of profiting from membership in what was now certain to be a victorious coalition, prompted Argentina to comply with the Chapultepec injunction and issue a belated declaration of war against Germany and Japan on March 27.

The most contentious topic at the Chapultepec Conference was the relationship between the nations of the Western Hemisphere and the new global security system that representatives of the United States, Great Britain, the Soviet Union, and China had officially endorsed at the Dumbarton Oaks Conference held in Washington from August 21 to October 21, 1945. The term "United Nations," originally employed to designate the Allied states at war with the Axis, was appropriated as the title of the new international organization. Devised by American devotées of the Wilsonian vision of world order that the United States had repudiated after the last war, this successor to the defunct League of Nations was intended to replace the discredited traditions of great power rivalries, balance of power, spheres of influence, and regional alliances with a global system of collective security. Comprising all sovereign states of the world, the organization would serve as a forum for the peaceful settlement of international disputes and, if the need arose, would become the instrument of collective security through the application of economic or military sanctions against an aggressor. During the debates within the Roosevelt administration over planning for the United Nations, a faction headed by the young and energetic Under-Secretary of State for Latin American Affairs Nelson A. Rockefeller expressed the fear that a global system of collective security might threaten the principle of hemispheric solidarity and weaken the bonds that had been forged between the United States and its neighbors to the south during the war. This group of U.S. officials urged that a provision be inserted in the UN Charter that would permit the development of regional security arrangements for the Western Hemisphere outside the proposed international organization.

In the meantime the Latin American representatives at the Chapultepec Conference had come to favor a regional security system for the Western Hemisphere for their own reasons: At a meeting of the foreign ministers of the American Republics in Rio de Janeiro in January 1942, Under-Secretary of State Sumner Welles had led the Latin American representatives to expect a massive program of U.S. economic assistance for their countries, a commitment that was subsequently reinforced by lavish U.S. government spending for the procurement of strategic raw materials from America's hemispheric allies. As victory in Europe approached, many Latin American statespersons hoped that the intensified U.S. interest in their region during the common effort against the Axis would result in a significant expansion of U.S. economic assistance after the war. By emphasizing the regional approach to peace and security in the Western Hemisphere, they expected to become privileged beneficiaries of U.S. foreign aid as active participants in the emerging postwar inter-American system. The interests of the United States and of Latin America therefore coincided as the Chapultepec Conference addressed the issue of the postwar international order. After perfunctorily endorsing the Dumbarton Oaks plan for a global security system under the auspices of the proposed United Nations organization, the delegates called for the creation of a "regional arrangement" to preserve peace and security in the Americas after the war.

At the founding conference of the United Nations that opened in San Francisco on April 25, 1945, the Latin American states boasted the largest voting bloc with nineteen out of the fifty countries represented. Argentina was conspicuously absent because of the adamant opposition of the Soviet Union, which proclaimed that Buenas Aires's pro-Axis sympathies during most of the war disqualified it from membership in the embryonic world body despite its last-minute, opportunistic declaration of war against Germany and Japan.* In line with the preferences expressed earlier at Chapultepec, the U.S. and Latin American delegations in San Francisco succeeded in securing approval of what would become Article 51 of the UN Charter, which reserved for each member "the inherent right of individual or collective self-defense." This critical provision authorized the formation of regional security systems outside the international organization that was being founded. Although few observers anticipated it at the time, Article 51 would later serve as the legal justification for the multitude of regional alliance systems that proliferated during the Cold War. The neo-Wilsonian dreams of an international system of collective security uniting all countries of the world faded as the wartime alliance disintegrated and the United States and the Soviet Union embarked on their global rivalry in the early postwar years.

The countries of Latin America were the first to press for a regional security system under the provisions of Article 51 of the UN Charter. As the war in Asia drew to a close in August 1945, Brazil offered to host a conference of the American states in Rio de Janiero to draft a mutual defense agreement covering the Western Hemisphere. The Truman administration initially hesitated to join a regional association that included Argentina. Toward the end of the war that country had fallen under the domination of Colonel Juan Perón, an avowed admirer of Hitler who permitted thousands of Nazi officers and officials to enter Argentina and establish false identities there. But the vitriolic campaign against Perón launched by U.S. Ambassador (and later assistant secretary of state for Latin American affairs) Spruille Braden backfired: Washington's attempt to expose Perón's pro-Nazi policies through the publication of incriminating documents enabled him to exploit public resentment against U.S. meddling in Argentina's domestic affairs. After Perón's election to the presidency in

---

*The U.S. and Latin American delegations eventually struck a bargain with Moscow whereby they would support the separate membership of the Ukrainian and Belorussian Soviet Socialist Republics in exchange for the admission of Argentina.

February 1946, the Truman administration reluctantly made its peace with Argentina, a shift in policy that was facilitated by Perón's fervent anti-Communism and his declaration of support for U.S. foreign policy objectives in the Cold War.

This rapprochement between Buenos Aires and Washington removed the major cause of Washington's reluctance to endorse Brazil's earlier invitation to an inter-American security conference. In August 1947, President Truman and his new secretary of state, George Marshall, arrived in Rio to participate in the long-postponed Inter-American Conference for the Maintenance of Continental Peace and Security. Having recently proclaimed the Truman Doctrine and the policy of containment, the president sought to enlist the Latin American states in the American global campaign to combat Soviet expansionism (just as Roosevelt had mobilized them against the presumed threat of Nazi Germany during World War II). Invoking Article 51 of the UN Charter, which authorized the establishment of regional security arrangements, the delegations at the Rio Conference unanimously approved the Inter-American Treaty of Reciprocal Assistance (which became widely known as the "Rio Treaty"). It defined an armed attack against any of the American states, from outside or inside the hemisphere, as an attack on all of them requiring collective measures to curb the aggression. The new pact in effect extended the hemispheric alliance system that had been forged during the war against the Axis.

The Rio Treaty was endowed with a permanent political structure at the next inter-American conference in Bogota, Colombia, in April 1948, when the delegates transformed the old Pan-American Union (a loose-knit, largely symbolic entity) into the Organization of American States (OAS). The charter of the new regional organization set up a permanent council with headquarters in Washington to handle day-to-day matters and stipulated the convocation of inter-American conferences every five years to address major issues facing the hemisphere. The OAS proved successful in resolving several minor disputes within the region, such as those between Nicaragua and Costa Rica in 1949, 1955, and 1959 and between Nicaragua and Honduras in 1957. But difficulties arose within the organization when the United States attempted to employ the inter-American security machinery on behalf of its global struggle with the Communist bloc. In the early stages of the Korean War, the Truman administration requested military support from Latin American states on the grounds that the Rio Treaty obligated them to defend the United States against North Korean (and later Chinese) aggression. None of the Latin American members of the OAS states responded to Washington's appeal save Colombia, which contributed one infantry battalion to the UN forces battling the Communist forces on the Korean peninsula. The ruling elites of those countries were much less concerned about Communism in Asia or Europe than they were about the threat of revolution at home. The United States could help them to avoid the revolutionary upheavals that were sweeping much of Asia in two ways. First, it could provide security assistance to strengthen the governments' ability to curb domestic unrest. Second, it could furnish economic aid to increase the standard of living of the population, thereby removing the sources of revolutionary discontent.

The Truman administration responded with alacrity to the Latin American governments' appeal for security assistance. In 1951 the U.S. government extended to Latin America the Military Security Program, which had been established in 1949 to facilitate the rearmament of Western Europe. During the first half of the 1950s Washington concluded bilateral mutual defense agreements with a number of Latin American states and supplied them with military equipment and advisers. The flow of U.S. military aid had the effect of rendering the Latin American armed forces increasingly dependent on the United States for weapons and ammunition. Many senior members of the officer corps received their training in the United States and developed close ties with their U.S. counterparts.

As we have seen, one of the principal motivations behind Latin American support for the regional security system of the Western Hemisphere was the anticipation of substantial economic assistance from Washington. The appearance of President Truman and Secretary of State George Marshall at the Rio Conference in August 1947 came just a month after the non-Communist nations of Europe had met in Paris to accept Marshall's historic offer of massive U.S. economic assistance. The Latin American delegates at Rio waited in eager anticipation for the president or his secretary of state to announce a "Marshall Plan" for the Western Hemisphere. But Truman made it abundantly plain in his speech in Rio that U.S. government aid would be restricted to countries recovering from the devastation of war. Latin America would have to turn to Wall Street rather than Washington for financial support. The Truman administration also steadfastly opposed Latin American proposals for international agreements to stabilize world commodity prices in order to prevent the drastic price fluctuations of the region's principal exports, insisting on the preservation of the free market as the price-setting mechanism.

The economic stagnation suffered by all Latin American countries after World War II, caused partly by long-term structural problems and partly by the abrupt termination of war-induced demand for their raw materials after 1945, exacerbated acute social tensions that stemmed from the extreme maldistribution of land and capital. The landowning, commercial, and financial oligarchies, in alliance with the military caste and the hierarchy of the Catholic church, maintained a monopoly on political power and resisted social and economic reforms that would curtail their privileges and prerogatives to the profit of the landless, impoverished peasantry in the countryside and the small but expanding working class in the cities. Such a volatile situation was a classic prescription for social instability; many of the republics of Latin America were shaken by a seemingly endless cycle of popular upheaval and savage government repression in the years after 1945. And in view of the extensive involvement of U.S. firms in the economies of the region, together with Washington's preoccupation with preventing the spread of Soviet influence there, it is scarcely surprising that the domestic turmoil there would eventually engage the attention of the authorities in Washington.

## The Revival of U.S. Interventionism: Guatemala, 1954

One of the most economically underdeveloped and socially retrograde countries in the Western Hemisphere at the end of World War II was the small Central American country of Guatemala. In this impoverished society just south of Mexico, a tight-knit elite of wealthy families dominated the government, controlled the army, and owned most of the country's land. Virtually the sole source of Guatemala's national income was tropical agricultural products such as bananas, which were exported mainly to the United States. Two percent of the population owned 70 percent of the land, which was cultivated by destitute peasants who scratched out a meager existence amid hopeless conditions of poverty, illiteracy, and disease. The landowners were largely of European stock while most of those who toiled in the fields were indigenous Mayans, which added a racial component to the country's sharp division between rich and poor.

Toward the end of World War II the political situation in Guatemala began to undergo a fundamental transformation. After a popular insurrection ousted the thirteen-year-old dictatorship of General Jorge Ubico, the country held its first free presidential elections in December 1944. The winner was a university professor named Juan Arévalo who had campaigned on a platform of moderate social and economic reform. In the course of the next six years Arévalo's government sponsored a series of measures aimed at alleviating the plight of the indigenous peasantry. This progressive legislation predictably antagonized the land-owning oligarchy, which feared the loss of its power and privileges, as well as its allies in the officer corps of the army.

But the relatively modest innovations undertaken by Arévalo were nothing compared to what was soon to come. The country's second free election in November 1950 brought to the presidency the following March the ruling party's most vociferous advocate of radical socioeconomic reform, a thirty-year-old former army colonel named Jacobo Arbenz Guzmán. During his campaign Arbenz had pledged to extend the government's campaign to narrow the gap between rich and poor by improving the lot of the impoverished Indians in the countryside. In June 1952 the Guatemalan congress approved and Arbenz signed into law the most sweeping land distribution scheme in the history of Latin America. It authorized the government to expropriate hundreds of thousands of acres, divide the huge tracts into small plots, and parcel them out to the people that had long been cultivating them. This revolutionary legislation predictably provoked the wrath of the wealthy families that owned most of the real estate earmarked for nationalization. They mounted a campaign to block the government's proposed program, and promptly discovered a powerful ally in this venture: The new laws threatened the economic interests not only of the Guatemalan landowning elite but of foreign-owned (mainly U.S.) operations as well. In February 1953 the Arbenz government notified the U.S.-owned United Fruit Company, the largest corporate landowner in the country, of its intention to expropriate 225,000 acres of the firm's uncultivated land as part of the nationwide redistribution scheme. Arbenz offered to compensate the company in the amount of $600,000, which was what United Fruit had declared to be the value of its property for tax purposes. The company countered with a demand for $15 million and appealed to Washington for diplomatic support. Lobbyists for the American banana concern, backed by the American ambassador to Guatemala, pointed out to the new Eisenhower administration that the Guatemalan Communist Party had supported Arbenz during his election campaign and that its officials had advised him during the drafting of the land reform laws. The presence of a few Communists in Arbenz's entourage inspired fears in Washington that he was becoming an unwitting stooge of the Kremlin who might permit his country to become the first Soviet client state in the Western Hemisphere. In October 1953 a high-ranking official in the State Department sharply criticized Guatemala for "openly playing the Communist game" and warned that it could expect no further assistance from the United States.

While the Eisenhower administration publicly squabbled with the Guatemalan government over the latter's threat to the United Fruit Company's property rights, the British government was facing a similar challenge to its economic interests in Iran. In the spring of 1951 the intensely nationalistic Iranian prime minister Mohammed Mossadegh, who (like Arbenz) enjoyed the support of the country's Communist Party, had nationalized the Iranian oil industry. This move enraged the management of the British-controlled Anglo-Iranian Oil Company, which produced, refined, and marketed most of the country's substantial petroleum resources. When Anglo-Iranian appealed to its government for support in the dispute, London turned in desperation to Washington for assistance. Alarmed at the prospect of a nationalistic Iran hostile to Western interests, President Eisenhower decided that Mossadegh had to go. Once ensconced in the White House, the organizer of the Allied invasion of Europe in World War II ironically was averse to the overt use of military force in support of important national objectives. Recalling the daring wartime exploits of the Office of Strategic Services (OSS) under its flamboyant chief, "Wild Bill" Donovan, Eisenhower preferred to rely on covert operations instead. He therefore instructed the Central Intelligence Agency (CIA), the successor to the O.S.S., to arrange for the removal of the Iranian prime minister without directly implicating the United States government. CIA operatives thereupon conspired with renegade officers of the Iranian army to foment an insurrection against Mossadegh in the summer of 1953, which resulted in his deposition and the restoration of a pro-Western government in Teheran.

The success of the covert operation against Mossedegh in Iran emboldened the Eisenhower administration to plan a similar campaign against Arbenz in Guatemala. After Washington terminated all economic assistance to his government, the CIA secretly began to train and equip a mercenary army of Guatemalan exiles in Honduras and Nicaragua that was headed by a dissident Guatemalan military officer named Lieutenant Colonel Carlos Castillo Armas. When the United States rejected the Guatemalan government's urgent request for military aid to defend itself, Arbenz turned in desperation to Moscow. Although the post-Stalinist leadership in the Kremlin had observed the political developments in Guatemala with only mild interest and exercised no influence on Arbenz, the opportunity to challenge the United States in its own backyard was too good to pass up. The Soviet government instructed its satellite Czechoslovakia to sell the Guatemalan government two thousand tons of old German rifles and machine guns that had been confiscated at the end of World War II.

The arrival of this cargo of obsolete Czechoslovak weapons on the Guatemalan coast in the spring of 1954 supplied the Eisenhower administration with the pretext it required for implementing the operation it had been planning for months. On June 18 Castillo Armas and some two hundred troops crossed into Guatemala from Honduras as the capital was being bombed and strafed by World War II vintage airplanes manned by CIA pilots. Abandoned by the high-ranking officers in his army, Arbenz abruptly resigned on June 27 and fled to Mexico in exile. After landing in Guatemala City in an American airplane, Castillo Armas elbowed his way into power at the head of a military junta that proceeded to revoke all the political, social, and economic reforms of the past ten years. The government banned opposition parties, jailed thousands of political dissidents, executed hundreds of suspected Communists, repealed Arbenz's land reform legislation, and restored expropriated lands (including United Fruit's) to their previous owners. In the ensuing wave of violence Castillo Armas was assassinated in 1957. The country was governed thereafter by a succession of right-wing dictatorships that retained close ties with Washington. In the last year of Eisenhower's term Guatemala provided training facilities for Cuban exiles who were preparing (with CIA assistance) an invasion of Cuba to overthrow Fidel Castro (see page 107). In the meantime Guatemalan security forces waged a ruthless counterinsurgency campaign against Arbenz's former allies and their new recruits, who conducted hit-an-run operations against the government from rural hideouts. For the next four decades, over one hundred thousand Guatemalans perished in this brutal civil war.

The covert operation that ousted Arbenz in 1954 was the first instance of a unilateral intervention by the United States in Latin America since the promulgation of Franklin Roosevelt's Good Neighbor Policy twenty-one years earlier. To some critics at the time it represented a violation of the august principle of nonintervention enshrined in the Charter of the Organization of American States (OAS). In anticipation of this objection, Dulles had taken the precaution of soliciting support for collective action against Guatemala from the hemispheric security organization. Appearing at an emergency meeting of the OAS in Caracas in March 1954, the U.S. secretary of state pressed for a resolution authorizing an immediate response to what he characterized as the acute threat of a Communist takeover in Guatemala. Faced with widespread opposition within the Latin American delegations to the use of military force, Dulles had to settle for a watered-down resolution (approved by a vote of 17 to 1—Guatemala opposed, with Argentina and Mexico abstaining) that bristled with anti-Communist rhetoric but made no reference to the need for prompt action against Arbenz. Even the innocuous anti-Communist language of the compromise resolution encountered some resistance in the OAS, whose Latin American members seemed more concerned about the revival of U.S. interventionism in the hemisphere than about the remote threat of Communism there.

## "Yankee, Go Home!"

Latin American reactions to the overthrow of the Arbenz government in Guatemala were mixed. Some of the military or civilian dictatorships with close ties to Washington, such as Nicaragua and Venezuela, openly supported the U.S. unilateral intervention. Other countries acquiesced in the apparent abrogation of the Good Neighbor Policy. But expressions of public outrage resounded throughout Latin America, particularly from university students and nationalist leaders who feared a revival of Washington's interference in their country's affairs. The conspicuous role played by the United Fruit Company in the Guatemalan episode also rekindled long-simmering resentments against the inordinate power exercised by U.S. firms in the region.

The extent of this growing anti-U.S. sentiment was graphically illustrated during Vice President Richard Nixon's good will tour to Latin America in the spring of 1958. Nixon's reputation as a staunch anti-Communist made him a natural target for student leftists in the various universities that he insisted on visiting against the advice of his security staff. Hecklers in Montevideo, Uruguay, and Lima, Peru, greeted him with jeers and insults whenever he spoke. The ugliest outburst of anti-Americanism took place in Venezuela, where the corrupt, repressive government of Marcos Pérez Jiménez had been overthrown in a military coup earlier in the year. Jimenez had been a staunch supporter of the United States during his seven-year reign, welcoming American foreign investment, cooperating with American oil companies, and backing Washington to the hilt in the Cold War. After his ouster the Eisenhower administration granted asylum to Jiménez and his detested police chief, generating a wave of indignation among those Venezuelans who had suffered at the hands of this brutal dictatorship. When Nixon's motorcade steered through the streets of Caracas it was blocked by angry, stone-throwing demonstrators, who broke the windows and smashed the fenders of his automobile as Secret Service agents drew their guns before the driver was able to extricate the vehicle from the angry mob.

The intensity of the anti-American sentiment that had turned Nixon's "good will" tour into a public relations disaster prompted officials in Washington to pay closer attention to the volatile political situation south of the border and to give careful consideration to possible remedies. It had become evident that one of the principal sources of political instability in the region was its economic backwardness. A few weeks after Nixon's trip came to its ignominious conclusion, Brazilian President Juscelino Kubitscheck floated the idea of a joint program of economic development for the hemisphere on the implicit assumption that most of the financing would come from the United States government. Shrewdly couching his proposal in Cold War language, the Brazilian head of state pleaded for a U.S. commitment of $40 billion in economic assistance to Latin America for the next twenty years as a means of combating Communist subversion. But this bid for the equivalent of a Marshall Plan for Latin America was given the cold shoulder by the Eisenhower administration, which remained wedded to the conviction that private lending and investment rather than governmental aid programs financed by taxpayers' dollars were the appropriate means of promoting economic development in Latin America.

One lone U.S. government initiative did emerge from the internal debates prompted by the Nixon tour: The U.S. government finally agreed to support the creation of an Inter-American Development Bank (IADB), a government-funded regional financing agency that several Latin American countries had been proposing for years. The new agency, to which the United States government contributed a paltry $500 million, disbursed its first development loans to Latin American countries in October 1960 as Eisenhower prepared to vacate the White House. Although a mere drop in the bucket compared to the region's desperate need for working capital, the IADB funds represented the first U.S. effort to promote Latin American economic development with public funds.

## Kennedy's Alliance for Progress

The incoming Kennedy administration completely transformed this modest Eisenhower initiative into a wide-ranging, ambitious program of hemispheric economic development closer to the spirit of Kubitschek's stillborn proposal of 1958. In his inaugural address on January 20, 1961, the new American president spoke of forging an "alliance for progress" between the United States and the other republics of the Western Hemisphere to lift them out of the economic misery to which they had been condemned for so long. In a follow-up speech on March 13 to a gathering of delegates from the Latin American states, Kennedy provided a detailed blueprint for a comprehensive project of U.S. foreign aid to the region. He called for "a vast cooperative effort, unparalleled in magnitude and nobility of purpose, to satisfy the basic needs of the Latin American people for homes, work and land, health and schools." At the Inter-American Economic and Social Conference in Punta del Este, Uruguay, the following August, Kennedy's secretary of the treasury, C. Douglas Dillon, formally unveiled the Alliance for Progress as the keystone of the new administration's economic policy toward the Western Hemisphere.

The advertised objective of the unprecedented U.S. aid program to Latin America was to eradicate illiteracy, hunger, and disease in the region as well as to promote an annual growth rate of at least 2.5 percent (about twice that of the 1950s). To reach this lofty goal Dillon pledged $20 billion over the next decade. These funds were to be provided by U.S. government grants, by multinational lending agencies such as the World Bank, and by private American investors and financial institutions. But Kennedy and his advisers realized that pouring dollars into Latin America would not cure its economic problems if the money were diverted into the pockets of the wealthy few. So the United States demanded, as a quid pro quo for the provision of development aid, that the recipient countries enact measures of land distribution and tax reform to reduce the notorious inequality of wealth that had long plagued the region. Kennedy also made it clear that he expected to deal with democratically elected governments rather than the military or civilian dictatorships that predominated there. The eloquent young president's insistence on linking U.S. economic aid to the cause of social and political reform evoked great enthusiasm among the masses in Latin America, who had grown accustomed to Washington's support for oligarchies and autocrats. On the other hand, it alienated the economic, political, and military elites of the recipient countries, which had the most to lose from the reforms envisioned by the Alliance. Yet the U.S. aid program received the official endorsement of all of the twenty republics of Latin America, save one. Ironically, it was the one whose history throughout the twentieth century had been most closely linked, economically, politically, and militarily, to the United States.

## The Challenge of the Cuban Revolution

Since the mid-1930s the island of Cuba had been single-handedly dominated by a former army sergeant named Fulgencio Batista. Originally aligned with a radical political movement that had ousted the despised dictator Gerardo Machado in 1933, Batista quickly acquired absolute power and proceeded to govern the little island, either directly or through hand-picked stooges, for the next quarter century. His power rested on the support of the Cuban business and agricultural elites, the army, and the American financial and commercial enterprises whose interests his regime protected. The government in Washington, although periodically afflicted with pangs of discomfort with the corrupt and repressive character of Batista's rule, was willing to tolerate the situation because of the Cuban dictator's friendly attitude toward foreign investment and his solid support of the United States in the Cold War.

Throughout the 1950s a revolutionary challenge to Batista's autocratic regime was mounted by a young middle-class revolutionary named Fidel Castro. The son of a prosperous Spanish immigrant born in 1927, Castro rebelled against his bourgeois upbringing (which included a Jesuit primary and secondary education followed by law school) to become a full-time revolutionary dedicated to the overthrow of the Batista dictatorship. After traveling throughout Latin America and observing movements of social and political protest in a number of countries, Castro mounted his first revolutionary operation on July 26, 1953, with an attack against a provincial army garrison in the city of Santiago. Captured, convicted, and imprisoned, he was amnestied after a year and fled to Mexico to plan a new revolutionary operation. With a tiny band of loyal followers (including a twenty-seven-year-old Argentine physician named Ernesto "Che" Guevara, who had witnessed firsthand the CIA-sponsored overthrow of Arbenz in 1954), Castro landed in Cuba in 1956 on a dilapidated yacht to incite what he hoped would be a full-scale insurrection in Cuba's major cities. When the anticipated urban uprising did not materialize, he fled to the Sierra Maestra mountains in the eastern part of the island and resumed his efforts to forge an effective rebel force. In this rugged redoubt Castro and his little contingent of middle-class revolutionaries came in contact for the first time with the destitute, landless peasantry. He promptly recognized the rural masses as potential recruits to the revolutionary cause. A series of laudatory accounts of the rag-tag group's honesty, bravery, and dedication by a *New York Times* reporter who had been smuggled into the rebels' mountain hideout instantly transformed the obscure rebel leader into an international hero. Castro's image of revolutionary idealism contrasted sharply with the reports in the world press of the Batista regime's venality, mismanagement, and repression.

As violent clashes between army troops and rebels in the Sierra Maestra multiplied, the Eisenhower administration came to regard the Batista regime as a liability. In March 1958 it imposed an arms embargo on both the government and the rebels, an ostensibly even-handed policy that redounded to Castro's benefit by signaling that Washington had lost confidence in the regime in Havana that it had supported for so long. Reading the handwriting on the wall, Batista abruptly abdicated on the last day of 1958 and flew off with a planeload of relatives and financial assets to the Dominican Republic. On New Years Day 1959 Fidel Castro triumphantly entered Havana, clad in the green fatigues that would become his signature. The following April the new Cuban leader visited the United States to reassure the Eisenhower administration of his good intentions. The apprehensive president avoided a direct meeting with the bearded revolutionary, delegating to Vice President Nixon the task of according the visitor a polite reception. Appearing on the popular television news program *Meet the Press,* Castro conveyed in halting English the unmistakable impression of a Cuban patriot. He emphatically denied the presence of Communists in his entourage and affirmed his friendship for the United States.

On returning to Cuba, however, Castro proceeded to launch a sweeping program of socioeconomic reform that was guaranteed to ruffle feathers in Washington. In the spring of 1959 he instituted a sweeping transfer of land ownership that made Arbenz's short-lived experiment in Guatemala five years earlier pale by comparison.

The Cuban government expropriated all estates larger than one thousand acres and announced plans to redistribute the nationalized landholdings to small farmers and cooperatives. As in the earlier Guatemalan land reform scheme, the former owners would be compensated in Cuban government bonds on the basis of the property values declared to the tax collector. Under the agrarian reform law, U.S. sugar companies in Cuba stood to lose over 1.6 million acres of land by the end of the year. The Eisenhower administration retaliated against this threat to American interests on July 6 by announcing a 95 percent reduction of the Cuban sugar quota, which had allowed the island's main cash crop to enter the United States at below-market prices. Castro then turned his attention to other sectors of the Cuban economy that were dominated by foreign companies: On October 14, 1960, he nationalized all foreign financial, industrial, and commercial enterprises, including U.S.-owned electricity and telephone companies, banks, oil refineries, and nickel mines. This measure prompted Washington to impose an embargo on all exports to the island except medical supplies and foodstuffs. When Castro angrily demanded that personnel at the American embassy in Havana be reduced to eleven persons, Eisenhower severed diplomatic relations with Cuba just before leaving office in January 1961.

The defiant anti-Americanism that Castro increasingly relied upon to win public support for his regime naturally caught the attention of the Soviet Union. The Cuban leader had held the country's small Communist Party at arm's length while he planned and executed his insurrection in the 1950s. But his brother Raul and his *compadre* Guevara had both been converted to Marxism-Leninism during the campaign against Batista. After taking power Castro abolished all political parties except the Communist Party, whose organizational expertise he would increasingly depend on to implement his agrarian reform program. As Washington applied economic sanctions on Cuba in the last year of the Eisenhower administration, Castro increasingly turned to America's Cold War rival for support. In February 1960 Anastas Mikoyan, the deputy chairman of the Soviet Council of Ministers, turned up in Havana at the government's invitation to negotiate the economic basis of the emerging partnership between the two countries. The Soviet visitor and the Cuban leader signed a trade agreement whereby Moscow granted $200 million in low-interest loans and agreed to purchase four million tons of sugar (roughly one-fifth of Cuba's sugar crop) in each of the next four years. The Soviet Union's willingness to replace the United States as the primary market for Cuban sugar and the island's major source of foreign credit undermined the U.S. economic sanctions imposed during the last year of the Eisenhower presidency. By the beginning of 1961, three-quarters of Cuba's foreign trade was being conducted with the USSR and Eastern Europe.

Cuba's growing economic links with the Communist bloc were complemented by an expanding military relationship between Moscow and Havana. The Soviet Union had been begun supplying arms to Cuba in the fall of 1959, even before Castro had broken with the United States. Throughout 1960 Soviet weapons, technicians, and military advisers arrived on the island, while Cuban airmen received training in Czechoslovakia to fly Soviet-built planes. Seizing an opportunity to announce his new alignment at an international forum, Castro traveled to New York City in September 1960 to attend the annual session of the United Nations General Assembly. There he met Nikita Khrushchev for the first time, not in some penthouse

*Fidel Castro and Nikita Khrushchev embracing each other in New York City while attending a session of the United Nations General Assembly, September 1960. (National Archives)*

suite in downtown Manhattan but in a third-class hotel in Harlem, where the Cuban delegation had ensconced itself to advertise its solidarity with the victims of American racism. At the UN General Assembly the Cubans wildly applauded each allusion to their revolution in Khrushchev's speech. Appearing at the podium in full battle dress, Castro delivered a four-and-a-half-hour harangue on September 26, inveighing against the evils of American imperialism and lavishing praise on his new patrons in Moscow.

## The Bay of Pigs Fiasco

The apparent emergence of a pro-Soviet client state ninety miles from the United States caused great anxiety in Washington. The CIA had already begun to consider recruiting Cuban exiles who were flooding into Florida for an invasion force to topple the Castro regime. In March 1960 Eisenhower formally authorized the agency to provide clandestine training for these anti-Castro emigrés in Guatemala and Nicaragua. During the 1960 presidential campaign, Kennedy had vigorously criticized Eisenhower (and by implication, Kennedy's opponent, Vice President Richard Nixon) for permitting a Soviet client state to be established in America's own backyard. Without knowing the specific details of the CIA invasion plan, Kennedy demanded that something be done to remove Castro from power. Shortly after his inauguration the new president overcame a last-minute bout of skepticism and approved the scheme he had inherited from his predecessor. He had received solemn assurances from the CIA that the arrival of the exile army on the island would incite massive defections from Castro's militia and a popular uprising against his rule. Memories of the ease with which a few hundred U.S.-trained Guatemalan exiles had toppled Arbenz in 1954 were still fresh in the minds of those responsible for covert operations in Washington.

On April 17 a brigade of about sixteen hundred Cuban exiles trained by the CIA in Guatemala disembarked from American ships at the designated landing site of Giron Beach in the Bahia de los Cochinos (Bay of Pigs) on the southern coast of Cuba. Instead of rising up against Castro, as the organizers of the operation had predicted, the local population as well as the military forces in the area remained loyal to their leader. At the end of three days all of the invaders were either dead or in jail. When the extent of the disaster became evident, Kennedy turned a deaf ear to the brigade's frantic pleas for American air support. He was unwilling to permit the United States to become involved directly in an operation that seemed likely to fail. The Bay of Pigs fiasco tarnished the shining image of the charismatic new American president only a few months after his inauguration. The resulting recriminations produced in Washington a kind of obsession with the Cuban leader, whose revolutionary regime came to be seen as a serious threat to the security of the United States in its own backyard. The heightened tension between the United States and the Soviet Union after the Berlin crisis in the summer of 1961 aggravated these anxieties about Castro, who openly declared his Marxist-Leninist sympathies at the end of the year. The CIA continued overtly and ostentatiously to train Cuban exiles in Florida for Bay of Pigs–type operations in the future. Covertly, but presumably well known to Castro's efficient intelligence services, it engaged in an elaborate campaign (code-named Operation Mongoose when it was formally authorized in November 1961) to destabilize the Cuban government through sabotage and even assassination plots against its head of state. In the spring and summer of 1962 the U.S. navy conducted extensive maneuvers in the Caribbean that must have appeared intimidating to the isolated, vulnerable regime in Havana.

In short, Fidel Castro had good reason to fear that the Bay of Pigs invasion was merely the first stage in the Kennedy administration's campaign to dislodge him. It seemed likely that Washington's next move would be much more dangerous than the landing of fifteen hundred amateur fighters on a beach without air cover. The Cuban leader therefore turned to the only possible source of protection against the formidable threat from the superpower to the north. Khrushchev's earlier warnings against any U.S. attempt to overthrow Castro were dismissed in Washington as hot air. By the summer of 1961 Kennedy knew how far the Soviet Union had fallen behind the United States in the nuclear arms race and therefore how difficult it would be for Khrushchev to back up his tough talk with military muscle (see page 78). But what the American president apparently failed to appreciate was the extent to which the defense of the Cuban revolution had become a preeminent goal of Soviet foreign policy. Washington had been willing to go to the brink of war to defend the isolated outpost of democratic capitalism in Berlin. For Moscow, Castro's island stood out as the Communists' only showcase in the West. The "loss" of Cuba would severely damage the international credibility of the Soviet Union as the patron of national liberation struggles against the capitalist imperialist powers. Already under fire from China and from critics at home for an insufficiently militant stance toward the West, the Soviet leader determined that Castro had to be provided with the protection he sought.

## To the Brink of Armageddon

In April 1962 the Soviet Presidium approved Cuba's urgent request for conventional weapons for its defense against a possible U.S. attack. This military aid package included a Soviet infantry regiment as well as 180 surface-to-air missiles (SAMs) for air defense. In late May Khrushchev obtained his colleagues' endorsement of a much more grandiose plan to ensure Cuba's security. The project included the construction of a base for Soviet submarines carrying ballistic missiles armed with nuclear warheads as well as the deployment of thirty-six medium-range (1,100-nautical mile) SS-4 and twenty-four intermediate-range (2,200-nautical mile) SS-5 missile launchers on the island. Nuclear weapons had not appeared on Castro's shopping list, but Soviet officials had no difficulty persuading the Cuban leader to accept them for the defense of his island. Never before had Moscow offered to transfer nuclear weapons outside its borders—not to its Eastern European satellites, not to China in the heyday of Sino-Soviet friendship during the fifties. Khrushchev apparently took this audacious step because he assumed that the delivery and installation of these missiles, which was scheduled to take place between August and November, would enable him to confront Kennedy with a fait accompli. The American president would have to adapt to the presence of the Cuban missiles, just as Moscow had learned to live with the thirty Jupiter IRBMs that the United States had placed in Italy in 1961 and the fifteen that had been installed just across the Soviet border in Turkey between November 1961 and March 1962.

The successful deployment of the Soviet missiles in Cuba would have brought Khrushchev two important advantages in the Soviet-American global rivalry. First of all, it would have greatly enhanced Moscow's credibility as the protector of countries threatened by the United States, countering Washington's reputation as the defender of the isolated, vulnerable city of West Berlin. Second, as we have seen, Khrushchev had been humiliated by the October 1961 speech by Deputy Secretary of Defense Roswell Gilpatric exposing the extent of America's superiority in strategic nuclear weapons (that is, warheads that could reach the territory of the adversary). By 1962 the United States had stockpiled some five thousand nuclear warheads compared to only several hundred for the Soviet Union. Worse, in the five years since Sputnik the Russians had lagged far behind the Americans in the construction of delivery systems for their long-range missiles: about twenty ICBMs capable of reaching U.S. territory, compared to a U.S. ICBM force of 180. In all of the other categories of strategic weapons the Russians suffered an overwhelming disadvantage: 200 Soviet versus 630 American long-range bombers; six Soviet ballistic missile submarines (SLBMs), whose base in the Kola Peninsula seven thousand miles from the United States prevented them from maintaining regular patrols within range of U.S. targets, compared to twelve Polaris submarines in the U.S. fleet (each carrying 12 missiles) that could constantly operate within range of Soviet targets. Since the MRBMs and IRBMs to be deployed in Cuba could reach targets almost anywhere in the continental United States—including the Strategic Air Command's bomber bases and other military targets—they would immediately function as substitute "strategic" missiles and thereby partially compensate for the Soviet Union's inferiority in ICBMs, SLBMs, and long-range bombers. After the midterm congressional elections in November, when Kennedy would presumably be less vulnerable to partisan political criticism from the Republican opposition for permitting a Soviet arms buildup in Cuba, Khrushchev would be free to reveal the existence of the missiles. From his newly acquired position of de facto strategic parity with the United States, he could extract concessions from Washington on Berlin, Laos, and other matters in dispute.

Why Khrushchev and his advisers were so confident that the deployment of the Cuban missiles could be accomplished without detection by American intelligence remains a mystery, even after the profusion of memoirs from participants and the opening of Soviet archives. In August CIA Director John McCone expressed his concerns to Kennedy about the unusually large shipments arriving on the island from the Soviet Union. American spies operating in the country filed reports of eighty-foot canvas-covered cylinders transported on trucks into remote palm forests. But although suspicions were mounting in Washington about the flurry of Soviet activity in Cuba, conclusive evidence of a nuclear arms buildup was lacking. Kennedy initially ruled out the most effective means of discovering what the Cubans and their Soviet patrons were up to—over-flights by high-altitude U-2 reconnaissance planes—for fear that one would be shot down (as had occurred over the Soviet Union in 1960 and more recently in early September over China). When he changed his mind and authorized a U-2 operation for October 14, the plane returned with unmistakable photographic evidence of Soviet missile sites under construction on the island.

After reviewing the reconnaissance photography on October 16, Kennedy convened in utmost secrecy a high-level team of officials in the White House to advise him on an appropriate response to the challenge. Formally known as the Executive Committee (or Ex Com) of the National Security Council, this small group conducted daylong meetings that Kennedy himself joined on October 20. The one option that the Ex Com ruled out from the very beginning was precisely the one that Khrushchev had assumed the U.S. government would adopt: the acceptance of the new strategic situation after the usual pro forma protests. All of Kennedy's advisers agreed that the only acceptable outcome to the crisis would be the removal of all of the missile launchers from the island.

Three alternative means of achieving that goal were under consideration. One faction dominated by high-ranking military officers proposed conventional air strikes to destroy the missile sites before they became fully operational. Kennedy vetoed such drastic action because of the grave risks entailed: A bombing campaign would inevitably cause casualties among the Russian technicians working on the sites and might stampede whoever had operational control of the missiles into retaliating with those that had already been armed with nuclear warheads. Another coterie within the Ex Com advocated an amphibious invasion of the island, this time by American (rather than Cuban exile) forces with full air support. But Kennedy also rejected this type of military operation because it too was likely to result in heavy Russian casualties and risked provoking Soviet nuclear retaliation. A third faction favored a purely diplomatic campaign in the United Nations to force the Russians to dismantle and remove the missiles. That option proved unacceptable because the delay caused by the diplomats' haggling would enable the Soviet workers to complete their work on the missile sites. The United States would be penalized for its patient diplomacy with the fait accompli that Khrushchev had envisioned, leaving the Soviet Union with a fully operational nuclear deterrent ninety miles from Florida.

Smarting from Republican congressional criticism of his botched Bay of Pigs operation and of his passivity during the expansion of Soviet military ties with Cuba, Kennedy was under enormous political pressure to take decisive action. In the end he chose a dual-track strategy that was designed to remove the offending missiles while minimizing the risks of a violent confrontation with the Soviet Union. He ordered a massive conventional military buildup in south Florida in preparation for an invasion of the island. Second, he resorted to the Defense Condition (DEFCON) alert system that Eisenhower had set up in 1959 after American territory had come within range of Soviet nuclear weapons. On October 22 Kennedy ordered the U.S. strategic forces shifted to DEFCON 3 and later to DEFCON 2, the highest alert level short of war. This action quintupled the number of B-47 and B-52 nuclear-loaded bombers of the Strategic Air Command (SAC) kept airborne; sixty-six SAC planes made daily flights across the Atlantic and, after refueling, prepared (if so ordered) to mount bombing raids in the Soviet Union; 182 of the new silo-based Minutemen ICBMs were prepared for firing. All of these measures were undertaken without the slightest effort at concealment in order to achieve two objectives. The first was to convey U.S. determination to remove the offending missile sites from Cuba. The second was to deter the Soviet Union from interfering with the American invasion of Cuba if such action were to become necessary.

On the evening of October 22, Kennedy publicly unveiled the second part of his dual-track policy in a nationally televised speech. After summarizing the U-2 photographic evidence of the missile sites under construction, he announced the imposition of a naval "quarantine" of the island—carefully avoiding the term "blockade" because it signified an act of war according to international law—to prevent the arrival of Soviet ships carrying additional parts for the missiles under construction. He warned Moscow that a nuclear missile launched from Cuba against any nation in the Western Hemisphere would be considered an attack on the United States and would trigger American nuclear retaliation against the Soviet Union. He demanded the prompt dismantling of the missile launchers already operational and the suspension of all construction work on the rest. Armed with the unanimous support of U.S. allies in NATO and the OAS, Kennedy ordered the naval quarantine to begin on October 24.

Eventually 180 U.S. warships established a quarantine line around the eastern tip of Cuba with instructions to intercept and search all vessels suspected of carrying the proscribed equipment. At the height of the confrontation thirty Soviet or Soviet-

chartered cargo ships were crossing the Atlantic en route to Cuba. Although unknown to the U.S. at the time, four of them were carrying IRBMs and a fifth bore
nuclear warheads. Also lurking in Cuban waters were four Soviet submarines armed
with nuclear-tipped torpedoes that could sink any U.S. naval vessels that interfered
with the Soviet shipments. After a decade of careless nuclear saber-rattling, the two
superpowers seemed locked in a collision course that might end in their first direct
military confrontation since the advent of the Cold War.

The first break in the tension-filled impasse came on the evening of the twenty-
fourth, when the four ships carrying the IRBMs stopped and reversed course (the
ship carrying the warheads had already arrived at a Cuban port). Moscow's decision
not to defy the American blockade failed to solve the problem of the missiles that
had already reached the island: Although unknown to U.S. officials at the time, the
thirty-six MRBMs along with their nuclear warheads had arrived. Two days after
Kennedy's public address on October 22, nine missile launchers had been assembled
and rendered operational. As the construction crews at the missile sites scrambled to
complete their work with the materials at hand, the American president made it clear
that military action would be forthcoming unless the construction was suspended
and the operational weapons dismantled and removed. Unwilling to risk nuclear war
on this issue, Khrushchev issued a compromise proposal that was delivered to the
American embassy in Moscow on October 26. In a long, rambling letter to Kennedy
he observed that if the United States were to pledge never to invade Cuba, the necessity for deploying the Soviet missiles on the island would disappear.

As Kennedy and his advisers pondered an appropriate response to this secret approach, a second letter from Khrushchev was broadcast by Radio Moscow the next
day that contained an additional condition: In exchange for the removal of the missiles from Cuba, the United States would not only have to issue a no-invasion pledge
but would also have to remove the fifteen Jupiter IRBMs that it had deployed in
Turkey between November 1961 and March 1962. In the summer of 1961 Kennedy
had almost canceled the plan to deploy the fifteen Jupiters, which many U.S. experts
judged to be inaccurate and obsolete.* In the end he reversed his decision in the face
of urgent appeals from the government in Ankara, which craved the Jupiters as politically potent symbols of America's commitment to Turkey's defense. By the time of
the Cuban crisis Kennedy had forgotten temporarily about the missiles in Turkey,
which had been slated for removal as soon as Polaris submarines with their SLBMs
were deployed in the Mediterranean, and had to be reminded of them by an aide. It
therefore would have been easy for Kennedy to acquiesce in Khrushchev's demand
for a policy that United States planned to pursue anyway.

But unlike Khrushchev's first message, which had been conveyed in utmost secrecy
to Washington, the second letter was broadcast to the entire world as it reached the
White House. The president was unwilling to give the appearance of bowing to Soviet

---

*It is worth noting that the Jupiters, unlike their cousins the Thor IRBMs deployed in Great
Britain and Italy, were semimobile and therefore very difficult to detect. There is some evidence that Soviet military officials were genuinely concerned that these missiles based in
Turkey could wipe out the country's command and control system without warning and therefore adamantly demanded their removal.

pressure as American voters prepared to vote in the midterm congressional elections amid Republican allegations that the Democratic administration was cowering before the Communist threat. He also feared that the acceptance of such an exchange under duress would damage the credibility of the United States in the eyes of its European allies, who might worry about similar tradeoffs at their expense in the future. So Kennedy responded favorably to the conciliatory portion of the first message and simply ignored the more belligerent second message (which some American officials suspected had been drafted by hard-liners in the Kremlin appalled by Khrushchev's willingness to compromise). In a letter to Khrushchev dated October 27, Kennedy pledged not to invade Cuba in exchange for the removal of all the missiles on the island. Through his brother, Attorney General Robert Kennedy, he privately assured the Soviet ambassador in Washington that while no written commitments concerning the Jupiters could be given for domestic political reasons, the Turkish missiles would be unobtrusively withdrawn once the crisis had subsided.* Kennedy accompanied his accommodating message with the stern warning that if the missiles in Cuba were not removed promptly, the United States would do the job itself and accept the consequences.

At this critical stage of the Cuban missile crisis, Fidel Castro became a participant in the drama for the first time. Assuming that an American invasion of his country was imminent and unaware of the secret dealings between Washington and Moscow, the Cuban leader entreated Khrushchev to launch a preemptive nuclear strike against the United States. Having accepted at face value the Soviet leader's extravagant claims about Soviet strategic superiority, Castro apparently assumed that the Russians possessed thousands of ICBMs that could devastate their Cold War adversary. Khrushchev, who knew better, was not prepared to plunge the world into a nuclear war he was bound to lose on behalf of his Cuban client. So he sent Kennedy a third and final letter on October 28 accepting the U.S. no-invasion pledge and offering in exchange to remove all the missiles from Cuba and return them to the USSR.

Castro was so enraged at Khrushchev for caving in to the American ultimatum that he refused to meet with the Soviet emissary, Anastas Mikoyan, until Moscow brought him to heel by threatening to cut off the Soviet oil supplies on which Cuba desperately depended. Unwilling to honor an agreement to which he was not a party, the Cuban leader petulantly refused to permit the prescribed verification of the missiles' removal by a UN inspection team. While the United States resorted to other satisfactory means of verification, Kennedy used the exclusion of the UN inspection team as an excuse to withold the formal issuance of the no-invasion pledge. Although Kennedy and his successors honored it in spirit, the committment remained nothing more than an informal understanding until Leonid Brezhnev finally secured from President Richard Nixon a written confirmation of the pledge in August 1970. There is no small irony in the fact that Fidel Castro, who denounced the settlement after those tension-filled thirteen days in October 1962 as a betrayal of the Cuban revolution, survived in power long enough to witness the demise of Kennedy, Khrushchev, the Cold War, and the Soviet Union itself.

---

*The Jupiter missiles were in fact removed from Turkey six months later with a minimum of fanfare.

# FIVE

# THE RISE AND FALL OF DÉTENTE, 1962–1979

## The Challenge of Arms Control

One of the most important lessons learned by both sides from the Cuban missile crisis was the need to improve the rudimentary communications network between Moscow and Washington, which had significantly increased the danger of accidental nuclear war. In one of the most critical moments in the crisis, the first letter from Khrushchev to Kennedy took eight hours to reach the White House after it had been delivered to the American embassy in Moscow. To prevent such inefficiency in communication during future crises, the two superpowers concluded the so-called hot line agreement of June 20, 1963, which established direct teletype contact between the White House and the Kremlin. From that point on the leaders of the two superpowers were able to consult with one another directly in times of international tension in order to avert misunderstandings that might lead to consequences neither side intended and both would deeply regret.

In addition to this progress in the prevention of accidental nuclear war, the most important diplomatic consequence of the Cuban missile crisis was a renewed interest in nuclear arms control. Since the end of World War II, this topic had been addressed by the two superpowers without success. Less than a year after Hiroshima and Nagasaki, the Truman administration unveiled an elaborate scheme for the international control of weapons of mass destruction that the United States alone currently possessed and whose destructive power had been so graphically demonstrated against Japan. Drafted by Under-Secretary of State Dean Acheson and the future chairman of the Atomic Energy Commission, David Lilienthal, the proposal was extensively modified and then presented to the United Nations in June 1946 by the distinguished presidential adviser Bernard Baruch. The Baruch Plan included what seemed to be a magnanimous pledge by the United States to give up its nuclear monopoly by agreeing to transfer all of its fissionable materials to the custody of the new international organization and, once a system of strict controls had been established, to destroy its small stockpile of nuclear weapons.

But the plan contained two qualifications that had been inserted by Baruch himself to allay concerns in the U.S. Congress that foreign powers might take advantage of this unprecedented offer by a sovereign state to sacrifice its military superiority: First, all other member-states of the UN would have to pledge to refrain from ever constructing nuclear weapons of their own. Second, they would have to submit to periodic on-site inspections by a UN agency charged with the responsibility of verifying compliance. Neither of these conditions was acceptable to the Soviet Union. Stalin was not prepared to suspend his country's own nuclear weapons program (which had been put into high-gear immediately after the American atomic bombs fell on Japan in the summer of 1945) so that the United Nations, which was at the time controlled by the United States and its client states in Western Europe and Latin America, could inherit the American nuclear monopoly. Nor would he ever agree to throw open his closed society to the prying eyes of UN disarmament inspectors. The Soviet Union therefore torpedoed the Baruch Plan, the first in a series of abortive attempts to control the powerful weapons that had ushered in the nuclear age.

Once the Soviet Union tested its first nuclear weapon in September 1949, it began to display greater interest in nuclear arms control. Stalin's death in March 1953 accelerated this trend, as his successors eagerly sought a relaxation of Cold War tensions. At the 1954 session of the UN General Assembly, the Soviet delegate proposed a moratorium on the manufacture of nuclear weapons and the establishment of a UN commission to consider means of controlling those already in existence. On May 10, 1955, Moscow called for a gradual reduction of conventional forces to fixed levels and the elimination of nuclear stockpiles once those levels had been reached. In his speech to the UN General Assembly in 1959, as we have seen, Khrushchev advocated general and total disarmament within four years. But all of these Soviet disarmament proposals in the fifties failed because Washington demanded on-site inspection to verify compliance while Moscow adamantly rejected the presence of foreign observers on its territory as a blatant violation of its national sovereignty. As we have seen, Khrushchev even vetoed Eisenhower's Open Skies scheme at the Geneva Conference in 1955, which offered the alternative of mutual aerial surveillance of the two superpowers' military installations (see page 68).

After the failure of these various efforts to control nuclear weapons during the 1950s, the threat of nuclear war during the Cuban missile crisis prompted the two superpowers to concentrate on two more modest and attainable objectives: the first was to prohibit those powers that possessed nuclear weapons from testing them in ways that endangered the environment and the health of the world's population. The second was to prevent the countries that did not possess nuclear weapons from acquiring them in the future.

## "Blowing in the Wind": The Bid to Limit Nuclear Testing

One of the most important issues at stake between the two blocs at the beginning of the 1960s was the question of how to prevent the dangerous effects of nuclear testing in the atmosphere. Public opposition to such tests had begun after the first U.S. hydrogen bomb test at Bikini island in the Western Pacific on March 1, 1954 (see page 76). The Bikini test (code-named BRAVO) yielded fifteen megatons, ten more than anticipated, generating radioactive fallout to a radius of several hundred miles. It spread downwind, contaminating the crew of the ill-named Japanese fishing boat, *Lucky Dragon*, causing severe illness and eventually one death. Elevated radiation levels were detected all along the Pacific rim after the BRAVO blast. For the first time people began to appreciate not only the destructive force of a nuclear explosion, but the serious environmental and health hazards of radioactive fallout as well.

The result was an international clamor for a halt to nuclear tests spearheaded by various nongovernmental organizations (NGOs), which eventually obliged world leaders to take notice. The Soviet arms control proposal of May 10, 1955, discussed in the previous section included a ban on all nuclear testing. The Eisenhower administration, which was committed to a new round of tests in order to perfect the new generation of nuclear weapons it was planning to deploy, rebuffed this Russian initiative. Each time Moscow offered to suspend its tests if the United States would do likewise, Washington suffered a public relations setback by failing to respond. Then, after completing a new series of nuclear tests, Khrushchev abruptly announced on March 31, 1958, a unilateral moratorium of testing and challenged Eisenhower to follow suit. The president countered with a proposal for a conference in Geneva at which the three nuclear powers (the United States, the Soviet Union, and Great Britain) would discuss a comprehensive test ban agreement. To set the stage for these negotiations, Eisenhower declared that the United States (which was about to complete its latest round of tests) would voluntarily abstain from further testing for a year after the opening of the conference. When Great Britain adhered to this voluntary understanding, the earth was free of nuclear tests for the first time since the advent of the atomic age.

The negotiations for a permanent test ban began on July 1, 1958, but dragged on inconclusively for the next three years. They were dealt a devastating setback on August 31, 1961, when Khrushchev (probably to reassure Soviet allies of his toughness and cover his retreat in Berlin), declared his intention to break the 1958 moratorium. On September 5 Kennedy responded by announcing the resumption of American tests, and Great Britain promptly followed suit. In the next two months the Soviet Union conducted a round of fifty atmospheric tests, capped by the largest nuclear explosion before or since: On October 30 the world's seismic detectors picked up a fifty-eight-megaton blast at a Soviet test site. Thirty-five hundred times larger than the Hiroshima explosion, it dwarfed the fifteen-megaton BRAVO test that had prompted the three nuclear powers to seek the test ban agreement that continually eluded them. The test ban talks in Geneva continually foundered on the issue of how to verify tests conducted underground: Although seismic stations located in foreign countries could detect explosions above twenty kilotons, the only reliable method of preventing small-scale cheating with low-yield underground tests was the type of intrusive on site inspections that the Soviet Union continually refused to accept.

The Cuban missile crisis in October 1962, which had generated the first overt threat of nuclear war and therefore sparked intense public interest throughout the world in reducing the threat of such a cataclysm, broke the logjam in the campaign to limit nuclear testing. The Soviet Union made the first move. Khrushchev sent Kennedy a letter on December 19, 1962, urging him to join in an effort to revive the long-stalled test ban talks. Six months later, in a major address at American University on June 10, 1963, Kennedy responded to Moscow's overtures by endorsing publicly a nuclear test ban treaty and announcing that the United States would refrain from conducting atmospheric tests if the Soviet Union would do likewise. On the nettlesome issue of verification for underground nuclear tests, Kennedy insisted on a minimum of six annual on-site inspections, while Khrushchev was prepared to accept no more than three. The two sides finally agreed to abandon these fruitless efforts to reach agreement on low-level underground testing, which required the deal-breaking on-site inspections to detect. The Americans and British devised a way to cut the Gordian knot and clear the way for intensive negotiations for a treaty: The proposed ban would be limited to tests in the atmosphere and those underground that were large enough to be detected by existing seismic equipment.

In August 1963 the United States, the Soviet Union, and Great Britain signed the Limited Test Ban (LTB) Treaty, which formally entered into effect on October 11 of the same year. During the moratorium on testing from 1958 to 1961, France had become the fourth member of the nuclear club on February 13, 1960, with its first successful atomic test at a Sahara Desert site in Algeria. Insisting that France's belated entry into the nuclear club required additional testing to perfect its nuclear weapons technology, President Charles de Gaulle refused to sign the LTB treaty. On losing its Sahara testing site after granting independence to Algeria in 1962, France resumed atmospheric testing on uninhabited atolls within its territories in the South Pacific (despite indignant protests from neighboring nations such as Australia and New Zealand). When China became the fifth member of the nuclear fraternity in October 1964, it declined to sign the LTB treaty for the same reason and defiantly conducted above-ground tests in its desert testing site in Xinjiang province.

But the environmental and health hazards of radioactive fallout declined dramatically with the suspension of Soviet, American, and British atmospheric testing. The LTB Treaty also served the important purpose of institutionalizing a mechanism for arms-control negotiations between East and West that had not existed before. On January 27, 1967, the three LTB signatories—this time joined by France—signed the Outer Space Treaty, which prohibited nuclear testing beyond the Earth's atmosphere as well as the placing of weapons of mass destruction into orbit around the Earth and their deployment in outer space or on celestial bodies such as the Moon.

## Preserving the Nuclear Oligopoly: The Non-Proliferation Treaty

In addition to imposing limits on testing by nuclear powers, Washington and Moscow cooperated in a campaign to prevent the spread of nuclear weapons to regions where they did not exist and to states that did not possess them. The precedent of regional denuclearization had been established by an obscure treaty of 1959 that declared Antarctica a nuclear-free zone. In 1967 most of the countries of Latin America signed the Treaty of Tlatelolco formally declaring that region off limits to nuclear weapons.* All five declared nuclear powers signed a protocol to the treaty,

---

*Argentina, Brazil, and Chile finally signed the treaty in 1994, and Cuba, the last holdout, signed in 1995.

which went into effect in 1968, pledging to respect Latin America's nonnuclear status and to refrain from using nuclear weapons against any of the treaty's signatories.

In the meantime Soviet and American negotiators were hard at work on a comprehensive agreement to prevent the spread of nuclear weapons to nonnuclear states. Great Britain had first tested an atomic device in 1952 and a hydrogen bomb in 1957, but the British nuclear deterrent was closely linked to that of the United States. It was evident that other countries possessed the scientific expertise to develop nuclear weapons and resented the determination of the two superpowers to preserve what was in effect a nuclear duopoly. Moscow's refusal to share its nuclear technology with Beijing had been one of the major causes of the Sino-Soviet split and China's determination to acquire an independent nuclear capability of its own. Similarly, Washington's reluctance to endorse France's nuclear conditions had driven de Gaulle to acquire for his country a nuclear capability independent of U.S. control (see page 127). What had been an exclusive club of two in the early 1950s expanded to five by the mid-1960s.

Once they had begun their joint campaign to place limits on the nuclear arms race, the two nuclear superpowers shared a common interest in preventing other countries from acquiring weapons of mass destruction that might upset the strategic balance. Accordingly, they joined with Great Britain to draft the Non-Proliferation Treaty (NPT), which was signed by those three powers on July 1, 1968. The NPT entered into force on March 5, 1970, when ninety-seven countries had signed and forty-seven (including the three original signatories) had ratified it. The three signatories possessing nuclear weapons pledged to refrain from supplying them or the technology to produce them to nonnuclear states, while the nonnuclear signatories promised never to produce or acquire them. Although France refused to ratify the treaty, it promised to abide by its provisions. China not only declined to ratify the NPT but also insisted that other countries were perfectly entitled to obtain weapons that the three nuclear powers had long possessed and continued to upgrade.* To meet the nonmilitary nuclear energy needs of the nonnuclear signatories, the nuclear states promised to supply them with commercial nuclear materials for civilian purposes. To ensure that these nuclear power facilities would not be diverted to military ends, the nonnuclear states were required to open their sites to periodic inspections by the Vienna-based United Nations International Atomic Energy Agency.

## Nuclear Parity and Mutual Assured Destruction

The agreements in the 1960s restricting the testing, development, and deployment of nuclear weapons constituted an unprecedented instance of international cooperation in the interests of global security. But these treaties did nothing to limit the expansion of nuclear warheads and the improvement of delivery systems by the two powers that alone possessed the capability of destroying the entire world. The principal roadblock to strategic arms control was the asymmetry of the two superpowers' nuclear forces. The Soviet Union had little interest in accepting limitations on strategic weapons as long as its nuclear arsenal remained decisively inferior to that of the

---

*France and China finally agreed to sign the NPT in 1992.

United States. On the contrary, Khrushchev had launched toward the end of the 1950s a crash program of nuclear modernization aimed at bridging the gap in ICBMs and SLBMs by the end of the decade.

As we have seen, Khruschev's bid to place intermediate-range nuclear missiles in Cuba was intended to compensate for this temporary inferiority in long-range missiles. His ignominious retreat from Cuba revealed to the world the extent of Soviet strategic inferiority and eventually contributed to his own political demise. On October 15, 1964, the Communist Party Central Committee forced him to retire and revived the tradition of collective leadership by separating the two offices of party secretary and prime minister that Khrushchev had combined. The new ruling duo of Party Secretary Leonid Brezhnev and Prime Minister Alexei Kosygin continued the military buildup that their predecessor had begun. This program included an expansion of the Strategic Rocket Forces and the Soviet navy's SLBMs, the restoration of Khruschev's deep cuts in Soviet ground forces, and the construction of a navy capable of a global presence. The principal objective of this massive rearmament campaign was the acquisition of strategic parity with the United States. In most of the relevant categories, the new leadership in the Kremlin met Khrushchev's end-of-the-decade target. By end of the 1960s the Soviet arsenal of ICBMs had expanded to 1,050 compared to 1,054 for the United States. During the same period the Soviets had surpassed the American submarine force of 656 SLBMs and were closing the gap in long-range bombers. This formidable increase in Soviet strategic capability occurred during the period when America's costly conventional military operation in Indochina, together with the domestic social reforms of Johnson's "Great Society," diverted funds from its nuclear program.

Amid this buildup of Soviet military power, officials in both Washington and Moscow began to revisit the long-deferred issue of nuclear arms control (see page 114). The Kremlin had expressed interest in beginning negotiations on strategic arms limitations as early as February 1967. By that time U.S. Secretary of Defense Robert McNamara had come to regard the emerging condition of nuclear parity between the two superpowers as a positive force for stability in the world: The completion of the Minuteman ICBM and Polaris SLBM deployment, in his view, rendered the U.S. strategic arsenal sufficiently menacing to deter a Soviet nuclear attack. The two superpowers had attained the condition of "mutual assured destruction" (MAD), that is, the ability to destroy more than a quarter of the enemy's population and over half of its industry in a retaliatory response to a first strike. By removing any incentive for either superpower to seek victory in nuclear war, this reciprocal vulnerability paradoxically provided the modicum of security for both parties that was required for genuine progress in arms control negotiations to be achieved.

But developments unrelated to the nuclear arms race intervened to prevent the advent of such discussions during Lyndon Johnson's tenure at the White House. The most significant of these was America's massive military intervention in Southeast Asia. Contrary to popular belief in the West, the Soviet government did not enthusiastically supply North Vietnam with arms to wage its war against the United States. It appears that Moscow was in fact quite resentful at having to compete with Beijing for Hanoi's favor. The Russians had poured about $3 billion worth of aid into North Vietnam between 1965 and 1971 (compared to about $1 billion that flowed from

China in the same period), yet the North Vietnamese continued to play one Communist power off against the other to extract more arms from each. The Kremlin could not afford to reduce the flow of aid to North Vietnam for fear of losing influence there to Beijing. But while continuing to support its Communist ally in Hanoi against the United States, Moscow issued periodic feelers to Washington about the possibility of discussing arms control.

President Johnson's decision in the spring of 1968 to suspend the bombing of most of North Vietnam and to seek a negotiated settlement in the peace talks that began in Paris in May removed one of the obstacles to strategic arms negotiations. On August 19, 1968, the Soviet government formally invited Johnson to a summit meeting in Moscow on September 30 to begin wide-ranging discussions on that subject. But the very next day an entirely unrelated episode intruded to prevent Johnson from crowning his presidency with a summit conference in Moscow that might set in motion the long-deferred negotiations to place limits on strategic arms. When Soviet tanks poured into Czechoslovakia to overthrow the reformist government of Alexander Dubcek, Johnson declined the invitation to the Moscow summit as a symbolic protest. But Washington's tacit acquiescence in the Soviet crackdown in Prague was greatly appreciated in Moscow and kept alive the hopes for bilateral discussions on strategic arms control as Johnson prepared to vacate the White House.

## The Road to SALT I

The simultaneous advent of the Nixon administration in Washington and Communist party boss Leonid Brezhnev's triumph over Soviet Premier Alexei Kosygin in their five-year rivalry for supremacy in the Kremlin in 1969 set the stage for significant progress in strategic arms control. Nixon and Brezhnev recognized that both of their countries would derive substantial economic benefits from the reductions in defense spending that would be facilitated by a mutually acceptable set of limits on a nuclear arms race which, in light of strategic parity and mutual assured destruction, neither superpower could win. Brezhnev made the first move. On January 20, 1969, as Nixon was taking the oath of office in Washington, the Kremlin unveiled a proposal calling for Soviet-American negotiations for a mutual limitation of intercontinental ballistic missiles. A week later the new occupant of the White House responded favorably to the Soviet initiative in a statement that cleared the way for substantive negotiations by accepting for the first time the principle of strategic parity. The first formal exchanges between Soviet and American delegates began in Helsinki on November 17, 1969, followed by six sessions held alternately in the Finnish capital and in Vienna for the next two and a half years under the formal title Strategic Arms Limitation Talks (SALT). While the Soviet delegation headed by Deputy Foreign Minister Vladimir S. Semenov met with the American delegation headed by Gerard C. Smith, Nixon's National Security Adviser Henry Kissinger and Soviet Ambassador Anatoly Dobrynin conducted "back channel" discussions in Washington as well.

There were three main issues in dispute during these negotiations, each of which was eventually resolved by compromise. First, the Soviets argued that the American intermediate-range missiles based in Western Europe should be counted as "strategic" weapons because they could reach targets in the Soviet Union. When the

*Soviet First Secretary Leonid Brezhnev and President Richard Nixon at the Moscow Summit, May 1972. This was the first visit of an American president to the Soviet Union since Roosevelt's trip to Yalta in 1945. (National Archives)*

United States refused to make this concession, the Russians finally agreed to postpone the issue of the European missiles for subsequent negotiations. The second controversy centered on a newly developed U.S. missile with multiple warheads capable of striking different targets, which was cursed with the inelegant designation multiple independently targetable reentry vehicle (MIRV). Both sides acknowledged the destabilizing character of MIRVs, which could severely upset the delicate balance of mutual deterrence, and both favored severe restrictions on their development. But as usual, the Americans insisted on verification procedures that the Russians were unwilling to accept. The Soviet negotiators again threw in the towel and agreed to exclude MIRVs from the discussions. Finally, Washington favored a comprehensive agreement linking the two offensive strategic systems that remained on the table (ICBMs and SLBMs) with the so-called anti-ballistic missile (ABM) defensive systems that both sides had begun to deploy (and which will be discussed later). The Russians pressed for and eventually won U.S. consent to draft a separate ABM treaty while seeking an agreement on the limitation of offensive strategic arms.

After two and a half years of official negotiations in Helsinki and Vienna, complemented by Kissinger's "back channel" talks with Dobrynin in Washington and Brezhnev in Moscow, an interim strategic arms control agreement was ready for signature when Nixon became the first American president since Roosevelt at Yalta to travel to the Soviet Union for a summit meeting. On May 26, 1972, the two leaders signed two separate documents customarily referred to collectively as the Strategic Arms Limitation Treaty (SALT). The first was the Interim Agreement on Strategic

Offensive Missiles, which dealt with the two types of delivery vehicles that could reach targets in the other country (ICBMs and SLBMs). Each side had worried that if the other ever achieved a significant numerical advantage in these two strategic weapons systems, it might be tempted to resort to a disarming first strike. To preclude such a dangerous possibility, the SALT agreement restricted the number of ICBMs and SLBMs that each side could deploy for a period of five years (October 3, 1972, to October 3, 1977). The treaty froze the existing number of American ICBMs at 1,054 while permitting the Soviet Union to expand its ICBM arsenal from 1,530 to 1,618; a ban on the construction of new SLBMs left the Soviet Union with 950 compared to 710 American missiles on submarines.

The second issue to be addressed at the SALT I talks was the ABM system that was designed to intercept and destroy incoming missiles before they reached their targets. The United States had conducted the first successful test of an interceptor missile in 1959, two years after the Soviets had tested their first ICBM. In 1962, Secretary of Defense Robert McNamara authorized research and development for a rudimentary ABM system consisting of a long-range, high-altitude missile (the Spartan) designed to intercept an incoming ICBM beyond the atmosphere, and a short-range missile (the Sprint) as a backup. McNamara was convinced that no antimissile system would ever be able to protect densely populated areas against the expanding Soviet ICBM force, since Moscow would easily be able to increase the number of offensive weapons needed to overwhelm the U.S. defensive system. But after China tested its first atomic bomb in 1964, the embryonic American ABM system was intended to defend population centers against the small nuclear arsenal and undeveloped delivery system of that new member of the nuclear club.

In the meantime the Soviet Union had begun to deploy its own ABM system (code-named "Galosh") to protect the city of Moscow, a development that greatly alarmed the Johnson administration when it learned of the system in 1966. Washington tried to persuade Moscow to accept a mutual ban on ABM systems in order to avoid a costly arms race in such defensive weapons systems, which were likely to be rendered obsolete by future offensive countermeasures such as the multi-warhead missiles (MIRVs) that were already on the drawing board.* But when Johnson raised the issue directly with Soviet Premier Alexei Kosygin at their brief summit meeting in Glassboro, New Jersey, in June 1967, the Soviet leader steadfastly defended the Soviet embryonic ABM program on the grounds that it was merely designed to protect civilian populations. Johnson thereupon followed McNamara's advice and ordered construction resumed on the American ABM system (renamed "Sentinel") to protect American cities against the minor nuclear threat from China. U.S. diplomats were at pains to assure their Soviet counterparts that Sentinel did not affect adversely the two superpowers' mutual deterrence.

But the incoming Republican administration in Washington had very different ideas about the purpose of anti-missile defense. Shortly after taking the reins of power, President Nixon announced on March 14, 1969, his intention to abandon

---

*The United States began tests of its Poseidon and Minuteman MIRVed missiles in 1968, and soon had MIRVs ready for deployment.

Johnson's Sentinel program for protecting cities against a Chinese nuclear attack in order to concentrate on the defense of America's Minuteman ICBM force against a disarming first strike by the much more formidable missile force of the Soviet Union. Housed in concrete underground silos and defended by an ABM system, the ICBMs could survive a nuclear first strike and deliver a devastating retaliatory counterblow. The Nixon ABM system, renamed "Safeguard" and partially operational by 1972, generated acute anxiety in the Kremlin. Officials in Moscow worried that what appeared to be a purely defensive weapons system threatened to neutralize the Soviet strategic nuclear forces and destabilize the system of mutual deterrence. If an effective ABM system were deployed to protect missile sites, it might be subsequently expanded to cover the country's major urban areas. With the assurance that its civilian population could be protected from a retaliatory strike, the superpower might succumb to the temptation to launch a surprise attack that would bring total victory against its Cold War adversary.

In recognition of this concern, the ABM treaty set a maximum of one hundred ABM launchers for the two sites that each signatory was permitted to deploy. Since the United States had already constructed a site to protect its ICBM silos located near Grand Forks, North Dakota, it was allowed to build another site around Washington, DC (the command and control center, thereby protecting the president's ability to order a retaliatory strike). Since Moscow was already covered by the Galosh system, the Soviet Union was permitted to construct a second ABM system to protect an ICBM site of its choosing. This arrangement was intended to enhance the credibility of mutual assured destruction in two ways: First, since it exposed the major population centers of both superpowers to utter devastation in a nuclear attack, it provided a powerful incentive for each to prevent a suicidal nuclear exchange. Second, by protecting one ICBM site on each side, it preserved the retaliatory capability of both and therefore removed the temptation for either one to launch a disarming surprise attack against the other power's land-based missiles.*

The quantitative limits on offensive strategic weapons that were codified in the SALT I treaty—1,618 Soviet versus 1,054 American ICBMs and 950 Soviet versus 710 American SLBMs—appeared at first glance to confer an advantage on the Soviet Union by allowing it to retain the lead in these two delivery systems that it had achieved in the 1960s. But in fact the United States enjoyed three other advantages that compensated for its inferiority in the number of missiles covered by the treaty. First, the Strategic Air Command possessed both a quantitatively and qualitatively superior fleet of long-range bombers capable of delivering nuclear warheads to Soviet targets. Second, the British nuclear deterrent, although small in comparison to the Soviet arsenal, was closely aligned with U.S. nuclear strategy, while the Russians could hardly depend on China's fledgling nuclear forces for support in a crisis.‡ Third, the United States enjoyed decisive technological superiority in the construction of warheads for several years. By the opening of the SALT talks in 1969, the

---

*In 1974 President Ford canceled plans to construct the second U.S. ABM site near the nation's capital for budgetary reasons.
‡The French nuclear deterrent was entirely independent of U.S. nuclear planning.

United States had begun to fit many of its land-based (Minuteman) and submarine-based (Poseidon) missiles with multiple warheads, each of which could be targeted for a different site. These missiles with MIRVs greatly increased the destructive power and reduced the vulnerability to interception of each American missile that was included in the SALT I numerical limitations. Although the Soviet Union successfully tested MIRVS in 1973 and began to deploy them in the mid-1970s, the United States enjoyed a lead in the production of this important category of offensive strategic weapons.

In sum, the two superpowers remained roughly equal in their strategic capability as a consequence of the SALT I treaty concluded in May 1972. Each side's ability to destroy the social system of the other remained unimpaired. The failure to limit long-range (or "heavy") bombers, MIRVs, intermediate- and medium-range missiles, and other important components of the strategic balance left the two superpowers free to expand their nuclear capability by those and other means. Yet for all of its weaknesses, the SALT I treaty represented the first successful limitation on the nuclear arms race since it had begun at the end of the 1940s. Moreover, SALT I was intended only as an interim agreement of five years' duration, to be succeeded by a more comprehensive treaty that would place limits on weapons systems not covered by its restrictions.

The remarkable progress in strategic arms control during the early 1970s dealt only with the *military* component of the East-West rivalry. It was evident that success in restraining the nuclear arms race would not lead to a genuine relaxation of tensions unless accompanied by a settlement of the *political* conflicts that had fueled the military rivalry between the two blocs. Those political conflicts had begun in Europe in the years after World War II and had divided that continent into two armed camps. Accordingly, the arms control negotiations between the two superpowers were complemented by a parallel movement in Europe to resolve the outstanding political disputes on that continent and improve relations between the two sides of the Iron Curtain.

### Europe between the Superpowers: De Gaulle's Grand Design

The First European statesman to devise a comprehensive plan to reduce the tensions caused by the Cold War in Europe was President Charles de Gaulle of France. The leader of the Free French government in exile during World War II, de Gaulle had abruptly resigned in 1946 when the French electorate voted to restore the prewar system of parliamentary supremacy rather than approve the strong executive authority he advocated. He was recalled to power in 1958 to rescue France from the political chaos caused by its disastrous and doomed effort to preserve control of Algeria (see page 86). Within four years de Gaulle had granted independence to Algeria and divested France of the remainder of its colonial empire in Africa. In the meantime he had established a new constitutional system in France that vastly increased the powers of the chief executive at the expense of the parliament. Both the policy of decolonization and the constitutional reforms were means to an end that de Gaulle assiduously pursued for the rest of his career: Freed from the burdens of colonial rule and insulated from interference by parliament, press, and people, the French president

*President Charles de Gaulle of France, who withdrew that country from NATO's integrated military command and sought to emancipate France and Western Europe from what he saw as United States military and economic domination. (Hulton Archive by Getty Images)*

was empowered to pursue two aspirations that he had cherished since the end of World War II. The first was to restore France to its rightful place as the preeminent power in Europe. The second was to emancipate Europe from what he regarded as the suffocating hegemony exercised by the two superpowers in order to restore the old continent to its former status as an independent, dynamic, powerful actor on the world stage.

De Gaulle was convinced that the United States and the Soviet Union had agreed tacitly to partition Europe into spheres of influence at the wartime conferences of Yalta and Potsdam, from which, he never forgot, France had been excluded. The political, economic, and military division of Europe during the Cold War froze the hegemonic position of the two non-European superpowers in their respective halves of the continent. The Soviet Union preserved its control of Eastern Europe by political pressure and, when necessary, military force. The United States maintained its preeminence in Western Europe in a much more benevolent fashion: It wielded its economic leverage to integrate Western Europe into an international economic order dominated by U.S. firms, while exploiting Western Europe's fears of Soviet aggression to keep it in a servile position of military dependence on the United States through the North Atlantic Treaty Organization.

De Gaulle regarded this condition of Western European subservience to the United States as entirely unsatisfactory for a number of reasons. First of all, it consigned these once powerful and independent states to the lowly status of compliant protégés, depriving them of the ability to pursue foreign policies that did not meet with the approval of their protector across the Atlantic. Although the principal objective of this ardent French nationalist was the restoration of *French* national independence and grandeur, de Gaulle also expressed two sentiments that were widely shared throughout Western Europe as a whole. The first was the emerging self-confidence resulting from the region's spectacular postwar economic recovery since World War II: By the early 1960s the European Economic Community was well on its way to becoming an economic powerhouse in the world, with an aggregate gross national product approaching (and soon surpassing) that of the United States. This impressive economic growth had effectively erased the feelings of inferiority of the early Cold War years, when the old continent depended so heavily on American military protection and financial assistance. Second, the growing asymmetry between Europe's economic power and independence, on the one hand, and its military weakness and dependence, on the other, played directly into de Gaulle's hands as he solicited support from other European states for France's challenge to American hegemony. The resentment against U.S. domination of NATO ran deep in the former great powers on this old and proud continent, and not only in France.

Another source of de Gaulle's criticism of Washington's foreign and defense policy were the growing doubts about the reliability of American's "nuclear umbrella" as protection for Western Europe. In light of NATO's failure to meet the ambitious manpower targets that had been set at the 1952 Lisbon Conference, U.S. ground forces stationed in Europe had ceased by the end of the 1950s to serve as a "shield" to slow up a Communist military advance as originally intended. They had become instead little more than a "trip wire" to ensure the early use of nuclear weapons at the beginning of a conventional war. But once American territory had been brought within range of Soviet nuclear weapons by the end of the 1950s, the credibility of the American pledge to employ nuclear weapons in a European war gradually began to erode. The Kennedy administration eagerly sought an alternative to the all-or-nothing obligation to unleash the American nuclear arsenal against the Soviet Union in response to a conventional attack in Europe. The new strategy that it embraced, which came to be known as "flexible response," repudiated the early recourse to strategic nuclear weapons in favor of a graduated response to a conventional Warsaw Pact attack. But what seemed to U.S. strategic planners as pragmatism and flexibility spawned anxiety among some of the European members of the Atlantic alliance. The Europeans' greatest fear, which de Gaulle shrewdly exploited for his own ends, was that the disappearance of the unconditional U.S. pledge of nuclear deterrence might tempt the Soviet Union to wage a conventional war in Europe that would devastate that continent but leave both American and Soviet territory unscathed.

Shortly after coming to power in June 1958, de Gaulle proposed a radical restructuring of NATO to enhance France's role in the alliance's decision-making apparatus. On September 25 he dispatched a memorandum to Washington and London proposing the creation of a tripartite "inner directorate" within the organization consisting of the United States, Great Britain, and France. These three governments would jointly develop a common diplomatic and strategic policy for the alliance and manage affairs not only within NATO but across the entire globe. France's bid for equality with the two English-speaking powers within NATO fell on deaf ears in Washington. Eisenhower politely but firmly turned down de Gaulle's proposal on October 20 with the observation that such an oligarchy of three would antagonize the alliance's other members, who would be excluded from decision-making that might affect their vital interests. What really prompted the president's rejection was his unshakable belief in the necessity for exclusive American control of the organization.

Rebuffed in his bid for a privileged power-sharing arrangement *within* NATO, de Gaulle promptly strove to enhance France's power and influence *outside* it. To pave the way for his country's independence from the American-dominated alliance system, de Gaulle set out to acquire for France the preeminent symbol of great power status in the postwar world: a nuclear deterrent force. On assuming office he accelerated the nuclear weapons program initiated by his predecessors in the Fourth Republic, which resulted in the successful test of an atomic weapon in 1960 (see page 158). The outgoing Eisenhower administration, although prevented by the McMahon Atomic Energy Act of 1946 from helping other countries to develop nuclear weapons*, was no more dismayed by the French atomic test in 1960 than it had been by Great Britain's entry into the nuclear club in 1952. But President Kennedy and Secretary of Defense Robert McNamara were intent on establishing close U.S. supervision of the Western alliance's nuclear forces to ensure a carefully calibrated mechanism of retaliation against Soviet aggression. To achieve this degree of centralized control, Kennedy sought to exploit a glaring weakness in the British and French nuclear forces: their lack of an effective delivery system. At a November 1962 conference in Nassau with British Prime Minister Harold Macmillan, Kennedy offered to provide Polaris missiles (which Britain could install on its submarines) to replace the aging British strategic bomber force. The upgraded British nuclear weapons system would be part of a proposed new "multilateral nuclear force" in NATO. Although the United States extended the same offer to France, it did so after the bilaterally negotiated Nassau Accord had been announced in the press. This slight infuriated de Gaulle, whose resentment against "Anglo-Saxon" high-handedness dated from his exclusion from Allied councils by Roosevelt and Churchill during World War II. He imperiously rejected the Nassau offer at a press conference on January 14, 1963, also taking the occasion to announce his intention to veto Great Britain's application for admission to the EEC (see page 336).

The American plan for a Multilateral Nuclear Force (MLF) that was finally unveiled in March 1963 was modified from a submarine fleet to a group of twenty-five surface ships armed with Polaris missiles under the joint control of the alliance member states. They would carry crews of mixed nationality, with commands assigned according to financial contribution (with a limit of 40 percent for a single nation). What Kennedy and McNamara saw as a magnanimous gesture to share decision-making authority with the European allies, de Gaulle disdained as a ploy to preempt France's plans to construct an independent nuclear force of its own. The MLF languished amid angry exchanges between Washington and Paris until Presi-

---

*In 1957 the act was amended to allow the sharing of nuclear technology with Great Britain, which had tested its first atomic bomb in 1952.

dent Johnson finally abandoned it at the end of 1964. By that time France had begun to build the first generation of its independent nuclear striking force (*force de frappe*), which consisted of sixty-two Mirage IV bombers. It would later add land-based MRBMs and a fleet of nuclear-powered submarines armed with SLBMs. De Gaulle's military theorists endowed the independent French nuclear force with elaborate strategic rationales: The theory of "multilateral deterrence" held that the proliferation of nuclear actors enhances global stability and reduces the chances of nuclear war by forcing the two superpowers to calculate the possible responses of third parties in the midst of a nuclear attack. The theory of "proportional deterrence" asserted that a middle-sized country like France needed only a nuclear force with sufficient destructive force to inflict unacceptable damage on the potential aggressor; that is, the prospect of significant death and destruction would offset any gains the enemy could conceivably acquire by defeating and conquering France. But the main objective of the *force de frappe* was political rather than military: It would be a tool to enhance France's prestige and power in Europe and in the world, enabling it to acquire a position of equality with the superpowers through the possession of nuclear weapons that it alone controlled. France could then assume the leadership of a Western Europe that was genuinely independent of U.S. control.

De Gaulle's vision directly clashed with the Kennedy administration's "grand design" for the future relationship between the United States and Europe (see page 335). Kennedy welcomed the emerging European Economic Community as a valuable trading partner of the United States. He secured congressional approval of the Trade Expansion Act of 1962, which foresaw reciprocal tariff reductions and the tightening of economic links between the two sides of the ocean. But de Gaulle feared that the United States was intent on using both the EEC and NATO as vehicles to perpetuate its domination of Western Europe. In vetoing the British application for admission to the EEC at his January 14, 1963, news conference, he warned that the inclusion of Great Britain would turn the old continent into "a gigantic Atlantic Community that would be dependent on and be run by America." Nine days after his announcement that France would not allow what he would later refer to as America's "Trojan Horse" into Europe, de Gaulle sought to strengthen France's ties with another European state on which he hoped to base his audacious project for European independence. On January 23 de Gaulle and West German Chancellor Konrad Adenauer signed what came to be known as the Elysée Treaty, which provided for Franco-German cooperation on security matters (including regular meetings of defense ministers, exchanges of military personnel, and cooperation in arms production). De Gaulle hoped that that by forging a Paris-Bonn axis, he could lure West Germany into a privileged bilateral link with France that would form the nucleus of an autonomous Western European bloc capable of dealing with the two superpowers from a position of strength for the first time. Since the Federal Republic had foresworn the right to acquire nuclear weapons of its own, the *force de frappe* and the political advantages that accompanied it would ensure France's dominant position in the relationship.

Adenauer responded favorably to de Gaulle's solicitation because he harbored doubts about Washington's reliability as a defender of West Germany's interests. The French president played on these fears during the Berlin crisis of 1961, when Kennedy's failure to contest the construction of the Berlin Wall left some nationalistic Germans fearful that U.S. policy would condemn Germany and Berlin to per-petual division. But the West German chancellor was unable to convince his own parliament that the uncertain new relationship with France was preferable to the tried-and-true partnership with the United States, which had resulted in the deploy-ment of U.S. combat forces in forward positions to defend Germany's eastern border. When the Bundestag in Bonn approved the Franco-German treaty in May 1963, it rendered it innocuous by adding a preamble reaffirming the Federal Republic's loy-alty to the Atlantic Alliance. After Adenauer retired five months later, the project for a Paris-Bonn axis lapsed into insignificance until West German Chancellor Helmut Kohl and French President François Mitterrand resurrected it in the 1980s.

Having failed to detach the Germans from the United States, de Gaulle resumed his assault on the American-dominated Atlantic Alliance. The central issue that de Gaulle seized on in this campaign against NATO was the unacceptable threat to France's national independence posed by its membership in an integrated military command headed by an American general and ultimately controlled by the American president. The French leader had already signaled his dissatisfaction with the inte-grated command structure of NATO by detaching France's Mediterranean and Atlantic fleets from the Alliance command in 1959 and 1963, respectively, and then by withholding French participation in NATO naval war games in 1964. He made his major move in a message to President Lyndon Johnson on March 7, 1966, announc-ing the withdrawal of French military and air forces from the NATO command, de-manding the removal of the Alliance's military headquarters from the Paris region, and requiring the departure of all U.S. military bases from French territory.*

After thumbing his nose at Washington, de Gaulle proceeded to pour salt on the wound by embarking in June on an official visit to Moscow, where he was invited to speak on Russian television and at the city's major university. He become the first Western leader to visit the top secret Baikonur cosmodrome in Kazakhstan, where he witnessed the launching of a space satellite. The Franco-Soviet joint declaration at the end of the visit alluded to future scientific and cultural exchanges and announced the establishment of a direct telecommunications "hot line" between the Kremlin and the Elysée Palace. In the same year French Foreign Minister Maurice Couve de Murville visited Prague, Bucharest, Budapest, and Sofia, as France expanded cul-tural contracts with all of the Soviet satellites in Eastern Europe. Soviet Premier Alexei Kosygin returned de Gaulle's visit in December, enthusiastically endorsing the improvement in Franco-Soviet relations amid a warm reception in Paris.

De Gaulle's bid for détente with the Soviet Union was designed to establish France as the "privileged spokesman" for the European allies in their relations with the Communist bloc. A French-dominated Western Europe detached from the United States would be well positioned to negotiate with Moscow over the remaining issues in dispute between the two blocs, especially those concerning a divided Germany and its eastern frontiers. With Washington no longer a dominant presence in Western Europe, the Soviet Union would be susceptible to French pressure to relax its

---

*The headquarters were transferred from Paris to Brussels in 1967. France remained a mem-ber of the purely political organs in the Alliance, such as the North Atlantic Council.

stranglehold on Eastern Europe. Paris's special relationship with Bonn would enable France to induce the Germans to settle their dispute with Poland over its western border (an issue that will be discussed later). De Gaulle's ultimate dream seems to have been a mutual disengagement of the two superpowers that would enable the two halves of Europe to reunite after so many years of division. The end of the Cold War in Europe would enable the old continent to regain its former authority and influence in the world. On occasion de Gaulle even left the impression—as in his provocative allusion to a "Europe from the Atlantic to the Urals"—that a cooperative, peace-loving Russia might some day be permitted to rejoin the European system in which it had played such an influential role under the Romanovs.

De Gaulle's bold bid to break up the bipolar international system failed because he had overplayed his hand. The French student rebellion in the spring of 1968, which was followed by massive labor unrest throughout the country, shook the Fifth Republic to its foundations. A serious economic crisis in the summer and a run on the franc in the fall exposed the constraints on de Gaulle's ambitions for France's role as an independent player between the two superpowers. To cope with its financial difficulties de Gaulle's government was obliged to accept emergency assistance from the United States and Great Britain, the two "Anglo-Saxon" powers he had been denouncing for their overbearing behavior toward continental Europe. The Warsaw Pact's invasion of Czechoslovakia in the summer of the same year also dealt de Gaulle's foreign policy a cruel blow: His strategy of loosening Western Europe's ties with the United States was predicated on the expectation that Moscow would be willing to loosen its iron grip on Eastern Europe. The Soviet tanks rolling into Prague disproved that assumption and forced NATO to close ranks. De Gaulle's resignation in April 1969 brought down the final curtain on his grandiose scheme for détente in a French-led Europe emancipated from the two superpowers.

## *Ostpolitik:* West Germany Looks East

As events were to prove, the key to a relaxation of East-West tensions in Europe was to be found not in Paris but in Bonn. The Cold War in Europe had begun over the question of the political status of Germany. The division of that country into Communist and non-Communist halves, as well as the anomalous status of its former capital Berlin, had kept the two blocs at loggerheads since the late 1940s. The West German state, under the stewardship of Chancellor Konrad Adenauer from 1949 to 1963, refused to acknowledge the existence of the Communist state of East Germany, claimed the exclusive right to represent its inhabitants abroad, and insisted on treating West Berlin as an integral part of West Germany. Adenauer's ultimate goal was the reunification of the country by free elections, which were certain to lead to the absorption of the Communist state in the east by the democratic, capitalist state in the west.

The strategy adopted by the fervently anti-Communist chancellor of the Federal Republic to achieve the ultimate goal of reunification was what he called a "position of strength": By joining a prosperous Western Europe under the protection of the United States, West Germany would be strong enough to pressure the Soviet Union into abandoning its East German client state to its inevitable fate. In the meantime the Federal Republic sought to isolate East Germany from the rest of the world by dint of the Hallstein Doctrine of 1955, which stipulated that Bonn would sever diplomatic relations with any state (except the Soviet Union) that recognized the illegitimate puppet state to the east. Bonn's treatment of East Germany as an international pariah and its persistent demand for German reunification through free elections remained a source of perpetual antagonism between the Federal Republic and the Soviet Union.

Another cardinal feature of West German foreign policy generated acute anxiety in the Communist state of Poland. This was Bonn's refusal to recognize the loss of German territory at the end of World War II after Poland, with the support of the Soviet Union, unilaterally extended its western border several hundred miles to what came to be known as the Oder-Neisse Line (see page 32). The advancing Soviet forces expelled almost all of the area's ten million German inhabitants, most of whom eventually settled in West Germany and formed a powerful political pressure group that demanded compensation for the possessions and property they had left behind. The West German government insisted that East Germany's acceptance of its border with Poland was meaningless and that only a united German government could enter into negotiations to settle this territorial dispute. Bonn's refusal to recognize East Germany's sovereignty and Poland's western frontier, together with its political claims on West Berlin, remained the principal sources of East-West friction in Europe. After Adenauer's resignation in October 1963, his successor Ludwig Erhard reaffirmed this "policy of strength" toward the Communist states to the east.

But in December 1966 a governing coalition was formed in West Germany that brought to the foreign ministry the Social Democratic leader Willy Brandt, who personified a bold new approach to foreign policy toward the Communist bloc. An increasing number of West Germans had grown disillusioned with Adenauer's hard-line stance, which had left Germany as divided as ever while poisoning relations between the Federal Republic and its Communist neighbors to the east. The radical new alternative that Brandt proposed was a relaxation of tensions with Eastern Europe as a prelude to settling the principal issues in dispute between the two Cold War blocs. To achieve that goal he was willing to jettison Bonn's sacrosanct doctrine that German reunification was a precondition for European détente. Brandt strove instead to reverse the priority: An improvement in relations between West Germany and the Communist bloc would pave the way for the reunification of the two German states on a stable, peaceful continent.

During the year 1967 the West German foreign minister took the first tentative steps in his new *Ostpolitik* (Eastern Policy) by restoring diplomatic ties with Romania and Yugoslavia despite their recognition of East Germany, a de facto repudiation of the hallowed Hallstein Doctrine. By 1968 West German trade missions were turning up in Eastern European capitals to negotiate contracts with government agencies. West German banks began to finance exports to the Communist countries with hard currency loans. These expanding diplomatic, commercial, and financial links between West Germany and Eastern Europe provoked strenuous opposition in East Germany. Ulbricht's hard-line Communist regime deeply resented the spectacle of its Warsaw Pact allies mending fences with its sworn enemy, which steadfastly refused to acknowledge the legitimacy of the East German state. Brandt's *Ostpolitik* also generated concerns in Moscow that West Germany's direct overtures to the satellites might lead to dangerous foreign meddling in the Soviet sphere. The military intervention in Czechoslovakia in the summer of 1968—which Communist bloc propaganda justified as a response to the penetration of that country by West German "revisionists"—temporarily sidetracked Brandt's opening to the east as Bonn joined other NATO nations in condemning the Warsaw Pact's action. But when the West German elections of October 1969 brought Brandt to power as chancellor in a center-left coalition, he resumed his *Ostpolitik* with a much more daring initiative: He abandoned the traditional policy of treating East Germany as a pariah, announcing plans to expand economic, cultural, and political contacts with its people. But Communist party boss Walter Ulbricht in East Berlin would have nothing to do with the West German state until it recognized East Germany as a sovereign state, something that no West German leader would ever be able to do because it would betray the cherished cause of German reunification. So Brandt decided to settle West Germany's differences with the Soviet Union in the hopes that Moscow could be induced to pressure East Germany to deal with the Federal Republic without insisting on preconditions Bonn could not meet.

Brandt signaled his good intentions toward the Soviet Union on November 28, 1969, by signing the Non-Proliferation Treaty, which the Russians had demanded as a precondition for an improvement of relations with West Germany. On August 12, 1970, the West German chancellor journeyed to Moscow to sign with Prime Minister Alexei Kosygin a bilateral nonaggression treaty, which included an explicit pledge to recognize the territorial status quo in Europe (including Poland's disputed western boundary and the boundary between the two German states). These two benevolent gestures allayed old Eastern European anxieties about an aggressive West Germany armed with nuclear weapons seeking to recover the territory it had lost at the end of World War II. Brandt's historic trip to Moscow also reassured the Kremlin that his opening to Eastern Europe would not threaten Soviet hegemony in that region. With Moscow's blessing he proceeded to open negotiations with Poland over the long-standing border dispute between Bonn and Warsaw. Once the details were worked out, Brandt traveled to the Polish capital on December 7, 1970, to sign a treaty confirming West Germany's recognition of the Oder-Neisse Line. In a poignant gesture he visited the memorial for the Warsaw ghetto and knelt in homage to the victims of Nazism, reinforcing the message that West Germany had repudiated its evil past and was committed to living peacefully with its neighbors.

West Germany's rapprochement with the Soviet Union and Poland was a remarkable achievement. But the issue of reconciliation with East Germany proved a much greater challenge for Brandt's new *Ostpolitik*. Adenauer had insisted on the reunification of Germany through democratic elections and refused to have anything to do with the East German state. Shortly after becoming chancellor in 1969 Brandt had attempted to break the ice in intra-German relations with the imaginative proposal that Germany be considered "two states within one nation." As a token of good will he became the first West German chancellor to visit East Germany by traveling to Erfurt in March 1970 and meeting with East German Prime Minister Willi Stroph. But Stroph was merely a figurehead in a state that had been tightly controlled almost since its creation by the omnipotent head of its Communist Party. Ulbricht's overriding obsession throughout his career had been to secure the international respectability that would be possible only if West Germany and its NATO allies formally recognized his regime. He therefore continued to demand, as a precondition to any improvement in relations between the two German states, the one concession that Brandt could not make. By this time, however, the Soviet Union had developed a strong interest in promoting a relaxation of tensions in Europe in order to obtain what it had craved for so long: Western acceptance of its political and territorial gains after World War II. Once the Soviet leadership had given its blessing to Brandt's opening to Eastern Europe, it decided to sacrifice Ulbricht in the interests of European détente. On May 3, 1971, the Kremlin engineered the replacement of the old East German hard-liner as Communist party leader by the more subservient Erich Honecker.

The new East German government proved amenable to Brandt's eager entreaties for a rapprochement. On December 21, 1972, the two states signed the so-called Basic Treaty, an agreement that fell considerably short of the formal diplomatic recognition that Ulbricht had craved desperately for so long. It provided for an expansion of cultural and economic relations between the two countries as well as the establishment of "permanent representative missions" in each capital that would function as de facto embassies. When the Basic Treaty was ratified by the West German parliament on May 11, 1973, East Germany had finally obtained the political respectability it had sought in vain since its creation: Most countries of the world accorded it diplomatic recognition (although the United States dragged its heels before finally taking the step on September 4, 1974). The culmination of this historic transformation came on September 18, 1973, when the two German states joined the United Nations.

One unresolved issue pertaining to the two German states could not be dealt with by them but had to be addressed by the four powers that retained residual occupation rights in the city of Berlin. In September 1971 representatives of the United States, the Soviet Union, Great Britain, and France signed an agreement recognizing each other's existing rights in their respective sectors of the city. The Soviet Union made two major concessions by guaranteeing West Germans unimpeded access to West Berlin and by formally accepting West Germany's claim to represent that portion of the divided city abroad. In December the two German states signed a transit agreement endorsing the Four-Power understanding on Berlin, finally and definitely terminating the controversy that had poisoned East-West relations since the advent of the Cold War.

Brandt had been careful to keep the Nixon administration informed of his overtures to the Communist bloc, but he neither consulted with Washington nor sought its prior approval of his ventures. Nixon and Kissinger were originally quite wary of the West German initiatives, fearing that Brandt's efforts to mend fences with the countries of the Warsaw Pact might ultimately dilute Bonn's commitment to the Atlantic Alliance. But as the United States began to undertake its own efforts to improve relations with the Communist bloc through arms control agreements and other means, it became evident that West Germany's *Ostpolitik* in Europe complemented the Nixon-Kissinger pursuit of détente between the two blocs across the globe.

## Helsinki: A European Security Agreement at Last

Because of the emerging conflict between East and West in Europe after World War II, a peace conference ratifying the territorial changes resulting from the Allied victory had never been convened. Since the Soviet Union was the principal beneficiary of those redrawn frontiers, the Kremlin had long pressed for the convocation of a Europe-wide security conference to give the international stamp of approval to the postwar European order. The United States and its Western European allies adamantly rebuffed these Soviet overtures. In light of what the Western powers perceived to be the overwhelming conventional military superiority enjoyed by the Communist bloc, NATO regarded any political settlement in Europe as meaningless unless accompanied by a mutual reduction of Soviet and American armed forces on the continent. Moscow just as adamantly resisted the idea of mutual military retrenchment, which might weaken its political control of Eastern Europe and might lead to a dangerous increase in West German military forces to compensate for the reduction in U.S. troop strength. The Soviet Union also insisted that a security conference for Europe ought to be confined to states located on that continent, which meant the exclusion of the Western European states' transatlantic ally and protector.

But events in the early 1970s led both sides to appreciate the advantages of both a mutual reduction of forces in Europe and an all-European security conference including the United States. Western Europe's interest in mutual force reductions on the continent was prompted by growing fears of a *unilateral* cut in American troop strength in NATO. Every year since 1966 Senate Majority Leader Mike Mansfield of Montana had introduced a resolution calling for a substantial reduction in American forces on the continent. Growing disillusionment with the war in Vietnam by the early 1970s caused an increase in public and Senate support for the Mansfield Resolution. Some critics of military spending in the United States wondered why the "Vietnamization" of the war in Southeast Asia should not be followed by the "Europeanization" of the Cold War in Europe. Nixon began to view mutual force reductions as a useful means of preempting the growing sentiment for unilateral American troop cuts as indicated by the increasing number of votes that Mansfield got for his resolution.

Brezhnev had also come to appreciate the advantages of reducing military tensions on the Soviet Union's European flank in order to cope with the growing conflict with China in the Far East (see page 213). In addition to favoring military détente in Europe to free up forces for redeployment on the long frontier with China, the Kremlin also worried about a precipitous American withdrawal from Western Europe: It might lead to the ultimate nightmare of a West Germany operating without restraint from Washington. For these reasons Brezhnev gave the prospects of military détente in Europe a powerful shot in the arm in July 1971. Five days before Mansfield's resolution calling for a 50 percent reduction in the three hundred thousand American military contingent stationed in Europe was expected to pass the Senate, the Soviet leader publicly called for negotiations on mutual and balanced force reductions on the continent. The White House was thereupon able to beat back the Mansfield Resolution with the persuasive argument that a *unilateral* cutback in U.S. forces would undercut a possible agreement on *mutual* force reductions of the two armies that faced each other along the Central Front.

In the meantime the Communist bloc had revived its old proposal for the convocation of an all-European security conference to confirm the political status quo on the continent. At a June 1970 meeting of the Warsaw Pact in Budapest, a new twist was added to the old scheme that rendered it much more attractive to the West: For the first time the Soviet Union and its Eastern European satellites formally invited the United States and Canada to join the European states at such a gathering. After NATO (in December 1971) and the Warsaw Pact (in January 1972) endorsed the proposals for a European security conference and for negotiations on mutual force reductions, Brezhnev and Nixon finally agreed at their Moscow summit meeting in May 1972 to proceed simultaneously with a Conference on Security and Cooperation in Europe (CSCE) and negotiations on Mutual and Balanced Force Reductions (MBFR). Exploratory talks on the CSCE opened in Helsinki on November 22, 1972, and on MBFR in Vienna on January 31, 1973.

The ceremonial opening of the CSCE took place on July 3, 1973, in Helsinki, attended by the foreign ministers of all European states (except for the renegade Communist state Albania), Canada, and the United States. While the serious negotiations got underway from September 1973 to July 1975 Richard Nixon and Willy Brandt, the two Western leaders who had initiated the movement for East-West détente, were forced from office by domestic scandals in 1974. But their successors resumed the commitment to a political settlement in Europe. President Gerald Ford and Communist Party Secretary Leonid Brezhnev, accompanied by their respective foreign ministers, Henry Kissinger and Andrei Gromyko, traveled to Finland on August 1, 1975, to sign the Final Act of the Conference on Security and Cooperation in Europe. The Helsinki Final Act became, in the eyes of many observers, the crowning achievement of détente.

The various proposals that the thirty-three European countries, Canada, and the United States had submitted to the conference were divided into three distinct categories (or "baskets," as they were quaintly called). Basket One comprised the set of interrelated principles that Soviet leaders from Stalin to Brezhnev had avidly championed as the key to political stability on the continent: formal recognition of the existing political frontiers in Europe as inviolable and of the territorial integrity of each sovereign state on the continent. The significance of the Basket One provisions was much greater than this formal and legalistic language implied: Basket One in fact represented a major triumph for the Communist bloc, which had finally obtained Western recognition of the postwar territorial gains of Poland, Czechoslovakia, and the Soviet Union as well as of the Soviet annexation of the Baltic states of Latvia, Lithuania, and Estonia in 1940. It also affirmed the sanctity of the border separating the two Germanies, thereby providing multilateral confirmation of the bilateral understanding previously reached between the two German states. The sense of security that resulted from this political agreement was enhanced by a set of "Confidence-Building Measures," such as advanced notification of and the exchange of observers at military maneuvers of more than twenty-five thousand troops conducted by the two alliance systems.

Basket Two of the Helsinki Final Act, which dealt with economic relations between the two blocs, proved to be the least significant of the three categories of agreements. It contained a set of provisions for the expansion of intra-European cooperation in trade, industry, science, and technology that were also designed to reduce tensions between East and West.

In exchange for obtaining its long-deferred objective of Western recognition of the European territorial status quo, the Kremlin was obliged (with great reluctance) to swallow the annoying language included in Basket Three. The provisions in this category comprised various commitments to preserve human rights (including a pledge by all signatories to respect freedom of expression and the right to emigration). Basket Three was reminiscent of earlier pledges by Stalin to respect political liberties, such as in the Atlantic Charter and the Declaration on Liberated Europe, which the Soviets had violated with impunity because of the absence of enforcement machinery. But unlike those wartime precedents, the human rights provisions of the Helsinki agreement did not vanish into irrelevance. The conferees at Helsinki established the CSCE as a permanent organization and scheduled a follow-up meeting two years later. The institutionalization of the Helsinki process encouraged dissidents in several Eastern European countries to submit formal complaints about human rights violations to the CSCE conference in Belgrade in 1977, to the acute embarrassment of the Communist bloc delegates. Those and later demands for political liberalization from Poland, Czechoslovakia, and other Soviet satellites had little effect in the short run. But many of the underground organizations that were inspired by the Helsinki process of the mid-1970s later would play important roles in the political revolutions that swept Eastern Europe at the end of the following decade.

Thirty years after the surrender of Nazi Germany, the signing of the Helsinki Final Act brought a formal end to World War II. The document fell short of a peace treaty, since it was merely a political statement of intent rather than a legally binding document that was not submitted to the national legislatures for ratification. But the political division of Europe that resulted from the rivalry between the two conquerors of Nazi Germany had finally—or so it seemed at the time—been recognized as permanent. By securing the West's de facto acknowledgment of their postwar political and territorial gains on the continent, the Soviet Union and its satellites obtained the international legitimacy that they had sought for so long. That sense of *political* security reinforced the sense of *military* security resulting from the achievement of strategic parity with the United States that was confirmed by the SALT treaty of 1972.

Complementing the political and military détente of the first half of the 1970s was an informal "economic détente," which the Soviet Union eagerly sought as a means of gaining access to Western trade and technology to shore up the deteriorating economic situation in the Communist world. In December 1970 violent protests in Poland against an increase in food prices reflected growing dissatisfaction behind the Iron Curtain with living conditions in the Communist bloc. To remedy the economic difficulties in the East European satellites and in the Soviet Union itself, Brezhnev solicited imports of food, manufactured goods, and technology from the capitalist West. During the 1970s the channels of trade and investment between the Communist and non-Communist world that had been clogged since the advent of the Cold War were opened up, with impressive results. Western European banks provided credits to the governments of Eastern Europe to finance imports from the West, while Western firms set up subsidiaries in Communist countries to take advantage of low labor costs and a largely untapped market for their manufactured goods. After the failure of the 1972 Soviet grain harvest, officials in Moscow cast covetous eyes on the enormous grain surplus produced by the American Midwest. To remedy the shortfall in Soviet grain production the Communist government indulged in some old-fashioned capitalist speculation by concealing the extent of its purchases of

American grain on the open market. This subterfuge resulted in secret deals struck by the Russians at bargain prices before the resulting surge in demand generated a one-third increase in the price of grain to American consumers. The angry reaction of American consumers to the food price increases (or the "Great Grain Robbery," as critics called it) prompted Washington to open negotiations with Moscow for an orderly, long-term marketing arrangement to prevent such precipitous price swings. On October 25, 1975, the two governments concluded a five-year sales agreement that provided for annual Soviet purchases of six to eight million tons of American grain. The United States thereby became the principal foreign supplier of grain to its longtime adversary in the Cold War. The Soviet-American grain deal provided handsome profits for American farmers, thereby adding an important American interest group to the pro-détente lobby in the United States.*

### The Failure of SALT II and the Renewal of the Arms Race

Richard Nixon's forced resignation in 1974 as a result of the Watergate scandal did not disrupt the progress of strategic arms control negotiations between the two superpowers. His successor, Gerald Ford, had little experience in foreign affairs and therefore retained and relied heavily on Secretary of State Henry Kissinger, who preserved continuity in U.S. foreign policy. In one of his first important decisions, the new president authorized his secretary of state to travel to Moscow in October 1974 to explore the possibility of jump-starting the stalled Geneva talks for a successor to the SALT Treaty that was due to expire in 1977. When Kissinger encountered a conciliatory attitude on the part of the Soviet leaders, it was hastily announced that Ford would extend a previously scheduled trip to Japan and South Korea to meet with Brezhnev at a military resort near the Russian port city of Vladivostok on November 23–24 to draft the outline of a ten-year strategic arms limitation agreement.

The Vladivostok interim agreement included numerical limits on MIRVs and "heavy" (that is, intercontinental) bombers—two categories that had been excluded from the SALT I treaty. It restricted each side to an aggregate limit of 2,400 missile launchers (ICBMs and SLBMs) and heavy bombers and confined each side to 1,320 launchers fitted with MIRVs. This interim arms control agreement reflected a substantial concession by the Soviet Union, since Ford and Kissinger were able to exclude from the Vladivostok restrictions the U.S. "forward-based" intermediate-range nuclear weapons systems in Western Europe, which could logically be defined as "strategic weapons" since they were capable of striking targets within the Soviet Union (see page 109). Since the Russians had no such forward-based delivery systems in the Western Hemisphere after Khrushchev's failure to place MRBMs and IRBMs in Cuba, the Vladivostok guidelines gave the United States a clear-cut advantage. On the other hand, Kissinger privately agreed to exclude the new Soviet Backfire bomber from the category of heavy bomber covered by the agreement even though

---

*When President Carter reduced grain sales to the Soviet Union in 1980 as punishment for its invasion of Afghanistan, the howls of protest from the American farm belt induced the anti-Communist Ronald Reagan to revive the grain sales to Moscow upon his arrival at the White House in 1981.

the newly deployed plane clearly possessed an intercontinental range. Both governments hailed the Vladivostok summit as a shining symbol of détente that should inspire the delegations in Geneva to fashion a SALT II agreement that would place effective limits on the nuclear arms race.

As the Geneva negotiators labored to convert the Vladivostok principles into a second strategic arms control treaty, domestic American political developments intervened to delay the diplomats' progress. The summit meeting at which Ford and Brezhnev were to affix their signatures to a SALT II treaty was repeatedly postponed because of an outburst of opposition to the pact in the United States. To the surprise and consternation of Ford and Kissinger, this domestic criticism of the arms control agreement centered on the seemingly unrelated issues of trade and immigration. In October 1972 Washington and Moscow had concluded a Soviet-American trade agreement that was intended to reinforce the emerging political and military détente by promoting the expansion of economic contacts between the two countries. The Soviet Union was unquestionably the principal beneficiary of the agreement, since it had a much greater need for American manufactured goods, high technology, and farm products than Americans had for anything the Russians could produce. In addition to granting the Soviet Union preferential or "most-favored-nation" (MFN) trade status,* the agreement also authorized credits to help the Soviet Union overcome its chronic shortage of hard currency, which was necessary to pay for imports. In December 1973 the U.S. House of Representatives passed the trade bill, but it was encumbered with an amendment requiring the reduction of Soviet restrictions on emigration as a condition for MFN trade status.

The passage of the so-called Vanik Amendment reflected the political clout of a strange coalition of U.S. interest groups: It included Jewish organizations outraged by the tax on immigration that Moscow had imposed in August 1972 to prevent large numbers of Soviet Jews from leaving the country, anti-Communist opponents of détente on the Republican right, and liberal critics of Kissinger's balance-of-power *Realpolitik.* Jewish emigration from the Soviet Union had increased from virtually nothing in 1970 to thirty-five thousand in 1973 during the heyday of détente, and the Kremlin provided Kissinger with private assurances that the relaxation of restrictions would continue. But the politically ambitious Democratic Senator Henry Jackson, who planned a run for the presidency in 1976, demanded an increase to sixty thousand and sponsored the restrictive Vanik Amendment in the Senate. The Jackson-Vanik Amendment passed the Senate on December 13, 1974, and President Ford signed the Trade Reform Act into law on January 3, 1975. During the congressional debate on the Jackson-Vanik Amendment, Moscow angrily denounced it as an intolerable interference in the internal affairs of the Soviet Union. The passage of the amended trade bill depriving the Soviet Union of MFN status provoked a furious response from the Kremlin. The Russians immediately canceled the 1972 trade agreement and turned for trade and credit to the advanced industrial countries of Western Europe, which did not permit concerns about human rights to interfere with prof-

---

*That is, its exports would receive the best tariff treatment the United States granted to its other trading partners.

itable economic relations. The Jackson-Vanik Amendment also led to unpleasant consequences for Soviet Jews: Jewish emigration dwindled from thirty-five thousand in 1973 to thirteen thousand in 1975.

Amid this tussle over trade and immigration, the centerpiece of détente remained strategic arms control. Kissinger flew to Moscow in January 1976 to present the final American proposal on the long-deferred SALT II Treaty. But the negotiations were soon sidetracked by a number of controversies unrelated to the topic at hand. Kissinger complained about the Soviet-Cuban presence in Angola, which Brezhnev brushed aside as irrelevant to the subject at hand (see page 295). When Kissinger pressed the point, Gromyko countered with Moscow's objections to being excluded from the peace negotiations in the Middle East (see page 390). When the U.S. secretary of state finally got around to presenting the Ford administration's arms control proposals, two of them proved unacceptable to the Soviets. The first was the demand that future production of the Backfire bomber (which Brezhnev continued to insist was a medium-range aircraft lacking an intercontinental range) be counted in the aggregate ceiling of twenty-four hundred strategic launchers. The second was a proposal to increase the limits on the ground-launched cruise missile, a pilotless miniature aircraft with its own guidance system that could slide beneath radar and reach Soviet targets undetected. The United States had already begun to perfect this technologically sophisticated, highly accurate new weapon system while the Russians lagged far behind.

On Kissinger's return from Moscow the domestic political situation within the United States began to heat up in such as way as to prevent the administration from risking further arms-control concessions. Within the Republican Party, former California governor Ronald Reagan began to denounce the "Ford-Kissinger" foreign policy for jeopardizing U.S. national security and ignoring Soviet aggressiveness across the globe. Stung by these attacks from the right wing of his own party and fearful of appearing weak in the face of a resurgent Soviet Union, Ford announced in March 1976 that he was abandoning the term "détente" as he prepared to launch his election campaign. It soon became evident that the hopes for the prompt conclusion of a second strategic arms limitation agreement had vanished. After fruitless attempts to surmount the stumbling blocks represented by the Backfire bomber and cruise missile, Ford decided in April 1976 to break off the SALT II negotiations for the remainder of his presidential term.

The election of Jimmy Carter as president brought to the White House someone with even less foreign policy experience than Gerald Ford had possessed. His selection of Cyrus Vance as secretary of state and Zbigniew Brzezinski as national security adviser set the stage for an internal split within the foreign policy–making apparatus of his administration that would produce an impression of vacillation and incoherence. Vance was firmly committed to resuming the Nixon-Ford policy of détente with the Soviet Union and was reluctant to damage that relationship by challenging Moscow in peripheral areas of the Third World. Brzezinski, a Polish émigré professor from Columbia University who regarded the Soviet Union as an inherently expansionist power, disdained détente as a delusion and pressed for a reversion to the old policy of global containment. President Carter began his term with a steely determination to institute a decisive break with the foreign policy tradition of his predecessors. First of all, he rejected the previous two administrations' preoccupation with the bilateral relationship between the two superpowers. Carter strove instead to promote a much more active American engagement in regions such as Africa, Latin America, and the Middle East that were only tangentially involved in the Cold War. Second, the born-again Christian in the White House repudiated the amoral approach of Kissingerian *Realpolitik* in favor of a neo-Wilsonian concern for human rights, which he pursued with a dogged determination for the remainder of his term.

During the 1976 U.S. presidential campaign, candidate Jimmy Carter had promised major reductions in the defense budget if elected. Once in office he made good on this pledge by scrapping two weapons systems inherited from the Ford administration. The first was the B-I bomber, a supersonic strategic aircraft to replace the obsolete B-52 that was much more capable of penetrating Soviet air defenses. The second was the so-called Enhanced Radiation Weapon that was often inaccurately referred to the "neutron bomb," a warhead for use on U.S. tactical nuclear weapons (eight-inch artillery and Lance short-range missiles) deployed in Europe. Its lethal short-range radiation effects combined with low heat and blast characteristics seemed an ideal means of blocking a conventional Soviet offensive in West Germany: It could destroy advancing enemy tank formations without causing extensive collateral damage to the territory one was trying to defend.* Carter determined that the B-1 bomber was too costly and the neutron bomb too controversial in the eyes of America's European allies, so he canceled the former in June 1977 and deferred deployment of the latter in April 1978.

In the meantime Carter had come under intense pressure to counter perceived Soviet strategic gains, not only from the Republican opposition but also from members of his own party such as Senator Jackson and a vocal band of conservative Democrats who dominated the ominously named Committee on the Present Danger. Despite Moscow's explicit acceptance of deterrence based on the assumption of strategic parity and mutual assured destruction, this growing chorus of Cassandras in the United States loudly proclaimed that the Russians had abandoned the principle of parity in favor of a bold attempt to attain decisive strategic superiority. Some also suggested that the Russians had never really accepted the doctrine of mutual assured destruction and were intent on developing a war-fighting capability (including the means of surviving a nuclear war). These American critics issued ominous warnings that the new Soviet ICBMs with MIRVS deployed in the mid-1970s, which had much greater accuracy than their single-warhead predecessors, could wipe out the entire American ICBM force (one thousand Minutemen and fifty-four Titans) in a "disarming first strike" that would confront the United States with a terrible choice: Either it could respond by obliterating the major population centers of the Soviet Union with its surviving SLBM and strategic bomber forces, thereby exposing American cities to destruction by the remaining Soviet ICBMs, or it could refrain from retaliating and permit the Soviet Union to exploit its new strategic advantage to obtain mastery in the world.

---

*Soviet propagandists had a field day denouncing the neutron bomb as a quintessentially "capitalist" weapon, one that kills people but spares property.

Reneging on his campaign pledge to cut military spending, the new president embarked on a sustained effort to accelerate the development of three new strategic weapons systems that would enhance America's "counterforce capability" (that is, the ability to destroy the Soviet land-based missiles). The first was the "Missile Experimental" (MX) ICBM, which was thought to be virtually invulnerable to a disarming first strike because the missiles could be continually shuttled along ten thousand miles of rails in and out of forty-six hundred shelters in a kind of nuclear shell game. The second was the "cruise" missile, the small, relatively inexpensive, computer-driven, pilotless aircraft on which the United States had already been significant progress. The third was the Trident II SLBM, a replacement for the aging Polaris that would combine invulnerability to detection with much greater accuracy.

While striving to modernize the U.S. strategic arsenal, Carter also attempted to revive the dormant negotiations for a SALT II agreement based on the Vladivostok guidelines, which had been 90 percent completed before Ford applied the brakes in March 1976. The new occupant of the White House wrote Brezhnev on January 26, 1977, calling for a "rapid conclusion" of the new strategic arms treaty, and dispatched Secretary of State Vance to Moscow in March to reactivate the stalled negotiating process. Before he could get down to business, Vance encountered a storm of Soviet complaints that had nothing to do with the new American negotiating positions but rather with the effects of Carter's human rights campaign on domestic Soviet politics. Within three months of taking office the State Department was publicly denouncing the harsh treatment of Soviet dissidents Andrei Sakharov, Alexander Ginzburg, and Yuri Orlov, while Carter entertained the exiled dissident Vladimir Bukovsky at the White House. This U.S. pressure on the Soviet Union to grant political liberties to its citizens was extended to the Eastern European satellites through provocative broadcasts on Radio Free Europe and the Voice of America.

After taking note of these Soviet complaints, Vance presented a U.S. arms-control proposal that went far beyond the Vladivostok guidelines. It included more stringent limitations on the number of ICBMs with MIRVs as well as a total ban on the development, testing, and deployment of new types of long-range missiles. Brezhnev rejected the new American proposal out of hand, both because it entailed much larger sacrifices on the Soviet side and because the Kremlin was intent on consolidating the agreements already reached in negotiations since Vladivostok before venturing into uncharted territory. For the next two years the two sides squared off in a complex set of exchanges, variously conducted in meetings between Vance and Soviet Ambassador Anatoly Dobrynin in Washington, between the two delegations in Geneva, and in sporadic correspondence between Carter and Brezhnev. After the SALT I Interim Agreement expired on October 3, 1977, the two sides continued to abide by its provisions as work on a successor agreement resumed. After all of the differences were ironed out, Carter and Brezhnev finally traveled to Vienna to sign the SALT II treaty on June 18, 1979.

The new pact confirmed the aggregate ceilings of twenty-four hundred long-range nuclear weapons tentatively approved at Vladivostok. But it also included limits on the number of ICBMs, on the number of missiles with MIRVs, and on the number of MIRVs per missile. It also took into account more recent weapon systems that caused concern on both sides: An additional protocol set limits on the air-launched

and ground-launched cruise missiles (ALCMs and GLCMs) that the United States
had begun to develop, while Brezhnev gave a written assurance that the Soviet Backfire bomber would not be used as an intercontinental aircraft. On ratification the
treaty was to remain in force until 1985, when it was expected to be superceded by a
successor agreement (SALT III).

SALT II contained a number of advantages for the United States and hardly represented a threat to its strategic position. But that is precisely how it was portrayed
by its opponents in the United States, who warned that a massive increase in Soviet
defense spending in the 1970s had created a dangerous "window of vulnerability"
that placed America's land-based strategic missiles at risk: In theory, the SALT II
ceilings allowed the Soviet Union to put enough missiles on its ICBMs to enable
them to destroy up to 90 percent of the U.S. ICBM silos in a "disarming first strike."
This pessimistic interpretation was based on an inaccurate intelligence assessment of
Soviet defense spending (which had actually leveled off in the 1970s) as well as a
wildly exaggerated opinion of Soviet technological capabilities. It also discounted
the crucial circumstance that less than a quarter of the total American strategic warheads were located in the allegedly vulnerable land-based ICBM force, whereas
three-quarters of Soviet warheads were in fixed silos against which the United States
was attempting to develop a counterforce capability of its own. The "window of vulnerability" controversy of the late 1970s, like the "bomber gap" and "missile gap"
alarms of the late 1950s, revealed how U.S. strategists consistently overestimated the
economic and technological capabilities of America's Cold War adversary.

This mounting anxiety in certain American circles about the prospect of Soviet
strategic superiority, together with a set of other disturbing developments throughout
the world, converged at the end of the decade to ruin the SALT II Treaty's chances of
passage in the United States Senate. Moscow's logistical support for Ethiopia in its
war with Somalia rekindled American fears of a Soviet-Cuban offensive in Africa
that had first emerged during the Angolan Civil War in the middle of the decade (see
pages 297). Two other developments entirely unrelated to the Soviet-American
global rivalry also damaged SALT II's chances by reinforcing the growing sense of
America's vulnerability and loss of prestige throughout the world. The first was the
Panama Canal Treaty, which Carter pushed through the Senate despite vociferous
Republican complaints of a demeaning and dangerous sacrifice of an important
national asset (see page 282). The second was the Iran hostage crisis, which seemed
to confirm the increasingly widespread image of the United States as a helpless
Gulliver being brought down by lowly Lilliputians (see page 398).

Even the most trifling incident fed this new insecurity about American's declining
position in the world. In the autumn of 1979, while the SALT II Treaty was under
consideration in the Senate Foreign Relations Committee, U.S. intelligence discovered the presence of some three thousand Soviet ground troops in Cuba. Secretary of
State Vance concluded that the Russian soldiers, who had been stationed on the island
since the mid-1970s, did not violate the understanding that Kennedy and Khrushchev
had reached when the Soviet missiles were removed in 1962. But President Carter,
eager to counter allegations that his administration had been too accommodating to
Moscow in the SALT II talks, began referring to the Soviet unit as a "combat
brigade" and declared its presence in Cuba unacceptable. Congressional critics of

détente thereupon put the administration in a tight spot by demanding the removal of the Russian units, in a farcical replay of the events leading up to Kennedy's ultimatum to Khrushchev in the autumn of 1962. When Carter urged Brezhnev to recall the brigade or at least to reduce its combat capability in order to smooth SALT II's path to Senate ratification, the Soviet leader indignantly refused: The three thousand-man contingent had neither air- nor sea-lift capabilities, lacked offensive weapons, posed no threat to the United States, and had gone about its business without incident for several years. By November 1979 the Cuban combat brigade fiasco vanished from public consciousness, but not without leaving a residue of anti-Soviet sentiment in the United States that added to SALT II's woes in the Senate.

In the meantime a development of much greater resonance became a subject of grave concern for the United States and its NATO allies. As the negotiations for SALT II resumed after Carter's election, the Soviet Union began to replace its obsolete SS-4 and SS-5 intermediate-range missile force with SS-20 land-based missiles whose three thousand-mile range covered all of Western Europe. Unlike the older missiles, the SS-20s had MIRVs, three 150-kiloton independently-targetable warheads that could reach West German targets in twenty minutes. They were also mobile, which made them much more difficult to locate and destroy than their stationary predecessors. When the first SS-20 unit became operational toward the end of 1977, European leaders led by West German Chancellor Helmut Schmidt complained that the new weapons system would give the Soviet Union a decisive advantage in the "theater" nuclear balance on the continent. America's NATO allies began to worry that the United States, faced with the condition of strategic parity with the Soviet Union, might be tempted to renege on its long-standing commitment to employ nuclear weapons in retaliation against a conventional Soviet attack on the continent. A Europe "decoupled" from the U.S. strategic deterrent would be vulnerable to Soviet intimidation.

To calm these Allied anxieties and reaffirm U.S. support for the defense of Western Europe, the Carter administration resolved to challenge the new Soviet buildup in theater nuclear weapons. With the full support of the American delegation, NATO's foreign and defense ministers meeting in Brussels decided on December 12, 1979, to deploy a new generation of intermediate-range missiles in Western Europe unless the Soviet Union would agree in arms control talks to eliminate the SS-20s. In the absence of such an agreement, 108 Pershing II missiles would be deployed in West Germany to replace the shorter range Pershing Is that had been there since 1969, while 464 ground-launched cruise missiles (GLCMs) would be deployed in Great Britain, Italy, Belgium, and the Netherlands as well as West Germany by the end of 1983. The new weapons would reduce the risk of nuclear blackmail from the SS-20s by removing Western European worries about being cut loose from the U.S. nuclear deterrent: Since the American-controlled missiles deployed in West Germany and the Low Countries would lay in the path of a Soviet invasion, the American president would be obliged to "use them or lose them" at the beginning of World War III in Europe.

NATO's decision to modernize its nuclear forces in Europe provoked a predictably indignant response from the Kremlin. The Soviet government totally ignored the fact that the initiative for the Pershing II and GLCM deployments had come not from Washington but from America's NATO allies, whose leaders were worried about the imbalance of theater nuclear forces caused by the SS-20 deployment. Instead, Brezhnev and company apparently suspected that the entire controversy had nothing to do with the balance of intermediate-range nuclear forces in Europe but had been manufactured by the Carter administration to create a pretext for shelving SALT II and expanding U.S. strategic capabilities. Although Moscow reluctantly entered discussions on theater nuclear forces in Geneva in October 1980, Soviet negotiators refused to even consider scrapping the SS-20 that were already deployed while demanding that NATO rescind its decisions to deploy the Pershings and GLCMs. The Russians complained that the Pershing II, ten times more accurate than the Pershing I with a flight-time of ten minutes compared to thirty minutes for an ICBM from the United States, possessed counterforce capabilities that would permit a disarming first strike against Soviet ICBM silos as well as command and control centers. The Soviet claim that Washington was behind the campaign to deploy the "Euromissiles," although entirely untrue, was bolstered by an eruption of popular protest in those Western European countries whose governments had agreed to receive them. This public opposition to the deployment increased in intensity after the accession of President Ronald Reagan in January 1981. The new U.S. head of state was thought to be much less interested in pursuing the "negotiating track" of the 1979 NATO ultimatum than in completing the missile modernization program.

The Reagan administration was concerned about the rising chorus of opposition in Western Europe to the intermediate-range nuclear forces (INF) deployment, which Brezhnev had effectively exploited with a proposal for a moratorium on new nuclear weapons systems on the continent that won widespread public approval in several NATO countries. To counter this European criticism, Reagan surprised many observers by dispatching a delegation to Geneva in November 1981 to participate in the INF talks with the Soviet Union. The U.S. delegation scored a formidable public relations coup in these negotiations by proposing a simple, definitive solution to the nuclear arms race on the continent. This was the so-called zero option, whereby the United States would cancel its plans to deploy the 572 cruise and Pershing II missiles in exchange for the dismantling of the 600 Soviet SS-20s. The American plan was disadvantageous to the Soviet Union for two major reasons. First, it would have required the Russians to scrap an already operational weapons system in exchange for a U.S. pledge not to deploy an untested system that had generated political opposition among America's European allies. Second, it excluded consideration of the British and French nuclear forces, which were slated to be equipped with more MIRVed warheads than the Soviet SS-20s possessed. Whenever the Russians broached the topic of including the British and French nuclear forces in the negotiations, the U.S. delegates to the INF talks protested that London and Paris would never allow their national nuclear deterrents to be bargained away by their transatlantic ally.

Although the Kremlin dismissed the "zero option" proposal out of hand, the Soviet negotiators at Geneva tried to find common ground with their American counterparts. The two negotiating teams reached a tentative agreement in July 1982, when the Soviet delegate proposed a reduction of the SS-20s to seventy-five while the United States would be permitted to deploy an equal number of GLCMs (but none of the much more destructive Pershing II ballistic missiles). But neither the White House nor the Kremlin was willing to endorse the compromise and it died. By the end of the year the Soviet Union hardened its position in the hope of exploiting the growing antinuclear sentiment in West Germany and Great Britain. As the United States began to deploy the first group of missiles in West Germany and Italy in the fall of 1983 to meet the deadline specified by NATO four years earlier, the Soviet delegates indignantly stormed out of the deadlocked talks in Geneva.

While the two superpowers failed to reach agreement on intermediate-range nuclear weapons in Europe, the complex issue of strategic arms control also continued to elude a mutually acceptable solution. The Reagan administration displayed an ambivalent attitude toward the SALT process. On the one hand, the new U.S. head of state presided over the largest peacetime military buildup in history to counter what he and his advisers appeared to believe was the Soviet Union's bid to achieve overwhelming strategic superiority. Reagan's defense planners devoted particular attention to the problem of how to protect America's land-based deterrent from a Soviet first strike: After a lengthy consideration of various basing schemes they finally secured congressional authorization in May 1983 of the MX missile, which would be based in existing hardened silos, as a replacement of the ostensibly vulnerable Minuteman ICBM force.

This concern about the survivability of America's land-based strategic forces inspired a revival of interest in some type of ABM system that would shield the ICBMs from a disarming first strike. The Soviet Union had deployed and expanded the minimal ABM system that was permitted under the SALT I treaty of 1972 (see page 122). Five years later the Pentagon, concerned about the vulnerability of the American ICBM force to a Soviet surprise attack, began to finance feasibility studies for the creation of a missile defense system employing a number of exotic products of high technology. The Reagan administration greatly expanded the scope of the top-secret ABM project that it had inherited. On March 23, 1983, the president publicly broached the idea of developing a missile defense system composed of satellite-launched laser beams that could intercept and destroy Soviet missiles before they reached the territory of America or its allies.

Most observers agreed that Reagan's new proposal—promptly dubbed the Strategic Defense Initiative (SDI) by its proponents and "Star Wars" (after the hit movie) by its critics—would violate the ABM provisions of the SALT I Treaty of 1972 (see page 123). It also directly contradicted the official American nuclear strategy of reciprocal deterrence. Opponents of the scheme charged that by removing the certainty of mutual annihilation, SDI would upset the "balance of terror" that had kept the peace during the Cold War and pave the way for all sorts of nightmare scenarios: The superpower protected by the missile screen might be tempted to disarm its rival with a surprise attack to gain mastery of the world; the unprotected superpower might be stampeded into a preemptive nuclear attack before the other had completed its own defensive system. The new U.S. missile defense plan, which was followed up by a projected $26-billion, five-year program to develop the necessary technology, set off alarm bells in the Kremlin. Soviet officials knew that their inferior economic base would be incapable of sustaining such a costly competition with their technologically advanced adversary. The SDI project threatened to neutralize the Soviet nuclear deterrent or to stretch the Soviet economy to the breaking point as it struggled to develop effective countermeasures.

The divisive issue of anti-missile defense was inextricably linked to the general subject of strategic arms control, which had been left unresolved by the failure of the U.S. Senate to ratify the SALT II agreement during the Carter years. The Reagan administration's emerging policy toward strategic arms control unexpectedly belied its reputation for unswerving opposition to any compromise with what the resolutely anti-Communist occupant of the White House had publicly castigated as the "Evil Empire." After criticizing the unratified SALT II agreement during the election campaign for freezing the United States into a dangerous position of strategic inferiority, the new president subsequently agreed to follow his predecessor's policy of abiding by the treaty's limitations as long as the Soviet Union did likewise. Reagan then surprised his critics by agreeing to a resumption of strategic arms negotiations with the Soviet Union. In a May 1982 speech he suggested that the new round of discussions be designated as Strategic Arms Reduction Talks (START) to signify a decisive break with the SALT II Treaty. The replacement of the word "Limitation" with "Reduction" expressed Reagan's hope for deep cuts in, rather than the imposition of upper limits on, the nuclear arsenals of the two superpowers. The START talks, which opened in Geneva on June 29, 1982, yielded no concrete results and were suspended in November 1983 when the Soviet delegates walked out in protest against the beginning of the American INF missile deployments in Western Europe. For the remainder of the first Reagan term and the beginning of the second, the earlier arms-control initiatives languished amid the deteriorating relations between Washington and Moscow.

# SIX

# REGIONAL RIVALRIES AND COLD WAR CONFLICTS IN THE MIDDLE EAST, 1945–1975

## The Establishment of the Jewish State

At the end of World War II the new Labour government in London prepared to grant independence to the subject populations of the British Empire. But Foreign Secretary Ernest Bevin was intent on preserving a British military presence in the Middle East, both to protect the country's oil fields and pipelines in the Persian Gulf as well as to support its remaining naval bases along the Red Sea and the Indian Ocean. He believed that the most suitable site for the retention of Britain's influence in this region was Palestine, which it had administered since the end of World War I under a mandate from the League of Nations. But this aspiration was frustrated by two contending forces in the area that were intent on replacing Britain as the sovereign authority there. The first was the mandate's roughly 1.3 million Arab inhabitants, supported with varying degrees of enthusiasm by the neighboring Arab states of Egypt, Syria, Lebanon, Iraq, and Transjordan (later renamed Jordan), who demanded an independent Palestine under their control. The second was the six hundred thousand Jews who had migrated to Palestine from Russia and Eastern Europe in five waves (or Aliyahs) from 1882 through the 1930s, some in a sentimental return to the land of their biblical forbears, others to escape anti-Semitic persecution in their countries of origin.

The Zionist movement, founded in the late nineteenth century to campaign for a Jewish homeland in Palestine, had secured British support for that goal during World War I in the form of the Balfour Declaration issued in November 1917. In the interwar period more than 100,000 European Jews immigrated to Palestine, expanding the Jewish population there, before a government White Paper imposed severe limits to the influx of Jews in 1939 as World War II began. At the end of World War II the official mouthpiece of the Zionist movement, the Jewish Agency, demanded that the British authorities permit unlimited Jewish immigration to Palestine to accommodate the roughly one hundred thousand survivors of the Nazi Holocaust who were languishing in displaced person (DP) camps in Europe. Since Arabs outnumbered Jews two to one in Palestine at the end of the war, the issue of Jewish immigration became the key to the territory's political future after the British departure. By retaining the monthly Jewish immigration quota of fifteen hundred that had been set by the government White Paper in 1939, Britain guaranteed that an independent Palestine would be dominated by an Arab population that was double that of the Jews.

This restriction on Jewish immigration prompted the Jewish Agency and its military arm, the Haganah, to launch in the autumn of 1945 an undeclared war against the British mandatory authorities in Palestine. By the end of that year eighty thousand British troops had been dispatched to enforce London's authority, while Bevin sought to enlist U.S. support. Reflecting intense political pressure from American Jews on behalf of their coreligionists in the DP camps of occupied Germany, President Truman had formally requested at the end of August 1945 that Britain permit the immediate admission of the 100,000 Jewish DPs to Palestine. By the end of 1946 the population of these camps had increased to 250,000, as Jews from Eastern Europe fled anti-Semitic outbreaks there. Britain's refusal to permit unrestricted Jewish immigration to Palestine, which resulted in many heart-rending scenes of boats crammed with Holocaust survivors being turned away from their destination, generated friction between London and Washington even as those two governments were joining forces against the Soviet Union at the beginning of the Cold War. Bevin denounced as hypocritical the Truman administration's pressure on Britain to allow 100,000 European Jews into Palestine while the U.S. Congress refused to modify its own restrictive immigration policies, which admitted less than six thousand Jewish refugees to the United States between May 1945 and September 1946.

Two Anglo-American committees proposed partial solutions to the dilemma in April and July 1946, but to no avail. In the meantime two Zionist underground organizations, the Irgun Zvai Leumi ("National Military Group") and LEHI ("Fighters for the Freedom of Israel"), were waging a bloody campaign of terror against British soldiers and administrators that severely undermined public support for the mandatory power's hopeless task in Palestine. Weary of the acrimonious exchanges with Washington over the issue and facing a severe economic crisis that made the nearly £40 million Britain spent annually to maintain its army in Palestine difficult to justify, Bevin announced on February 25, 1947, that he was washing his hands of the entire problem and was dumping it in the lap of the new United Nations.

In April the world organization promptly formed a United Nations Special Committee on Palestine (UNSCOP), composed of representatives from eleven nations,* which conducted on-site investigations and issued a report to the UN General Assembly at the end of August. The UNSCOP report unanimously recommended the termination of the British mandate and the creation of an independent Palestine after a two-year transitional period. But the committee was divided on the key question of the political structure of the future state. A majority of eight called for partition into a Jewish and Arab state and the internationalization of Jerusalem, which contained

---

*Australia, Canada, Czechoslovakia, Guatemala, India, Iran, the Netherlands, Peru, Sweden, Uruguay, and Yugoslavia.

holy sites of the world's three major monotheistic religions. The Jewish state would comprise roughly 56 percent and the Arab state about 43 percent of mandate Palestine's ten thousand square miles.* A minority of three (India, Iran, and Yugoslavia) called for a single independent federal state, which would have contradicted the tenets of Zionism by consigning the Jews to minority status in the proposed Jewish state.

The Jewish Agency promptly endorsed the majority report and mounted an energetic campaign on behalf of partition. Virtually all the Palestinian Arabs and their supporters in the neighboring Arab states rejected the recommendation and declared that they would not be bound by a UN decision to approve it. They complained that it gave the Jews, most of whom had arrived in the last thirty years and who were outnumbered by the Arabs two to one, more territory than was allotted to the people that had inhabited Palestine for centuries. On November 29, 1947, the UN General Assembly narrowly approved the recommendation for partition by the required two-thirds majority (33 to 13 with ten abstentions). To the surprise of many observers, the Soviet Union and its Eastern European satellites voted with the United States and its Western partners on behalf of the resolution, marking one of the few instances in which the two rival blocs in the emerging Cold War supported the same policy in the UN.

For the next six months Arab and Jewish militants in Palestine jockeyed for position in anticipation of the British withdrawal. The cause of the Palestinian Arabs was gravely undermined by intense intra-Arab rivalries: Egypt supported a faction controlled by Haj Amin al-Husseini, the grand mufti (highest Muslim religious official) of Jerusalem, who hoped to control the Palestinian resistance to the Zionists and disburse the funds provided by the Arab states for that purpose. The Arab League refused to provide financial assistance to the mufti or to create a Palestinian government-in-exile, preferring to back one of his rivals, Fawzi al-Qawuqii, who led a group of non-Palestinian Arab volunteers intent on defeating the Zionists when the British mandate ended. King Abdullah of Jordan, who threw his support to still another rival Palestinian faction, planned to annex Jerusalem and central Palestine to his own state. As a result of this internecine bickering, the Arabs were unable to create a unified military command or to devise a coherent military strategy.

On May 14, 1948, the British mandate formally came to an end as the head of the Jewish Agency, David Ben-Gurion, proclaimed in the coastal city of Tel Aviv the establishment of the state of Israel. The next day the United States became the first foreign power to accord the Jewish state de facto recognition, and the Soviet Union promptly followed with de jure recognition. In the meantime Arab armies from Iraq, Syria, Lebanon, Egypt, and Jordan had invaded the new state from all directions. Abdullah's Arab Legion, the best organized and equipped of the Arab forces, moved into the part of Palestine allocated to the Arab state in the UN partition resolution that would later be known as the West Bank of the Jordan River and occupied the eastern half of the city of Jerusalem. But that proved to be the only military success recorded by the enemies of the Jewish state. The Jewish Haganah units, better trained and more highly motivated than their faction-ridden, mutually suspicious

---

*According to official estimates, the proposed Jewish state would have contained about 498,000 Jews and 407,000 Arabs (before further Jewish immigration). The proposed Arab state would have contained about 725,000 Arabs and 10,000 Jews.

*Zionist officials display the proclamation announcing the establishment of the state of Israel, which was issued by David Ben-Gurion (left) at a hotel in Tel Aviv on May 14, 1948* (National Archives)

enemies, inflicted crushing defeats on all fronts. By the end of 1948 the Israeli forces had thoroughly trounced the Arab armies, paving the way for a series of armistice agreements negotiated on the island of Rhodes during the first half of 1949.

As a result of the Armistice of Rhodes, the territory of Israel was increased by about one-fifth of the area assigned to it by the UN partition plan. Its Jewish population had been augmented by the influx of the 100,000 survivors from the DP camps in Germany. They were followed by emigrants from Eastern Europe and from Arab countries, so that by the beginning of 1950 the Jewish population of Israel had reached one million. By the same year its Arab population had dwindled to about 150,000. The reason for that dramatic decline was that some 750,000 Palestinian Arabs, about 70 percent of the Arab population of mandate Palestine, had either fled or were expelled from their homes during the 1948 war and were prevented from returning by the Israeli government. Of those refugees, about 470,000 settled in squalid camps set up in the Egyptian-controlled Gaza Strip and the Jordanian-controlled West Bank. The remainder ended up in Syria, Lebanon, Jordan, Egypt, and Iraq. Only Jordan granted its Palestinian population citizenship. The rest were condemned to the humiliating condition of statelessness, nurturing a passionate desire to return to their homes that was encouraged by the propaganda agencies of the Arab countries that remained (despite the armistice of 1949) in a state of war with the Jewish state. To prevent a renewal of hostilities, the United States, Great Britain, and France issued in May 1950 the so-called Tripartite Declaration. The three signatories affirmed their commitment to promote peace and stability in the region by preserving a military balance between Israel and the Arab states so that neither side would be capable of defeating the other. But the war of 1948 would not be the last military confrontation between the Jewish state and its Arab neighbors.

## The Road to Suez

Israel's complete triumph in the 1948 war severely undermined the prestige of the Arab leaders whose armies had been routed by the military forces of the new Jewish state. In Syria, Jordan, and Egypt reform-minded young officers rebelled against their governments, which they blamed for the recent national humiliation. While the Syrian and Jordanian regimes foiled the coups and clung to power, the corrupt, British-subsidized monarchy of King Farouk in Egypt was overthrown in July 1952 by a group of "Free Officers" under the titular leadership of General Mohammed Neguib. The new military government promptly abolished the monarchy, sent the playboy king into exile, and purged the army of its royalist sympathizers. On April 17, 1954, the brains behind the military revolt, Colonel Gamal Abdel Nasser, replaced Neguib as head of the ruling junta in Cairo. By the end of the year Nasser had acquired absolute power and began to unveil an ambitious program to modernize Egypt's antiquated economic system and rejuvenate its battered military forces.

The dynamic new Egyptian leader became a founding member of the nonaligned movement and soon perfected a remarkable capacity for playing the two super-powers against one another in order to obtain from both the economic and military assistance that his campaign of national regeneration required. But Egypt's quest for military aid in Washington was rebuffed by the Eisenhower administration, which was bound by the Tripartite Declaration of 1950 to preserve a military balance be-tween Israel and the Arab states. Frustrated in his bid for arms deliveries from the United States, Nasser later turned to the Soviet bloc for support. Although an im-placable foe of Communism at home, he was perfectly happy to receive whatever as-sistance Moscow was willing to offer. The leadership in the Kremlin was displeased by Nasser's repressive measures against the Egyptian Communist Party, but it was tempted by the opportunity to extend Soviet influence to the Middle East. So First Secretary Nikita Khrushchev responded sympathetically to the Egyptian leader's entreaties. The first concrete results of this Soviet-Egyptian rapprochement came on September 27, 1955, when Nasser announced with much fanfare the conclusion of a bilateral barter arrangement whereby the Soviet Union promised to provide arms to Egypt via Czechoslovakia in exchange for payment in cotton and rice.

Egypt was at the time one of the most arid countries in the world. Its thirty million people had no fertile land beyond the Nile Delta and the thin strip along both banks of the river. To alleviate this difficult situation Nasser eagerly embraced a proposal from his economic advisers to construct a dam near the city of Aswan on the Upper Nile, which would provide irrigation to some ten thousand square kilometers of desert and increase Egypt's arable land by a third. As an added bonus the hydroelec-tric power generated by the new dam would expand Egypt's electricity output by one half. Lacking sufficient capital for his pet project, Nasser approached the World Bank on September 26, 1955, for a $240 million loan. After careful consideration the

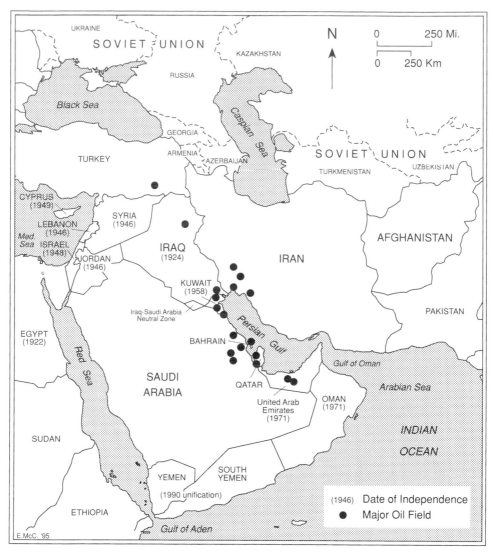

*The Middle East after World War II*

international lending institution consented to the request, on the condition that the United States and Great Britain contribute $70 million to the loan package. But as is its custom, the World Bank attached a number of restrictions to the proposed loan on how the proceeds might be spent.

Bristling with indignation at this infringement of Egypt's freedom of action, Nasser decided to cover his bets by seeking an alternative source of financing as well. Before formally accepting the World Bank's offer, he sought and obtained from the Soviet Union an agreement in principle to grant Egypt a loan of $200 million to help finance the construction of the dam. Moscow's offer came with no strings attached and on very attractive terms: repayment over thirty years by the usual means of cotton and rice deliveries at the rock-bottom interest rate of 2 percent. The prospect of Soviet financial assistance to Egypt, coming on the heels of Nasser's arms deal with Czechoslovakia, suddenly sparked anxiety in Washington that Egypt might be gravitating to the Communist camp. Secretary of State Dulles hastily persuaded President Eisenhower to allocate $54 million in aid to Cairo for the dam project. Once British Prime Minister Anthony Eden had agreed to kick in $16 million, the loan package had reached the $70 million required by the World Bank for the first stage of the dam's construction.

While the feverish negotiations over the financing of the Aswan Dam continued behind closed doors, the Egyptian government suddenly and unexpectedly announced on May 16, 1956, that it had decided to accord diplomatic recognition to the People's Republic of China. The establishment of diplomatic ties between Cairo and Beijing was hardly a newsworthy event. Many European states, including Great Britain, had recognized the People's Republic shortly after the Communist victory in the Chinese Civil War and conducted normal relations with it for years. But Nasser was not content with simply opening an Egyptian embassy in Beijing. He also announced plans to send a high-level military mission to China and dropped hints that he might seek arms from the Chinese Communist regime to supplement the deal he had recently struck with the Soviet satellite Czechoslovakia. As always, the Egyptian leader liked to keep all options open to maximize the potential benefits for his own country.

As he resumed his customary gambit of pitting the two blocs against one other in search of military and economic aid from the highest bidder, Nasser began to focus his attention on the last remnant of European imperialism on Egyptian territory. This was the presence of British military forces in the Suez Canal Zone. In 1875 Britain had acquired majority control of the company that operated the vital waterway, which had been built by the French in the 1860s to connect the Mediterranean to the Red Sea. After landing military forces in Egypt in 1882, Britain established a protectorate over the country at the beginning of World War I. The explosion of Egyptian nationalist resentment at the country's colonial status after the war finally forced Britain to sign a treaty with Egypt in 1936 that converted the protectorate into a bilateral alliance between two sovereign states. British military forces, previously entitled to operate throughout the entire country, were confined to the Canal Zone where they protected Britain's important strategic and economic interests at this vital choke-point on the British "lifeline" to Asia.

The presence of these British soldiers along Egypt's most valuable economic asset represented a humiliating constraint on the country's sovereignty that sparked sharp protests from patriotic Egyptians. A year before the overthrow of King Farouk in 1952, the Egyptian parliament had defiantly demanded the revision of the Anglo-Egyptian Treaty of 1936. As the new military junta increased the pressure on London to relinquish this last vestige of European imperial authority in the country, the new administration in Washington supported the Egyptian position. Eisenhower and Dulles hoped that by siding with the forces of anticolonialism in the Middle East, the United States stood to gain not only a valuable ally in Egypt but also friends throughout the Third World. Deprived of Washington's support, London caved in and signed an agreement with Cairo on October 19, 1954, that provided for the removal of all

British military forces from the Canal Zone by the summer of 1956. In exchange Egypt promised to preserve freedom of navigation through the canal and to allow British military forces to return if any Arab state or Turkey came under attack from a foreign power.

The Anglo-Egyptian agreement of October 1954 set the stage for the termination of Britain's longstanding imperial presence in the Middle East. Then in the following month, the insurrection mounted by the Arab majority in Algeria against French rule threatened the position of the other European imperial power in the Arab world (see page 86). Nasser offered full support to the Algerian rebels, including a safe haven in Egypt for those obliged to flee the French counterinsurgency forces. Officials in Paris deluded themselves into believing that the Egyptian leader was one of the driving forces behind the Algerian revolution and therefore that his removal from power would greatly enhance the prospects of preserving French rule. In fact, Nasser was restricted to offering mostly rhetorical support to the anti-French movement in Algeria, since that country did not share a common border with Egypt. But the charismatic leader in Cairo was in a much better position to intervene in another conflict that had been brewing along Egypt's eastern frontier since the end of the Arab-Israeli war of 1948.

To the new generation of Arab leaders, the emergence of a state dominated by citizens of European descent* in the very heart of the Arab world represented an intolerable affront to Arab dignity and a reminder of the humiliating legacy of colonialism. By the mid-1950s Nasser had assumed de facto leadership of the Arab-Palestinian cause against the new Jewish state. The influx of Jews to Israel on the basis of the "Law of Return" (which guaranteed automatic citizenship to all Jews of the diaspora), together with the Israeli government's refusal to readmit the Arab inhabitants who had been evicted or fled during the 1948 war, condemned the Palestinian refugees to an exile status that they steadfastly refused to accept. The Egyptian president became their most vociferous public advocate: Radio Cairo flooded the airwaves of the Arab world with impassioned rhetoric denouncing Zionism as a new form of colonialism and calling for the destruction of the Jewish state and the return of the Palestinian diaspora.

Even before Nasser, Egypt had played a prominent role in the low-level conflict waged by the Arab states in the Middle East to prevent Israel from consolidating its control of territory it had won in 1948. Palestinian guerrillas (or *Fedayeen*) were permitted to mount raids into Israel from the Gaza Strip, a small portion of mandate Palestine that Egypt had annexed after the war. Merchant ships en route to Israeli ports were denied use of the Suez Canal and the Strait of Tiran at the mouth of the Gulf of Aqaba, which provided Israel's only outlet to the Red Sea. By the year 1956 Israeli Prime Minister David Ben-Gurion had concluded that the only means of achieving Israel's two major foreign policy objectives—the termination of the commando raids from Gaza and the assurance of free passage through the Suez Canal and the Red Sea—was a preemptive military operation against Egypt.

---

*The vast majority of Jews who had settled in Israel were Ashkenazi, or European, Jews, mostly emigrants from Russia and Eastern Europe.

Amid these disparate developments—Soviet-American competition for influence in the Middle East, the Egyptian-supported Algerian insurrection against France, and the simmering tension between the Egypt and Israel—Great Britain formally terminated its seventy-year military occupation of the Suez Canal on June 13, 1956, as stipulated in the October 1954 agreement. The British departure from Suez left Egypt with full responsibility for the defense of the country's economically important waterway, through which much of the world's trade passed. But by that time the U.S. government had become thoroughly disenchanted with the foreign policies of Gamal Abdel Nasser. Eisenhower and Dulles had earlier cultivated the Egyptian leader in the hopes that he would become a pro-American, anti-Communist successor to the departing European colonial power in this vital part of the world. But the arms deal with Communist Czechoslovakia, the courting of Communist China, and the bid for Soviet financing of the Aswan Dam prompted a reconsideration in Washington of the commitment to assist Egypt in its ambitious construction project. Domestic political forces in the United States also began to work against the Egyptian leader. Jewish Americans vigorously objected to the provision of funds to a country that supported Palestinian raids against Israel from Gaza, denied it access to the Suez Canal and the Red Sea, and openly called for its destruction. Defenders of American cotton interests on Capitol Hill, which wielded inordinate influence because of the overrepresentation of Southern legislators in the congressional power structure, opposed the use of taxpayers' money to finance a dam that would help Egypt increase its cotton exports to the detriment of cotton farmers from the American South.

This mounting American disenchantment with Nasser finally burst into the open on July 20, 1956, when Secretary of State Dulles abruptly and tactlessly informed the Egyptian ambassador that the U.S. government had decided to withdraw its offer to help finance the construction of the Aswan Dam project. Within hours the British government revoked its pledge of financial support as well. The World Bank then withdrew its financial aid package of $240 million, which had been offered contingent on the Anglo-American contribution. Nasser's pet construction project suddenly seemed doomed, causing him acute embarrassment and a terrible loss of face. But not for long. He announced to a cheering crowd on July 26, 1956, that his government had assumed control of the Suez Canal Company and would employ the revenues from the tolls paid by ships using the canal to finance the construction of the dam.

Egypt's nationalization of the Suez Canal Company was perfectly in accord with international law. The waterway was located on Egyptian territory and was therefore subject to Egyptian control. The company's concession to operate the canal was due to expire in twelve years. In canceling the concession Nasser solemnly pledged to compensate the dispossessed shareholders, the majority of whom were British and French citizens, for the generous dividends they would no longer receive. While London and Paris howled in protest, Washington (whose citizens had no significant financial stake in the company) responded with greater restraint. Acknowledging that Egypt was entitled to nationalize the firm, Dulles devoted his renowned diplomatic skills to organizing a "users' committee" that would secure an iron-clad commitment from the government to preserve the right of free passage through the canal by the merchant ships of the world. Although this right was guaranteed by a 1888 treaty,

Egypt had violated it by banning Israeli ships from using the waterway and could therefore do so against other nations as well.

In the meantime the French government had become so exasperated with Nasser for his support of the Algerian rebels and his peremptory treatment of French holders of Suez Canal Company bonds that it decided to resort to force. Officials in Paris therefore established clandestine contact with representatives of the only other country whose hostility to Nasser was equal to their own: the state of Israel. By the end of September Paris and Tel Aviv had reached a top secret agreement to mount a joint military operation against Egypt. They then approached London, which had grievances of its own against the Egyptian leader, about joining the plot.

Although fully receptive to these Franco-Israeli overtures, British Prime Minister Anthony Eden was reluctant to act in concert with Israel for fear of alienating pro-British Arab states such as the Hashemite monarchies of Jordan and Iraq. So Eden and a small group of advisers concocted an elaborate hoax that would conceal Britain's cooperation with Israel while achieving the result that all three conspiring countries sought, which was the overthrow of Nasser: Israeli military forces would launch an offensive across Egypt's Sinai Peninsula toward the Suez Canal. Great Britain and France would jointly issue an ultimatum warning that if both belligerents did not halt their military operations the two European powers would occupy the canal to ensure its security. Israel would accept the ultimatum and suspend its advance toward the canal; when Egypt rejected the ultimatum, as it was fully expected to do, the Anglo-French planes would bomb Egyptian airfields preparatory to an Anglo-French joint landing to seize control of the canal and overthrow the man who had nationalized it.

The hair-brained scheme unfolded according to plan in its early stages. The Israeli army launched its surprise attack across the Sinai on October 29. Within a few days its armored columns had smashed through the Egyptian defenses and then halted ten miles short of the canal in compliance with the pre-arranged Anglo-French ultimatum. The Israelis thereupon concentrated on achieving their two principal objectives, which were to clear out the Palestinian guerrilla bases on the Gaza Strip and to capture the Egyptian base at Sharm-al-Sheikh that enabled Nasser to bar the Strait of Tiran to Israeli shipping. After several days of bombing Egyptian positions, British and French ground troops that had been assembled on the island of Malta staged successful amphibious and paratroop landings at Egyptian ports on both banks of the canal. Their announced purpose was to separate the two belligerents and keep the vital waterway open to traffic. But both of these objectives had become moot by the time the operation got under way: The fighting between Israeli and Egyptian forces had virtually ceased. The canal had been rendered totally unusable when Egyptian militiamen sank ships weighted with concrete across the entire width of the waterway.

It soon became evident that the real aim of the operation was not the protection of the canal but the deposition of Nasser. Eden and French Prime Minister Guy Mollet were both obsessed with the historical lessons of the 1930s. They conjured up in their minds the absurdly distorted image of Nasser as an incarnation of Adolf Hitler who had to be removed from power to prevent a repetition of the craven policy of appeasement that they had witnessed earlier in their careers. The replacement of Nasser with a more moderate leader would enhance British interests by curbing the poisonous brand of anti-Western Arab radicalism he personified; it would bolster France's counterinsurgency campaign against the Algerian revolutionaries by depriving them of their main source of foreign support; and it would enhance the security of Israel by depriving the Palestinian guerrillas of their principal patron and protector.

The Anglo-French-Israeli intervention in Suez was a temporary military success. The Soviet-equipped Egyptian army proved no match for the Israeli forces in the Sinai and could not prevent the Anglo-French occupation of the nation's major ports. But it was a diplomatic disaster in the long run because of the unexpected and vigorous opposition of the United States. Eden and Mollet had not given Eisenhower advance warning of their secret scheme. Both assumed that Washington would prefer to be left in the dark about, but would tacitly approve of, their plan to topple the man who had accorded the Soviets entrée to the Middle East, embraced Communist China, and threatened the state of Israel. But from the American perspective the Anglo-French intervention at Suez could not have come at a more inopportune time: Eisenhower was winding up his reelection campaign on the theme that he had ended the Korean War and presided over four years of peace and stability in the world. Now America's two closest allies in NATO were engaged in an unprovoked surprise attack against a sovereign state. Moreover, the Anglo-French operation gave off the pungent odor of old-fashioned colonialism at a time when Dulles and Eisenhower were attempting to counter Khrushchev's new diplomatic offensive in the Third World by advertising U.S. support for national self-determination. To add insult to injury, the attack against Nasser in Egypt coincided with the Soviet intervention in Hungary. How could the United States condemn the appearance of Russian tanks in Budapest while tolerating Israeli tanks in the Sinai and Anglo-French paratroops along the Suez Canal?

So the Eisenhower administration energetically opposed the Anglo-French-Israeli operation in Egypt. The U.S. delegate introduced a resolution in the UN Security Council demanding an immediate withdrawal of the invasion forces. The Treasury Department conducted a selling operation against the pound sterling on international money markets, causing a run on the British currency and a sharp drop in its value. The collapse of sterling coincided with a severe shortage of British oil supplies caused by the blockage of the Suez Canal and the diversion of tankers around South Africa's Cape of Good Hope. The painful economic penalties that Britain was obliged to pay as a consequence of the Suez operation revealed how weak and vulnerable that once formidable imperial power had become.

The Soviet Union was able to reap a number of diplomatic advantages from the Suez affair. It served to distract world attention from the embarrassing events in Hungary. It enabled the Kremlin to win widespread respect in the Arab world by supporting an embattled Arab state against the European imperialists and their Zionist ally. On November 5 Moscow had proposed a joint U.S.-Soviet intervention to block the Anglo-French invasion. Prime Minister Bulganin dashed off a menacing letter to Eden that included a veiled threat of rocket attacks against the United Kingdom. The Soviet proposal for joint military intervention with the United States was a meaningless gesture, since Moscow knew that it would be rejected in Washington. Bulganin's implied hint of nuclear retaliation against Great Britain was empty bravado, since the Russians would never risk nuclear war over an issue so unrelated to their vital interests. Nevertheless, Moscow was able to pose as the defender of the cause of anti-imperialism in the Arab world without lifting a finger. In fact, it was the firm diplomatic and financial pressure from Washington that induced London and Paris to accept a cease-fire on November 6. By that time the Anglo-French forces had only managed to secure control of half of the canal, so they had little bargaining power when negotiations for a final settlement got underway. The British, French, and Israeli troops were obliged to evacuate the Egyptian territory they had occupied. On November 15 a United Nations Emergency Force (UNEF) arrived in the Canal Zone to supervise the cease-fire and maintain the security of the waterway. The following May Israel agreed to withdraw its military forces from the Sinai in exchange for Egypt's acceptance of a UN force on the border between the Gaza Strip and Israel and at the town of Sharm al-Sheikh on the southern tip of the Sinai peninsula. The UN force in Gaza protected Israel from raids mounted by Palestinian militants who temporarily resided there, and the UN contingent at Sharm al-Sheikh protected Israeli shipping's freedom of passage through the Gulf of Aqaba.

The Soviet military intervention in Hungary and the American diplomatic intervention in Suez in November 1956 demonstrated two important and interrelated truths about the bipolar international order during the Cold War. Hungary revealed that Moscow's Warsaw Pact allies in Eastern Europe would have to toe the Kremlin line or suffer painful consequences. Suez proved that America's NATO allies in Western Europe, while enjoying much more latitude than the Communist satellites to pursue their own national goals, would not be permitted to do so if those goals met with disapproval in Washington. While Great Britain licked the wounds inflicted at Suez and accepted its subordinate status, French officials began—even before the return of Charles de Gaulle—to explore ways of reducing their country's security dependence on the United States.

## Nasserism and the Crises in Lebanon, Jordan, and Iraq

Before the Suez episode neither of the two superpowers had been directly involved in the political conflicts of the Middle East. In the aftermath of Suez, American officials worried that Moscow, either directly or indirectly through Nasser's increasingly pro-Soviet Egyptian government, would attempt to fill the vacuum created by the recession of British and French power in the Arab world. The objects of greatest American concern were the pro-Western regimes in Lebanon, Jordan, and Iraq. After gaining its independence from France in 1946, Lebanon represented something of an anomaly in the predominantly Muslim Middle East with its Maronite Christian community, which constituted roughly half of the country's population. To avert religious tension between these Christians and the Sunni and Shiite Muslims who comprised the other half, the three confessional groups devised an intricate power-sharing arrangement: The president would always be a Maronite Christian, the prime minister a Sunni Muslim, and the speaker of the parliament a Shiite Muslim. Since the Christian president was responsible for the conduct of foreign relations, Lebanon pursued a pro-Western policy in the years after independence: The Maronites looked to the West for help in preserving their political power, which was increasingly threatened by the demographic trend toward a Muslim majority.

The two other enclaves of Western influence in the Middle East were Jordan and Iraq. Both had been established as British mandates under the League of Nations after World War I and had received financial and military support from London ever since. Both were ruled by monarchs of the Hashemite dynasty, which served as the agent of British imperial influence in the region. Although Iraq and Jordan acquired political independence in 1932 and 1946, respectively, the two states remained closely linked to Great Britain, politically, economically, and militarily. Jordan's King Hussein and his young cousin Feisal II of Iraq had both been educated in British schools and relied heavily on British officials for advice.

It was largely to ensure the security of these three pro-Western regimes in the region that the American president promulgated on January 5, 1957, the Eisenhower Doctrine, which pledged American military assistance (including the use of combat forces) to any nation in the Middle East that was threatened by "International Communism." The anti-Communist rhetoric of this puzzling pronouncement irritated Arab nationalist opinion. There were no indigenous Communist parties in the Middle East that posed any threat to existing regimes. The Soviet Union was geographically separated from the region by Turkey and Iran, two non-Arab, staunchly pro-Western states that formed what was often referred to as the "Northern Tier" of the anti-Soviet bloc. Critics of Western influence in the Middle East suspected that the Eisenhower Doctrine was directed less at the nonexistent threat of Communism than at the radical brand of Arab nationalism championed by the president of Egypt.

Nasser had acquired a loyal following among Arab opposition groups throughout the region, particularly in the pro-Western states of Jordan, Lebanon, and Iraq. In the meantime the government of Syria had begun to echo Nasser's strident criticism of Western interference in the Arab world and had followed Egypt into the Soviet orbit. In July 1957 Damascus concluded a major economic and military assistance agreement with Moscow that caused grave concern in Washington as well as in the conservative, pro-Western regime in neighboring Lebanon. Then the revelation of American political intrigue in Syria incited an outburst of anti-American sentiment in that country: Ever since the leftward turn of the Syrian government in the mid-1950s, U.S. intelligence agents had been actively conspiring with dissident members of the Syrian officer corps to mount a coup against the regime. When Syrian counterintelligence agents uncovered the plot in August 1957, the government angrily denounced Washington's intervention in its internal affairs and accelerated its orientation toward Moscow.

Syria's three pro-Western neighbors thereupon hatched a complex scheme to topple the left-leaning regime in Damascus with the covert encouragement of the Eisenhower administration. Iraq prepared for a military offensive against Syria, while Lebanon and Jordan pledged to mobilize their armies to force a dispersal of Syrian forces and facilitate a rapid Iraqi victory. The United States secretly promised to prevent the Soviet Union from assisting its newly acquired Syrian client. But Washington's three co-conspirators lost their nerve at the last minute and aborted the operation. In the meantime Nasser ostentatiously airlifted Egyptian troops to Syria in October and pledged his full support to the embattled regime. The Syrian government reciprocated the Egyptian assistance by becoming Nasser's most vocal supporter in the Middle East.

The apex of Syrian-Egyptian cooperation came in February 1958, when Cairo and Damascus proclaimed the political union of the two noncontiguous countries as the United Arab Republic. The new political union became the focal point for radical Arab opposition to the Baghdad Pact, the alliance of the conservative, anti-Communist states in the region (Turkey, Iran, and Iraq) that, along with the pro-Western regimes in Lebanon and Jordan, were widely reviled as tools of Anglo-American imperialism (see page 75). The emergence of Syria as a proponent of pan-Arabism was no coincidence: That increasingly popular ideology had been championed by a group of intellectuals from that country long before it took root in Egypt. Two Syrian schoolteachers, a Greek Orthodox Christian named Michel Aflaq and a Muslim named Salah al-Din Bitar, established an Arab Renaissance (Baath) party in 1943 under the slogan "unity, liberty, and socialism." The Baath party advocated an Arab cultural renaissance as well as the unification of the entire Arab world under a single political authority. Following a succession of military coups beginning in 1949, the Baathists became a powerful force in the Syrian parliament after that country's first genuinely free elections in 1954 (the very year that Nasser took power in Egypt).

By 1958 the Middle East had therefore split along Cold War lines. The Western client states of Lebanon, Jordan, and Iraq faced the Soviet client states of Egypt and Syria (which had merged politically in the first concrete achievement of the pan-Arab movement). It was not long before the increasingly tense political situation in the region exploded in a chain reaction of political instability with far-reaching consequences. The first eruption occurred in Lebanon, which was dominated by the conservative, pro-Western, Maronite Christian President, Camille Chamoun. The Muslim population of Lebanon deeply resented Chamoun for a number of reasons: He had refused to break diplomatic relations with Great Britain and France during their attack on Egypt in the fall of 1956. He had publicly endorsed the Eisenhower Doctrine and its implied threat of American military intervention in the Arab world. He had skillfully preserved the political dominance of the Christians in Lebanon even though they had come to be outnumbered by the Muslims.

This Muslim discontent with Chamoun reached a fever pitch when he seemed intent on manipulating the parliamentary elections scheduled for June 1957 to ensure the election of his henchmen, which would enable him to amend the constitution to permit his reelection when his term expired in September 1958. After the rigged 1957 elections in Lebanon returned many Chamoun supporters to the parliament, the Muslims suspected a constitutional coup. They received the support of many Druze* and dissident Christians (including even the Maronite patriarch) in protesting the electoral irregularities. Since Egypt was funding the opposition to Chamoun while the latter's party had received American financial aid, the domestic political showdown in Lebanon had begun to assume international significance. When Chamoun refused to rule out a constitutional amendment to permit his reelection, the opposition took to the streets to thwart what it viewed as a plot to retain power. In the meantime Radio Cairo excoriated the government in Beirut as a lackey of foreign imperi-

---

*The Druze sect is an eleventh-century offshoot from the Fatidmid Ismailis, a dissident Shiite group, whose followers settled in the slopes of Lebanon's Mount Hermon.

alists. Giving as good as he got, Chamoun branded his domestic opponents "Nasserites" and accused them of plotting to absorb Lebanon into the United Arab Republic that had been formed by the merger of Egypt and Syria in February 1958.

The simmering conflict in Lebanon might have subsided in June 1958, when Chamoun finally promised to step down at the end of his term. But the small country was suddenly swept up in a violent political explosion that shook Iraq on July 14. The pro-British King Faisal II in Baghdad had ordered a contingent of his army to advance into Jordan in support of his Hashemite cousin Hussein, who was coming under attack from Arab nationalists for his pro-Western policies. Nasser denounced the Iraqi troop movements not only as a bid to bail out Hussein in Jordan but also as a prelude to an intervention in Lebanon on behalf of Chamoun and in Syria to topple its anti-Western regime. As the Iraqi units commanded by Brigadier Abd al-Karim Kassem passed near Baghdad on their way to the Jordanian border, they seized the opportunity to overthrow the Hashemite monarchy. While the army seized control of the government, the Iraqi people took control of the streets. Mobs massacred the entire royal family and the Anglophile prime minister, Nuri al-Sa'id.

The new military junta in Baghdad promptly proclaimed a republic with Kassem as president and launched a campaign to eradicate Western (and especially British) influences in the country. The Iraqi coup of 1958 dealt a severe blow to the Baghdad Pact, the British-sponsored anti-Communist alliance that included Iraq, Iran, Turkey, and Pakistan. Its member states prudently decided in October 1958 to transfer the alliance's headquarters from the Iraqi capital to Ankara, Turkey, renaming it the Central Treaty Organization (CENTO) to emphasize its geographically central location between NATO and SEATO. The new Iraqi republic finally withdrew from the organization in March 1959. To the outside world it appeared that the pillar of British influence in the Middle East had been toppled by a group of young officers who resembled those who surrounded Nasser in Egypt. Radical Arab nationalists throughout the region applauded the coup in Baghdad in the expectation that post-Hashemite Iraq would soon join Egypt and Syria in an expanded United Arab Republic.

Fearful that the threat of Nasserism would spread to his own country, President Chamoun of Lebanon reacted to the Iraqi coup by issuing on July 14 a desperate appeal to Washington for military protection. The next day American marines waded ashore on the bathing beaches of Beirut for the ostensible purpose of rescuing Lebanon from the threat of "International Communism" as prescribed by the Eisenhower Doctrine. By the end of the summer the size of the marine contingent had expanded to fourteen thousand. In the meantime King Hussein, anxious to avoid the tragic fate of his cousin in Baghdad, appealed to London for assistance and welcomed some two thousand British paratroops to Jordan on July 17. The U.S. marines in Lebanon and the British army units in Jordan forestalled any pro-Nasserite agitation that might have been developing against Chamoun and Hussein.

The political firestorm that swept across the Middle East in the summer of 1958 rapidly died out. President Chamoun honored his pledge to step down and was replaced in September after a free election by the Maronite Lebanese army commander, General Fu'ad Chehab. By the end of the year the American marines withdrew from Lebanon and the British paratroops from Jordan. Contrary to the Western powers' worst fears, the new Iraqi government proved entirely cooperative with its neighbors. All talk of Iraq's joining the United Arab Republic came to an end when Brigadier Kassem made it clear that he had no intention of deferring to Nasser. On the contrary, the Iraqi Republic resumed the propaganda war against Egypt that the Hashemite monarchy had begun, while Kassem suppressed both the Nasserite and Communist opposition in the country.

Notwithstanding these disappointing setbacks in Iraq, Jordan and Lebanon, the Egyptian leader resumed his campaign for Arab unity under Egyptian leadership. Soon after the Suez affair he had secretly turned to Washington for support, hoping that American opposition to the Anglo-French-Israeli attack might translate into an improvement of Egyptian-American relations. But Eisenhower and Dulles spurned Nasser's overture because they were committed to supporting the conservative Arab regimes he was seeking to undermine. The U.S. government suspended grain and food shipments that had previously gone to Egypt, and for the remainder of 1957 Washington irritated Cairo by continuing the freeze on Egyptian assets in the United States that had been imposed during the Suez crisis. The enraged Egyptian strongman turned to Moscow for the economic and diplomatic assistance that was unavailable from Washington. In October 1958 the Soviet government finally agreed to replace the United States, Great Britain, and the World Bank as the source of funds for the construction of the Aswan Dam.

The continuing flow of Soviet arms to Egypt, coupled with the arrival of Soviet officers to train the Syrian army, provoked concern in Washington about the prospect of Syrian-Egyptian regional dominance. This concern proved unfounded. The Syrian-Egyptian union collapsed in September 1961 with Syria's abrupt secession from the United Arab Republic in reaction to Nasser's insistence on imposing Egyptian personnel and policies on his partners. The formation of a new Syrian government from which the pro-Nasser Baath party was excluded further embittered relations between Damascus and Cairo. Then two developments in 1963 seemed to favor the resumption of efforts on behalf of pan-Arabism. In February pro-Nasser officers in the Iraqi army ousted and murdered Brigadier Kassem, who had kept his distance from the Egyptian leader. A month later a similar coup overthrew the Syrian government that had severed the union with Egypt. But the prospect of Arab unity was continually hampered by the intense rivalry among the leftist regimes that ruled in Cairo, Damascus, and Baghdad. All three regimes sought to win the support of the Arab masses by championing the cause of progressive Arab nationalism against the conservative, pro-Western monarchies of Saudi Arabia and Jordan. In pursuit of this objective Nasser had dispatched Egyptian military forces to support the young officers that had rebelled against the reactionary Islamic regime in Yemen, which was backed by the pro-American kingdom of Saudi Arabia. During the first half of the 1960s Egypt's increasingly strident campaign against the conservative Arab monarchies aligned with the United States overshadowed even its opposition to Israel.

## The Renewal of the Arab-Israeli Conflict after Suez

The most vocal opponent of Israel in the years after the Suez crisis was Syria, which nurtured two major grievances against the Jewish state. The first was anger at Israel's plans to divert water for irrigation purposes from the Jordan River, whose headwaters crossed Syrian territory. The second was outrage at Israel's harsh treatment of the Palestinians, whose insistent demand for the establishment of a state of their own at Israel's expense received strong support from Damascus.

The status of the 2.75 million stateless Palestinian Arabs, half of them refugees from the area incorporated in the new Jewish state after the 1948 war, would remain the central issue in the perpetual conflict between Israel and its Arab neighbors for decades to come. The refusal of Israel to let them return and the unwillingness of all neighboring Arab states except Jordan to grant them citizenship condemned most of the Palestinians to "temporary" refugee camps in Syria, Lebanon, Jordan, the Jordanian-controlled West Bank, and the Egyptian-controlled Gaza Strip, where they nursed their resentment amid poverty, idleness, and squalor. In 1964 the Arab League formally acknowledged their political grievances by sponsoring the creation of the Palestinian Liberation Organization (PLO). Its first leader, Ahmad al-Shuqayri, was an attorney who was closely aligned with Nasser. In time the new organization formed its own military force, which was integrated into an Arab unified command under an Egyptian officer.

Nasser hoped to control the PLO and its military wing in order to restrain it from provoking a confrontation with Israel that would drag Egypt into a potentially premature military showdown with the Jewish state. Since the government of Syria favored just such a confrontation with Israel, Damascus shifted its support from the Egyptian-controlled PLO to a rival Palestinian organization named al-Fatah ("conquest") that had been created in the late 1950s by Palestinian students in Cairo, including an engineering graduate named Yasser Arafat. In 1966 a coup in Damascus brought to power a radical Baathist government that was determined to replace Egypt as the leader of the Arab cause. It stepped up support for al-Fatah's raids from the West Bank and Gaza against Israel. It also unleashed a propaganda campaign against King Hussein, who (although he could not prevent al-Fatah from operating in the West Bank) had banned the radical Palestinian organization from the refugee camps in his kingdom east of the Jordan River.

Hussein's hostility to radical Palestinian nationalism was understandable: Palestinians comprised roughly 60 percent of Jordan's population and therefore posed a potential threat to his political authority. The West Bank, which was under Jordanian control and played an important role in the Jordanian economy, was being openly discussed by al-Fatah militants as the nucleus of a future Palestinian state. In the midst of this mounting tension, Nasser moved closer to Syria for fear of losing the support of the Palestinians and their radical Arab supporters. On November 7, 1966, Egypt and Syria concluded a mutual defense pact and set up a joint military command. In the months to come Nasser struggled to preserve his credibility as spokesman for the Arab cause by stepping up his rhetorical attacks on Israel for its maltreatment of the Palestinians within its borders and its refusal to permit the refugees outside them to return to their homes.

In the meantime the United States had begun to become involved more actively in the turbulent political situation of Middle East than ever before. The Kennedy administration had supplied Hawk antiaircraft missiles to Israel to counter the Soviet deliveries of aircraft and other military equipment to Egypt, Syria, and Iraq. The Johnson administration expanded the list of military hardware delivered to the

Jewish state. The United States also shipped arms to conservative Arab regimes such as Jordan and Saudi Arabia that were seen as useful allies against the radical Arab states and their Soviet patron. In the mid-1960s Moscow increased its military assistance to its Arab clients, profiting from Washington's distraction in Vietnam to expand Soviet influence in the Middle East. The two superpowers were thus gradually being drawn into the escalating regional conflict between Israel and its Arab neighbors.

At the beginning of 1967 al-Fatah stepped up its raids from the Gaza Strip into Israel, while skirmishes along the Israeli-Syrian border intensified. The government in Damascus began to criticize Nasser for failing to take a sufficiently militant stand against Israel. Syrian radio broadcasts taunted the Egyptian leader for hiding behind the UNEF that had been deployed on the border between the Egyptian-controlled Gaza Strip and Israel and at Sharm al-Sheikh at the southern tip of the Sinai peninsula after the Suez war as a buffer between the two powers. Stung by these Syrian allegations of passivity, Nasser pursued a more aggressive policy toward the Jewish state. After Israel sent tank forces to the Syrian border in April, Nasser mobilized the Egyptian army and moved troops into the Sinai on May 14. Four days later he took the provocative step of requesting the removal of the UNEF from the Gaza Strip and Sharm al-Sheikh. With no attempt to negotiate or probe the Egyptian leader's intentions, UN Secretary General U Thant hastily complied and ordered the peacekeeping contingent to withdraw. Once Egyptian forces had replaced the departing UN contingent at Sharm al-Sheikh overlooking the Strait of Tiran on May 21, Nasser announced the next day that the Strait would be closed to all shipping headed for Israel. On May 29 Jordan's King Hussein agreed to conclude a mutual defense pact with Egypt and to place his military forces under Egyptian command. By evicting the UN forces from the Sinai, blocking Israel's access to the Red Sea, and forming a military alliance with Jordan, Nasser apparently hoped to silence his Syrian critics who had been complaining about his insufficiently militant stance toward Israel.

Israeli Prime Minister Levi Eshkol responded to the entry of Egyptian forces into the Sinai by decreeing a total mobilization and to the closure of the Strait of Tiran by calling up the reserves. Israeli military leaders lobbied strenuously for a preemptive strike against Egypt to remove the threat to the Jewish state on its western border. Right-wing parties in the Israeli parliament welcomed war as a means of acquiring East Jerusalem and the West Bank from Jordan, so that the territory of modern Israel would approximate that of the ancient Hebrew state of biblical times. Although the cautious Eshkol hoped for a diplomatic settlement of the escalating crisis, he bowed to the pressure on June 1. He appointed Moshe Dayan (hero of the 1956 Suez campaign and the most vociferous advocate of a military action) as defense minister and brought into his government Menachem Begin (leader of the right-wing Gahal party and passionate advocate of territorial expansion). On June 4 the Israeli cabinet approved Dayan's carefully crafted plan for a preemptive war against Egypt.

On the morning of June 5, 1967, Israeli air raids against Egyptian airfields in the Sinai peninsula destroyed most of the Egyptian air force on the ground. This surprise attack deprived the Egyptian army in the Sinai of air cover, exposing it to Israeli bombing and tank assaults that completely destroyed its effectiveness as a fighting force. When Jordan honored its alliance with Egypt by opening up an artillery barrage against Israeli positions, Dayan launched the second stage of his war plan by hurling Israeli units into the Jordanian-controlled West Bank. By the end of June 7 the Israeli army had captured East Jerusalem and was driving across the West Bank when King Hussein hastily accepted the Israeli offer of a cease-fire. The next day Nasser followed suit to prevent the Israeli forces crossing the Sinai from seizing the Suez Canal and completely destroying the Egyptian army. Syria, which had not been actively involved in the war, called for a cease-fire on June 9 after witnessing the disarray of the Egyptian and Jordanian armies. But Dayan ignored the Syrian appeal and ordered an offensive into the Golan Heights, the barren plateau overlooking Israel at its northeastern corner. Dayan's lunge for the Golan was prompted by both military and economic considerations: For years Syria had used the plateau to shell Israeli settlements in Galilee. The Golan also controlled the headwaters of the Jordan River, a waterway that carried a scarce resource in the arid Middle East that Israel regarded as vital to its future prosperity. When the Israeli offensive on the Syrian front halted on June 10, Dayan's forces occupied the entire Golan Heights with the Syrian army in full retreat.

The United States, distracted by its deepening military involvement in Vietnam and therefore reluctant to be drawn into a second conflict with Soviet client states on the other side of the world, remained aloof during the Six Day War. The "hot line" that had been set up by Kennedy and Khrushchev after the Cuban missile crisis was used by President Johnson and Soviet Premier Alexei Kosygin for the first time to prevent this regional conflict in the Middle East from escalating into a dangerous confrontation between Moscow and Washington. After Nasser had expelled the UN forces in the Sinai and blockaded the Strait of Tiran, Washington urged the Israeli government to postpone a military response to the Egyptian provocation pending U.S. diplomatic efforts to arrange for a reopening of the Strait. At the same time the Johnson administration insisted on solemn assurances that if the crisis degenerated into armed conflict, any territories conquered by Israel would be evacuated as part of a comprehensive set of peace settlements with individual Arab states that would terminate the state of war that had continued since the armistice of 1949.

But the extraordinary extent of the Israeli victory against the three Arab states emboldened Tel Aviv to lock in the recently acquired territorial gains beyond the 1949 armistice lines. Muslims residing in the neighborhood of the Wailing Wall in old Jerusalem were promptly evicted to permit Jews to worship at the holiest site in Judaism. Over one hundred thousand Palestinians fled from Israel and the West Bank to Jordan, after which most of their homes were demolished to dissuade them from returning. Basking in the euphoria of military triumph, the Jewish state peremptorily declared the 1949 armistice agreements invalid and announced its refusal to evacuate any of the territories occupied without iron-clad peace agreements with the individual Arab states that would guarantee Israel's security.

Although the United States voted for the resolution in the UN Security Council condemning Israel for unilaterally annexing East Jerusalem, Washington refrained from exerting pressure on Israel to return the occupied territories. In December 1967 the Johnson administration sold fifty F-4 Phantom jets to Israel, a transaction that inaugurated a new stage in Washington's engagement in the Arab-Israeli conflict. France, Israel's principal arms supplier and diplomatic supporter since the mid-1950s, had abruptly reversed its policy just prior to the Six Day War when President

*Israel and Its Occupied Territories after the Six Day War*

Charles de Gaulle suspended military assistance to Israel and began to court the Arab states. The United States would thereafter replace France as the principal source of arms and diplomatic support for the Jewish state, which Washington increasingly viewed as a valuable ally in the campaign to prevent Soviet penetration of the Middle East through Moscow's radical Arab clients.

The Israeli government officially regarded the newly occupied territories (the Sinai Peninsula, the Gaza Strip, the Golan Heights, and the West Bank) as valuable bargaining chips to obtain peace settlements with the Arab states, giving rise to the slogan "land for peace." But some Israeli military strategists who disdained the 1949 frontiers as indefensible viewed the occupied territories as a source of "security in depth" that should never be abandoned. They were complemented by an increasingly vocal minority, led by right-wing political leader Menachem Begin, who saw the recent territorial gains as the fulfillment of the two-thousand-year-old dream of restoring the biblical land of Israel. In the following years private citizen groups in Israel mounted an intensive campaign to convert the conquests of the Six Day War into permanent acquisitions by establishing isolated Jewish settlements in the West Bank and to a lesser extent in the Sinai, Gaza, and the Golan Heights. While the Israeli government publicly affirmed that the future political status of the occupied territories was negotiable as part of a comprehensive peace settlement, the Jewish settlers who established what they expected to be permanent residence in these areas often acted with the tacit support of some cabinet ministers and military commanders on the spot.

Nasser resigned from office in disgrace after the humiliating rout of his military forces and the loss of Egyptian territory during the Six Day War. Although he quickly reversed himself and reassumed power on a wave of popular support, his reputation as the foremost defender of the Arab cause in the Middle East had been damaged beyond repair. The Soviet Union also suffered a severe political setback as the Egyptian army it had equipped and the Syrian army to which it had sent advisers crumbled ignominiously before the Israeli onslaught. But although its Egyptian and Syrian clients had been humbled by superior Israeli military power in June 1967, the Soviet Union harvested a number of advantages from Nasser's debacle. Half of the Arab states had severed diplomatic relations with Washington during the Six Day War, and several of them promptly granted the Soviet navy access to their ports in retaliation against America's support for Israel.

Just as the Soviet Union was obtaining these footholds in the Arab world, Great Britain was preparing to evacuate the last remnants of its empire "east of Suez." The British tried in vain to transfer political authority in the strategically situated port of Aden on the Arabian peninsula to conservative, pro-Western sheiks. But the People's Republic of South Yemen that received its independence in November 1967 promptly gravitated to the Soviet orbit and granted the Russian navy access to the old British port. In January 1968 London announced its intention to withdraw all of its military forces from the Arab sheikdoms along the Persian Gulf. The evacuation of the last British units from this strategically and economically vital region on December 2, 1971, marked the end of an imperial presence that had begun in the last century.

In the aftermath of the Six Day War, the chastened Nasser sought to repair his tattered relations with the moderate regimes in the Arab world. He desperately needed financial assistance from the oil-producing states of Saudi Arabia, Kuwait, and Libya, all of which were ruled by conservative monarchies aligned with the West. In August 1967 Egypt reached a settlement of its conflict with Saudi Arabia in Yemen, and Saudi financial aid began to flow to Cairo. In the meantime Nasser and King Hussein secretly expressed interest in negotiations with Israel through the intermediary of the United Nations that would lead to an Israeli evacuation from the Sinai and the West Bank in exchange for recognition of Israel's sovereignty. Syria continued to refuse all compromise, as did the Palestinians, who feared that their own interests would be sacrificed in any state-to-state deal between Israel and one or more of the Arab states. On November 22, 1967, the UN Security Council approved Resolution 242, which called for Israel's withdrawal from territories occupied in the Six Day War as part of a comprehensive settlement providing for the recognition of the sovereignty and territorial integrity of each state in the region. While Resolution 242 prescribed a framework for multilateral negotiations under the auspices of the United Nations, the Israeli government preferred direct bilateral talks with each Arab government. When the Arab states predictably refused to enter directly into such discussions with a country whose very right to exist they were not prepared to concede, the United Nations negotiator, Sweden's Gunnar Jarring, was prevented from making any progress toward a Mideast peace settlement.

In the meantime the Palestinian movement stepped up its militant opposition to Israel. Al-Fatah leader Yasser Arafat secretly entered the West Bank in July 1967 to organize the million Palestinians who had just come under Israeli rule there into a revolutionary movement of national liberation. After failing to incite a popular insurrection against the Israeli occupation, Arafat turned in desperation to Jordan's King Hussein for support. The Palestinian al-Fatah guerrilla leader and the Jordanian monarch shared an interest in preventing Israel from annexing the West Bank, Arafat because he regarded the region as the nucleus of a future Palestinian state, Hussein because he hoped to restore it to Jordanian sovereignty. The king agreed to permit al-Fatah guerrillas in Jordan to mount raids into the West Bank and Israel to keep the pressure on the Israeli government to withdraw from the occupied territory. But Hussein's hopes of controlling al-Fatah and using it for his own purposes were dashed as its fighters operated with impunity throughout the West Bank, ignoring Jordanian advice on strategy and tactics.

As Israel tightened its control of the occupied territories, an ideological split within the Palestinian movement emerged. Fatah faced challenges from more radical movements such as Dr. George Habash's Popular Front for the Liberation of Palestine (PFLP) in late 1967 and Nayif Hawatmah's Popular Democratic Front for the Liberation of Palestine (PDFLP) in early 1969. Al-Fatah bent all of its efforts to the single goal of forging a Palestinian state and was willing to make common cause with conservative Arab regimes such as Hashemite Jordan to achieve that result. Although Habash and Hawatmah were both Christians—whereas al-Fatah was dominated by Sunni Muslims—the PFLP and the PDFLP leadership spoke the language of Marxist-Leninism and regarded the liberation of Palestine as merely part of a broader mission of radicalizing the entire Arab world at the expense not only of the despised Zionist entity but also of the conservative Arab monarchies. In December 1967 the colorless Ahmad al-Shuqayri was ousted as head of the umbrella organization of the Palestinian cause, the PLO. After a year of infighting Yasser Arafat was elected head of the organization in February 1969. But the two rival groups continued to press for their radical agendas and prevented the new PLO leader from exercising undisputed control of the Palestinian national movement.

While the Palestinians and Jordanians concentrated on organizing resistance to the Israeli occupation of the West Bank, the armies of Egypt and Israeli faced each other warily across the Suez Canal. Israel obtained decisive military superiority over Egypt after the delivery of Skyhawk and Phantom jets from the United States toward the end of the 1960s. It constructed a formidable defensive fortification called the Bar-Lev Line on the Israeli side of the Canal to protect the newly acquired Sinai buffer zone against a surprise attack. In the meantime Nasser sought to restore his country's military capability that had been shattered during the Six Day War. From March 1969 to August 1970 Egypt engaged in a series of intensive artillery barrages against Israeli positions across the Canal in the hopes of softening up the enemy for an offensive that would establish Egyptian bridgeheads on the Israeli side of the waterway.

Amid this "war of attrition," as it came to be called, Nasser responded to Israeli retaliatory bombing raids by turning to Moscow for assistance in rectifying Egypt's vulnerability to Israeli air power that had been demonstrated in the Six Day War. In early 1970 he pressured Brezhnev into supplying Egypt with some three hundred surface-to-air missiles (SAMs) by threatening to resign to make way for a pro-American successor if his demands were not met. Moscow also sent twenty-one thousand advisers and technicians to man the SAM sites and reorganize Egypt's shattered armed forces. Soviet pilots in Egypt began flying bombing missions against Israel while Soviet economic aid to Egypt continued to flow. In exchange for these services, the Soviet Mediterranean fleet obtained facilities at the Egyptian ports of Alexandria, Port Said, and Mersa Matrûh while the Soviet air force used an Egyptian airfield near Cairo for reconnaissance flights along NATO's southern flank.

The massive influx of Soviet military forces into Egypt greatly alarmed the Nixon administration and prompted Secretary of State William Rogers to seek a diplomatic settlement to the undeclared war along the Suez Canal. Rogers dispatched a note to the interested parties calling for a cease-fire and negotiations based on UN Security Council Resolution 242, including its requirement of Israeli evacuation of the occupied territories. Egypt and Jordan promptly endorsed the Rogers note. Israeli Prime Minister Golda Meir, after intense pressure from Washington coupled with assurances of continued American military support, accepted the American proposal (which included the implicit agreement to negotiate a withdrawal from some of the territories occupied in the Six Day War). In the meantime the United States and the Soviet Union had conducted intensive discussions throughout 1969 aimed at reaching a settlement of the conflict along the Suez Canal that each superpower could sell to its regional protégé. The Israeli government energetically opposed these bilateral negotiations between Washington and Moscow, which it feared would lead to a joint proposal for a pullback from some of the occupied territories without adequate security guarantees. When these Soviet-American talks failed to produce a joint settlement, the State Department unveiled its own proposal in December 1969 for separate Israeli-Egyptian and Israeli-Jordanian agreements, which the Meir government rejected out of hand. The Nixon administration finally forced Israel to join Egypt and Jordan in accepting a temporary cease-fire in August 1970, although no progress on a comprehensive diplomatic settlement was forthcoming.

The Palestinian leadership was enraged that Nasser and Hussein had consented to a cease-fire with the state that the PLO viewed as the sole obstacle to the creation of a Palestinian homeland. The Jordanian king in particular had become the object of Palestinian wrath for his apparent willingness to betray the interests of his large Palestinian population. The cease-fire and the prospects for peace talks without the Palestinians provoked a round of airplane hijackings in Jordan engineered by the PFLP, the most radical faction of the PLO. Hussein used this wave of unrest as a pretext for cracking down on the Palestinian guerrilla movement in his country. From September 16 to 25, 1970, a full-fledged civil war raged in Jordan between the Palestinian organizations and Hussein's troops, leaving three thousand dead and over eleven thousand injured. The result was a decisive military triumph for the Jordanian monarch, whose army successfully suppressed the insurrection while his air force repulsed a Syrian tank invasion in support of the Palestinians.

But Hussein's victory over the Palestinians in his country was tempered by constraints that were imposed upon him by the other Arab heads of state, who had engaged in a round of emergency negotiations so exhausting that Nasser died of a heart attack in the midst of one of the sessions on September 28, 1970. The most galling of the compromises that Hussein had to swallow was the requirement that he recognize the PLO as the representative of the Palestinian people, a concession that theoretically negated his political authority over the Palestinian majority in his own country. But with the renewal of Palestinian-Jordanian fighting in July 1971 Hussein finally expelled the PLO leadership for good. With his administrative infrastructure and about fifteen thousand fighters in tow, Arafat transferred the organization's headquarters to Lebanon where they joined roughly two hundred thousand Palestinian refugees who already resided there.

Lebanon was the only country in the region that had somehow managed to remain aloof from the Arab-Israeli struggle that raged across its southern frontier. But that isolation came to an end in the early 1970s. Even before the arrival of the PLO, the more radical factions of the Palestinian movement had begun to use the territory just north of the Israeli border as a base of operations for commando raids and artillery barrages against the Jewish state. Under pressure from other Arab countries, the Lebanese government permitted the PLO to control the camps that had been set up in the country to accommodate the stream of Palestinian refugees from Jordan after Hussein's crackdown. But the arrival of Arafat and his entourage exacerbated the religious tensions that had simmered in Lebanon since the late 1950s. The Maronite Christians resented the influx of the predominantly Muslim Palestinians and began to form paramilitary groups to deal with them. Most of the Sunni Muslims in Lebanon welcomed the Palestinians (whose leadership was largely Sunni), regarding them as allies against the Christian factions that continued to dominate the Lebanese political system. The relative calm and stability that Lebanon had enjoyed since its independence from France at the end of World War II would not survive the confluence of these divergent ethnic, political, and religious forces. After its eviction from

Jordan and its relocation to Lebanon, the PLO resorted in desperation to a series of terrorist acts to dramatize its people's plight. These included the kidnapping and murder of Israeli athletes at the 1972 Olympic Games in Munich and terrorist attacks against Israeli officials. This upsurge of violence provoked Israeli retaliatory raids against PLO positions in southern Lebanon as well as the assassination of Palestinian officials in Beirut. And much worse was yet to come.

The replacement of Nasser by his long-time lieutenant Anwar al-Sadat in September 1970 seemed to confirm Egypt's traditional policy of friendship with the Soviet Union. The new leader in Cairo made a determined effort to strengthen his country's links to its Soviet patron. In March 1971 Sadat made his first trip to Moscow with a long shopping list of military hardware to enable Egypt to resume the "war of attrition" along the Suez Canal. What he received the following month fell far short of expectations: SAM missile batteries but not the missile-equipped aircraft he had earnestly sought. The following month Sadat signed a fifteen-year Treaty of Friendship and Cooperation with the Soviet Union in the expectation of obtaining additional military assistance to bolster Egypt in what he called its "year of decision" concerning the lost land in the Sinai. But despite three more trips to Moscow in October 1971 and February and April 1972, the Egyptian leader failed to obtain the military hardware he felt his military needed to reconquer the lost territory. He implored Brezhnev to take a hard line with Nixon on Middle East questions at their Moscow summit meeting in July 1972. But the joint communiqué issued at the end of the conference revealed that Moscow's interest in East-West détente far outweighed its concern for clients in peripheral regions. Sadat's mounting disappointment with the level of Soviet support led him to consider a drastic reorientation of Egyptian foreign policy that Nasser had long pondered but never succeeded in implementing: the development of close ties with the United States.

Sadat's new interest in cultivating better relations with Washington fortuitously coincided with a new orientation of U.S. policy toward the Arab-Israeli conflict. During the first two years of the Nixon administration, Secretary of State William Rogers had strongly supported the efforts of UN Ambassador Gunnar Jarring to seek a Mideast settlement based on Resolution 242 (see page 168). While Nixon clearly sympathized with Israel and continued to supply it with arms, he was in hot pursuit of détente with the Soviet Union and therefore prodded Jerusalem* to seek a peaceful resolution of its conflict with Moscow's client state in Cairo. Sadat came to realize that Washington alone was in a position to lean on the Israelis to reach a settlement with Egypt that would enable it to regain the Sinai. He also understood that the United States would not play an active role in the dispute between Cairo and Jerusalem as long as Egypt retained its close military ties to Moscow. A reversal of alliances seemed in the offing.

---

*After the Israeli seizure of the West Bank in the Six Day War of 1967, the capital of the Jewish state was transferred from Tel Aviv to the newly reunited city of Jerusalem. Several foreign powers (including the United States) refused to recognize Israeli sovereignty over all of Jerusalem pending a formal peace treaty and maintained their diplomatic representation in the former capital.

The Egyptian leader conveyed his first signal of displeasure to Brezhnev on July 18, 1972, by expelling most of the twenty-one thousand Soviet advisers and technicians from his country, although he allowed the Russian navy to retain access to Egyptian ports. This defiant gesture had the intended effect in both Moscow and Washington. Beginning in February 1973 the Soviets began to supply Egypt with the arms that they had previously withheld for fear of encouraging an Egyptian attack against Israel. In the fall of 1972 the Nixon administration responded gratefully to Sadat's eviction of the Soviet personnel with an intimation that it would undertake a diplomatic initiative in the Middle East after the presidential election. But while the Soviet weapons continued to arrive in Egypt during the spring and summer of 1973, Nixon was so distracted by the Watergate crisis that his Middle East policy was left in limbo. In the meantime the Israeli government of Prime Minister Golda Meir, reacting to pressure from its right-wing opposition, authorized the construction of Israeli settlements in the territories captured in the 1967 war. By the beginning of 1973 forty-four settlements had been established on the West Bank, the Golan Heights, and the northern part of the Sinai Peninsula while an additional fifty were planned by the end of the year. Minister of Defense Moshe Dayan unveiled a scheme to partition the Sinai by establishing permanent Israeli control over a southeastern portion along the Gulf of Aqaba.

Emboldened by the flow of Soviet weaponry, disappointed by American diplomatic inaction, and worried about losing part of the Sinai to permanent Israel control, Sadat opted for military action as a means of breaking the stalemate. On October 6, 1973, the Jewish holy day of Yom Kippur (when many Israeli soldiers were on holiday leave), Egypt joined Syria in launching a carefully planned surprise attack against Israel. Egyptian forces crossed the Suez Canal and poured into the Sinai Peninsula, demolishing Israel's renowned Bar-Lev Line, which had been deemed impregnable, as Syrian armored divisions rumbled into the Golan Heights. After two weeks of the fiercest tank battles since World War II on the Sinai and the Golan, Israel gained the upper hand: Israeli forces drove the Syrians off the Golan Heights and advanced to within twenty miles of Damascus. On the Egyptian front the counterattacking Israeli forces crossed the canal and proceeded to destroy most of the Egyptian armor, while the Egyptian Third Army was encircled and trapped in the western Sinai.

In the meantime the two superpowers had been drawn into the escalating conflict in the Middle East. The Soviet Union organized a massive airlift of military supplies to Egypt and Syria. U.S. Secretary of State Henry Kissinger, who was operating on his own because of Nixon's preoccupation with his domestic political scandal, had originally withheld arms deliveries to Israel to force it to accept a cease-fire that would preserve some of Egypt's gains and facilitate peace talks that might break the diplomatic stalemate. But when Sadat rejected the U.S. cease-fire proposal in the hopes of seizing more Sinai territory, Kissinger released the U.S. weapons that had been withheld. In the meantime Sadat reacted to the Israeli army's crossing of the Suez Canal and the threat to the isolated Egyptian Third Army by issuing an urgent plea for a joint Soviet-American intervention to enforce a cease-fire. Although Washington adamantly rejected a proposal that would have allowed Soviet forces into the Middle East, Moscow warned that it might respond unilaterally to Sadat's invitation.

Nixon promptly placed U.S. military forces on nuclear alert (DEFCON 3), and Brezhnev followed suit. Suddenly it seemed that Soviet-American détente might be unhinged by the escalating confrontation between the two superpowers' clients in the Middle East.

But the crisis was nipped in the bud when the United States persuaded Sadat to revoke his request for superpower intervention in favor of an appeal to the United Nations. On October 24 the two belligerents accepted a Soviet-American cease-fire proposal that the Security Council had approved two days earlier, which provided for the deployment of a seven-thousand-person UN peacekeeping contingent between the two armies. Israel was the clear victor in the war, but it owed that victory to the massive airlift of American military supplies. Israel's total dependence on the United States for its security enabled Washington to intervene directly in the Arab-Israeli conflict for the first time in an effort to induce the two sides to accept a negotiated settlement. In the spirit of détente, the Nixon administration agreed to a Soviet proposal for the convocation of a Middle East peace conference at Geneva. In the presence of American and Soviet officials, Israel officials met face-to-face with delegates from the Arab states of Egypt and Jordan—Syria refused to attend—for the first time since the creation of the Jewish state. But the Geneva Conference became bogged down in details and became irrelevant, which enabled U.S. Secretary of State Kissinger to bypass both the United Nations and the Soviet Union in search of an American-brokered bilateral peace settlement between Egypt and Israel.

For the next two years the peripatetic American secretary of state shuttled between Egypt and Israel in search of a bilateral peace settlement, effectively freezing the Soviet Union out of the negotiations. In January 1974 Kissinger induced the two sides to sign a Disengagement of Forces Agreement, which led to the withdrawal of the Israeli army from the west bank of the Suez Canal and delineated the territory there where Egyptian troops would be permitted to remain. In September 1975, Egypt and Israel signed a disengagement agreement that stipulated Israel's withdrawal from the strategic passes it occupied in the Sinai and set up a buffer area manned by U.S. and UN observers to detect violations of the cease-fire. Both the Soviet Union and the United Nations were thus elbowed out of the Israeli-Egyptian negotiations by the crafty Kissinger, who single-handedly set in nation what would come to be known as the "peace process" in the Middle East.

Despite Israel's military victory in 1973 and America's emergence as the only credible broker of a Mideast peace, the Yom Kippur War and its aftermath resulted in a serious setback for the Jewish state and its U.S. patron. On October 17 the oil-producing states of the Arab world, led by Washington's long-time friend Saudi Arabia, retaliated against the American airlift of military equipment to Israel by imposing a total embargo on petroleum exports to the United States and a partial embargo on other countries based on the extent of their support for the Jewish state. The Organization of Petroleum Exporting Countries (OPEC), the oil-producing cartel dominated by the Arab oil-producing countries, announced on December 23 a fourfold increase in the posted price of crude oil. The successive shocks of the embargo (which remained in force for five months) and the quadrupling of crude oil prices caused severe gasoline shortages and long lines at filling stations in the United States. The drastic price increases of this essential commodity precipitated the worst downturn of the world economy since the Great Depression, dramatically revealing the extent of the industrial world's dependence on the developing world for energy supplies. The United States imported 40 percent of its petroleum in the mid-1970s; Western Europe and Japan satisfied over 80 percent of their energy needs through purchases abroad. OPEC's success in boosting the price of its precious product with impunity also set an instructive precedent for other commodity cartels that might be tempted to exploit the industrial world's dependence on a wide range of raw materials to increase their world prices. For the first time in history, the impoverished countries of the developing world seemed to have acquired an economic weapon that could be used against the wealthy nations of the industrial world to effect a massive redistribution of wealth.

# SEVEN

# Asia Recuperates from the Ravages of War

As World War II drew to a close, the two most important countries in Asia lay in ruins. Japan had been defeated militarily, its major cities had been destroyed by American air power, and it was obliged to endure the humiliation and hardship of Allied (but in effect American) military occupation. China had been devastated by the Japanese invasion, the wartime fighting, and the beginning of the civil war between the Nationalist government and its Communist adversaries. Yet within four decades both of these countries recovered from the depths of national ruin. By the time of the death of Emperor Hirohito in 1989, Japan had achieved through entirely peaceful means an economic preponderance in Asia far greater than that acquired by military force during the earlier period of his reign from 1931 to 1945. The small island nation had surpassed the Soviet Union to become the second economic power of the world. Although China would endure several internal crises and external threats on its road to recovery, the most populous country in the world also emerged from its postwar plight to become a major actor on the world stage. When Deng Xiaoping, the architect of China's modernization, died in 1997, the country he left behind qualified as East Asia's premier military power and was poised to become a major participant in the international economy in the coming century.

The United States had become a transpacific power in the closing years of the nineteenth century when it acquired the Philippines from Spain and Hawaii from its indigenous inhabitants and then demanded that the "door" to China be open to its export trade. After single-handedly thwarting Japan's bid for hegemony in East Asia during World War II, the United States reasserted its strategic and economic interests in the region. Its immediate objective after the war was to ensure that Japan would never again seek to dominate China and its other neighbors by force of arms. But by the end of the 1940s that concern would be superceded by a new preoccupation with the threat of Communism in the region: During the next two decades the only two "hot wars" the United States would wage in its global confrontation with the Communist bloc would take place on the mainland of Asia. The struggle for control of the Korean peninsula, and then for the successor states of the French Empire in Indochina, would become entangled with Washington's determination to "contain" Communism in Asia after successfully containing it in Europe.

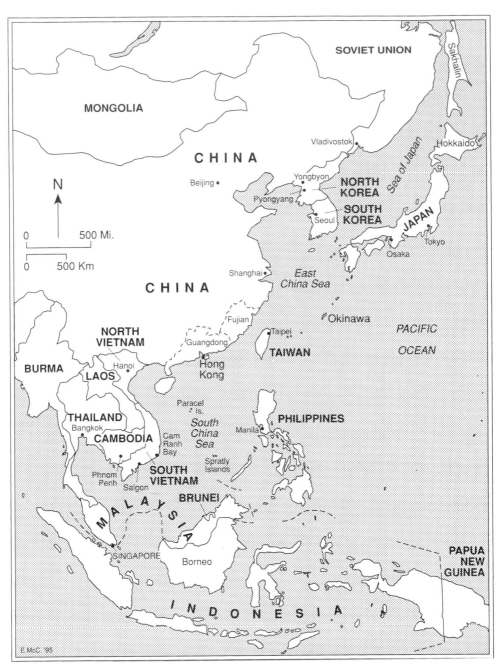

*East Asia after World War II*

Before World War II, the peoples of East Asia had submitted to the political, economic, and military domination of three European imperial powers—Great Britain, France, and the Netherlands—as well as an emerging indigenous imperial power—Japan. The United States played a subsidiary role in the region by virtue of its modest military and naval presence in the Philippines. Japan succeeded in expelling the Western imperial powers from their East Asian possessions during its aggressive bid for dominance in the region. The behavior of the Japanese forces throughout the areas that they occupied from 1937 to 1945 was abominable. The legacy of indiscriminate rape, pillage, and destruction from this tragic period of Asia's history serves as an indelible stain on Japan's reputation that still inspires apprehension in its neighbors about the prospect of a Japanese military revival. But Japanese propaganda during the war employed the rhetoric of anticolonialism to justify its quest for regional hegemony in the eyes of the very indigenous populations it was subjugating. Slogans such as "Asia for the Asians" and the "Greater East Asia Co-Prosperity Sphere" concealed Japan's own imperial designs beneath a seductive appeal to ethnic and racial resentment against the Caucasian imperial powers. Some Asian opponents of colonialism, such as the Vietnamese nationalist Ho Chi Minh in French Indochina, spurned this racially tinged appeal and joined forces with the non-Asian opponents of Japan. Others, such as the Indonesian nationalist leader Achmed Sukarno in the Dutch East Indies, were tempted by Tokyo's anti-European rhetoric and welcomed the Japanese occupiers as allies against European colonial domination. Japan's unexpectedly swift surrender in the summer of 1945 brought to the fore the question of Asia's political future. Would the European powers return to Asia and regain the political authority and economic privileges the Japanese had wrested from them? Or would the explosive forces of nationalism thwart the restoration of European rule and result in the creation of independent states?

## The Chinese Civil War

The biggest question of all in postwar Asia was the political fate of China, its most populous country and one of the few in the region that had escaped direct imperial rule from Europe. From 1937 Japanese military forces overran the major port cities of China and occupied the eastern third of the country. The Nationalist (Kuomintang, or KMT) government of Generalissimo Chiang Kai-shek (Jiang Jieshi) abandoned its capital of Nanking (Nanjing) and regrouped in the southwestern city of Chungking (Zhongking). Riding a wave of sympathy generated by the brutal behavior of the Japanese forces along the Chinese coast, Chiang Kai-shek's government won strong public support in the United States during the war. Roosevelt lavishly supplied Chiang with military equipment and advisers in the hopes that the Nationalist army could break the Japanese military's stranglehold on coastal China. Vastly overestimating the strength and popularity of the KMT among the Chinese masses, Roosevelt expected liberated China to join the United States, Great Britain, and Soviet Russia as one of the world's "Four Policemen" by replacing Japan as the dominant power in Asia. The American president saw to it, over the objections of a skeptical Churchill, that China was awarded a permanent seat on the Security Council of the new United Nations. The KMT's cause was backed in the United States by an influential group of Americans with familial ties to the U.S. missionary effort in China, such as Henry Luce, publisher of the influential newsweekly *Time*. This so-called "China lobby" hailed the Generalissimo, who had been converted to Methodism by his American-educated wife Soong Mei-ling, as the best hope for creating a Westernized, Christian China after the war.

But the Chungking government's ambition to acquire total political control of China after the Japanese surrender was forcefully contested by the Chinese Communist Party (CCP), which had spent the war in the city of Yenan in the northeastern province of Shensi. The Communist forces had arrived at this remote outpost in the mid-1930s, when a young political organizer named Mao Zedong led them on a yearlong retreat of over six thousand miles to escape the Nationalist armies that were attacking them in the coastal cities. Of the one hundred thousand Communist militants who began what came to be known as the "Long March," only about thirty thousand made it to Yenan. There they established their own primitive form of government and began to recruit supporters among the landless peasantry in the impoverished province. When Japan launched its war against China in 1937, these hardy survivors of that long and arduous journey developed into a disciplined force intent on expelling the Japanese from China. Mao and Chiang agreed to shelve their political differences to form a United Front against the invader.

The United States, which had been the major source of military and economic assistance to the Nationalist Chinese government during its wartime struggle with Japan, confronted an agonizing policy dilemma in China as the war in Asia drew to a close. Some officials in Washington wanted to increase American support for Chiang Kai-shek's government, fearing that the Communists in Yenan would attempt to seize power in the rest of the vast country. This group regarded Mao and his followers as Asian counterparts of the Communist forces in Eastern Europe that operated as stooges of the Soviet Union. But another faction challenged this view of the Chinese Communist movement as a compliant creature of Moscow. The band of two dozen military advisers and foreign service officers that had been sent to Yenan in the summer of 1944 to make contact with Mao's guerrilla forces were highly impressed by what they saw there. Calling themselves the "Dixie Mission" because they were operating in "rebel" territory, these American officials came to regard Mao and his followers as an indigenous political movement that had sprung from the social conflicts of the Chinese countryside rather than as part of an international Communist conspiracy hatched in the Kremlin. Their reports to Washington celebrated the Communists' fighting spirit, cohesion, and popularity among the peasant masses as they did their best to harass the Japanese invaders.

As this glowing praise for the CCP poured into the State Department from the Dixie Mission in Yenan, the reports arriving from the Nationalist regime's wartime capital of Chungking told a different tale. The American diplomats attached to Chiang's government were aghast at the corruption, nepotism, and inefficiency they observed. Many had come to the conclusion that the United States was pouring its money down a rat hole in China and did not hesitate to express that opinion in their cables to the State Department. These complaints from the political and economic officers in the American mission were confirmed by the blistering broadsides from General Joseph Stilwell, whom Roosevelt had sent to Chungking as Chiang's chief military adviser. The tough-talking, no-nonsense "Vinegar Joe" had lost all confidence in the Nationalist Chinese leader, whom he disdained as an incompetent strategist who surrounded himself with fawning officers promoted on the basis of loyalty rather than merit and who spent more time worrying about the political challenge from the Communists in Yenan than the military threat from the Japanese on the coast. Chiang used his contacts in Washington to get Stillwell recalled when he learned of these unflattering reports. But doubts about the Nationalists' reliability as an ally had been firmly planted in Washington.

In September 1944 Roosevelt sent Patrick Hurley, a flamboyant Republican lawyer and former secretary of war under Herbert Hoover, as his special envoy to evaluate the political situation in China and attempt to reconcile the KMT and the CCP. After conferring with Mao in Yenan, Hurley secured what he deemed a workable arrangement for a coalition government. But when he returned to Chungking accompanied by Mao's right-hand man Zhou Enlai in November 1944 to secure Chiang's approval of the compromise, the KMT leader sabotaged the deal by insisting that the Communist armies disband and accept the authority of Nationalist officers in exchange for token representation in the Nationalist-controlled government. When Hurley revoked his earlier endorsement of the compromise agreement and backed Chiang's demand for what would have been political suicide for the CCP, Zhou angrily returned to Yenan with empty hands. On January 9, 1945, he and Mao got the Dixie Mission to transmit an urgent message to the State Department requesting American support for their military effort against the Japanese. The two Communist leaders even offered to travel to Washington to negotiate an agreement. In the meantime Hurley had concluded that Chiang deserved full American support against the Communists. When he got wind of the CCP's back-channel bid for U.S. support, he fired off a message to Roosevelt warning that the State Department's agents in Yenan had been seduced by the Communists and were undermining the Nationalist cause. By that time Hurley had come to detest the two principal CCP leaders, whom he contemptuously referred to in public as "Moose Dung" and "Joe N. Lie."

While the Roosevelt administration grappled with these conflicting signals from its agents in China, the Soviet Union began to formulate its own policy toward the political situation there. It rapidly became evident that policy would be dictated not by ideological affiliation but rather by cold calculations of Soviet national interest. At the Yalta Conference in February 1945, Stalin informed Roosevelt that he would support the Nationalist Chinese government in Chungking rather than the Communist movement in Yenan. He demanded as a reward the reestablishment of Russian control of the railroad network and two major seaports of Manchuria, which had been lost to Japan after its military victory over the tsarist empire in 1905. From the American point of view the restoration of these old imperial privileges was a small price to pay for ensuring that Soviet military power, which would be hurled against Japan after the end of the war in Europe, would not be used to undermine the Nationalist government and bolster the Communist movement in China.

These provisions of the Yalta agreement were implemented on August 14, 1945, the day before Japan announced its decision to surrender, when Stalin signed a treaty of friendship and alliance with the Chinese prime minister, Chiang's brother-in-law T. V. Soong. By its terms Moscow formally recognized the KMT as the sole legitimate government of China and pledged to send it military and economic aid. Stalin obtained joint Sino-Soviet management of the Manchurian railroad system and the commercial port of Dairen (Dalny), the right to construct a Soviet naval base at Port Arthur (Lüshun), and Chinese recognition of the "independence" of Mongolia (which had seceded from China and become a Soviet client state in the mid-1920s). In the meantime the Kremlin advised the Chinese Communists to dismantle their independent military apparatus and merge with the KMT as junior partners in a governing coalition.

After Japan's surrender the new American president, Harry S. Truman, issued an order specifying that all Japanese military forces in China surrender only to the armies of the KMT. To assist in this effort, Truman rushed sixty thousand U.S. Marines from the Pacific to occupy strategic positions and ports in North China, while the U.S. Navy and the Army Air Force transported Nationalist troops to the same destinations. The Soviet units that poured into Manchuria after Stalin's declaration of war against Japan on August 8 proceeded to play a double game: On the one hand they turned over captured Japanese weapons to Mao's partisans in the region, while at the same time allowing KMT troops to arrive in force to take up their positions in the areas surrendered by the Japanese. It seemed as though Stalin was intent on playing off the two rival Chinese political factions in order to forestall what he wanted most to avoid: the establishment of a unified China under a single political authority, Nationalist or Communist. In the meantime the Russian army in Manchuria concentrated on its one overriding mission: the confiscation and removal to the Soviet Union of the province's portable industrial assets.

Abandoned by his ideological brethren in Moscow, spurned by his ideological adversaries in Washington, Mao faced the prospect of defeat at the hands of the more numerous, better equipped KMT forces that were reoccupying large parts of northern China with the active support of the Americans and the tacit acquiescence of the Russians. He therefore put out feelers for a negotiated settlement with the Nationalists. But Chiang (with the encouragement and support of Patrick Hurley, who had since acquired the rank of ambassador) blocked an agreement by reissuing his old deal-breaking demand for the demobilization of the Communist army. By the autumn of 1945 Washington was prepared to renew the stalled diplomatic efforts to secure a genuine power-sharing arrangement between the two Chinese political forces whose troops were jostling for advantage in North China. But Hurley unexpectedly threw a monkey wrench into the negotiating process on November 27: After denouncing unnamed "traitors" in the State Department for undermining the Nationalists and indirectly assisting their Communist rivals, the American ambassador angrily resigned.

In one final bid to broker a cease-fire in the Chinese Civil War and promote the formation of a KMT CCP coalition government, Truman dispatched one of his most trusted advisers, Army Chief of Staff General George C. Marshall, on a mission of mediation. On his arrival in Chungking in December 1945 Marshall met with representatives of the Nationalist government as well as with Mao's personal delegate, Zhou Enlai. After an exhaustive round of negotiations, he persuaded both sides in January 1946 to accept a truce in North China and Manchuria and to open talks on the establishment of a coalition government. In the following July Marshall arranged for a suspension of U.S. arms deliveries to the KMT and the removal of all American

Marines from China, while the Soviet forces evacuated Manchuria. Both super-powers were therefore spared a direct confrontation in the Far East as the Cold War began to unfold in Europe.

But the temporary cease-fire broke down, as Chiang decided to mount an all-out campaign to eliminate his Communist adversaries. The bloodiest fighting took place in Manchuria, where the Nationalists (who had transferred their capital from Chung-king to Nanking in May 1946) controlled the cities while the Communists dominated the rural areas. Within a year the larger and better equipped Nationalist army became overextended and suffered a serious decline in morale in the lower ranks. The latter problem arose from the widespread corruption in the officer corps, insufficient rations, and the raging inflation that wiped out the purchasing power of the troops. By November 1948 the Communist forces, their ranks swollen with discontented desert-ers from the Chiang's armies and their arsenals replenished with captured American weapons, had conquered all of Manchuria and most of northeast China. They then began a southward advance in pursuit of the retreating Nationalist forces.

The Truman administration had long since lost all confidence in Chiang and re-fused to resume arms shipments to his army after the breakdown of Marshall's truce. The general returned to Washington in January 1947 to become secretary of state, thoroughly disillusioned with the Chinese Nationalist leader because of his refusal to reform his own government and make the necessary concessions to end the civil war. U.S. strategists were beginning to write off China and to focus on the offshore is-lands of East Asia—including Japan—as America's line of defense in the Far East (see page 189). Although American surplus war stocks in China had been turned over to the KMT, U.S. officials decided not to squander additional assets in a lost cause. Then the rough and tumble of domestic politics began to impinge on the conduct of U.S. foreign policy in Asia. Ambassador Hurley's acerbic accusations that the admin-istration was selling out the Nationalists were taken up by the China Lobby. After the president promulgated the Truman Doctrine in March 1947, his political critics began to ask why the United States should assist the Greek government against a Communist-dominated insurgency while denying aid to the Chinese government, which faced an even greater Communist threat. Bowing to this political pressure from the Republican right, Truman approved the sale of light arms and ammunition to the Nationalists in May 1947, and then $125 million in financial assistance in April 1948.

The resumption of American aid to the KMT proved too little and too late, as it continued to squander its original military advantage. Chiang also alienated the peasant masses by refusing to enact land reforms, which would have dispossessed the landowning elite on which he continued to rely for support. In August 1949 the Truman administration finally decided to cut its losses and suspended all economic and military aid to the doomed Nationalist government. Amid Republican com-plaints that the Democratic president was abandoning China to Communism, the State Department issued a "White Paper" to demonstrate that direct U.S. interven-tion in the Chinese Civil War would be an exercise in futility: Unlike the democratic countries of Western Europe that were suitable partners in a campaign to contain Communist expansion, the Chinese government had alienated its own people and squandered the $3 billion in economic aid that Washington had already provided since the end of World War II. It is ironic that just as Washington was washing its hands of the Chinese Nationalists, Moscow was attempting to restrain the Chinese Communists. As Chiang's forces in northern China suffered setback after setback throughout 1948, Stalin advised Mao to halt his southward advance at the Yangtze River and to accept the establishment of a non-Communist enclave in southern China. After the Chinese Communist leader rejected that advice and ordered his troops to seize the southern cities in early 1949, the Soviet ambassador remained with the retreating Nationalist government to the bitter end. Stalin's refusal to back Mao to the hilt reflected his distaste for a unified Communist government in China that might be beyond his control.

The Communist forces captured Beijing in January 1949 and devoted the rest of the year to extending their control over the entire country. On October 1 Mao stood

*The recently victorious Chinese Communist leader Mao Zedong during his visit to Moscow in December 1949–February 1950. This was the only personal encounter between Mao and Josef Stalin and led to the signing on February 14, 1950, of a Sino-Soviet treaty of alliance between the two Communist powers. (National Archives)*

in Beijing's Tiananmen Square to proclaim the establishment of the People's Republic of China (PRC) as the defeated Nationalist army and political leadership fled to the offshore island of Formosa (Taiwan). Having established a Communist government in the world's most populous country with minimal assistance from Moscow, Mao was in a much stronger position than the Communist party bosses in Eastern Europe—who had been installed and were kept in power by Soviet military might— to pursue an independent course in the Cold War. A year earlier Yugoslavia had set the precedent for a nonaligned Communist regime that was able to maintain cordial relations with the West. Some U.S. officials entertained the hope that Mao, once he had consolidated his power, would become the Tito of Asia.

As final victory loomed in the summer of 1949, the Chinese Communist leader became extremely apprehensive about two threats to the country he was about to lead. The first stemmed from the deplorable economic conditions in China that resulted from the Japanese occupation and the civil war. The country desperately needed a massive infusion of capital and technology from abroad to rebuild its shattered infrastructure. There was only one country in the world capable of providing such economic assistance. It had recently demonstrated its willingness to spend vast sums of money to finance the economic recovery of its former adversaries, Germany in Europe and Japan in Asia. But the Marshall Plan and the bilateral U.S. aid program for Japan had been proffered to countries with democratic political systems and capitalist economies. A devout adherent of Marxist-Leninist doctrine, Mao was determined to install a Communist political and economic system in China that was bound to prove unacceptable to the Americans. Mao's second concern was that the United States might intervene militarily in China to reverse the outcome of the civil war. (While there is no evidence that the Truman administration contemplated such an action, the Chinese leadership apparently deemed it a distinct possibility). Assuming the unavailability of U.S. economic assistance and worried about the potential menace of American military power, Mao concluded that the only hope of enhancing his country's future prosperity and security was to approach Moscow. On June 30, 1949, as Communist troops were pushing back the Nationalist forces on all fronts, he publicly revealed for the first time the international orientation of the new state he was about to establish: The new China must "unite in a common struggle with those nations of the world which treat us as equal," he announced in a dramatic public statement. Lest there be any doubt about the nations to which he was alluding, he specified that the Chinese people must "ally ourselves with the Soviet Union, with the People's Democratic countries. . . . We must lean to one side." In this way Mao signaled to Moscow (and to Washington) that he would be no Asian Tito, that he accepted Soviet leadership in the international Communist movement, and that he would look to Stalin for guidance and support.

Two days after Mao's famous "lean to one side" speech, a Communist Chinese delegation headed by Mao's close collaborator Liu Shaoqi set out for Moscow. There the Chinese negotiators held four cordial meetings with Stalin to lay the groundwork for future cooperation between the two Communist powers. In an entirely uncharacteristic mea culpa, the Soviet leader apologized to his guests for his inadequate support for the Chinese Communist movement during the Civil War. He encouraged them to set up a central government as soon as possible, implying that the new regime would receive prompt recognition and assistance from the Soviet Union. He was even prepared to assign China an important role in the world Communist movement: Moscow would remain the beacon of the international proletarian revolution, but Beijing could assume primary responsibility for promoting Communist revolutions in Asia. The day after Mao announced the formation of the PRC on October 1, the Soviet Union dutifully severed relations with KMT and extended formal recognition to the new government in Beijing. This was Moscow's public response to the Chinese "lean to one side" declaration that Mao had eagerly awaited. The last link between the Soviet Union and his longtime adversaries in China had been severed.

Flush with victory over the KMT, Mao Zedong himself boarded a train on December 6, 1949, and left China for the first time in his life on a ten-day journey across Siberia to confer with the Soviet leader in Moscow. In a round of intensive discussions, the two men agreed to replace the Sino-Soviet Treaty of Friendship and Alliance that Stalin had concluded with the Chinese Nationalist government at the end of the war with a new pact between the two Communist governments. On January 20, 1950, Premier Zhou Enlai arrived to negotiate the details of the new agreement. The Chinese delegation persuaded their Soviet hosts to accept a clause stipulating that if one party were attacked by a third country the other would intervene militarily on its behalf. They also extracted a pledge of Soviet economic aid for the reconstruction of China (although the commitment bore humiliating neo-imperialist overtones, as in the creation of joint-stock companies to develop the natural resources of Manchuria). In exchange for these favors Mao reaffirmed the concessions that Stalin had wrung from the KMT in the original Sino-Soviet treaty: China recognized the Soviet client state in Mongolia and acknowledged Soviet control of the Manchurian railroad and rights to the two Yellow Sea ports of Dairen (Dalny) and Port Arthur (Lüshun), although Mao secured a Soviet promise to restore the ports to Chinese control by 1952. Three days after signing the thirty-year Treaty of Friendship, Alliance, and Mutual Assistance on February 14, 1950, Mao and Zhou left Moscow with what seemed to be a solid Soviet pledge of military protection and economic assistance for their newly created state.

The West's initial reaction to the Communist victory in China was tepid and restrained. Great Britain promptly adapted to the fait accompli by extending diplomatic recognition to the PRC in January 1950. London's principal motivation for such hasty recognition was the desire to protect its crown colony of Hong Kong, that anomalous relic of British imperialism off the Chinese coast whose special status Mao pledged to respect. At the other extreme, France adamantly refused to recognize the PRC because Mao was providing military aid to the Viet Minh in its bid to expel the French from Vietnam (see page 220). The United States originally steered a middle course in its official policy toward the new Chinese government. On the one hand, the Truman administration refused to follow Great Britain's lead in establishing formal diplomatic relations with Beijing. The ostensible reason for the delay was the maltreatment of U.S. consular officials in Chinese port cities and the seizure of American-owned property throughout the country. The real reason was that Truman and his new secretary of state, Dean Acheson, feared the political outcry that an exchange of ambassadors with Mao's government would generate among Republicans on Capitol Hill who had been castigating the administration for the "loss of China."

But the State Department patiently prepared for a politically opportune moment when the United States could join the Scandinavian countries, Switzerland, and Great Britain in recognizing the PRC. In January 1950 Truman reaffirmed the Allied declarations at Cairo and Potsdam that Taiwan was an integral part of China. In the meantime, the People's Liberation Army prepared to complete its victory in the civil war by invading the island, where Chiang had set up a government-in-exile as the Republic of China. The president also declined to resume the flow of U.S. military aid to the KMT that had been suspended the previous summer and refused to promise assistance to Chiang in the event of an invasion from the mainland. The unmistakable message emanating from Washington in the first half of 1950 was that the United States was preparing to make its peace with the new Communist regime in Beijing after a suitable interval.

## The Korean War and Its Repercussions for the Far East

The development of normal relations between Washington and Beijing was to be postponed for what turned out to be two and a half decades because of the sudden and unforeseen outbreak of armed conflict on the Korean peninsula in the summer of 1950. By the end of that year half a million Chinese and American troops would be fighting each other in a full-scale war that would drag on for another two-and-a-half years. The importance of the Korean War as a catalyst for rearmament and remobilization in the United States and Western Europe has already been treated (see page 45). Let us now turn to the causes and consequences of that conflict in Asia.

Korea had long been known as the "hermit nation" because of its isolation from the rest of the world. That solitude was shattered in 1905 when Japan defeated Russia in a war that had been fought in part to determine which of those two powers would control the Korean peninsula. After occupying Korea for five years, Japan annexed the country outright in 1910 and proceeded to subject its population to political subjugation and economic exploitation for the next three decades. During World War II the Allied powers agreed that after Japan's defeat it should be compelled to relinquish control of Korea. At the Cairo Conference in 1943 Roosevelt, Stalin, and Churchill pledged that the country would achieve self-rule "in due course." At Yalta Stalin accepted Roosevelt's suggestion that a tripartite trusteeship composed of the three Allied powers be established to prepare the country for eventual independence.

After the Soviet Union's intervention in the war against Japan on August 8, 1945, the Red Army poured into the Korean peninsula in pursuit of the disintegrating Japanese forces there. This rapid Soviet military advance caused concern in Washington that the invading Communist forces would occupy the entire country before American troops could arrive to play their rightful role in receiving the surrender of the defeated Japanese military units there. Truman therefore hastily obtained Stalin's consent on August 14 to the provisional partition of Korea along the 38th parallel of latitude into a Soviet occupation zone in the north and an American occupation zone in the south. This agreement between Washington and Moscow left the northern Soviet zone in possession of most of the peninsula's heavy industry and raw materials, while the southern American zone inherited most of its light industry and arable land together with about two-thirds of its population. True to his word,

Stalin ordered Soviet ground forces to halt their southward advance at the 38th parallel, even though American troops would not arrive in their designated occupation zone until early September.

Since the days of the tsars, Russia had always sought to prevent any other great power from gaining control of the Korean peninsula. That objective had been thwarted after Russia's defeat by Japan in the war of 1904–1905. Thirty years later, Japan was on the verge of a devastating military defeat that would free the peninsula of its armed forces as Russian soldiers moved in to replace them. Why did Stalin so readily consent to the interim arrangement allowing U.S. forces to land in southern Korea, when Soviet troops were in position to occupy the entire country? Since the United States had never expressed the slightest interest in Korea, it is likely that the Soviet leader agreed to the temporary partition of the country on the assumption that it would inevitably fall within the Russian sphere of influence once the proposed joint trusteeship had expired and the two occupation forces had withdrawn.

After Japan's formal surrender on September 2, 1945, an American Military Government (AMG) was established in the southern half of Korea under the command of General John Hodge. The AMG was immediately confronted with a bitter dispute between indigenous political organizations that vied for predominance in their newly liberated country. One of these groups, a loose-knit coalition of Communists and leftists of various tendencies, precipitously announced on September 6 the creation of a Korean People's Republic. The AMG ignored this unilateral declaration and shunned the political movement that had issued it, which the Americans suspected of harboring sympathies for the Soviet Union. Instead, the U.S. military authorities cultivated amicable relations with other political factors that could be relied on to facilitate the occupation. These included a small coterie of English-speaking, foreign-educated Koreans from the upper classes; former Korean functionaries in the Japanese colonial service widely resented as collaborators; and even a handful of former Japanese colonial administrators who chose to remain after their government's surrender. What all of these groups shared in common, apart from a willingness to cooperate with the American military authorities, was the absence of close ties to the Korean masses.

As the U.S. authorities in the south struggled to put together an indigenous coalition to assist them in the occupation, the Allied powers were still officially committed to the Yalta scheme for a trusteeship to prepare all of Korea for eventual independence. Accordingly, the Allied foreign ministers agreed at their December meeting in Moscow to establish a provisional government that, in cooperation with a Soviet-American joint commission, would make arrangements for a Four-Power trusteeship that would operate for a period of five years. At the expiration of the trusteeship, nationwide elections would be conducted to permit the Korean people to choose a government for the entire peninsula.

Amid the intense political jockeying in preparation for the designation of the provisional government, a seventy-year-old Korean politician in the American zone named Syngman Rhee began to pull away from the pack. In 1904 Rhee had traveled to the United States, where he converted to Christianity and received a Ph.D in international law from Princeton University. On returning to his homeland he began agitating for independence from Japan and was forced to flee the country in 1910 to elude the Japanese police. Rhee spent the next thirty-five years in the United States, tirelessly soliciting American support for an independent Korea under his leadership. When he turned up in the U.S. occupation zone on the peninsula in October 1945, this English-speaking, U.S.-educated, Christian gentleman seemed a godsend to American officials in Seoul who were searching for indigenous political leaders: Here was a staunch anti-Communist whose impeccable nationalist credentials would enable him to win much broader popular support than other prominent right-wing personalities, most of whom had been tainted by their collaborationist links to the Japanese colonial administration. The AMG accordingly threw its support behind the Representative Democratic Council that Rhee and his conservative allies had founded in February 1946. The leftist groups, thwarted in their bid to create an independent republic and ignored by the American occupation authorities, reacted to this overt intervention by the AMG in domestic political affairs by staging a general strike the following September. A bloody confrontation that ensued between right-wing and left-wing forces left a thousand dead or seriously injured and dozens of left-wing militants in prison.

Negotiations in the Joint Soviet-American Commission in Seoul in the early months of 1946 were hampered by the fact that the Korean Communist Party was the only political group in the south that supported the decision by the Moscow Foreign Ministers' Conference to establish a trusteeship for the peninsula. All the non-Communist parties, with Rhee's right-wing coalition leading the way, angrily rejected the trusteeship plan and demanded immediate independence for their country. The opposition to the trusteeship plan by the non-Communist parties in the south provided Moscow with a valuable weapon that it brandished in the meetings of the Joint Commission. The Soviet delegation insisted that only those parties that supported the trusteeship plan be permitted to participate in the preparations for the elections for a provisional government. The American delegation rejected this proposal, which would have meant that only the Communists in the south would be eligible. With each side refusing to budge, the Joint Commission adjourned *sine die* on May 8, 1946.

In the meantime the Soviet occupation authorities in the north had begun to transfer administrative authority and supply weapons to a band of Korean Communists operating in the northern city of Pyongyang, whose leader was a fiery young militant named Kim Il Sung. Born to a peasant family in 1912, Kim went to Manchuria in 1932 to fight alongside the Chinese Communist partisans against the Japanese military forces that had recently occupied that province. In 1941 Kim crossed the border into Siberia to enlist in the Red Army. By August 1945 the thirty-two-year old soldier was back in his homeland with the Soviet forces that drove into northern Korea after Stalin declared war on Japan. In the months following the Japanese surrender, Kim caught the attention of the Kremlin and was placed in charge of the Communist political apparatus that was emerging in northern Korea under the watchful eyes of the Soviet occupation forces.

With the collapse of the trusteeship project in the spring of 1946, the Truman administration submitted the question of Korea's political future to the United Nations. With U.S. support the UN decided to conduct elections to form a single government for the entire peninsula. Since the United States and its clients in Western Europe and Latin America dominated the new world organization, the Kremlin opposed the plan for UN-supervised elections. With Moscow's blessing Kim Il Sung excluded the United Nations Temporary Commission on Korea (UNTCOK) from the Soviet occupation zone and refused to allow the proposed elections to be held there. Stymied in its efforts to conduct elections in the north, UNTCOK proceeded to schedule elections for a national constituent assembly in the south. The UN monitoring commission certified the elections that were held in South Korea on May 10, 1948, as free and fair, although they were disrupted by leftist demonstrations that resulted in five hundred deaths and the imprisonment of ten thousand protesters. Since North Korea refused to participate and the leftist parties in the south boycotted the elections, the right-wing coalition won a comfortable majority. The newly created National Assembly meeting in Seoul issued a proclamation on August 15 establishing the Republic of Korea (ROK) with Syngman Rhee as its president. On September 9 Kim Il Sung announced in Pyongyang the creation of the People's Democratic Republic of Korea. Kim promptly transformed the new North Korean state into a rigid Communist dictatorship, banning all opposition parties and centralizing political power in his own hands. In Seoul the authoritarian Rhee cracked down on his domestic opposition, jailing almost ninety thousand people during his first year in office. Although the Communist regime in the north and the anti-Communist regime of the south were sworn enemies of each another, they shared two deeply held convictions: The first was that the division of Korea was inadmissible; the second was that it must be reunified forthwith.

After the partition of Korea into two mutually antagonistic regimes, the two occupying powers proceeded with their plans to evacuate their respective zones. The last contingent of Soviet troops left North Korea in December 1948. In the meantime the forty-five-thousand-man U.S. army had begun a gradual withdrawal from South Korea that was finally completed in June 1949. The Pentagon had determined that the peninsula was of minimal strategic value to the United States and that the military units stationed there could be put to much better use elsewhere. Neither Kim Il Sung in Pyongyang nor Syngman Rhee in Seoul made a secret of his ambition to preside over the reunification of the peninsula, by force if necessary. The departing Soviet army had left behind a formidable arsenal of airplanes, tanks, and artillery as well as several thousand military advisers to bolster the North Korean regime. After Rhee repeatedly threatened to send his army north to unify Korea under his authority, the Truman administration became worried that the South Korean leader's bellicosity might drag the United States into an unwanted conflict on the peninsula. Washington accordingly refused to supply the South Korean army with the kinds of advanced military equipment, such as tanks and aircraft, that would be required to mount an offensive military operation against the North. Instead, the United States restricted its aid to small arms and light artillery, which would enable South Korea to maintain domestic order and repel an attack from the north, as well as a five-hundred-man military advisory group to train the inexperienced South Korean army.

The Korean peninsula thus became a site of potential instability after the withdrawal of the occupation forces of the two superpowers: two independent Korean governments, a Communist dictatorship in the north and an authoritarian anti-Communist state in the south, each claiming sovereignty over the territory ruled by

the other. The border separating them across the 38th parallel was an entirely artificial one that had been provisionally established by the two occupying powers for
their own convenience. There were no natural markers such as wide rivers or high
mountains to separate the two states, which had been arbitrarily carved out of a relatively homogenous population that shared a common language, ethnic identity, and
historical experience. Amid this volatile situation along the parallel, border patrols
from each side clashed repeatedly throughout the year following the withdrawal of
U.S. forces in the summer of 1949. Each of the two Korean governments periodically renewed its claim of sovereignty over the entire peninsula and hinted at the im-
minence of military action to achieve that goal.

As we have seen, the Soviet Union had facilitated the return of Kim Il Sung to
North Korea and helped him to establish a one-party Communist state there before
removing its own occupation forces. Documentary evidence in the Kremlin archives
suggests that Stalin's interest in maintaining control of northern Korean through a
"friendly" government in Pyongyang reflected his appreciation of both the strategic
significance and valuable natural resources of the country. But Moscow required the
North Korean government to pay for the economic assistance proferred by its superpower patron. Stalin also refrained from signing a bilateral military alliance with
Kim Il Sung's government on the model of the mutual defense pacts that had been
concluded with the Soviet satellites in Eastern Europe in 1948. Although the North
Korean leader owed his position to Stalin's patronage, Kim had no reason to consider
Moscow a generous benefactor or a reliable supporter of his goal of reunification.

The archives in Moscow that were made available to researchers after the collapse
of the Soviet Union have afforded historians a rare glimpse into the decision-making
process in North Korea, the Soviet Union, and Communist China during the first half
of 1950. What these long inaccessible records reveal is that the North Korean leader
was overtaken by a powerful temptation to achieve unification of the peninsula that
was inspired by developments in the military, diplomatic, and political realm. From
the military perspective, the North Korean People's Army (NKPA) enjoyed a decisive advantage over its counterpart in the south: The NKPA had 135,000 soldiers (of
which 10,000 were battle-seasoned veterans of the fighting in Manchuria during the
Chinese Civil War) and was well equipped with Soviet T-34 tanks and heavy artillery. By contrast, the South Korean army was half as large and possessed only light
arms. North Korea's military advantage was reinforced by the total diplomatic isolation of the South Korean government. With the departure of the American occupation forces from South Korea in June 1949, the United States had no residual obliga-
tions to the new regime it left behind. President Truman had withheld offensive
weapons from Rhee for fear that they would be used for an invasion of the north.
Secretary of State Dean Acheson confirmed in a well-publicized speech in Washington on January 12, 1950, that the Korean peninsula lay outside a U.S. "military defense perimeter" in Asia that included the offshore islands from Japan to the Philippines but no territory on the mainland. Rhee's government had no reason to believe
that its erstwhile patron would lift a finger to defend it. South Korea's military weakness and diplomatic isolation were aggravated by an acute domestic crisis in the
spring of 1950 as the country suffered a severe bout of unemployment and inflation.
Leftist groups that had been excluded from political power clashed with the govern-

ment's increasingly repressive security forces. The national elections in May revealed the sharp decline in Rhee's popularity when his ruling party lost several seats in the parliament.

These mounting internal tensions within South Korea appear to have persuaded Kim Il Sung that his embattled rival in Seoul would be unable to mobilize public support in the event of a military showdown between the two states. The North Korean leader therefore decided to strike while the iron was hot. Just as Rhee had sought American blessing for a military action against the North to reunify the peninsula under his rule, Kim repeatedly had badgered the Kremlin to support an attack against the South that would yield a reunified Communist Korea. In the fall of 1949 and in February 1950, Kim journeyed to Moscow to make his case directly to Stalin. Whereas the Truman administration never gave in to Rhee's requests for military support for an invasion of the North, Kim eventually persuaded the Soviet leader that the unpopular regime in Seoul would collapse like a house of cards from the combined pressure of a North Korean military assault and the anticipated uprising by two hundred thousand Communist sympathizers in the south. In a final face-to-face meeting in Moscow in April 1950, Stalin approved the North Korean plan to reunify the country by military force. There is evidence that the Soviet Union had been transferring some military equipment to North Korea even before Kim pressed Stalin to give him the green light. The Soviet leader now authorized the acceleration of these deliveries to ensure victory for the North Korean army. But Stalin apparently gave Kim his assent only after obtaining assurances that the proposed operation would be completed before American troops stationed in nearby Japan could be drawn into the conflict. Kim's hasty consultation with Mao on his way back from Moscow elicited a cautious Chinese endorsement of the North Korean plan. Both Communist leaders expected the projected war on the peninsula to be over quickly. Even if it dragged on, they apparently assumed that the United States would refrain from interfering in a purely internal Korean dispute just as it had remained aloof from the civil war in China and permitted a Communist victory there.

Bolstered by this support from Moscow and Beijing, Kim Il Sung launched his bid to "liberate" the other half of the peninsula. In the early morning of June 25, 1950, the NKPA unleashed a heavy artillery barrage against the South Korean lines along the 38th parallel. Within hours some ninety thousand infantry troops, accompanied by 150 tanks and more than 100 airplanes, burst across the border at eleven points. As the outmanned and outgunned forces of the ROK fell back in full retreat, NKPA troops advanced virtually unopposed toward the South Korean capital as Rhee issued frantic appeals to Washington for help. President Truman responded to the Korean emergency with an improvised policy in the remaining five days of June that would have lasting repercussions for America's future role in Asia. First, he requested an emergency meeting of the United Nations Security Council to deal with the crisis. In the absence of the Soviet delegate, who had been boycotting its sessions since January to protest the exclusion of Communist China from the world organization, the Security Council approved a resolution demanding the immediate withdrawal of the North Korean army from South Korea. As NKPA forces continued their advance and occupied Seoul on June 27, the Security Council passed a U.S.-sponsored resolution urging all member states of the UN to furnish military assistance to South Korea. Even before the passage of the UN resolution, Truman had ordered U.S. military forces on occupation duty in Japan to launch air and naval attacks against the North Korean invasion forces, which began the next day. Then Truman ordered the immediate transfer of two U.S. infantry divisions stationed in Japan to assist the retreating South Korean army. Instead of going to Congress with a request for a declaration of war, he circumvented that constitutional requirement by designating the Korean operation a "police action." This would set the precedent for subsequent U.S. military interventions in various parts of the world.

To implement its June 27 resolution the Security Council, still in the absence of the Soviet delegate, voted on July 7 to set up a United Nations command to coordinate the military operations of those member states willing to contribute troops. Since U.S. forces would be doing the bulk of the fighting, Truman was authorized to appoint the commander of the UN expeditionary force. He predictably chose General Douglas MacArthur, the commander of U.S. occupation forces in Japan whose soldiers had already been rushed to South Korea and were being directed from his headquarters in Tokyo. Within a few months U.S. pressure had induced twenty other states to join the American units in the UN expeditionary force. But the eighty-three thousand U.S. troops bore the main brunt of the fighting, accounting for half of the ground forces (compared to 40 percent contributed by South Korea, whose army had immediately been placed under MacArthur's command), 86 percent of the naval forces, and 93 percent of the air forces.

Truman's decision to intervene militarily in Korea had little to do with the perceived strategic significance of the peninsula, which (as we have seen) had earlier been excluded from American defense planning for East Asia. Rather, it was prompted by his conviction that the North Korean attack was a Soviet-inspired test of U.S. credibility in Asia much more daring and dangerous than the probes in Europe that had given rise to the American doctrine of containment there. What we now know from the declassified archives of the former Soviet Union, as indicated in the earlier summary of the decision-making process before the invasion, reveals a much more nuanced and ambiguous Soviet role. The Korean War began as a regional conflict between two rival governments for control of the peninsula they shared. Stalin and Mao acquiesced in rather than orchestrated Kim II Sung's scheme for military action, and only after it seemed certain of success and devoid of risks. But U.S. officials were not privy to the top secret deliberations in Moscow, Beijing, and Pyongyang. They simply assumed that the North Korean aggression represented a shift in tactics by the Communist bloc from subversion to armed invasion as a means of conquering independent non-Communist nations.

The early stages of the war did not go well for the American and South Korean armies. By the beginning of August, the NKPA had driven the U.S. eighth army and its ROK allies into a small corner around the port of Pusan on the southeast coast. But the North Korean forces had suffered heavy casualties and lost two-thirds of their T-34 tanks in the process. The U.S. and ROK forces dug in around a five-thousand-square-mile area bounded by what came to be known as the "Pusan Perimeter" and finally halted the enemy advance. While the North Koreans tried in vain to break through this impregnable bastion and drive the UN forces into the sea, MacArthur decided to execute the strategy that he had devised in the early stages of the war.

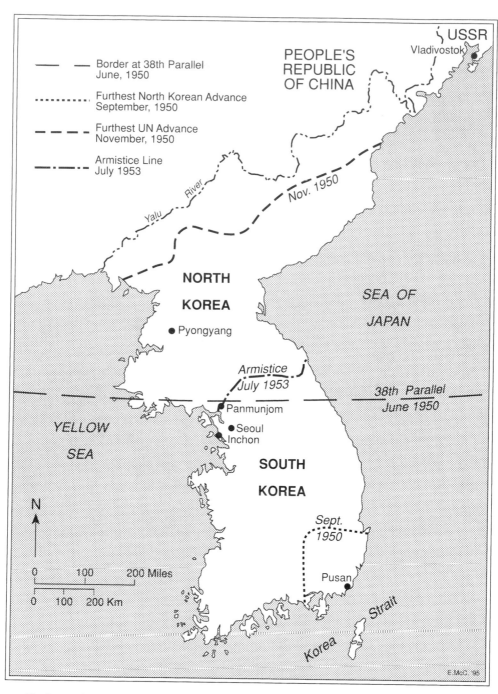

*The Korean War 1950–1953*

While the defenders of Pusan engaged the forward echelons of the North Korean army, MacArthur dispatched a huge naval strike force of 269 ships carrying seventy thousand men up the west coast of Korea. On September 15 a contingent of U.S. marines waded ashore on two beaches behind enemy lines at Inchon, the port of Seoul. This amphibious landing caught the North Koreans completely by surprise. Within four days fifty thousand Americans troops were ashore and began to advance toward the occupied South Korean capital. In the meantime the U.S. eighth army was breaking out of the Pusan Perimeter, stampeding the NKPA into a hasty retreat northward. At the end of September the marines driving inland from Inchon liberated Seoul as U.S. and ROK forces from Pusan reached the 38th parallel and the North Korean army disintegrated.

The daring debarkation at Inchon, and the prompt liberation of South Korea that followed it, fulfilled the UN mandate to "repel the armed attack" by restoring the military status quo ante. MacArthur's accompanying instructions to "restore international peace and security" seemed to suggest as the next step the opening of negotiations with North Korea for a cease-fire and some kind of political settlement. But after his stunning triumph at Inchon and the disorganized retreat of the North Korean invasion force, MacArthur was in no mood to halt his army's northward advance in the interests of international diplomacy. The general's prestige and popularity at home were such that President Truman did not dare to object when MacArthur unveiled a plan to pursue the retreating North Koreans deep into their own territory, punish them for their aggression, and obtain the kind of unconditional surrender that he had received from the Japanese five years earlier. Indeed, the White House itself succumbed to the temptation to exploit the favorable military situation to topple the North Korean regime and erase the artificial dividing line that neither of the two Korean regimes nor the United Nations had ever recognized as permanent. On September 27 the Joint Chiefs of Staff in Washington secretly authorized MacArthur to carry the war into North Korea, pending approval of the new policy by the United Nations. In the meantime Syngman Rhee, sensing that his cherished goal of a unified peninsula was at hand, ordered ROK troops to prepare for an invasion of the north.

The swift and massive intervention of the American-dominated United Nations army in Korea in the summer of 1950 had caught the Kremlin completely off guard. Its failure to wield its veto in the Security Council to prevent the authorization of such an action was obviously a serious tactical blunder. Stalin finally realized his error and on August 1 ordered the Soviet delegate to resume his seat and block any resolution that might threaten his North Korean ally. Faced with the certainty of a Soviet veto in the Security Council, the Truman administration persuaded the British government to introduce on October 7 a new resolution in the General Assembly, which was not bound by the rule of unanimity and where the United States commanded a solid majority of votes. It instructed MacArthur to take all appropriate measures to restore "stability throughout Korea" so that the peninsula-wide elections called for in the 1947 UN resolution could be held. Acting on the authority of this resolution, which was legally dubious because the UN Charter does not endow the General Assembly with such decision-making power, MacArthur ordered his troops across the 38th parallel on October 9. By the end of the month they had captured the northern capital of Pyongyang and were approaching the Yalu River on the Chinese border in hot pursuit of the retreating North Korean forces. In the meantime President Truman had summoned MacArthur to a brief meeting at Wake Island in the western Pacific, where the commander in chief received the general's confident assurances that total victory over the Communist enemy was in sight.

The extension of the war to North Korea in the autumn of 1950 inevitably raised the question of China's reaction to the bloody conflict that was raging across its Manchurian frontier. Excluded from membership in the United Nations by the American veto and elbowed out of North Korea by the Soviet Union, Beijing had taken no part in the flurry of diplomatic activity during the early stages of the war. But the PRC rapidly recognized the potential threat to its interests posed by America's expanding military activities in East Asia: On June 26 Truman had ordered the U.S. seventh fleet into the Taiwan Strait to prevent the rivalry between the "two Chinas" from complicating the military situation in Korea. Although ostensibly an even-handed attempt to separate the two belligerents, the U.S. naval deployment ruined the PRC's plans to complete its victory in the civil war by capturing Chiang Kai-shek's offshore haven. Moreover, Washington's assertions of impartiality between Beijing and Taipei were contradicted by the provocative behavior of General MacArthur in the early stages of the Korean War. After Chiang publicly offered to contribute thirty-three thousand Chinese Nationalist troops to the UN war effort in Korea, MacArthur paid a lavishly publicized visit to the Generalissimo on Taiwan in late July. At a press conference MacArthur implied that the United States was prepared to defend the island in the event of an invasion from the mainland. Truman, who had spurned Chiang's offer of combat units in Korea and had no intention of becoming embroiled in a conflict in the Taiwan Strait, privately upbraided his arrogant commander for exceeding his authority. But since the president was not yet prepared to criticize the popular general in public, the Communist leadership in Beijing had no reason to doubt that MacArthur's embrace of Chiang represented official U.S. government policy.

There is no evidence from Soviet and Chinese memoirs or archival sources of a bellicose Chinese attitude in the early stages of the Korean War. Mao had cautiously endorsed Kim's plan to attack the south, but only on the assumption that it would result in a speedy victory without provoking a U.S. military intervention. The relationship between Beijing and Pyongyang was cordial but hardly intimate. Mao had not even bothered to send an ambassador to North Korea until the war began. Only a single Chinese army corps was stationed along the Yalu River border with North Korea at the time. But as the fighting on the peninsula intensified, Beijing prudently began to take precautionary measures. By early August more than 250,000 regulars of the People's Liberation Army had been redeployed along the border with North Korea. Later in the month Mao issued instructions to prepare for possible military action on the peninsula by the end of September if the North Korean government requested assistance.

Since Kim Il Sung preferred to win the war on his own, he refrained from appealing to Beijing for help while his troops had the South Korean army on the run. But MacArthur's landing at Inchon in mid-September and the northward advance of the UN forces in the next two weeks incited panic in both Pyongyang and Beijing. On October 1 Kim urgently requested the dispatch of the Chinese thirteenth army corps to Korea. The next day Mao convened an emergency meeting of the Party Politburo Standing Committee, which ordered preparations for military intervention by mid-October. In the meantime assurances were forthcoming from Moscow that, in the spirit of the Sino-Soviet Treaty of February 1950, Russian aircraft would provide air cover for Chinese land forces if they intervened in Korea. Faced with the harrowing prospect of a U.S.-controlled armed force approaching the Chinese border, the re-unification of Korea under a fervently anti-Communist regime, and a Nationalist Chinese attack against the mainland from Taiwan, Mao and his associates were pre-pared to risk all-out war with the United States. On September 30, with South Korean troops poised to advance into North Korea, Chinese Foreign Minister Zhou Enlai publicly announced that his country would not tolerate an invasion of its neigh-bor by "the imperialists." A few days later he conveyed an explicit private warning to Washington through the Indian ambassador to China that if any military forces other than South Korean units crossed the 38th parallel, China would be obliged to inter-vene in defense of its vital interests. MacArthur contemptuously dismissed this signal as a bluff and ordered his forces into North Korea on October 9. Seven days earlier, Mao had issued the order for Chinese military intervention in the Korean War by the middle of October.

In the meantime Zhou Enlai and a high-level Chinese delegation had flown to the Soviet Union to complete the arrangements for the deployment of Soviet fighters and bombers to support the Chinese infantry in Korea. In a marathon ten-hour meeting with Stalin at a Black Sea villa on the night of October 9–10, the Chinese officials were dismayed to learn that the Soviet leader had changed his plans. Although promising to send military equipment for Chinese use, Stalin rescinded his earlier offer of air support on the spurious grounds of insufficient preparation. After an ago-nizing overnight meeting of the CCP Politburo in Beijing on October 13–14, the Chinese leadership reaffirmed its decision to intervene despite the disappointing news from the Soviet Union. Mao had evidently concluded that the potential damage to the PRC's credibility as the defender of the revolutionary cause in Asia, together with the threat to Chinese security posed by the advancing American troops, required a vigorous response. But the Chinese leader must surely have begun to entertain sec-ond thoughts about the reliability of Moscow as an ally.

On October 19 almost two hundred thousand Chinese "volunteers" (who were actually regular units of the PLA) began pouring across the Yalu River into North Korea. They traveled stealthily at night to avoid detection by UN forces and hid dur-ing the day in the rugged Korean mountains. They clashed with UN forces in sharp, brief attacks in the first week of November, apparently to reinforce Zhou's earlier warning that a UN advance north of the parallel would not be tolerated, and then re-turned to their hidden positions. The Chinese tactical retreats lulled MacArthur into overconfidence and prompted him to resume his northward march, which brought one of his advance units to the banks of the Yalu River on November 21. Truman and his military advisers, still reluctant to interfere with what appeared to be a spectacu-larly successful military operation, ignored the Chinese warnings and hit-and-run probes in the north.

Flushed with an uninterrupted string of successes in the field, MacArthur renewed a full-scale offensive on November 24. His goal was to achieve total victory and, as he incautiously boasted in public, to bring the boys home by Christmas. But on the next day the Chinese army, swollen to 300,000 battle-hardened veterans of the civil war, joined the 80,000 survivors of the North Korean army to launch a massive counteroffensive against MacArthur's widely dispersed UN force of 150,000. As the front lines of the U.S. eighth army disintegrated, MacArthur anxiously cabled Washington on November 28 that "We face an entirely new war." By the end of the year the counterattacking Chinese and North Korean forces had crossed the 38th parallel. On January 4, 1951, the southern capital of Seoul fell for the second time to the northern invaders. After the Chinese intervention Stalin overcame his initial hesitation and dispatched two air force divisions to defend the Yalu bridges in November 1950. But he went to extraordinary lengths to conceal evidence of Russian participation in the war. Soviet aircraft bore North Korean markings while their pilots wore Chinese uniforms and were instructed to speak Korean in their radio communications. By the spring of 1951 these camouflaged Soviet planes were engaged in intensive air combat with U.S. fighters, although they were prohibited from operating over enemy-held territory to prevent their pilots from being taken prisoner and identified if shot down. In the meantime Truman had grown weary of the war in Korea and American diplomats were prowling the corridors of the United Nations to drum up support for a cease-fire. But China, emboldened by its success on the battlefield in the winter of 1950–1951, defiantly refused to negotiate unless the United States agreed to withdraw all of its ground forces from Korea, remove the seventh fleet from the Taiwan Strait, and lift its veto of Beijing's application for UN membership.

As his forces retreated before the Communist onslaught, MacArthur urgently requested extreme measures to remedy the deteriorating situation. He sought authorization from Truman to carry the war directly to the new enemy's territory by bombing Chinese facilities across the Yalu, imposing a naval blockade on the PRC, and unleashing the Nationalist forces on Taiwan to open another front on the Chinese mainland to divert PLA troops from Korea. While his commander pressed for all-out war, Truman was coming under increasing pressure from America's allies in Europe to seek a negotiated settlement of a regional conflict that risked escalation into a world war in view of China's alliance with the Soviet Union. In early March the president decided to confine UN military operations to Korea while simultaneously pursuing a negotiated settlement that would restore the division of the peninsula at the 38th parallel. Then the Chinese spring offensive in South Korea petered out when it outran its supply line and communications network, and the UN forces again counterattacked and crossed into North Korea. MacArthur thereupon issued on his own authority a provocative proclamation that in effect presented Beijing with the ultimatum of accepting an armistice at the parallel or enduring attacks on its own Manchurian territory across the Yalu. On April 5 the Republican leader of the U.S. House of Representatives caused a sensation in Washington by reading on the floor of Congress a letter from MacArthur implying that Nationalist Chinese troops should be unleashed against the Chinese Communists. The letter concluded with the pungent observation that "There is no substitute for victory," a direct criticism of Truman's decision to wage a limited war and seek a negotiated settlement.

Stung by this insulting challenge to his presidential authority by his independent-minded proconsul in Asia, Truman dismissed MacArthur on April 11 and replaced him with General Matthew B. Ridgway (the commander of the eighth army that was advancing into North Korea.) MacArthur's departure cleared the way for the opening of armistice talks. Both the United States and the Soviet Union had come to realize that the risk of escalation was too great to allow the conflict on the Korean peninsula to continue. In June Washington discreetly approached Moscow about the possibility of armistice negotiations, and both the Soviet and Chinese governments responded favorably. Representatives of the UN Command met with their Chinese and North Korean counterparts for the first time on July 10, 1951, in the Communist-controlled South Korean city of Kaesong at the 38th parallel. After months of bickering the Communists broke off the truce talks in August, but they were resumed the following October in the nearby farm village of Panmunjom. By November the parties had reached agreement on an armistice line along the existing front that was slightly more advantageous to South Korea than the original border at the 38th parallel. But the negotiations dragged on for another two years in a hopeless deadlock over the contentious issue of the repatriation of the 170,000 Chinese and North Korean prisoners of war (POWs) that were held by UN forces on an island off the southeast coast of South Korea. About 50,000 of the Communist (including two-thirds of the Chinese) POWs in UN custody refused to return to their homelands and requested political asylum. Recalling the tragic fate of the Soviet soldiers in Nazi POW camps who had been forcibly repatriated after World War II only to perish at the hands of Stalin's executioners or in Siberian prison camps, U.S. negotiators demanded that all prisoners held by both sides be given the choice of whether to return. The Chinese were willing to allow the North Korean prisoners to remain in the south if they chose to do so but insisted on getting all of theirs back.

During the American presidential campaign of 1952 the Republican candidate, General Dwight D. Eisenhower, capitalized on the growing public weariness with the war in Korea. He promised that, if elected, he would travel to the front to seek ways of bringing the seemingly interminable conflict to an honorable end. The month after his landslide electoral triumph in November, the president-elect redeemed his campaign pledge by visiting the freezing U.S. troops (who were spending their third Christmas in Korea with no end in sight). It became evident that none of the belligerents had anything to gain from a continuation of this ruinous conflict. China was devoting over half of its annual revenue to the war, the United States was footing the lion's share of the bill for the UN military operation, the two Korean armies had suffered horrendous casualties, and the fighting had ground down to a hopeless stalemate. Once in the White House Eisenhower sought to jump-start the peace process by issuing veiled threats to resort to nuclear weapons and to expand the conflict beyond the Korean peninsula if a diplomatic solution were not forthcoming.

While this nuclear saber-rattling may have pressured the Communist side to work harder for a negotiated settlement, it was the death of Josef Stalin on March 5, 1953, that broke the ice in the long-stalled peace talks. The much more conciliatory "collective leadership" in the Kremlin, eager to bring the pointless war on the Korean peninsula to an end, induced the Chinese to make a key concession: On March 28 Foreign Minister Zhou Enlai offered for the first time to reconsider Beijing's policy on the repatriation of POWs, which had long represented the major stumbling block to an agreement. In early June the two Communist governments finally accepted the principle of voluntary repatriation, on the condition that those prisoners refusing to return be interviewed by military observers from neutral India to verify that they were acting on their own free will. With this final obstacle overcome, the armistice was finally signed at Panmunjom on July 26, 1953, and went into effect the next day. It established a demilitarized zone between the two Korean states and set up a joint UN-Communist military armistice commission to meet periodically for the purpose of resolving matters in dispute. After three years of warfare, the political situation on the Korean peninsula was virtually unchanged: The armistice line was drawn roughly alone the same line where it had existed when the fighting began. Kim Il Sung remained in power in Pyongyang and Syngman Rhee still ruled in Seoul.

The human costs of the Korean War were high for all participants: The United States lost 54,246 soldiers (of whom 33,629 died on the battlefield); over a half million Chinese fighters perished; the combined total of military and civilian deaths in the two Koreas topped two million. The Korean War had long-term repercussions in Asia that were far out of proportion to its trivial political outcome on the peninsula.* First of all, it solidified the relationship between the Soviet Union and the recently established People's Republic of China. As noted earlier, Stalin had given minimal assistance to Mao during the latter's contest with Chiang for supremacy in China. But after an initial hesitation Moscow furnished sorely needed military assistance to Beijing when it intervened in Korea, while machinery and industrial technology flowed from Russia to China and Chinese students traveled to the USSR for training. Whatever reluctance Stalin may have had about supporting the new Communist regime in China was overcome when U.S. military forces approached his ally's Yalu frontier. What began as a regional rivalry between two third-rate powers for control of the Korean peninsula ended in the extension of the Cold War to the entire area of East Asia and the western Pacific. The United States, confronted by what it viewed (incorrectly, as it turned out) as a calculated bid by a monolithic Communist bloc to expand into the power vacuum of an Asia recently liberated from Japanese domination, hastened to reengage its power in the region by extending military protection and economic assistance to many of its non-Communist states.

The first beneficiary of this new American commitment to the containment of Communism in Asia was South Korea itself. Although the armistice mandated negotiations for a peace treaty, such talks never got off the ground and the two Korean states remained in a state of war. To ensure the security of South Korea, a force of fifty thousand American soldiers remained in that country. A bilateral security treaty committed the United States to defend South Korea against another attack from the north, the first such obligation to a country on the mainland of Asia. The perpetual threat of invasion also furnished a convenient pretext for the maintenance of an authoritarian political system in the south. Rhee browbeat the South Korean parliament in 1952 into ratifying constitutional amendments that granted him quasidictatorial

---

*The UN intervention in the Korean War did not establish a precedent for coercive military action by the international body in response to aggression. It would take another forty years and the end of the Cold War before another UN military force, again led by the United States, would intervene in response to Iraq's invasion of Kuwait.

power. Although the United States continued to regard the autocratic South Korean leader as a political embarrassment, Washington refrained from interfering with his increasingly repressive domestic policies for fear of undermining the South Korean state and inviting another North Korean attack. From an insignificant, unknown country excluded from the U.S. defense perimeter in Asia, South Korea had become the preeminent symbol of America's military reengagement in the Far East.

The American security pledge to South Korea was followed by a succession of military agreements with island nations in the western Pacific that were designed to protect them from Communist aggression. On August 30, 1951, a treaty with the Philippines (which had obtained its independence from the United States in 1946) reaffirmed the U.S. air and naval base rights in that country that had been granted in March 1947 and committed the United States to its defense. On September 1, 1951, Washington concluded a tripartite security agreement with Australia and New Zealand known as the ANZUS Pact, thereby replacing Great Britain as the protector of those two transplanted European societies in the South Pacific. As will be seen, the Korean War also led the United States to provide military aid and offer protection to the Nationalist Chinese government on Taiwan against the threat of invasion from the mainland (see page 209).

## From Hiroshima to Japan, Inc.: The Asian Model for Economic Growth

The most important participant in the American-sponsored East Asian security system that began to emerge in the early stages of the Korean War was the country whose military aggression had brought the United States into the Far Eastern war a decade earlier. When General Douglas MacArthur assumed the title of Supreme Commander of Allied Powers (SCAP) in Japan, the Truman administration was preoccupied with affairs in Europe. He therefore received only a vague set of directives concerning the treatment of America's recently defeated enemy in Asia. The imperious American proconsul was given virtual carte blanche not only to manage the military occupation but also to shape the political and economic future of the country. In contrast to the situation in defeated Germany, the American conquerors had permitted a democratically elected Japanese government to operate alongside the military occupation from the very beginning of the postwar period. But there was no doubt about who possessed the exclusive power to render decisions that would determine the fate of the country.

On October 11, 1945, MacArthur publicly elaborated a list of general principles to guide him as he pursued his preeminent objective, which was to eradicate the last vestiges of the old imperial traditions from Japanese society and to lay the basis of an entirely new political, social, and economic order. These included the emancipation of women, the protection of labor's right to organize and bargain with management for higher wages and improved working conditions, the breakup of the old zaibatsu industrial conglomerates that had promoted and profited from the seizure of the markets and resources of the "Co-Prosperity Sphere" in East Asia, the purging of public officials and business leaders who had cooperated with military leaders in planning and waging the recent war, and the establishment of a Western-style system of representative government. The American plan also called for the imposition of restrictions on Japan's economic recovery and the supervision of reparation payments to those countries in Asia that had suffered the consequences of Japanese aggression. These abstract goals would be converted into practical policies by the roughly fifteen hundred American military and civilian members of the American occupation regime. The only compromise with the old order in Japan was the U.S. government's decision to retain the emperor. Fearing an outbreak of social and political unrest in response to the humiliation of the occupation, MacArthur appreciated Hirohito's value as a source of national cohesion. Shorn of all but ceremonial power and forced to forfeit his claim to divinity, the very man whom U.S. propaganda had reviled as the incarnation of evil during the war became a useful instrument for the preservation of social order during the American occupation of Japan.

The postwar Japanese political elite attempted to draft a new constitution that would have retained many of the familiar features of the imperial system enshrined in Meiji constitution of 1890, which was based on the Imperial German model. But MacArthur preempted this bid to preserve the old order and took matters into his own hands. Citing provisions of the Potsdam declaration demanding the elimination of the sources of Japanese aggression, the supreme commander resolved to impose on the occupied country a new constitution based on Anglo-American principles of liberal democracy. In February 1946 he secretly instructed his staff to prepare a text based on three broad principles: preservation of the emperor as constitutional monarch, disarmament and the repudiation of war, and the abolition of the feudal system. A committee of twenty-four SCAP officials set up shop in a Tokyo office building with instructions to produce a draft constitution within a week. Six days later, on February 10, the finished product landed on MacArthur's desk. After making only one minor change he approved his staff's handiwork for presentation to the Japanese government, which had been completely unaware of the weeklong "constitutional convention." Forcing the surprised Tokyo officials to abandon their hopes of retaining the old system, SCAP unveiled the new constitution on March 6, 1946.

After almost a year of discussion and debate within Japan, the new constitution entered into effect on May 3, 1947. It established a parliamentary system on the British model; outlawed discrimination based on religion, race, or sex;* recognized organized labor's right to collective bargaining; guaranteed civil liberties; and formally renounced war and the means of waging it. The socioeconomic reforms decreed by the Japanese constitution, reinforced by statutes subsequently enacted by parliament, were breathtaking in their scope. The government purchased every parcel of land larger than ten acres and resold it on credit to tenant farmers on very favorable terms. Compulsory primary education was extended from six to nine years. Eighty-three of the largest zaibatsu industrial cartels were earmarked for dissolution, while stringent new antitrust laws were enacted to prevent the revival of these discredited relics of the imperial past. A sustained campaign was undertaken to purge

---

*The provision affirming "the essential equality of the sexes," inserted by a twenty-two-year-old woman member of the drafting team named Beate Sirota, went far beyond the U.S. constitution (which includes no provision for equal rights based on gender).

Japan of those responsible for the country's aggression before and during the war: Some two hundred thousand officials who had served the old regime were dismissed. High-ranking military and political leaders were tried at a war crimes tribunal that convened in Tokyo on May 3, 1946, and met for thirty-one months. Sixteen were sentenced to life imprisonment, one was sentenced to twenty years, and seven were executed in January 1948.*

By the autumn of 1948 the emerging Soviet-American confrontation in Europe prompted the Truman administration to reevaluate its severe occupation policy in Japan. U.S. officials began to worry that a disarmed, destitute Japan would present a tempting target for Soviet meddling after the departure of American occupation forces. These Cold War anxieties inspired a high-level decision in Washington to promote the economic recovery of America's erstwhile enemy in Asia. In October the White House instructed MacArthur to draw up a set of sweeping new policies that contradicted many of his earlier reforms. These included the end of requisitions of capital equipment for reparation payments, which removed a potentially damaging claim on Japanese production that might well have discouraged domestic savings, investment, and entrepreneurial activity; the removal of restrictions on Japanese industrial production and the encouragement of exports; the imposition of wage controls; and sharp reductions in government spending to achieve a balanced budget.

After his election in November 1948, Truman dispatched to Tokyo a banker named Joseph Dodge with instructions to supervise this radical reorientation of U.S. occupation policy. Dodge abruptly terminated SCAP's project for the compulsory decentralization of Japanese industry, which had succeeded in dismantling only eleven of the eighty-three zaibatsu cartels on MacArthur's "hit list." Within a few years several of the old conglomerates (such as Mitsubishi, Mitsui, and Sumitomo) had been reconstituted, and new ones (such as Hitachi, Toshiba, Toyota, and Nissan) were formed on the zaibatsu model. New legislation curtailed the rights of organized labor and encouraged savings and investment. The repeal of MacArthur's earlier restrictions on Japan's industrial recovery represented such a drastic departure from previous policy that it came to be known as the "reverse course." It reflected the Truman administration's determination to fortify Japan against the threat of Communism in Asia, a concern reinforced by the establishment of the People's Republic of China in 1949.

The Korean War also demonstrated the strategic importance of Japan to the United States. Concerned that the island nation might be tempted to develop trade links and eventually political ties with Communist China, Washington worked hard to integrate the recently defeated enemy into the U.S.-dominated economic and security system in East Asia. But Japan could hardly be expected to serve as a partner of the United States in its struggle against Moscow and Beijing while American troops still occupied the country. So the Truman administration pressed for the conclusion of a peace settlement with Japan that would terminate its status as an occupied enemy, restore it to full political sovereignty, and preserve the right of the

---

*Five of the convicted war criminals died in prison; the rest were either paroled or granted clemency before serving out their terms.

United States to maintain military bases there. To negotiate such an agreement Truman enlisted the services of the Republican attorney and foreign policy specialist John Foster Dulles. In early 1951 Dulles and Japanese Prime Minister Yoshida Shigeru prepared a draft document that was presented to the fourteen cobelligerent powers (including the Soviet Union) on March 29. On September 8, 1951, delegates of the United States and forty-eight other nations signed a peace treaty with Japan in San Francisco. The Soviet delegation boycotted the final session of the conference and refused to sign the treaty, which it had played no role in drafting.

On the same day that the Japanese peace treaty was signed, Washington and Tokyo concluded a bilateral security pact that authorized the indefinite retention of U.S. military forces in Japan and the maintenance of a major base under direct American administration on the Japanese island of Okinawa in the Ryukyu chain. Since two rival governments claimed to represent China, neither was invited to the San Francisco conference. The peace treaty left to Japan the choice of which China it would deal with, but Dulles made it unmistakably clear to Yoshida that Washington would not look favorably on Japan's recognition of the People's Republic. Unwilling to displease its new ally, Tokyo signed a peace treaty with Chiang Kai-shek's government on April 28, 1952. By that time America's former enemy Japan, like its former enemy in Europe, had become an indispensable asset in the campaign to contain Communism across the globe.

The constitutional requirement of Japanese disarmament became an early casualty of the expansion of the Cold War to the Far East. As U.S. occupation forces in Japan were being rushed to Korea in the summer of 1950, the Truman administration responded favorably to Tokyo's request for authorization to create a seventy-five-thousand-member National Police Reserve to maintain internal order in the absence of the GIs. The Japanese peace treaty of 1951 contained a provision that explicitly authorized rearmament with certain restrictions. A rudimentary Japanese navy was created in August 1952 to ensure coastal defense. In February 1954 the existing ground and naval forces were expanded and a small air force was brought into being. All of these units were designated as "self-defense" forces in deference to the constitutional renunciation of war and the means of waging it. But whatever their euphemistic designation, they formed the nucleus of Japan's rearmament as it became a valuable ally of the United States in the Asian theater of the Cold War.

The Japanese-American security treaty of 1951 granted the United States the right to maintain military forces on Japanese territory, but it did not include an explicit American commitment to defend the country. When the treaty came up for renewal in 1960, its revised version included such a pledge, but it also obligated Japan to cooperate with the United States if the security of East Asia were threatened. Leftist groups in Japan vociferously opposed the latter provision on the grounds that it would subordinate Japanese military power to America's aggressive policies in Asia. The opposition to the renewal of the security treaty turned so violent that it led to the cancellation of the proposed visit of President Eisenhower to Tokyo in June 1960 and caused the premature resignation of the prime minister who had signed it. But the pro-American Liberal Democratic Party won the national elections later in the year and preserved the privileged bilateral security relationship with the United States. The Japanese-American security treaty was again renewed in 1970, despite vigorous domestic opposition and public protests, this time in reaction to the American invasion of Cambodia (see page 236). These periodic expressions of opposition to the security treaty reflected widespread resentment in Japan against that country's military dependence on the United States and the irritating presence of U.S. military personnel in Japan and especially on the island of Okinawa. But in fact Japan derived a substantial economic benefit from the American security guarantee: It enabled Tokyo to allocate less than 1 percent of its gross domestic product to defense, freeing up funds to finance economic modernization and promote foreign trade.

When the U.S. occupation of Japan began in the summer of 1945, the country lay in ruins. Its major cities had been leveled by either conventional or (in the case of Hiroshima and Nagasaki) atomic bombardment. Its internal transportation network was in shambles. It lost the vast colonial empire that it had acquired over the past fifty years, which had provided the resource-poor country with the raw materials, energy supplies, and food that it required. The provision of almost $2 billion of American aid—mostly in the form of food and raw materials, which were in dangerously short supply—rescued Japanese society from the immediate consequences of its wartime devastation. Capital investment and technology transfers from the United States enabled Japanese industry to replace its war-damaged or obsolete equipment with modern machinery. By the end of 1949 Japan had already attained its prewar level of productivity, owing in large part to the benevolent economic policy pursued by the U.S. occupation authorities. Then the outbreak of the Korean War in the summer of 1950 accelerated the transformation of the Japanese-American relationship from an adversarial to a cooperative one. Because of its strategic location opposite the Korean peninsula, Japan was ideally situated to provide the supplies and equipment required by the UN military forces in their conflict with the North Korean and Chinese armies. The expansion of Japanese production of war-related materials during the Korean War set in motion what would later be called "the Japanese miracle," which would propel the former defeated power to the highest standard of living in Asia by the end of the 1950s.

It would be inaccurate to attribute Japan's stunning postwar economic recovery solely, or even primarily, to external forces such as the provision of U.S. aid or the demand for Japanese goods stimulated by the Korean War. Major credit for that growth belongs to the active, interventionist role assumed by the state in the promotion of industrial production and foreign trade. The Japanese government, acting through bureaucratic agencies spearheaded by the powerful Ministry for International Trade and Industry (MITI), skillfully employed monetary incentives such as subsidized interest rates on loans and preferential tax treatment to encourage the diversion of the country's productive factors—labor, capital, and raw materials—to firms producing for export. The state also encouraged the high level of concentration that characterized Japanese industry in general and the export sector in particular. The goals of achieving economies of scale, avoiding duplication, and discouraging destructive competition resulted in the establishment of ten gigantic foreign trade cartels that collectively accounted for more than half of Japan's total exports. That strategy of export-oriented growth reflected Japan's shrunken geopolitical status in the postwar world: Deprived of its colonial empire and the economic resources it had supplied to Japanese industry, the small island-nation was obliged to ship finished manufactured goods to foreign markets in order to pay for the imports of food, fuel, and raw materials that were unavailable at home. The results of this export drive were extraordinary: Japanese exports, which were negligible in 1949, would rise to 3.2 percent of total world exports in 1961 and 10 percent of the total by 1986.

Japan's foreign trade boom depended on two advantageous characteristics of the postwar international economic order. The first was the relatively unimpeded access to foreign markets that had been facilitated by the periodic tariff reductions negotiated under the auspices of GATT (see page 25). By targeting a handful of potentially lucrative markets and flooding them with manufactured goods priced slightly above or, in some cases, even at the cost of production, Japan succeeded in underselling foreign competitors in their own domains. As a consequence, the United States would become Japan's major foreign customer, taking more than a third of its exports by the mid-1980s, while Europe occupied a distant second place. By that period an astonishing 22 percent of all U.S. imports came from the small island-nation across the Pacific. The second key to Japan's export growth was the assured availability of relatively inexpensive raw materials, food, and, above all, energy. From the end of World War II through the early 1970s, commodity and energy prices remained at bargain levels relative to the prices of finished manufactured products. This disparity represented an extremely important advantage to Japan, which was deeply dependent on foreign sources of minerals, agricultural products, and fuel.

The aforementioned internal and international trends are insufficient in themselves to account for Japan's phenomenal postwar recovery. What had also been required was a strategy for exploiting the advantages and compensating for the disadvantages of the country's particular economic situation. In retrospect, it is difficult to recall a country with greater economic disabilities than Japan confronted in the years after World War II: insufficient arable land, raw materials, and energy; a severe shortage of investment capital due to heavy expenditures during the war and an epidemic of inflation after it; and the curse of overpopulation, aggravated by the return of six million soldiers and settlers from China, Korea, and the islands that had been conquered and colonized in the years of imperial expansion.

But what might seem at first glance to be a severe handicap—a population too large for the available land, food, and fuel—in fact resulted in a hidden advantage: a large, compliant labor force willing to work longer hours at lower wages than their counterparts in the Western industrialized world. Japanese employers, therefore, had the edge on competitors in the United States and Europe, whose higher labor costs led to higher prices for the finished product. In short, Japan compensated for its comparative disadvantage of insufficient natural resources and investment capital by successfully exploiting its comparative advantage of low labor costs to produce labor-intensive manufactured goods (mainly in the textile industry), which it exported at competitive prices to high-wage foreign markets.

By the late 1950s, as the profits from foreign sales of its labor-intensive manufactured products accumulated, the second, or capital-intensive, phase of Japan's postwar economic development began. The Japanese citizens' renowned ethic of austerity and frugality, which emphasized production over consumption and deferred over instant gratification, had resulted in one of the highest savings rates in the world. The country's comparative advantage no longer lay in low labor costs—as we shall see, other East Asian nations were beginning to produce labor-intensive goods at lower prices than Japan as its workers began to demand higher wages—but rather in its growing reserves of capital that was available for productive investment. The Japanese government shrewdly responded to this evolution in the country's comparative advantage by shifting resources from the labor-intensive to the capital-intensive sector of the economy. Accordingly, Japanese textile exports were replaced by iron and steel products, ships, petrochemicals, television sets, transistor radios, motorcycles, and, eventually, automobiles, of which Japan became the world's leading producer in the year 1980.

By the decade of the 1970s, another shift in Japan's comparative advantage prompted a further change in the structure of its export trade: Having produced an ample supply of well-educated, highly skilled technicians, scientists, and engineers, Japan began to redirect its economic resources from the capital-intensive to the technology-intensive sector. At first the country had concentrated on importing foreign technology and adapting it to its particular requirements, but soon it began to promote domestic research and development that would generate homegrown production techniques and technologies. As a result, the label "made in Japan," once associated with cheap manufactured goods of dubious quality, came to designate state-of-the-art products of highly sophisticated design. World markets were soon being flooded with technology-intensive products from Japan such as telecommunications equipment, office machines, electrical machinery, computers, and precision instruments. By the early 1980s, this small, resource-poor, overpopulated island off the coast of China had overtaken its gigantic neighbor, the Soviet Union, to become the second economic power of the world.

As we have seen, Japan's export-driven industrial growth depended to a large extent on the availability of cheap energy supplies and raw materials from abroad as well as the guaranteed entrée to foreign markets for manufactured products that had been fostered by the postwar international trading system. In the course of the seventies, both of these advantageous conditions were endangered, with serious consequences for Japan. The sharp increase in world oil prices and the prospect of petroleum producer cartels, embargoes, and supply disruptions represented a grave menace to a country that possessed no oil reserves of its own. Equally as ominous was the mounting threat of protectionism in the industrial world: Japan's enormous annual trade surplus with the European Community (EC), which ballooned from $506 million in 1970 to $12.2 billion in 1975 to $22.5 billion in 1986, generated angry allegations of "dumping" and pleas for protection in many European countries. By the early 1980s the EC was erecting selective barriers against Japanese imports while some member-states, such as France, were harassing Japanese firms with cumbersome customs procedures. In the meantime, American manufacturers of automobiles, television sets, video equipment, and other products that were increasingly undersold by their Japanese competitors pressured Washington into insisting that Tokyo agree to "voluntary export restraints." The combined result of the oil price increases and the emergence of protectionism in the developed world was a precipitous drop in Japan's growth rate, from an average of about 10 percent (from the mid-1950s to the mid-1970s) to 5 to 6 percent for the rest of the 1970s and 3 to 4 percent in the early 1980s.

2

06                *A World of Nations*

In the face of escalating costs of energy imports from the Middle East and protectionist threats to its export trade from the United States and Europe, Japan initiated a compensatory strategy of intensifying its economic links with the developing countries within its own region. Tokyo began to target East Asian countries for massive development assistance as part of a deliberate policy to promote regional economic cooperation. Private Japanese firms followed the government's lead by making substantial direct investments in mining and petroleum facilities in Southeast Asian countries for the purpose of securing reliable supplies of inexpensive raw materials and fossil fuels, while at the same time developing new markets for Japanese manufactured products as a hedge against American and European protectionism. Meanwhile, Japanese companies that had abandoned labor-intensive production at home invested their retained earnings in light manufacturing concerns operating in low-wage East Asian countries in order to export low-priced goods to markets in the developed world.

The other nations of the region derived reciprocal benefits from Japan's financial and commercial expansion along the western rim of the Pacific: They received desperately needed capital to finance their own industrial development and obtained access to the Japanese market for their exports. By the 1980s Japan had dispelled the residual feelings of distrust in its neighbors and had become not only their premier trading partner but also a model for economic development that many of them had begun to emulate. After decades of third-class status in the international economic order dominated by the Western industrial powers, the countries of East Asia had decided to "look East" and follow the example of the only non-Western country that had reached the pinnacle of economic development. So well did they learn that lesson, and so successfully did they apply it to their own particular circumstances, that they became major trading powers in their own right by the 1980s.

The earliest Asian imitators of the Japanese example—South Korea, Taiwan, Singapore, and Hong Kong—were so effective in their bid for rapid economic development that they quickly earned the sobriquet "Asian Tigers." In common with the Japanese prototype, all four countries shared a set of characteristics—or what economists call "factor endowment"—that would scarcely seem conducive to economic growth: Like most other developing nations, they suffered from overpopulation and a shortage of investment capital, but unlike many Third World societies they also lacked natural resources such as minerals, fossil fuels, and arable land. These four Asian Tigers converted such apparent disadvantages into advantages as they followed the path of export-driven industrialization that Japan had blazed a generation earlier. The shortage of mineral wealth, energy supplies, and fertile agricultural land—which precluded options such as mining and farming, that were available to other developing countries—provided a strong incentive to export finished manufactured products to pay for essential imports of raw materials, fuel, and food. The common cultural heritage based on Confucianism that these four countries shared—which emphasized the virtues of frugality, industry, self-discipline, and hierarchy—was ideally suited to the type of production in which they specialized. They relied on a docile workforce willing to toil long hours at tedious, low-paying tasks, such as fabricating ready-to-wear garments or assembling discrete components of intricate machines.

The four Asian Tigers enjoyed the latecomer's advantage in their relationship with Japan: Once Japan had launched a new product and created a new market for it, South Korea, Taiwan, Hong Kong, and Singapore would move in and undercut the Japanese with their cheaper version of the original item. The Tigers launched their earliest export drives in the 1960s with low-cost textiles just as Japan was abandoning the production of such labor-intensive products. In the following decade, as the profits generated by low labor costs enabled them (again, like Japan) to attract foreign capital to supplement domestic savings, they purchased more sophisticated machinery and equipment in a successful adaptation to the shift in comparative advantage from labor-intensive to capital-intensive production. Their export trade advanced up the product scale to radios, televisions, sewing machines, and motorcycles as Japan moved into high-technology products. By the 1980s, the advanced educational systems and technical training programs of the Four Tigers had begun to produce such a highly skilled, experienced workforce that some of them even began to compete with Japan in technology-intensive industries such as computers and biotechnology.

Amid the numerous similarities among the four East Asian Tigers, one notable difference between them was the role of the state in promoting economic development. At one extreme South Korea developed a brand of "state capitalism" in which the government actively intervened in the economy by providing tax incentives and subsidies to encourage production in certain sectors, by protecting favored firms while allowing others to decline, and by maintaining government ownership of some basic industries. The ruling elites of Taiwan and Singapore, although less committed to the principle of state control of the economy, also stressed central planning and used public funds to promote private economic development in selected sectors. At the other end of the spectrum was Hong Kong, a haven of unfettered laissez-faire capitalism with low taxes, minimal government spending, and private ownership of business. But despite such differences in emphasis, all four countries displayed a preference for letting the invisible hand of world market forces rather than the heavy hand of government planning dictate the allocation of resources within their economies.

The extent of the East Asian economic achievement is revealed in one remarkable statistic: With a combined population of only 3 percent of the total population of the developing world, the Four Tigers accounted for over half of its total manufactured exports by 1976. In the first decade after World War II, the United States and Great Britain had been obliged to supply economic aid to the resource- and food-poor countries of South Korea and Taiwan, and Singapore and Hong Kong, respectively. By the mid-1980s, the Western world found it difficult to sell manufactured goods to East Asia and faced stiff competition from East Asian manufactured exports in other markets. Canada, Australia, and the United States had settled into a paradoxical kind of neocolonial relationship with the region, importing its manufactured products in exchange for food and raw materials while running up huge annual trade deficits with it.

As had been the case with Japan's earlier experience, the crash program of industrialization undertaken by the four Asian Tigers depended on a number of conditions in the international system: In the security sphere, they had all benefited in varying degrees from U.S. military protection, with South Korea and Taiwan owing their very national existence to the projection of U.S. military and naval power across the Pacific. In the financial realm, all four had received massive infusions of Western capital, originally in the form of U.S. or British government aid, then through commercial loans from American and European banks or direct investments from Western-controlled multinational corporations. But the most significant form of these four countries' dependence on extrinsic economic forces was to be found in the sphere of international trade: Two-thirds of their manufactured exports went to the countries of the industrialized world, primarily to the United States and the members of the EC.

This dependence on the Western-dominated international economic system developed into a potentially serious liability in the early 1980s as a result of three trends that threatened the continuation of East Asia's economic growth. The first was the international debt crisis, with its flurry of defaults and reschedulings, which reduced the amount of capital available for foreign lending while inspiring caution in the foreign loan departments of Western banks. The second was the severe recession in the industrialized world that caused a reduction in demand for East Asian exports. The third was the upsurge in protectionist sentiment in the United States and the EC, already noted in connection with its potentially hazardous effect on Japan's foreign trade. These three trends confirmed what had first been brought to light during the oil shocks of the 1970s—that the booming East Asian economies suffered from a disadvantage typical of the developing world that international economists call an "extraregional bias": The economic performance of each Asian country depended much more heavily on developments outside the region than on those within it, leaving it vulnerable to trade disruptions and monetary instability caused by distant forces beyond its control. This preference for trade and financial ties with the developed world precluded the formation of an intraregional economic bloc (such as the EC) as a buffer against adverse trends in the international economic order.

One of the principal obstacles to the forging of such intraregional economic links was the intense commercial rivalry that had developed among the four Asian Tigers and between each of them and Japan. Since these five industrial dynamos of Asia possessed essentially the same factor endowment, produced the same products, and exported to the same markets, competition rather than mutually profitable exchange characterized their economic relations with one another. But the threat of interruptions in the deliveries of raw materials and energy, followed by the erection of protectionist barriers in the industrialized world, had obliged Japan and the Four Tigers to look for markets and natural resources closer to home. What they found was the prospect for intensive regional economic cooperation with the organization known as the Association of Southeast Asian Nations (ASEAN). Formed in August 1967 by the states of Indonesia, Malaysia, Thailand, and the Philippines—and later joined by Brunei after its independence from Britain—ASEAN comprised economies that admirably complemented those of Japan and the Four Tigers: Deficient in investment capital and industrially undeveloped, they were richly endowed with many of the natural resources (such as petroleum, natural gas, wood, and foodstuffs) that Japan and the Four Tigers lacked.

Responding to this golden opportunity, Japan, South Korea, and Taiwan began to export finished manufactured goods and technology to these ASEAN countries in exchange for raw materials and fuel while investing heavily in the oil, mining, forest, and agricultural sectors of their economies. The result of this exchange of capital, manufactured products, and raw materials was the emergence of an economic sub-system in Asia that in some respects resembled the neocolonial nexus between the United States and Latin America or between the EC and Africa. Or, as some ob-servers recognized, it represented a benevolent version of the old imperial Japanese dream of the Greater East Asia Co-Prosperity Sphere, based on reciprocal economic interchange rather than unilateral military domination.

By the end of the 1970s, the countries of ASEAN had grown dissatisfied with the role of commodity-producing junior partners of the dynamic industrialized Asian economies to the north. They opted instead for the low-skilled, low-cost, labor-intensive, export-oriented strategy of industrialization that had previously en-riched Japan and then the Four Tigers. Many ASEAN countries were soon recording annual growth rates of between 6 and 8 percent in a period when most developing countries were mired in recession and foreign indebtedness. They began to make sig-nificant inroads in markets for low-cost manufactures in the industrialized world by edging out the Four Tigers with cheaply made, inexpensive textile products. Once again, the law of comparative advantage operated with predictable regularity on the Asian stage as the ASEAN countries made a determined bid for rapid industrializa-tion to escape their long history of economic backwardness and dependence.

## The United States and the "Two Chinas"

During the Korean War, as we have seen, the United States abandoned its even-handed policy toward the "two Chinas" by resuming the deliveries of economic and military assistance to the Nationalist government on Taiwan that had been discontin-ued toward the end of the Chinese Civil War. Throughout the 1950s American aid to Taiwan averaged $250 million per year. In early 1953 President Eisenhower an-nounced that the U.S. seventh fleet, which continued to patrol the Taiwan Strait, would no longer interfere with Chiang's efforts to "liberate" the mainland. In time Nationalist planes conducted raids against the Chinese coast and commandos mounted forays to the mainland. On December 2, 1954, the United States concluded a mutual defense treaty with Taiwan (which continued to be recognized by most non-Communist countries as the Republic of China [ROC] and retained the Chinese seat in the United Nations). Unlike its behavior during the Chinese Civil War, the Nation-alist government on Taiwan put the U.S. military and financial aid to good use. Pro-tected by American naval power and the 1954 security pledge, the ROC developed an impressive defense capability and, as we have seen, became a major economic power in the world by the 1960s (see page 206). But Taiwan's military security and economic development were continually threatened by the sword of Damocles wielded by Beijing, which continually reasserted its claim to the island. Because of its 1954 security commitment to the ROC, the United States was directly implicated in this bitter quarrel across the Taiwan Strait.

The first in a long series of confrontations between the "two Chinas" concerned three small island groups off the Chinese coast that had been occupied by the Nationalist forces as they retreated to Taiwan: Quemoy (Jinmen), opposite the port city of Xiamen (Amoy); Matsu (Mazu), opposite Fuzhou (Foochow); and the Tachen

Islands to the north. Intent on seizing these Nationalist outposts, units of the PLA assembled on the coast opposite Quemoy and on September 3, 1954, opened an artillery barrage against the large Nationalist garrison there. In January 1955 mainland Chinese commandos overran one of the Tachen Islands, demonstrating that this island chain was too far from Taiwan to be given air cover by Nationalist planes. Anxious about the prospect of a military showdown with the mainland, President Eisenhower persuaded Chiang Kai-shek to abandon the militarily indefensible Tachens in exchange for a secret pledge that U.S. forces would intervene in response to a Communist assault on Quemoy or Matsu. Secretary of State Dulles privately warned Beijing through third parties that Washington would not rule out the use of nuclear weapons if the two islands were attacked, while the chairman of the Joint Chiefs of Staff, Admiral Arthur Radford, publicly discussed the possibility of a nuclear confrontation over these obscure Nationalist Chinese outposts in the Taiwan Strait.

In the spring of 1955 Eisenhower sent a top secret mission to Taipei offering to institute a naval blockade of the Chinese coast opposite Taiwan if the ROC would abandon Quemoy and Matsu. Chiang indignantly refused, declaring that his decision to abandon the Tachens was the last time he would surrender Nationalist-held territory to Communist rule. While Washington was secretly urging Taipei to compromise in the interests of averting a conflict in the Taiwan Strait, Moscow was applying behind-the-scenes pressure on Beijing for the same purpose. When the Soviet government informed Mao that it was unwilling to risk a nuclear war with the United States over mainland China's bid to dislodge the Nationalists from the two offshore islands, the Communist Chinese leader was forced to back down. In April 1955 Chinese Foreign Minister Zhou Enlai offered to negotiate the dispute in the Taiwan Strait, declaring for the first time that China would pursue by peaceful means the recovery of Taiwan and the small offshore islands its troops occupied.

After three years of relative calm, the volatile situation in the Taiwan Strait was reignited in the late summer of 1958. On August 23 the Chinese Communists renewed their heavy shelling of Quemoy, attempted to blockade the island, and broadcast provocative warnings of an imminent invasion. As in the earlier offshore island crisis in 1955, the United States publicly announced its full support for Chiang Kai-shek. This time the dispute assumed more ominous overtones, however, because Eisenhower had concluded an agreement with Chiang in May 1957 to supply Taiwan with Matador missiles armed with nuclear warheads that were capable of reaching the Chinese mainland. Although these nuclear weapons were never brought into play, the Nationalist forces relied on American Sidewinder missiles armed with conventional warheads to achieve control of the airspace in the Taiwan Strait. To break the Communist blockade Eisenhower ordered ships from the seventh fleet to convoy Nationalist merchant vessels supplying the beleaguered island. At the height of the second Quemoy crisis in 1958, Beijing was displeased to note the absence of support from Moscow. As in the offshore island crisis three years earlier, the Soviet leadership reiterated the warning that it was not prepared to risk a nuclear confrontation with the United States on China's behalf. Faced with Washington's display of force and Moscow's counsels of restraint, Mao was again obliged to beat a hasty retreat. China suspended the shelling of Quemoy in October and agreed to open discussions with U.S. representatives in Warsaw to seek a peaceful resolution of the dispute.

Washington publicly hailed this latest triumph against what it viewed as a coordinated campaign of Communist intimidation of strategically vulnerable outposts of the "free world": Just as the Soviets had failed to dislodge the Western allies from Berlin, the Chinese Communists had failed to evict America's Nationalist Chinese allies from Quemoy. Privately, however, Eisenhower was developing second thoughts about his government's open-ended endorsement of Nationalist China's foreign policy goals, just as Khrushchev was busy watering down the Soviet Union's security pledge to the PRC. Dulles flew to Taipei and urged Chiang Kai-shek to recognize the fait accompli of Mao's victory in the civil war. Bowing to this pressure from his patrons and protectors in Washington, Chiang publicly renounced the use of force to regain power on the mainland on October 23, 1958. This declaration by the Nationalist Chinese regime, together with the suspension of the PRC's shelling of the coastal islands, brought about a notable reduction of tension across the Taiwan Strait by the end of the fifties. But the settlement of the offshore islands dispute did not lead to an improvement of relations between the PRC and the United States. Washington continued to withhold diplomatic recognition; to prohibit its citizens from trading with, investing in, or traveling to China; and to block Beijing's annual application for admission to the United Nations.

## The Disintegration of the Sino-Soviet Alliance

After the victory of his Communist forces in the Chinese Civil War, Mao's decision to throw in his lot with the Soviet Union was made under the tyranny of necessity: No other power in the world was prepared to assist the new regime in Beijing as it sought to rebuild China's devastated socioeconomic system. No other power was willing to offer support against the new state's adversaries in Taipei and Washington. True, the economic aid that Stalin proffered to Mao was less than had been desired. True, Soviet military support for the fledgling Chinese Communist regime during the Korean War and the crises in the Taiwan Strait fell short of expectations. But Beijing had nowhere else to turn for the assistance that it required in the regime's formative years. This dependence on and alignment with the Soviet Union continued after Stalin's death and the end of the Korean War in 1953. In September of that year the post-Stalinist leadership signed an agreement for the provision of Soviet economic assistance and technical advisers to China to promote that country's modernization. Moscow loyally lead the annual campaign in the United Nations Security Council to transfer the Chinese seat from the Nationalist government on Taiwan to the Communist regime on the mainland. In short, Beijing's subservience to Moscow seemed so pronounced that American policymakers during the Eisenhower years, led by Secretary of State John Foster Dulles, continued to view mainland China as nothing more than what a high-level Truman administration official had labeled it in 1951: a "Slavic Manchukuo."*

---

*The author of the remark was Assistant Secretary of State (and future Secretary of State) Dean Rusk. Manchukuo was the vassal state established by the Japanese in Manchuria after occupying the Chinese province in 1931.

But the strong relationship between the two Communist powers gradually deteriorated during the second half of the 1950s, for a number of reasons. First, The Chinese government began to express dissatisfaction with the cavalier treatment it was receiving from its Russian benefactors. China's disappointment with the amount of Soviet economic assistance, a sentiment dating from the Stalin years, evolved into deep resentment when Khruschev's campaign to win support among the nonaligned countries of the Third World led him to provide more aid to non-Communist countries such as Egypt and India than to Moscow's loyal Communist ally in Beijing. By the end of the 1950s Mao seemed to have lost all confidence in the USSR as China's foreign economic benefactor and reached the conclusion that the Soviet model was inappropriate for China's long-term development needs. He embarked on a massive program to forge Chinese economic self-sufficiency that was hailed as the Great Leap Forward. Although it proved a disaster and was abandoned after a few years, the Great Leap definitely severed the already tenuous economic ties between the two giants of the Communist world.

The salient issue of nuclear weapons also played a significant role in disrupting the cooperative relationship between China and the Soviet Union. Since the mid-1950s Khrushchev had continually decried the dangers of a nuclear holocaust and repudiated the doctrine of the inevitability of war between the Communist and capitalist blocs. By contrast Mao seemed willing to accept the risk of nuclear war and endure its terrible consequences in pursuit of a Communist victory against the "imperialist powers" in the West. He boasted that China's enormous population would leave enough survivors to rebuild the country after a full-scale nuclear exchange that had wiped the enemy off the face of the earth. When the Russians warned that they would not employ their nuclear weapons to deter an American nuclear strike against the mainland during the Chinese shelling of Quemoy in September 1954, Mao recognized the extent of his country's dependence on the USSR for its security and resolved to remedy the situation. On January 15, 1955, he ordered a crash program to develop for his country an independent Chinese nuclear force.

In light of the primitive character of Chinese expertise in nuclear physics, however, Mao was obliged to turn to the Soviet Union for the technical knowledge that would be required to construct a nuclear weapons system. On October 15, 1957, Khrushchev reluctantly agreed to provide a limited amount of technical assistance to the embryonic Chinese atomic program. The Soviet leader also promised to deliver a prototype of an atomic bomb to assist the Chinese scientists in their nuclear research, but only on the condition that Moscow retain exclusive control of the warheads on any weapons produced. As Soviet technicians prepared the sample bomb for delivery, Mao reiterated his blood-curdling observations about China's ability to survive a nuclear war and then resumed the shelling of Quemoy and Matsu in August 1958 without a word of warning to the Kremlin (see page 210). The Chinese leader later informed the startled Soviet foreign minister Andrei Gromyko that he had considered using the offshore islands dispute to lure the United States into a war on the mainland, adding that he was counting on a massive Soviet nuclear response if the Americans resorted to atomic weapons. This belligerent Chinese behavior during and after the second Quemoy crisis in 1958 prompted Khrushchev to postpone delivery of the long-overdue prototype of an atomic bomb. In June 1959 the Soviet government finally confirmed what the Chinese had doubtless long suspected: The sample bomb would not be sent, and no further Soviet assistance to the Chinese nuclear program would be forthcoming. If Mao wanted to join the nuclear club, his country would have to do so on its own.

Amid these mounting disputes between Moscow and Beijing, the Chinese became extremely apprehensive about the prospect of a Soviet-American rapprochement based on the two superpowers' mutual interest in averting nuclear war. Such a development would leave an economically underdeveloped, militarily weak, diplomatically isolated China to fend for itself. Khrushchev's visit to the United States in 1959 fed these fears of a superpower accommodation at China's expense, as photos of the Soviet and American leaders engaged in friendly conversation dominated the world press. The Soviet leader seemed to justify these Chinese anxieties when, on what turned out to be his final visit to Beijing after his U.S. tour, Khrushchev bluntly advised Mao to avoid conflicts with the United States over Taiwan or any other issue. In the meantime, Moscow's policy toward the long-standing border dispute between China and India in the Himalayas had aggravated the growing rift between the two Communist powers (see page 257). Just before Khruschev left for his American trip in September 1959, the Kremlin enraged the Chinese by announcing Moscow's neutrality in its fraternal Communist ally's conflict with non-Communist India and then added insult to injury by announcing another huge loan to New Delhi.

The growing rift between Moscow and Beijing reached the point of no return throughout the year 1960 in a series of tit-for-tat gestures. In April of that year the Chinese government lashed out in public against its unreliable Soviet patron in a series of declarations in April 1960, accusing Moscow of betraying the Marxist-Leninist doctrine of world revolution by promoting Khruschev's timid doctrine of peaceful coexistence with the capitalist-imperialist camp. At a congress of the Romanian Communist Party the following June, the Chinese delegate repeated the charge before the assembled comrades, reaffirming the orthodox doctrine of the inevitability of war between the two camps. In August Khrushchev retaliated by withdrawing the 1,390 Russian technicians who were working on economic development projects in China. He later cut off all economic assistance to Albania, which had became the only member of the Communist bloc to side with Beijing in this public row.

For the remainder of the 1960s, the Sino-Soviet split widened, with each side exploiting conflicts across the globe to gain points in the ongoing dispute with its Communist rival. Having suspended all military assistance to China, Moscow supplied the Indian air force with advanced jet engines and then reaffirmed its neutrality during the latest Sino-Indian border conflict in the autumn of 1962. Mao castigated Khrushchev's retreat during the Cuban missile crisis in the same period as yet another example of the Soviet Union's unreliability as an ally. At the same time, clashes broke out between Soviet and Chinese forces on the border of the Chinese province of Xinjiang. As China spun out of the Soviet orbit, Mao's associates began raising territorial claims all along the country's forty-five-hundred-mile border with the Soviet Union: That country contained almost a million square miles of former Chinese territory that the Russian Empire had annexed from China's impotent Manchu dynasty in the nineteenth century. The historic rivalry between these two old neighbors appeared to develop a momentum of its own that was entirely unrelated to orthodox Communist doctrine.

Beijing actively sought to attract supporters and allies in its emerging struggle with Moscow, both within the Communist world and among revolutionary movements in the Third World. The former goal proved elusive: Leftist fringe groups in Western Europe and the United States, disillusioned with the bureaucratic sclerosis of the Soviet Union and its subservient Communist parties, raised the banner of their own idiosyncratic versions of "Maoism." Devotées of what came to be called the "New Left" in the industrial world were inspired by what they imagined to be China's purer form of revolutionary idealism. But all of the existing Communist states save Albania reaffirmed their allegiance to Moscow. Two of the Soviet satellites in Eastern Europe sought to exploit the Sino-Soviet split for their own advantage: Romania's strongman Nicolae Ceauçescu managed to conduct a relatively independent foreign policy that sometimes clashed with official Kremlin doctrine, establishing diplomatic relations with West Germany and maintaining them with Israel in 1967 while declining to permit Warsaw Pact military maneuvers on Romanian soil. In the spring of 1968 the new reform-minded government in Czechoslovakia under Alexander Dubcek launched a set of sweeping socioeconomic and political reforms that directly contradicted Soviet orthodoxy: These included assaults on the twin Communist principles of centralized control of the economy and the suppression of domestic opposition to the Communist Party.

Brezhnev was willing to tolerate Ceaucescu's apostasy in foreign policy because the Romanian autocrat maintained an iron grip on domestic affairs, brutally suppressing the slightest signs of anti-Communist activity that might spread to the other Soviet satellites in Eastern Europe. But Dubcek's relaxed policy toward political dissent threatened to undermine the dominant position of the country's Communist Party and set a dangerous precedent for other Warsaw Pact states, so the leadership in the Kremlin as well as the heads of its hard-line Warsaw Pact allies decided that his liberal Communist regime had to go. As Soviet tanks rumbled into Prague on August 20–21, 1968, to terminate Czechoslovakia's brief experiment with political and economic liberalism, the Chinese government was confronted with a dilemma: It loathed the liberal principles that inspired the reformist government in Czechoslovakia and hardly wished to endorse the kinds of socioeconomic and political reforms that had unfolded during the "Prague Spring." But Moscow's brutal suppression of the Czechoslovak experiment in the summer of 1968 sent an ominous signal to Beijing, which was also engaged in pursuing its own unorthodox brand of Communism. Mao's regime therefore joined the Western powers in roundly condemning the Soviet intervention as a violation of national sovereignty. The following November the Warsaw Pact adopted at Moscow's behest the so-called Brezhnev Doctrine, which justified the use of armed force by the Soviet Union and its allies to intervene in the internal affairs of any Communist country threatened by foreign or domestic forces deemed "hostile to Socialism." Directed at prospective dissidents in Eastern Europe who might be tempted to follow the Czechoslovak precedent, it also seemed applicable to China's evolving domestic situation as well: The so-called Cultural Revolution that Mao had instigated in 1966, although directed at the entrenched leadership of the Chinese Communist Party and the state planning bureaucracy, assumed an anti-Soviet character that greatly concerned observers in Moscow.

The Johnson administration in Washington fully appreciated the opportunities for American foreign policy offered by the widening conflict between the Soviet Union and the PRC. Ever since the early 1950s U.S. officials had been seeking ways of cracking the monolithic Communist bloc and profiting from tensions between its two most important members. But while the Sino-Soviet split reached its point of no return in the second half of the 1960s, Washington was prevented from exploiting for its own benefit the turmoil within the Communist bloc because of its all-consuming military involvement in Southeast Asia, which would take precedence over everything else.

### The Agony of Indochina: The French Phase

During the second half of the nineteenth century France acquired imperial control of a territory sandwiched between China and Siam (later renamed Thailand) on the southeast corner of the Asian mainland. It included Cambodia, Laos, and three provinces on the Pacific coast—Tonkin, Annam, and Cochin China—which would collectively come to be known as Vietnam. The French were drawn to Indochina for economic, strategic, and religious reasons: Daring entrepreneurs established plantations in the verdant jungles to harvest rubber, a precious product that would soon become an essential component of the automobile and other inventions of the industrial age; others dug mines to extract valuable industrial raw materials such as tin and tungsten. Military leaders established army garrisons and naval bases to support France's imperial ambitions in the contest among the great powers of Europe for preeminence in Asia. Catholic missionaries were drawn to the region by the prospect of bringing the word of the Christian God to peoples of other faiths who might be susceptible to conversion. In general terms, the French arrived in Indochina imbued with what they conceived of as their "civilizing mission" to provide the indigenous inhabitants they encountered with the superior political, economic, cultural, and religious practices of the metropole.

Sporadic opposition to French rule in Indochina had emerged soon after the region was formally incorporated into the French Empire. This inchoate resistance developed into an organized political force after World War I under the leadership of a charismatic Vietnamese nationalist whose family name was Nguyen Sinh Cung but who later adopted the pseudonym Ho Chi Minh. Born to an impoverished family in 1890, Ho had briefly taught elementary school before signing on as a steward for a French ocean liner in 1912 to see the world. After working in a variety of odd jobs in New York, Boston, London, and other foreign cities, he moved to Paris in 1918. Taking the name Nguyen Ai Quoc (Nguyen the Patriot), he joined a group of nationalistic Vietnamese emigrés who were agitating for an end to French domination of their country. Inspired by Woodrow Wilson's wartime rhetoric in support of national self-determination, Ho hoped that the American president could be induced to apply that principle to the Vietnamese just as it was being applied to the subject peoples in Europe such as the Poles, Czechoslovaks, and Yugoslavs. The young Vietnamese militant drew up an eight-point memorandum demanding civil liberties, legal equality, and political rights for his compatriots and submitted it to the peace conference that was meeting in Paris in 1919 to draft the treaties ending the Great War.

Once it became evident that the Wilsonian principle of national self-determination was reserved for white people only (the inhabitants of the defunct empires of Germany, Austria-Hungary, and Russia in Europe), the disillusioned Vietnamese patriot turned to an alternative vehicle for the liberation of his people. On reading the anti-imperialist writings of the Bolshevik leader Vladimir Lenin, Ho Chi Minh was converted to the Marxist-Leninist faith. After helping to found the French Communist Party in 1920, he spent the years 1923–1924 in Moscow immersing himself in the strategy and tactics of revolution. Following clandestine visits to China, Hong Kong, and Thailand during the 1920s, Ho founded the Indochinese Communist Party in 1929. He remained in exile in China throughout the 1930s, while his small band of followers in Vietnam were ruthlessly suppressed by the French colonial authorities.

The defeat of France in June 1940 electrified the Vietnamese nationalists by revealing the vulnerability of the formerly invincible colonial overlord. But a new obstacle to Vietnamese national liberation promptly appeared on the scene. In September 1940 Japanese military forces poured out of southern China into Tonkin, the northernmost province of Vietnam. By July 1941 the Japanese had advanced southward into Annam and Cochin China to occupy the remainder of the country. The French colonial administration in Indochina collaborated with the Japanese occupiers just as their superiors in France collaborated with the German occupiers there. Ho secretly returned to his homeland after almost thirty years of absence to organize the resistance to both the Japanese and the French. In May 1941 he founded the Viet Nam Doc Lap Dong Minh (the League for the Independence of Viet Nam), or Vietminh. Still known to his followers as Nguyen Ai Quoc, he changed his name one final time to Ho Chi Minh ("He Who Enlightens"). In 1943 Ho established contact with the wartime U.S. intelligence organization, the Office of Strategic Services (OSS), offering to provide information on Japanese troop movements in Vietnam and requesting arms shipments to his resistance fighters who were operating in the jungles and mountains. Although the OSS officers knew of Ho's Communist background, they valued his services in the struggle against the Japanese. The OSS airlifted five thousand guns to the Viet Minh and received reports from Ho's underground apparatus about Japanese military activities. Commanding the Vietminh's military organization from a hidden mountain cave was a brilliant strategist and tactician named Vo Nguyen Giap, a French-educated lawyer from a wealthy family whom Ho had recruited in China in 1939.

The abrupt end of the Asian war in the late summer of 1945 left a vacuum of political power in Vietnam as the Japanese military occupation came to an end. On August 25 the Viet Minh forced the abdication of Bao Dai, the emperor of Annam whom the Japanese had retained as a figurehead ruler in the ancient imperial city of Hue, as Ho Chi Minh entered the Tonkinese capital of Hanoi to supervise the replacement of Japanese officials by Viet Minh agents. A week later, as General MacArthur was receiving the Japanese surrender on the battleship *Missouri* in Tokyo Bay on September 2, Ho appeared in public in Hanoi to declare the independence of the Democratic Republic of Vietnam. U.S. military officers stood at attention beside General Giap on the Vietminh military reviewing stand while American aircraft flew overhead to celebrate the event. Ho delivered a stirring speech that included the declaration (presumably added to please his American audience) "that all men are created equal, that they are endowed by their Creator with certain inalienable rights, among these are life, liberty, and the pursuit of happiness." He then cabled an urgent appeal to Washington requesting recognition of Vietnam's independence on the basis of the neo-Wilsonian principles of national self-determination that President Roosevelt had reaffirmed in his wartime speeches.

Ho had some reason to expect a favorable response in Washington to his bid for U.S. recognition. French authority in Indochina had been completely discredited when the colonial administration there collaborated with the Japanese occupation forces. Whenever President Roosevelt addressed the issue of Indochina during the war, he vigorously opposed the reintroduction of French colonial power there after the defeat of Japan. In 1943 FDR raised with British Foreign Secretary Anthony Eden the possibility of placing Indochina under an international trusteeship to prepare it for eventual independence. When Churchill denounced the U.S. proposal as a dangerous precedent that might undermine Britain's own colonial position in Asia, the trusteeship idea disappeared from sight. But the Vietminh's wartime cooperation with the OSS in clandestine operations against the Japanese led some American foreign service officers and intelligence agents to regard Ho as a potential ally after the war. President Truman spurned France's appeals for assistance in transporting French troops to Vietnam after the Japanese surrender. With the abdication of the Vietnamese puppet emperor, the departure of the Japanese occupation forces, and the reluctance of the United States to help the French reestablish their colonial authority in Southeast Asia, the fulfillment of Ho's dream for independence of his country seemed imminent.

But the postwar power vacuum in Indochina would soon be temporarily filled by two other forces. At the Potsdam Conference in July 1945 the Allied leaders had designated the Nationalist Chinese army to receive the Japanese surrender in Vietnam north of the 16th parallel in the province of Tonkin, while British units transferred from liberated Malaya would perform the task in the southern administrative districts of Cochin China and Annam. On September 13, 1945, British General Douglas D. Gracey entered the southern city of Saigon at the head of two thousand Indian soldiers, with another eighteen thousand British and colonial troops on their way. A few weeks after his arrival, Gracey decided to supply weapons to the several thousand unarmed French troops remaining in the south so that they could protect French citizens from harassment by the Viet Minh. On September 20 the Nationalist Chinese General Lu Han led two hundred thousand troops into the northern district of Tonkin. Within a few weeks the Chinese forces were evicting the Viet Minh from their administrative offices and supporting their non-Communist rivals. When the British army finished disarming the Japanese and evacuated the two southern administrative districts in December 1945, it turned over military authority to French troops and political authority to French colonial officials who assumed their old posts in Saigon and the provincial capitals of Annam and Cochin China. The Nationalist Chinese occupation forces in the north reached an agreement with French officials in February 1946 and returned to China in October after transferring administrative control of Tonkin to the French.

Stung by the reappearance of French military and political authorities in the country whose national independence he had recently declared, Ho Chi Minh attempted to reach an accommodation with the imperial power. On March 6, 1946, he signed an agreement in Hanoi with French government representative Jean Sainteny, according to which France formally recognized the Democratic Republic of Vietnam as a sovereign state with full control over its internal affairs. With Cambodia and Laos it would form a new "Indochina Federation" as a self-governing member of the French Empire, which was later renamed the French Union to remove the old colonial connotations. Sainteny promised free elections in the southern district of Cochin China, where political opposition to the Vietminh and pro-French sentiment was the strongest, to allow its citizens to decide whether they wished to join the new state. In exchange for recognition and the prospect of national unification, Ho accepted the presence of twenty-five thousand French soldiers in Tonkin to replace the departing Nationalist Chinese troops for five years. Both agreed that Ho would lead a Viet Minh delegation to Paris to work out the details of a final settlement.

While Ho was en route to Paris in June 1946, the new French High Commissioner for Indochina abruptly preempted the elections promised by Sainteny in the south by announcing the creation of an independent Republic of Cochin China within the French Union. In negotiations conducted throughout the summer of 1946 in the Château de Fontainbleau outside Paris, Ho labored in vain to win unconditional French acceptance of Vietnamese independence. The most he could obtain was a pledge to conduct a unification referendum in Cochin China by 1947. Ho returned to Hanoi in mid-September resentful at his cavalier treatment in France and apprehensive about his country's future. During a bitter dispute between French and Viet Minh officials in Hanoi over authority to collect customs in the port of Haiphong, skirmishes broke out in the city. Alarmed at this outburst of violence, the French High Commissioner decided to show the Viet Minh who was in charge. On November 23, after a two-hour warning to evacuate Haiphong, French tanks and infantry units stormed into the city while a French cruiser in the harbor shelled its residential neighborhoods. When the smoke had cleared almost six thousand Vietnamese lay dead. On December 19, the day after French military authorities ordered General Giap to disarm his troops in Hanoi, the Vietminh retaliated for the Haiphong massacre by blowing up Hanoi's electrical power station and assassinating several French administrative officials. Ho and his entourage slipped out of the city and relocated in the jungle sixty miles to the east, where he commanded a force of about forty thousand Viet Minh guerrillas. The Franco-Viet Minh war had begun.

The two sides each pursued a military strategy that reflected its particular historical experience. Ho and Giap borrowed heavily from the doctrines of guerrilla warfare that Mao Zedong's Communist forces were currently employing with remarkable success against the KMT in China: Avoid pitched battles with the enemy at all costs and concentrate on hit and run attacks; ambush government convoys, destroy transportation and communication systems, and assassinate administrative officials; when faced with superior firepower, melt into the countryside where sympathetic peasants can provide sustenance and hiding places. The French strategy in the war against the Vietminh was based on the lessons they had learned from World War II in Europe. By the autumn of 1947, one hundred thousand French infantrymen supported by air power and heavy artillery had arrived in Vietnam. In control of the major cities in all three administrative districts, the French constructed isolated military outposts in the countryside from which seasoned troops conducted search-and-destroy missions to flush the Viet Minh out of their rural hiding places. Forced into open terrain, the guerrillas would be exposed to annihilation by the superior firepower of the French in a World War II–type conventional battle that would end the insurgency.

In a bid to compete with the Viet Minh for the loyalty of the population, the French sought to de-emphasize the colonial aspects of the conflict. On March 8, 1949, France recognized the independence of Vietnam within the French Union. A month later the long-postponed elections in Cochin China, which were boycotted by the Vietminh and in which only seventeen hundred voters participated, resulted in an overwhelming vote in favor of joining Tonkin and Annam in the new sovereign state. On June 14 its first government was established in Saigon under the leadership of Bao Dai, the deposed figurehead emperor under the Japanese occupation who had returned from his exile in Hong Kong.

The policy of the United States toward the Franco-Vietminh conflict underwent a radical evolution during the second half of the 1940s. The Truman administration originally adopted an even-handed approach toward the war in Southeast Asia as it concentrated on the deteriorating political situation in Europe. On the one hand, the United States had refused to assist the return of French military forces to Vietnam and continued to prod Paris to grant greater political liberties to the Vietnamese. On the other hand, Washington had rebuffed all of Ho's diplomatic overtures in the early postwar years. During his trip to Paris in the summer of 1946 to negotiate a settlement with the French government, the Viet Minh leader had approached the U.S. embassy with an offer to welcome American foreign investment and to lease the port of Cam Ranh Bay for a U.S. naval base in exchange for recognition. This last Viet Minh bid for U.S. support against France fell on deaf ears. Washington's wariness of the Vietnamese nationalist movement reflected the increasing tensions with the Soviet Union in Europe. Despite the fact that Stalin had given little support or encouragement to the Vietminh, Ho's record as a dedicated Communist came back to haunt him.

The defection of Yugoslavia from the Soviet bloc in 1948 led some in Washington to see Ho as a potential Tito in Asia whose independent brand of Communism might merit American support. But the establishment of the PRC in October 1949 and its alignment with Moscow in early 1950 raised the alternative possibility that the Vietminh leader might follow Mao into the Soviet camp. The wave of anti-Communism that swept the United States after the "loss" of China dashed Ho's hopes of securing support from the Truman administration. Secretary of State Dean Acheson had come to fear that a Vietminh triumph in Vietnam would be followed by the absorption of the two other constituent states of Indochina, Cambodia and Laos, into a unified Communist power. American officials began to view the Vietminh struggle against the French in the context of Communist-backed insurgencies in the Philippines, Malaya, and Burma. All of this unrest seemed part of a Communist advance throughout Southeast Asia masterminded by Moscow and supported by Beijing.

The French government skillfully exploited these American fears by representing its military effort in Vietnam as the Asian counterpart of the policy of containment that the United States was conducting in Europe. In the course of 1949 officials in Washington began to view the war in Indochina less as an anticolonial struggle than as the Far Eastern theater of the Cold War. Then on January 15, 1950, Ho proclaimed from his jungle hideout the reestablishment of the "Democratic Republic of Vietnam" that had effectively ceased to exist after his escape from Hanoi in December 1946. Moscow and Beijing promptly extended formal diplomatic recognition to this "virtual government," a slap in the face to Bao Dai's French-controlled regime in Saigon. This diplomatic charade prompted Washington to issue its first overt expression of support for France's war against the Vietminh: The U.S. extended formal diplomatic recognition to the royalist governments of Laos and Cambodia as well as Bao Dai's regime in Vietnam as "Associated States within the French Union." The two superpowers had thus been indirectly drawn into the Franco-Vietminh conflict for the first time.

After the establishment of the PRC in the fall of 1949, Mao began to provide more than rhetorical support to the Vietminh in its struggle against France and its Vietnamese allies. China sent supplies and weapons to Giap's guerrillas and provided military training for his officers in Chinese camps. Not to be outdone, the Soviet Union also began to send arms to the Vietminh. Fortified by this assistance from his two Communist patrons, Giap was able to form five fully equipped infantry divisions and one artillery division. His guerrilla army had increased in size from about forty thousand in 1945 to more than one hundred thousand by early 1950. Since the French government was legally prohibited from sending draftees to this foreign war, the French professional army never exceeded the size of its enemy forces. To counterbalance the Chinese aid to the Vietminh, President Truman announced on May 15, 1950, the provision of $15 million to support the French war effort. This modest expenditure was the first in a long series of outlays by the American government to thwart Ho Chi Minh's relentless campaign to achieve independence for Vietnam. The outbreak of the Korean War a month later led to a dramatic increase in American assistance. In the following autumn $150 million in U.S. military equipment together with the first contingent of American military advisers arrived in Saigon to assist France's counterinsurgency campaign.

In a replay of the Chinese Civil War, the Vietminh gained and retained effective control of the countryside. while French authority was confined to the major cities. In the autumn of 1953 the French military commander, General Henri Navarre, concluded that France was squandering its manpower and equipment in an endless game of cat-and-mouse with scattered guerrillas who vanished at the first hint of combat. He devised an audacious strategy for a decisive encounter with the Vietminh that would bring a speedy French victory in the war. Navarre ordered the construction of a large French military base in the remote village of Dien Bien Phu three hundred miles northwest of Hanoi near the Laotian border. The garrison was built in the center of a broad valley surrounded by mountains that were known to be honeycombed with Vietminh hideouts. The objective of the Navarre Plan was to lure the elusive enemy into a frontal attack against the fortress in the valley below so that French tanks, artillery, and aircraft could finish them off in a decisive engagement in open terrain. The 13,500 crack paratroops in the French garrison could be continually resupplied by air from Hanoi on a landing strip constructed in the valley. Since there were no roads up the mountains to the Vietminh positions above Dien Bien Phu, Navarre assumed that they would be unable to employ artillery against the French forces in the fortress below.

In early 1954 Giap sent 47,000 of his best soldiers up the mountains encircling the improvised French garrison at Dien Bien Phu. The Chinese then supplied the Viet Minh with American-built howitzers and mortars that had been captured in the Korean War. Each artillery piece was torn apart, carried up the mountains by porters, and then painstakingly reassembled. From their commanding heights the Vietminh opened up a massive artillery barrage against the French units pinned down in their self-made trap in the valley below. The incessant shelling destroyed the French artillery bases and put the airstrip out of commission, so the garrison could be resupplied with food, weapons, and ammunition only by inaccurate and risky parachute drops. The Vietminh then launched a ferocious infantry assault across the valley on March 13. They promptly seized two forward French outposts and threatened to engulf the demoralized French soldiers in their besieged fortress.

French Chief of Staff General Paul Ely hastily flew to Washington on March 20 to plead for immediate military assistance from the United States, which by then was paying almost 80 percent of the cost of the French war effort in Vietnam. Ely and his political superiors in Paris desperately hoped that the Americans would be willing to supplement dollars with airmen. The French general's initial soundings in Washington gave some reason for optimism: Acting without presidential approval, Chairman of the Joint Chiefs of Staff Admiral Arthur Radford presented the French general with a plan (code named Operation Vulture) for the use of twenty-five American B-29s from the Philippines and aircraft carriers in the South China Sea to break the siege by destroying the Vietminh artillery positions. Radford also hinted that if conventional bombing did not do the trick, nuclear weapons might be considered as a last resort.

The Eisenhower administration had recently unveiled its "New Look" in U.S. defense policy, which relied on air power as a safer and cheaper alternative to the deployment of ground forces abroad. So the French request for air support in Vietnam seemed fully compatible with current American strategic doctrine. But Eisenhower refused to commit himself to any action on behalf of the beleaguered French before sounding out congressional opinion. Recalling the three-year stalemate in Korea that had ended less than a year before, legislative leaders were in no mood to be dragged into another conflict on the mainland of Asia. Led by the Senate Democratic floor leader, Lyndon B. Johnson of Texas, they unequivocally opposed an American military intervention in Vietnam. Eisenhower thereupon rejected the French request for immediate U.S. air support, but sent Dulles on a whirlwind tour of European capitals to sound out America's allies about the alternative of collective action to rescue the endangered defenders of Dien Bien Phu. In London Dulles hinted that the United States might be willing to give the French military assistance if Great Britain and perhaps other NATO powers would join the effort. But the Conservative government of Winston Churchill, convinced that the French campaign in Indochina was doomed, declined to become implicated in a lost cause. In an April 7 press conference Eisenhower warned of the serious consequences of a French defeat by comparing the situation in Southeast Asia to a line of dominoes: If Vietnam were to fall to the Vietminh, the other countries of Southeast Asia would topple one by one until the entire region was lost to Communism. But faced with congressional opposition and the British refusal to participate, Eisenhower had to inform the French that they were on their own in their bid to prevent the first domino from falling.

At a Four-Power conference in January 1954, French Foreign Minister Georges Bidault had persuaded Dulles to support the convocation of a Five-Power conference in Geneva in the following spring to address the deteriorating military situation in Indochina. The U.S. secretary of state originally demurred because the fifth power Bidault proposed to invite was the People's Republic of China, with which neither the United States nor France had diplomatic relations and which Dulles reviled as an illegitimate regime. But he finally relented in exchange for a tacit pledge from the French government to bring the long-deferred European Defense Community Treaty to a vote in the French National Assembly (see page 57). The decision to convene a Five-Power conference on Indochina in the spring of 1954 provided Ho and Giap with a powerful incentive to present the diplomats with a military fait accompli. As the delegates gathered in Switzerland in preparation for the critical meeting, the Vietminh forces dug trenches and tunnels along the valley of Dien Bien Phu through which they advanced inch-by-inch toward the hapless French paratroops in their fortress of doom. The day before the Geneva conference opened on May 8, the garrison capitulated and the eleven thousand surviving French soldiers marched off in humiliation to Vietminh POW camps.

The fall of Dien Bien Phu shattered whatever hope France entertained of preserving its colonial authority in Indochina. After the resignation of the Laniel government on June 12, the new French premier, Pierre Mendès-France, announced on July 20 that he would travel to Geneva and obtain a cease-fire within a month or resign. Invitations to the high-level gathering had been issued to the Vietminh, as well as to the French-backed governments of Vietnam, Laos, and Cambodia. The Viet Minh delegation at the Geneva Conference, headed by Ho's long-time comrade and confidant Pham Van Dong, was in a strong position to achieve its goals: Its military forces had just defeated the French in a decisive encounter on the battlefield. The new government in Paris had announced its intention to terminate a war it no longer wished to fight and set a deadline for an agreement to permit its troops to withdraw. The foreign ministers of Ho Chi Minh's two Communist allies, China and the Soviet Union, were seated at the conference table to support his cause. The Viet Minh delegation pursued a simple and straightforward objective at the talks: the removal of French colonial authority and its replacement by an Indochinese Federation in which the neighboring states of Laos and Cambodia, ruled by Vietminh–backed "resistance governments," would eventually fall under the domination of a Communist Vietnam.

But these various Indochinese representatives would not make the crucial decisions at Geneva. Acting as his own foreign minister, Mendès-France went straight to the delegates of the two powers that counted—Soviet Foreign Minister Vyacheslav Molotov and China's Zhou Enlai to enlist their support for a face-saving settlement that would allow France a graceful exit from its Indochina nightmare. As it turned out, the post-Stalinist leadership in the Kremlin was anxious to preserve its new reputation for moderation and conciliation. So Molotov and his associates, instead of supporting Ho Chi Minh's delegation to the hilt, urged caution on their Vietminh colleagues. The Chinese government, whose military forces had just spent three years fighting the Americans in Korea and which was rechanneling its energies into economic recovery, apparently worried about a possible U.S. military intervention in Vietnam and did not want to give Washington any pretext for such an operation.

Mao's subsequent remarks about the inevitability of war between the communist and capitalist worlds and China's ability to survive and win it served as a rhetorical smokescreen for what was in fact a relatively cautious Chinese foreign policy in Asia after the Korean armistice.

So Zhou Enlai joined forces with Molotov to pressure Pham Van Dong into shelving the original plan for a federation of the three states of Indochina under the effective control of the Viet Minh. He was also induced to drop the demand that the "resistance governments" of Laos and Cambodia be admitted to the conference in place of the French-backed royalist regimes that ruled those two countries. Finally, the Soviet and Chinese foreign ministers even persuaded the Vietminh delegation to abandon its call for the immediate independence of Vietnam under its control and to tolerate the temporary presence of a non-Communist entity in the south. China apparently did not look forward to a strong, united Vietnam, emboldened by its stunning military victory over the French and poised to dominate the rest of Indochina. A temporary and perhaps even permanent partition of Vietnam seemed a preferable alternative, provided that the non-Communist regime to be set up in the south did not become, like South Korea, a vehicle for the projection of U.S. military power on the Asian mainland.

On July 20, the deadline that Mendès-France had set for reaching a settlement, the diplomats finally hammered out the details of the Geneva Accords terminating the eight-year war in Southeast Asia. Vietnam was to be temporarily partitioned along the 17th parallel of latitude. The Vietminh would administer the northern zone from their capital in Hanoi, while Bao Dai's non-Communist regime in Saigon would govern the south. Both governments were forbidden to join alliances with foreign powers or receive military assistance from abroad. At the end of two years the entire country would be reunited on the basis of a free election under the supervision of a United Nations Control Commission. French and Viet Minh troops would be evacuated from Laos and Cambodia, whose royalist governments were recognized as fully independent by all signatories to the accords. Like the two Vietnams, Laos and Cambodia were required to adhere to a strict neutrality.

The Vietminh's military triumph in the shell-strewn valley of Dien Bien Phu had thus been transformed into a diplomatic defeat at the conference table in Geneva. In deference to his Soviet and Chinese patrons, Ho Chi Minh had to swallow a peace settlement that denied him the fruits of victory against an exhausted European colonial power that was eager to withdraw. He was obliged to surrender about 20 percent of the territory that his army had conquered to a hostile regime in the south controlled by former servants of the French. Even before the haggling diplomats had announced the final settlement in Geneva, the anti-Communist government in Saigon began to take shape. On June 14 Emperor Bao Dai selected as his prime minister a French-educated Catholic mandarin named Ngo Dinh Diem. When he learned of the provisions of the Geneva Accords, Diem angrily denounced them for condemning the northern half of country to Communist rule. Ignoring the prohibition against foreign military ties, the new prime minister of what came to be known as South Vietnam looked abroad for support against the new Communist regime that was being installed in the north. With the French busily preparing to evacuate their military forces from the country, he turned to the only other foreign power in a position to render assistance to his fledgling regime: the United States of America.

Diem had good reason to expect a sympathetic response from the Eisenhower administration to his request for emergency aid. Washington's attitude toward the Geneva Conference and the agreements it had produced was hardly enthusiastic. Before the debacle at Dien Bien Phu the United States had agreed to participate in the conference in the expectation of masterminding a settlement in Indochina that would exclude the Viet Minh from political power. When the extent of Ho's military triumph became evident, American enthusiasm for the Geneva meeting evaporated. Secretary of State Dulles, for whom the prospect of face-to-face encounters with Communist leaders was a source of great distaste, abandoned the conference after a few days without even making contact with the Soviet and Chinese delegations. During a chance encounter in a hotel lobby he even refused to shake the outstretched hand of Chinese Foreign Minister Zhou Enlai. Dulles instructed his delegate, Walter Bedell Smith, who remained as an observer at the conference, to refrain from signing the Geneva Accords and to offer instead an innocuous pledge that the United States would not violate their provisions. The U.S. secretary of state particularly disliked the neutralization portion of the Accords, which left the three weak non-Communist states of the former French Indochina exposed to the superior military power of the triumphant regime in Hanoi.

Since the United States decided not to rescue the French at Dien Bien Phu, it was in no position to prevent Mendès-France from cutting whatever deal he could at Geneva. But Washington had no intention of being bound by the provisions of the Geneva Accords if they interfered with its objective of containing Communism in Asia. A CIA sabotage team was dispatched to the new state of North Vietnam to engage in the type of covert action on behalf of U.S. foreign policy goals that the Eisenhower administration had successfully executed in Iran and Guatemala. The peripatetic Dulles flew to Manila and on September 8 presided over the creation of the South East Asia Treaty Organization (SEATO), a regional security system that he hailed as the Far Eastern counterpart of NATO. In fact, as we have seen, few of the newly independent states in the region showed any interest in SEATO. Dulles was able to induce only three Asian countries (the Philippines, Thailand, and Pakistan) to join the United States, France, Australia, and New Zealand in the new security organization (see page 74). Although the Geneva Accords forbade Laos, Cambodia, and South Vietnam from adhering to such an alliance, a subsequent protocol to the SEATO treaty committed its members to protect the three Indochinese states against the threat of Communism. By the end of 1954 Washington had replaced Paris as the spearhead of the anti-Communist cause in Indochina. U.S. military advisers arrived in Saigon to train the South Vietnamese army while $400 million in U.S. financial aid flowed into Diem's coffers. It soon became evident that China had lost one of the major advantages Zhou Enlai thought he had gained at Geneva: the exclusion of American power and influence from Southeast Asia, a region that the leaders in Beijing hoped would eventually fall under Chinese domination.

### The Agony of Indochina: The American Phase

Soon after the Geneva Accords entered into force, the Communist regime in Hanoi began to wage a relentless campaign against "rich peasants" and Catholics (from

N

| 0 | 100 | 200 Miles |
| 0 | 100 | 200 Km |

PEOPLE'S REPUBLIC OF CHINA

BURMA

NORTH
VIETNAM

●Dienbienphu    ●Hanoi

●
Haiphong

LAOS

Gulf of
Tonkin

Hainan

●Vientiane

Demilitarised Zone

●Hue

THAILAND

Da●
Nang

●Pleiku

●Bangkok

CAMBODIA

Phnom
Penh ●

SOUTH
VIETNAM

●Cam Ranh
Bay

●Saigon

Gulf of
Thailand

SOUTH CHINA SEA

MALAYSIA

E.McC.'95

*Indochina, 1954–1975*

families that had been converted by French missionaries over the years). Thousands of "landlords" (a category that included farmers who owned only a few acres) were executed or sent to "re-education camps" by hastily convened tribunals. These brutal measures incited a revolt in the countryside that North Vietnamese security forces quelled with great ferocity. In response to this repression more than six hundred thousand Catholics fled the north to South Vietnam, with the active encouragement of the Catholic-dominated regime in Saigon. In the meantime, Ho had ordered most of the Viet Minh guerrillas who lived south of the 17th parallel to leave their families behind and move north until the scheduled reunification elections in 1956. About ten thousand of them remained in South Vietnam with orders to seek popular support in preparation for the elections Ho fully expected to win. But since South Vietnam had not signed the Geneva Accords, Diem felt under no obligation to abide by their provisions for nationwide elections for reunification. In the summer of 1955 he twice rebuffed requests from Hanoi to designate representatives to the proposed electoral commission. The Eisenhower administration, convinced that Ho would prevail in all-Vietnamese elections, exerted no pressure on the anti-Communist leader in Saigon to participate in a procedure that was likely to result in his political demise. As the deadline for the projected elections expired in the summer of 1956, the provisional demarcation line along the 17th parallel, like the 38th parallel in Korea, hardened into a de facto political frontier separating two ideologically antagonistic states.

In the meantime Diem had taken several steps to consolidate his power in the south. In October 1955 a fraudulent referendum dethroned Emperor Bao Dai and established the Republic of Vietnam with Diem as president with virtually dictatorial power. His security forces waged a ruthless campaign to extirpate through executions and imprisonment the Communist cadres that had remained in the south. The cancellation of the unification elections, the establishment of one-man rule in Saigon, and the efforts to eradicate the Vietminh in the south prompted a sharp reaction in Hanoi. In December 1956 Ho instructed his cadres in the south, whose numbers had been depleted by Diem's repressive tactics, to organize the rural masses against the Saigon government. Between 1957 and 1960 they assassinated hundreds of South Vietnamese government officials in remote villages. Both the government and the insurgents waged a campaign of terror against each other for the remainder of the 1950s. South Vietnamese security forces also moved against a number of powerful non-Communist groups in the south that posed potential threats to the state: the Cao Dai, a schismatic Catholic sect; the mystical Buddhist Hoa Hao; and the mafialike Binh Xuyen (which controlled gambling, narcotics and prostitution in Saigon). Diem made a half-hearted attempt to enact land reform, but he soon antagonized local peasants with corrupt schemes of land redistribution that favored Catholic refugees from the north. He also managed to alienate career government officials by placing his relatives in high administrative posts.

Anxious to avoid a Korea-type U.S. military response to the civil war in the south, Hanoi had originally assumed that the unpopular regime in Saigon would succumb to the mounting political opposition it faced. But the crackdown by Diem's police threatened to decimate North Vietnam's sympathizers in the south. Jailings and executions caused the membership of the Communist Party in South Vietnam to decline from about fifty-five thousand in 1954 to about five thousand by the end of the decade. In the summer of 1959 the North Vietnamese government decided that in order to topple the Saigon government, the guerrillas in the south would require its direct assistance. By the beginning of the 1960s, southerners who had fled north in 1954 were being infiltrated back into the south along a primitive path cut through the jungles of eastern Laos popularly known as the Ho Chi Minh Trail. Once ensconced in their rural hideouts, these cadres renewed the hit-and-run tactics they had used against the French, striking at South Vietnamese units near the cities and then vanishing into the countryside.

In September 1960 the ruling party of North Vietnam formally endorsed the goal of overthrowing the Saigon regime and unifying the two halves of the country. On December 20 agents from Hanoi secretly assembled in a remote rural camp in South Vietnam and set up the National Liberation Front (NLF), a political arm of the guerrilla movement in the south that Diem promptly stigmatized as "Viet Cong" (Vietnamese Communists). In the meantime the United States had stepped up its military assistance to Saigon. The 275 American military advisers attached to the South Vietnamese army shortly after partition had grown to almost 900 by the end of the 1950s. Between 1954 and 1961 the United States spent over $1.5 billion in military and economic assistance to South Vietnam. During the same period the Soviet Union, the Eastern European satellites, and China managed to contribute only about $570 million worth of weapons and supplies to the Communist regime in Hanoi.

As the Kennedy administration took office in January 1961, its principal foreign policy concern in Southeast Asia was not Vietnam but rather the landlocked kingdom of Laos. The Geneva Accords of 1954 had acknowledged the independence of this backward, isolated country on the condition that it remain neutral, a compromise that Kennedy and his foreign policy advisers were willing to accept. But the royalist government in the Laotian capital of Vientiene had to cope with the Communist Pathet Lao movement that controlled large parts of the country with active assistance from neighboring North Vietnam. There followed a confusing succession of coups, countercoups, and palace revolutions in Vientiene, as Washington dispatched covert aid and advisers to various right-wing factions while Moscow and Beijing backed a coalition of neutralists and the Pathet Lao. Faced with a rightist insurrection led by Phoumi Nosovan with clandestine support from the United States, the neutralist prime minister Souvanna Phouma aligned with the Pathet Lao and began to receive arms deliveries from the Soviet Union. The anti-Communist government of Thailand, which was secretly working with the CIA in support of the rightist rebellion against Souvanna Phouma, warned the United States that a Communist takeover in Laos would directly threaten its own security.

To sort out the complicated political conflicts in Laos, the great powers reconvened the Geneva Conference on Indochina in May 1961. After a year of disputatious wrangling, an agreement was finally reached in the summer of 1962. It ostensibly guaranteed the neutrality of Laos—by prohibiting it from signing alliances with, furnishing bases for, or receiving military aid from foreign powers—under a coalition government composed of the pro-Western, pro-Communist, and neutralist factions. But by late 1962 the United States had resumed arms shipments to the coalition government in violation of the neutralization agreement. Soon American planes were conducting clandestine bombing raids against the Pathet Lao insurgents, who had abandoned the tripartite coalition in power as it increasingly turned to Washington for support.

The collapse of the Laos accords was inevitable because this isolated country, which shared a long common border with Vietnam, could not avoid being dragged into the escalating conflict in that country. Hanoi informed Souvanna Phouma in the summer of 1962 that, although willing to tolerate a neutralist regime in Vientiene, it reserved the right to continue using the Ho Chi Minh Trail in eastern Laos to supply the Communist guerrillas in South Vietnam. This caveat violated the neutrality provisions of the 1962 Geneva Accords, but there was nothing that the weak Laotian government could do about it. In subsequent years some sixty-seven thousand North Vietnamese soldiers patrolled the Ho Chi Minh Trail in eastern Laos in cooperation with their Pathet Lao allies. In the meantime the United States had been waging a clandestine bombing campaign against the trail with the tacit agreement of the neutralist government. On the ground the CIA recruited a nine-thousand-man mercenary army from the Hmong (or Meo) ethnic minority to fight the Pathet Lao guerrillas and attack the North Vietnamese supply routes.

The world scarcely took notice of the civil war in Laos because of its preoccupation with the much more visible and overt struggle across the border in Vietnam. The Communist-dominated National Liberation Front that had been formed in South Vietnam during the transition from the Eisenhower to the Kennedy administration won support from a broad range of non-Communist opponents of the Diem regime. Kennedy and his advisers interpreted the unrest in the south in purely Cold War terms: It was seen not as a civil war between antagonistic factions within the country, but rather as part of the Soviet strategy of promoting "wars of national liberation" in the Third World. To combat this Communist-led insurrection Washington persuaded Diem to adopt and implement the so-called Strategic Hamlet Program, which was loosely modeled on two successful counterinsurgency operations in the 1950s. The first was the British relocation program for the ethnic Chinese squatters in Malaya run by Robert Thompson, which had helped to crush an insurrection during the so-called Malayan emergency (see page 251). The second was the suppression of the Huk rebellion in the Philippines, which had been masterminded by a swashbuckling CIA operative named Edward Landsdale and executed under the auspices of the progressive Philippine statesman Ramon Magsaysay (see page 254).

The legendary Landsdale had been transferred to Saigon as CIA station chief in 1954, and Thompson arrived in 1961 as head of the British mission to advise the South Vietnamese government. The Strategic Hamlet Program was designed to shield peasants from the Viet Cong by relocating them to villages protected by barbed wire and land mines. But the Vietnamese rural population, which was far more attached to its home villages than were the Chinese squatters whom the British had successfully relocated in Malaya, bitterly resented being evicted by the government from their ancestral lands. Moreover, the program was supervised by Diem's corrupt, autocratic, opium-addicted younger brother, Ngo Dinh Nhu, the head of South Vietnam's secret police and one of the most unpopular officials in the nepotistic regime. The peasants herded into the fenced, fortified compounds by Nhu's detested agents were thoroughly alienated from the Saigon government and became tempting targets for Viet Cong recruiters who easily infiltrated the strategic hamlets.

Kennedy's hopes that Diem could combine the reformist dedication of Magsaysay in the Philippines with the efficient relocation program of the British administration in Malaya were gravely disappointed. The South Vietnamese president isolated himself from the rural masses, increasingly relying on a small coterie of people like himself: urban, upper class, French-speaking Catholics who were out of touch with the squalid poverty and acute social tensions in the countryside. The Catholics' virtual monopoly on high government posts in Saigon and the provincial capitals bred resentment among the Buddhist majority of South Vietnam. This religious discontent reached a fever pitch on May 8, 1963, when the government prohibited Buddhists from flying their flags to celebrate Buddha's birthday in the city of Hue (where one brother of Diem's served as archbishop and another as provincial military commander). When a thousand Buddhists took to the streets in protest against these restrictions on their freedom of worship, troops of the Army of Republic of Viet Nam (ARVN) opened fire on the demonstrators, killing eight and wounding dozens more. Two months after the riot in Hue, the protests against religious discrimination burst onto the streets of Saigon. As South Vietnamese police raided pagodas and arrested fourteen hundred Buddhist clerics, five Buddhist monks committed suicide by setting fire to themselves in public. Diem declared martial law throughout the country on August 20, 1963, but the social and religious unrest in the south continued. As the Strategic Hamlet Program unraveled amid a veritable civil war between the Catholic minority in power and the restive Buddhist majority, the Kennedy administration began to reevaluate its unswerving support for Diem's government.

Shortly after taking office Kennedy had dispatched another 500 American military advisers to Vietnam, bringing the total to 1,400. By the end of 1961 that number had increased to about 2,600; by the end of 1962 it stood at 11,300; at the time of Kennedy's assassination in November 1963 it had swollen to 16,500. In the meantime the amount of U.S. financial aid to Saigon continued to increase during Kennedy's final year in office. Amid this escalating American involvement, the administration vainly attempted to prod the increasingly dictatorial Diem to institute land reform to appease the impoverished peasantry, grant greater political freedom to the non-Communist opposition groups, and accord religious toleration to the discontented Buddhists. But the South Vietnamese leader, convinced that the mounting political and religious opposition was instigated by Hanoi and its agents in the south, turned a deaf ear to Washington's pleas for conciliation in favor of even more repressive policies that only served to incite greater opposition to his regime. In response to Diem's crackdown on the Buddhists in the spring and summer of 1963, American officials publicly criticized Diem's policies for the first time. Kennedy's ambassador in Saigon, Henry Cabot Lodge, and his agents discreetly revealed to South Vietnamese military officers that the South Vietnamese leader had lost favor in the White House.

These signals from Washington inspired a conspiracy among senior ARVN officers to remove Diem from office. When rumors of the U.S.-backed plot reached the president and his brother and confidant Nhu, the two toyed with the idea of breaking with the United States, inviting the Viet Cong into a governing coalition, and approaching Hanoi for a negotiated settlement. But before this bizarre scheme for a political turnabout could proceed any further, the conspirators staged their coup on November 1. After declining Ambassador Lodge's offer of American protection,

Diem and Nhu fled to the Saigon suburb of Cholon. Cut off from all of their customary sources of support, the two brothers reluctantly surrendered to the security forces
of the new military junta that had taken power. Both were promptly murdered by the
personal bodyguard of the new government's strongman, General Duong Van Minh.
Minh and his colleagues attempted to conciliate a broad range of disaffected groups
within South Vietnam, especially the Buddhists and the Cao Dai and Hoa Hao sects.
They also developed plans to appease the rural peasantry by terminating the detested
Strategic Hamlet Program. But a group of disgruntled officers led by General
Nguyen Khanh toppled Minh in January 1964. This new coup had been organized
with the acquiescence of the new American administration of Lyndon B. Johnson,
which suspected Minh of planning to stem the influx of U.S. military personnel and
open negotiations with the Viet Cong. The Khanh government reversed Minh's conciliatory approach toward the Buddhists and the sects while welcoming the expanding American military presence in South Vietnam.

After the assassinations of Ngo Dinh Diem and John F. Kennedy in November
1963, South Vietnam experienced great political instability as the various contending
factions in the military jockeyed for positions of power. Hanoi decided in the spring
of 1964 to exploit this political uncertainty in Saigon by training and equipping for
the first time northern-born Vietnamese regulars for redeployment south to fight
alongside the Viet Cong. At the same time the new Johnson administration in Washington was making plans for a major expansion of the American military commitment to South Vietnam. The president had been persuaded by Secretary of Defense
Robert McNamara and National Security Adviser McGeorge Bundy that the only
hope of winning the war in South Vietnam was to make Hanoi suffer for its support
of the insurgency there. They proposed the launching of a gradually escalating series
of bombing raids against targets in North Vietnam in retaliation against Viet Cong attacks in the south. The poor showing by the ARVN troops against the rebels also
convinced policymakers in Washington that American ground forces in the south
would be required to suppress the insurgency. This inclination toward escalation was
reinforced by domestic political considerations: Johnson began to come under intense criticism from his Republican opponent in the forthcoming presidential election, Senator Barry Goldwater, for pursuing a "no win" policy in Vietnam. But the
White House was unwilling to approve such a drastic expansion of the U.S. military
commitment without the approval of Congress. So a draft resolution was prepared by
McGeorge Bundy's brother William, an official in the Pentagon, according the president carte blanche to deal with the situation. All that was lacking was a pretext for
seeking such authorization from the legislators on Capitol Hill.

Johnson was handed that pretext on the evening of August 4, 1964, by a murky incident in the Gulf of Tonkin off the coast of North Vietnam. The radar operators on
two American destroyers that were collecting electronic data on North Vietnamese
ship movements saw blips on their screen that they took to be North Vietnamese pa-
trol boats. The sonar operator on one of the destroyers thought that he detected
sounds of incoming torpedoes. Although no damage was found on either ship, President Johnson immediately ordered a retaliatory raid on torpedo boat bases in North
Vietnam by carrier-based aircraft. On August 7 the administration submitted to Congress a modified version of the draft resolution that had been prepared before the

incident in the Gulf of Tonkin, authorizing the president to respond to North Vietnamese aggression by all appropriate means. The so-called Tonkin Gulf Resolution
passed unanimously in the House of Representatives and sailed through the Senate
by a vote of 88 to 2. The president had thus obtained a blank check to pursue the undeclared war in Vietnam as he saw fit.

Following his landslide victory in the presidential election of November 1964,
Johnson prepared to take the two steps that his closest advisers deemed essential for
victory in the escalating conflict across the Pacific: a U.S. bombing campaign against
North Vietnam and the deployment of American ground troops in the south. On
February 7, 1965, the Viet Cong gave the American president the provocation he
required by launching its first major offensive against U.S. facilities in South Vietnam, a night raid on the barracks of an American airfield at Pleiku that resulted in
nine American deaths and over a hundred casualties. Johnson ordered retaliatory air
strikes against North Vietnam from carriers of the seventh fleet in the South China
Sea as part of a massive bombing campaign code-named "Rolling Thunder." After
originally prohibiting the bombing of densely populated urban areas of the north, the
president gradually lifted the restrictions until U.S. aircraft began targeting industrial
facilities in Hanoi and Haiphong. To cope with the bombing campaign the North
Vietnamese developed an effective air defense system consisting of Soviet surface-
to-air missiles, anti-aircraft batteries, and MiG fighters. In the course of the war more
than nine hundred American planes were shot down over North Vietnam, and the
hundreds of pilots who were taken prisoner were used by Hanoi for propaganda
purposes.

The North Vietnamese army was able to repair its destroyed communication system with relative ease. The thick vegetation that covered much of the country, together with the cloudy weather during the monsoon season, facilitated the clandestine movement of troops despite the bombing campaign. Operation Rolling Thunder
did not destroy or even disrupt for long North Vietnam's war-making capability and
its political infrastructure. The government simply evacuated its officials from targeted cities such as Hanoi and Haiphong and reassembled them in safe rural hideouts. The strategic bombing of North Vietnamese cities, like the German Luftwaffe's
raids on British cities in the autumn of 1940, had the opposite effect of the one intended: Instead of destroying morale they stiffened popular resistance. Intent on
avoiding any incident that might provoke China into intervening in the war, Johnson
forbade bombing raids near the Chinese border. He also limited the war in a number
of other ways: by refraining from mining Haiphong harbor to disrupt the flow of
Soviet and Chinese aid to North Vietnam; by permitting the North Vietnamese to
send supplies to the south through Cambodia; and by allowing the Viet Cong to use
that neighboring country as a sanctuary from search-and-destroy sweeps by ARVN
and later American troops.

The air war in the north was complemented by an aggressive American effort to
bolster the South Vietnamese army's counterinsurgency operation against the Viet
Cong. Shortly after the beginning of the bombing campaign, Washington announced
on March 10, 1965, that two battalions of marines were being dispatched to the city
of Da Nang in South Vietnam to help the ARVN cope with the increasingly daring
attacks by the Communist guerrillas in the south. The three thousand marines that

disembarked in Da Nang represented the first contingent of regular combat troops sent to Vietnam. On July 28, 1965, the president who had promised during his election campaign the previous year that he was "not going to send American boys 15,000 miles away from their homes to do what Asian boys should do for themselves" approved the recommendation of the U.S. commander, General William Westmoreland, to dispatch 180,000 American ground forces to Vietnam to shore up the sagging Saigon army. That number of American combat troops would reach 385,000 by the end of the following year, 535,000 by the beginning of 1968, and a high point of 540,000 by the end of Johnson's presidential term in January 1969.

While the air war in the north failed to bring Hanoi to its knees, the "search-and-destroy" campaign in the south was also falling for short of its objective to route the Viet Cong from its rural hideouts. To remove the natural camouflage that protected the guerrillas in the south from U.S. air power, American transport planes sprayed a number of chemical agents, such as the dioxin-laced "Agent Orange," to defoliate the forests in Viet Cong–controlled areas. The nineteen million gallons of these herbicides that were dropped over about a fifth of the territory of South Vietnam ravaged the natural environment and had detrimental health effects on both Vietnamese civilians and U.S. servicemen. But American units on the ground could neither locate the rural bases of the enemy nor impede its activities beyond the confines of the government-controlled towns and villages. The pacification program in South Vietnam, instituted to win the support of the peasantry, proved a total failure.

The one bright spot in the American war effort was the development of relative political stability in Saigon during the second half of the 1960s. In February 1965 the last in a series of military coups by ambitious ARVN officers brought to power a junta dominated by Nguyen Van Thieu and Nguyen Cao Ky. In 1967 the two men decided to legitimize the political power that they had usurped by conducting a nationwide election. After an American-style political campaign with rallies, handshaking, and lavish promises, Thieu was elected president and Ky vice president. Although the election was plagued by voting irregularities and instances of outright fraud, the two military officers-turned-statesmen acquired a measure of legitimacy that promised to bring an end to the political chaos that had plagued South Vietnam since the demise of Diem.

But that legitimacy was soon challenged by Hanoi. Ho and his colleagues remained convinced that the South Vietnamese government would collapse like a house of cards without American military forces there to prop it up. In early 1968 North Vietnam decided to mount a major offensive in the south in the hope of sparking a mass uprising that would prove to the American public that the Thieu-Ky regime was no longer worth supporting. On January 30, 1968, the first day of Tet, the festival that the Vietnamese celebrate at the beginning of the lunar New Year, half the South Vietnamese army was on leave after Hanoi and Saigon had jointly agreed to a holiday truce. Shortly after midnight some thirty thousand Viet Cong guerrillas, joined by forty thousand North Vietnamese regulars who had secretly massed throughout South Vietnam, launched a well coordinated surprise attack against thirty-six of the forty-four provincial capitals of the country. The Viet Cong had even succeeded in infiltrating five armed battalions into the capital city itself. Early in the morning of January 31 Communist soldiers penetrated the grounds of the presidential palace, the radio station, the airport, and the heavily fortified American embassy. Seventy-five hundred North Vietnamese regulars captured the imperial city of Hue, while North Vietnamese and Viet Cong forces attacked five of the six major cities in the south.

This abrupt switch from hit-and-run guerrilla tactics to conventional warfare proved a military disaster, as the North Vietnamese and Viet Cong fell before the superior firepower of the enemy. From January to March over fifty thousand Viet Cong fighters and North Vietnamese regulars perished compared to some four thousand South Vietnamese and two thousand Americans. The Communist forces had failed to hold any of the cities they had overrun once American and Vietnamese units mounted a counterattack. Hue was the last Communist stronghold to fall, after over three weeks of American and ARVN artillery fire reduced the city to rubble and killed over half of the invaders. As a result of the disastrous Tet offensive, the Communists suffered a serious manpower shortage that hampered their ability to mount attacks on South Vietnamese strongholds for the next several years. The assault also resulted in an embarrassing political failure, since the inhabitants of the South Vietnamese cities refused to rise up in support of the North Vietnamese regulars and Viet Cong guerrillas who apparently expected to be greeted as liberators.

Despite the Communists' military reverses during the Tet offensive, Hanoi and its supporters in the south won a powerful psychological victory by demonstrating that no part of South Vietnam was secure—not even the government buildings and diplomatic compounds in the capital. The offensive exposed the hollowness of the Johnson administration's wildly optimistic assertions that victory was just around the corner, that North Vietnam was on the verge of collapse because of the American bombing campaign, and that the Viet Cong were about to slink back into the jungles in defeat. During the Tet offensive the North Vietnamese and Viet Cong proved their willingness to endure horrendous casualties and still continue to fight. The United States was put on notice that it too would have to adapt to the reality of a long, deadly war of attrition. But the American people were gradually coming to the conclusion that the conflict in Vietnam was not worth the sacrifices that would be required to achieve a clear-cut victory.

As the stalemate in the south continued, U.S. public opinion became disillusioned with the war effort and began to favor a negotiated settlement. Signs of dissatisfaction had begun to surface on American college campuses in response to the beginning of the bombing campaign in 1965. The most vociferous domestic opposition developed in the next three years, when the incapacity of the South Vietnamese army required the deployment of large numbers of American draftees. The horrors of combat in the jungles of Southeast Asia were brought home to the living rooms of America through the daily reports of television news correspondents, who were permitted to accompany American troops during their combat operations. In the spring of 1966 the Senate Foreign Relations Committee conducted hearings that turned into an informal trial of the Johnson administration, whose optimistic assessments of the war encountered increasing skepticism from legislators.

To counter criticism that was emanating from members of his own party, Johnson tried on several occasions in 1966–1967 to induce Hanoi to accept a negotiated settlement by temporarily suspending the bombing of North Vietnam. But Ho Chi Minh's preconditions for peace talks were totally unacceptable: a permanent halt to the bombing campaign against the north, the evacuation of all American ground troops from the south, and the replacement of the Thieu-Ky government with a coalition including representatives of the National Liberation Front. After each bombing "pause" failed to lure the North Vietnamese to the conference table on American terms, Johnson resumed the attacks in an effort to force them to negotiate. The Tet offensive revealed that the bombing of the north had neither stemmed the flow of North Vietnamese men and materiel to the south nor brought Hanoi any closer to negotiations. The choice Johnson faced was a stark one: Accede to General Westmoreland's urgent request for another two hundred thousand ground troops and authorization to carry the ground war to North Vietnam and the enemy sanctuaries in Laos and Cambodia, or meet enough of Hanoi's conditions to bring it to the bargaining table so that the United States could extricate itself from the quagmire in Southeast Asia.

The mounting public opposition to Johnson's Vietnam policy in the United States was graphically revealed in the first state primary election of the 1968 presidential campaign. The antiwar Senator Eugene McCarthy of Minnesota stunned the nation by winning 42 percent of the vote in the New Hampshire Democratic primary on March 12. When Senator Robert Kennedy of New York, the younger brother of the slain president, plunged into the race for the Democratic nomination on an antiwar platform, private polls commissioned by the White House revealed that Johnson would lose the next primary in Wisconsin. The president thereupon summoned a group of trusted advisers on March 25 for consultations. This select group of "wise men," a veritable Who's Who of the American military and political establishment, persuaded Johnson to reject Westmoreland's plea to widen the war. They also induced him to move closer to the North Vietnamese conditions for peace negotiations. In a nationally televised address on March 31, the demoralized chief executive announced his decision to confine the bombing of North Vietnam to the sparsely populated region below the 20th parallel and to send only token reinforcements of ground troops to the south. He asked Hanoi to enter peace talks to end the war and declared that he would not accept his party's renomination for the presidency. A few days later he recalled Westmoreland from his Vietnam command to underline his sincerity about seeking a nonmilitary solution to the conflict.

On May 3, 1968, the North Vietnamese government finally agreed to send a delegation to meet with U.S. negotiators in Paris. For the remainder of that fateful year the peace talks bogged down over procedural issues such as the shape of the conference table as the American presidential campaign unfolded. The Democratic presidential candidate, Hubert Humphrey, who had loyally supported the war as Johnson's vice president, openly advocated a negotiated settlement. Johnson suspended all bombing of North Vietnam on October 31 in a last-ditch attempt to break the logjam in Paris (and to improve Humphrey's chances of winning the election). But the Republican presidential candidate, Richard Nixon, secretly conveyed a message to South Vietnamese President Thieu urging him to boycott the Paris talks and await a Republican administration that would be more sympathetic to his interests. Thieu thereupon dug in his heels and refused to participate in the peace negotiations, ensuring that no progress would be made in Paris for the remainder of Johnson's term.

Richard Nixon was a longtime anti-Communist who had staunchly supported the U.S. military intervention in Vietnam. But by the end of the 1960s he had concluded that the war was unwinnable short of a massive increase in American troop strength. An avid reader of public opinion polls, he recognized that the American people would never consent to such an expansion of the war. During the campaign he had made veiled references to a "peace plan" that he had devised to bring an end to America's long nightmare in Indochina. There was no such plan. But after winning the election the new president and his national security adviser, Henry Kissinger, concocted a twofold strategy to extricate U.S. combat forces from Vietnam without having to suffer the dishonor of a military defeat. Kissinger had concluded that the war was a waste of American manpower and resources. Both he and Nixon intended to improve relations with the Soviet Union and China. They realized that Vietnam stood in the way of such a rapprochement with the two major Communist powers.

Nixon revealed his Vietnam strategy during a trip to the Pacific in the spring of 1969. He met with South Vietnamese President Thieu on the island of Midway and bluntly informed him that the ARVN would have to assume the major burden of the war effort. He then flew to the island of Guam and unveiled the so-called Nixon Doctrine: The United States would henceforth reduce its combat forces in Vietnam while increasing logistical support for the South Vietnamese army. This strategy of "Vietnamization" was inherently risky, since the South Vietnamese army had never developed into an effective fighting force. But Nixon made good on his pledge to terminate active U.S. involvement on the ground in Vietnam. The number of GIs stationed in the country dropped from 540,000 when Nixon entered the White House to 139,000 by the end of 1971 and to 25,000 by the end of his first term.

While they presided over the pullout of U.S. ground forces, Nixon and Kissinger were at pains to avoid the humiliation of a North Vietnamese military victory over South Vietnam. Like every recent American president, Nixon was unwilling to endure the political repercussions of "losing" Vietnam as Truman had "lost" China. He was willing to remove American forces only in exchange for Hanoi's solemn pledge to halt its military aggression against South Vietnam and accord the Saigon government a decent opportunity to survive. North Vietnam depended on the Soviet Union for a wide variety of vital economic resources, most notably oil. Nixon and Kissinger therefore tried to persuade the Kremlin leadership, as part of their new policy of détente with the other superpower, to coerce Hanoi into accepting a compromise settlement in the Paris talks that would enable the United States to exit with honor from Vietnam and preserve the Saigon regime. But unlike the situation at the Geneva Conference in 1954 (when the Russians and Chinese induced the Vietminh to accept a compromise settlement to give the French a graceful way out), the Soviet Union refrained from pressuring its ally in Hanoi to accommodate the United States. Soviet military aid continued to flow to North Vietnam well into the Nixon presidency, which eventually enabled the North Vietnamese to renew their offensive against the Saigon regime in 1972.

While Nixon began to withdraw U.S. ground forces from Vietnam, Hanoi continued to pursue the war in the south and instructed its negotiators in Paris to rebuff all American bids for a diplomatic settlement. Even top secret, "back channel" talks between Kissinger and North Vietnamese delegates in Parisian suburbs went nowhere.

The North Vietnamese had little incentive to compromise at the peace table because they knew that Nixon would not dare to reverse the course of de-escalation he had set in motion for fear of inflaming the war-weary American public. They also knew that the South Vietnamese army was incapable of winning the war on its own. Time was clearly on Hanoi's side. All it had to do was stall in Paris while the U.S. army completed its phased withdrawal from South Vietnam, leaving the fragile Saigon regime and its ineffectual army to fend for itself.

In the face of Hanoi's intransigence at the Paris peace talks, Nixon decided to subject the enemy to two final blows in an effort to force it to negotiate in good faith. The first victim of this expanded U.S. military activity was not North Vietnam but the neighboring country of Cambodia. Since obtaining its independence in 1954, Cambodia had clung to a precarious neutrality under the tutelage of its monarch, Prince Norodom Sihanouk. Expecting North Vietnam to win the war, the wily prince in Phnom Penh had refused to cooperate with the U.S.-sponsored regional security organization SEATO, withstood pressure from Washington to support the American war effort in Vietnam, and announced in 1964 his refusal to accept any further American aid. In 1966 he bowed to pressure from China and allowed the Cambodian port of Sihanoukville to be used to supply Viet Cong units in South Vietnam. He also tacitly permitted the North Vietnamese army to use his country's territory as staging areas for its campaign in South Vietnam. Whereas President Johnson had consistently prohibited his generals from expanding military operations into Cambodia against North Vietnamese units stationed there, Nixon ordered a secret bombing campaign within Cambodian territory in April 1969. Sihanouk looked the other way rather than challenge this blatant infringement of his country's sovereignty, as he had when North Vietnamese units operated within it. But he refused to permit U.S. or ARVN ground forces to pursue North Vietnamese troops across the Cambodian border.

Sihanouk's juggling act finally came to an abrupt end on March 18, 1970, when he was overthrown in a military coup during his annual vacation on the French Riviera. The new head of state in Phnom Penh, General Lon Nol, had been secretly encouraged by U.S. intelligence officials to move against the slippery Sihanouk. Lon Nol promptly reversed the deposed monarch's policy of placating Hanoi and submitting to pressure from Beijing. The removal of Sihanouk afforded a golden opportunity to Nixon, who had concluded that the bombing of the North Vietnamese sanctuaries in Cambodia was ineffectual and that the introduction of ground troops was necessary to deliver a knockout blow against the enemy forces there. He therefore announced on April 30 that American and South Vietnamese ground forces had crossed the border into Cambodia with the approval of the new regime in Phnom Penh to wipe out the North Vietnamese and Viet Cong sanctuaries in the country.

Nixon's Cambodian operation proved a total failure. All U.S. soldiers were withdrawn in a month without having located a single North Vietnamese or Viet Cong hideout. But the brief raid into Cambodia had several unintended consequences: Protests on American college campuses against the expansion of the war led to the killing of four students at Kent State University in Ohio by national guardsmen. After American forces withdrew from Cambodian territory, South Vietnamese soldiers lingered long enough to engage in a rampage of murder and looting that inflamed Cambodian opinion against them. In the meantime Sihanouk established a coalition government-in-exile in Beijing including representatives of the indigenous Cambodian Communist movement, the Khmer Rouge, which had begun to receive aid from North Vietnam and China. The Khmer Rouge proceeded to mount a full-scale insurgency against the American-backed regime of Lon Nol. The result was a bloody civil war in Cambodia, which Sihanouk had so skillfully kept out of the Vietnam conflict until his ouster.

After a lull in the fighting in South Vietnam, Hanoi decided in May 1971 to prepare for another major offensive within a year, confidence that U.S. public opinion would not permit the reintroduction of ground forces. In the meantime Nixon had decided to employ air power to prevent a North Vietnamese victory. On December 26, 1971, he resumed the bombing of North Vietnam south of the 20th parallel to deter another offensive, but to no avail. The long-planned North Vietnamese attack began on March 30, 1972, when infantry units spearheaded by tanks burst through the demilitarized zone along the border separating the two Vietnams. Within a month the president responded to this direct threat to his policy of "Vietnamization" by taking a step that Johnson had never dared to contemplate: He ordered the mining of Haiphong harbor in order to halt the flow of weapons to Hanoi from the Soviet Union. The mining operation was a short-term success: Moscow did not challenge the de facto blockade, which was an act of war according to international law. In the meantime the most intensive bombing campaign of the war did not halt the North Vietnamese advance in the south, but it began to stall in the middle of June. The resulting stalemate on the battlefield finally prompted both parties to seek a negotiated settlement. Hanoi had good reason to fear losing the hitherto unconditional support of its patrons in Moscow and Beijing. Despite some collateral damage to Soviet ships docked in Haiphong harbor and the continued bombing of North Vietnam, Brezhnev had warmly welcomed Nixon on the American president's historic state visit to Moscow in May 1972. It became clear to Hanoi that Moscow was giving top priority to its pursuit of détente with Washington. Nixon's invitation to China the previous February suggested that Beijing was also eager to improve relations with Washington (see page 243). Neither event inspired confidence that North Vietnam could continue to rely on the unwavering support of its two Communist patrons.

By September 1972 only thirty-nine thousand U.S. military personnel remained in South Vietnam. It was evident that Nixon would easily defeat the Democratic presidential candidate, George McGovern, who was running on a platform of immediate and unconditional withdrawal from Vietnam. With nothing to gain by delay, North Vietnamese representative Le Duc Tho resumed negotiations with Kissinger in Paris. These intensive discussions finally resulted in a breakthrough when each side made a crucial concession: Hanoi dropped its demand for the removal of the Thieu regime and the creation of a coalition government including the NLF. Kissinger promised the total withdrawal of American forces within two months, accepted the stipulation that the Saigon government enter into discussions with the NLF, and agreed to a cease-fire in place instead of the total withdrawal of North Vietnamese forces from the south that the United States had long demanded.

Nixon was denied a peace treaty by election day when Thieu adamantly refused to endorse the compromise settlement that Kissinger and Le Duc Tho had approved in Paris. After Nixon's reelection by a landslide, he decided to use a combination of the carrot and the stick to assure the South Vietnamese president's acceptance of the draft agreement. The carrot consisted of an eleven-day bombing campaign against Hanoi and Haiphong in late December, which was designed to strengthen Saigon's bargaining position in the projected peace talks with its Communist adversaries. Kissinger followed up this demonstration of U.S. support for Saigon with a private commitment to reintroduce American ground troops if Hanoi violated the agreement. The stick consisted of a threat to cut off American aid and make a separate peace with Hanoi if Thieu refused to accept the deal. After the South Vietnamese president caved in and endorsed the Paris accords, Le Duc Tho and Kissinger signed the cease-fire agreement on January 27, 1973, shortly after Nixon began his second term. The United States pledged to remove all of its armed forces from South Vietnam within sixty days. The two sides agreed on an exchange of prisoners of war. The ambiguous political terms of the accord—which were never carried out—provided for negotiations between the two contending factions in the south to organize democratic elections.

Although the United States was the principal foreign power engaged in the war in Vietnam, its Cold War adversary played an indirect role as well. The expansion of the American commitment to South Vietnam in 1965 was matched by an increase in the Soviet Union's assistance to North Vietnam. Khrushchev had drastically reduced Soviet military aid to Hanoi in 1964 after Ho Chi Minh had declined to give unequivocal support to Moscow in its escalating dispute with Beijing. But Ho's refusal to take sides in the rift between his two Communist patrons also irritated Mao, who kept Chinese assistance to North Vietnam at a low level. After deposing Khrushchev in October 1964, the new leadership in the Kremlin sought to mend fences with North Vietnam to secure its unequivocal support. Soviet Prime Minister Alexei Kosygin visited the North Vietnamese capital in February 1965 and concluded a mutual security pact with Ho Chi Minh, coincidentally just as the American bombing campaign against the North began. Moscow indignantly denounced the American air strikes and stepped up its deliveries of military equipment to Hanoi. The flow of Soviet arms continued well into the Nixon presidency, enabling the North Vietnamese to drive a hard bargain at the Paris peace talks. Soon thereafter the Soviet Union began to provide training for North Vietnamese regulars and to send Giap's army an increasing amount of military aid, including airplanes, antiaircraft batteries, artillery, machine guns, and rifles. China provided North Vietnam with only about a quarter of the aid sent by the Soviet Union and its Eastern European satellites. About sixty thousand Chinese operated in North Vietnam as railway maintenance workers, warehouse personnel, and antiaircraft crews. But the provision of combat troops was out of the question. The "Cultural Revolution" that began in the spring of 1966 absorbed the energies of the Chinese for the next several years and prevented them from playing a major role in support of North Vietnam.

The United States persuaded a number of its allies in the Far East, including South Korea, Thailand, the Philippines, Australia, and New Zealand, to contribute to the South Vietnamese war effort. The U.S. naval and air bases in the Philippines provided crucial repair stations and staging grounds for American ships and planes. While politely declining Chiang Kai-shek's offer of Nationalist Chinese units for fear of provoking Beijing into a more active intervention on Hanoi's behalf, the

United States induced South Korea to contribute fifty thousand combat troops to the war. Japan sent medical teams and over $50 million in economic aid to South Vietnam. American military bases in Japan and Okinawa served the American war effort pursuant to the Japanese-American security treaty, despite vociferous protests that erupted in several Japanese cities in 1967–1968. As in the Korean War, the Japanese economy benefited handsomely from the U.S. military involvement in Vietnam. Japan's export trade with South Vietnam expanded significantly during the conflict, while American soldiers on leave poured dollars into the Japanese economy. South Korea's and Taiwan's export boom during the 1960s was fueled in part by the demand for textile products induced by the war.

As the last remnants of the huge U.S. expeditionary force departed from South Vietnam in early 1973, the Saigon regime was left in an exceedingly advantageous position vis-à-vis its Communist adversaries. The ARVN had become the fifth largest military force in the world, fortified with a formidable cache of weapons and ammunition left behind by the Americans. In addition to its advantages in manpower and firepower, South Vietnam had been privately assured by the Nixon administration of prompt American military intervention if the North Vietnamese violated the Paris peace agreement. But the promise of U.S. support vanished into thin air in November 1973 when the U.S. Congress overrode President Nixon's veto to enact the War Powers Act. This legislation stipulated that American military personnel sent into combat overseas be repatriated within two months in the absence of explicit congressional approval. It was unmistakably evident that American public opinion would not permit the return of U.S. military forces to the land they had recently evacuated. Thus was born what later advocates of American intervention elsewhere in the world would lament as the "Vietnam syndrome": the reluctance to use military force abroad in pursuit of American interests.

After rebuilding its armed forces Hanoi concluded in January 1975 that, in light of the drastic reduction in U.S. military aid to Saigon and the continuing weakness of the ARVN forces, the time was ripe to resume the military pressure on South Vietnam. On March 9 North Vietnamese units opened a series of offensives against South Vietnamese military positions from the Central Highlands toward the sea with the objective of slicing the country in half. After the fall of the key ARVN outpost of Ban Me Thuot, President Thieu decided to abandon the Central Highlands and pull back his military forces to protect the embattled country's major cities. But to no avail. By the last week of March the cities of Hue and Danang—which had become household words to American television viewers—fell to the North Vietnamese as thousands of desperate refugees clogged the roads and demoralized ARVN units surrendered. In the meantime the other two pro-Western regimes of Indochina teetered on the verge of collapse: In Laos the Communist Pathet Lao mounted a major offensive against the government of Souvanna Phouma on March 27 and approached the capital city of Vientiene. In Cambodia the Khmer Rouge Communist guerrilla forces controlled 80 percent of the country and besieged the capital city of Phnom Penh. After the pro-American Cambodian head of state General Lon Nol resigned and fled the country, Khmer Rouge military units entered the capital on April 17 and took control. As eighteen divisions of the North Vietnamese army prepared to mount the final assault on Saigon and the ARVN began to disintegrate, South Vietnamese President Nguyen

Van Thieu resigned on April 21. Eight days later the U.S. ambassador launched a massive evacuation operation that airlifted seventy-one hundred U.S. and South Vietnamese military and diplomatic personnel from Saigon and sea-lifted over seventy thousand South Vietnamese nationals to U.S. ships offshore. On April 30, 1975, a North Vietnamese armored column entered the city and smashed through the gates of the presidential palace to raise the Viet Cong flag. Three divisions of the victorious army were promptly redeployed to Laos, where they helped the Pathet Lao drive the final nail into the coffin of that country's non-Communist regime in late August.

When historians evaluate a major war, it is customary to assess the benefits and the costs that flowed from the conflict. North Vietnam, the victor, obtained the ultimate reward of sovereignty over the southern part of the country that the government in Hanoi had always insisted should and would be united under its aegis. Ho Chi Minh, who died in 1969, did not live to see his country's military triumph in 1975 and the reunification of the two Vietnams that formally took place the following year. But his political and military advisers who had fought beside him against the Japanese, the French, the Americans, and the South Vietnamese had cause for celebration. The social, economic, and psychological costs of that victory were enormous, however, and would be paid by succeeding generations for decades to come.

For the United States, the loser, there were no discernible benefits from what had become America's longest war. The human costs included the approximately fifty-eight thousand U.S. servicepeople who lost their lives and the hundreds of thousands of survivors who coped with wounds or long-term physical disabilities. The economic costs of the war, which had risen to $50 billion a year at its height, were profound: Refusing to increase taxes or reduce spending for his "War on Poverty" at home, President Johnson financed the military operation in Southeast Asia by borrowing. The result of these expanding budget deficits was a chronic inflation that undermined the American economy and helped to destroy the international monetary system that had been created at the end of World War II. The collapse of the gold standard, the end of the system of fixed exchange rates, and the ballooning balance-of-payments deficits of the United States in the early 1970s were all partly traceable to the financial burden of the Vietnam War. Finally, its social consequences within the United States were also profound and long-lasting. Two of them stand out as fundamental: public cynicism about the government generated by the exaggerations and misstatements concerning the progress of the war and a generation of disaffected veterans, some afflicted with crippling psychological disabilities as well as bitter memories of a war that (unlike the one their fathers had waged against Hitler and Hirohito) had lost the support of the people at home.

## China Turns to the West

Despite their joint efforts on behalf of North Vietnam during its military struggle with the United States, the rift between the Soviet Union and China continued to widen during the second half of the 1960s (see page 213). On March 2, 1969, the war of words between Moscow and Beijing degenerated into a war of bullets. Chinese and Soviet military forces exchanged gunfire on the Damansky (or Chenpao) island along the course of the Amur and Ussuri rivers that separate the two countries, a border clash that resulted in several casualties on both sides. After other border incidents in the following summer and a revival of Chinese territorial claims, the Soviet Union transferred from Europe several combat divisions and bomber units armed with nuclear weapons and began to stockpile tactical nuclear weapons in the Soviet satellite of Mongolia adjacent to China. Soon after the Nixon administration took power in Washington, the Kremlin secretly inquired about its reaction—which turned out to be decidedly negative—to a preemptive Soviet strike against the small but growing nuclear forces that China was developing in its testing site in Xinjiang province since joining the nuclear club in 1964. Soviet diplomats then approached the governments of India, Thailand, and Indonesia in the summer of 1969 with a proposal—which was promptly rejected by all three—for a quadripartite military alliance directed against China. Although these projects for nuclear intimidation and diplomatic encirclement both fizzled, the Kremlin kept up the pressure on its antagonist in Asia. By the beginning of the 1970s Soviet troop strength on the Chinese border approached the Red Army's contribution to the Warsaw Pact's forward forces in Eastern Europe. Mao urged his countrymen to "store grain and dig tunnels deeply" in preparation for war against either the former ally in Moscow or the longtime adversary in Washington. China suddenly found itself squeezed between two superpowers armed with advanced nuclear weapons that could devastate its territory with impunity; the rudimentary Chinese delivery system provided no credible deterrent against either threat.

This growing tension between the two Communist powers obviously presented a tempting opportunity for the United States to move into the breach. A direct approach to Beijing was out of the question because the United States steadfastly refused to accord diplomatic recognition to the PRC. Notwithstanding the absence of formal diplomatic relations, desultory conversations between U.S. and Chinese representatives had taken place in Geneva and Warsaw since the mid-1950s. Mao suspended these informal contacts in the second half of the 1960s because of the massive American bombing campaign against neighboring North Vietnam. But the channel of communication between Washington and Beijing was not closed down completely during the Vietnam War. With France serving as an intermediary, the two governments privately agreed in 1965 to avoid a repetition of the Sino-American clash fifteen years earlier, when MacArthur's aggressive strategy had provoked Chinese military intervention in the Korean War. The United States informally promised not to invade North Vietnam and to refrain from bombing near the Chinese border. But a genuine improvement in Sino-American relations was precluded by China's internal chaos during the Cultural Revolution of 1966–1969, when Mao purged his putative enemies at home and suspended the PRC's contacts with most foreign governments.

As U.S. intelligence soon discovered, the Cultural Revolution was largely directed at Chinese supporters of the Soviet Union, which by the late sixties Mao had come to regard as the main threat to China's security. In the meantime President Johnson's decision to seek a negotiated settlement in Vietnam at the end of his term calmed Chinese fears about the expansion of American power on the mainland of Asia. Then Nixon and Kissinger sensed that Beijing might be willing to settle its differences with the United States in order to concentrate on dealing with the Soviet threat from the north. Soon after his inauguration Nixon began to send friendly signals to Beijing with the French government serving as the intermediary. The first public gesture from Washington came in July 1969, when the State Department announced a relaxation of travel restrictions to China dating from the Korean War. In January 1970 Beijing reciprocated by proposing the resumption of the ambassadorial talks in Warsaw that had been broken off because of the American bombing campaign in Vietnam. After two such Sino-American meetings the U.S. invasion of Cambodia in the spring of 1970 once again interrupted the discussions, as Beijing sharply criticized the most recent U.S. military action.

Yet positive signals continued to issue from both capitals. In an October 1970 press conference, Nixon used the term "People's Republic of China" (rather than "Red China" or "Communist China") for the first time. Two months later Mao told the visiting American journalist Edgar Snow that he hoped to discuss solutions to Sino-American difficulties with the new president. In March 1971 the State Department removed all remaining restrictions on travel to China, paving the way for Beijing's first public expression of good will toward Washington: In the following month the Chinese government invited an American table tennis team competing in Japan to play against the championship Chinese team. While newspaper columnists joked about Beijing's circuitous "Ping Pong diplomacy," the U.S. athletes were greeted by Premier Zhou Enlai with a friendly speech about the need to expand people-to-people contacts between the two countries. Within a few months American students, scholars, and journalists were visiting the exotic country that had been off limits for two decades. In June Nixon did his part to preserve the momentum of the thaw in Sino-American relations by revoking the twenty-year-old trade embargo on China and encouraging U.S. firms to seek customers there. The advent of tourism and trade between the two countries highlighted the anomalous absence of official links between the two governments. After communicating with Chinese authorities through Pakistan (which enjoyed cordial relations with both the United States and China), Kissinger secretly flew to Beijing on July 9 to confer with Zhou Enlai. On receiving assurances that the United States was prepared to establish some type of government-to-government relationship with the PRC, Zhou issued a formal invitation for a presidential visit to his country. On July 15, 1971, Nixon astonished the world by revealing Kissinger's exploratory mission and announcing his intention to travel to China.

The announcement of the Nixon trip precipitated a ferocious power struggle within the Chinese leadership. Lin Biao, head of the People's Liberation Army and Mao's presumptive heir, headed a radical faction that opposed a Sino-American rapprochement and favored repairing relations with Moscow. When Mao openly sided with the moderates led by his longtime associate Zhou, Lin allegedly planned a coup in September 1971 to reverse the emerging détente with the United States. After the plot was uncovered the rebellious military leader vanished from public view. He was later reported to have perished with several co-conspirators in a suspicious airplane crash while seeking asylum in the Soviet Union. Mao and Zhou exploited the alleged conspiracy to mount a wholesale purge of the PLA officer corps in order to remove known or suspected opponents of the new line. Nixon facilitated Mao's internal campaign by inaugurating a major reversal of American foreign policy that was warmly received in Beijing. On October 25, 1971, the United States stood aside as the United Nations voted to admit the PRC, expel the Chinese Nationalist government, and transfer to Beijing China's permanent seat on the Security Council.*

In February 1972 Richard Nixon journeyed over twenty thousand miles across the Pacific to become the first American president in history to visit China. In addition to a historic hour-long meeting between Nixon and the ailing seventy-eight-year-old Mao Zedong, the two historic adversaries engaged in intensive discussions of the major points of dispute between them. On February 27 Nixon and Premier Zhou Enlai signed a joint communiqué in Shanghai that candidly recorded the differences that continued to separate the two countries. China demanded an end to all U.S. military assistance to Taiwan and reaffirmed its intention to support "the struggles of all oppressed peoples" (an unmistakable reference to the North Vietnamese). The United States acknowledged that the PRC was the sole government of China and that Taiwan was a part of China, but insisted that the longstanding dispute between Beijing and Taipei be resolved by peaceful means. Nixon pledged to reduce the U.S. military presence on Taiwan as tensions in the area diminished, but reaffirmed the 1954 mutual defense treaty with the island in the absence of adequate guarantees against an invasion from the mainland. Both governments condemned the quest for "hegemony" in East Asia (a term China usually employed against the USSR and pledged to oppose any other nation's efforts to that end (an unmistakable warning to Moscow). Indeed, the principal victim of the emerging Sino-American rapprochement was the Soviet Union. By "playing the China card," Nixon and Kissinger hoped to induce the Kremlin to adopt a more cooperative attitude toward strategic arms control and political détente in Europe (see page 121). The U.S. military withdrawal from Vietnam currently being negotiated in Paris was also bound to increase pressure on Moscow by releasing Chinese military forces in the southern region for redeployment along the Soviet frontier. The PRC chose to "play the American card" for similar reasons: The same Chinese leader who had earlier criticized Khrushchev for his policy of peaceful coexistence with the capitalist-imperialist bloc was now sidling up to the United States to counterbalance Soviet power in Asia.

Economic considerations played an important role in the Sino-American rapprochement as well. Since the nineteenth century the lure of the "China market" had exerted a powerful attraction on the American business community. For two decades this vast country comprising a quarter of the world's population had been off limits to U.S. exporters. The prospect of sales to this previously inaccessible market proved particularly attractive at a time when the U.S. economy had begun to falter after a quarter century of expansion in the face of stiff competition from Japan and the European Economic Community. After Nixon's trip had broken the ice, representatives of American firms rushed to China in search of deals to make. U.S. exports to China soared from a paltry $5 million in 1969 to almost $1 billion by the mid-1970s,

---

*Washington had tried to arrange a compromise that would have permitted the PRC to take the Chinese seat on the Security Council while allowing the "Republic of China" on Taiwan to retain membership in the General Assembly. But a majority of the United Nations voted to expel Taiwan from and admit the PRC to both bodies.

with grain shipments accounting for most of these early sales. The Chinese government relished the opportunity to develop commercial relations with the United States to replace the trade links with the Soviet Union that had been severed in the 1960s.

The emerging Sino-American rapprochement in the early 1970s stopped short of the establishment of formal diplomatic relations. Nixon dropped hints to his Chinese hosts that he was prepared to consider recognizing Beijing and severing ties with Taiwan after the 1972 elections. But he got cold feet after his landslide reelection. Although the old "China lobby" was all but defunct, there were still enough sympathizers of Nationalist China in the right wing of the Republican Party to make it politically inexpedient to take the ultimate step of formal recognition. The best that the Chinese could get was an agreement in May 1973 to establish "liaison offices" that would serve as unofficial embassies in the two capitals. But this awkward "two Chinas policy" kept the flame of the Sino-American rapprochement alive while preserving Washington's traditional ties with Taipei. All of the old assumptions about great power relations in the Far East had been brought into question. The American withdrawal from Southeast Asia and the simultaneous expansion of Soviet military power along China's northern border in the early 1970s radically transformed the geopolitical situation in that part of the world. The Cold War in Asia receded in importance as Washington, Moscow, and Beijing pursued a complex triangular diplomacy that had nothing to do with ideological loyalties and everything to do with the pursuit of their respective national interests.

## Indonesia's Bid for a Regional Role

On August 17, 1945, two weeks before Ho Chi Minh surfaced in Hanoi to declare Vietnam's independence from France, a nationalist leader on the island of Java named Achmed Sukarno had appeared in the city of Jakarta to announce the transformation of the Dutch East Indies into the independent Republic of Indonesia. But unlike Ho and his associates in the Viet Minh, Sukarno and his co-leader of the Indonesian national cause, Muhammed Hatta, had no ties to the international Communist movement. On founding the Indonesian Nationalist Party (PNI) in 1928 to agitate for independence from the Netherlands, Sukarno and Hatta both rejected Communism as a suitable vehicle for the achievement of national liberation. After two years in jail for anticolonial activities, they were released and exiled in 1933. During the Japanese occupation of the Dutch East Indies, the two nationalist leaders were permitted to return to Java and resume their anticolonial activities. Toward the end of 1944, Japanese occupation officials began to seek the support of the indigenous peoples of the Dutch East Indies against the advancing U.S. military and naval forces by promising them full independence. In May 1945 Sukarno, Hatta, and their followers were permitted to draw up a constitution for an independent Indonesian Republic.

The East Indies had long represented an important source of rubber, tin, and especially oil for the Netherlands. So the postwar Dutch government was as intent on regaining control of its Southeast Asian colony as the government of liberated France was on returning to Indochina. Just as British military forces had been delegated to receive the Japanese surrender in the southern half of Indochina, British units

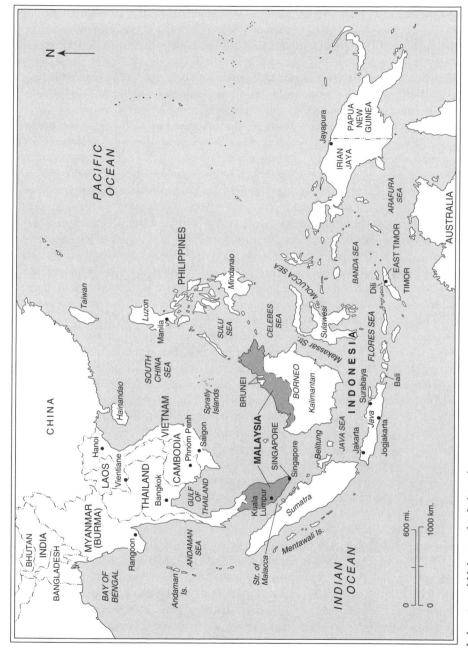

Indonesia and Malaysia after Independence

disarmed the Japanese forces in the Dutch East Indies. But unlike British General Douglas Gracey in southern Indochina, who permitted French colonial forces to return to the territory under his control, the commander of British forces in Southeast Asia, Lord Louis Mountbatten, prevented Dutch troops from returning on his arrival in the East Indies in September 1945. He did so to avert a violent clash between the colonial power and the newly established Indonesian Republic, which possessed a military force that had been trained and armed by the Japanese before their departure.

But when negotiations between the Dutch and Indonesian authorities stalled after several months of bitter wrangling, the financially strapped British decided to extricate themselves from the sticky situation. Mountbatten removed most of the British troops from the islands in April 1946, transferring administrative authority not to representatives of the Indonesian Republic but rather to the Dutch colonial officials who had been allowed to return. Under strong pressure from London and Washington, representatives of the two parties initialed a compromise arrangement known as the Cheribon Agreement in November 1946. It provided for Holland's recognition of an Indonesian Republic comprising the islands of Java, Sumatra, and Madura, which would be combined with the remaining islands under Dutch control to form a federal United States of Indonesia under the nominal jurisdiction of the Dutch crown. But after the agreement was signed on March 25, 1947, attempts to carry it out were stymied by sharp differences of opinion between the two parties. Repeated armed clashes between them prompted the one hundred thousand Dutch troops stationed on the island of Java to mount a "police action" on July 20 against the military forces of the fledgling Indonesian Republic. Responding to harsh criticism in the United Nations, the two sides agreed to a cease-fire in January 1948. But continual skirmishes between Dutch and Indonesian units resulted in a second "police action" on December 18 of that year, during which the Dutch overtly attempted to topple the Indonesian government that had been established in Java. This campaign failed to achieve its objective, as the Indonesian army dispersed into the interior and mounted a campaign of guerrilla warfare against the Dutch-controlled cities.

Unlike the conflict that was simultaneously raging in Indochina, the national liberation movement in Indonesia remained untainted by Communist affiliations. In fact, Indonesian military forces ruthlessly crushed a Communist uprising in September 1948. The United States therefore did not view the struggle against the Dutch through the prism of the Cold War, as it increasingly came to do in Indochina. Worried that the Dutch attempts to suppress Indonesian nationalism might play into the hands of Asian Communists, the Truman administration temporarily suspended Marshall Plan aid in an effort to pressure Holland into reaching a settlement with the rebels. Dutch and Indonesian representatives met in The Hague during the fall of 1949 and finally reached what appeared to be a mutually satisfactory compromise: Both parties recognized the United States of Indonesia with the Dutch queen as titular head of state, Sukarno as president, and Hatta as prime minister. The agreement postponed the controversial issue of the political status of the hotly contested territory on the western half of the island of New Guinea (widely known as West Papua). On December 27, 1949, Holland formally transferred political authority over the rest of the Dutch East Indies to the new Indonesian Republic while retaining control of West Papua.

The multiethnic, multireligious, multilingual republic of Indonesia that obtained its independence at the end of 1949 boasted a large and expanding population as well as vast reserves of petroleum, tin, and rubber. The opposition Communist Party of Indonesia (the PKI), which had declined into political insignificance at the time of independence, rallied to win 16 percent of the vote in the elections of 1955. Heartened by this remarkable electoral comeback, the PKI sought to mend its fences with the ruling party of President Sukarno. By that time the flamboyant Sukarno had become a statesman of world renown, joining with India's Nehru, Egypt's Nasser, and Yugoslavia's Tito to form the nonaligned bloc of newly independent states that refused to take sides in the Cold War. In April 1955 he hosted a historic meeting of Afro-Asian states in the Javanese city of Bandung, which denounced the surviving remnants of colonialism in the world and advocated disengagement from the East-West conflict. But for all his impassioned rhetoric about nonalignment in the Cold War, Sukarno began to respond favorably to the political overtures from his country's Communist Party and began openly to criticize Indonesia's socioeconomic elites for their close ties to Western commercial and financial interests.

Sukarno's turn to the left antagonized anti-Communist regional military commanders on the island of Sumatra, who sought financial assistance from American oil companies and military aid from the U.S. government for a planned insurrection against the government in Jakarta. The Eisenhower administration, alarmed at the growing influence of the PKI within Sukarno's entourage, began in 1956 to deliver arms to the Sumatran military rebels. CIA pilots were soon conducting bombing missions against Indonesian government forces on behalf of the insurgents. Sukarno responded to this challenge to his political power by proclaiming martial law, imposing on the compliant Indonesian parliament an authoritarian system of "guided democracy," and tightening his links with the PKI. In 1957 the Indonesian government confiscated all remaining Dutch-held properties and expelled Dutch personnel from the country, to the satisfaction of its Communist allies and to the consternation of its anti-Communist critics in Washington.

The increasingly contentious political situation in Indonesia soon attracted the attention of foreign powers, both within and outside the region, which sought to profit from the simmering conflict between the government and its opponents. The newly independent states of Malaysia and Singapore, which retained close ties to their former British colonial masters, actively supported the Sumatran military insurrection and served as conduits for foreign weapons deliveries to the rebels. Sukarno thereupon turned to the Soviet Union and Eastern Europe for military and economic assistance to counter the intervention of neighboring states that he reviled as lackeys of British imperialism. As part of Khrushchev's campaign to woo non-Communist nations in the Third World, Moscow extended a $117.5 million credit to Indonesia in 1959 and an additional outlay of $250 million in January 1960. Communist China intensified its already intimate ties with the ostensibly nonaligned regime in Jakarta.

Bolstered by this expanding support from the two Communist powers, Sukarno successfully suppressed the rebellion in Sumatra by the beginning of the 1960s. He then turned his attention to the western half of the island of New Guinea that remained under Dutch control. After obtaining warships, aircraft, and military technicians from the Soviet Union, Sukarno dispatched a contingent of "volunteers" in 1962 to organize a popular insurgency against Dutch rule in the territory (which he henceforth referred to as Irian Jaya). The Kennedy administration regarded Indonesia, with its hundred million people and its abundant supplies of oil, tin, and rubber, as a valuable prize in the Cold War. Unwilling to be identified with European colonialism as he courted public opinion in the Third World, Kennedy successfully pressured the Netherlands into relinquishing its last colonial foothold us the region. In September 1962 the Dutch government agreed to transfer Irian Jaya to Indonesian control by May 1, 1963, on the condition that a UN-supervised plebiscite be conducted by 1969 to determine the territory's political future. In 1965 the Papuan inhabitants of the territory, who are ethnically distinct from their Indonesian neighbors, launched a guerrilla war against Sukarno's occupation forces with World War II–vintage weapons and, in some cases, bows and arrows. The Indonesian air force responded by bombing Papuan villages, the army executed suspected ringleaders of the revolt, and a rigged plebiscite in 1968 produced an overwhelming vote in favor of annexation by Indonesia. Hordes of refugees fled across the border to the independent state of Papua New Guinea, whose government had refrained from supporting the Papuans in Irian Jaya for fear of provoking Indonesian retaliation. The newly enlarged Indonesia, a sprawling nation of over thirteen thousand islands with a population of over one hundred million, had become a major power in Southeast Asia. The United States and its most important ally in the region, Australia, were so reluctant to antagonize the populous, strategically situated, resource-rich country that they turned a blind eye to Sukarno's brutal suppression of the Papuan insurgency.

Indonesia's effortless absorption of Irian Jaya inspired Sukarno to assert similar territorial claims against the newly independent state of Malaysia, which (with British approval) had annexed the former British colonies of Sabah and Sarawak in northern Borneo. Denouncing Malaysia as a neocolonial creature of Great Britain, Sukarno decided to launch a military expedition against Sabah and Sarawak from Indonesian territory in southern Borneo. A convenient pretext for action arose in December 1962 when British troops intervened to crush a leftist insurrection against the Sultan of Brunei, whose small oil-rich state in northern Borneo had refused to follow its neighbors Sabah and Sarawak into the the Malaysian federation (see page 252). Sukarno thereupon dispatched Indonesian "volunteers" to Sarawak and Sabah in April 1963 in a blatant bid to destabilize the new Malaysian state. The Indonesian military campaign—widely known as the Konfrontasi ("Confrontation")—also began to receive assistance from indigenous Chinese guerrilla fighters in the contested territory who were loyal to the PRC.

Malaysian defense forces, openly assisted by British, Australian, and New Zealander units, clashed with Indonesian forces in Sarawak, while Sukarno received strong diplomatic support from Beijing and military assistance from Moscow. Increasingly opposed to the Indonesian leader's quest for regional hegemony, the Johnson administration in Washington supplied credits to Malaysia for arms purchases and suspended all economic and military aid to Jakarta in 1964. Indonesia's case against Malaysia was much weaker than its earlier claims to the Dutch-controlled Irian Jaya. Malaysia was a newly independent sovereign state governed by Asians, whose annexation of Sabah and Sarawak had received the formal approval of the United Nations.

Sukarno therefore found it increasingly difficult to secure domestic and foreign support for his Malaysian policy. When Malaysia was elected to the UN Security Council in 1965, Indonesia withdrew from the organization in protest. After abandoning the United Nations, Sukarno turned to the one great power that had been excluded from the world body and which shared his antipathy for the "neo-imperialist" state of Malaysia: Jakarta and Beijing began to explore the possibility of forming a vast Asian bloc to operate outside of the UN, which both governments disdained as a tool of the Western powers and their lackeys in the Third World.

As Sukarno's campaign to destabilize Malaysia bogged down into a hopeless stalemate, the upper echelons of the Indonesian army became increasingly disenchanted with his policy of confrontation. As Sukarno tightened his domestic political links with the PKI and his external links with the PRC, anti-Communist officers began to conspire against the government. In September 1965 a group of left-wing junior officers linked to the PKI kidnapped and assassinated several American-trained generals, whom they suspected of opposing the Konfrontasi with support from the CIA. The staunchly anti-Communist General Raden Suharto used the murders of his senior colleagues as a pretext to crack down on the PKI and rein in Sukarno. After initiating a reign of terror that resulted in the deaths of more than three hundred thousand leftists in the country, Suharto wrested de facto control of the government from Sukarno (whom he suspected of complicity in the abortive coup) in 1966. Suharto promptly terminated the Konfrontasi (for which the army had never developed much enthusiasm) over the indignant protests of the increasingly powerless president, reestablished friendly relations with Malaysia, and severed diplomatic relations with China. In 1967 Suharto finally replaced Sukarno as president and accelerated the political transformation of Indonesia into a bastion of anti-Communism in Southeast Asia and a staunch supporter of the United States in the Cold War. The bloody turmoil in Indonesia in 1965–1966 was almost entirely overshadowed by the contemporaneous conflict in Vietnam. Unlike the situation in Vietnam, the great powers did not become directly involved in the struggle between Sukarno and his foreign and domestic opponents. Washington's and Beijing's intervention on opposite sides in Indonesia was so indirect and surreptitious as to escape public notice. But in fact the stakes were much higher in the populous, resource-rich, strategically situated Indonesian archipelago than in Vietnam. The eventual "loss" of South Vietnam to Communism had much less geopolitical resonance than Indonesia's abrupt shift from a pro-Communist to a pro-American orientation.

Within a few years the Suharto regime in Jakarta renewed Sukarno's policy of exploiting European decolonization in Southeast Asia to promote Indonesia's territorial expansion. In the heyday of European imperialism the tiny island of Timor in the East Indies was divided between Holland and Portugal. The Dutch-controlled western half was absorbed by Indonesia at the time of its independence in 1949. The eastern half of the island remained one of the last relics of the fading Portuguese Empire, with an indigenous population comprising impoverished peasants of Malay-Melanesian stock. When the Portuguese dictatorship of Marcello Caetano was overthrown in 1974, the successor regime promptly announced its intention to grant independence to the country's remaining possessions in Africa and Asia. As was the case in the Portuguese African colonies of Angola and Mozambique, the nationalist movement in East Timor splintered into feuding factions. The Revolutionary Front for an Independent East Timor (Fretlin) represented the small but articulate urban intellectual elite, including a minority that openly embraced the ideology of Marxism. While Fretlin demanded immediate independence, a more conservative party called the Timorese Democratic Union (UDT) sought autonomy within a revamped Portuguese Empire. A third movement known as the Timorese Popular Democratic Association (Apodeti) represented the small Muslim minority that favored union with the predominantly Muslim state of Indonesia.

Ever since its acquisition of independence from the Netherlands at the end of 1949, Indonesia had to cope with the threat of separatism throughout the ethnically heterogeneous archipelago. The sudden emergence of the small independent state of East Timor amid an ethnically, linguistically, and religiously diverse region threatened to set a dangerous precedent that might lead to the disintegration of the polyglot Indonesian state. The anti-Communist government of Suharto therefore provided clandestine support for the Timorese factions opposing Fretlin, which Jakarta denounced as a Communist-controlled stalking horse for China. In the summer of 1975 a civil war erupted in East Timor between these contending factions. Indonesian military units crossed the border from the Indonesian territory of West Timor to harass the Fretlin forces, in a repetition of Sukarno's "Confrontation" with Malaysia in the sixties. By November 1975 Fretlin had defiantly declared the independence of East Timor and hurled its ragtag army against the Indonesian units in the country.

Determined to unburden itself of this distant remnant of its overseas empire, Portugal washed its hands of the escalating conflict in East Timor. The United States was the only foreign power in a position to dissuade Indonesia from meddling in the affairs of its small neighbor. But American firms enjoyed profitable economic relations with Indonesia, the government in Washington valued it as a bulwark of anti-Communism in the region, and the U.S. navy depended on access to Indonesian ports to accommodate its vessels operating in the Indian Ocean and the Western Pacific. The Suharto government therefore felt free to launch on December 7, 1975, a full-scale invasion of East Timor, which resulted in some two thousand deaths, the imprisonment of thousands of Fretlin supporters, and widespread looting and rape. After Indonesia formally annexed the eastern portion of the island in 1976, Fretlin continued to wage an underground guerrilla campaign that attracted the sympathy and support of human rights groups throughout the world. But Jakarta maintained an iron grip on the former East Timor for the next two decades.

One of the major reasons for the establishment of the Association of Southeast Asian Nations (ASEAN) in August 1967 was to involve Indonesia in a multilateral system of regional cooperation that would curb its hegemonic ambitions, just as the European Economic Community was set up in part to harness West Germany's energies for the greater good of the region. Apart from its occupation and annexation of East Timor in the mid-1970s, Suharto's regime maintained a low profile in Southeast Asia compared to Sukarno's aggressive policies during the 1960s. Jakarta refrained from meddling in the affairs of its neighbors, became a cooperative participant in ASEAN's annual meetings, and directed its energies inward to concentrate on economic development. By the 1980s Indonesian economy was recording impressive growth rates, and the country seemed poised to become the next "Asian Tiger."

## From the Emergency in Malaya to the Emergence of Malaysia

In contrast to attempts by the French and Dutch colonial authorities to regain their Southeast Asian possessions, the restoration of British authority in Malaya received the general approbation of the local population. As a result of massive migration from the Asian mainland, ethnic Chinese had become about 45 percent of the population compared to 44 percent for the indigenous Malays and 10 percent for those of Indian descent. The leading nationalist movement in the colony, the Malay Association, comprised conservative members of the socioeconomic elite who favored the continuation of British rule. A more radical nationalist organization, the Kesatuan Malaya Muda (KMM), enjoyed little popular support. The Malayan Communist Party (MCP) that had been formed in 1930 was composed mainly of Chinese migrant laborers imported to work in the tin mines and on rubber plantations, who clashed with the indigenous Malays in ugly incidents of racial violence. Emulating the successful model of Mao's revolutionary movement in China, the MCP launched a guerrilla campaign against the British authorities in 1948. Much of the support for this insurgency emanated from groups of unemployed Chinese workers who had relocated to rural areas and took possession of unoccupied tracts of land. In response to the murder of British planters by a group of MCP guerrillas in the summer of 1948, the British government declared a state of emergency and sought to quell the rural rebellion.

The insurrection in Malaya received the active support of a newly established foreign power in the region. Military officers from China's PLA secretly infiltrated Malaya in the early 1950s to work with the MCP to organize the country's ethnic Chinese minority into a revolutionary movement, which proceeded to carry out attacks on government officials and British planter families. But the absence of a common border with China denied the MCP the kind of direct assistance from Beijing that the Communist forces in the adjacent states of Korea and Indochina were receiving. Moreover, the Communist-led rebellion in Malaya was weakened by the MCP's failure to broaden its appeal beyond its ethnic base in the ethnic Chinese minority to attract support within the majority Malay population. British counterinsurgency experts profited from these weaknesses to mount a successful campaign to snuff out the rebellion. Lieutenant General Sir Harold Briggs arrived in Malaya in April 1950 with an elaborate plan to relocate the Chinese squatters to new villages. Soon the sharp increase in demand for tin and rubber caused by the Korean War sparked an economic boom in the colony, which created employment opportunities that helped to ameliorate many of the social tensions that had fed the rebellion. Robert Thompson directed an elaborate counterinsurgency operation designed to win the allegiance of the peasants by promoting land reform and economic development while protecting them from the guerrillas. By the mid-1950s the insurgent movement had dwindled to a few thousand members. British authorities relaxed their repressive policies toward the insurgents, although the state of emergency was not formally lifted until 1960. As we have seen, the successful British police operation during the Malayan emergency became a model for the counterinsurgency campaign that the United States would later wage (with much less favorable results) in Vietnam (see page 228).

The defeat of the Malayan insurgency enabled Great Britain to transfer governing authority in Malaya to a reliable surrogate, Tunku (or Prince) Abdul Rahman. The British-educated Tunku became the country's first prime minister in 1957, after it united with the former British colony of Singapore. From the very beginning the Malay political elite that dominated the new state faced the prospect of eventually being outnumbered by the Chinese immigrants who had been brought in by the British during the colonial period to work in the islands' tin mines and rubber plantations. The Tunku sought to ensure a non-Chinese majority in 1963 by proposing the expansion of a reorganized Malay Federation to include the British colonies of Sarawak, Sabah, and Brunei on the island of Borneo (see page 248). Although the Sultan of Brunei stayed out of the proposed federation for fear of losing control of his vast oil wealth, the neighboring British colonies of Sarawak and Sabah joined the Malay peninsula to form the new Federation of Malaysia on September 16, 1963. Great Britain warmly applauded this complex political arrangement, which left the former colonial power with residual military basing rights as well as considerable economic influence in the newly independent country.

The patriotic euphoria surrounding the creation of Malaysia concealed an ominous internal threat to the new country's political cohesion: The island of Singapore did not fit in comfortably with the remainder of the Federation: Singapore's ethnic Chinese majority, which constituted 75 percent of the city's 1.7 million population, resented the Malays' political domination of the new state. Moreover, Singapore's urban, cosmopolitan, entrepreneurial lifestyle shared little in common with that of its predominantly rural, economically underdeveloped partner. An outbreak of ethnic tension between Chinese and Malays in Singapore during the summer of 1964 prompted concern among officials in the Malaysian capital of Kuala Lumpur that the assertive Chinese minority would undermine the stability of the federation. To avert this threat, the government of Tunku Rahman expelled Singapore and its Chinese majority from the federation in August 1965. Cut off from its traditional markets, the densely populated, economically advanced little city-state had to look elsewhere for customers. The escalation of the American military campaign in Vietnam fortuitously provided an alternative source of demand for its exports. As we have seen, Singapore would rapidly become one of the economic success stories in Asia, while its former partners in the Malaysian Federation continued to languish in economic backwardness (see page 206).

## Insurgency and Counterinsurgency in the Philippines

In 1934 the administration of President Franklin Roosevelt announced that the Philippines, which had been acquired from Spain after the Spanish-American War of 1898, would be granted full independence at the end of twelve years. In 1936 America's sole possession in the western Pacific was granted Commonwealth status, which accorded its indigenous inhabitants the right to elect their own president and occupy most of the administrative positions in the government. The enthusiasm for Philippine independence was stronger among the colonizers than among the colonized. In a period of severe economic crisis, the U.S. Congress wished to rid itself of the financial burden of governing the far-off islands. Organized labor wanted to end the Filipinos' right of free immigration to the United States, which threatened the jobs of American workers during the Great Depression. U.S. sugar interests wanted to suppress the right of Philippine sugar to enter the American market duty-free and undersell their own product. By the end of the 1930s fewer than nine thousand U.S. military and administrative personnel remained in the Philippines, which was slated to receive its independence in 1946.

Economic power in the Philippines was monopolized by a close-knit oligarchy of wealthy landowners residing on the island of Luzon. Throughout the 1930s this most densely populated island of the archipelago was plagued by an acute shortage of arable land. This disagreeable condition was the result of overpopulation and the maldistribution of agricultural real estate, which pitted a small landowning elite against the mass of destitute peasants in an increasingly acrimonious class struggle. The Philippine Communist Party (PKP), which had failed to attract much of a following on the islands and was largely confined to the major cities, had little to with this rural conflict. During World War II, however, the PKP leader, a young tenant farmer named Luis Taruc, gained control of the guerrilla movement that was spearheading Filipino resistance to the Japanese occupation on Luzon. The Hukbalahaps, or Huks, as they were widely known, waged an energetic campaign of sabotage and harassment against Japanese troops while promoting a sweeping program of land reform to alleviate the distress of their peasant followers. By the autumn of 1944 the Huks' organization, led by a coalition of Communists and non-Communist partisans, had grown to over ten thousand guerrilla fighters who had accumulated a formidable cache of captured Japanese arms. These rural rebels fought bravely alongside the U.S. military forces under General Douglas MacArthur that had returned to the islands, temporarily shelving their radical program of land redistribution in the common interest of expelling the Japanese invaders.

The former American Commonwealth of the Philippines became an independent republic on July 4, 1946, according to plan. The elections held the previous April, which would determine the political orientation of the first postindependence government, resulted in a narrow victory for the conservative, pro-American Liberal Party. The new government in Manila proceeded to pursue policies that were clearly designed to satisfy its former colonial master: It granted ninety-nine-year leases for U.S. air and naval bases on the islands; it provided extensive economic concessions to private U.S. investors, which brought an influx of American capital; and it ordered the Huks to surrender their arms to government forces in deference to U.S. complaints about the presence of Communists in the movement's leadership. The Huks responded by staging an uprising in central Luzon against the government and its allies among the landed elite. Armed with their captured Japanese weapons, the rebels won widespread support among the impoverished tenant farmers of Luzon and conducted a campaign of harassment against the government in Manila well into the 1950s. Although Taruc and the other Huk leaders were idealistic social reformers rather than orthodox Marxist revolutionaries, Washington denounced the Huk insurrection as Communist-inspired and provided financial assistance to equip the Philippine police and security forces that were endeavoring to suppress it.

The Philippine government's counterinsurgency campaign only served to radicalize the leadership of the Huks, whose moderate leader Taruc was replaced by two committed Marxist revolutionaries, the brothers Joseph and Jesus Lava. Although they unleashed a series of hit-and-run attacks against government facilities throughout the islands, the Huks never succeeded in expanding beyond their base of operations in central Luzon. Nor, despite the Lava brothers' Marxist rhetoric, did they manage to attract support from the Soviet Union or China for their revolutionary struggle. But by tapping the wellsprings of rural discontent on Luzon, the Huks remained a thorn in the side of the U.S.-backed regime in Manila. In the early 1950s the Philippine government finally abandoned repression for an enlightened policy of conciliation. An official in the Department of National Defense named Ramon Magsaysay, the son of a schoolteacher who had been raised among the indigent peasantry of central Luzon, introduced a series of measures to address the grievances of the insurgents' peasant clientele. These programs of rural development and land reform, which were accompanied by an offer of amnesty to the Huk militants, attracted widespread support and helped to sweep Magsaysay into the presidency of the Philippines in 1953 on a wave of popular enthusiasm. By the time of his death in March 1957, Magsaysay's reforms had successfully co-opted the Huks and led to their demise (although the moderate measures he had initiated left intact the political and economic power of the wealthy landowning class of central Luzon). The defeat of the Huks through a combination of the carrot (rural development, land reform, amnesty for rebels) and the stick (tough measures against the guerrillas who refused to surrender) became, with the British suppression of the rebellion in Malaya, a model for the subsequent American counterinsurgency operation in Vietnam (see page 228).

## India's Quest for a "Third Way"

The "crown jewel" of the British Empire, the Indian subcontinent furnished important economic and military advantages that greatly enhanced the mother country's global power. Its served as an enormous guaranteed market for British manufactured goods and a reliable source of valuable raw materials. It provided an abundant supply of able-bodied young men who replenished the depleted ranks of the British army in both world wars and defended British imperial outposts across the globe. After World War I a nationwide movement of opposition to the British Raj (or rule) in India emerged in the form of the Indian National Congress, which drew its inspiration from an attorney-turned-Hindu spiritual leader named Mohandas K. "Mahatma" Gandhi. Committed to the belief that nonviolent resistance was both the most ethical and the most effective means of achieving the cherished goal of independence, Gandhi and his disciples waged a low-intensity campaign of harassment throughout the interwar period that included noncooperation with colonial authorities and the boycott of British goods. The charismatic Indian holy man was imprisoned several times for his acts of civil disobedience, only to be released on humanitarian grounds when his health deteriorated as a result of the hunger strikes that he invariably staged. The most promising opportunity for the Indian National Congress to rid the country of British rule came during World War II. While its colonial overlord was fully engaged in a fight for its very survival against Hitler's bombers in Europe and submarines in the North Atlantic, Japanese military forces overran Britain's other

Asian colonies by the spring of 1942. As Japanese troops driving across Burma approached the Indian frontier, the government in Tokyo issued seductive appeals to the Indian population to rebel against the British Raj and join Japan's campaign to eradicate European imperialism from Asia. While a few die-hard Indian nationalists were attracted to this siren song from Tokyo, Gandhi and his followers resisted the temptation to align with the Japanese against the British. But Gandhi's insistent demand that Britain withdraw from India and allow its people to cope with the Japanese threat by themselves landed him back in jail as the British forces in India concentrated on repulsing the Japanese advance.

By the end of World War II two developments within Great Britain itself contributed to the demise of that country's colonial rule in India. The first was the economic crisis that had resulted from six years of warfare, which severely constrained Britain's ability to bear the onerous costs of empire. The second was the national election of July 1945, which replaced the Conservative government of Winston Churchill that was intent on retaining the empire with a Labour government of Clement Attlee that was committed to decolonization. The renamed All-India Congress under Gandhi and his loyal disciple, a Cambridge-educated lawyer named Jawaharlal Nehru, turned down the new British government's opening proposal for autonomy. When London finally offered on March 14, 1946, to begin discussions with Indian representatives leading to full independence, the serious business of arranging the end of British colonial authority in India began.

As these negotiations proceeded, it became evident that the achievement of Indian self-rule was complicated by a seemingly intractable problem that had long plagued the subcontinent. From the very beginning of the Indian struggle for liberation after World War I, the opposition to the British Raj had been split along religious lines. The Indian National Congress of Gandhi and Nehru was composed almost entirely of the spokesmen for the colony's three hundred million Hindus. Representatives of the country's one hundred million Muslims formed a separate organization known as the All-India Muslim League. Although the two organizations occasionally worked together against the British authorities, the two religious communities that they represented continually clashed at the local level. The announcement of Britain's intention to withdraw removed the sole raison d'être for cooperation between these two rival groups. Negotiations between British and Indian officials in the spring of 1946 broke down because of acrimonious conflict between the Congress Party and the Muslim League. The leader of the latter group, Mohammed Ali Jinnah, demanded the creation of a separate Muslim state in all parts of British India with a Muslim majority. The Congress Party defiantly clung to Gandhi's vision of a united India embracing all faiths.

To break this logjam, the British government decided to issue a dramatic ultimatum to the two rival claimants to the colonial succession. Prime Minister Clement Attlee declared on February 20, 1947, his intention to grant full independence to India no later than June 1948. He appointed as viceroy Lord Louis Mountbatten, commander of British military forces in Southeast Asia during the war, with instructions to supervise an intensive round of negotiations leading to the transfer of power by the prescribed deadline. Once in Delhi, Mountbatten succeeded in getting the two sides to accord the elected parliaments of India's thirteen provinces the opportunity to decide between a single unitary state or two separate ones. The predominately Muslim provinces of Sind, Baluchistan, and the North West Frontier voted for accession to a separate Muslim state. So did the eastern, predominantly Muslim part of the province of Bengal, which meant that it would be separated by thousands of miles of Indian territory from the larger portion of the new Muslim state. Within a ten-week period during the summer of 1947, Mountbatten, Nehru, Jinnah, and their advisers painstakingly delineated the frontiers and divided the financial assets of British India between the two prospective successor states. The formal termination of British colonial authority on August 15, 1947, brought into being the predominantly Hindu state of India and the predominately Muslim state of Pakistan as self-governing dominions within the British Empire.

The British withdrawal did not result in immediate peace and tranquillity on the Indian subcontinent because the border that had been hastily drawn between the two successor states had left millions of Hindus in Pakistan and millions of Muslims in India. Neither of the two new governments was willing to cope with large, restive religious minorities that were unlikely to recognize its authority. They preferred instead the expedient solution of organizing in the autumn of 1947 a massive population exchange, during which some two million people relocated amid terrible acts of violence committed by and against Hindus, Muslims, and Sikhs.* Two months after independence, the Hindu Maharaja Sir Hari Singh of Kashmir belatedly brought his predominantly Muslim state into the Indian Union. Kashmir's Muslim majority protested vehemently and received strong support from the adjacent Islamic state of Pakistan. Sporadic fighting continued between the two successor states of British India from October 1947 until a UN-brokered cease-fire took effect in January 1949. A so-called Line of Control was established between the eastern part of Kashmir that was occupied by Pakistan and the western part that became the Indian state of Jammu and Kashmir. A UN resolution called for a referendum to permit the Kashmiris to decide their political future. But India refused to consider allowing such a procedure to take place in its predominantly Muslim province of Jammu and Kashmir for fear that a vote to secede would set a dangerous precedent for the ethnically and religiously heterogeneous country.

In the course of the 1950s and 1960s the Indian subcontinent was drawn into the East-West global struggle, although regional conflicts over disputed territory between India and Pakistan and between India and China always took precedence over Cold War issues. The two states carved out of British India did not hesitate to forge opportunistic relationships with Washington and Moscow in order to bolster their respective positions in the region. Pakistan aligned with the United States and its allies against the Communist bloc, joining SEATO in 1954 and Baghdad Pact (later the Central Treaty Organization, or CENTO) in 1955. By contrast Pakistan's regional

---

*Sikhism is a religion founded in the fifteenth century that combines elements of Islam and Hinduism. The Sikh kingdom in the northwestern corner of the Indian subcontinent was conquered by the British in 1847 and transformed into the Indian province of Punjab. On the eve of Indian independence in 1947 it was split in two, with East Punjab joining India and West Punjab joining Pakistan.

rival initially refused to take sides in the early years of the Cold War. Jawaharlal Nehru, India's popular prime minister from independence in 1947 to his death in 1964, sought to mobilize the newly independent nations of Africa and Asia into a nonaligned bloc that would offer a "third way" between Washington and Moscow. Like Egypt's Nasser, Nehru did not hesitate to exploit India's nonaligned status to play each superpower against the other to maximize the economic benefits for his own country. In 1952 he concluded with the United States a five-year "Point Four" program of development assistance, a precursor of the elaborate foreign aid programs that would flourish under the Kennedy and Johnson administrations in the 1960s as part of the American campaign to win the "hearts and minds" of the former colonial peoples in the Third World. To balance this turn to the West, Nehru signed a trade pact with the Soviet Union in December 1953 and with the PRC in 1954. He traveled to Moscow in June 1955 to conclude an agreement for Soviet economic and technical assistance with Khrushchev and Bulganin, who were about to launch their bid to win support among the newly independent countries of the world.

In the 1960s India's ability to abstain from the hurly-burly of international politics was severely tested when a long-standing territorial dispute with China escalated into armed conflict. In 1914 the mountainous, isolated kingdom of Tibet, which had been ruled by China for centuries, profited from the political chaos caused by the Chinese revolution of 1911 to declare its independence under its divine ruler, the Dalai Lama. Thirty-five years later, as Chinese troops poured into North Korea to engage MacArthur's UN force in October 1950, Mao sent the PLA into Tibet to reclaim it for China. In the spring of 1951 Beijing granted the isolated country high in the Himalaya Mountains internal autonomy within the People's Republic, allowing the Dalai Lama to remain as its figurehead leader on the condition that the Chinese government would handle Tibet's relations with foreign powers. After a decade of increasingly tense relations between Tibet's Buddhist population and Chinese authorities, fighting erupted in the capital of Llasa in the spring of 1959. Chinese Premier Zhou Enlai responded to the rebellion by dissolving the government headed by the Dalai Lama, who fled with thousands of his subjects across the border to India. As the outspoken Tibetan spiritual leader appealed to the United Nations for support against China's campaign to eradicate the Buddhist religion in his country, the Indian government granted the Dalai Lama asylum and openly supported the Tibetan cause.

Deeply resentful of the Indian government's hospitality to the Dalai Lama and his entourage, Beijing began to challenge the border between Tibet and India that had been drawn by a British commission headed by Sir Henry McMahon before World War I. The Chinese Republic had never recognized the McMahon Line, but it was too weak to contest it and had no legal standing to do so as long as Tibet remained independent. But once Beijing assumed control of Tibet's foreign and military affairs and directly administered it as a Chinese province after 1950, it revived the old challenge to the British-drawn frontier. Periodic border clashes between Chinese and Indian units in the Himalayas erupted into open warfare in October 1962, coincidentally at the height of the Cuban missile crisis. As Chinese troops poured across the Indian frontier Nehru issued a frantic appeal for U.S. military assistance to President Kennedy, who was preoccupied with his impending showdown with Khrushchev in the Caribbean. After the settlement of the Cuban crisis President Kennedy responded to Nehru's request by dispatching transport planes with U.S. crews to assist the Indian army that was retreating before the Chinese onslaught. Then the Chinese government abruptly announced a cease-fire and withdrew its troops from the disputed region. After Nehru's death in 1964 his successors, profiting from the widening rift between Moscow and Beijing, turned to the Soviet Union for support against their common Chinese adversary. The Sino-Indian conflict over Tibet and the McMahon Line cemented relations between Moscow and New Delhi, while China forged close ties with Pakistan on the basis of their shared hostility to India.

While India struggled to strengthen its defenses against its powerful neighbor to the north, the tensions over Kashmir increased when the Pakistani government stepped up its support for the Muslim opponents of Indian rule in the disputed province. The simmering conflict in Kashmir boiled over into brief wars between India and Pakistan from April to June 1965 and from September 1965 to January 1966. Tank battles spread to the Punjab region of India before the two belligerents reached agreement on a cease-fire and troop withdrawal. In the following years discontent grew among the Bengali-speaking inhabitants of East Pakistan, who accused the government in the capital city of Karachi in West Pakistan of economic exploitation and linguistic discrimination. In December 1970 the military government permitted the first free elections in a decade. They were won by the Bengali-based Awami League, which gained a majority in the new National Assembly and developed a set of demands for greater Bengali autonomy. But the head of the outgoing military regime, General Yahya Khan, intervened to prevent the parliament from holding its first meeting in March 1971. When protest demonstrations engulfed the cities of East Pakistan, Pakistani military forces poured into the Bengali capital of Dacca and began to massacre suspected supporters of the Awami League. As East Pakistan seethed with insurrection against West Pakistan, India seized the opportunity to strike a blow against its rival on the subcontinent. New Delhi permitted officials of the Awami League to set up a government-in-exile for West Pakistan in Calcutta, while India openly backed the Bengali insurrection against the Pakistani government. In December 1971 India bolstered its political support for the Bengali insurgency with military force. Indian troops swept into East Pakistan and routed the Pakistani army, leaving India free to reorganize the region as the independent state of Bangladesh.

India managed to inflict this humiliating defeat on its regional adversary without interference by the great powers, although China's intervention to preserve Pakistan's territorial integrity remained a possibility to the end of the war. Beijing had cautioned New Delhi against invading East Pakistan during the 1965 war and reiterated that warning in 1971. India responded to the renewal of Chinese pressure in August 1971 by concluding a treaty with the Soviet Union, which committed Moscow to intervene on India's behalf in the event of war with a third party. China placed its forces on alert along the Indian frontier as a gesture of support for Pakistan, while the Soviet Union shifted troops to its long border with China. The United States was caught on the horns of a dilemma by the Indo-Pakistani war of 1971: The Nixon administration had already taken steps to reverse two decades of American foreign policy and seek better relations with China (see page 234). It wanted to avoid having to choose between the equally unpalatable alternatives of tolerating a Chinese military intervention against India or of incurring Beijing's wrath (and possibly derailing the emerging Sino-American détente) by opposing it. To avoid this Hobson's choice, Washington privately pressed Moscow to induce its new Indian ally to forswear any territorial annexations in East Pakistan. While the United States remained publicly neutral in the brief Indo-Pakistani war in 1971, Nixon and Kissinger had thus decided to "tilt" toward Pakistan (in part to facilitate the planned opening to China, preparations for which were well underway).

India's regional conflicts with Pakistan and China continued at a low level of intensity without provoking the intervention of either superpower. To strengthen its position India tightened its links with the Soviet Union, abandoning Nehru's policy of nonalignment in the Cold War. In the meantime Pakistan drew closer to the United States, receiving extensive U.S. military aid and helping to facilitate the improvement in relations between its two allies, the United States and China, the following year. By the mid-1970s the two competitors on the Indian subcontinent had been drawn into the triangular relationship between the United States, the Soviet Union, and China. The increasingly intimate Sino-Pakistani-American relationship reached its apex after the Soviet invasion of Afghanistan in 1979. In the next decade these three powers would jointly supported the Islamic insurgency within Afghanistan against the Soviet forces and their Afghan collaborators (see page 361).

# EIGHT

# The Inter-American System since the Cuban Missile Crisis

### The Specter of Castro and the Demise
### of the Alliance for Progress

The Latin American states rallied behind President Kennedy in his showdown with Khrushchev during the Cuban missile crisis of 1962. The OAS unanimously supported the U.S. blockade of the island to force the removal of the Soviet missiles and then accepted the settlement that had been reached between Washington and Moscow, even though America's hemispheric neighbors had been largely ignored throughout the crisis. Once it was clear that Castro's position was secure as a result of Kennedy's no-invasion pledge, the countries of Latin America were forced to define their relationship with the one-party Communist state in Cuba that seemed here to stay. One by one they decided to cut their ties with the island in an effort to isolate it in the hemisphere. Toward the end of 1963 the discovery of three tons of weapons that Castro had shipped to guerrillas in Venezuela prompted that country's government to press for sanctions against the Havana government. When further evidence of Cuban arms turned up in several Latin American countries, the OAS voted in July 1964 to break diplomatic relations with the island and to suspend all trade and sea communications with it. Mexico was the lone dissenter, and the Havana–Mexico City flight remained Cuba's only direct air link to the rest of the Western Hemisphere for many years to come. In the face of this economic boycott by Cuba's traditional trading partners, the new pariah in the Caribbean was obliged to increase its economic dependence on the Soviet Union. The Russians continued to purchase most of the Cuban sugar crop and to provide Castro with oil and other raw materials at subsidized prices. In exchange the Cuban leader loyally supported the foreign policy goals of his benefactors across the globe. By the mid-1970s, as we have seen, Cuba was even venturing beyond the hemisphere to assist Soviet-backed forces in various parts of Africa (see page 295).

Moscow's ally in the Caribbean was singularly ineffectual in its campaign to export the Cuban brand of revolution to the rest of Latin America. Since Castro had launched his own successful insurrection against Batista with about twenty dedicated disciples, he apparently assumed that a small band of guerrillas could replicate his success against other dictatorial regimes in the region. But Cuban-supported rebellions in Venezuela, Peru, and Guatemala were crushed in the 1960s by state security forces that had been trained and armed by the United States as part of the counter-insurgency program initiated by President Kennedy and expanded by his successor. The daring attempt by Castro's agent Ernesto (Che) Guevara to establish a "continental command" in Bolivia failed when the Bolivian army captured and killed the charismatic revolutionary leader in 1967.

The official policy of the United States toward Latin America during the 1960s was symbolized by Kennedy's Alliance for Progress. The original plan envisaged a $20 billion government aid program over the next decade to promote land and tax reform, affordable housing, improvements in public health and primary education, and economic development (see page 103). From the standpoint of expenditure, the Alliance lived up to its promise: Over the prescribed ten-year period the U.S. government provided some $18 billion in foreign aid to Latin America, either directly or through multinational institutions such as the World Bank, and arranged for an additional $3 billion in private investment. But from the perspective of its effect on the standard of living of Latin American people, the Alliance did not come close to achieving the ambitious goals of its founders for a number of reasons. First, the recipient governments borrowed heavily abroad, so that in the early years about 90 percent of the U.S. aid was spent to service that foreign debt rather than to alleviate the poverty of the people or stimulate economic growth. Second, the amount of new private investment that accompanied the Alliance's public funds was exceeded by the amount of profits repatriated to the United States and Europe by companies operating in Latin America. Third, in many countries the entrenched landed oligarchies blocked the sweeping social reforms that were supposed to accompany the American aid program, so that the campaign against poverty, illiteracy, and disease never got off the ground. Finally, the governments of many of the recipient states diverted a substantial proportion of the American government funds, either through waste, mismanagement, or corruption, from their intended purposes. The result was that the wide gap between rich and poor in Latin America remained what it had been for decades. Aggregate economic growth for the region during the 1960s was 1.5 percent per year, well below the Alliance's 2.5 percent target and no improvement over the 1950s.

Another feature of the Alliance for Progress that fell far short of expectations was the proviso that economic development be accompanied by the spread of political democracy. It proved a bitter irony that while several Latin American dictators had been overthrown during Eisenhower's second administration, six popularly elected presidents were toppled in military coups during Kennedy's abbreviated term in office. This trend toward authoritarian rule provoked only mild rebukes and the temporary suspension of aid from Washington: The Kennedy administration was so concerned about the possible spread of Castro's revolution to the rest of Latin America that it was unwilling to challenge the autocratic but staunchly anti-Communist military regimes that seized power in the region.

The administration of President Lyndon Johnson had inherited from its predecessor a top secret campaign to overthrow Castro by covert means, which had been

*South America*

initiated after the Bay of Pigs fiasco and continued even after Kennedy's "no invasion pledge" to Khrushchev in the autumn of 1962. Code-named Operation Mongoose, it included plans to destroy the Cuban sugar crop as well as hair-brained schemes to assassinate Castro with cigars laced with LSD, poison-tipped pens, and exploding clamshells as he snorkled. Once in the White House Johnson ordered an end to all such efforts to unseat the Cuban leader. But the termination of Operation Mongoose did not mean that the new president had abandoned his predecessor's obsession with preventing Cuban-style revolutions in Latin America. On the contrary, the Johnson administration became even more preoccupied with the threat of Communism in the Western Hemisphere than Kennedy had been. Washington quietly abandoned the Alliance for Progress's proviso that political democracy accompany the economic growth that the American funds were designed to foster. U.S. government aid increasingly was diverted from the economic to the military sector in order to bolster the counterinsurgency campaigns that several Latin American governments were waging against domestic guerrilla movements that were widely thought to be inspired and financed by Havana.

The Brazilian government of President Joaõ Goulart hardly qualified as anti-American. On the contrary, it had enthusiastically supported the U.S. position during the Cuban missile crisis. But Goulart was a radical populist who supported redistributionist economic policies that alarmed the entrenched oligarchy and its supporters in the military. In 1963 the Brazilian government permitted the formation of labor unions in the countryside, which put pressure on large landowners to grant higher wages to farm workers and led to some seizures of land by impoverished peasants. On March 1, 1964, a carefully organized conspiracy of army generals forced Goulart into exile and established an authoritarian military dictatorship. The American ambassador and military attaché had been in touch with the plotters and later conveyed Washington's approval of the coup. U.S. dissatisfaction with Goulart stemmed from his failure to deal with the mounting financial difficulties that plagued Brazil as well as his populist attempts to mobilize the lower classes that might play into the hands of Castro and his sympathizers in the country.

This heightened concern about the threat of Communism in the Western Hemisphere prompted the Johnson administration to undertake the first overt United States military intervention in the region since the 1920s. It took place in the Dominican Republic, a small Caribbean country that, like pre-Castro Cuba, had been a virtual United States protectorate since the early part of the century. When the long-time Dominican dictator Raphael Trujillo was assassinated in May 1961, his aide (and the country's nominal president) Joaquin Balaguer assumed control of a transitional government. Under intense pressure from Washington, Balaguer organized the country's first free elections for December 1962. The winner of the elections, a radical reformer named Juan Bosch, initially received strong support from the Kennedy administration because his imaginative plans to address the social and economic problems of the impoverished Caribbean country fit in well with the objectives of the Alliance for Progress. But Washington eventually came to view Bosch as too weak to prevent a Castro-type revolution, so the United States refrained from opposing a military coup that toppled him in September 1963. Although obtaining prompt recognition from the United States, the new military regime failed to win popular support at home. On

April 24, 1965, pro-Bosch rebels took up arms against the ruling junta, plunging the little country into chaos. Four days later President Johnson, without consulting the other member-states of the OAS, dispatched U.S. marines to the Dominican capital of Santo Domingo for the ostensible purpose of protecting American residents of the country. Within a few months the American military force had expanded to twenty-five thousand. U.S. officials expressed retrospective fears that the rebellion had been instigated by Cuba or by pro-Castro elements on the scene.

Even if there had been a genuine threat of Communism in the Dominican Republic, the unilateral American military operation represented a patent violation of the nonintervention provision of the OAS charter. For the first time since the advent of Franklin Roosevelt's Good Neighbor Policy in 1934, U.S. marines were on occupation duty in a sovereign state in Latin America. Nevertheless, most of the other Latin American governments acquiesced in this unilateral American military operation. Indeed, many of them contributed troops to an inter-American peacekeeping force in the Dominican Republic that supervised nationwide elections in June 1966, which were won by Trujillo's former associate Balaguer. In September the U.S. marines together with the other contingents of the inter-American peacekeeping force withdrew from the country, as Balaguer and his conservative allies consolidated their power. By the end of the decade Bosch and his leftist supporters had receded into political insignificance. In the meantime the Dominican episode had demonstrated Washington's determination to intervene, unilaterally if necessary, when political instability in Latin American threatened to set the stage for a Castro-type revolution.

## Marxism and Despotism in Chile

The Nixon administration initially displayed very little interest in Latin American affairs. Its priorities lay elsewhere: an honorable exit from Vietnam, détente with the Soviet Union, and an opening to China. Nixon and Kissinger considered Latin America entirely peripheral to their geopolitical conception of a "pentagonal" world order comprising the United States, the USSR, the EEC, China, and Japan. But their attention was drawn south of the border in the early 1970s by dramatic political developments in Chile, a country that had long boasted one of the most stable and democratic political cultures in Latin America. The presidential elections of 1964 had provided the Chilean electorate with a stark choice between two radically different prescriptions for the country's future. One alternative was represented by the only significant coalition of left-wing political parties in the entire Western Hemisphere. The Socialist-Communist Alliance (FRAP), headed by a physician-turned-politician named Salvador Allende Gossens, advocated a series of extensive socioeconomic reforms: These included the breakup of the large landed estates in the countryside, redistribution of small tracts to the destitute peasantry, and the nationalization of the American-owned copper companies that had long dominated the Chilean economy. The FRAP was opposed by Eduardo Frei's Christian Democratic Party (PDC), which campaigned for a set of moderate social reforms aimed at alleviating the deplorable conditions of the ill-fed, ill-housed, ill-educated majority without disturbing the existing power relations in Chilean society. Although the PDC favored reformist measures (such as the expropriation of unused land) that antagonized the conservative parties, the latter groups threw their support to Frei's Christian Democrats as the only viable alternative to Allende's much more radical proposals. The U.S. government supported Frei for the same reason, despite the PDC's call for Chilean part ownership of the American copper companies to assure greater national control of the nation's natural resources. With the CIA secretly covering more than half of Frei's campaign expenses, the Christian Democratic candidate won handily in the 1964 elections with 56 percent of the vote compared to Allende's 39 percent.

During the next six years the Christian Democratic government made good on its campaign promises for moderate social reform. The Chilean state acquired 25 percent ownership of the Anaconda Copper Company and 51 percent ownership of its rival Kennecott. A land reform act of 1967 ordered the expropriation of uncultivated farmland and its redistribution to one hundred thousand propertyless peasants. In many ways Frei's Christian Democratic government seemed a throwback to the original spirit of the Alliance for Progress and its prescription for piecemeal social reform and political democracy. But during the presidential election campaign of 1970, in which Frei was constitutionally banned from participating, Allende's Socialist-Communist alliance denounced the ruling Christian Democrats' moderate reforms as insufficient. The left-wing coalition renewed its demand for the total nationalization of the copper firms and other American-controlled enterprises in the country. The blatant anti-American rhetoric of Allende's party prompted the Nixon administration to order the CIA to spend lavishly to prevent a left-wing electoral victory. But Allende profited from a split between his right-wing and reformist opponents to win a razor-thin plurality of 36 percent compared to 35 percent for the conservative candidate and 29 percent for the Christian Democrat. As required by the Chilean constitution, his election would have to be confirmed by the parliament after a two-month interregnum.

Alarmed at the prospect of radical economic reforms that would jeopardize U.S. commercial interests in Chile, the Nixon administration pulled out all the stops in a determined campaign to block Allende's road to the presidential palace. The CIA developed plans to destabilize the Chilean economy, to bribe legislators to vote against Allende, and, according to some observers, to provoke the Chilean military to intervene. When the chief of the Chilean general staff, General René Schneider, expressed his opposition to military interference in politics, U.S. officials developed contacts with dissident officers who later kidnapped and then assassinated Schneider. But this economic pressure and these contacts with Chilean officers hostile to Allende failed to prevent him from becoming the first democratically elected Marxist head of state in the Western Hemisphere. Once ensconced in the presidential palace, he proceeded to inaugurate a far-reaching program of socioeconomic reform in an effort to redeem his campaign pledges to urban workers and rural farm laborers. The new president secured legislative approval for the total nationalization of the copper companies. Other American multinational corporations, such as the International Telephone and Telegraph Company and Ford Motor Company, were slated for similar treatment. He also nationalized the domestic coal and steel industries and over half of the private banks. Since his government had no way of obtaining the foreign currency required to compensate the nationalized foreign firms, Allende peremptorily announced that no compensation was due to the American firms because of the enormous profits they had extracted from Chile over the years.

The denial of compensation for the nationalized American firms afforded the Nixon administration, which had been the subject of aggressive lobbying by the aggrieved companies, to impose retaliatory sanctions on Chile's Marxist regime. These included an informal loan embargo by the World Bank, the Inter-American Development Bank, and the Export-Import Bank as well as the suspension of all American private direct investment in Chile. The CIA secretly subsidized strikes by truckers and other antigovernment forces. These policies were designed to implement Nixon's instructions to "make the economy scream." While the country suffered from a severe shortage of working capital, Allende stepped up his land reform measures in response to pressure from militant peasants and agricultural laborers. Some of them had begun to seize land on their own, prompting the proprietors to hire armed guards to protect their property. To satisfy the demands of the urban workers, the government raised wages and imposed price controls: These policies resulted in inflation, shortages of basic goods, the emergence of a vast black market, and the flight of capital to foreign havens. By early 1973 the inflation rate in Chile had climbed to 150 percent, the balance-of-payments deficit skyrocketed, and the decline in world copper prices depressed export earnings. Supporters and opponents of the government regularly took to the streets in noisy demonstrations, while strikes and boycotts in several key sectors paralyzed the Chilean country.

The powerful political opposition to Allende in the parliament began to pose a major obstacle to further socioeconomic reforms. The radical fringe of the governing coalition therefore urged the president to abandon the legal road to socialism: Leftist firebrands demanded that he use the police against recalcitrant legislators, rule by presidential decree, and accelerate the nationalization and land redistribution policies. Ironically, the Chilean Communist Party counseled caution and restraint, fearing that such radical measures would provoke a violent reaction from the right that might overturn the recent gains. Although Allende had given Fidel Castro a rousing welcome when the Cuban leader visited Chile in 1971, he remained committed to the democratic path to socialism and refrained from using force to crush his opponents and implement his reforms.

Amid this spreading economic chaos and political unrest, disgruntled members of the Chilean officer corps decided to act. The military conspiracy unfolded on September 11, 1973. The navy seized the port of Valparaiso while the air force unleashed a rocket attack against the presidential palace in central Santiago, which army units invaded in search of the besieged head of state. Allende perished in the coup, either by his own hand or by gunfire from the soldiers. The Nixon administration, which had waged a sustained campaign to destabilize Allende's government and actively encouraged the military conspirators, promptly recognized the new military junta headed by General Augusto Pinochet Ugarte. Pinochet proceed to wage a brutal campaign of repression against leftist groups within the country that left at least three thousand Chileans dead and thousands in prison or exile. In September 1976 Chilean government agents planted a car bomb in Washington that killed Orlando Letelier, a former Allende ambassador to the United States who had become an outspoken critic of the military regime. Pinochet ruled with an iron fist until 1988, when the Chilean dictator finally caved in to international pressure for political liberalization and risked a plebiscite on his one-man rule that he lost by a margin of 55 percent to 43 percent. In 1989 an impeccably democratic presidential election brought to power the Christian Democrat Patricio Aylwin, who headed a coalition of center and center-left parties.

## Dictatorship, Development, and Human Rights

While the Pinochet regime was suppressing domestic opposition during the 1970s and 1980s, military governments throughout South America dashed the hopes for democracy in the region. After the overthrow of President Joaõ Goulart in 1964, Brazil was ruled for the next twenty-one years by a succession of military governments. They pursued a policy of rapid economic development based on the repression of labor unions to ensure low wages, the encouragement of foreign lending and investment, and an expansion of exports. Throughout the 1970s Brazil experienced a remarkable economic boom that lasted until the early 1980s, when its enormous foreign debt forced it into de facto default along with other Latin American countries that had borrowed excessively to finance their crash programs of modernization. Brazil's traditional rival Argentina experienced a similar combination of political autocracy and economic growth. After an Argentine military coup in March 1976 ousted Isabel Perón (wife of the late revered dictator Juan Perón), a succession of generals occupied the presidency and waged what its critics dubbed a "dirty war" against Peronistas and Marxist guerrillas in which at least fifteen thousand people were killed or disappeared without a trace. Not until December 1983 did the military government give way to civilian rule, after its humiliating defeat by Great Britain in the brief war over the Falkland (Malvinas) Islands in the previous year.

The long period of military rule in Latin America coincided with an impressive record of economic growth. From 1960 to 1973 the economies of Latin America grew at an average annual rate (after inflation) of almost 6 percent, far surpassing the real growth rates of the rest of the developing world. This economic dynamism continued well into the 1980s, despite temporary setbacks such as the oil shock of 1974 and the debt crisis of the early 1980s (see page 273). Several aspects of the sustained expansion in this traditionally backward region are worthy of note. First of all, it was export driven: Foreign trade as a percentage of GNP more than doubled between 1970 and 1980 in Brazil, Mexico, Argentina, Chile, Ecuador, and Venezuela and substantially increased in other Latin American countries. Total Latin American exports increased by over 10 percent a year from 1965 to 1973, compared to a 3.6 percent annual rate for the previous fifteen years. This expansion of Latin America's trade reflected a historic shift from its traditional reliance on commodity exports—primarily minerals and tropical foodstuffs—to its newly acquired capability to sell manufactured goods abroad. The proportion of manufactures in Latin America's total exports increased from 3.6 percent in 1960 to 17.2 percent in 1970. The region's exports of manufactured goods grew at an annual rate of 26.5 percent, compared to a 16.4 percent increase for the entire world during the same period. Manufactured goods replaced coffee as Brazil's leading export in the early 1970s. By 1979, the manufacturing sector in Argentina, Brazil, Uruguay, and Mexico accounted for over a quarter of those countries' GNPs. The export-led economic dynamism of these newly industrializing countries of Latin America in turn attracted foreign investment on a major scale. By the end of the 1970s, many experts were predicting a glorious economic future for a region that had for so long languished in poverty and underdevelopment.

At the height of this remarkable economic expansion in the 1970s, the new Carter administration in Washington had begun to de-emphasize the counterinsurgency features of U.S. policy toward Latin America and attempted to resurrect the commitment to political liberalization, social reform, economic development, and hemispheric cooperation that had originally inspired Kennedy's Alliance for Progress. While Carter refrained from subjecting strategically important countries such as China and South Korea to the stringent requirements of human rights, he exerted strong pressure on Latin American autocracies to loosen their iron grip. He suspended military assistance to several right-wing dictatorships south of the border; as a result U.S. military aid to Latin America declined from $234 million in 1976 to $54 million in 1979. The goal of the new policy was to win favor among progressive, democratic forces in the region and to reestablish the reputation of the United States as a champion of representative government.

The first beneficiary this new orientation of American policy was the Latin American country whose sovereignty had been most blatantly compromised by its historic relationship with the United States. America's ownership of the Panama Canal and the five-mile-wide zone surrounding it had long been a source of friction with Panama. In 1952 the Panamanian president, Colonel José Antonio Remon, persuaded Washington to renegotiate the 1903 treaty that had granted the United States perpetual sovereignty over the zone. Three years later a revised treaty increased annual U.S. payments to the Panamanian government and curtailed economic privileges for U.S. citizens in the zone. In 1964 widespread rioting in response to a perceived insult to the Panamanian flag by American high school students in the zone led to more intensive negotiations concerning the future of the canal. In 1968 a coup by the Panamanian national guard brought to power Brigadier General Omar Torrijos Herrera, who was determined to bring the seemingly interminable talks to a successful conclusion. After nine years of tortuous negotiations with the Nixon, Ford, and Carter administrations, Torrijos finally achieved his goal. Despite howls of protest from the Republican right that the termination of United States sovereignty over the canal and the zone would constitute an intolerable threat to American security interests in the Western Hemisphere, the Carter administration won Senate approval of a new treaty in 1977. The landmark agreement transferred to Panama immediate legal jurisdiction over the Canal Zone and full control of the canal itself at the end of 1999. The demise of the most egregious symbol of "Yankee imperialsm" in the Western Hemisphere reflected the increasing willingness of Washington to deal with Latin America on its own terms rather than as a theater of East-West rivalry.

## The Nicaraguan Revolution and Its Consequences

The Carter administration's new policy of promoting democracy and human rights in Latin America was put to its severest test in Nicaragua, a Central American country that had long been under the sway of American economic and military power. Since the mid-1930s Nicaragua had been run either directly or through hand-picked surrogates by the family of General Anastasio Somoza Garcia, a ruthless tyrant who had

*Members of the Sandinista rebel army manning a Russian AGS-17 automatic grenade launcher during the rebellion that overthrew the dictatorship of Anastasio Somoza Debayle in 1979. (Hulton Archive by Getty Images)*

amassed a huge personal fortune before succumbing to an assassin's bullet in 1956. After his eldest son and heir Luis died of a heart attack in 1963, power passed to his younger son, Anastasio Somoza Debayle. A West Point graduate with an American wife, Somoza the younger resumed his father's policy of supporting Washington's anti-Communist policies in Central America in exchange for the continual flow of U.S. military and economic aid. But he also continued his father's policy of repressing political opposition, accumulating a huge fortune for himself and his family while defending the privileges of the destitute country's small oligarchy of landowners and businesspeople.

By the end of the 1960s the corruption and brutality of the Somoza regime had spawned an opposition movement that, in the absence of political institutions through which its grievances could be expressed, went underground and increasingly turned to violence as a tactic to win power. This broad coalition of anti-Somoza militants adopted the name of the martyred hero General Augusto César Sandino, the leader of the resistance to the U.S. occupation forces in the 1920s who had been murdered by Somoza senior's national guard in 1934. The Sandinista National Liberation Front escalated its guerrilla attacks until the Somoza regime finally collapsed in 1979. With Somoza in exile, the new Sandinista government that assumed power in Managua proclaimed that it would pursue a nonaligned foreign policy and implement a program of fundamental socioeconomic reform at home.

The Nicaraguan rebels had taken over a poverty-stricken country that desperately needed economic assistance from abroad. Once in power the Sandinista leaders first

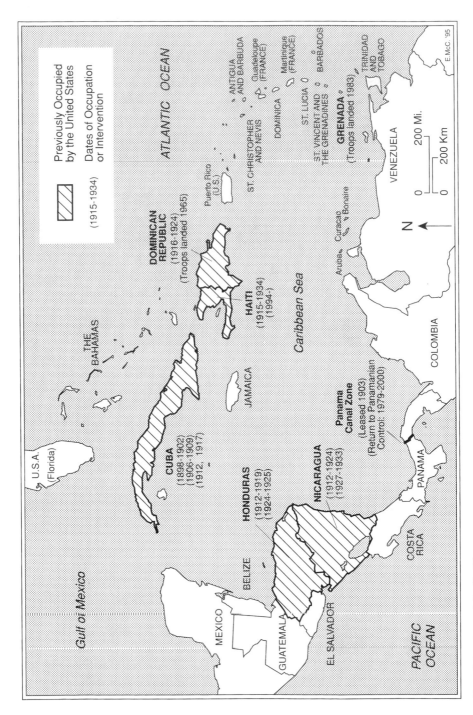

Central America and the Caribbean

appealed to the champion of human rights in the White House, who had signaled his distaste for the Somoza dictatorship by suspending U.S. military aid to the regime in 1978 and economic aid in early 1979. The Carter administration promptly provided the Sandinista government with $8 million in emergency aid, and Congress later appropriated $75 million in long-term assistance. Western European countries dispatched even more economic assistance than the Americans did, while other Latin American countries such as Venezuela, Costa Rica, and Panama expressed their strong diplomatic support. In the meantime Fidel Castro announced his enthusiastic endorsement of the new left-wing regime in Managua and sent twenty-five hundred Cuban medical personnel, school teachers, and engineers to participate in the Sandinistas' ambitious program of social reform and economic development. For a brief moment in seemed that the Nicaraguan revolutionaries who had ousted Somoza would manage the remarkable feat of maintaining friendly relations with both Washington and Havana.

But the Sandinistas' honeymoon with the United States was cut short as a result of the political chaos and social unrest that erupted in the neighboring country of El Salvador. The Salvadoran dictatorship of General Carlos Humberto Romero had been overthrown in October 1979 by a group of reform-minded junior army officers who announced their intention to address the concerns of the landless peasantry and reached out to popular organizations that had been suppressed by the previous regime. But the reformist junta's mild attempts to reduce the country's huge disparity between rich and poor were cut short by determined opposition from the landowning oligarchy and senior military officers who supported it. In the following year a number of Salvadoran guerrilla organizations went underground and joined forces to form both a unified military command called the Farabundo Marti National Liberation Front (FMLN) and a broad coalition of civilian supporters called the Democratic Revolutionary Front (FDR). In the winter of 1980–1981 the government uncovered evidence that the FMLN guerrillas were receiving weapons from the Sandinista regime in Nicaragua that had originated in Cuba. The outgoing Carter administration, which had earlier suspended military aid to El Salvador in response to its human rights violations, reacted with panic and resumed arms deliveries to the government. American officials had also become increasingly wary of the Sandinistas, noting that many officials in Managua were beginning to employ incendiary rhetoric studded with favorable references to the Cuban revolution.

During his successful presidential campaign in 1980, Ronald Reagan strongly denounced the "Marxist" regime in Nicaragua as a threat to the security of all Central America. He also blamed Carter's obsession with human rights for hastening the demise of Somoza's autocratic but pro-American regime. Shortly after taking office in January 1981, Reagan and his advisers crafted a coordinated campaign to combat what they viewed as the spread of Cuban and Soviet influence in the region and to strengthen America's anti-Communist allies there. He removed most of the restrictions on U.S. military assistance to those Latin American governments that had been found by his predecessor to be in violation of human rights. He also strongly denounced the flow of Cuban arms to Nicaragua and Nicaraguan arms to the Salvadoran guerrillas.

In the spring of 1981 the Reagan administration escalated its campaign against the spread of Communist influence in Central America by ordering the CIA to furnish financial and logistical support to a loose-knit coalition of former national guardsmen under Somoza and disenchanted Sandinista supporters who had organized to overthrow the left-wing regime in Managua. Widely known as the "Contras" because of their counterrevolutionary goals, this fighting force set up bases in neighboring Honduras and Costa Rica, both of which received U.S. government funds as compensation for their services. From these staging grounds, the Contras mounted periodic raids into Nicaragua to destabilize the left-wing government in Managua. The Reagan administration supported the Contra's war against the Sandinistas in a number of ways. It ordered the CIA to mine Nicaragua's harbors and to conduct bombing raids on its oil storage depots. When the CIA funds supporting the Contras ran out, Reagan secured congressional authorization for tens of millions of dollars to resume the flow of weapons and ammunition to the anti-Sandinista forces. Because of concerns about both the methods and the goals of the Contras, the U.S. Congress cut off all but nonmilitary aid in 1984 and 1985. The White House proceeded to circumvent these congressional restrictions by covertly financing the Contra war effort with funds raised from foreign governments, private organizations, and the proceeds of secret arms sales to Iran. The United States also waged economic warfare against the Sandinistas by cutting Nicaragua's sugar quota, imposing a trade embargo, and pressuring the World Bank and other multilateral lending agencies into withholding loans and credits to the capital-starved country.

In the meantime the civil war in El Salvador continued to attract the attention of officials in Washington concerned about the spread of Cuban (and, by implication, Soviet) influence in Central America. As the Salvadoran rebels mounted what they confidently hailed as their "final offensive" in January 1981, the incoming Reagan administration promptly moved to bolster the embattled government against the spreading insurgency. American military aid to that small country ballooned from $35.5 million at the beginning of Reagan's first term to over $1 billion at the beginning of his second term. When Congress threatened to cut off the funds because of the Salvadoran government's appalling human rights record, the White House pressured the regime into holding what turned out to be relatively free elections and actively supported the presidential candidacy of the moderate Christian Democrat José Napoleon Duarte. Duarte's election in the spring of 1984 removed U.S. congressional objections to the provision of military assistance, thereby ensuring a steady stream of money to finance the Salvadoran army's counterinsurgency campaign. Duarte's attempt to implement a modest land reform program to consolidate his popular support ran into a buzz saw of opposition in the Salvadoran congress, which was dominated by representatives of the landowning elite. The moderate government in El Salvador was caught in the crossfire between the leftist guerrillas of the FMLN and right-wing "death squads" closely linked to the army, whose dominant position in the society was reinforced by the steady influx of military aid from Washington.

The Reagan administration's determination to eradicate the threat of Communism in the Western Hemisphere finally led to the direct use of military force in an unlikely locale. In 1979 the pro-American government on the tiny Caribbean island of Grenada had been ousted by a revolutionary group known as the New Jewel Movement. Maurice Bishop, the president of the newly established People's Revolutionary Government of Grenada, identified himself as a Marxist, declared his admiration for

Fidel Castro, and began to denounce the role of American imperialism in the Caribbean. Whereas the Carter administration had ignored the rhetorical posturing by the little island's leftist regime, Reagan assailed the Grenadan government as a Soviet-Cuban client state that was part of the larger campaign of communist subversion in the region. Castro seemed to confirm Reagan's suspicions by providing Bishop with small arms and a construction crew to help build an airport to serve the island's tourist industry. Washington expressed its displeasure at Grenada's increasingly intimate ties with Cuba by suspending economic aid and mobilizing opposition to the revolutionary government among neighboring islands in the eastern Caribbean. When Bishop subsequently toned down his revolutionary rhetoric and seemed prepared to mend his fences with the United States, a radical faction of his own movement overthrew and murdered him on October 12, 1983. The Reagan administration responded to these events two weeks later by reviving the old policy of unilateral intervention last employed by President Johnson in the Dominican Republic in 1965. Warning that the airport runway the Cubans were constructing in Grenada could accommodate Soviet military aircraft, Reagan ordered a U.S. military landing on the island. After three days of combat with the Grenadan army and the Cuban construction crews, the nineteen-hundred-strong U.S. invasion force removed the New Jewel government and laid the groundwork for the election of a pro-American government. The invasion of Grenada and the overthrow of its left-wing regime was clearly intended to intimidate the Sandinistas into suspending their military aid to the Salvadoran rebels by raising the specter of a similar operation in Nicaragua.

## The Latin American Debt Crisis of the Eighties

While the Reagan administration was reasserting U.S. prerogatives in the Caribbean basin during the early 1980s by brandishing the big stick against the governments of Nicaragua and Grenada and the insurgents in El Salvador, all of Latin America was suddenly engulfed by a severe financial crisis that dramatically increased its financial dependence on the United States. During the second half of the 1970s, U.S. and European banks had begun to lend to the governments of the region billions of "petrodollars" that had been deposited by the oil-exporting countries after the run-up in oil prices began in 1973. As a result of this borrowing binge, the total foreign debt of Latin America skyrocketed from $2.3 billion in 1970 to $75 billion in 1975 to $229 billion in 1980. By the early 1980s the region accounted for over 60 percent of the world's total foreign debt. Of the seventeen less developed countries with the highest external debt in 1982, twelve were located in Latin America. This heavy indebtedness became a serious problem when the world slid into a deep recession at the end of the 1970s. The decline in the export earnings of the Latin American countries made it impossible for them to continue the interest payments on their foreign debt. The first sign of trouble came when the government of Argentina, reeling from its humiliating defeat by Great Britain in a war over control of the Falkland (Malvinas) Islands in 1982, announced that it was suspending payment on its $37 billion external debt. Argentina's de facto default sent a shock wave of anxiety through world financial markets, which responded by shortening maturities on new loans and demanding repayment of existing ones when they came due. But that ominous episode was merely a foretaste of the much more serious crisis that was ignited by events in Mexico during the summer of the same year.

Throughout the 1960s Mexico had experienced a spectacular economic takeoff, recording an annual growth rate of almost 7 percent and becoming the most highly developed industrial economy in Latin America. Then during the second half of the 1970s exploration in the country's oil-producing region identified vast new reserves of petroleum. This discovery could not have come at a more propitious time for Mexico, since the production quotas set by the OPEC oil cartel between 1974 and 1979 had caused the world price of its precious product to soar. Mexico's petroleum export earnings skyrocked from $500 million in 1976 to more than $18 billion in 1981, while the future looked incredibly bright: The value of proven oil reserves in the country increased from $80 billion in 1976 to almost $900 billion in 1979. The dream of rapid economic growth financed by the steady flow of revenues from oil exports inspired Mexican President José Lopez Portillo to undertake a massive program of public investment in manufacturing, agriculture, and transportation. When these outlays began to outstrip the country's financial resources in the early eighties, the Mexican chief of state refused to end the spending spree for fear of alienating a public that had become accustomed to his government's largesse. Instead, he resorted to the less politically unpopular expedient of foreign borrowing to bridge the gap. Once again the Mexican government's timing seemed perfect: American, European, and Japanese banks aggressively sought customers for their expanding capital reserves, enabling Mexico to run up a foreign debt of more than $85 billion by 1982. But in the previous year an unanticipated surplus of oil production had caused a sharp decline in oil prices for the first time since the 1974 price increases. The resulting drop in the value of Mexico's oil exports, which by then accounted for 75 percent of its total export earnings, forced the country to default on its enormous foreign debt in the summer of 1982.

The Mexican debt crisis of 1982 posed a serious threat not only to the debtor countries but to the international banking system as well. Since American banks held almost 40 percent of Latin America's total foreign debt and most of the loans were denominated in dollars, the U.S. government and U.S. financial institutions had considerable leverage over the economies of the region as they sought to solve the crisis. The Treasury Department in Washington stepped in to arrange for a $1 billion "bridge loan" from several central banks to tide the defaulting debtor over while its principal foreign creditors agreed to defer interest payments for three months. Washington pressed the Mexican government to begin negotiations with the IMF to seek a long-term solution to the problem. In November 1982 the international lending agency put together a bailout package consisting of $3.84 billion in credits to Mexico between 1983 and 1985. But the IMF exacted a high price for its rescue operation: It required the Mexican government to implement a strict austerity program that included slashing appropriations for public works programs and raising taxes to eliminate the budget deficit, phasing out popular but costly government subsidies for food and public utilities and instituting a tight monetary policy to curb inflation (which had reached almost 60 percent at the height of the crisis). The fund also required that Mexico reduce its tariffs to stimulate greater efficiency and thus greater competitiveness in foreign trade.

The problem of unsustainable foreign indebtedness spread throughout the rest of Latin America, as country after country was obliged to suspend payment on its foreign debt. By the end of 1983 most of the hard-pressed governments had avoided bankruptcy by signing rescheduling agreements with their foreign creditors that extended the maturities and reduced the annual interest payments. In exchange for this stay of execution the debtors were required by the banks to adopt a set of deflationary policies (including cuts in government spending and higher interest rates) that put a brake on Latin America's economic growth for the rest of the decade. In the meantime the anxious executives of the U.S. financial institutions that had imprudently poured so much of their clients' savings into Latin America during the past decade abruptly turned off the faucet, further aggravating the debtor governments' plight. Worried about the prospect of a massive default that could severely damage the U.S. banking system, the Bush administration unveiled a government-backed rescue operation known as the Brady Plan (after Treasury Secretary Nicholas Brady) in the spring of 1989. This imaginative scheme encouraged the banks to exchange their old loans for new bonds with either a reduced principal or lower interest rate. To minimize the risks to the lending institutions, the new debt instruments would be guaranteed by a pool of funds raised by the IMF, the World Bank, and the governments of advanced industrial states. The Brady Plan required all parties to share the costs of recovery from the international debt crisis. The banks were protected from default in exchange for accepting lower returns on their loans. The debtor countries got lower interest charges in exchange for commitments to implement the customary deflationary policies required to restore their capacity to service their foreign debt. By the early 1990s several Latin American governments had concluded debt reduction agreements with their foreign creditors based on the Brady Plan, which afforded them relief from the threat of default and enabled them to concentrate on getting their financial house in order.

## The Turn toward Liberalism and Regional Economic Cooperation

In the hopes of breaking out of the depressingly familiar cycle of unemployment, low productivity, inflation, and foreign debt, the governing elites of most Latin American countries were converted to the model of export-oriented, marked-driven growth that had been popularized by such East Asian economic powerhouses as Taiwan and South Korea. The unlikely pioneer of this radical new approach to economic development was Chile's General Augusto Pinochet. The strongman in Santiago called in a team of free-market economists from the University of Chicago to recommend a set of structural reforms that succeeded in curbing that country's rampant inflation and ushered in a remarkable period of economic growth. When Pinochet stepped down in 1989 after losing a referendum, his democratically elected successor Patricio Aylwin preserved the former dictator's free market policies, and Chile's impressive economic performance continued. In the same period President Carlos Salinas de Gotari of Mexico, who negotiated a comprehensive settlement with the country's creditors in 1990 that freed up funds for urgent domestic needs, embraced the same neoliberal techniques that Chile had so successfully employed and reversed his country's slide into economic chaos. By the mid-1990s the model of market-oriented growth had become the watchword for most of the rest of Latin America as well. The old traditions of state ownership, government subsidies, tariff protectionism, and import substitution succumbed to the new enthusiasm for privatization, competition, and free trade that was sweeping the globe in the post–Cold War era.

Washington responded with enthusiasm to Latin America's widespread acceptance of neo-liberal economic principles with a dramatic proposal to tighten the economic bonds between the United States and its neighbors to the south. In June 1990 President George H. W. Bush launched the "Enterprise for the Americas" initiative, a grandiose scheme for a vast free trade zone encompassing the entire Western Hemisphere. When it soon became evident that he had overreached, Bush retreated to the more limited goal of tightening the economic links between the United States and the two countries beyond its northern and southern borders. The United States and Canada, which had long been each other's most important trading partner, had concluded a free trade agreement in 1987 that removed all trade barriers between the two neighbors by the beginning of 1989. That same year President Salinas of Mexico, the United States's third most important trading partner, sought a similar bilateral trading arrangement as part of his campaign to dismantle the remainder of Mexico's protectionist economic system. He hoped to gain access to the American market for Mexico's embryonic light manufacturing industry as well as to secure direct investment from businesses and loans from banks in the United States.

The heads of American corporations responded with enthusiasm to the Mexican initiative, perceiving the opportunity to relocate their production facilities south of the Rio Grande to take advantage of lower labor costs there. After Canadian representatives were brought into the bilateral U.S.-Mexican free trade talks, the three North American countries signed an agreement in October 1992 to remove all trade barriers among them within twenty years. When the North American Free Trade Agreement (NAFTA) entered into operation on January 1, 1994, it experienced some rough sledding: Strong resistance was forthcoming from U.S. labor unions, which feared the loss of jobs to Mexican workers willing to work for much less than their American counterparts, as well as from environmentalists who worried about Mexico's lower standards for air quality, toxic wastes, and pesticides used in food production. It helped to provoke a peasant uprising in the southern Mexican state of Chiapas that was timed to coincide with the activation of the free trade agreement, which the rebel leaders feared would further erode the living standards of their destitute followers. But the governments of all three countries remained committed to the ultimate goal of full economic integration.

During the tripartite negotiations that produced NAFTA in the first half of the 1990s, the countries of Latin America hastened to conclude subregional economic agreements of their own that were designed to promote productivity through economies of scale. In March 1991 Argentina, Brazil, Paraguay, and Uruguay signed the Southern Cone Common Market Treaty creating a regional common market known by its Spanish acronym MERCOSUR. By the beginning of 1995, these four countries had dismantled tariffs against each other's products and created an enormous free trade zone embracing almost two hundred million people. Boasting extensive mineral and agricultural resources, an embryonic industrial base, a growing entrepreneurial class, and a combined gross domestic product of over $420 billion, MERCOSUR seemed poised to become an economic giant in the twenty-first century.

As the Southern Cone countries intensified their economic ties in the first half of the 1990s, smaller regional blocs coalesced throughout the rest of Latin America. In 1992 Bolivia, Colombia, Ecuador, Peru, and Venezuela revived the old Andean Pact that had languished since the early 1970s, slashing regional tariffs and prompting a surge in trade among the signatories. In the same year thirteen Caribbean islands united to create a regional common market known as Caricom. The following year Guatemala, Honduras, El Salvador, Nicaragua, and Costa Rica resuscitated the moribund Central American Common Market formed in 1964 with the goal of removing trade barriers and promoting economic integration among its five members. This headlong plunge into regional economic integration caused the value of trade among Latin American countries, which had long been overshadowed by their trade with countries outside the region, to expand from $12 billion in 1988 to more than $30 billion by the mid-1990s.

Recognizing the growing importance of the Latin American market for U.S. exports, the Clinton administration in Washington responded to this trend toward regional economic integration by dusting off President Bush's old project for a trade agreement embracing the entire hemisphere. In December 1994 Clinton hosted in Miami the first summit meeting of the thirty-four nations of the hemisphere since 1967. At this historic gathering the assembled heads of state endorsed the ambitious goal of creating a vast free trade bloc from Alaska to Argentina by the year 2005.

The optimistic expectations for sustained economic growth that swept Latin America during the first half of the 1990s had to be lowered by the end of the decade, as the negative effects of globalization that battered the newly industrializing powerhouses of East Asia reached the Western Hemisphere (see page 383). Those hardest hit were the remnants of the inefficient sectors of the economy that had benefited from state protection, as the influx of cheap foreign goods and the end of government subsidies forced marginal firms into bankruptcy and their workers into unemployment. Even Brazil, South America's largest, most populous, and most economically advanced country, suffered a destructive run on its currency by foreign speculators in 1998–1999 that required a bailout by the IMF and the adoption of painful austerity measures. In the meantime the lesser economies of the region, despite a decade of efforts at trade diversification, remained dependent on the fluctuating prices of a few commodity exports and therefore vulnerable to foreign exchange shocks when those prices headed south.

One commodity produced in abundance in the Andean region of South America retained a high price on the world market because of the seemingly insatiable demand for it in the developed world: Enterprising entrepreneurs in Peru and Bolivia bought coca leaves from destitute farmers, reduced them to a paste, and sent it by airplane to factories in Colombia. There it was refined into pure cocaine in factories set up in the cities of Medellin, Cali, and Cartegena by powerful drug cartels for distribution in the United States, where cocaine had become a favorite recreational drug in the 1980s. The street price for the product in American cities was ten thousand times what the poor Andean peasant had received for his crop. The huge profits earned by the drug lords, which were laundered by banks in the Caribbean, enabled them to wield enormous political power at all levels through bribery of police, military, and government officials. The cocaine trade accounted for a substantial portion of the GNP of Bolivia, Colombia, and Peru, leading one observer to remark that the cocaine cartels represented the most profitable multinational corporations owned by Latin Americans.

To stem the flow of narcotics into the United States, the Bush administration unveiled a $2.2 billion economic assistance program in 1989 known as the Andean Plan, which financed efforts by local security forces to suppress the supply. The Clinton administration sought to cut off the coca producers in Bolivia and Peru from the refining facilities of the drug barons in Colombia by helping the Peruvian and Colombian air forces intercept planes carrying the partially refined product. When this intervention succeeded in reducing coca production in Peru and Bolivia by half, farmers in Colombia began cultivating the valuable cash crop to meet the continuing demand in the United States. By the beginning of the twenty-first century Washington was providing lavish military assistance to the Colombian government, which was conducting an aggressive campaign against the cartels and their leftist guerrilla allies, the Revolutionary Armed Forces of Colombia (FARC). The issue of narcotics control generated resentment against the United States in the Andean countries, whose officials complained that the key to the problem was demand rather than supply: As long as Americans were willing to pay high prices for high-grade cocaine on the streets of Miami and New York, the impoverished Colombian peasant would plant the crop that earned a much higher return than any conceivable alternative.

## The Advance of Democratic Institutions

The spread of economic liberalism throughout Latin America in the last two decades of the twentieth century was accompanied by the notable progress of political democracy, first in the larger nations of South America and then in the countries in the Caribbean basin. Military dictatorships surrendered power to civilian governments in Argentina, Brazil, and Chile during the 1980s. The end of the Cold War reinforced this democratic trend by removing the incentive for Washington to support repressive regimes in the name of anti-Communism. The collapse of the Soviet Union and China's repudiation of world revolution demoralized the Marxist-Leninist guerrilla movements that had waged low-intensity insurgencies since the 1960s. The termination of Soviet subsidies and below-market oil sales to Cuba as the Soviet economy disintegrated wreaked havoc on the Cuban economy, which had already been debilitated by the U.S. trade embargo that no president dared to lift for fear of alienating the anti-Castro Cuban American voting bloc in Florida. The aging revolutionary leader in Havana compromised his orthodox Marxist principles in the mid-1990s by soliciting direct foreign investment from Europe and Canada to reverse Cuba's economic decline. But the combination of a one-party state and rigid government control of the economy left Cuba something of an anomaly in a region that had apparently been converted, at least in principle, to the practices of representative democracy and market capitalism.

Perhaps the most striking example of democratization in Latin America occurred in a country that had long maintained the façade of representative government to conceal what had become a de facto one-party state. Despite the democratic guarantees enshrined in the 1917 constitution of Mexico, the Institutional Revolutionary Party (PRI) had ruled that country through an uninterrupted string of electoral victories since 1929. The PRI's monopoly on political power, which was facilitated by a vast patronage machine, manipulation of the mass media, and outright electoral fraud, began to unravel in the 1990s after President Salinas brought the country into the NAFTA trade pact with the United States and Canada. In 1994 the peasant uprising in Chiapas reflected mounting dissatisfaction with the PRI's corruption of the Mexican political process as well as apprehension about the negative effects of globalization. A run on the peso later in the year prompted a precipitous capital flight that caused Mexico's most serious financial emergency since the debt crisis of 1982. When the Clinton administration stepped in with a bailout in 1995, the imposition of deflationary requirements (including a sharp increase in interest rates and sales taxes) aggravated the mounting disapproval with the PRI's traditional stranglehold over the Mexican political system. In 1997 the world's longest ruling party lost control of the lower house of the parliament. The final blow came in the summer of 2000, when the center-right opposition candidate Vicente Fox staged an electoral upset to become the first non-PRI president of Mexico in over seventy years. At the beginning of the twenty-first century the expanding economic cooperation between the United States and Mexico under NAFTA, together with Washington's approval of the return to a genuine multiparty system south of the Rio Grande, was offset by two sources of tension between the two neighboring countries. The first was illegal immigration, which generated intense opposition in the U.S. border states in the southwest. The second was Mexico's role as transit point for the influx of illegal drugs from production facilities in Colombia, Peru, and Bolivia. During the negotiations on the U.S. financial bailout in 1994–1995 the Clinton administration extracted from the Mexican government a pledge of cooperation in the war on drugs. But corruption among Mexican law enforcement officials hamstrung the campaign from the very beginning.

The emerging conviction in Latin America that political and economic freedom would improve the lives of the common people did not produce the miraculous results anticipated and led to disillusionment with democracy as a panacea for the region's socioeconomic ills. This sense of frustration did not lead to a return to the military strongman by the customary unconstitutional means. Instead, populist politicians took power through the ballot box in several countries in the 1990s by exploiting public concern about government corruption or the violent activities of armed guerrilla bands that still roamed the countryside. The perfect embodiment of this new brand of authoritarian populism in Latin America was Alberto Fujimori of Peru, an engineer of Japanese descent who had been elected president in 1990. Once in office Fujimori sold state enterprises to private investors and ended food subsidies in what turned out to be a successful program of shock therapy to revitalize the declining Peruvian economy. When the Peruvian Congress balked at these radical reforms, the flamboyant president assured himself the support of the army and then simply shut down the parliament in 1992 and proceeded to rule by decree. Declaring a state of siege, he launched a nationwide counterinsurgency campaign against an antigovernment guerrilla movement known as Sendero Luminoso (Shining Path), which controlled vast portions of the Peruvian highland and enjoyed profitable relations with the coca-producing farmers there. After Peruvian security forces captured the movement's leader in 1993, it began to decline as a viable force. Fujimori's success in reviving the Peruvian economy and suppressing the Shining Path won him strong support among the population, which tolerated his undemocratic methods because of the concrete results he delivered. After getting the obedient Peruvian Congress to amend the constitution to permit him to run again, Fujimori was reelected in 1995 and 2000. But at the beginning of his third term, evidence of electoral fraud generated such potent public opposition to his one-man rule that the Peruvian autocrat fled to Japan, where he announced his resignation and sought permanent residence. The Peruvian showcase of what might be called modern enlightened despotism gave way to a system of representative democracy that proceeded to purge Fujimori's henchmen from the country's political and military institutions.

## The Return of Regional Stability to Central America

Latin America's great success story during the 1990s was the termination of the two bloody civil wars that had wracked Central America throughout the previous decade. The return of stability to that inflamed region was facilitated by the winding down of the civil war in Nicaragua as the Cold War came to an end. As Moscow reduced oil deliveries to Managua and urged restraint on the Sandinistas, Washington suspended aid to the Contras in 1987. This disengagement of the two superpowers from the Nicaraguan civil war shifted the burden of peacemaking to neighboring countries. Attempts at a regional settlement had come to naught ever since the advent of the Contadora group's mediation efforts in 1983. But the peace plan drafted by Costa Rican President Oscar Arias Sanchez and endorsed by five Central American heads of state in August 1987 offered a workable solution in the form of a cease-fire, the end of all external military aid to the belligerents, and the holding of free democratic elections in Nicaragua. The Sandinista government of President Daniel Ortega Saavedra made the first moves toward a settlement by instituting a unilateral cease-fire in March 1988 and then pledging in February 1989 to hold the free elections called for in the Arias Plan within a year. Deprived of their U.S. aid, the Contras agreed to demobilize their military forces and participate in the forthcoming electoral process while Washington ended its economic embargo of Nicaragua.

The Sandinista regime's willingness to hold elections was prompted by two considerations: The first was the reduction of Soviet aid, which aggravated the deteriorating economic conditions of the country that included an annual inflation rate of over 3,000 percent, severe shortages of many essential commodities, massive unemployment, and a defense burden that consumed over half of the national budget. The other was the optimistic expectation that the Sandinista party would win handily against its political opposition. But to the surprise of most observers, the free elections held on February 25, 1990, resulted in the triumph of a motley coalition of opposition groups ranging from Somoza supporters on the extreme right to democratic socialists on the left that had been formed in June under the name National Opposition Union (UNO). In April 1990 Violeta Barrios de Chamorro, who had served in the Sandinista government in the first nine months of the revolution before resigning in disillusionment, replaced Ortega as president of Nicaragua in the first democratic, peaceful transfer of power in that country within recent memory. The Sandinistas honored their pledge to preserve the cease-fire in the civil war, while the Contras continued to disband in the expectation of participating in the political system of which their ideological confrères had recently gained control.

The tenuous truce between Chamorro's center-right governing coalition and the Sandinista-controlled military survived despite periodic clashes between reconstituted Contra and Sandinista guerrilla groups in the countryside as well as continual verbal sniping from parliamentary critics at both extremes of the political spectrum. Chamorro's inclusion of Sandinista representatives in her cabinet and her retention of the former president's brother Humberto Ortega as army chief alienated her right-wing allies in parliament and antagonized the United States. When she finally yielded to right-wing and U.S. pressure in the autumn of 1993 and promised to replace Ortega within a year, she predictably enraged her Sandinista coalition partners. But the two sides did not revert to the type of violent behavior that had devastated the country during the 1980s.

The political defeat of the Sandinistas in Nicaragua dealt a crushing blow to their ideological allies in El Salvador, the Democratic Revolutionary Front (FDR) and its military wing, the Farabundo Marti National Liberation Front (FMLN), which had been engaged in an insurgency against the central government throughout the eighties. In March 1989 the right-wing Nationalist Republican Alliance (ARENA) won the elections in El Salvador and its leader, a pro-American businessman named Alfredo Cristiani, replaced the ailing Christian Democratic President Jose Napoleon Duarte (who had attempted in vain to steer a middle course between ARENA on the right and the FMLN on the left). The ARENA government expanded and intensified its predecessor's counterinsurgency campaign against the rebels. But pressure from Washington to seek a negotiated peace and curb its hard-liners in the military forced the Salvadoran government to the conference table, while the collapse of the Sandinistas and the crisis in the Soviet Union deprived the FMLN of external support.

Peace talks under the auspices of the United Nations began in April 1990, and in January 1992 they produced a cease-fire in the struggle between the Salvadoran government and the FMLN. By the end of that year the reciprocal demobilization of government and rebel forces under the supervision of a United Nations observer force (ONUSAL) formally terminated the fourteen-year civil war, which had caused seventy-five thousand deaths and massive socioeconomic dislocation. Despite occasional instances of rebel terrorism and government repression, the cease-fire held. The FMLN began to operate as a political party rather than a revolutionary movement, and the Cristiani regime abandoned the excesses of its predecessors. In elections in 1997 the FMLN won a third of the seats in the parliament, as did the ruling ARENA party; thus these two former enemies became political competitors willing to play by the rules of the game. As the bloody civil wars in Nicaragua and El Salvador faded into sporadic spasms of low-level violence, Central America entered into a period of relative peace and stability after a decade and a half of ideological strife.

## The Reluctant Gendarme of the Hemisphere after the Cold War

The Reagan administration's aggressive policy toward the Sandinistas in Nicaragua and the leftist regime in Granada during the 1980s had been prompted by an obsessive concern about the spread of Soviet-Cuban power and influence in the Western

Hemisphere. With the end of the Cold War, the basis of U.S. policy toward Latin America shifted from ideological combat to more mundane concerns, such as the war on drugs and the promotion of democracy, regional stability, and economic development. These new preoccupations led to two U.S. military interventions in Latin America that belied the widespread expectation of American disengagement from the hemisphere in the post–Cold War era.

The first of these pertained to Washington's expanding campaign to stem the influx of drugs from Latin America to the streets of U.S. cities. By the end of the 1980s the Bush administration faced a delicate diplomatic situation when a Florida grand jury indicted the Panamanian head of state, General Manuel Antonio Noriega, for smuggling cocaine into the United States. Once employed by the CIA to funnel aid to the Contras in Nicaragua, the corrupt, autocratic Noriega was exposed as a significant player in the deadly narcotics trade that the U.S. government was ostensibly attempting to curb. After Noriega rejected the results of a free election that repudiated his hand-picked candidate to succeed him, the Panamanian opposition appealed to Washington for support. When a CIA-sponsored military coup against the defiant Panamanian strongman failed, President Bush decided to take direct action. In blatant disregard of the principle of national sovereignty as well as of the nonintervention provisions of the OAS charter, Bush dispatched more than twenty thousand U.S. military forces to Panama City in December 1989, ostensibly to protect American soldiers in the Canal Zone but in reality to capture the indicted head of state. Within a few days American forces surrounded Noriega's refuge in the Vatican embassy and blared rock music, which he was known to hate, twenty-four hours a day until he finally surrendered on January 3, 1990. After the U.S. invasion force installed a successor regime, Noriega was extradited to Florida, where he was subsequently tried, convicted, and imprisoned for drug trafficking. Only twenty-three American soldiers and fifty-five members of the Panamanian National Guard died during the fighting. But between five hundred and a thousand civilians were killed in the crossfire.

Most Panamanians originally favored the U.S. invasion and the overthrow of Noriega, hoping for lavish U.S. economic assistance to rebuild their devastated country. But Washington proved unwilling to back up its military action with financial aid once Noriega had been apprehended, and Panama suffered a severe economic downturn throughout the first half of the 1990s. But the U.S. military intervention did not derail Washington's commitment to the agreement signed in 1977 by President Jimmy Carter to evacuate the Panama Canal Zone and turn over the U.S.-owned waterway to Panamanian control. On the last day of 1999 the American flag was lowered for the last time in the Panama Canal Zone. In the meantime the United States Southern Command, which supervised U.S. military activities in the Central American–Caribbean region from Panama, had relocated to Miami. These two events as the twentieth century drew to a close symbolized the end of the era of U.S. unilateralism in the Western Hemisphere that had opened with the defeat of Spain as the previous century approached its end.

But another development in the mid-1990s suggested that America's penchant for acting as the policeman of the hemisphere had not disappeared. While preparing for the seizure of Noriega as part of the U.S. war on drugs in the late 1980s, the Bush administration also began to pay attention to the deteriorating domestic situation in

Haiti. In the mid-1980s nationwide protests had erupted in that impoverished Caribbean country against the brutal and corrupt government of Jean-Claude ("Baby Doc") Duvalier, who had succeeded his father François ("Papa Doc") in 1971. The combination of U.S. pressure and mounting public opposition forced the despot into exile on the French Riviera in 1986 and set the stage for the country's first free presidential election in decades in 1990. The winning candidate, a popular Catholic priest named Father Jean-Bertrand Aristide, had campaigned on a program of radical socioeconomic reform that alienated the wealthy urban elite and its allies in the Haitian officer corps. Before the new president could implement his ideas, however, Aristide was overturned by a military coup in September 1991 and forced into exile to the United States.

Even before this fleeting experiment in democracy, destitute Haitians had been crowding into makeshift boats and crossing the Caribbean toward Florida in search of political asylum. With the deposition of Aristide the flow of refugees from the islands became a flood, posing an embarrassing problem for the U.S. government. After an initial attempt to set up refugees camps on the U.S. naval base at Guantanamo in Cuba, the Bush administration ordered the coast guard to intercept the boats and return them to Haiti. Incoming President Bill Clinton reneged on his campaign promise to permit the Haitians to enter the country as political refugees, deciding instead that the only viable solution to the refugee problem was the establishment of a stable democratic government in Haiti under Aristide. Washington thereupon orchestrated a set of economic sanctions in partnership with the UN and the OAS that eventually compelled the ruling junta in Haiti to sign an agreement in July 1993 allowing the deposed leader to regain power within three months. When the foot-dragging officers in charge failed to meet the prescribed deadline for restoring the legally elected head of state, Clinton dispatched a contingent of Marines in the fall of 1994 to occupy the country and reinstate Aristide. Its mission accomplished, the U.S. intervention force handed over authority to a UN peacekeeping force in March 1995 and evacuated the island. The UN and the OAS supervised legislative elections as well as a presidential election to replace Aristide, whose term had expired and who was constitutionally prohibited from seeking reelection. Despite his undiminished popularity and the fact that most of his presidency had been spent in exile, the charismatic cleric-turned-politician willingly transferred power to his elected successor in February 1996. This was the first successful transition from one democratically elected leader to another in Haiti's long history of despotic rule. Aristide returned to the presidency through a free election in 2001. Although Haiti remained the poorest country in the Western Hemisphere and one of the poorest in the world, it joined the other Latin American states in an impressive commitment to democratic rule.

# NINE

# AFRICA: THE TRAVAILS
# OF INDEPENDENCE

Practically the entire continent of Africa had been carved up among the European powers during the era of imperial expansion in the second half of the nineteenth century. By the end of World War II the only independent African states admitted to the new United Nations organization were Liberia, Ethiopia, Egypt, and South Africa.* But in the years to come the European colonial powers recognized the impossibility of retaining their holdings in Africa in a period when the two superpowers, amid their sharp ideological differences on most other matters, were both opposed to the continuation of colonial rule. The history of the African continent since 1945 has therefore been dominated by the phenomenon of decolonization, a process that occurred in three great waves: The 1950s saw the independence of the former Italian colony of Libya (1951), of the former British possessions of Sudan (1956) and Ghana (1957), and the former French colonies of Morocco and Tunisia (1956) and Guinea (1958). The second great wave came in the early 1960s, when Great Britain, France, and Belgium divested themselves of their remaining African possessions. The third wave came in the mid-1970s, when Spain and Portugal repudiated the autocratic regimes that had clung tenaciously to their African empires and withdrew from the continent. By 1985, the centenary of the Act of Berlin that had partitioned the continent into European spheres of influence, forty-five African countries operated as sovereign political units in the postcolonial world.

Amid the second great wave of national independence, representatives of the new states met in Addis Ababa, Ethiopia, in 1963 to establish the Organization of African Unity (OAU) as a vehicle to promote peace, stability, and economic development on the continent. The delegates immediately recognized that those laudable goals were

---

*Among those four states only Liberia, set up as a haven for freed American slaves before the Civil War, escaped European colonial domination because of the informal protection of the United States. Great Britain granted independence to Egypt in 1936; Italy occupied Ethiopia from 1936 to 1941; and South Africa was a self-governing dominion of the British Empire (later Commonwealth) until its white-only government declared independence in 1960.

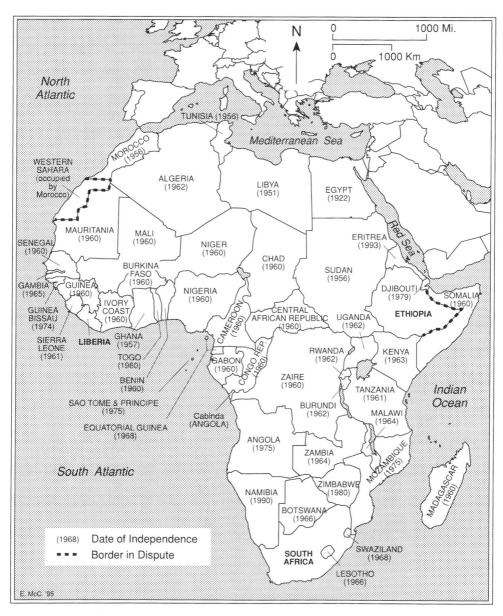

*Africa after World War II*

gravely threatened by a tragic curse of the colonial legacy: The European powers that convened at the Conference of Berlin in 1884–1885 to divvy up the continent had failed to delineate their respective colonial holdings according to principles of ethnicity. They preferred instead to draw the map of Africa in such a way as to accommodate their own strategic and economic interests as well as to enable them to manipulate tensions between the indigenous tribes as a means of discouraging united resistance to colonial rule. The result was a collection of colonies comprising ethnic groups with a long history of animosity toward one another, enclosed by borders that separated peoples who shared a common sense of ethnic identity. This state of affairs was a recipe for political instability and interstate conflict once these colonies gained their independence: As the citizens of each newly sovereign state lost the only source of cohesion that united them—the struggle against the common oppressor from Europe—the heightened sense of ethnic identity across the continent threatened to undermine the integrity of states and inviolability of the borders that separated them.

To avert the twin dangers of secession and boundary disputes, the OAU enshrined in its charter a stipulation that the national borders inherited from the colonial powers (with all of their egregious flaws) must be deemed sacrosanct. At the same time the charismatic prime minister of Ghana, Kwame Nkrumah, won widespread support within the OAU for his radical vision of pan-Africanism: It envisioned a continent insulated from foreign interference, by the former colonial powers as well as by the two superpowers, united in the common pursuit of political stability, regional cooperation, and economic growth. Alas, none of these ambitious goals for independent Africa would be realized for the remainder of the twentieth century. Instead, the continent would be torn apart by violent ethnic conflicts within states as well as by destructive wars between them. This continual turmoil would in turn leave Africa vulnerable to direct and indirect foreign intervention by former colonial powers and eventually by the two superpowers, cripple its capacity for economic development, and leave it desperately dependent on the outside world for the modest degree of security and economic growth it was able to achieve. As the noble dream of pan-African unity vanished, a handful of large states on the continent—Nigeria in the west, Libya in the north, Congo/Zaire in the center, and South Africa in the south—projected their power into neighboring countries in an effort to achieve hegemony in their respective regions. For different reasons these assertive bids for regional leadership fell far short of their goals, leaving the African continent weak, balkanized, and therefore tempting targets for external meddling.

During the 1960s intense ethnic strife within two newly independent African states set the precedent for internal political conflict that would plague the continent for the rest of the century. We have seen how the struggle in the former Belgian Congo between the central government and a secessionist movement in the mineral-rich province of Katanga during the early sixties drew the attention of the two superpowers to the heart of Africa (see page 88). In the second half of the decade acute tribal conflict in Nigeria, Africa's largest and wealthiest state, prompted the Ibo people in the eastern part of the country to secede and establish on May 30, 1967, the independent "Republic of Biafra." In the ensuing civil war of 1967–1970, which pitted the Ibos against the Hausa-Fulani group in the north and its Yoruba allies in the west, the central government ruthlessly suppressed the Biafran secessionist movement. As in the Congo crisis earlier in the decade, foreign powers jockeyed for advantage amid the Nigerian turmoil by supporting one or the other of the contending parties. The international politics of the Nigerian Civil War made strange bedfellows, revealing the extent to which the rigidly bipolar international system had broken down by the late 1960s: Great Britain, the former colonial authority, joined the Soviet Union in supplying arms to the central government. France, Portugal, and China supported the Biafran secessionists. The United States remained largely on the sidelines, distracted by its deepening involvement in Vietnam.

The failure of the secessionist movements in the former Belgian Congo and Nigeria in the 1960s and the preservation of the territorial integrity of those two multiethnic states seemed to vindicate the OAU's principle of the inviolability of the borders inherited from the colonial powers. But the intervention of foreign powers, directly in the Congo crisis and indirectly in the Nigerian Civil War, revealed the fragility of independent Africa's aspiration to free itself from interference by former colonial powers and to remain nonaligned in the Cold War. It rapidly became evident that contending political factions in Africa would not be able to resist the temptation to seek external support for their political goals. Even the most ardent African advocate of nonalignment in the Cold War—Ghana's Nkrumah—succumbed to this temptation: Once in power he declared his country a Socialist state and welcomed Soviet, East German, and Chinese instructors to train his military, security, and intelligence services. Washington responded to this provocation by supporting a military coup in 1966 whose leaders ousted Nkrumah, expelled his Communist-bloc advisory personnel, and transformed the country into a pro-Western outpost in West Africa.

## The Curse of Underdevelopment

The African continent was blessed with a wide range of industrial raw materials, minerals, and tropical agricultural products, which had attracted the attention of the colonial powers. But the Europeans had simply extracted these natural resources without investing in an infrastructure that would support long-term economic development. Moreover, they refrained from educating and training indigenous African elites to assume political, military, and economic authority after decolonization. The result was that at the time of independence the economic advantage conferred by Africa's substantial endowment in natural resources was totally erased by the absence of sufficient capital, technology, entrepreneurial skills, and managerial expertise to develop those resources. Africa's conundrum was that while its only hope for preserving its recently gained political independence was to lift the continentwide curse of economic backwardness, the sole means of doing so was to depend on external powers for the assets that it lacked: foreign investment, loans, technology, technical expertise, and guaranteed markets for its exports. This *dependence* on external economic assistance conflicted with the overriding objective of political *independence* from foreign domination or preponderant influence. Beginning in the 1980s, Africa was hit by a new curse that would soon erase the small gains in economic development that were recorded: the spread of the AIDS epidemic. Of the world's twenty-five most AIDs-afflicted countries, twenty-four are in Africa. By the end of the twentieth century the deadly disease was already causing shortages of skilled workers in several African countries. It was overwhelming the primitive medical and public health services and producing a sharp decline in African life expectancies. Medical authorities predict that a quarter of the continent's population will die of the disease.

During the period of global economic expansion in the 1960s, many of the newly independent African countries developed advantageous links with the global monetary and trading system of the non-Communist world. The two principal international lending agencies, the IMF and the World Bank, provided infusions of capital to help hard-pressed countries balance their international accounts and finance long-term construction projects. Under the Kennedy and Johnson administrations the United States provided development assistance, while Peace Corps volunteers flocked to Africa with valuable technical and managerial skills. The economic expansion during the sixties generated ample reserves of capital in U.S., European, and Japanese banks for investment and loans to Africa. It also stimulated demand in the industrialized world for the raw materials and tropical agricultural exports Africa possessed in abundance. Many African states participated in the successive rounds of tariff negotiations sponsored by GATT and developed some mutually profitable trading relationships with the developed world on the basis of the exchange of their primary products for its manufactured goods. But the booming sixties gave way to the global recession of the 1970s caused by the skyrocketing world price of oil. This severe economic downturn had a devastating impact on all African countries (save the oil-producing states of Algeria, Nigeria, Libya, Gabon, Congo, and Cameroon), plunging them into a prolonged economic crisis that continued well into the 1980s.

In the meantime, Africa began to suffer from the economic disability that had long afflicted the independent republics of Latin America: Each country's reliance on a single cash crop or mineral for its export earnings proved catastrophic, as the recession in the industrial world caused a drastic drop in demand for (and therefore the prices of) Africa's nonpetroleum commodity exports. Strapped for funds to purchase essential imports of food and oil, many African nations were forced to borrow heavily from the international lending agencies as well as Western banks. Africa's total external debt soared from $14.2 billion in 1973 to $42 billion in 1976 to over $150 billion by 1984, while the average ratio of debt to GNP of all countries on the continent doubled from 1973 to 1984 (when it reached an ominous 40 percent). The fatal combination of explosive population growth, drought, and decline in food production (due in part to the rural population's flight to the cities in search of higher living standards) caused famine in many African countries. The international lending agencies and foreign banks predictably required the debtor governments to reduce domestic spending and curtail imports as a condition for future loans, which aggravated the continent's economic decline.

At its annual conference in Addis Ababa in 1973, the OAU had unveiled a radical proposal to cope with the spreading crisis through the creation of a New International Economic Order (NIEO): The industrialized countries of the north were called upon, in the interests of justice and in expiation for the past sins of colonialism, to transfer a substantial proportion of their wealth to the impoverished countries of the south through development assistance, debt cancellation, commodity price stabilization agreements, and the reduction of tariffs against exports from the developing world. Although this bold project for the redistribution of global wealth was approved by the UN General Assembly in 1974, the NIEO died when the governments of the industrial world predictably refused to ask their electorates to endure the fiscal sacrifices that would have been required. Thereafter Africa would have to live with the humiliating condition of having to rely on the willingness of foreign powers, including those that had controlled its destiny in the imperial era, to help it achieve its goal of economic growth.

## The Persistence of "Neo-Imperialism"

As Great Britain divested itself of its African colonies in the early 1960s, its attempt to reorient its foreign policies toward the emerging European Economic Community that it hoped to join caused a loosening of its ties with its former overseas possessions. London did strive to preserve a modicum of influence in its former African colonies by providing military support for established governments in its former empire: In 1964 British commandos were dispatched to rescue the governments of Kenya, Tanzania, and Uganda from army mutinies. Although refraining from direct military intervention in the Nigerian Civil War of 1967–1970, Britain provided military assistance to the central government as it suppressed the Biafran secession (see page 286). British banks and businesses retained important economic stakes in the former African colonies, while London preserved substantial cultural influence on the continent through the Commonwealth (an organization of former British dependencies dominated by the anglophone African states). In contrast to this informal, indirect British attempt to preserve influence in Africa after decolonization, the other major colonial power intervened so blatantly and overtly in the affairs of its former African possessions that critics began to refer to France's role in postindependence Africa as "neo-imperialism."

On withdrawing from French West Africa and French Equatorial Africa in 1960, France concluded mutual defense treaties with twelve of the successor states (Cameroon, the Central African Republic, Chad, Congo, Dahomey [later renamed Benin], Gabon, Ivory Coast, Niger, Madagascar, Mauritania, Senegal, and Togo). By virtue of these agreements France provided the armies of the newly independent states with weapons, equipment, and military advisers; maintained major French bases in Ivory Coast, Senegal, Gabon, and the Central African Empire; and reserved the right of military intervention. On June 27, 1977, France belatedly granted independence to its small enclave of Djibouti, wedged precariously between Ethiopia and Somalia on the Horn of Africa at the confluence of the Red Sea and the Gulf of Aden. The former colonial power retained use of the airfields and port facilities of the fledgling mini-state as well as the right to station forty-five hundred French troops there and to intervene militarily if it faced an external threat from its two warring neighbors Ethiopia and Somalia. In 1978 a group of mercenaries led by former French soldiers overthrew the leftist government of the Comoro Islands off Madagascar. They proceeded to set up a puppet regime that allowed France to retain control of the island of Mayotte, the site of France's only naval base on the Indian Ocean. To back up its extensive network of air, naval, and military bases across the continent, France retained on its territory a forty-seven-thousand-man Rapid Reaction Force prepared for prompt deployment to Africa in an emergency. On a number of occasions Paris exercised behind-the-scenes influence to rescue protégés threatened by internal insurrection as well as to hasten the downfall of long-time enemies (such as Mali's Modibo Keita in 1968) or former protégés who had fallen from grace (such as Mauritania's Moktar Ould Daddah in 1978 and Jean-Bedel Bokassa of the Central African Empire, which was renamed Central African Republic after his deposition in 1979).

In addition to protecting African clients from internal insurgencies, France did not hesitate to shield them from external threats as well. The former French colony of Chad faced both types of challenges, and the former colonial power acted with determination to bail it out. When Chad obtained independence in 1960, the settled Christian inhabitants in the south antagonized the nomadic Muslims in the north by monopolizing the high-level positions in the army and civil service. Anticipating a northern backlash against southern dominance, France retained a large military contingent in the northern part of the country for five years after independence to preserve order and protect the successor regime. This lingering French presence strengthened the position of President N'garta Tombalbaye, a southerner who transformed the arid, impoverished, land-locked country into a one-man dictatorship until his overthrow in 1975 by a group of dissident military officers from his own part of the country.

In the meantime an external threat to the unity of the country arose from the assertive behavior of President Muammar el-Qaddafi of Libya, Chad's neighbor to the north. After overthrowing the pro-Western Libyan monarchy in 1969, Qaddafi nationalized the American companies that exploited the country's vast oil reserves, closed the U.S. and British air bases in the country, and turned to the Soviet Union for economic and military support. Intent on transforming Libya into the dominant power in North Africa, he exploited the political turmoil in Chad by sending Libyan troops southward to bolster his country's historic claim to the northern part of the country known as the Aouzou Strip. The government in Chad appealed for and obtained the intervention of French military forces against the Libyans, who had advanced beyond the Strip to threaten the rest of the country. Paris eventually threw its support behind a Chadian military leader named Hissène Habré, who waged a long campaign throughout the 1980s against the Libyan army and its Muslim allies in the north. While attempts by the OAU to mediate the dispute failed, Chad's dependence on the military forces of the former colonial power to contain Libya dramatically exposed the limits to Africa's ability to manage its own affairs. The conflict also acquired Cold War overtones, as Moscow backed Libya with arms and diplomatic support while Washington, Paris, and the French African client states supported Habré until his overthrow in 1990.

In addition to its activist policies in the former French African colonies, France also replaced Belgium as the principal foreign defender of the pro-Western regime of Mobutu Sésé Sékó in the former Belgian Congo (that had been renamed Zaire). After seizing power in 1965 Mobutu converted Zaire, with its strategic location and valuable mineral resources, into a bastion of anti-Communism on the continent. The Zairean strongman succeeded in suppressing all internal opposition to his autocratic, corrupt regime, with the approval and covert support of the West. But he faced an external threat from the former security forces of Zaire's mineral-rich province of Katanga, which had fled to neighboring Angola after Katanga's bid for secession had been crushed in the early 1960s. In March 1977 some two thousand former Katangan gendarmes in northern Angola, who had been given refuge and encouragement by the pro-Soviet government there, launched a raid into their home province (which had since been renamed Shaba). As the Zairean army retreated in disarray, Mobutu desperately appealed for a Western-backed rescue operation. On April 7 French aircraft rushed fifteen hundred Moroccan troops accompanied by French military advisers to expel the invaders.

In May 1978 about four thousand Katangan émigrés mounted a second invasion from Angola that overran the copper mining center at Kolwezi, threatening the six hundred European residents who supervised the mining operations there. In an impressive display of Western military cooperation, U.S. planes airlifted French and Belgian troops to the troubled area to rescue the Europeans and foil the efforts by the invasion force to gain control of the province. In May 1978 Paris arranged for the Franco-Belgian units to be replaced by an all-African peacekeeping force comprising fifteen hundred troops from the pro-Western African states of Gabon, Ivory Coast, Morocco, Senegal, and Togo. The affair of the two Shaba invasions petered out amid angry charges from Washington that the Katangan gendarmes had been supported by Cuba and the Soviet Union and their client Angola, while Moscow denounced Mobutu as a Western puppet.

France's extensive military involvement in postcolonial Africa was complemented by the retention of intimate economic ties between that country and its former colonies on the continent. At France's insistence, the 1957 Treaty of Rome creating the European Economic Community incorporated a system of preferential trade and economic aid arrangements between the six members of the EEC and their African territories. After achieving independence in 1960, eighteen former African dependencies of the EEC states (fourteen French, three Belgian, and one Italian) sought to lock in the special trade and aid benefits that they had acquired in the Treaty of Rome while still colonies of the community's member states. The Yaoundé Convention that was signed in 1963 and would remain in force from 1964 to 1969 preserved and extended the special commercial ties between former colonizer and colonized. It allowed almost all of the agricultural exports of the African members (mainly coffee, cocoa, bananas, and pepper) to enter the EEC duty-free. The Yaoundé Convention set up a Development Fund (to which France and West Germany each contributed about a third) that disbursed $730 million in economic assistance to the eighteen African member-states. Since Great Britain was not yet a member of the EEC, its former African colonies were excluded from this preferential trade and aid relationship. France's former colonies received the lion's share of both advantages conferred by the Yaoundé system: duty-free access to the huge European market for their agricultural products as well as economic aid from the Development Fund. Since most of the African states continued to direct their foreign trade to their former colonial master, France retained guaranteed access to strategic raw materials and tropical foodstuffs that did not compete with French domestic products. The powerful bilateral commercial connection that France maintained with its former African dependencies was reinforced by a French-controlled monetary arrangement known as the "franc zone." This closed monetary system united the currencies of most of the former French colonies of sub-Sahara Africa in a single currency known as the African Financial Community (CFA) franc, which was freely convertible to the French franc at a fixed exchange rate. French banks and firms were therefore free to invest

in franc-zone African countries without fear of currency devaluations, foreign exchange losses, or exchange controls, which accorded them a substantial advantage
over foreign competitors.

France's privileged and profitable relationship with its former African colonies
antagonized its longtime rival and EEC partner, West Germany. Lacking residual
colonial ties in Africa to exploit for its own economic benefit, the Federal Republic
had minimal commercial interests in francophone Africa. Yet Bonn was obliged to
match Paris's contribution to the EEC's Development Fund, which benefited France's
West African clients states (and indirectly, France itself). West Germany's trade with
Africa was centered on Great Britain's former African colonies. But since the African
members of the Commonwealth had been excluded from the Yaoundé regime at
France's insistence, their commodity exports to Europe were hit with high duties
while the primary products from francophone Africa entered duty-free. When Great
Britain belatedly gained admission to the EEC in 1972, it vigorously supported the
bid by Nigeria and other anglophone African states to obtain the same preferential
trade and aid benefits that the Yaoundé eighteen had enjoyed for almost a decade.
With West Germany's support, Britain finally forced the EEC to accept the expansion of the Yaoundé regional arrangements to a global system embracing not only the
rest of Africa but the entire former colonial world: In 1975 the newly expanded nine-
member EEC concluded the so-called Lomé Convention with some fifty-four former
European dependencies in Africa, the Caribbean, and the Pacific (the so-called ACP
countries).

The Lomé system was hailed by most African leaders as a vast improvement over
the Yaoundé regime for a number of reasons: First, all manufactured exports and
96 percent of commodity exports from the ACP countries were admitted duty-free to
the EEC, which gave the former European colonies a tariff advantage over other developing countries in Latin America and Asia that were not parties to the Lomé
arrangement. Second, the ACP countries were allowed to maintain high tariffs against
manufactured goods from Europe to protect their "infant industries," which encouraged the development of a manufacturing sector. The most innovative feature of the
Lomé agreement was the establishment of a commodity stabilization fund set up by
the wealthy EEC states: Known as STABEX, this fund provided low-interest loans
and outright grants to ACP countries whose export earnings were dependent on a single commodity when the price of that commodity dropped below a specified level. A
second Lomé Convention, which was concluded in 1980 and remained in force until
1985, expanded the number of products covered by the STABEX scheme and doubled the annual contributions from the Development Fund. This trend toward the increase in Europe's commitment to promote the economic development of the former
colonial world continued with Lomé III (1986–1990) and Lomé IV (1990–2000).

Nevertheless, the Lomé system came under criticism from some African leaders
for its inadequacies. The EEC's acceptance of African tariff protection against Europe's manufacturing products proved a meaningless concession, since the African
states had no "infant industries" to nurture. African critics complained about insufficient outlays from the Development Fund, the stringent conditions attached to the
loans, and the minimal African participation in the fund's policymaking. For the advocates of African self-determination, the Lomé system represented little more than

a neo-imperialist scheme to perpetuate Africa's dependency: By according Africa's commodity exports preferential entrée to the European market, it discouraged the development of alternative markets. It also inhibited the kind of industrial production that had enabled impoverished East Asian countries such as Taiwan and South Korea to break out of their condition of economic backwardness to export labor-intensive manufactured goods to the world market. Instead, Africa remained locked in a neo-colonial relationship of dependency with Western Europe, exporting the tropical food-stuffs and minerals required by the former colonial powers and their EEC partners.

### Competing Territorial Claims in the Sahara

One of the longest and most intractable territorial disputes in postcolonial Africa was the bitter struggle that erupted in the mid-1970s over the Spanish Sahara, which the new democratic government in Spain had decided to evacuate after the death of that country's longtime dictator Francisco Franco. In the autumn of 1975 King Hassan of Morocco assembled some 350,000 of his subjects along his kingdom's southern border to conduct a peaceful march of unarmed civilians into this arid domain to press Morocco's historic claim to the territory, which contained valuable reserves of phosphates. In the meantime a competing claim had emanated from neighboring state of Mauritania on the basis of the undisputed ethnic, cultural, and religious similarities between the Mauritanians and the indigenous nomadic peoples of the Spanish Sahara. The Spanish government had originally planned to conduct a plebiscite in the area, which would henceforth be known as the Western Sahara in recognition of its postcolonial status, to enable its Saharawi inhabitants to determine their own political future. But in the face of bitter opposition from the two African claimants to the territory, the Madrid government signed an agreement with Morocco and Mauritania in November 1975 transferring the northern two-thirds of the country to Morocco and the southern third to Mauritania. As the Spanish colonial forces withdrew in the winter of 1975–1976, Moroccan and Mauritanian troops moved in to occupy their respective portions of the partitioned country.

But the Moroccan and Mauritanean forces encountered a vigorous guerrilla resistance by the indigenous inhabitants, who had not been consulted in the partition negotiations and had no intention of acquiescing in an arrangement that replaced one foreign ruler with two others. In 1973 Saharawi militants had established a national independence movement named Polisario (a Spanish acronym for the Popular Front for the Liberation of the Western Sahara) to wage guerrilla war against Spanish colonial authorities. After the last Spanish troops departed in February 1976, Polisario proclaimed the independence of the Saharan Arab Democratic Republic. It promptly secured diplomatic recognition from most member-states of the OAU and began to harass the Moroccan and Mauritanian forces that had arrived to stake the territorial claims of their governments. The conflict in the Sahara soon attracted the interest of other foreign powers. Algeria, which had a long-standing border conflict with Morocco, provided sanctuary for the Polisario leadership and supplied Soviet-made weapons to the guerrilla forces in the Western Sahara. Morocco and Mauritania turned to their traditional patron France for support in their campaign to suppress the insurrection. French Jaguar jets based in Senegal provided air support for the Mauritanian forces and eventually French officers advised Mauritanian ground forces fighting Polisario. France furnished Morocco with advanced Mirage aircraft and helicopter gunships as well as direct air support.

In the summer of 1979 a military coup in Mauritania prompted that impoverished country to renounce its territorial claims to the southern third of the Western Sahara and pull back its troops, which were promptly replaced by Moroccan forces from the north. For the remainder of the 1980s Morocco and Algeria resumed their acrimonious dispute over the Western Sahara while Polisario continued its insurgency. By the mid-1980s some 120,000 Moroccan troops were tied down in the Sahara fighting about 20,000 Polisario guerrillas. In the meantime Hassan had begun to construct a defensive wall to enclose the valuable phosphate deposits and main areas of human settlement, leaving the economically worthless and uninhabitable desert area to the rebels. The costs of maintaining the army and constructing the wall imposed a heavy financial burden on the Moroccan treasury, which had to be alleviated by massive infusions of French and U.S. military and financial aid to Hassan's pro-Western regime. The struggle faded into a low-intensity conflict, with the weakened remnants of the guerrilla movement struggling in vain to prevent the consolidation of Moroccan control.

### The Cold War and the End of the Portuguese African Empire

In April 1974 the forty-two-year-old dictatorship in Portugal was toppled by a group of reform-minded military officers who were intent on divesting the country of the remnants of its colonial empire in Africa. The new left-wing regime in Lisbon promptly laid the groundwork for the granting of independence to the colonies of Mozambique and Angola, both of which would eventually fall under the control of national liberation movements that openly described themselves as Marxist. The leftist FRELIMO* movement in Mozambique received more aid from China than from the Soviet Union, so the United States did not actively oppose its accession to power or support its non-Marxist rivals. But Angola, Portugal's most prosperous African colony located on the west coast, was to be drawn into the Cold War struggle with devastating consequences for the process of East-West détente.

The Angolan resistance movement split into three tribal-based factions, each of which carved out an ideological niche for itself and promptly solicited and received assistance from various foreign patrons. The Marxist-oriented Popular Movement for the Liberation of Angola (MPLA), headed by Agostinho Neto and dominated by the mixed-race, urbanized, educated elite, had long received support from Castro's Cuba as well as rather tepid backing from the Soviet Union. The National Front for the Liberation of Angola (FNLA), headed by Holden Roberto and dominated by the Bakongo tribe in the east, was sponsored by President Mobutu Sésé Sékó of Zaire and received covert funding from the CIA. The FNLA also received arms and military advisers from China, which had developed close links with Zaire after Mobutu sought to reduce his dependence on the United States. The National Union for the

---

*Portuguese acronymn for Frente de Libertaçao de Moçambique.

Total Independence of Angola (UNITA), headed by Jonas Savimbi and dominated by the Ovimbundu tribe in the south, also received military aid from Beijing. When the new left-wing Portuguese government suspended counterinsurgency operations against all three factions of the resistance movement in the spring of 1974, each group set up offices in the country's capital of Luanda in November to jockey for position as the colonial power prepared to withdraw.

On January 15, 1975, the three rival leaders signed a tripartite agreement in Alvor, Portugal, which approved the creation of a transitional coalition government that would replace the deporting colonial power the following November. But an increase in covert CIA funding to the FNLA emboldened Roberto to violate the Alvor accord in a brazen bid for exclusive control of the government-to-be: In March his forces invaded Angola from their Zairean bases, besieged the MPLA headquarters in Luanda, and began to cooperate with UNITA against their common Marxist rival. The embattled MPLA began to receive large quantities of Soviet arms from the leftist People's Republic of the Congo (Congo Brazzaville) to the north. Moscow's major motivation for backing the MPLA appears to have been a desire to counter China's influence with the FNLA and UNITA. In the spring Neto appealed to Castro for emergency aid, and by the summer more than 200 Cuban military advisers had arrived in Luanda to assist the MPLA. Neto's forces thereupon succeeded in evicting the FNLA and UNITA from the capital, the former regrouping in the north, the latter in the south. In the meantime U.S. Secretary of State Kissinger got President Ford to approve funding for a covert operation to rescue the two non-Marxist factions that seemed in danger of losing to the Soviet- and Cuban-supported MPLA.

In the meantime other foreign powers were sucked into the Angolan quagmire as the November 11, 1975, independence date approached. Mobutu transfered to the FNLA arms he had earlier received from China in a frantic effort to shore up his protégé Roberto's faltering forces; as Zairean troops poured into Angola from the east, South Africa joined the fray by supplying arms and military advisers to UNITA in its southern enclave. In the fall of 1975 Cuba dispatched hundreds of military advisers and (for the first time) about seven hundred combat troops to the MPLA, while South Africa sent some three thousand soldiers deep into Angola to fight alongside FLNA and UNITA units in a bid to expel the MPLA from the capital. To support its embattled Angolan ally, Cuba mounted a major military operation against the two non-Marxist groups in November, originally in Cuban aircraft and ships but soon by a hastily organized Soviet airlift. The MPLA profited from the massive Cuban intervention to decimate the FNLA and Zairean forces north of Luanda and to halt the UNITA and South African advance from the south. In the meantime each of the three Angolan factions had issued separate declarations of independence on November 11 and established rival governments, the MPLA in Luanda and the FNLA and UNITA in the provincial town of Huambo. But the FNLA-UNITA "government" promptly disintegrated, and by February 1976 the OAU and Portugal formally recognized the MPLA as the government of Angola. South African forces withdrew from the south in March, leaving the MPLA and the Cuban military contingent, which had grown to about 17,000 troops, in control of most of the country.

The Cuban intervention in the Angolan Civil War was mounted entirely on Havana's initiative, although Castro prudently sought and obtained Moscow's approval of the operation. China quickly disengaged from the Angolan morass once it observed the weakness of the FNLA and UNITA and realized that its association with white-ruled South Africa would tarnish its reputation among the African states that it was avidly courting. By contrast, the Ford administration privately welcomed the South African intervention in the Angola Civil War after the Cuban troops had begun to arrive. When the secret CIA discretionary funds ran out in November 1974, Kissinger had to go hat in hand to Congress for a new appropriation. But the bitter memories of Vietnam had soured the legislators on foreign military entanglements in far-off, obscure regions of the Third World. In December 1975 and January 1976, respectively, the Senate and House rejected the administration's urgent pleas and voted overwhelmingly to prohibit further American covert aid for Angola.

The new People's Republic of Angola proudly advertised its Marxist orientation and on October 8, 1976, signed a twenty-year Treaty of Friendship with the Soviet Union. The Cuban troops joined MPLA fighters to drive the UNITA guerrillas into the southeastern corner of the country, from which they would harass the government in a low-level insurgency for decades to come. But the establishment of a self-professed Marxist state in Angola did not necessarily represent a Soviet victory and a U.S. defeat. The Neto government permitted American oil firms to resume operations in the Angolan enclave of Cabinda on the Atlantic coast, while the companies continued to pay royalties to the central government. The investments of other American multinational firms were left untouched by the new "Marxist" regime in Luanda. The Soviet Union, a belated and rather reluctant supporter of the MPLA, failed to gain strategic advantages in the country such as naval or air bases. Yet the Ford administration chose to interpret the political outcome of the Angolan Civil War in the worst possible light: Washington repeatedly portrayed the Cuban expeditionary force as a "proxy" of Moscow and denounced Soviet encouragement and logistical support for the MPLA government as a violation of the spirit of détente. The United States stubbornly refused to follow other Western countries in granting recognition to and establishing trade links with the new regime.

The American reaction to events in Angola betrayed a certain degree of hypocrisy. During the period that the United States was covertly assisting the FNLA, it regarded this kind of competition with the Soviet Union in the Third World as a normal exercise that was perfectly compatible with détente. It was the U.S.-backed FNLA that had violated the Alvor power-sharing agreement in March 1974 in a daring bid to seize total control of the state apparatus. The first foreign combat forces to enter Angola were the Zairean units that invaded in July 1975 in support of the FNLA with the tacit support of Washington. The United States did not object to the intervention of South Africa beginning in August. Until 1975 the Soviet Union had been a desultory supporter of the MPLA. When the two U.S.- and Chinese-backed factions began to falter and Cuba began providing hundreds of advisers to the MPLA in the autumn of 1975, Moscow saw the opportunity to help a national liberation movement come to power in Africa and threw its support to the probable winner. The United States began to complain about foreign interference in the Angolan Civil War only after the tide had turned against the faction it had been covertly backing since the beginning of the conflict.

The United States regarded the triumph of the Marxist MPLA in Angola as a major turning point in the Soviet Union's strategic position in the world. For the first time Moscow had helped to install a friendly government thousands of miles beyond its own borders by employing the air capabilities it had acquired by the early 1970s (see page 295). Prevented by Congress from intervening in Angola, the Ford administration could only issue ineffectual diplomatic protests as a west African state seemed to fall under the sway of Moscow and Havana. Kissinger and Ford worried that the Soviet success in Angola would encourage other "liberation movements" to seek Soviet support elsewhere in the Third World. It might also embolden Moscow to use its Cuban "surrogates" to perform similar tasks in regions where Soviet military forces could not be employed.

## The Cold War and Interstate Conflict on the Horn of Africa

Another important source of Soviet-American friction during the second half of the 1970s was the conflict that erupted in the summer of 1977 between Ethiopia and Somalia on the Horn of Africa. The Ethiopian Emperor Haile Selassie, a longtime supporter of the United States, had been overthrown by a military coup in September 1974. The new ruling junta, or Dergue, veered sharply to the left after Lieutenant Colonel Mengistu Haile Mariam took power in February 1977 and began to make overtures to Moscow and Havana for support. In the meantime the multiethnic country, which had been held together by Selassie's autocracy, began to disintegrate along tribal lines. The contiguous state of Somalia decided to exploit its neighbor's chaotic situation to assert a longstanding territorial claim to the Ethiopian desert province of Ogaden, which was inhabited by an ethnic Somali majority. After seizing power from a pro-Western regime in 1969, Somali General Mohammed Siad Barre announced the creation of a "Marxist" state and promptly obtained Soviet and Cuban aid. In 1974 he concluded a treaty of friendship with the Soviet Union. Seizing this opportunity for the extension of its influence, Moscow promised arms and military advisers for the Somali army in exchange for access to naval facilities at the Somali port of Berbera on the Red Sea as well as the use of two Soviet-constructed airfields in the country. Siad Barre subsequently solicited Cuban and Soviet support for his claim to the Ogaden and began to prepare for military action there.

After Castro and Soviet President Nikolai Podgorny tried in vain to broker a settlement between these two rival "Marxist" regimes, Havana and Moscow were left in the embarrassing position of backing both sides in the escalating conflict on the Horn of Africa. When Somali irregulars invaded the Ogaden in the spring of 1977, the Soviet Union began emergency arms shipments to Ethiopia while Cuba (with Moscow's approval) dispatched a small group of military officers to advise the Ethiopian army. In the summer Siad Barre sent regular army troops into the Ogaden to bolster the Somali guerrillas that had been marauding throughout the Ethiopian province. The outbreak of a full-scale war there forced the Soviet Union to choose between its two allies in the region. Brezhnev opted for Ethiopia, presumably because of its greater size and population. In August Moscow suspended arms deliveries to Somalia and expanded its military assistance to Ethiopia. By the winter of 1977–1978 Mengistu's regime in Addis Ababa was gravely threatened, not only by the Somali occupation of almost the entire Ogaden region in the south but also by a resurgence of secessionist agitation in the northern province of Eritrea.

The Soviet Union responded to Mengistu's frantic pleas for assistance by airlifting some fifteen thousand Cuban troops and shipping about $1 billion worth of weapons to Ethiopia. In the meantime Siad Barre had approached the United States with a request for military aid, hinting that he was prepared to sever Somalia's ties with Havana and Moscow. In retaliation against the Soviet Union's active support of Ethiopia and in the hopes of inducing Washington to provide the arms that were no longer available from Moscow, the Somali leader executed an abrupt foreign policy reversal in November 1977. He expelled all Cuban and Soviet advisers from the country, repudiated the Somali-Soviet treaty of friendship of 1974, and revoked the Soviet navy's access rights to the Red Sea port of Berbera. Although pleased by this development, the Carter administration hesitated to support Somalia's aggressive pursuit of its territorial claims against Ethiopia, partly in deference to the OAU's hallowed principle that the postcolonial borders on the continent could not be changed by force. While the United States continued to rebuff the Somali requests for arms, Ethiopian troops accompanied by two Cuban combat brigades and equipped with Soviet-made tanks, aircraft, and weapons mounted a counteroffensive in late January 1978 that drove the Somalis out of the Ogaden. Under prodding from Moscow, which was loath to antagonize other African states by violating the principle of territorial integrity, the Ethiopian forces halted their counteroffensive at the border and refrained from penetrating Somali territory. The Soviet military advisers attached to the Ethiopian army then helped Mengistu suppress the Eritrean secessionist campaign in the north, which had exploited Ethiopia's conflict with Somalia in the Ogaden to seize control of about 90 percent of the province. By the early spring of 1978, the Somali-Ethiopian conflict on the Horn of Africa had come to an end with both regimes still in power and no territory exchanged.

Washington refused to be dragged into a confrontation with Moscow on the Horn of Africa. President Carter rejected the proposal of his National Security Adviser Zbigniew Brzezinski for the dispatch of a naval task force to the region and rebuffed Siad Barre's plea for arms until Somali troops evacuated the Ogaden. But this did not mean that the U.S. government was unconcerned about the Soviet-Cuban intervention on Ethiopia's behalf. On the contrary, it provoked a sharp reaction in Washington that undermined the already deteriorating relations between the two superpowers. Carter and Brzezinski focussed on the geopolitical significance of the Soviet airlift of Cuban "mercenaries" in support of the victors, which set a dangerous precedent for Communist meddling in other unstable regions in the world. The Soviet and Cuban interventions on behalf of the winning side in the Angolan Civil War of 1975–1976 and the Somali-Ethiopian War of 1977–1978 were interpreted in Washington as evidence of a master plan to surmount the wall of containment that had been erected against Soviet expansion in Europe and Asia. American concern about the successful airlifts to the west and east coasts of Africa was heightened by the simultaneous expansion of Soviet naval power in the Mediterranean Sea and the Indian Ocean. The Russians had obtained bases in the Ethiopian port of Massawa and in South Yemen's port of Aden (through an agreement with the revolutionary regime that had been established in 1967 after the end of British colonial rule). In comparison with the earlier part of the Cold War, when the Soviet fleet was little more than a coastal defense force without overseas bases to support it, the modernized Soviet navy of the late 1970s had become an instrument for the projection of influence far beyond the shores of the USSR.

## The Collapse of White Minority Rule in the South

By the beginning of the 1980s, Africa's long struggle for independence from the handful of European colonial powers that had partitioned the continent a century earlier was over. The disintegration of the Spanish and Portuguese African empires in the mid-1970s left only two remaining bulwarks of European dominance on the continent. One was the former British colony of Rhodesia. Its white settler population had defiantly declared independence from Great Britain in 1965 rather than follow the rest of the British colonies in submitting to black majority rule. Rhodesian Prime Minister Ian Smith, representing the wealthy white landowners who owned the country's productive agricultural property and controlled its political system, attempted to preserve white minority rule in the face of strong pressure (including economic sanctions) from the former colonial power as well as the independent African states. For the next fifteen years Rhodesian security forces waged a relentless counter-insurgency campaign against the Zimbabwe African National Union (ZANU) led by Joshua Nkomo and Robert Mugabe's much more radical Zimbabwe African People's Union (ZAPU). Finally bowing to diplomatic pressure from abroad and military pressure from within, Rhodesian delegates to the Lancaster House Conference in London in 1980 reluctantly agreed to hold the free elections that were certain to result in the end of white minority rule. After ZAPU won the 1980 elections in a landslide, Robert Mugabe became prime minister of a government committed to removing the last vestiges of white colonialism in the newly renamed country of Zimbabwe.

The advent of black majority rule in Rhodesia/Zimbabwe in 1980 focused attention on the last country on the continent of Africa that remained under the control of its white minority. Originally settled by Dutch, French, and German Protestant refugees from the European religious wars of the seventeenth century, the Union of South Africa became a self-governing dominion of the British Crown in 1910 after its white settler population had been defeated by the British in the Boer War of 1899–1901. Beginning in 1948 the right-wing National Party instituted a new legal system known as apartheid (meaning "separateness" in the Afrikaans language spoken by the descendents of the original settlers), which strictly segregated the country's white and nonwhite citizens in land ownership, residence, work, education, religion, athletics, and public services. As Great Britain was preparing to grant independence on the basis of black majority rule to the rest of its African colonies independence in 1960, South Africa's white minority government moved resolutely to suppress the emerging force of black nationalism there. On March 21 police opened fire on a peaceful demonstration in the township of Sharpeville, killing 67 and wounding 186 black protesters. In response to international condemnation of the Sharpeville massacre and pressure to grant majority rule, South Africa withdrew from the Commonwealth and became an independent republic in May 1961.

Black resistance to white minority rule in South Africa was spearheaded by the African National Congress (ANC), a politically moderate organization founded in 1912 to promote the interests of the country's nonwhite majority. Outlawed by the

*Nelson Mandela, president of the African National Congress (left) during a discussion with a Cape Town Teacher. (Hulton Archive by Getty Images)*

government in 1960, the ANC went underground to wage its campaign for a multi-racial, democratic South Africa. One of its prominent officials, a young lawyer named Nelson Mandela, was arrested in 1962 and two years later received a sentence of life imprisonment. The remainder of the ANC leadership fled into exile to sympathetic neighboring countries. Prevented from engaging in legal political activity, the movement resorted to armed struggle as the only means of achieving its goals and urged its followers to revolt. The government in Pretoria responded with an intimidating show of force. When schoolchildren in the black township of Soweto southwest of Johannesburg demonstrated in 1976 against legislation making Afrikaans the compulsory language of instruction, police intervened with guns and tear gas setting off a wave of rioting. By the end of the year more than five hundred nonwhites had been killed. Each anniversary of the demonstration was marked by further violence, which in turn prompted police repression. International organizations such as the Commonwealth and the UN strongly condemned these repressive policies, imposing economic sanctions and diplomatic isolation that condemned South Africa to the status of an international pariah.

The collapse of the Portuguese African empire in the mid-1970s and the white minority regime in Rhodesia in 1980 removed the three buffer states that protected South Africa from a black-controlled continent. The newly independent Marxist states of Angola and Mozambique provided sanctuary and support to ANC guerrillas as they waged their war of liberation, while Zimbabwe's President Robert Mugabe became black Africa's most vociferous critic of apartheid. To compensate for the loss of this protective shield of white-controlled neighboring states to the north, South Africa endeavored to tighten its hold on South West Africa (a former German colony which it had administered since 1920 under a mandate from the League of Nations). In 1971 the International Court of Justice ruled that South Africa's mandate over South West Africa (renamed Namibia by the United Nations in 1967) had expired. In the meantime a national liberation movement for Namibia called the South West Africa People's Organization (SWAPO) was waging a guerrilla campaign against South African forces from neighboring Angola under a militant leader named Sam Nujoma. The expanding conflict in Namibia finally induced the United States to intervene diplomatically to try its hand at bringing an end to the unstable situation in Southern Africa. Whereas President Jimmy Carter had displayed unremitting hostility to South Africa because of its blatant violation of human rights, the new Reagan administration sought to promote gradual reform in the country through a so-called policy of constructive engagement. Its principal goals were threefold: to end the guerrilla war in Namibia and reestablish a stable political situation there; to get the Cuban troops out of Angola, where they remained to support the MPLA regime against the insurgency of Jonas Savimbi's South African-backed UNITA movement; and to induce South Africa to loosen the racist restrictions on its black majority.

This U.S. preoccupation with promoting stability in southern Africa was inspired by Cold War concerns: Reagan administration officials feared that the mounting turmoil in the mineral-rich, strategically located region might tempt the Soviet Union to intervene as it had earlier in Angola and Ethiopia. Under gentle prodding from Washington, South African president P. W. Botha agreed to enter into what proved to be prolonged and complex negotiations with his country's sworn enemies. In December 1988 the South African government and SWAPO finally agreed to a cease-fire in Namibia to be followed by a UN-supervised election to determine the political future of that country. The Angolan government consented to the phased withdrawal of the Cuban troops stationed there by the summer of 1991 in exchange for the evacuation by the end of the summer of 1988 of the South African troops that had remained in southern Angola to bolster UNITA. The mutual withdrawal brought a formal end to the foreign intervention that had plagued Angola since its independence in the mid-1970s, although the UNITA insurgency resumed despite numerous failed attempts at a cease-fire. After SWAPO won the Namibian elections held in November 1989, Nujoma was installed as president of the newly independent country in March 1990. South Africa remained the sole remnant of white European privilege on a continent of independent states ruled by their black majorities.

In the meantime the political situation in South Africa itself underwent a radical transformation at the turn of the decade. F. W. de Klerk, the new president who had replaced the ill Botha in the fall of 1989, stunned members of his National party by repealing many of the laws segregating the races. In 1990 de Klerk removed the ban on the African National Congress, released the imprisoned ANC militant Nelson Mandela, and opened negotiations with the organization in search of a peaceful resolution of the decades-long conflict. On March 17, 1992, a two-thirds majority of the white electorate approved a referendum endorsing de Klerk's policy of negotiating with the ANC. As the audacious head of state proceeded to dismantle the remaining vestiges of apartheid, the international community repealed most of the international sanctions that had been imposed on South Africa in the mid-1980s. After tortuous negotiations throughout the following year, an interim constitution was drafted on November 18, 1993. It scheduled the country's first free elections for a parliament that would be empowered to choose a new president and draft a permanent constitution by the end of the century.

The elections in South Africa transpired peacefully and on schedule at the end of April 1994. After the ANC won control of the new legislative body, the white minority that had enjoyed a political monopoly for so long was obliged to share power with its longtime adversaries. Mandela became president and de Klerk deputy president of a new multiracial, democratic country that had endured Africa's longest and bitterest civil strife. For the remainder of the 1990s Mandela encouraged the white professionals, businesspeople, and farmers of South Africa to repudiate the precedent of white minorities elsewhere on the continent and remain with their skills and wealth to promote the country's economic development. Although de Klerk later resigned after bitter disputes with the ANC and some whites chose to emigrate to Europe or the United States, many stayed behind and made their peace with the newly empowered black majority. When Mandela stepped down in June 1999 after the country's second post-apartheid election, his legacy was the only workable multiracial society on the continent. His successor, the ANC candidate Thabo Mbeki, preserved political continuity and set about tackling South Africa's economic problems (notably the soaring unemployment rate for young black workers) and social problems (notably an increase in urban crime and violence).

## Disorder on the Horn

The conflict between Ethiopia and Somalia on the Horn of Africa in the late 1970s had attracted the attention of the two superpowers. The Soviet Union (with its Cuban ally) helped Ethiopia expel Somali military forces from its Ogaden province and then suppress a secessionist movement in its northern province of Eritrea, prompting anxious concern in the United States about the spread of Communist influence to Africa (see page 298). The end of the Cold War and the Soviet disengagement from Africa at the beginning of the 1990s deprived the Ethiopian strongman, Mengistu Haile Mariam, of his foreign benefactor and protector. His corrupt, despotic regime was overthrown in May 1991 by a movement called the Ethiopian People's Democratic Revolutionary Front, which was based in the northern province of Tigre. The front's leader, Meles Senawi, assumed the leadership of a fractured country whose sixty-four ethnic groups demanded and obtained political automomy for, and the right to speak the local language in, the regions they inhabited. The northern province of Eritrea, which had failed to achieve by force of arms under Mengistu the much more ambitious goal of independence, won that prize under Meles in a referendum in May 1993. The secession of Eritrea, which deprived Ethiopia of its ports on the Red Sea and condemned it to the status of a landlocked country, represented the first violation of the old OAU principle affirming the sanctity of the post-colonial borders. It established a dangerous precedent that threatened to undermine the national unity of other multiethnic states on the continent.

Ethiopia's regional rival Somalia suffered an even more traumatic experience after the collapse of the dictatorship of Mohammed Siad Barre in January 1991. Whereas Ethiopia was plagued by ethnic antagonism, the ethnically homogeneous Somalia was torn apart by violent clashes between more than a dozen clans and sub-clans headed by powerful military commanders whose militias operated with impunity. The reigning warlord in the capital city of Mogadishu, Ali Mahdi Mohammed, from the Abgal lineage of the Hawiye clan, was incapable of imposing any semblance of law and order beyond his own bailwick as the authority of the central government vanished and the economy collapsed. Ali Mahdi's fall from power in Mogadishu in the autumn of 1992 removed the last trace of central political authority as terror, disease, and starvation (made worse by a severe drought) swept the country. When several Non-Governmental Organizations (NGOs) hastened to provide emergency assistance to the suffering masses of Somalia, convoys delivering food and medicines were periodically looted or forced to pay "protection" money by armed gangs. To provide genuine protection for the international relief effort the UN Security Council set up the United Nations Operation in Somalia (UNOSOM), the first specifically humanitarian mission in the history of the international organization.

But while 400,000 Somalis perished from the famine in the course of 1992, UNOSOM proved utterly incapable of offering effective security for the relief convoys because of bureaucratic infighting and red tape. At the end of the year UN Secretary General Boutros Boutros-Ghali persuaded the United States to take charge of an expanded humanitarian operation to ensure that the food and medicines got through. After successfully opening up most of the supply routes for the humanitarian convoys, the U.S.-led Unified Task Force (UNITAF) turned over its responsibilities to a beefed-up United Nations force (UNOSOM II) of 20,000 members that included a 4,000-person American unit. But the hopes that this expanded operation could serve as a successful precedent for a UN international police force were dashed in the Somali capital of Mogadishu in October 1993: U.S. Rangers and Special Forces were in hot pursuit of the warlord General Mohammed Farah Aideed of the Habr Gedir lineage of the Hawiye clan, whose gunmen had murdered UN peacekeeping troops in June. After they were surrounded by Aideed's supporters, two U.S. helicopter gunships were shot down and a rescue force was ambushed on the ground, resulting in the deaths of eighteen American soldiers. President Clinton promptly ordered the U.S. military contingent from Somalia to withdraw by March 1994 and announced that American participation in future UN peacekeeping operations would be severely restricted. UNOSOM II closed up shop in March 1995, abandoning the devastated country to its squabbling warlords as the civilian death toll continued to mount.

Sudan, Africa's largest country, is divided in half along religious, ethnic, and cultural lines. The north is predominantly Muslim and Arabic-speaking with close ties to the Arab world, while the south is predominantly Christian and animist and identifies with Black Africa. Sudan had been a close ally of the United States during the Cold War, providing the U.S. Central Command with access to its military facilities and receiving U.S. military and economic assistance. But when General Omar Hassan al-Bashir seized power in a military coup in 1989, Washington suspended all aid to Sudan. The end of the Cold War had reduced the country's strategic value to the United States, while the mounting influence of Islamic fundamentalist groups on the new government prompted concern in Washington. The Bashir regime proceeded to antagonize the United States by supporting Iraq in the Gulf War of 1991, cultivating warm relations with Iran and Libya, and allowing the Saudi fugitive Osama bin Laden to set up training camps for Islamic militants in the country (see page 364). In the meantime the government intensified a campaign launched in the early 1980s to impose the Sharia (Islamic law) on the Christian and animist south, a provocative policy that had incited a full-scale civil war. John Garang's Sudan People's Liberation Army in the south, which had been fighting the government for a decade, joined forces with the dissident Sudan Alliance Forces of Abdel Aziz Khalid Osman in the north. Accusing the Sudan of sponsoring terrorist activities abroad, the United States provided military support to the neighboring countries of Eritrea, Uganda, and Ethiopia that were providing sanctuary for the opposition forces. The violence that wracked the country for the rest of the decade contributed to the deaths from hunger and disease of more than a million Sudanese.

## War and Genocide in Central Africa

Rwanda and Burundi are tiny, densely populated, impoverished states situated between Zaire and Tanzania in the Great Lakes region of Central Africa that became independent from Belgium in 1962. The ethnic breakdown in both countries consists of roughly 85 percent Hutu and 14 percent Tutsi, two groups that have been in almost constant conflict since the departure of the colonial power. The Belgians favored the Tutsi minority, according it priority in educational opportunities and government employment. The Hutu majority, predominantly poor peasants, were poorly educated and entirely excluded from political power. After independence both groups pursued a systematic campaign to exterminate members of the other group to preserve or acquire a numerical advantage. The most recent of these instances of ethnic slaughter occurred in the spring of 1994 in Rwanda, where the Hutu majority had secured control of the government. When an airplane carrying the Hutu presidents of Rwanda and Burundi was shot down by unidentified assailants, the Hutu in Rwanda exploded in an orgy of violence that eventually took the lives of almost 800,000 Tutsi and sympathetic Hutu. Despite much hand-wringing and expressions of concern, the United Nations and the international community did not intervene to prevent or curb what had become the most blatant act of genocide since the Khmer Rouge killing grounds in Cambodia in the late 1970s.

When the Tutsi-dominated Rwandan Patriotic Front took control of the country in the summer of 1994 and halted the killing, about 1.5 million Hutu fled to refugee camps in neighboring Zaire to escape the wrath of their ethnic enemies. Fearing that the refugees were plotting to return to their homeland and regain power with the acquiescence of the Zairean regime of Mobutu Sésé Sékó, the Rwandan government developed an audacious plan to replace Mobutu with someone willing to move against the Hutus along the border. In 1996 the Rwandan Tutsi regime selected a long-time opponent of Mobutu from Zaire's Shaba province named Laurent Kabila to lead an opposition movement called the Alliance for Democratic Forces for the Liberation of Congo (ADFL). Such a hair-brained scheme would have been unthinkable in the heyday of the Cold War, when the staunch anti-Communist Mobutu enjoyed the firm support of the United States, France, and Belgium. But the collapse of the Soviet Union removed the Zairean dictator's usefulness to his Western patrons, who began to pressure him to introduce democratic reforms. The deterioration of his country's economic situation in the mid-1990s eroded his traditional support in the army and the civil service and left him vulnerable to the type of insurrection that the Rwandan regime was plotting. The pretext for action came in the fall of 1996, when a group of ethnic Tutsis called the Banyamulenge who inhabited Zaire's eastern province for generations but were denied citizenship and harassed by the Zairean army took up arms against Mobutu with Rwandan support. As the ADFL military force that Kabila had organized drove across the country to link up with the Banyamulenge rebels, it met only token resistance from Mobutu's demoralized and underpaid troops. When the ADFL forces entered Kinshasha on May 17, 1997, Kabila was greeted with an outburst of popular enthusiasm for having cashiered the hated 32-year dictatorship. Many hoped that this mineral rich country of 45 million inhabitants in the center of Africa could finally achieve the economic prosperity that had been promised but never delivered since independence because of Mobutu's kleptomaniac rule.

These high hopes for post-Mobutu Zaire, which Kabila renamed the Democratic Republic of Congo (DRC) after taking power, were soon dashed by what would become the biggest African war in modern times. The Rwandan government expected to be rewarded for its sponsorship of the ADFL by a determined campaign by the new government in Zaire to move against the Hutu refugee camps along the country's eastern border that were launching operations into Rwandan territory. But Kabila proved unable or unwilling to bring the militias in the camps under control. The new Zairean leader also began to assert his independence from his patrons by placing people from his home province of Shaba in positions of power and ignoring the advice of the Rwandan officials who had remained in the country to help reorganize his army. Fearful that the cabal of Rwandan advisers might seek to topple him, Kabila expelled them from the country in the summer of 1998. The Rwandan government felt totally betrayed by its former protégé. Taking advantage of an uprising by dissident elements in the eastern part of the DRC, Rwanda launched a joint military operation with Uganda (which shared its concern about incursions from the Hutu refugee camps) to depose Kabila and replace him with a more reliable ally.

Instead of leading to a speedy military triumph, the Rwandan-Ugandan offensive against the DRC unexpectedly plunged Central Africa into an armed struggle that involved eight countries, leading some observers to compare it to the First World War. The three states of Angola, Namibia, and Zimbabwe intervened militarily on Kabila's behalf in pursuit of their own special interests, which included economic designs on the substantial resources of cobalt, copper, timber, and oil in the DRC. From the north, Chad sent military forces and Sudan dispatched advisers to bolster Kabila's regime. When outside pressure by the United States, France, and Belgium finally brought about a cease fire in the summer of 1999, the country was in shambles. The central government was incapable of providing a modicum of services, while five foreign armies and numerous armed militias roamed the country. In the meantime Kabila antagonized many of his supporters by accumulating absolute power in the manner of his predecessor Mobutu. Amid growing internal opposition the new Congolese autocrat was assassinated in January 2001. He was promptly succeeded by his son Joseph, who launched an energetic quest for foreign mediation to end the violence in his country. In February the United Nations Security Council approved a resolution providing for the withdrawal of all foreign troops, which began to be implemented in the spring of 2001. But the withdrawal plan did not apply to the various irregular fighting units from foreign countries that remained in the DRC. It seemed certain that this vast and economically valuable country the size of Western Europe would take decades to recover from the military conflict and political instability that engulfed it at the end of the twentieth century.

The overthrow of Mobutu tipped the balance in the Angolan Civil War against the UNITA rebel movement of Jonas Savimbi, which had received strong support from the Zairean strongman in its campaign against the MPLA government of José Eduardo dos Santos. As we have seen, the withdrawal of foreign military forces (Cubans supporting the government, South Africans backing UNITA) at the end of the 1980s paved the way for a settlement of the destructive conflict that had torn the country apart since its independence from Portugal in 1975 (see page 294). A historic peace agreement signed by the two rivals on May 31, 1991, in Bicesse, Portugal, had established procedures for an immediate cease fire; the simultaneous demobilization of the two armies and the creation of a single national army composed of equal numbers of soldiers from each side; and the preparation for elections under the supervision of a UN observer team. The election was finally held in September 1992 with an extraordinary 90% voter turnout and was certified as free and fair by observers from the United States and the European Community. But when the governing MPLA-won 54% of the votes to UNITA's 34% and dos Santos defeated Savimbi in the first round of the presidential elections, UNITA denounced the elections as fraudulent and refused to abide by the results. Savimbi's forces, which had only partially demobilized under the Bicesse provisions, launched attacks on government positions and seized control of about 70 percent of the country within six months.

The United States formally recognized the MPLA government in Luanda (which had repudiated its Marxist ideology), suspended all aid to its former ally UNITA, and pressured Savimbi to reach a settlement. The old war horse was able to finance his insurgency without the support of his former superpower patron through the sale of diamonds mined in UNITA-held territory and smuggled to foreign buyers through Zaire. But the fall of Mobutu in 1997 deprived Savimbi of his last foreign source of support. As the Angolan government extended its control over former UNITA-held areas, its military forces cornered and killed the guerrilla leader in February 2002. Savimbi's death severely weakened the UNITA leadership, which caved in to international pressure and agreed to a cease-fire agreement with the government in March that included an amnesty for UNITA rebels accused of crimes and offered a glimmer of hope that the twenty-seven-year-old civil war would finally come to an end.

## Nigeria's Bid for Regional Leadership in West Africa

Nigeria, with its vast oil reserves and a quarter of Africa's population, had long been regarded as a potential force for political stability and economic development in its region of West Africa. But throughout the 1990s Nigeria occupied an anomalous position in the eyes of the international community. On the one hand, it came under intense pressure from the United States and the European Union to abandon its tradition of military government and return to civilian rule. One the other hand, it earned lavish praise from Western powers for its valuable role as peacekeeper in the bloody civil wars that engulfed West Africa in the last decade of the twentieth century.

After nine years of military rule, Nigeria held presidential elections in June 1993 that turned out to be the fairest ever held in the country. But when the apparent winner of the elections, Chief Moshood K. O. Abiola, prepared to take office, the ruling military leader General Ibrahim Babangida declared the elections null and void because of procedural flaws. Later in the year the military-dominated provisional government transferred power to General Babangida's protégé, General Sani Abacha, amid a nation-wide protest at the military's high-handed flouting of the popular will. A strike by oil workers which temporarily paralyzed Nigeria's most important industry provoked a wave of repression, including the detention of the opposition leader Chief Abiola. The military regime outraged international opinion in 1995 by executing the writer Ken Saro-Wiwa and eight associates for anti-government activities. The widespread political corruption made possible by petroleum revenues fueled public cynicism and siphoned off funds that might otherwise be used to finance much needed social services. The death of General Abacha and the accession of the progressive General Abdusalam Abubakar in 1998 finally led to the legalization of political parties and the freeing of political prisoners. A relatively free and fair presidential election that was held in the following year brought to power General Olusegun Obasanjo, a reform-minded military leader who became the first democratically elected leader in Nigeria in seventeen years. But the prospects for a stable democratic system were always limited by the behind-the-scenes power and influence exerted by a military class that had ruled the country for most of its post-independence history.

The international community was constrained from applying too much pressure on Nigeria to reform its autocratic political system because of its willingness to act as an agent of regional stability in West Africa throughout the decade of the 1990s. One of the consequences of Nigeria's long period of military rule was that it created the largest and best equipped army of West Africa. For the first three decades after independence, this formidable military force was employed to preserve order in the sprawling nation of two-hundred different ethnic groups. But in 1990 the sixteen-member Economic Community of West African States (ECOWAS) called upon Nigeria to lead a five-nation peacekeeping force that was sent to Liberia; that small country had lapsed into a brutal civil war between the forces of rebel leader Charles Taylor and the government troops of President Samuel Doe, who was captured and executed by the insurgents. The Nigerian-led West African Cease-fire Monitoring Group (ECOMOG) remained in Liberia for seven years until the civil war, which decimated the country's economy and left more than 150,000 dead, was terminated by a cease-fire. Having been prevented by ECOMOG from seizing power in Liberia by force of arms in 1990, Taylor gained power by the ballot box when he won 75 percent of the vote in elections conducted in the summer of 1997.

After shouldering the burden of peacekeeping in Liberia for seven years, Nigeria responded to the appeal from ECOWAS that it lead a 15,000-man ECOMOG peacekeeping force in the neighboring country of Sierra Leone, which was torn apart by murderous violence after a rebel group called the Revolutionary United Front (RUF) had overthrown President Ahmed Tejan Kabbah in May 1997. ECOMOG originally succeeded in driving the insurgents from the capital and restoring a semblance of order. But the RUF continued to wage a brutal campaign against the reinstalled civilian government, which included the killing or maiming of unarmed civilians. When the February 1999 elections in Nigeria brought to power the civilian government under former General Obasanjo, the new regime's desire to concentrate on domestic reform prompted it to turn over ECOMOG's peacekeeping duties in February 2000 to a UN Mission in Sierra Leone (UNAMSIL). But the underfunded, ill-equipped UN mission required an emergency military intervention by Great Britain to compel the RUF to surrender and disarm by January 2002. In the meantime Liberian President Charles Taylor had been exposed as the foreign patron of the RUF, which he provided with weapons in exchange for diamonds mined in the sector of Sierra Leone under rebel control. Taylor was finally subdued by intense international pressure, including UN resolutions imposing an arms embargo and urging all nations to ban imports of diamonds from Sierra Leone.

The eruption of violence and instability in Liberia and Sierra Leone in the 1990s demonstrated the importance of establishing a regional security system in West Africa. Nigeria's assumption of the principal responsibility for preserving order during the civil wars in those two countries seemed to suggest that it was willing and able to act as the dominant power in a region plagued by political instability and conflict. The transformation of ECOMOG into the permanent military arm of ECOWAS during the intervention in Sierra Leone provided a multilateral institutional framework for the employment of Nigerian military power in the interests of regional stability. The necessity of summoning Great Britain to bail out the ineffectual UN force in Sierra Leone represented an embarrassing regression to neo-colonial dependency. But apart from the brief British rescue operation in Sierra Leone, the former colonial powers as well as the United States displayed little inclination to become embroiled in African conflicts in general and West African troubles in particular. On the contrary, the United States, Great Britain, and France all developed elaborate plans to train African military forces in peacekeeping skills. For better of for worse, the African states would be left to their own devices to preserve peace and security in their neighborhood. In the increasingly unstable region of West Africa, Nigeria (working through ECOMOG) seemed the only power capable of fulfilling that role.

## The Algerian Crisis in the 1990s

The Arabic term Maghreb refers to the westernmost extension of the Arab Islamic empire along the southern shore of the Mediterranean Sea during the century after Mohammed's death. In the modern world, the former French colonies of Algeria, Tunisia, and Morocco constitute the three core states of the region, which also includes Mauritania to the east and Libya to the west. Perhaps the most salient fact about the three core states of the Maghreb during the three decades after they achieved independence from France was the rapid growth of their population and the inability of the economic systems of the three states to provide sufficient employment for the expanding labor force. The expanding pool of unemployed youth in the larger cities was swollen by the influx of immigrants from declining rural areas in search of jobs. The presence of these idle, dissatisfied job seekers in the large cities of North Africa began to constitute a potential threat to the existing political system. With no hope for a better future and nothing to lose, many of them proved susceptible to the appeal of a new type of Islamic fundamentalism that combined a radical critique of the existing order with promises of personal salvation.

Since the mid-1980s both Morocco and Tunisia faced Islamic protest movements whose messianic zeal appealed to discontented parts of the population and threatened to undermine the legitimacy of the governments. The Moroccan monarchy and the Tunisian republic were able to fend off the challenge with a minimum of difficulty. But Algeria, the largest, wealthiest, and most powerful of the North African states, confronted an Islamic opposition movement whose extraordinary popularity shook the post-independence state to its very foundations. The National Liberation Front (FLN) that had led the movement of national independence from France ruled Algeria as a secular, one-party state until President Chadli Bendjedid launched a sweeping constitutional reform in 1989 that created a multiparty democracy. One of the several political parties that were legalized in that year was the National Salvation Front (FIS), which openly called for the creation in Algeria of an Islamic state. The FIS astonished everyone by winning 54 percent of the vote in the first freely contested municipal elections in the summer of 1990. Its dramatic 44 percent showing in the first round of the nationwide elections in December 1991 left little doubt that the Islamic party would trounce the FLN in the run-off scheduled for mid-January 1992 and take control of the state.

Before Algeria could be converted into an Islamic Republic, the army intervened to foreclose that possibility. Claiming that an FIS-led government would threaten the country's embryonic democracy, a committee of top military officers forced the president to resign, cancelled the scheduled general election, and declared a state of emergency. The new military regime outlawed the FIS, imprisoned its leaders, and waged a brutal war of repression against the Islamic opposition. The FIS and its military wing, the Islamic Salvation Army (AIS) fought back with a campaign of violence against government officials and institutions, while a separate terrorist group known as the Armed Islamic Groups (GIAs) carried out bombings, assassinations, and kidnappings against innocent civilians in an effort to destabilize the regime. By the time that the violence tapered off toward the end of the decade, more than 60,000 lives had been lost. The response of the European Union to the wave of violence in Algeria during the 1990s revealed two contradictory impulses. On the one hand, the Western powers were embarrassed by the FLN's blatant violation of democratic principles when it annulled elections that the Islamists were virtually certain to win. On the other hand, European countries directly across the Mediterranean such as France, Spain, and Italy worried that the emergence of an Islamic state in Algeria would cause a stampede of illegal immigration that would have dire economic and political consequences at home.

# TEN

# The Decline and Fall of the Soviet Empire

## Economic Restructuring, Political Reform, and Arms Control

After two strokes in 1975 and 1978, Leonid Brezhnev's health deteriorated markedly over the next few years. Before his death in 1982, he tried in vain to anoint his loyal disciple Konstantin Chernenko as the next general secretary of the Communist Party. But Yuri Andropov, the chief of the KGB since 1967, outmaneuvered Chernenko and his Brezhnevite allies in the Politburo to secure the succession. Accurately suspected by the old guard of harboring reformist sentiments, Andropov recognized that the Soviet economy had begun to collapse under the weight of the disastrous policies of the Brezhnev years, which critics began to refer to as the "era of stagnation." Sensing the potentially disastrous political and military consequences of the country's economic downturn, the new general secretary set out to shake up the system. He mounted an energetic campaign to eliminate corruption and inefficiency in the regime's swollen bureaucracy and attempted to improve labor productivity. But before his economic reforms had a chance to take effect, Andropov himself fell ill and died in 1984. This time the entrenched forces succeeded in installing Chernenko as party leader. He surprised no one by giving every indication of reverting to the corruption, incompetence, and inefficiency associated with his deceased patron. But Chernenko in turn died in March 1985 before he could reverse the reformist policies that his predecessor had set in motion. The new general secretary—the fourth in three years during this prolonged leadership crisis in the Kremlin—was Andropov's hitherto obscure young disciple Mikhail Gorbachev.

Khrushchev used to taunt Western leaders during the fifties with the boastful prophecy that "We shall bury you!" Contrary to the widespread misinterpretation of this declaration in the West, the bombastic Soviet leader was not referring to a Soviet military triumph over the West. He meant instead that the spectacular economic achievements of the USSR eventually would demonstrate the indisputable superiority of Socialist principles. The peoples of the Third World and, eventually, of the capitalist countries themselves would embrace the tried-and-true practices of

Communism in the USSR, while the discredited nostrums of capitalism would be interred for good. Mikhail Gorbachev recognized that if the current economic malaise of the Soviet Union were allowed to continue, Khrushchev's provocative prediction would be turned on its head: Unless radical surgery were performed on his country's failing industrial and agricultural system, it was socialism rather than capitalism that would be "buried": The credibility of Marxist-Leninist ideology would be damaged beyond repair in the eyes of the rest of the world.

Gorbachev also shared the concern of his patron Andropov that the decay of the Soviet economy in the Brezhnev era posed a serious security threat: It undermined the country's capability to sustain the costs of the nuclear and conventional arms race with the United States. These costs had begun to increase after the collapse of détente at the end of the 1970s. They escalated beyond all measure after President Ronald Reagan took office in 1981 with an iron determination to restore American military power, which he believed had been permitted to wither under his predecessor, Jimmy Carter. During his first term, the new occupant of the White House launched the most formidable peacetime military buildup in American history to rectify what his secretary of defense, Caspar Weinberger, ominously described as the "descent from a position of clear strategic superiority to the present perilous situation." The five-year, $1.5 trillion defense program for 1982–1986 included two strategic weapons systems inherited from the Carter administration that had a "counterforce" capability (that is, the ability to strike the Soviet ground-based missile force): the MX ICBM, which would eventually be based in fifty hardened silos, and the Trident II SLBM. Reagan's budget also resumed production of the B-1 bomber, which Carter had canceled for budgetary reasons. It established the goal of a six-hundred-ship navy by the end of the decade. It included funds for the Strategic Defense Initiative (SDI), which the Kremlin dreaded as a possible threat to the retaliatory capacity of its long-range missile force (see page 145).

Recognizing the impossibility of matching this formidable rearmament program amid the pervasive signs of Soviet economic decline, Gorbachev eagerly embraced the alternative means of diplomacy to limit an arms race he knew his country could not win and feared would drive it into bankruptcy. The new Soviet general secretary therefore launched an international political offensive on two fronts in an audacious bid to improve relations with the Western world. On the political front Gorbachev strove to settle all of the Cold War conflicts across the globe that had contributed to the disintegration of détente by the end of the 1970s. On the military front he sought a comprehensive set of arms-control agreements that would terminate Soviet-American competition in conventional and nuclear weapons. The resulting improvement in East-West relations and the reduction in arms spending would enable the Soviet government to devote its attention, energy, and resources to desperately needed internal reforms.

Although Gorbachev would remain a devout Communist for the rest of his public career, he fully appreciated the endemic weaknesses of the Soviet economic system and displayed a willingness to experiment with radical cures. The result was an ambitious scheme of economic restructuring, or *perestroika,* whose goals included the decentralization of decision-making and self-management in industry, the encouragement of private initiative, and the introduction of a modified market economy to stimulate productivity and satisfy the long-ignored demand of Soviet citizens for consumer products. Faced with formidable opposition from the entrenched defenders of the old ways within the bureaucracy, the Communist Party, the intelligence services, and the military, Gorbachev mobilized public support for his radical economic proposals by introducing a set of political reforms—collectively designated by the slogan "*glasnost,*" or "openness"—that promoted greater public participation in the political life of the nation. *Glasnost* and *perestroika* were intended not to destroy the Soviet political and economic system but rather to reform it in order to ensure its survival.

While pursuing these internal political and economic innovations, Gorbachev waged a vigorous campaign to reduce tensions with the United States. He was particularly intent on pursuing a negotiated settlement to the most complicated and dangerous feature of the Cold War—the nuclear arms race. Even before his accession, the two superpowers had taken steps to breathe new life into the stalled strategic arms-control process. Shortly after Reagan's reelection in November 1984 the White House jointly announced that American Secretary of State George Shultz and Soviet Foreign Minister Andrei Gromyko would discuss the resumption the Strategic Arms Reduction Talks (START), which the Russians had unilaterally suspended in the fall of 1983 in protest against the impending deployment of the U.S. intermediate-range missiles in Europe (see page 145). In deference to Soviet concerns the negotiations would include the topic of "space weapons," a reference to Reagan's 1983 speech on missile defense that had caused such consternation in Moscow. In March 1985 high-level negotiations between the United States and the Soviet Union opened in Geneva, just as Gorbachev took power in Moscow. In the meantime Reagan's effort to increase military spending while cutting taxes had saddled him with an enormous budget deficit and inspired a bipartisan congressional resolution requiring budgetary balance. This pressure from Capitol Hill to cut federal spending thus made Reagan receptive to Gorbachev's overtures for negotiations to limit the nuclear arms race.

The new man in the Kremlin signaled his sincerity in pursuing strategic nuclear arms race by unilaterally announcing in the summer of 1985 a temporary moratorium on nuclear testing and challenging the United States to follow suit. In July he replaced the long-time Soviet Foreign Minister Andrei Gromyko, the preeminent symbol of Soviet toughness in the Cold War era, with the reformist party leader from Georgia, Eduard Shevardnadze. To the surprise of many observers, Reagan responded with enthusiasm to these conciliatory gestures from Moscow. The ardent anti-Communist in the White House and the new head of the "Evil Empire" met for the first time the following November in Geneva and quickly developed a strong rapport. While the START talks in Geneva dragged on inconclusively, Reagan and Gorbachev agreed to meet in Reykjyavik, Iceland, in October 1986 to prepare the ground for a projected summit conference in Washington that would to strive to break the logjam in strategic arms negotiations.

The Reykjavik meeting counts as a unique episode in the annals of great power diplomacy. To pave the way for a strategic arms agreement, Gorbachev made sweeping concessions in the Soviet negotiating position in the deadlocked talks on intermediate-range nuclear forces (INF) in Europe: He dropped the Soviet demand that the British and French nuclear forces be counted in NATO's total. He accepted Reagan's "zero option" plan, whereby all Soviet SS-20 intermediate-range missiles based in Europe would be dismantled in exchange for the removal of the Pershing IIs and GLCMs that NATO had recently deployed. Turning to the topic of long-range nuclear weapons, the two leaders agreed in principal to a 50 percent reduction in all ballistic missiles (ICBMs and SLBMs) within five years and to their total abolition within ten. Gorbachev's only nonnegotiable demand was the one concession that Reagan was unwilling to make: the scrapping of the SDI missile defense program, which the Soviet leaders feared would neutralize their country's nuclear deterrent. Reagan's refusal to sacrifice his pet project for protecting the American homeland against incoming ballistic missiles torpedoed the conference and rendered moot the sweeping measures of nuclear disarmament that the two leaders tentatively had endorsed.

Unable to break the deadlock on strategic arms reduction, the two sides shifted their attention to other matters in dispute after the failure of the Reykjavik summit. Gorbachev finally abandoned his quest for a comprehensive nuclear arms reduction package and offered in February 1987 to consider separately the more circumscribed issue of INF in Europe. After one last abortive bid to slip SDI into the discussions, Gorbachev threw in the towel and accepted a modified version of Reagan's 1981 "zero option" solution to the INF dispute. He traveled to Washington on December 8, 1987, and cosigned with Reagan the INF Treaty, which provided for the destruction of all of NATO's Pershing IIs and GLCMs and all of the Soviet SS-20s by the end of 1991. Although the INF agreement affected only about 5 percent of the nuclear arsenals of the two sides, it nevertheless represented a milestone in the history of nuclear arms control: Whereas the SALT process had imposed limits on the future deployment of certain types of strategic weapons, the INF Treaty decreed the total elimination of an entire class of nuclear weapons that were already operational. The final text reflected three major concessions by the Soviet Union that qualified the pact as a major diplomatic defeat for Gorbachev. First, he was obliged to swallow a drastically asymmetrical reduction of theater nuclear weapons (the destruction of 851 Soviet launchers and 1,836 missiles compared to 283 American launchers and 867 missiles). Second, he agreed to include in the category of weapons to be eliminated the SS-20 missile force that had been deployed in Asia, which weakened the Soviet nuclear posture vis-à-vis China. Finally, he abandoned the traditional Soviet opposition to adequate verification procedures, accepting a remarkably intrusive monitoring system that included short-notice, on-site inspections by the other signatory.

The Soviet leader accepted the agreement on intermediate-range nuclear weapons because he hoped that it would provide a new impetus for the negotiations on strategic arms reduction that had shown no progress since the Reykjavik meeting. At the Washington summit the two sides did record substantial progress on a START Treaty, tentatively agreeing to a ceiling on delivery vehicles for each side and applying to strategic weapons some of the verification procedures that had been included in the INF pact. But the stumbling block that prevented the adoption of a START agreement to match the INF breakthrough was the U.S. plan for strategic missile defense. In the meantime the audacious Soviet leader had determined that the only means of maintaining the momentum of arms control, which he continued to regard as an essential component of his goal of shifting Soviet spending priorities from a militarized to a consumer economy, was to mount a bold unilateral act of his own.

*President Ronald Reagan and Vice-President (and President-Elect) George H. W. Bush meet with Soviet General Secretary Mikhail Gorbachev on Governor's Island, New York, December 1988. Reagan had earlier denounced the Soviet Union as the "Evil Empire," and Bush was president during its collapse in 1991. (Courtesy Ronald Reagan Library)*

After purging his enemies from the Communist Party Central Committee, winning election as president of the Supreme Soviet, and pushing through electoral and constitutional reforms to consolidate his personal power, Gorbachev appeared at the United Nations in December 1988 to deliver the first address by a Soviet leader to the world organization since Khrushchev's memorable oration in 1960. The contrast with his predecessor's shoe-banging harangue could not have been more vivid: The Soviet president called for a new approach to international relations based on the principles of global security and interdependence, declaring that the increasingly warm relations between Moscow and Washington had set an excellent example of constructive dialogue free of ideology. He then proceeded to announce a unilateral reduction of Soviet armed forces by half a million men in the next two years. He specifically singled out Eastern Europe for substantial cuts in tanks, artillery pieces, and combat aircraft, signalling thereby not only a reduction of the Soviet military threat to NATO but also a new approach to Moscow's relations with its satellites.

Gorbachev's historic address at the UN was clearly intended as a nostalgic celebration of his fruitful collaboration with Reagan as the latter prepared to leave the White House. It also represented an appeal to President-elect George H. W. Bush for a continuation of the Soviet-American dialogue. Gorbachev's unilateral cuts in

Soviet military power in Eastern Europe helped to energize the convention arms control negotiations between NATO and the Warsaw Pact. The Mutual and Balanced Force Reduction (MBFR) talks between the two alliances had dragged on without significant progress in Vienna since the heyday of the Nixon-Brezhnev détente in 1973. In March 1989 the moribund MBFR discussions were supplanted by a new negotiating forum under the auspices of the Conference on Security and Cooperation in Europe (CSCE). Designated as the Conventional Armed Forces in Europe (CFE) talks, it included all member states of NATO and the Warsaw Pact. On November 19, 1990, the twenty-three participants signed the CFE Treaty, which established a balance of conventional forces in Europe by prescribing substantial reductions in Soviet conventional weapons such as tanks, combat aircraft, and artillery from the region west of the Ural Mountains. For the first time since the early 1950s, the two alliance systems that had confronted each other with the world's highest concentration of military hardware had agreed to reduce the size of their arsenals of conventional arms.

## The Liberation of the Satellites

This astonishing progress in conventional arms reduction in Europe was overtaken by a series of revolutionary political changes within the Communist half of the continent. In his historic speech at the UN in December 1988, Gorbachev had endorsed the principle of "freedom of choice" for citizens throughout the world. Many observers interpreted these words as a signal that Moscow was prepared to loosen its iron grip on its satellites in Eastern Europe. His progressive political and economic innovations at home inspired dissident groups in that region, who began to realize that they now had a friend in Moscow, to demand similar reforms of the Communist leadership in their own countries.

The first Soviet bloc country to test the Kremlin's willingness to tolerate the extension of *glasnost* and *perestroika* to Eastern Europe was Poland, which of all of the Communist satellites in Eastern Europe was the most ripe for a radical political transformation. The origins of Poland's volatile political situation may be traced to the summer of 1980, when the Communist government's decision to increase food prices provoked a massive protest demonstration and strike by trade unionists at the Lenin Shipyard in the port city of Gdansk. The shipworkers at Gdansk, led by a charismatic electrician named Lech Walesa, demanded and obtained from the embattled Communist prime minister the right to form a trade union free of government control. Known as Solidarity, this first free trade union in the Communist world attracted millions of members and increasingly came into conflict with the authorities in Warsaw. Fearing that this domestic turmoil would give rise to a Soviet military intervention (as it had in Poland in 1956 and Czechoslovakia in 1968), the head of the Polish army, General Wojciech Jaruzelski, declared marshal law with Moscow's blessing. He proceeded to outlaw Solidarity, arrest thousands of its members, and assume the offices of prime minister and party leader. After their release from prison with the suspension of marshal law in 1982, Walesa and his comrades in Solidarity operated as a kind of unofficial political opposition to the Communist regime. This spreading anti-Communist campaign received the active support of the former archbishop of Krakow, Karol Wojtyla, who in 1978 had become the first Roman Catholic Pope of Polish nationality as John Paul II. He also became the first Pope to visit a Communist country when he received a tumultuous welcome in his native land from its predominantly Catholic population a year later. The growth of anti-Communist opposition within Poland, led by the Solidarity trade union movement and the Catholic church, undermined the authority of Jaruzelski as his government struggled to cope with the domestic repercussions of Gorbachev's "new thinking" in Moscow. Bowing to intense political pressure in February 1989, Jaruzelski lifted the ban he had imposed on Solidarity seven years earlier and opened negotiations with its leadership for political reforms. When free elections were held in June for a third of the upper house and the entire lower house of the Polish parliament, Solidarity candidates won almost all of the contested seats. In August a Solidarity-led coalition took power in Warsaw, the first non-communist government in Eastern Europe since the advent of the Cold War.

While Poland was throwing off the shackles of Communist rule, Hungary's reformist Communist party was rushing to refurbish its image while anti-Communist opposition mounted throughout 1989. It formally abandoned the ideology of Leninism, changing its name to the Hungarian Socialist Party and the country's name to "the Republic of Hungary" from the Soviet-style "Hungarian People's Republic." The remains of Imre Nagy, the prime minister who had been overthrown and executed after the 1956 revolution, were reinterred with full national honors amid outpourings of popular emotion. Hungary took the first step in dismantling the Iron Curtain by opening its barbed-wire border with Austria to permit free circulation of people. In January 1990, the government in Budapest asked the Soviet Union to remove all of its military forces from Hungary, which the following March the Kremlin agreed to do by the summer of 1991.

After the collapse of the Communist regimes in Poland and Hungary the rest of the hard-line regimes in Eastern Europe fell like dominoes. In November Bulgaria's Communist boss Todor Zhivkov, who had ruled that country since 1954, was ousted by a coalition of reformists. Later in the month his Czechoslovak counterpart met a similar fate, as opposition groups agitated for the end of Communism and the removal of Soviet troops from the country. In late December the playwright Vaclav Havel, the country's most famous dissident, was elected president, while the parliament chose as its speaker former prime minister Alexander Dubcek, who had been ousted by the Russians after the "Prague Spring" of 1968. The "Velvet Revolution" in Czechoslovakia, like the political changes in the rest of Eastern Europe, occurred in a peaceful manner as the Communist regimes relinquished power without a fight. The single exception to the rule was Romania, whose Communist dictator Nicolae Ceauşescu ordered his troops to fire on demonstrators in December and promptly was overthrown and executed. The successor government removed the remnants of Ceausescu's political apparatus and developed plans for the country's first free elections.

This sweeping political transformation in Eastern Europe throughout the revolutionary year of 1989 transpired with the full acquiescence of the Kremlin. Not only did Gorbachev refrain from interfering in the movement toward liberalization and popular rule; he also warned the old-line Communist officials that they had better adapt to the new political conditions or lose their positions. He apparently did not foresee the possibility that the kind of reformist Communism he welcomed in Eastern Europe would be swept away by the escalating force of anti-Communism among the population. But when this trend became unmistakable throughout the region, Moscow did nothing to reverse the course of history. In response to requests by Czechoslovakia and Hungary for the removal of Soviet troops, Gorbachev's agreement in February and March 1990, respectively, to a total military withdrawal from the two countries by the end of June 1991 sounded the death knell of Moscow's hegemony in Eastern Europe. Poland, after a long delay caused by skepticism about German acceptance of the Oder-Neisse Line, reached agreement with the Soviet Union in October 1991 for the withdrawal of Soviet troops by October 1992. Moscow's acquiescence in the loss of political and military hegemony in Eastern Europe was apparently prompted by two considerations, one in the military sphere and the other in the economic: Khrushchev and Brezhnev had considered the satellites vital to the Soviet Union's security interests in Europe and had therefore intervened in Hungary and Czechoslovakia, respectively, to preserve Soviet control. For Gorbachev, the security value of the region had dwindled amid the relaxation of political tensions with the West and the mutual reductions of conventional arms on the continent. Second, there appears to have been an element of economic self-interest involved in the Kremlin's willingness to relinquish its Eastern European empire: Whereas the satellites had once served Moscow's economic interests, they had long since become an economic burden because of the special trade arrangements that guaranteed them energy supplies and raw materials from the Soviet Union at prices well below the world market price.

## The Reunification of Germany and the Breakup of the Warsaw Pact

As the former Soviet satellites cashiered their Communist governments throughout 1989, the tumultuous political developments in East Germany confronted the Soviet leadership with an unexpected challenge that tested Gorbachev's tolerance of the cataclysmic changes that were underway: Massive antigovernment demonstrations in the streets of Leipzig and other East German cities throughout October 1989 provoked the aged Communist Party boss Erich Honecker to order a crackdown. But his security forces refused to fire on the demonstrators, while many soldiers and police began to fraternize with the angry crowds. On October 17 Honecker's own hand-picked Politburo replaced the old hard-liner with the more pragmatic Communist functionary Egon Krenz. In the meantime East German citizens had been flocking to Hungary and crossing the border into Austria, which the reformist government in Budapest had thrown open in September. After an initial hesitation Krenz yielded to intense popular pressure by revoking all travel restrictions to the West and opening the checkpoints along the Berlin Wall. The notorious symbol of the Iron Curtain dividing Europe receded into history, as joyous East Berliners streamed through the barbed wire and concrete barrier and joined their West Berlin counterparts in raucous demonstrations. When the reformist Communist government in East Germany was compelled by the momentum of events to conduct the country's first free elections on March 18, 1990, the Communists won only 16 percent of the vote against two non-Communist electoral groups. The next month the East German parliament formed a non-Communist government for the first time in the country's forty-one-year history.

With both German states in the hands of non-Communist governments, the long-dormant issue of the country's political division became the principal topic of discussion. The only historical rationale for Germany's partition had been the ideological incompatibility between the Western and Soviet occupation zones, and then between the two independent states that had been established after the foreign troops withdrew. As they were preparing for their challenge to the fading Communist Party in the March 1990 elections, all of the non-Communist political groups in East Germany publicly endorsed the cause that their West German counterparts had long embraced: the reunification of the two states. They spoke for an expectant East German population that, amid the exhilaration following the opening of the Berlin Wall, longed for the economic benefits that would result from their absorption by the prosperous West German state. Once in power, the center-right coalition in East Berlin opened discussions with the government of Chancellor Helmut Kohl in Bonn about the proper means of managing the political reunification that the populations of both Germanies earnestly desired.

Whereas Gorbachev had accepted with equanimity the loss of the Soviet satellites throughout 1989, he viewed with alarm the prospect of a renascent, reunited Germany amid the disintegration of the Eastern bloc. The day after the opening of the Berlin Wall, the Soviet president forcefully expressed his concerns to President Bush, British Prime Minister Margaret Thatcher, and French President François Mitterrand (who represented the three other powers with residual occupation rights in Germany and Berlin). Gorbachev found a sympathetic ear in London and Paris, for Thatcher and Mitterrand both privately worried that a powerful, prosperous, united Germany might upset the European balance of power and dominate the continent. But Bush and his secretary of state, James Baker, shared none of the atavistic apprehensions of the European leaders about a united Germany throwing its weight around. Their main concern was to ensure that it remain within NATO, which Gorbachev adamantly opposed as a grave threat to the East-West strategic balance. But the Soviet president finally recognized that he was powerless to prevent German reunification and that a Germany constrained by its NATO membership was preferable to an unbridled Germany operating as a loose cannon on the deck. He therefore agreed to submit the sensitive issue to what came to be known as the "2 + 4" talks (referring to the two German states and the four World War II victors: the United States, Great Britain, France, and the Soviet Union). Kohl eventually provided the assurances required to allay Soviet concerns: He reaffirmed the sanctity of Germany's eastern borders; pledged to honor its commitment not to acquire nuclear, chemical, or biological weapons; promised that no other NATO military forces would be stationed in eastern Germany, which would be evacuated by Soviet troops by 1994; and agreed to reduce German armed forces to 370,000 men. On September 12 the 2 + 4 talks ended with an agreement whereby the four occupying powers relinquished their residual occupation rights in Germany. This paved the way for the reunification of the country on October 3, 1990.

The recession of Soviet power from Eastern Europe and the reunification of Germany in 1989–1990 terminated the Cold War that had begun in the second half of the 1940s with the partition of Europe into two hostile blocs and the partition of Germany into two hostile states. The institutional instruments for the maintenance of

Soviet hegemony in Eastern Europe disappeared one by one as the new era opened: In January 1990 the Soviet prime minister announced to a meeting of Comecon—the Communist bloc's economic organization—that Soviet trade with the other members would be conducted at world market rather than Soviet-subsidized prices beginning January 1991. Thus deprived of its raison d'être as the nexus of a preferential trading system, Comecon itself was disbanded on June 28, 1991. By the end of the year, Soviet trade with Eastern Europe had declined by 60 percent as the former satellites eagerly turned to the West for their foreign economic links. The Warsaw Pact, which had also been rendered obsolete by the earthshaking political changes in its Eastern European member-states, was formally dissolved on July 1, 1991.

Before acquiescing in the dismantling of Soviet political and military hegemony in Eastern Europe, Gorbachev had already begun to disengage from other foreign undertakings inherited from the Brezhnev era that had perpetuated Cold War tensions with Washington: As part of his bold campaign to improve relations with the United States, Gorbachev would draw down Soviet military power or political influence in all the places that Washington was citing as unacceptable instances of Soviet expansionism: Afghanistan, Cambodia, Nicaragua, Cuba, and Angola. Never before in history had a great power willingly sacrificed its extensive global interests with such rapidity and with such equanimity. By the beginning of the last decade of the twentieth century, the country that under Stalin had become one of the world's two superpowers and under Brezhnev had acquired nuclear parity with the United States and developed a world-class navy to support its global ambitions was retreating from its forward positions everywhere in the world.

## The Disappearance of the Soviet Union

But the worst was yet to come. As Moscow relinquished control of Eastern Europe and scaled back its commitments abroad throughout 1989, Gorbachev began to face mounting political unrest at home. The radical restructuring of the Soviet economy and the public relations hoopla that accompanied it had stimulated a sharp increase in expectations on the part of Soviet consumers, who had endured so many years of deprivation and desperately craved a better life. Unfortunately for Gorbachev, the economic conditions in the country not only failed to improve but deteriorated even further. The Soviet economy's output of agricultural goods, oil, and coal fell far short of government targets. By the beginning of the 1990s the country's gross national product had declined by 2 percent, the government's foreign debt skyrocketed, and both the national budget deficit and the foreign trade deficit widened. Already endemic corruption became rampant and extended to all levels of Soviet society, shortages in basic commodities led to rationing, and the black market in high-priced goods flourished. These bleak economic conditions led to growing disillusionment with *perestroika,* whose meager results scarcely seemed an improvement over the much-maligned "period of stagnation" under Brezhnev.

The faltering economy in turn generated an unprecedented wave of political discontent, which Gorbachev hoped to contain through a number of gestures toward greater democratization. In June 1988 the old rubber stamp Supreme Soviet was replaced by a new Congress of People's Deputies, two-thirds of whose members would be chosen through direct election while the remaining third would be selected by official organizations. This superlegislature of 2,250 members met in May–June 1989 to elect the country's first parliament, a Supreme Soviet of 542 members with Gorbachev as its chairman. The proceedings of the Congress of People's Deputies were broadcast live on television, giving the Soviet people an unprecedented experience in democratic politics as spokespersons for "liberal" and "conservative" factions took the floor to criticize the government and even Gorbachev personally. The telecasts finally had to be discontinued amid reports of worker absenteeism and productivity declines, as enthralled citizens sat glued to their television sets watching the spectacle of deep-seated national problems being aired for the first time.

As the old restrictions on political activity disappeared, the long-suppressed aspirations of the USSR's subject nationalities boiled over in several of the non-Russian republics. Religion, Marx's "opiate of the people" that had supposedly vanished in the workers' paradise, resurfaced as a source of mounting unrest in the Caucasus and Central Asia: Throughout 1990 Christian Armenians battled Muslim Azeris in the Armenian enclave of Nagorno-Karabakh within Azerbaijan, while violent demonstrations staged by Muslims in the republics of Kirgizia, Tajikistan, and Uzbekistan required the intervention of Soviet troops to restore order. In the meantime the non-Russian republics in Europe seethed with separatist discontent. The three Baltic republics, the last to be annexed by the Soviet Union in 1940 after two decades of experience as independent states, led the way. Lithuania defiantly declared its independence in March 1990 and elected a non-Communist as president. In May Latvia announced its intention to secede, and Estonia soon followed suit. The demand for national self-determination had also spread to two republics with a much longer history of Russian domination: Georgia (the homeland of Stalin and Gorbachev's foreign minister Eduard Shevardnadze) and Ukraine (where secessionist fervor was fed by the incompetence and indifference of Soviet authorities in response to the radioactive contamination caused by an explosion in a nuclear power plant in Chernobyl in 1986). Two years after the Chernobyl disaster Moscow's failure to furnish prompt assistance to the victims of an earthquake in Armenia fanned the flames of rebellion there as well.

In his determination to loosen up the Soviet political system and promote greater popular participation, Gorbachev had vastly underrated the explosive power of ethnic nationalism in the Soviet republics. The declaration of independence by the Baltic states in 1990 finally led him to conclude that the situation had gotten out of hand and required remedial action. This judgment reflected the growing pressure on him by officials in the military and security forces to curb the centrifugal forces that threatened to destroy the country's national unity. In his first attempt to reverse the trend toward disintegration, Gorbachev dispatched Soviet military units to the Baltic states in early 1991 as the separatist agitation there continued unabated. Having assumed the Soviet presidency the previous year and vastly increased his personal powers, he forged a tactical alliance with defenders of the old system in the army, the KGB, and the Communist Party in a desperate bid to stem the secessionist tide. When his liberal Foreign Minister Eduard Shevardnadze resigned in protest against the new repressive policy in December 1990, Gorbachev reshuffled his government to include several notorious hard-liners. It appeared to many observers that the new

Soviet leadership's commitment to political and economic reform was coming to a screeching halt.

In the meantime the standard of reform had been taken up by an opposition politician named Boris Yeltsin, whom Gorbachev had dismissed from his government in 1987. Running on a platform calling for a radical restructuring of the Soviet economic and political system that went far beyond Gorbachev's *perestroika* and *glasnost,* Yeltsin was elected to the new Congress of People's Deputies from a Moscow constituency. His big chance came in May 1990, when he became chairman of the Supreme Soviet of the Russian Republic. From this new forum Yeltsin launched a vigorous campaign on behalf of the full democratization of the Soviet political system, the establishment of a market economy, and the recognition of a greater autonomy for the Soviet republics (including his own). In June 1991 Yeltsin was elected president of the enormous Russian Republic by popular vote, a position that endowed him with a greater claim to political legitimacy than Gorbachev himself enjoyed. It also afforded this ardent advocate of reform the opportunity to practice what he preached within his own political domain. Yeltsin promptly unveiled an ambitious scheme to dismantle the command economy and expose it to the operation of the free market. In a spectacular blow against the old order, the new president outlawed the Communist Party within the Russian Republic. It was evident that Yeltsin's revolutionary plans for Russia had nothing in common with Gorbachev's cautious campaign to renovate the Soviet Union. In a word, the latter sought to save the Communist system by reforming it. The former sought to bury it and start afresh.

The indefatigable Gorbachev's campaign to steer a middle course between the hidebound defenders of the old order and the impatient champions of the new had finally run its course. His acquiescence in the military's crackdown in the Baltic states signified his determination to employ force to prevent the dissolution of the Soviet Union into its various national components. In one last desperate gamble to hold the country together through peaceful means, he had presented to the Supreme Soviet in November 1990 the draft of a so-called Union Treaty that accorded much greater autonomy to the republics. But the forces of disintegration had already gone too far: The three Baltic states and Georgia refused to have anything to do with the proposed pact, while Ukraine, Belorussia, Armenia, and Yeltsin's Russia reserved the right to create their own armed forces and conduct relations with foreign states. When unrest in Latvia and Lithuania flared up again in early 1991, Gorbachev was persuaded by his military and security advisers to authorize another show of force in the Baltics until protest demonstrations in Moscow forced him to back down. When he took the gamble of announcing at the end of 1990 a nationwide referendum to secure public approval of the reformed union structure the following spring, several republics signaled their intentions to opt out of the Union by withholding two-thirds of their contributions to the Soviet budget in the first quarter of 1991. Although the nationwide referendum that was conducted on March 17, 1991, recorded a countrywide vote of 76 percent in favor of a renewed union, the vast majority of voters in the three Baltic republics, Georgia, Armenia, and Moldovia (renamed Moldova) stayed home. The leaders of these six nonunion republics refused to participate in Gorbachev's preparations for a formal signing of the Union Treaty, which had to be postponed several times until it was finally set for the summer of 1991.

In the meantime a clique of conservative hard-liners within Gorbachev's inner circle, who had strongly opposed the Union Treaty as an unacceptable sacrifice of central authority, learned of the president's plans to replace some of them with liberal supporters of the new concessions to the republics. Concluding that the time had come to halt the country's slide toward anarchy, they decided to mount a preemptive strike to forestall the signing of the treaty. A delegation of officials arrived at Gorbachev's vacation villa on the Crimean peninsula on August 18, 1991, to place him under house arrest. The next day a "State Committee on National Emergency" including Prime Minister Valentin Pavlov, Defense Minister Marshal Dmitry Yazov, and KGB Chairman Vladimir Kryuchkov seized power in Moscow. The new ruling clique declared a six-month state of emergency, during which it pledged to resume the program of gradual reform within the Union structure that the deposed president had initiated in the mid-1980s. In the meantime an interim government under Gorbachev's conservative vice president, Gennady Yanayev, was formed to restore social order and preserve the country's political unity. But before the new government could impose its authority on the population, a warning from dissident elements in the KGB enabled Yeltsin to evade arrest and make his way to the Russian parliament building. The president of the Russian Republic denounced the coup and rallied public support against the conspirators, winning over the rank and file and several loyalist officers in the military. When the government set up by the conspirators unaccountably failed to seize control of telecommunications facilities in the Soviet capital, Yeltsin was able to broadcast decrees as the Russian president and to rally domestic and foreign support. Within three days the coup had collapsed and its perpetrators were arrested.

Although Gorbachev promptly returned to Moscow and sought to reassume his presidential duties, the fact that most of the conspirators had been members of his own government had damaged his credibility beyond repair. Yeltsin successfully exploited the public acclaim he had earned in his central role in foiling the coup to usurp the powers of the Soviet government within the Russian Republic. When party leaders in the other republics followed suit, it was evident that Gorbachev's hopes of preserving the heritage of the Bolshevik Revolution while radically reforming the party of Lenin and Stalin were definitively dashed. In the meantime his plan for a refurbished Union was also dealt a crushing blow when Ukraine, originally a supporter of the Union, voted for independence on December 1. The next week the presidents of the three Slavic republics—Russia, Ukraine, and Belorussia (renamed Belarus)—effectively buried Gorbachev's Union Treaty by announcing the formation of an alternative organization of sovereign states loosely tied together in a cooperative arrangement and inviting all of the other republics to join. The leaders of eleven of the fifteen successor states met on December 21 to launch the Commonwealth of Independent States (CIS), declaring that the Union of Soviet Socialist Republics had ceased to exist.* On December 25 Gorbachev resigned as president of the defunct

*The three Baltic states (Latvia, Lithuania, and Estonia) declined membership in the new body. Georgia deferred its approval because of acute ethnic conflict within its borders, finally joining the CIS in 1993.

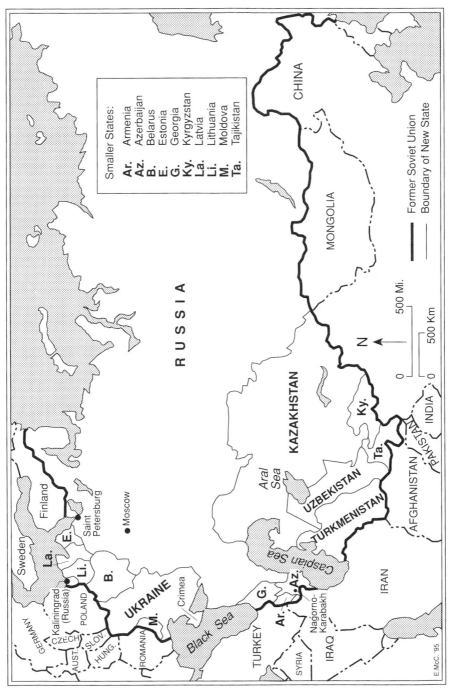

Smaller States:
**Ar.** Armenia
**Az.** Azerbaijan
**B.** Belarus
**E.** Estonia
**G.** Georgia
**Ky.** Kyrgyzstan
**La.** Latvia
**Li.** Lithuania
**M.** Moldova
**Ta.** Tajikistan

CHINA

MONGOLIA

RUSSIA

KAZAKHSTAN

Ky.

Ta.

INDIA

Aral Sea

UZBEKISTAN

TURKMENISTAN

AFGHANISTAN

PAKISTAN

Caspian Sea

IRAN

Finland

Sweden

Saint Petersburg

Moscow

La.

E.

Li.

B.

Kaliningrad (Russia)

GERMANY

POLAND

CZECH

AUST.

SLOV.

HUNG.

ROMANIA

UKRAINE

M.

Crimea

Black Sea

TURKEY

G.

Ar.

Az.

Nagorno-Karabakh

SYRIA

IRAQ

—— Former Soviet Union
—— Boundary of New State

500 Mi.

500 Km

N

0

0

E.McC. '95

*The Successor States of the Former Soviet Union*

323

USSR, turning over to his rival Yeltsin all of his official functions (notably including the control of the former Union's nuclear weapons).

One of the first decisions of the new loose-knit Commonwealth was to recommend that Russia—the largest, most populous, and most powerful of the successor states—inherit the Soviet seat on the United Nations Security Council. In the ensuing months Russia also absorbed most of the assets of the former Soviet Union while decisively repudiating its Marxist-Leninist heritage. In the meantime Washington reacted to the final agony of its long-time global rival by keeping its distance from those explosive internal political developments. But in the autumn of 1991 (between the failed coup attempt and Gorbachev's resignation), the United States and the Soviet Union succeeded in settling or seriously addressing a long list of disputes that had separated the two superpowers for years: The Kremlin announced that it would withdraw the twenty-eight-hundred-man brigade from Cuba that had ruffled American feathers during the Carter years (see page 142). Washington and Moscow jointly announced the suspension of arms supplies to the contending factions in the Afghan civil war, which would lead to the collapse of the pro-Soviet regime in Kabul seven months later (see page 363). The two governments jointly convened a Middle East peace conference in Madrid to address the Arab-Israeli conflict and joined China and other states in promoting peace settlements in the civil wars in Cambodia and El Salvador (see page 378). The most spectacular achievement of this period was the flurry of competitive arms-control initiatives, during which Bush and Gorbachev pledged to eliminate all their ground-launched tactical nuclear weapons as well as to remove all strategic bombers from alert status. It almost seemed as though the two superpowers were rushing to resolve as many of the items on their negotiating agenda as possible before one of them disappeared from the world scene.

After the disintegration of the USSR into fourteen sovereign political entities, the Bush administration immediately became preoccupied with the formidable arsenal of nuclear weapons that the Soviet Union had stockpiled during the Cold War. The issue of the roughly seventeen thousand short-range or tactical nuclear weapons (TNWs) that were dispersed among the fourteen former Soviet republics was promptly and efficaciously resolved: Since Gorbachev and Bush had agreed in the autumn of 1991 to dismantle all of these weapons, the successor states readily agreed to transfer theirs to Russia for eventual destruction. Of much greater concern to Washington was the status of the former Soviet Union's land-based strategic nuclear force and the massive reductions in those weapons that Gorbachev had agreed to before his fall. At their Moscow meeting in July 1991—which turned out to be the last Soviet-American summit—Bush and Gorbachev signed the Strategic Arms Reduction Treaty (START) that had been under negotiation since 1982. The START Treaty mandated deep cuts in ballistic missile warheads and the ICBMs that carried them, effectively reducing by about a third the two superpowers' land-based strategic nuclear forces. But with the collapse of the USSR, the twelve thousand Soviet nuclear warheads were inherited by the four republics—Russia, Ukraine, Belarus, and Kazakhstan—in which the ICBMs carrying them had been based.

Washington's anxieties about the unresolved status of these weapons were finally relieved in May 1992, when the four former Soviet republics that possessed them signed the Lisbon Protocol affirming their adherence to the START I Treaty.

Under intense U.S. pressure the three non-Russian republics (Ukraine, Belarus, and Kazakstan) that possessed almost a third of the former Soviet Union's strategic nuclear arsenal also agreed to sign the Non-Proliferation Treaty (NPT) as nonnuclear weapons states together with a protocol pledging to transfer all of their warheads to Russia within seven years. After all the other signatories had ratified the treaty and the protocol, Ukraine delayed ratification as a ploy to secure U.S. economic assistance to finance the costly process of dismantling its nuclear warheads and shipping them to Russia as well as security guarantees against a resurgent Russia. When a satisfactory agreement was concluded in January 1994, the Ukrainian parliament finally ratified the NPT by the end of the year as the START I Treaty entered into force.

In the meantime Yeltsin's newly independent Russian Federation, the sole heir to the Soviet Union's nuclear arsenal, avidly resumed the process of strategic arms negotiations with the United States that had been foreseen by the START I Treaty. The replacement of the Soviet Union with a Russian state that sought friendly relations with the United States and NATO radically reduced the threat of nuclear war and led many observers to conclude that the nuclear arms race had lost its rationale. At their first summit meeting in the summer of 1992, Bush and Yeltsin therefore jointly launched an initiative for a successor to the START Treaty that would mandate much deeper cuts in the two countries' strategic arsenals. Unlike START I, which had taken almost ten years to negotiate, the second Strategic Arms Reduction Treaty (START II) was signed by the two presidents in Moscow on January 3, 1993. It cut each signatory's strategic forces by a fourth over ten years (to 3,000–3,500 warheads for each side), which represented a return to the levels reached by the United States and the Soviet Union in the mid-1960s and mid-1970s, respectively. Most importantly, the treaty provided for the total elimination of a weapons system that had long eluded arms control negotiators: the famous multiwarhead (or MIRVed) land-based missiles. As we shall see, however, the path from signature and ratification of START II would be a long and tortuous one, in part because of increasing tensions between Moscow and Washington.

## The Ordeal of the Successor States

When Stalin drew the map of the Union of Soviet Socialist Republics in the 1920s, he followed the example of the European colonial powers in Africa by adopting the principle of "divide and rule": Instead of consolidating natural regions, he set boundaries that left large irredentist populations in each republic. This inhibited the emergence of a national identity that might threaten Moscow's hegemony. When the multiethnic successor states emerged from the wreckage of the former USSR, many were plagued by explosions of ethnic unrest and secessionist challenges. Such conflicts were particularly virulent in the Caucasus and Central Asia. The Caucasian republics of Georgia, Armenia, and Azerbaijan became embroiled in ethnic strife from the moment they achieved independence from Moscow. Georgia was beset by such seething secessionist agitation in the provinces of South Ossetia and Abkazia that its president, Gorbachev's former foreign minister Eduard Shevardnadze, had to request Russian military assistance in the fall of 1993 and to tolerate the deployment of twenty thousand Russian "peacekeeping" forces in his newly independent country. The secessionist fervor in the Armenian enclave of Nagorno-Karabakh within Azerbaijan, which had surfaced even before the disintegration of the Soviet Union, increased in intensity as the insurgents began to receive economic and military aid from the newly independent republic of Armenia.

The five predominantly Muslim republics of Central Asia—Kazakhstan, Kyrgyzstan (formerly Kirghizia), Tajikistan, Turkmenistan (formerly Turkmenia), and Uzbekistan—also faced the prospect of internal instability as the strong hand of Moscow was removed. The Soviet regime had energetically suppressed expressions of ethnic and linguistic affiliation between the inhabitants of the five Muslim republics and the neighboring states of Turkey and Iran. It also sought to curb the emergence of pan-Islamic sentiment connecting them with each other and with neighboring Islamic states. With the recession of Soviet power in the early 1990s, the resulting strategic vacuum in Central Asia unleashed all three of these forces. Regional powers sought to promote their interests in the region by exploiting ethnic, linguistic, or religious ties with the populations of the newly independent states. Iran touted its brand of Islamic government as a model that all of them might follow, while profiting from its ethnic and linguistic connections to Tajikistan (whose inhabitants are culturally Iranian and speak an eastern dialect of Persian). Turkey, which lost its significance to NATO as a front-line state on the Soviet Union's southwestern frontier and failed in its bid for prompt admission to the European Union, discovered a new arena for the expansion of its influence in Central Asia. The government in Ankara patronized the Turkic speaking populations of Kyrgyzstan, Turkmenistan, and Uzbekistan, prompting fears in Russia and elsewhere of a resurgence of the ideology of pan-Turkism that had once thrived in the region. The Turkish Republic also offered as a competitive alternative to the Iranian-Islamic model its own unique tradition as a secular state with a Muslim population. This attracted many of the former Communist leaders who remained in office in the new republics and worried about the threat posed by Islamic fundamentalism to their political power.

The Central Asian republic that suffered the greatest instability in the aftermath of the Soviet Union's collapse was Tajikistan. Of all the Muslim republics that had been created by the Soviet government in Central Asia, Tajikistan was the most artificial. The Persian-speaking Tajiks and the Turkic-speaking Uzbeks had been bitter rivals ever since the mid-1920s, when Stalin partitioned the territory that both groups had inhabited for centuries in such a way as to leave the Tajiks with the poorest and most mountainous portion. Soon after independence a bitter armed struggle developed between the old secular Communist ruling elite and a Muslim opposition movement that agitated for the creation of an Islamic state. The secularist government of neighboring Uzbekistan, fearing the spread of Islamic fundamentalism across its border, sought Russian assistance to crush the insurrection against its fellow secular regime in Tajikistan. Concerned about the effect of a fundamentalist Tajikistan on the twenty million Muslims citizens of the Russian Federation, Yeltsin ordered Russian infantry units that had remained in Tajikistan to cooperate with the Uzbek air force in suppressing the Islamic insurgency there. After defeating the opposition forces in the winter of 1992–1993, a Russian peacekeeping force remained in Tajikistan to bolster the secular government of what had become a Russian client state.

*The Central Asian Republics of the Former Soviet Union*

The governments of the other Muslim republics cooperated closely with Russia, regarding it as the ultimate source of protection against the threat of Islamic fundamentalism that had become more acute after the triumph of the Mujaheddin in Afganistan in 1992 (see page 363). The Central Asian republic that retained the closest ties to Russia was Kazakhstan. Subjected to intensive Russian settlement for over a century, its ethnic Russian community constituted 38 percent of the population, almost as large as the indigenous Kazakh population's 40 percent. The presence of the large Russian minority, coupled with the fact that it was the richest, largest, and most strategically located of the republics (between Russia and China), guaranteed that Moscow would pursue a special relationship with Kazakhstan. By the mid-1990s the principal external challenges to Russia's hegemony in Central Asia had fizzled. The specter of pan-Turkism dissipated once it became evident that Turkey lacked the economic resources and political influence required to translate its cultural and linguistic connections with Kyrgyzstan, Turkmenistan, and Uzbekistan into geopolitical advantage. Iran also failed to make significant inroads in the region, both with the bid to offer its Shiite version of Islamic government as a model for the predominantly Sunni populations of Central Asia and with the campaign to exploit its ethnic links with Tajikistan. As the presumptive heir of the Soviet legacy, Russia emerged victorious, at least for the foreseeable future, in the modern version of what the British poet Rudyard Kipling had called the "Great Game" for predominance in this remote part of the world.

In the meantime the stability of other Soviet successor states was challenged by the roughly twenty-one million Russians who had been left outside the borders of the Russian Federation after the breakup of the Union and looked to Moscow for protection and support. When the Moldavian Soviet Socialist Republic became the independent Republic of Moldova, some of its leaders openly discussed the possibility of uniting with Romania (with whom its majority population shared ethnic and historic ties). In response to this threat, the large Russian minority east of the Dniester River broke away from Moldova to form a separate republic with the tacit support of the renegade commander of the Russian fourteenth army that remained there. As in Georgia, the weak Moldovan government was obliged to accept a temporary Russian peacekeeping force to supervise a cease-fire between the two contending parties. The Russian majority in the Crimean Peninsula, which Khrushchev had transferred to Ukrainian sovereignty in the mid-1950s, agitated for independence while Moscow and Kiev squabbled over custody of the former Soviet Black Sea fleet based in the Crimean ports of Sevastopol and Odessa. (They finally agreed to a joint command over the fleet for five years, after which it was divided up between them). Twelve million Russians lived in the eastern Ukraine. Russians constituted 30 percent of Estonia's population and more than a third of Latvia's. As the governments of these new states began to display favoritism toward their ethnic majorities, public opinion within Russia naturally began to sympathize with the travails of the Russian minorities in the "near abroad"—an increasingly popular term for the collection of newly independent states that had once belonged to the old Soviet Empire.

The economic crisis that had set in at the beginning of the 1990s under Gorbachev worsened during the first several years of the Russian Federation's existence as an independent republic. Committed to liberal economic reform, Yeltsin followed the advice of economists from the West and officials of the International Monetary Fund by privatizing some state firms, closing others that were inefficient money-losers, and allowing the market to set wages and prices. This "economic shock therapy" caused acute social distress, as food and fuel prices soared, shortages of basic commodities developed, and unemployment spread. A new entrepreneurial class rose from the ranks of the defunct Communist Party, the KGB, and other agencies of the old regime to gain control of the newly privatized enterprises and their economic assets. This sudden acquisition of great wealth by the favored few engendered a culture of speculation and corruption that prompted widespread cynicism and dissatisfaction in the general population. Popular resentment at the the new elite's shameless looting of the country's valuable resources amid the deepening economic crisis spawned a vigorous political opposition to Yeltsin, who rapidly squandered the prestige he had earned during his dramatic showdown with the coup plotters in 1991. The anti-Yeltsin coalition was a motley crew, spanning the political spectrum from unreconstructed Communists yearning for the order and stability of the Soviet era to right-wing Russian nationalists intent on protecting the interests of their kinsmen in the "near abroad." When Yeltsin's former vice president joined forces with the parliamentary speaker in a plot to oust him, the president dissolved the parliament on September 21, 1993, and assumed emergency powers in order to salvage the democratic political reforms he had implemented. Two weeks later Yeltsin ordered the parliament building surrounded by tanks, which opened fire until all of the conspirators surrendered and were led off to prison. To the president's dismay, the legislative elections held the following December recorded a surprise swing to the extreme right-wing party of Vladimir Zhirinovsky, who had conducted a chauvinistic campaign calling for the restoration of the historic Russian Empire. Nostalgia for the glory days when the Soviet Union was one of the world's two superpowers and resentment at the territorial losses after the Union imploded fed the fires of Russian nationalism. The flames of those fires were kept burning by some emotionally charged controversies that emerged in the mid-1990s and remained red-hot issues into the next century.

The first was the on-again, off-again war between the Russian army and insurgent forces in Chechnya, one of the eighty-nine constituent republics and regions of the Russian Federation that had long resisted Moscow's authority. A predominantly Muslim, mountainous region that had been brought under Russian control in the 1870s, Chechnya declared its independence at the end of 1991 after the breakup of the Soviet Union. When Russian troops intervened to restore Moscow's authority in this rebellious region of the newly formed Russian Federation, the fierce Chechen resistance forced them to withdraw. But Yeltsin became increasingly concerned about the loss of the region's substantial oil reserves and about the dangerous precedent for the multiethnic Russian Federation's eighty-eight other constituent republics and regions. In late 1994, forty thousand Russian soldiers returned to Chechnya with orders to stamp out the insurgency. Fortified by volunteers and diplomatic support from neighboring Islamic countries, the Chechen guerrillas fought the Russian forces to a draw. By the autumn of 1996 Moscow was obliged to remove its troops a second time after the conclusion of an armistice agreement that deferred for five years the issue of independence for the rebellious province. But an outbreak of violence against Russians in Chechnya and bombings in several Russian cities in 1997–1998 enraged public opinion and led to demands for action. Then a band of Chechen Muslim fighters, some of whom were veterans of the successful anti-Soviet insurgency in Afghanistan, mounted an attack against Russian military units in the adjacent (and predominantly Muslim) Russian republic of Dagestan in the summer of 1999. In response to this latest outbreak of violence, a Russian force poured into Chechnya for the third time in the decade. Under the supervision of President Vladimir Putin, who replaced Yeltsin at the beginning of the twenty-first century, they expelled the rebel forces from the country's major cities and reasserted Russian control in the year 2000.

The resurgence of a potent brand of Russian patriotism in response to the threat of secession in Chechnya was fortified by increasing public resentment at the United States over two contentious issues. The first was the Clinton administration's sympathetic response to the applications of fifteen former Warsaw Pact states and Soviet republics for membership in the North Atlantic Treaty Organization as protection against a future security threat from Russia. Moscow vigorously opposed the expansion of the U.S.-dominated alliance up to its own borders as a provocative and unacceptable form of encirclement. To calm these Russian fears, NATO rebuffed the former Communist states' bids for immediate membership while Clinton unveiled an innocuous alternative in January 1994 called the Partnership for Peace, which proposed various types of military cooperation between NATO and former Communist or neutral countries on the continent. But after a relentless campaign waged by the leaders of Poland, Hungary, and the Czech Republic, U.S. Secretary of State Madeleine Albright announced in May 1997 that those three applicants would be admitted to the alliance. This unilateral American decision was ratified by the European allies at NATO's Madrid summit in July. In one of the notable reversals in modern diplomatic history, those three former stalwarts of the Warsaw Pact formally joined the U.S.-dominated alliance in March 1999 while the Russians fumed in impotent rage.

The second source of tension between Washington and Moscow during the second half of the 1990s was the renewal of American interest in proceeding with an updated version of the old Strategic Defense Initiative that had first been proposed by President Reagan in 1983. Charging that the construction of a national missile defense system in the United States would degrade the retaliatory capability of Russia's nuclear arsenal, Yeltsin and then his successor Vladimir Putin vigorously opposed the U.S. plan. After some unsuccessful tests of the anti-missile system the Clinton administration deferred a final decision on deployment, which would require the abrogation or modification of the Anti-Ballistic Missile Treaty signed by Nixon and Brezhnev in 1972. But the incoming administration of George W. Bush unequivocally endorsed the project and proceeded with plans to develop and deploy a workable national missile defense (NMD) system. In December 2001 the president formerly declared that the United States would abrogate the ABM Treaty and deploy an NMD system. Russian president Putin reluctantly accepted the decision as a fait accompli, apparently accepting U.S. assurances that the proposed missile defense system would be designed to protect against the small nuclear arsenals of "rogue states" (such as Iran, Iraq, or North Korea) rather than to neutralize the formidable strategic deterrent of Russia.

## The Fading Dream of Arms Control

Russian-American tensions over NMD at the beginning of the twenty-first century transpired amid a general decline in enthusiasm for arms control, which had played such an important role in bringing the Soviet-American conflict to an end. The initial expectation after the end of the Cold War was that the spectacular arms control achievements during Gorbachev's tenure would lead to further breakthroughs. The movement to limit nuclear testing received a shot in the arm in 1992, when the United States, Russia, and France (later joined by Great Britain) unilaterally suspended all nuclear tests and called for a comprehensive test ban treaty that would bring a permanent end to the practice. Of the five declared nuclear powers only China refused to participate in the voluntary moratorium, conducting a series of underground tests in 1993 and 1994 at its Lop Nor testing site in Xinjiang. Beijing claimed that the glaring inferiority of its strategic forces compared with those of the other nuclear powers required further testing to assure a satisfactory level of performance before agreeing to a moratorium.* Asserting the same justification, France also broke its self-imposed moratorium with six underground tests on the Mururoa atoll in the South Pacific in 1995–1996. In the meantime the ongoing disarmament conference in Geneva had issued a formal call in the summer of 1993 for negotiations to extend the old Limited Test Ban Treaty, which had prohibited nuclear tests in the atmosphere and in the sea, to cover underground blasts as well. But in November 1999 the United States Senate declined to ratify the Comprehensive Test Ban Treaty, citing old concerns about insufficient inspection procedures to monitor compliance and new scientific doubts about the reliability of computer simulation—the only known alternative to the actual testing of new weapon designs.

As the declared nuclear powers attempted (with varying degrees of success) to reduce their own nuclear stockpiles and limit nuclear testing during the 1990s, they also made a concerted effort to prevent the spread of these weapons of mass destruction to nonnuclear states. The Non-Proliferation Treaty (NPT) that entered into force in March 1970 prohibited the nonnuclear signatories from acquiring nuclear weapons and the nuclear signatories from assisting other states in joining the select nuclear club. While most countries had signed the NPT by the mid-1990s, some that had not (such as India, Pakistan, and Israel) were known either to have manufactured nuclear weapons or to have acquired the capability of doing so on short notice. Moreover, several signatories (including Iran, Iraq, Libya, and North Korea) were widely suspected of conducting clandestine nuclear programs in violation of the treaty. As we shall see, the efforts by the United States and other major powers, in partnership with United Nations agencies, to verify compliance by North Korea and Iraq with the NPT would prove frustrating and fruitless (see pages 380, 403).

In the meantime the international efforts on behalf of nonproliferation resumed and reached their apex in the mid-1990s. Ever since entering into force in 1970, the NPT had been extended for five-year periods after which a review conference met and renewed the treaty for another term. But at the fifth review conference in May 1995 in New York City, the 5 nuclear and 160 nonnuclear signatories voted to extend the treaty indefinitely. In the face of strenuous objections from nonsigners such as India, which argued that it was patently unfair for the five nuclear powers to retain their nuclear capability while others were prohibited from acquiring one, the extension of the treaty included a nonbinding provision encouraging nuclear disarmament

---

*China finally did adhere to the voluntary moratorium after conducting its final test in July 1996.

and the universal adoption of the Comprehensive Test Ban Treaty (CTBT). The failure of the five nuclear powers to move toward a radical reduction of their own nuclear weapons systems elicited allegations of hypocrisy from several nonnuclear
states. This made it easier for India and Pakistan to repudiate the nonproliferation
principle and conduct nuclear tests in the spring of 1998 (see page 388). The U.S.
Senate's refusal to ratify the CTBT in the autumn of 1999 added another weapon to
the arsenal of the NPT's critics, who argued that restrictions on nuclear power should
apply to all countries or be scrapped.

One of the major concerns about nuclear proliferation centered on the fate of the
huge stockpiles of nuclear waste materials located in the territory of the former
Soviet Union. Worried that criminal groups might obtain supplies of weapons-grade
uranium and plutonium and sell them to unfriendly states or terrorist organizations,
the Clinton administration initiated a program in 1994 whereby the United States
would purchase highly enriched uranium that was removed from dismantled nuclear
warheads and convert it to low-enriched uranium for use in nuclear power stations.
Since the safe disposal of weapons-grade plutonium posed a much greater challenge
for complicated technical reasons, efforts were undertaken to ensure the safe storage of Russian stockpiles of that material. The transfer to Russia of all weapons-
grade nuclear material from the three other nuclear-armed Soviet successor states,
Belarus, Kazakhstan, and Ukraine, was completed in late November 1996. But the
collapse of the Russian economy during the second half of the 1990s raised the possibility that some of its unemployed or underpaid nuclear scientists and engineers
would be tempted to sell their services to aspiring nuclear states such as Iran, Iraq, or
North Korea, which U.S. officials began to refer to as "rogue states." To discourage
such a dangerous brain drain, the United States allocated funds to Russian research
centers that hired former employees of the nuclear weapons industry.

In the meantime serious obstacles arose to block the prompt implementation of
START II, which had been signed by presidents Bush and Yeltsin in January 1993.
START II required the two countries to reduce their strategic warheads to below
thirty-five hundred by 2003 (later extended to 2007) and banned multiple warheads
on ICBMs. Although the U.S. Senate approved the treaty in January 1995, the
Russian Duma dragged its feet because of mounting resentment at the Clinton administration's plans for NATO enlargement and its willingness to consider an NMD
system. Russian second thoughts about START II also reflected dissatisfaction with
a perceived inequity in the treaty itself caused by its prohibition of all ICBMs with
MIRVs: This meant that Russia would have to destroy a large portion of its strategic nuclear force, which was dominated by land-based missiles with MIRVs. The
United States, which had more warheads on its submarine-based missiles, would
therefore enjoy a numerical advantage in warheads when START II entered into
force. Though Russia would have the right to bridge that gap by constructing five hundred new single-warhead missiles, many Russian legislators doubted that the deteriorating Russian economy could bear the costs of such a program.

While START II languished in Moscow, Clinton and Yeltsin looked farther into
the future at their Helsinki summit in March 1997: They agreed that when and if
START II entered into effect, the two states would promptly implement a successor
treaty (START III) that would reduce their strategic warheads to below twenty-five

hundred. But a succession of bitter political disputes with the United States intervened to sidetrack the START II ratification process in the Russian Duma as the twentieth century came to an end: The first was the Anglo-American bombing of Iraq in 1998 in response to Baghdad's refusal to permit UN inspections of its suspected nuclear weapons facilities; second was the announcement by U.S. Secretary of Defense William Cohen in January 1999 that the United States would seek amendments to the ABM Treaty of 1972 to permit the deployment of an NMD system; and finally the NATO bombing campaign against Serbia in 1999. These conflicts between Moscow and Washington were exacerbated by the freefall of the Russian economy that began in the summer of 1998, which led to a 30 percent devaluation of the ruble, a three-month default on Russia's domestic and foreign commercial debts, the bankruptcy of the country's major banks, and a 90 percent inflation rate. At the beginning of the twenty-first century, more than a decade after the end of the Cold War, the strategic arsenals of the United States and Russia were still legally limited only by the first START Treaty that had been proposed by President Ronald Reagan during his first term.

With the START II Treaty dead in the water, Russian President Vladimir Putin and U.S. President George W. Bush agreed to a simple, straightforward means of reducing the roughly 6,000 nuclear warheads that each of the former Cold War adversaries possessed. At a summit conference in the Kremlin in May 1992 (almost exactly thirty years after Richard Nixon and Leonid Brezhnev signed the original Strategic Arms Limitation Treaty), the two heads of state put their signatures on a pact that committed each signatory to reduce its deployed nuclear warheads to no more than 2,200 by the year 2012. But this seemingly spectacular reduction in strategic arms was full of qualifications and escape clauses: Each signatory was entitled to withdraw from the treaty with only a three-month notice; the weapons would not be destroyed but simply deactivated, which would enable each country to accumulate huge stockpiles of warheads that could promptly be reattached to missiles; and on the expiration of the treaty in 2012, both parties would be free to rearm unless the treaty were extended. These conditions had been inserted at the behest of the Bush administration, which was concerned about the future threat from hostile third parties armed with nuclear weapons and the ballistic missiles to deliver them to American territory. Critics of the new pact complained that it gave only the illusion of strategic arms reductions and, worst of all, left Russia with a stockpile of thousands of deactivated nuclear warheads that might fall into the hands of terrorist groups.

The campaign to limit the development, testing, and proliferation of nuclear weapons during the 1990s was complemented by contemporaneous efforts to impose restrictions on the two other weapons of mass destruction: chemical and biological weapons. Revulsion against the use of phosphene and mustard gas on the western front during World War I had resulted in the first chemical weapons arms control treaty, the Geneva Protocol of 1925, which prohibited the use (although not the possession) of all chemical weapons. During the Cold War many countries, including the two superpowers, accumulated vast stores of chemical weapons but did not employ them in combat. Negotiations to limit the production and stockpiling of chemical weapons that began in 1960 remained deadlocked until the end of the Cold War. Iraq's use of chemical weapons against Iran and its own Kurdish citizens during the

1980s, followed by its threat to use chemical weapons during the Gulf War of 1991, gave new impetus to the stalled talks. The Chemical Weapons Convention (CWC) was finally completed and opened for signature at the beginning of 1993 and entered into force in 1997. The CWC supplanted the old Geneva Protocol by prohibiting the production, stockpiling, and use of chemical weapons and required that all signatories destroy their chemical weapons stocks and production facilities within ten years of the convention's being implemented. It also provided for unrestricted, short-notice inspections to verify compliance with the convention, which began to be carried out toward the end of the century by monitoring teams of the Organization for the Prohibition of Chemical Weapons (OPCW).

Efforts to enforce the Biological Weapons Convention (BWC) of 1975, which prohibited the production and possession of germ warfare agents, proved ineffective because of the absence of reliable verification procedures. In the meantime several states, notably Iraq and North Korea, were widely suspected of acquiring the capability of producing such weapons. In 1994 the signatory powers established an ad hoc group in Geneva to negotiate and develop a set of legally binding and effective inspection procedures for the convention. After the group conducted several sessions in the closing years of the twentieth century, the new Bush administration in Washington threw a monkey wrench into the process: In July 2001 the United States withdrew from the negotiations for a BWC inspection regime, complaining that the proposed inspection procedures would not be thorough enough to detect illegal biological weapons production but would be intrusive enough to threaten the proprietary business information of American companies whose laboratories were under inspection.

All in all, it was evident by the beginning of the twenty-first century that arms control had had lost its salience as a means of enhancing international security, as reflected in the set of developments described in this chapter: the refusal of the U.S. Senate to ratify the Comprehensive Test Ban Treaty; the Russian Duma's refusal to ratify START II and then the highly qualified character of the strategic arms reductions codified in the 2002 Treaty of Moscow; the failure to devise effective means of monitoring the production of weapons of mass destruction in Iraq and North Korea; the expansion of the nuclear club to include India and Pakistan; the U.S. insistence on proceeding with the development of NMD; and the difficulties in developing iron-clad verification procedures for the Biological Weapons Convention, followed by the U.S. withdrawal from the negotiations for fear that the proposed inspections would represent a threat to trade secrets of American companies. Despite the end of the global conflict between the two superpowers and the dwindling threat of nuclear war, the advent of the new millennium seemed to herald a much more dangerous international environment than had existed during the good old days of the Cold War.

# ELEVEN

# EUROPEAN UNITY AND DISUNITY

As we have seen, the bold initiative during the second half of the 1950s toward European economic integration was dealt a severe setback when Great Britain refused to join the six continental European states (France, West Germany, and Benelux) that formed the European Economic Community (EEC) in 1958. Clinging to the twin illusions that its "special relationship" with the United States and its preferential trade ties with its former empire would enable it to prosper outside the emerging European entity, Britain joined Austria, Denmark, Norway, Portugal, Sweden, and Switzerland to form a loose-knit competitor to the EEC known as the European Free Trade Association (EFTA) in 1960 (see page 63). The emergence of the British-led EFTA greatly irritated the Kennedy administration in Washington, which had warmly endorsed the EEC's commitment to economic integration as a perfect complement to the new president's "Grand Design" for a tighter transatlantic partnership in the political, economic, and security fields. American opposition to EFTA reinforced other developments that prompted Harold Macmillan's government in London to reconsider its refusal to join the EEC. First, since Britain's trade with the EEC countries remained greater than with its EFTA partners, Britain would suffer severe economic consequences from the common external tariff that the Six were intent on erecting. Second, the major consideration that had kept Britain out of the negotiations that produced the Treaty of Rome—its unique cultural and economic ties to the anglophone world beyond Europe—had lost much of its significance by the early 1960s. The preferential trading arrangements with the Commonwealth were declining in importance as Canada, Australia, New Zealand, and other former colonies sought to diversify their foreign trade. The "special relationship" with the United States, which had begun to unravel with the showdown between London and Washington during the Suez fiasco in 1956, received the coup de grâce from the Kennedy administration when it embraced the EEC as the European pillar of its own "Grand Design."

Confronted with these new circumstances, the Macmillan government reversed its course and applied for admission to the EEC on August 10, 1961. Britain was soon followed by its EFTA partners Denmark and Norway as well as by Ireland. Throughout the year 1962 the British negotiator, Edward Heath, smoothed the path toward an agreement by gradually giving way on most of his original demands concerning such matters as protection for British agriculture and the retention of preferential ties to the Commonwealth. By the end of the year the prospects of expanding the EEC from six to ten seemed exceedingly bright.

## France's Campaign to Lead a "Europe of States"

But British hopes for entry into the Six were abruptly and unexpectedly dashed on January 14, 1963, when President Charles de Gaulle of France announced at a press conference that his government would veto Britain's application for admission to the Six. Although de Gaulle specifically cited Britain's insistence on privileged treatment for its farmers and the maintenance of its preferential trade ties with the Commonwealth as justification for his refusal, the real reasons were related to his own plans for the political future of Europe. De Gaulle envisioned France as the leader of the EEC, with West Germany serving as the junior partner in a projected Paris-Bonn Axis. He did not want London in the organization to challenge French predominance (see page 128). Moreover, he regarded Great Britain as a "Trojan horse" of the United States that would facilitate America's economic penetration of Europe to complement the military dominance it already exercised through NATO. When the new Labour government in London renewed the application for EEC membership in 1967, de Gaulle cast a second veto on November 27 for the same reasons he had done so four years earlier.

De Gaulle's vision of the EEC stood in marked contrast to that of the original proponents of European integration. A staunch opponent of federalism and a dogged defender of national sovereignty, he favored what he called a "Europe of States," by which he meant a loose-knit organization of six sovereign states marked by political cooperation at the intergovernmental level. In 1961–1962 he tried in vain to get the other five to accept a draft treaty drawn up on his instructions by the French diplomat Christian Fouchet. It envisioned a council of heads of government that would meet regularly and make the most crucial decisions, a permanent secretariat in Paris composed of foreign ministry officials from each member-state, and a European parliament whose members would be appointed by the national legislatures. The Fouchet Plan for an intergovernmental association of sovereign states foundered because, in the eyes of the five other members, it was incompatible with the federalist principles of the EEC. The French project would have created a set of parallel institutions in competition with the European Commission, the Community's administrative organ on which the ardent federalists pinned their greatest hopes.

The failure of the Fouchet Plan, together with de Gaulle's veto of Britain's application for membership, set the stage for a bitter confrontation in the EEC between the French president's intergovernmental philosophy and the federalist principle championed by the West German president of the European Commission, Walter Hallstein. In the mid-1960s the Commission sought to gain control of the revenue raised from customs duties imposed on imports from outside the Community in order to free itself from financial dependence on the contributions of the individual members' treasuries. Recognizing that this attempt to strengthen the supranational features of the EEC directly contradicted de Gaulle's plans for a "Europe of States," the shrewd Hallstein linked his bid to increase the powers of the Commission with another proposal before the EEC that France strongly supported: the extension of the 1962 agreement to establish a Common Agricultural Policy (CAP), which would benefit French farmers but was anathema to their West German counterparts, who feared the adverse effects of the CAP on their smaller and less efficient farms.

Unwilling to accept an expansion of the supranational powers of the European Commission as the price for its cherished CAP, France walked out of the EEC's Council of Ministers in June and continued to boycott it for the next seven months as the other five members struggled to resuscitate the European idea. In January 1966 the so-called crisis of the "empty chair" was resolved when the delegates of the six member-states hammered out a mutually acceptable settlement in Luxembourg. But the so-called "Luxembourg Compromise" was in fact a victory for France and de Gaulle's conception of Europe: The Council of Ministers would require unanimity before taking any action that affected the vital interests of any member state, and the Commission was obliged to consult and cooperate with the Council of Ministers on a regular basis. Hallstein's campaign to enhance the supranational character of the EEC had foundered on the shoals of national sovereignty championed by Charles de Gaulle.

## The Expansion and Deepening of the Community

The imperious French president's departure from office in 1969 removed the last obstacle to the expansion of the EEC. His successor Georges Pompidou lifted the French veto to Great Britain's membership shortly thereafter, enabling the leaders of Great Britain, Ireland, Norway, and Denmark to sign a Treaty of Accession in January 1972. After the Norwegian electorate narrowly voted against accession in a referendum, Great Britain, Ireland, and Denmark formally joined the EEC on January 1, 1973. Almost sixteen years after the signing of the Treaty of Rome, the Six had expanded to Nine.

The expansion of its membership did not lead to a deepening of the economic and political relations among the members of the European Community (as the EEC, ECSC, and EURATOM were collectively called after 1967). On the contrary, the EC remained little more than an intergovernmental association of sovereign states cooperating on economic matters, a far cry from the original vision of the idealistic federalists. But each year more and more impediments to the free circulation of goods, capital, and labor within the Community were eliminated, keeping alive the original vision of an economically integrated Europe. The Treaty of Rome had set a deadline of twelve years for the gradual elimination of all barriers to a common market. Although that deadline was not met, the EEC members did agree in 1968 to a common external tariff, a customs union for industrial goods, and a common agricultural policy. In 1975 the regular meetings of the nine heads of government (the Council of Ministers), which had functioned as the ad hoc decision-making group of the organization, was institutionalized as the European Council. Four years later a fully functioning European Parliament (EP), which had been envisaged by the Treaty of Rome but long remained a dead letter, was established in Strasbourg after the direct election of delegates by universal adult suffrage from the nine member-states. This embryonic legislative body of the Community lacked three crucial powers of a national legislature—the authority to introduce and enact legislation and to raise revenue directly through taxation. But the 518-member EP acquired the power to delay and even reject proposals submitted by the European Commission, the executive power of the Community headquartered in Brussels that enjoyed the sole prerogative of introducing legislation. The Parliament in Strasbourg also procured coequal authority with the European Council over the community's budget.

In the course of the 1980s, the nine-member EC was expanded to twelve with the admission of three Mediterranean states that had previously been excluded because of their underdeveloped economies and undemocratic political systems. Once representative government was restored to Greece in 1974 after seven years of military rule, that country was admitted as the EC's tenth member in 1981. The overthrow of the Caetano dictatorship in Portugal in 1974 and the advent of a constitutional monarchy in Spain following the death of its long-time dictator Francisco Franco in 1975 paved the way for the expansion of the EC to twelve with the admission of the two Iberian countries in 1986. As was the case with the first wave of expansion in 1973, however, the second wave was not accompanied by a deepening of integration among the member-states of the Community. On the contrary, since the mid-1970s terms like "Europessimism" or "Eurosclerosis" competed with the more optimistic slogans ritualistically reiterated by the proponents of federalism.

The European federalists had long recognized that the goal of full economic integration as a step toward political integration would remain a pipe dream until the members of the EC succeeded in developing an instrument for controlling the fluctuations in the value of their currencies against one another. At their summit conference in the Hague in 1969, the EC leaders formally endorsed the priority of managing intracommunity currency fluctuations in order to facilitate the ultimate objective of economic and monetary union (EMU). But the Nixon administration's abandonment of the gold standard, the collapse of the Bretton Woods system of fixed exchange rates, and the inflationary consequences of the global oil crisis during the first half of the 1970s generated such acute turbulence in the international monetary system that the movement toward EMU was derailed. Beginning in 1972 the currencies of the member-states of the EC were floating in value against the dollar as well as against the most stable currency among them, the German deutsch mark (DM). Eventually the EC nine devised a joint float against the dollar that was nicknamed "the snake": Each member-state pledged to keep its currency floating within a narrow range against the floating American currency. In the course of the 1970s several member-states had to move in and out of the "snake" to avoid the danger of seriously overvaluing their currencies, which would cause them to suffer balance of trade and balance of payments deficits. The "floating snake" slithered along until 1979, but its membership had dwindled to West Germany and the four countries (Belgium, the Netherlands, Luxembourg, and Denmark) that were able to keep the value of their currencies close enough to the DM.

When the international monetary disruptions began to moderate at the end of the turbulent decade of the 1970s, the EC leaders launched at their Brussels Summit of December 1978 a new initiative to stabilize Community exchange rates known as the European Monetary System (EMS). It established a so-called Exchange Rate Mechanism (ERM) founded on the European Currency Unit (ecu), a unit of account whose value was calculated on the basis of a basket of the participating national currencies and was intended to replace the "snake" as a more effective version of the joint float against the dollar. The member-states pledged to intervene in world money markets to maintain the value of their currencies within a narrow band relative to the ecu, creating a zone of exchange rate stability within the EC. The architects of the ERM hoped that this fictitious monetary unit would become the normal means of settling international accounts among the Community members, preparing them psychologically for the day when they would be willing and able to adopt the ultimate solution to the problem: a single currency for all member-states.

## The Relaunching of the European Idea

Although several EC members proved incapable of keeping their currencies within the prescribed range relative to the ecu, the EMS preserved a remarkable degree of exchange rate stability throughout the 1980s that fostered impressive economic growth within the Community. In the spring of 1989 the French president of the European Commission, Jacques Delors, endeavored to jump-start the stalled process of European integration with a three-stage proposal for the gradual achievement of total economic and monetary union the audacity of which was nothing short of breathtaking: The first stage envisioned the acceleration of economic and monetary coordination to bring all twelve EC currencies within the ERM. The second prescribed the establishment of a European Central Bank empowered to set a Community-wide monetary policy that would be implemented by the twelve national central banks. In the third stage the exchange rates would be irrevocably fixed, the national central banks would give way to the European Central Bank, and a single European currency would replace the national currencies of the member-states.

Delors's excessively optimistic set of deadlines for the establishment of fixed exchange rates, a European Central Bank, and a common currency was derailed in the early 1990s as speculators attacked the EC currencies, Great Britain and Italy withdrew from the ERM, and Ireland, Spain, and Portugal devalued their currencies. But the momentum toward complete economic integration was preserved by a process that had been revived by the passage of the Single European Act (SEA). Approved in December 1985 and formally signed by the EC leaders at their Luxembourg summit in February 1986, the SEA entered into force in July 1987. It stipulated the removal of all remaining barriers to trade among EC members (such as import quotas, passport controls, divergent levels of indirect taxation, and conflicting laws and regulations). The goal of these sweeping measures was the creation of a single market by midnight on December 31, 1992.

The adoption of the SEA was initially prompted by concerns in Europe about the damaging effects of economic competition with the gigantic multinational corporations based in the United States and Japan. A single unified market of 380 million consumers would enable European firms to meet these foreign threats by profiting from economies of scale to consolidate their operations and expand production. But another set of totally unexpected developments that burst onto the world scene in the late 1980s and early 1990s lent an air of urgency to the movement toward a single market and rekindled the old aspirations for a political union: The end of the Cold War, the liberation of Eastern Europe from Soviet control, and the reunification of

Germany in 1989–1990 yielded a new set of challenges and opportunities to the movement toward European integration. German reunification in October 1990 sparked fears, particularly in France, that this powerful, prosperous, newly enlarged state in the center of Europe would upset the balance of power on the continent by joining forces with the newly independent former Soviet satellites to the east. The best way to dissuade a united Germany from going off in adventuresome directions to the east and becoming too big and powerful for its neighbors in the west was to lock it into a set of regional linkages that would dilute the sentiment of German nationalism that all European countries feared. The renewed impetus toward integration in the early 1990s thus reflected the same concern that had originally inspired Jean Monnet and the other founding fathers of the movement four decades earlier: The "Europeanization" of Germany would prevent the "Germanization" of Europe.

With political union back on the agenda after so many false starts, the member-states recorded astonishing progress in ironing out difficulties that had stymied their negotiators for decades. In December 1991 a summit meeting of the European Council in the Dutch city of Maastricht approved a Treaty on European Union, which was signed by the foreign and economics ministers of the Twelve in February 1992. The common thread running through the Maastricht treaty was the strengthening of Community institutions at the expense of the member-states. It confirmed the deadline set by Delors in 1989 for the creation of a common currency by 1999; increased the powers of the European parliament; defined the principle of a "common European citizenship," which included the right to live, work, and even run for political office anywhere in the Community; and called for the development of a Common Foreign and Security Policy (CFSP) for the twelve member-states.

Before this bold new experiment could be implemented, the framers of the treaty had to test the extent of public support within the member-states through referenda or parliamentary ratification. What they discovered was widespread suspicion and resentment of the anonymous bureaucracy in Brussels, which reflected lingering anxieties about the prospect of losing national sovereignty. The optimism engendered by the stunning breakthrough at Maastricht turned to nervous apprehension when the treaty was narrowly rejected by Danish voters in June 1992 and then barely squeaked by in France, where right-wing opponents exploited public fears of immigrants armed with the proposed "common European citizenship" pouring into the country to take jobs from French workers. In the meantime opinion polls in Germany revealed widespread opposition to sacrificing the strong and stable deutsch mark to an untested European currency at a time when the country was enduring acute financial sacrifices to absorb the new citizens from the east.

The faltering movement eventually got back on track after various escape clauses were appended to the Maastricht treaty to make it more palatable. The Danes tendered their approval in a second referendum in May 1993, enabling the treaty to become operational the following November. In the meantime the single European market had gone into effect on schedule at the beginning of 1993, completing the drive toward economic unity begun by the ECSC four decades earlier. The Treaty of Rome had been so substantially amended by the Single European Act and the Maastricht treaty that a new name for the organization was in order: The European Community became the European Union (EU) in recognition of the remarkable

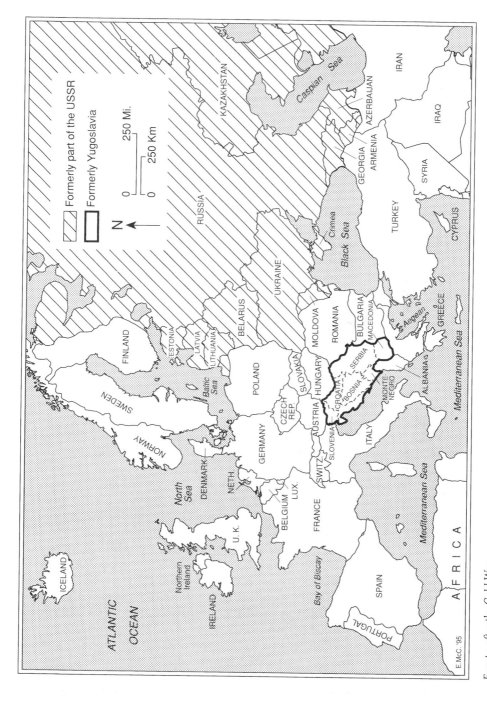

*Europe after the Cold War*

progress toward full economic and political integration that had been recorded since the beginning of the decade.

Amid this deepening of the integrationist links among the twelve members of the new European Union, the perennial issue of broadening its membership became a principal topic of discussion. The remaining members of the old European Free Trade Association (Austria, Finland, Norway, and Sweden), which London had masterminded in 1960 as a rival to the EEC, promptly applied for membership in the EU in 1993 to avoid missing the Maastricht Express. Negotiations with these four applicants were successfully completed in the course of 1994. All but Norway, whose voters rejected membership for a second time, joined the EU on January 1, 1995. The expansion of the EU from twelve to fifteen with the accession of Austria and the two Nordic neutrals transpired without major difficulty. The three new members easily met the principal criteria for admission that had been laid down at the Copenhagen summit of the European Council in 1993: geographical location, a democratic political system, and a market economy.

A much more daunting challenge was posed by the candidacies of the former Soviet satellites to the east. In the course of the 1990s these countries underwent a sweeping economic transformation from a command to a market-based system of production and distribution. The dismantling of the old statist system of government subsidies and price controls led to severe short-term hardships in the form of high unemployment and inflation. The erstwhile members of the Communist economic bloc, which had rapidly reoriented their foreign trade from the Soviet Union to Western Europe, understandably looked to the EU for economic assistance to mitigate the pains of readjustment to a capitalist system. No one could deny that these countries were historically and culturally part of Europe. They now asked to join their Western neighbors in the final stage of the long march toward economic and political unification that had begun just as they were emancipating themselves from Soviet domination. With the fall of the Iron Curtain it seemed entirely fitting that the two halves of Europe would reunite after four decades of separation. But as the applications for admission arrived at Brussels from the Eastern European capitals, some officials in the EU countries began to express misgivings about the prospect of expansion to the east. Opponents of eastward expansion in the EU voiced the fear that the underdeveloped economic systems of the former Soviet satellites would serve as a drag on the Union's budget, crowding out other programs in which several member-states were vitally interested because of the economic benefits they provided. One of these was the CAP, the complex set of price supports that subsidized farmers (especially in France) and ate up a large portion of the EU's annual budget. Another was the budgetary category known as "structural funds," outlays that were designed to reduce regional economic disparities within the Union by assisting the less developed agricultural countries (such as Greece and Portugal) as well as others with regions suffering from industrial decline (such as the United Kingdom). The impoverished new members from Eastern Europe posed a serious threat to the beneficiaries of this largesse.

Notwithstanding these concerns about the budgetary costs of eastward expansion, the EU was determined to encourage the democratization and economic liberalization of its newly emancipated neighbors to the east in order to promote peace and stability in the region. In December 1989 it took the initiative to create a European

Bank for Reconstruction and Development (EBRD) on the model of the World Bank, which provided loans to and encouraged capital investment in the Eastern European countries to facilitate their transition to market economies. In 1997 the European Commission's "Agenda 2000" specified the budgetary innovations that would be required before the EU could hope to absorb the Eastern European states without overwhelming its finances. These included a reform of the structural funds and a reduction in the outlays from the CAP. The following year negotiations began with six candidates that were expected to participate in the first wave of enlargement: five Eastern European states (the Czech Republic, Estonia, Hungary, Slovenia, and Poland) as well as the island of Cyprus (see later). A second group of applicants—Bulgaria, Latvia, Lithuania, Romania, and Slovakia—were led to believe that they would be next in line once they had met the specified criteria. But progress on re-forming the CAP was blocked by France, always deferential to its politically power-ful farmers, while the EU's poorer members resisted reductions in their coveted structural funds. The battle over the EU budget continued to complicate the Eastern European states' bid to join the European club as the twenty-first century began.

The candidacy for EC membership that provoked the most controversy was that of Turkey, which had originally applied in 1987. Three years later the European Com-mission declined to enter into accession talks with the government in Ankara, citing as impediments to admission Turkey's underdeveloped economy, the restrictions on civil liberties in its constitution, and its checkered record on human rights. Even if all of the accession criteria were met, it was evident that Greece would veto the applica-tion of its long-time adversary in light of acrimonious Greco-Turkish conflicts over Cyprus, territorial waters, Aegean airspace, and other matters. Turkey was deeply of-fended by the European Council's decision to omit it from the next round of enlarge-ment negotiations that opened in 1998 with the five Eastern European countries and Cyprus. The inclusion of Cyprus caused particular resentment in Ankara. The island had been partitioned into Turkish and Greek zones in 1974 and, since the Turkish part had not obtained international recognition, the accession talks were conducted only with the Greek representatives. Turkey's claim to be a part of Europe rested on history and geography. It had joined all the Western European intergovernmental or-ganizations, beginning with the Organization for European Economic Cooperation in 1948, the Council of Europe in 1949, and NATO in 1952. It had become an asso-ciate member of the EU and the Western European Union in 1963 and 1992, respec-tively. Some Turkish critics began to allege that the real reason for the country's exclusion had to do more with religion and culture than with politics and economics.

As the EU grappled with the issue of enlargement, progress toward full economic and monetary union proceeded without a hitch. At its December 1995 meeting in Madrid the European Council formally designated the projected new currency as the "euro," set a three-stage timetable for full monetary union, and reaffirmed the Maas-tricht criteria for participation in the single currency: These included a national bud-get deficit and public debt below 3 percent and 60 percent of gross domestic product, respectively; an inflation rate within 1.5 percent of the average in the three countries with the lowest rates; and a long-term interest rate within 2 percent of the average in the three countries with the lowest rates. The participating members would perma-nently fix their exchange rates on January 1, 1999, when the new European currency would begin to be employed in all bank and credit card transactions. Euro notes and coins were scheduled to enter into circulation on January 1, 2002, and to replace all national currencies the following July 1. The first stage in this gradual process arrived in the spring of 1998, with the certification of the member-states' compliance with the stringent Maastricht conditions. Although all fifteen countries had satisfied the budget deficit requirement, the European recession produced some bad news for the architects of "euroland": Interest rates in Greece remained too high, Germany and Ireland had failed to reach the inflation rate target, and only seven countries had met the public debt limit. Employing a loophole in the Maastricht treaty, eleven of the fifteen member states (excluding Great Britain, Denmark, Sweden, and Greece) opted for the euro.*

The second stage passed without incident on January 1, 1999, when the eleven participating countries fixed their exchange rates, the new European Central Bank began to assume control of a single monetary policy, and the new European currency began to be employed in bank and credit card transactions and to appear on restaurant menus and in shop windows alongside prices denominated in the national currencies. The new euro notes and coins entered into circulation on schedule on January 1, 2002, and a few months later the national currencies of the twelve participating countries ceased to be legal tender. But several obstacles to full economic integration for the European Union remained. First, the abstention of three states from participation in the common currency was an embarrassing reminder of the persistence of national sentiment. Second, the reluctance of workers in EU countries with high unemployment rates to relocate to those with better job opportunities because of linguistic and cultural preferences severely restricted the type of labor mobility that a fully integrated economic system ought to enjoy. Third, the failure to equalize tax rates and social welfare spending among the member-states imposed a competitive disadvantage on firms located in countries with high taxes and costly social welfare programs. Intensive efforts were underway to remove those remaining roadblocks to the achievement of the old dream that had begun fifty years earlier.

## The Elusive Quest for Security Cooperation

If control of the money supply is one of the principal hallmarks of national sovereignty, two equally important ones are the management of relations with foreign states and authority over the military forces that protect the security of the nation. While the national governments of the EU proved astonishingly nonchalant about sacrificing monetary sovereignty to the untested euro throughout the last decade of the twentieth century, the development of a common European foreign and security policy encountered much rougher sledding. The idea of a distinctively European foreign policy and a single military arm to back it up was as old as the idea of European economic unity itself. As we have seen, the French project in 1950 for a European

---

*Although Greece's economy had failed to qualify for admission to the "eurozone" on January 1, 1999, it was admitted on January 1, 2001. Great Britain, Sweden, and Denmark continued to opt out of the new monetary system.

Defense Community (EDC) envisioned a common European army with a European chain of command that would report to a European minister of defense (see page 47). But when the EDC went up in flames on the floor of the French National Assembly in 1954, the European federalist movement abandoned the security component of its campaign to concentrate exclusively on laying the groundwork for economic integration. The Treaty of Rome made no mention of the goal of coordinating foreign and defense policy because such an idea had come to be regarded as hopelessly utopian compared to the incremental and largely invisible sacrifice of sovereignty entailed in the move toward a common market. In any case the loss of control over the national army was patently unnecessary, since the North Atlantic Treaty Organization reinforced by the American nuclear guarantee provided all the security protection that the Europeans required.

In the mid-1980s the long-dormant cause of European security cooperation resurfaced in the form of a campaign to revitalize a largely forgotten institution known as the Western European Union (WEU). A revised version of the Brussels Treaty Organization of 1948, the WEU had been created in May 1955 after the failure of the EDC to facilitate the integration of West Germany into NATO (see page 58). But it promptly fell into complete disuse and played no role in the subsequent movement toward European integration. Then in 1984 French President François Mitterrand persuaded the other EC members that the WEU should be resurrected as a potentially useful security component to the emerging European economic and political entity. At its summit in the Hague in October 1987 the European Council endorsed the concept of the WEU as the "European pillar" of the Atlantic Alliance, recognized the role of the French and British nuclear forces in deterring aggression against the member-states of the EC, and called for closer military and diplomatic coordination to deal with "out of area" crises beyond Europe. In its first modest foray into actual military operations, the WEU coordinated mine-sweeping operations by its members in the Persian Gulf during the Iran-Iraq War of the 1980s.

The reemergence of the WEU and the resulting discussions of European defense cooperation during the second half of the 1980s remained a largely academic enterprise until the end of the Cold War gave the matter a new sense of urgency. The disintegration of the Warsaw Pact and the disappearance of the Soviet threat raised the possibility that the "decoupling" of American military power from the continent, which European Cassandras had been nervously predicting for decades, might finally become a reality. As domestic political groups in the United States clamored for economic rewards represented by the "peace dividend," the signs of American military retrenchment began to appear: The Bush administration announced in 1991 its intention to remove all U.S. short-range nuclear weapons from Europe and President Clinton decided in 1993 to cut U.S. ground forces in Europe to one hundred thousand by the end of 1996. As the EU marched triumphantly toward full monetary and economic union and made impressive strides toward political cooperation in the course of the last decade of the twentieth century, the long-deferred, unresolved question of how to endow the emerging European entity with a security dimension could no longer be ignored.

Another powerful impetus to greater European coordination of foreign and defense policies was the disappointing performance of the EU during the Persian Gulf

War of 1991. Although the European countries were much more dependent on the oil resources of the Gulf than was the United States, Europe's reaction to the unfolding crisis was hesitant and ineffective. The president of the WEU Assembly promptly condemned the Iraqi invasion of Kuwait, but it took almost three weeks for representatives of the organization's member-states to convene for a discussion of the crisis. By that time the United States had assumed the diplomatic initiative to organize and manage the multinational coalition that waged the successful six-week air campaign and four-day ground war to evict the Iraqi army from Kuwait (see page 402). Although WEU members Great Britain, France, and Italy contributed substantial military forces to the coalition's war effort, Germany was prevented by its constitution from sending troops abroad while Belgium, Spain, and Portugal managed only token participation in mine-sweeping operations and the naval blockade of Iraq. The forty-five ships that the WEU dispatched to the Gulf were scarcely more than a symbolic bid to show the flag in an American-dominated operation. The embarrassing lesson of the Gulf War for Europe was that it possessed neither the institutional machinery nor the military power to manage a unified and effective response to a direct threat to its vital interests. As the Belgian foreign minister lamented, Operation Desert Storm against Iraq revealed that the European Community was "an economic giant, a political dwarf, and a military worm."

In recognition of this glaring deficiency, the Maastricht treaty of February 1992 mandated the development of a Common Foreign and Security Policy (CFSP) and formally recognized the WEU as the prospective military wing of the emerging European Union. Three months later, France and newly united Germany took the initiative to create what French President François Mitterrand and German Chancellor Helmut Kohl hoped would become the nucleus of a future WEU defense force. Those two former adversaries created a European Army Corps (Eurocorps) to replace a small, experimental Franco-German brigade that had been formed two years earlier. The fifty-thousand-person Eurocorps established headquarters in Strasbourg in November 1993 and became fully operational by November 1995 as contingents from Belgium, Spain, and Luxembourg joined the original Franco-German core.

The embryonic security component of the EU faced its first test in the early 1990s with the breakup of Yugoslavia and the advent of bloody Balkan civil wars in Croatia and Bosnia (see page 349). Although the EU took an early and active role in sponsoring peace negotiations between the contending parties in both conflicts, it was the United States that eventually took the lead in initiating and orchestrating the NATO air strikes against Serb positions that paved the way for the American-brokered peace settlement for Bosnia in 1995 (see page 353). European diplomatic interventions in the Balkan conflict were conducted by individual countries (primarily Germany, Great Britain, and France) in pursuit of their particular national interests outside the EU structure. Once again, the prospects for developing a common foreign policy and an autonomous military instrument for the European Union seemed as remote as ever.

These first tentative steps toward greater defense cooperation in the 1990s were complicated by two thorny issues. The first had to do with the relationship between a future European defense force and the U.S.-dominated North Atlantic Treaty Organization. Washington initially endorsed the EU's new Common Foreign and Security Policy in 1991 as a welcome sign of the European allies' willingness to strengthen the "European pillar" of the Atlantic alliance. The WEU returned the compliment at the beginning of 1993 by transferring its headquarters from London to Brussels to facilitate liaison between the old Atlantic and the new European security organizations. But American satisfaction with Europe's apparent willingness to shoulder a greater share of the defense burden was tempered by mounting concerns that a separate European security architecture under the WEU would overlap with and possibly detract from NATO, producing a wasteful duplication of effort and generating transatlantic tensions. The second difficulty was in sorting out the relationship between the WEU and the EU, two parallel organizations with different memberships.* France backed by Germany proposed in 1997 the gradual merger of the two organizations so that the WEU would eventually become the military arm of the EU. But London opposed what it saw as a renewal of the old Gaullist ploy to build up a European defense capability at the expense of NATO and the United States. The four EU neutral states (Austria, Finland, Ireland, and Sweden) which were unprepared to join any military alliance conspired with Great Britain to block the proposal. These developments left the relationship between the EU and its prospective armed force undefined and uncertain.

Then the recently elected British prime minister, Tony Blair, executed a sharp reversal of his government's traditionally cautious policy toward European defense cooperation. Chafing at the marginalization of Europe in the Bosnian conflict and in the preparations for possible intervention in the Kosovo crisis, he declared that the EU would have to develop a future military capability without relying on the United States so that it could respond to international crises that affected its (as opposed to Washington's) vital interests. These words were music to the ears of French President Jacques Chirac, who met with Blair in Saint Malo on December 4, 1998. The two leaders issued a joint communiqué endorsing a European Security and Defense Policy (ESDP) and proposing the creation of an autonomous EU armed force capable of mounting military operations abroad. A few months later the deficiencies in existing European defense capabilities were graphically revealed during the NATO air war against Serbia in the spring of 1999, when inadequate military transport, surveillance, intelligence collection, and radio communication on the part of the European NATO members' forces elicited reactions of contempt and resentment within the U.S. command. The embarrassing European performance during the Kosovo campaign gave added momentum to the movement launched at Saint Malo. Shortly after NATO celebrated its fiftieth anniversary in April 1999 as its bombs fell on Serbia, the WEU revived and approved the French plan for a gradual merger with the EU. At its Helsinki Conference in December 1999 the European Union unveiled an ambitious plan to field by 2003 an autonomous rapid reaction force of more than fifty thousand troops capable of intervening in world trouble spots.

Fifty years after the proposal for a multinational European military force was first broached by the French at the middle of the twentieth century, the concept finally

---

*While assuming the role of observers in the WEU, Austria, Finland, Ireland, and Sweden retained their traditional status of neutrality in declining to become full members of the military organization.

seemed to have a decent chance of becoming a reality in the first decade of the twenty-first century. The big unanswered question concerning the emerging ESDP remained the following: Would EU taxpayers be willing to accept the substantial increase in defense spending—in peacetime, with no foreign threat in sight—that would be required to field the projected rapid reaction force and to finance the research, development, and procurement costs associated with the conversion of Cold War–era national fighting forces into a post–Cold War supranational military entity? Transnational mergers of European aerospace firms at the turn of the century seemed to herald a genuine determination to pool national resources in order to compete effectively with the gigantic U.S. defense contractors Boeing and Lockheed Martin in the scramble to sell weapons and equipment to the projected European military force. In March 2000 an EU interim military staff began consulting with NATO, the WEU, and national delegations, which some observers took to mean the advent of an effort to create an autonomous command staff separate from the Atlantic Alliance. But at the Nice summit in December 2000, Great Britain resisted France's campaign to weaken the links between the embryonic ESDP and NATO. It was agreed that the EU would not develop a defense planning capability of its own, but would continue to rely on NATO as the keystone of European defense. After the September 11, 2001, attacks on the U.S., Washington (with the support of London) pressed for the transformation of NATO into a global alliance against terrorism and "rogue states" intent on developing weapons of mass destruction. But to support its military interventions in Afghanistan in 2001–2002, the Bush administration preferred to bypass the alliance entirely and form a "coalition of the willing" including individual European states such as Great Britain and France (see page 365).

## The Resurgence of Ethnic Conflict

The multitude of advantages that the people of Eastern Europe gained from the disintegration of the Communist bloc were accompanied by one notable disadvantage that some came to regard as a curse: This was the reappearance of ancient ethnic antagonisms that had been submerged or suppressed during the four decades of Soviet domination. As the coercive power of the ruling Communist parties was lifted from the former satellites at the end of the 1980s, nationalist aspirations and resentments promptly filled the vacuum left by the disappearance of the socializing force of Marxist-Leninist ideology. We have already seen how the Soviet Union dissolved into its constituent ethnic components as the cause of national self-determination spread like wildfire from the Baltic to Central Asia, inspiring nationality groups to rediscover their distinctiveness. The revolutionary idea that a group of people sharing a common language and national identity deserves to have a sovereign state of its own had found fertile ground in that bubbling cauldron of ethnicity between Germany and Russia a century earlier. Many historians hold that potent sentiment responsible for the outbreak of the two world wars of the twentieth century. Ethnic nationalism returned with a vengeance at the end of the Cold War to threaten the stability of the newly emancipated states of Eastern Europe. Most states managed to preserve their national unity by retaining the acquiescence if not the loyalty of the restive ethnic minorities in their midst, but two that had been established at the end of World War I were broken apart. The first, Czechoslovakia, experienced a relatively painless division negotiated amicably at the bargaining table. The second, Yugoslavia, disintegrated into its constituent ethnic components amid an explosion of savagery and strife not seen in Europe since 1945.

The founders of the state of Czechoslovakia labored to fashion a unified national identity from the country's two largest ethnic groups, the Czechs in the west and the Slovaks in the east. At the end of the Cold War that experiment ended in failure. Despite the similarity of the two languages, despite the two peoples' recent history of shared oppression at the hands of the Russians, it had become apparent that the Czechs and Slovaks could no longer coexist comfortably within the same state. Age-old Slovak grievances about Czech domination of the political and economic life of the country, aggravated by the painful short-term effects of the transition from Communism to market capitalism, prompted the Slovak leadership to demand the partition of the unitary Czechoslovak state. The Czech-dominated government in Prague responded by conducting a set of cordial conversations with Slovak representatives that resulted in what came to be known as "the velvet divorce." The formal division of the country into the Czech and Slovak Republics on January 1, 1993, left two sets of problems that took longer to sort out: The first was an equitable division of the former Czechoslovakia's military and economic assets by the two successor states. The second was the presence of a discontented Hungarian minority in Slovakia and a smaller German-speaking minority in the Sudeten region of the Czech Republic. But these challenges were nothing compared to the trauma that had already begun to afflict the multinational, multireligious, multilingual country on the northern portion of the Balkan peninsula.

Yugoslavia achieved its national independence at the end of World War I after the disintegration of the two imperial powers that had vied for predominance in the Balkans, the Austro-Hungarian and Turkish empires. Originally known as the Kingdom of the Serbs, Croats, and Slovenes, its name was changed to Yugoslavia (the land of the Southern Slavs) in 1929 to acknowledge the existence of the country's other national minorities, notably the Bosnians, Albanians, Montenegrins, and Macedonians. The politically dominant Serbs, who had enjoyed national independence since 1878 and took the lead in liberating the southern Slav nationality groups from foreign rule, tended to regard the new state as a "Greater Serbia." The Catholic Croats and Slovenes and the Muslim inhabitants of Bosnia-Herzegovina thought otherwise, and resisted domination by the Orthodox Christian Serbs. The failure to develop a civic culture and a shared sense of patriotic loyalty to the Yugoslav state set the stage for a wave of internecine ethnic conflict during World War II, when the German army defeated the Yugoslav army and occupied a large part of the country. Many of the Croats, who resented Serbian domination of the prewar political system, welcomed the Germans as liberators and collaborated with them in a bloody campaign against the resistance movement that had emerged in opposition to the German occupation. The leader of that partisan movement, a Croat Communist militant named Josip Broz Tito, drew support from all ethnic groups and in late 1944 succeeded in expelling the Germans from the country. By the end of the war Tito had become the undisputed leader of a liberated Yugoslavia.

As we have seen, Tito's most memorable foreign policy accomplishment in the years after World War II was the transformation of Yugoslavia from a Soviet satellite into an independent Communist state that refused to take sides in the Cold War (see page 8). His greatest domestic political achievement, which passed largely unnoticed by foreign observers at the time, was to remove the nationality question as a threat to the unity of the country. The recipe for this remarkable feat was the combination of a rigidly centralized Communist bureaucracy superimposed on a federation of six Republics (Bosnia-Herzegovina, Croatia, Macedonia, Montenegro, Serbia, and Slovenia) and two autonomous provinces within Serbia (Vojvodina and Kosovo). In a shrewd bid to co-opt mounting demands for a devolution of political authority, Tito drafted a new constitution in 1974 that transferred substantial power from the federal government to the six constituent republics and Serbia's two autonomous provinces. By the time of his death in May 1980, the central government of the Yugoslav federation controlled foreign affairs and the national armed forces but little else.

The disappearance of the unifying symbol of Yugoslav identity opened a Pandora's box from which sprang the poisonous forces of ethnic nationalism that had been relatively quiescent during the thirty-five years of Tito's one-man rule. In 1987 a forty-six-year-old former banker named Slobodan Milosevic assumed control of the Serbian republic and promptly tried to reverse these centrifugal trends by strengthening the central power of the Serb-dominated federal institutions. He also waged a relentless campaign to promote Serbian nationalism, which threatened the integrity of several of the republics because of the presence of large Serb minorities in their midst. The paradoxical result of the new Serbian strongman's attempts to restore the central authority of the Yugoslav federal institutions was political fragmentation and civil war, as the other republics sought to emancipate themselves from the authority of Belgrade.

Slovenia and Croatia, the two most economically advanced members of the Yugoslav federation, had long complained of being economically exploited to the profit of the poorer federal units. Accordingly, they were the first to secede from the Yugoslav federation on June 25, 1991. Members of the Serb minority in both countries had already risen in revolt and proclaimed their intention to promote Serbia's annexation of the territory they inhabited. The Serb-controlled federal Yugoslav army openly lent its support to the well-armed militias that had been formed by the Serb minority in Slovenia and Croatia. When a UN-sponsored and monitored cease-fire finally brought an end to the fighting in February 1992, half a million people had been driven from their homes by the armed conflict in both republics. By that time Yugoslavia had in effect ceased to exist: All of the republics save Serbia and Montenegro had either declared their independence or were preparing to do so, although the Serbia-Montenegro remnant continued to retain the antiquated title "Federal Republic of Yugoslavia." By accepting the cease-fire with Croatia in early 1992, Milosevic had condemned the Croatian Serbs to the tenuous status of a despised minority in a state run by their traditional adversaries. But when the government of the newly independent republic of Bosnia-Herzegovina (hereafter Bosnia for short) sought to consolidate control over its polyglot population, the Serbian response would be much more defiant.

Bosnia comprises a hodge-podge of three principal ethnic and religious minorities that had coexisted in relative harmony for centuries. The largest among them, with 44 percent of the population, were those who had been converted to Islam. Together with their coreligionists in Albania, Montenegro, and Serbia's automomous province of Kosovo, these Muslim's constituted the most durable legacy of the long imperial

N

| 0 | 100 Miles |
| 0 | 100 km |

Former Yugoslavia
New National Boundary
Autonomous Region within Serbia

SLOVAKIA
UKRAINE
MOLDOVA
AUSTRIA
HUNGARY
SLOVENIA
Zagreb
CROATIA
ROMANIA
VOJVODINA
Novi Sad
Belgrade
BOSNIA-HERZEGOVINA
Sarajevo
S E R B I A
ADRIATIC
SEA
MONTE-NEGRO
Pristina
KOSOVO
Dubrovnik
Titograd
BULGARIA
BLACK SEA
Skopje
MACEDONIA
ITALY
ALBANIA
TURKEY
GREECE
AEGEAN SEA
E. McC. '95

*The Balkan Peninsula after the Breakup of Yugoslavia*

presence of the Ottoman Turks on the Balkan peninsula. The Bosnian Serbs, practitioners of the Orthodox Christian faith with close kinship ties to the inhabitants of Serbia proper, accounted for almost a third of the republic's population. Roman Catholic Croats who identified with the newly independent republic of Croatia represented 17 percent. As the predominantly Muslim government in the Bosnian capital of Sarajevo prepared to follow Slovenia and Croatia out of the crumbling Yugoslav federation in the summer and autumn of 1991, the Bosnian Serbs began to arm themselves with weapons obtained from the federal Yugoslav army. In the meantime their leader, a psychiatrist-turned-politician named Radovan Karadzic, conferred with Serbian president Milosevic in Belgrade to coordinate plans for joint military action against the emerging Bosnian political entity.

After the Bosnian Serbs established an autonomous enclave in the western part of the country in January 1992, Bosnian President Alija Izetbegovic formally announced the independence of his country the following March. Although the federal Yugoslav army evacuated the country as a result of international pressure two months later, it left behind most of its Bosnian Serb officers to bolster their kinsmen's escalating campaign against the Sarajevo regime. With the covert support of the Serbian government in Belgrade, the Bosnian Serb irregulars and former Yugoslav army troops launched a major offensive against non-Serb populations in the spring of 1992. By the end of the year the Bosnian Serbs controlled 70 percent of the newly independent country's territory.

The ensuing civil war in Bosnia would become the worst explosion of violence in Europe since the end of World War II. Muslim, Croat, and especially Serb irregulars violated most of the accepted rules of war: Bosnian Serb units launched mortar attacks on the besieged city of Sarajevo that caused widespread death and injury to the civilian population. Serb soldiers herded thousands of Muslim women into "rape camps," where they were sexually violated with impunity. Observers coined the term "ethnic cleansing" for the campaign by the Bosnian Serbs to confiscate the property and possessions of non-Serbs and force them into exile. All sides set up detention camps for prisoners-of-war where torture was regularly practiced and substandard conditions prevailed.

The initial response of the international community to the bloodshed in the former Yugoslavia was half-hearted and ineffective. The European Community, which was struggling with the challenge to develop a common foreign policy and defense identity, initially saw this conflict in its own backyard as an opportunity for a decisive assertion of its emerging political role. But the energetic attempts by its representatives to arrange for cease-fires in the summer and fall of 1991 failed in rapid succession. An EC-sponsored Yugoslav Peace Conference at The Hague in the autumn of 1991 collapsed without result. The Slovenian and Croatian declarations of independence and requests for European recognition in the summer shattered the unity of the EC and made a mockery of the mounting hopes for a common European foreign policy. The German Christian Democratic government of Helmut Kohl eagerly recognized the two Catholic secessionist republics, while France pursued its traditional pro-Serbian policy and initially supported the doomed cause of Yugoslav unity. When France and Germany proposed the dispatch of peacekeeping forces to the former Yugoslavia under the aegis of the Western European Union, the plan crashed on the shoals of British government opposition.

With the inability of the EU to devise a common policy toward the Balkan crisis, the United Nations stepped into the breach. The Security Council had imposed an arms embargo on all of the Yugoslav successor states on September 25, 1991, in an attempt to limit the violence. In the spring of 1992, two months after the advent of full-scale hostilities, the Security Council approved trade sanctions against Serbia and ordered a UN Protective Force (UNPROFOR) to the war-torn country to shield foreign humanitarian aid missions and guard designated "protected areas" in Croatia and Bosnia. In the meantime the already chaotic situation in Bosnia had degenerated into a three-cornered struggle when the government of Croatia, which had initially backed the Bosnian government against the Serb insurgency, decided to pursue its own ambitions by seizing Croat-inhabited sections of Bosnia that amounted to about 20 percent of the country's territory. Mediators Cyrus Vance (representing the UN) and Lord David Owen (representing the EC) finally came up with a peace plan that would have effectively partitioned Bosnia into a Swiss-type confederation of ten eth-nically based cantons. It was accepted by the Bosnian Croats and, after considerable hesitation, by the Bosnian Muslims, but was rejected by the Bosnian Serbs in early 1993 because it would have deprived them of the 70 percent of Bosnian territory they had won on the battlefield. Even the generous proposal unveiled in July 1994 by the so-called Contact Group (the United States, Russia, Great Britain, France, and Germany), which awarded the Bosnian Serbs roughly half of Bosnian territory, was turned down for the same reason.

The Bush administration in Washington had refused to be drawn into the Balkan imbroglio, preferring to rely on the European Community to take remedial action. But after the failure of the EC mediation efforts, the Clinton administration that took office in January 1993 decided to employ the military assets of NATO to protect the embattled Bosnian government (which had lost control of 90 percent of its territory to the Bosnian Serbs and Bosnian Croats). Resisting British and French pressure to commit American ground troops to the UN peacekeeping force in Bosnia (of which British and French contingents accounted for about a third of the total), Clinton chose to rely on the less risky alternative of air power. In February 1994 U.S. airplanes began to attack Serbian aircraft that were violating the "no fly zone" over Muslim areas that the UN protection force had earlier designated. The threat of NATO air strikes against Bosnian Serb military units besieging Sarajevo brought an end to the mortar strikes against that city's civilian population. Washington also employed co-ercive diplomacy to improve the military position of the besieged Bosnian Muslims. In March 1994 diplomatic pressure from Washington induced Croat President Franjo Tudjman to suspend his annexationist ambitions in western Bosnia and join a Muslim-Croat federation against Serbia. But U.S. Secretary of State Warren Christo-pher's earnest efforts to secure European participation in the U.S. air campaign against Bosnian Serb positions failed because of British and French fears that their own troops on the ground in UNPROFOR would be jeopardized.

The arms embargo that the UN Security Council had imposed an all former Yugoslav republics in September 1991 proved a godsend to the Bosnian Serbs, who received clandestine deliveries of weapons from the Yugoslav army and later from Russia while the Bosnian Muslims had to scramble for what they could get on the international arms market and later from sympathetic Islamic states such as Iran, Pakistan, and Sudan. Critical comment had been raised in the U.S. Congress and elsewhere about the unfairness of the general embargo to the struggling Muslim gov-ernment. When the Bosnian Serbs rejected a third partition plan that had been crafted by UN and EC mediators and secured the endorsement of the United States and Russia, President Clinton finally suspended U.S. participation in the embargo en-forcement task force in the Adriatic in November 1994. By the end of the year, the United States had dispatched a military mission and CIA operatives to train Bosnian government troops. Washington's open support for the Muslims generated acute tensions with Paris and London, which continued to oppose resolute military action against the Bosnian Serbs.

When the Bosnian Serbs accompanied their offensive in the spring and summer of 1995 with artillery barrages against Muslim cities that had been designated as "safe havens" by the UN, NATO mounted a retaliatory bombing campaign at the end of

August against Bosnian Serb positions. By that time the British and French had been persuaded to participate in the NATO air strikes because of the utter ineffectiveness of the UN protection force, 370 of whose members had briefly been taken hostage by the Bosnian Serbs and used as human shields for military sites targeted by the allied bombers. As a newly cohesive NATO increased its pressure on the Bosnian Serbs, the Croatian government finally redeemed the alliance it had concluded with Bosnia in the spring of 1994. In May 1995 Croatian troops advanced into the eastern portion of their own country that had been occupied by Croatian Serbs since the brief Serb-Croat war in 1991. By the end of the summer Croatian forces had reconquered most of the national territory, killing thousands of Serbs and expelling some 150,000 to Bosnian Serb territory or Serbia itself.

As the Bosnian Serbs reeled from the Croat-Muslim offensive and the NATO bombing, their fate was finally sealed by a horrendous incident that occurred on August 28, 1995: Bosnian Serb forces surrounding Sarajevo fired off a 120-mm mortar into the city's market place, killing thirty-seven civilians and wounding more than eighty. Amid the international outrage that this dastardly deed provoked, NATO aircraft began an intense bombardment of Bosnian Serb military positions such as army barracks, artillery sites, communications facilities, and ammunition dumps. This escalation of the NATO air war finally forced the Serbian government to the conference table.

The peace talks that terminated the war in Bosnia were conducted at a U.S. military base near the city of Dayton, Ohio, in November 1995. The three crucial participants—Bosnian President Izetbegovic, Serbian President Milosevic, and Croatian President Tudjman—met face-to-face to hammer out an agreement that would terminate the three-and-a-half-year conflict that had cost at least 215,000 lives, created almost 2.5 million refugees, and destroyed half of the schools, two-thirds of the houses, and most of the transportation and communication facilities of Bosnia. The Dayton Peace Accords preserved the sovereignty and territorial integrity of the devastated country while partitioning it into a Bosnian-Croat Federation and a Bosnian Serb Republic. A central government was to exercise sovereignty over the two ethnic-based entities, which would enjoy a considerable degree of autonomy. A NATO-controlled multinational peace implementation force (IFOR) of sixty thousand troops replaced the departing units of UNPROFOR with a one-year mandate to enforce the agreement and provide stability and security in the country. A year later IFOR was replaced by a NATO-led Stabilization Force (SFOR), whose membership was scaled back to thirty-five thousand. Although the Dayton Accords guaranteed the right of refugees to return to their homes, less than a fifth availed themselves of the opportunity and those that did tended to settle in areas where their kinsmen predominated.

In the meantime the United States had begun to provide arms and training to the Bosnian-Croat Federation Army to enable it to survive a future conflict with the Bosnian Serbs and their Serbian allies. The original objective was to create a rough balance of power in the region that would permit SFOR to withdraw by the June 1998 deadline that President Clinton had set. But the breakdown in cooperation among the two ethnic-based enclaves in Bosnia obliged Washington to retain its troops in the NATO stabilization force indefinitely. Although the foreign policy advisers of U.S. presidential candidate George W. Bush occasionally made noises during his successful electoral campaign of 2000 about bringing the men and women home from the Balkans, once in office the new American chief executive prudently preserved his predecessor's commitment to participate in the peacekeeping operation. Meanwhile, an international campaign was underway to bring the perpetrators of the gross human rights violations in Bosnia to justice. In response to early reports of deportation of civilians, torture, gang rapes, and other atrocities during the Bosnian civil war, the UN Security Council adopted a resolution on February 22, 1993, to create an International Criminal Tribunal for the Former Yugoslavia to consider allegations against individuals. After a slow start the tribunal that was set up in The Hague handed down its first prison sentence in November 1996, and many more followed in subsequent years. But the high officials who were indicted, such as Bosnian Serb leader Radovan Karadzic and his military chief, Ratko Mladic, went underground and evaded arrest. In the meantime the world's attention had already shifted from Bosnia as it labored to recover from its recent trauma to Serbia's southernmost province of Kosovo, where the curse of ethnic warfare returned to haunt the Balkan peninsula.

The Kingdom of Serbia had seized Kosovo from the decaying Ottoman Empire during the First Balkan War that erupted in 1912. As a result of the northward migration of Serbs from the province at the end of the nineteenth century and subsequent Albanian migrations into it in the intervening years, Kosovo had acquired an Albanian majority by the time the Turks withdrew. But the European powers rebuffed attempts by the newly independent state of Albania to absorb the province, preferring to support its transfer to Serbian control. Throughout the interwar period the Yugoslav government sought to eradicate Albanian culture in Kosovo by prohibiting the use of the Albanian language in schools and newspapers while encouraging ethnic Serbs to colonize the province in a campaign to reverse the demographic imbalance. During World War II the Albanians exploited Yugoslavia's defeat by Germany to take revenge on their ethnic adversaries, murdering or evicting Serbs from the homes. After the war Tito's policy of decentralization elevated Kosovo to the status of an autonomous region. In 1968 the Yugoslav Communist leader granted a number of sweeping concessions to the Kosovars, including greater use of the Albanian language and increased power for the autonomous region. After Tito's death in 1980 Serb nationalists began to complain about the continuing exodus of ethnic Serbs from the province and their maltreatment at the hands of the Albanian majority, which by then constituted 90 percent of Kosovo's population.

On his accession to power in Belgrade in 1987, Slobodan Milosevic quickly tapped into his countrymen's lingering resentments against the Kosovar Albanians as part of his nationalist campaign on behalf of a Greater Serbia. In the early 1990s he abolished the province's autonomy, replaced Kosovar Albanian officials with Serbs, terminated Albanian-language instruction at all levels of education, and even ordered Albanian town and street names changed to Serbo-Croatian. By the middle of the decade Serb settlers were being lured into Kosovo with promises of free land that had been confiscated from Albanians. Angered at the absence of any reference to Kosovo in the Dayton Accords, an increasing number of Kosovar Albanians began to support a militant group called the Kosovo Liberation Army (KLA), which burst on the scene at the end of 1997 with a series of terrorist assaults on Serbian security forces in the province. Throughout 1998 the KLA mounted a full-scale insurrection against the government in Belgrade with weapons procured from neighboring Albania, winning the support of many Kosovar Albanians who had been converted to the cause of secession. Milosevic responded by beefing up the Serb military presence in Kosovo, where ferocious assaults on Albanian villages killed innocent civilians and caused a flow of homeless refugees to improvised camps in rural areas. As the bloody scenario of Croatia and Bosnia seemed about to repeat itself, the United Nations Security Council issued sharp protests to the Belgrade government and demanded an end to hostilities. But when it became evident that historically Serbophile Russia would veto the use of force that might undermine the sovereignty its fellow Slavic state in the Balkans, the Clinton administration mounted a diplomatic offensive of its own to resolve the Kosovo conflict. In October U.S. envoy Richard Holbrooke negotiated an agreement with Milosevic that provided for the removal of Serb forces by a stipulated deadline as well as eventual autonomy and free elections for the province.

When the deadline expired, Serb military strength in Kosovo greatly exceeded the restrictions of the Holbrooke-Milosevic pact and continued to grow. The regular army was bolstered by Serb paramilitary units that terrorized Albanian villages and towns in a deliberate effort to frighten as many Kosovar Albanians as possible into leaving the country. Amid this deteriorating situation Great Britain and France cosponsored peace negotiations between Albanian and Yugoslav authorities under the auspices of the so-called Contact Group (which also included the United States, Germany, and Russia) in Rambouillet, France, in early February 1999. With Washington pressuring the Albanians to settle for something less than total independence and Russia leaning on the Yugoslavs to meet them halfway, an agreement emerged: Milosevic accepted the Albanian demand for a referendum in Kosovo after three years of autonomy to determine the province's political future, a concession that presumably reflected confidence in his ability to manipulate the voting procedures to ensure a favorable outcome. But he predictably rejected the military protocol attached by the West to the political arrangement, which provided for the deployment of thirty thousand NATO troops in Kosovo to monitor compliance with the agreement. When Russia backed Yugoslavia in this dispute, Milosevic exploited this split within the Contact Group and refused to sign the Rambouillet agreement that the Albanians had accepted. During this impasse in the negotiations Serbian tanks and artillery resumed their assault against the Albanians, driving thousands from their villages and burning the houses they abandoned. This latest instance of ethnic cleansing in the Balkans was apparently intended to empty the northern part of Kosovo of Albanians and partition the province along ethnic lines.

Recognizing the failure of the Contact Group and the UN Security Council to reach consensus on how to deal with the deteriorating situation in Kosovo—both because of Russian opposition—the United States and Great Britain decided to resort to military force with the only available instrument: the North Atlantic Treaty Organization. On March 24, 1999, NATO launched an intensive air campaign against Yugoslav military units in Serbia and Kosovo, command and control centers, supply routes, oil refineries, and other strategic targets. Instead of suspending their attacks on Albanian civilians to concentrate on defending against the aerial bombardment, Serb regular forces and paramilitary militias in Kosovo escalated their brutal campaign against the Kosovars. They eventually drove more than a million ethnic Albanians out of the province, most of them fleeing to nearby Albania. The destructive air war came to an end on June 10, when the battered Yugoslav government agreed to remove all military forces and equipment as well as civilian personnel from Kosovo and to permit the deployment of a NATO ground force to provide security for the province and supervise the return of the Albanian refugees.

The seventy-nine-day air campaign in Yugoslavia during the spring of 1999 was the first war in history in which one of the belligerents—NATO—emerged without a single casualty. The alliance had ruled out a ground offensive from the very beginning and ordered the bombing to be conducted at such high altitudes that only one plane (whose crew parachuted to safety) was brought down by Yugoslav antiaircraft fire. After the twenty-two-thousand-person NATO peacekeeping force (KFOR) began to take up its positions in Kosovo on June 12, 1999, almost three-quarters of the one million Albanian refugees returned to their villages while ethnic Serbs fled north to escape retribution. Vengeful attacks by Albanians on the dwindling Serb minority tested the peacekeeping skills of KFOR and of the province's new civil administration. A UN Interim Administration in Kosovo (UNMIK) set up shop in Kosovo to provide a modicum of political administration, supervise the disarmament of the paramilitary forces on both sides, and promote reconciliation between ethnic Albanians and Serbs. The European Union accepted primary responsibility for providing financial aid for the reconstruction of the devastated province, while hundreds of NGOs arrived to pursue humanitarian projects of relief and rehabilitation. In the meantime a fundamental political transformation unfolded in Serbia (or Yugoslavia, as it was still formally known): A year after his military defeat in Kosovo, Milosevic staged presidential elections in the autumn of 2000 to demonstrate his legitimacy and public support. When opposition candidate Vojislav Kostunica appeared to win the most votes, Milosevic sought to declare the results null and void. But massive public protests in Belgrade prompted the two pillars of the regime—the military and the police—to withdraw their support for the embattled head of state. After negotiating his departure from office, Milosovec went underground until he was arrested by Yugoslav police in June 2001 and transferred to the International Criminal Tribunal for the Former Yugoslavia in The Hague, where his trial as a war criminal began in February 2002. The advent of democratic rule in Serbia portended the end of a decade-long nightmare of brutality and conflict on the Balkan peninsula.

Developments in two other war-torn territories in the region also seemed to portend a new era of peace and stability. In March 2001 a new government in Kosovo headed by the moderate Ibrahim Rugova took power in an area that, although legally a part of Serbia, enjoyed *de facto* independence under the supervision of a European representative of the UN Secretary-General. In Bosnia the complicated arrangements of the 1995 Dayton Accords, which had partitioned the war-torn country along ethnic lives, resulted in a relatively stable political situation in which Muslims, Croats, and Serbs coexisted without violence. The EU agreed to replace the small UN International Police Task Force (IPTF) that worked alongside the much larger NATO Stabilization Force (SFOR) to preserve order in the country. This expanding European security involvement, together with the presence of European administrators representing the UN in Bosnia and Kosovo, signified that the Europeans were finally shouldering the responsibility of promoting peace and stability in their Balkan backyard.

# TWELVE

# ECONOMIC DEVELOPMENT AND STRATEGIC EVOLUTION IN ASIA

## Afghanistan under Siege

As the United States saw its longtime ally in Iran transformed throughout 1979 into a center of anti-American agitation, it was confronted with another crisis in the adjacent country of Afghanistan at the end of that turbulent year. Like its neighbor Iran, Afghanistan had been the site of intense competition between the Russian and British empires before World War I. With Great Britain and the new Bolshevik government both weakened by the war, these two historic rivals ended their "Great Game" for control of the forbidding mountainous terrain between Russia and India. In 1919 London renounced all claims to Afghanistan, recognized its full independence, and terminated the annual subsidy that it had long provided to the government in Kabul. In 1921 the Afghan ruler, Amir Amanullah, signed a treaty of friendship with the Soviet Union to provide insurance against a revival of British imperial ambitions in his kingdom and to secure Russian funds to replace the British subsidy. After a period of acute political instability Amanullah's teenage son, Mohammed Zahir Shah, was elevated to the throne in 1933. For the next forty years this Afghan monarch labored to preserve the independence and neutrality of his isolated mountain kingdom.

With the British withdrawal from India in 1947, Soviet Russia remained the only foreign threat to Afghanistan's independence. In an effort to balance his longstanding connections with his powerful neighbor to the north, King Zahir sought closer economic and military ties with the distant and disinterested United States. But Afghanistan's bid for Washington's support against possible Soviet pressure clashed with a competing American policy objective in South Asia: The new state of Pakistan that had been carved out of British India inherited territory inhabited by the Pashtun ethnic group that predominated in Afghanistan. King Zahir's regime refused to recognize the border between the two countries and cast the only vote against Pakistan's admission to the United Nations. Once the Eisenhower administration had decided to include Pakistan in the anti-Soviet alliance systems SEATO and the Baghdad Pact in the mid-1950s, it rebuffed the overtures from Kabul. Washington's cold shoulder

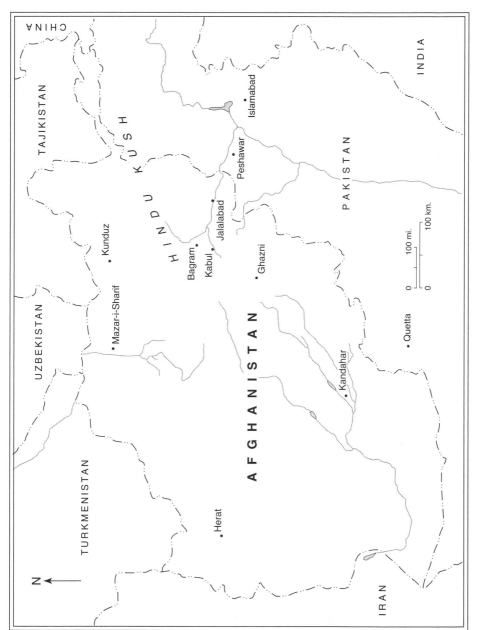

*Afghanistan*

forced Afghanistan by default to solicit further economic and military assistance from Moscow. In contrast to its neighbor Iran, which had severed all of its old links to the Soviet Union and became a staunch American ally in the Cold War, Afghanistan gravitated closer and closer to the Soviet orbit. In time it became what some Western observers began to describe as the Finland of Asia: a non-Communist neighbor of the Soviet Union that remained ostensibly neutral in the Cold War but prudently refrained from taking foreign policy positions that were unacceptable to Moscow.

The political stability of Afghanistan was shaken in the summer of 1973 when Prince Mohammad Daoud Khan, a cousin of the king and former prime minister, ousted the aged monarch with the support of the officer corps of the army. Daoud brought into his government a pro-Moscow faction of the indigenous Communist Party known as Parcham ("The Banner"), which was headed by a long-time party operative named Babrak Karmal. The more militant wing of the Afghan Communist movement, called Khalq ("The Masses") and led by Nur Mohammad Taraki and his disciple Hafizullah Amin, refused to support the new ruling elite and began to recruit allies in the armed forces. Then in the mid-1970s Daoud executed a dramatic shift in Afghan foreign policy in an attempt to compensate for his country's growing dependence on Moscow. He sought closer relations with China and the neighboring Islamic countries of Iran and Pakistan, all three of which were on exceedingly unfriendly terms with the Soviet Union. When this new orientation sparked opposition within the Afghan Communist movement in April 1978, Daoud arrested several Parcham and Khalq leaders (including Karmal, Taraki, and Amin). Communist sympathizers in the army thereupon overthrew and killed Daoud on April 27, released the imprisoned Communist leaders, and installed them in power. But the new ruling clique was torn apart by a bitter feud between the Parcham and Khalq, which the latter faction finally won. Although Amin was ostensibly Taraki's deputy, he became the de facto head of the new government in Kabul. Karmal and the Parcham were temporarily relegated to the sidelines.

The Taraki-Amin regime proceeded to institute a radical program of social, economic, and political reform that was designed to modernize the semifeudal structures of the country and centralize political power in the capital. These measures antagonized the provincial tribes that had long resisted domination from Kabul and provoked widespread unrest in rural areas. In the meantime the government's campaign of secularization and the expansion of educational opportunities for women sparked violent protests from the Muslim clergy and its fundamentalist followers. The overthrow of Daoud had been engineered by leftist officers with no connection to the Soviet Union. Indeed, the coup in Kabul had taken the Kremlin completely by surprise. But once the new "Communist" government began to encounter resistance to its reforms from Muslim and tribal militants, Taraki and Amin appealed to Moscow for military advisers to cope with the spreading insurgency and political advisers to assist with the implementation of the planned reforms.

When the Soviet officials arrived in Kabul, they promptly hatched a plot to unseat Amin and then work with Taraki to moderate the regime's unpopular reform program and to bring Karmal's pro-Soviet Parcham faction into his government. Amin preempted such a move by having Taraki arrested and then executed on October 8.

Although he continued to receive Soviet aid and advice, Amin revived Daoud's opportunistic overtures to the Islamic Republic of Pakistan in an apparent attempt to reduce his government's dependence on Moscow. By that time the Kremlin had become thoroughly disenchanted with Amin for two principal reasons. First, his campaign of secularization had instigated a wave of Islamic fervor that could spread across Afghanistan's fifteen-hundred-mile border with the USSR and undermine Moscow's authority in its predominantly Muslim Central Asian Republics. Second, the Afghan leader's cultivation of Pakistan, a staunch ally of the United States and close friend of China, fed Soviet fears that Amin might eventually turn on his Soviet benefactors and shift his allegiance to Moscow's two principal adversaries.

To remove these various threats, the USSR launched its first overt military operation outside its Eastern European satellite empire since the end of World War II. On December 27, 1979, Soviet airborne troops landed in Kabul, seized government buildings and communications facilities, and toppled Amin (who was killed in the fighting). The next day Soviet agents installed a new government led by the Parcham leader Babrak Karmal, as four Soviet motorized divisions poured across the frontier to occupy the major cities and airfields. Within a month seven divisions comprising some eighty-five thousand military personnel had taken up positions in the mountainous country. In the meantime a loose coalition of Islamic fundamentalists and tribal militants organized an insurrection against Karmal's regime and the Soviet forces that had created it and kept it in power. In the next several months, the Afghan army of ninety thousand lost almost a third of its membership to desertion or defection to the rebels. This required the deployment of additional Soviet troops into the country until they numbered almost one hundred thousand by the spring of 1980.

The U.S. government responded with indignation to the Soviet occupation of Afghanistan. President Carter immediately informed Brezhnev that the continued presence of Soviet forces in the country would fatally damage what remained of the spirit of détente. The Kremlin ignored these warnings, apparently assuming that the United States would acquiesce in the operation (as in Hungary in 1956 and Czechoslovakia in 1968) because Washington had no vital interests in a distant country that had already become a Soviet client state long before the invasion. In fact, the Soviet occupation of Afghanistan at the end of the 1970s drove the final nail into the coffin of the Soviet-American rapprochement established in the early years of that decade. When it became clear that the Russians were there to stay, the United States joined Egypt, Pakistan and China (with Saudi Arabia contributing financial support) in supplying covert military assistance to the Islamic resistance to the Soviet occupation. Carter imposed a number of sanctions on the Soviet Union, including an embargo on grain exports in excess of the minimum quantities specified in the 1975 agreement, restrictions on access to American fishing waters and high-technology exports, and a U.S. boycott of the Moscow Olympic Games in July 1980. He also increased the 1981 defense budget and asked the Senate to delay consideration of the SALT II Treaty that languished unratified in the upper house of the U.S. Congress.

Jimmy Carter interpreted the Soviet invasion of Afghanistan not within the context of the political, social, and religious complexities sketched out here, but rather from the broad geopolitical perspective emphasized by his National Security Adviser Zbigniew Brzezinski: The American president regarded the military operation as the last straw in a succession of aggressive acts through which the Soviet Union sought to exploit the "era of good feeling" between the two superpowers for its own selfish interests. The earlier operations had been executed by Moscow's reliable "surrogates": the Cubans in Angola and Ethiopia, the Vietnamese in Cambodia. Carter and Brzezinski viewed the overt use of Soviet military power in Afghanistan as a bid to profit from America's humiliating expulsion from Iran by driving toward the oil resources of the Persian Gulf and the Arabian peninsula as well as the warm waters of the Indian Ocean.

To cope with this perceived threat of Soviet expansion in South Asia, the American president unveiled in his January 1980 State of the Union Address what came to be known as the "Carter Doctrine": The United States considered the Persian Gulf so vital to its security that it would henceforth deny a foreign power control of the region "by any means necessary, including military force." To furnish this bold declaration with the requisite credibility, Carter ordered the creation of a rapid deployment force for use in the Persian Gulf–Red Sea area. Washington also sought new base facilities for American air and naval forces to compensate for the loss of the Shah of Iran's services as the policeman of the region. In June 1980 Oman and Kenya granted the United States access to naval and air facilities at Masirah Island and the port of Mombasa, respectively. In August Somalia agreed to receive American warships at its ports that had formerly been used by the Soviet fleet. The American naval base on the British-owned island of Diego Garcia in the Indian Ocean was upgraded to accommodate an expanded American naval presence to offset increased Soviet naval power in the region. Carter's determination to strengthen the American position in South Asia to contain the Soviet Union there forced him to compromise his commitment to human rights: In appreciation for Pakistan's valuable contribution to the Afghan resistance movement, Washington was obliged to tone down its customary criticism of the Pakistani dictator, General Zia ul-Haq. By the time he left the White House in 1981, Jimmy Carter had been converted from an earnest champion of human rights and détente to a staunch opponent of what he regarded as the new threat of Soviet expansionism across the globe.

In the meantime the one hundred thousand Soviet troops in Afghanistan became bogged down in a hopeless military stalemate with the Muslim Mujaheddin, who continued to receive U.S. and Chinese weapons via Pakistan. In March 1986 the Reagan administration intensified Washington's military engagement in the country by supplying the Afghan resistance with America's most advanced hand-held anti-aircraft missile, the Stinger, which enabled the Afghan insurgents to shoot down many Soviet and Afghan government aircraft and helicopters. With escalating Soviet casualties and reports of returning servicemen addicted to drugs, many observers began to refer to the Soviet Union's ordeal in Afghanistan as its "Vietnam." During his first year in power, Mikhail Gorbachev began to develop an exit strategy as part of his campaign to reduce tensions with the United States. Gorbachev privately informed Reagan of his intention to withdraw from Afghanistan during their first meeting at the Geneva summit in November 1985. In September 1987 Foreign Minister Shevardnadze confirmed to Secretary of State George Shultz that the decision had been made to leave by the end of the Reagan administration at the latest. He requested Washington's help in facilitating an orderly withdrawal and in preventing a

*Jubilant Afghan guerrillas on a captured Soviet armored personnel carrier during the Soviet military occupation of Afghanistan from 1979 to 1989. The Afghan guerrillas received substantial military assistance from the United States, Pakistan, and Saudi Arabia. (Hulton Archive by Getty Images)*

radical fundamentalist Islamic regime from seizing power in Kabul. In the meantime the Kremlin had been issuing blunt warnings to Afghan President Babrak Karmal and then his successor, Ahmedzai Najibullah, that the Afghan Communist leadership had better broaden its base of support in preparation for the day when it would have to defend itself against the Mujaheddin. In February 1988 the Kremlin publicly announced the plan to withdraw from Afghanistan within a year, and in February 1989 the last Soviet soldier left the country.

The abandoned Najibullah clung to power for another three years by exploiting the internecine rivalries among the insurgent Islamic factions. When the Mujaheddin finally occupied Kabul on April 25, 1992, and attempted to establish an Islamic state, the victorious coalition rapidly disintegrated along ethnic lines. Among other linguistic and tribal conflicts, the Pashto-speaking Pashtuns clashed with the Persian-speaking Tajiks, the Turkic-speaking Uzbeks, and a Persian-speaking Shiite group known as the Hazaras that received backing from Iran. The result of this ethnic strife was widespread death and destruction in Kabul and its environs for the next several years, as regional military commanders competed for territory and loot. Then in the middle of the 1990s a band of young Sunni Pashtuns called the Taliban began to win widespread public support in the southern part of the country by combating corruption, challenging the authority of the local warlords, and imposing a semblance of social order in the territories they occupied. The government of neighboring Pakistan, sensing the opportunity to extend its influence deep into Afghanistan, threw its support to the Taliban as it mounted a military offensive against the other armed groups vying for power. In September 1996 the Taliban entered Kabul and took control of the central government apparatus. The armed forces of the Tajik, Uzbek, and Hazara ethnic minorities, which comprised less than a third of the country's population, fell back to a mountain stronghold in the northwest corner of Afghanistan. Occupying less than 10% of the country, they formed what would later be called the Northern Alliance and conducted a rear-guard struggle against the new Pashtun-dominated Taliban. Their only foreign support came from Iran and Russia. Iran's assistance for the anti-Taliban coalition was a continuation of Teheran's long-standing patronage of the Shiite Hazara group of central Afghanistan. Russia provided the northerners with arms and ammunition at the insistent urging of the three predominantly Muslim but secular former Soviet republics of Central Asia bordering on Afghanistan—Turkmenistan, Uzbekistan, and Tajikistan—that faced insurgencies by their own Islamic fundamentalist groups that received support from the Taliban.

In the meantime the new rulers in Kabul had begun to subject the Afghan population under their control to strict codes of dress and behavior, based on their fundamentalist interpretation of the Koran. This included the eradication of all "decadent" cultural norms imported from the West, such as the right of women to receive an education, work outside the home, or appear in public without the traditional head-to-toe garment with narrow slits for the eyes. The Afghan government also banned Western music, television, films, and the Internet. The powerful Interservices Intelligence (ISI) agency of Pakistan continued to provide the Taliban with weapons, ammunition, and logistical support for their ongoing war with the Northern Alliance. The other principal foreign supporter of the Islamic resistance to the Soviet occupation in the 1980s—the United States—was originally favorably disposed toward the Taliban for reasons directly related to the politics of energy. After the breakup of the Soviet Union it was discovered that the Soviet successor states along the Caspian Sea possessed enormous reserves of fossil fuels. The U.S. oil company Unocal developed a plan to construct a pipeline to transport natural gas from the landlocked country of Turkmenistan through Afghanistan to ports in Pakistan for export. The Clinton administration enthusiastically supported the pipeline project through Afghanistan because it would circumvent Iran, with which the U.S. continued to remain on bad terms. From the perspective of this project to use Afghanistan as a conduit for the exploition of the Caspian natural gas reserves, the Taliban regime impressed Washington officials with its success in restoring political stability and social order to the war-torn country. But despite strenuous efforts by Pakistan to persuade the U.S. to accord diplomatic recognition and give its full support to the Taliban so that Unocal could complete its negotiations over the gas pipeline, Washington began to cool on the new rulers of Afghanistan in 1997 for two reasons. First, the Clinton administration had come under strong pressure from American feminists to repudiate the Taliban for their abominable treatment of Afghan women. Second, American officials became increasingly resentful at the Taliban's hospitality to the Saudi fugitive millionaire Osama bin Laden.

This tall, wealthy, charismatic young Muslim militant from a prominent Saudi family had operated in Pakistan during the 1980s, delivering donations of money and equipment from wealthy Saudi sympathizers to the Afghan mujaheddin to support their insurgency against the Soviet occupation. After the departure of the Soviet forces in 1989, bin Ladin set up an organization known as al-Qaeda ("Military Base") to unite the thousands of Arab volunteers who remained in Afghanistan after their successful *jihad* against the Russians. A year after bin Laden returned to his homeland to work in his family's business, King Fahd invited the United States to use Saudi Arabia as a staging ground for the planned military offensive against Iraq after Saddam Hussein's invasion of Kuwait in 1990. The arrival in his country of 540,000 "infidel" troops, followed by the Saudi government's decision to permit 20,000 of them to remain in Saudi bases to protect the desert kingdom after the Iraqi army was evicted from Kuwait, converted the enraged bin Laden into a fanatical enemy of the United States and the Saudi regime that allowed it to despoil the sacred land that contained the Muslim holy places of Mecca and Medina. After several years of self-imposed exile as a guest of the radical Islamic regime in Sudan (during which he began to transform al-Qaeda into a global network of Islamic militants), bin Laden returned to Afghanistan in 1996. A year later he forged a strong alliance with the Taliban's leader Mullah Mohammed Omar. Al-Qaeda set up training camps in the mountains of Afghanistan for young volunteers who had arrived from Arab countries to fight alongside the Taliban against the Northern Alliance. But the "Arab-Afghans" trained in these camps and assigned to clandestine cells throughout the world were also hard at work planning terrorist attacks against the interests of the United States in retaliation against its military presence in Saudi Arabia and its unswerving support for Israel. In 1998 al-Qaeda masterminded the bombing of the American embassies in Nairobi, Kenya and Dar-es-Salaam, Tanzania that killed two hundred twenty people and in 2000 organized a daring attack against the U.S.S. *Cole* at the port of Aden in Yemen that left seventeen American sailors dead. Apart from launching seventy cruise missile against some of bin Laden's training camps in Afghanistan as punishment for the African embassy bombings, the Clinton administration refrained from resorting to military action against al-Qaeda and its Taliban hosts.

This indulgent U.S. policy underwent a radical transformation after the hijacked airplane attacks on the World Trade Center in New York and the Pentagon in Washington on September 11, 2001, which killed more than 3,000 people and sent a shock wave of insecurity across the American homeland. When U.S. intelligence confirmed that the nineteen hijackers who had carried out this murderous assault on the two preeminent symbols of U.S. economic and military power belonged to the al-Qaeda network, President George W. Bush demanded that the Taliban regime surrender bin Laden and his associates to the United States for punishment. When the Afghan regime refused to comply, the president ordered the preparation of a military campaign to overthrow Mullah Omar's government and capture or kill the top al-Qaeda officials it sheltered. The United Nations Security Council promptly approved a resolution authorizing the retaliatory use of force. The European members of NATO invoked article five of the North Atlantic Treaty defining the attack against the United States as an attack on all signatories. But the Bush administration, while grateful for these expressions of support from the international community and its European allies, insisted on managing the military campaign unilaterally rather than submit to the cumbersome decision-making procedures of coalition warfare.* Since Afghanistan is a landlocked, remote country far from the centers of U.S. military power, Washington sought and obtained base facilities and overflight rights from neighboring states such as Uzbekistan and Tajikistan. It also induced President Musharraf of Pakistan, whose cooperation was essential to a successful military operation in Afghanistan, to repudiate the pro-Taliban faction in his military and intelligence services and lend logistical support to the U.S. military operation. Musharraf's reward for this abrupt foreign policy reversal was a massive influx of U.S. economic aid, the reduction in Pakistan's foreign debt, and the suspension of U.S. economic sanctions that had been imposed on Pakistan after its nuclear tests in 1998.

The war against the Taliban and al-Qaeda (code-named Operation Enduring Freedom) began on October 7, 2001, with an air campaign conducted by four aircraft carrier battle groups and surface ships and submarines armed with cruise missiles operating in the Arabian Sea as well as by long-range bombers based in the United States. In addition to destroying the Taliban's primitive air defense system, air bases, and military headquarters, the bombing and cruise missile attacks strengthened the position and bolstered the morale of the Northern Alliance forces after years of defeat and retreat. But as the Northern Alliance began to break out of its mountain redoubt in the northeast corner of the country and advance southward in the first week of November, Pakistan's President Musharraf warned Washington that the occupation of the capital city of Kabul by the Tajik-Uzbek-Hazara forces would antagonize the Pashtuns in the south and east and possibly throw them into the arms of the Taliban. The arrival of Northern Alliance troops in Kabul on November 12 set in motion a mad scramble for political advantage among the various Afghan warlords and their ethnic-based forces as it became evident that the Taliban's days in power were numbered. The Tajik former president Burhanuddin Rabbani reoccupied the office from which he had ousted by the Taliban in the mid-1990s and attempted to reassert his authority, prompting bitter complaints from the Pashtuns in the south and their Pakistani patrons. It momentarily seemed that the disintegration of the Taliban might revive the old ethnic rivalries that had torn the country apart in the first half of the 1990s.

Although they often disparaged the concept of "nation building," President Bush and his advisers recognized the importance of reconciling the contending political factions in post-Taliban Afghanistan to provide the order and stability required for the country to recover from its devastation. While supporting the military forces of the Northern Alliance, Washington had assiduously cultivated anti-Taliban Pashtun leaders in the south who were loyal to the exiled former king Mohammed Zahir Shah, widely regarded as a valuable symbol of national unity after the fighting was over. In December representatives of the various Afghan factions attended a UN-

---

*Small forces from Great Britain, France, and other countries eventually participated in the U.S. -led military operation.

sponsored conference in Bonn, Germany to lay the foundation for the country's political future. After much horse trading the conference established an interim administration that was carefully calibrated to create a balance the power among the contending factions. It's chairman was Hamid Karzai, a Pashtun supporter of the exiled king who was acceptable to the Northern Alliance as well as to U.S. intelligence officials (who recalled him as a consultant for the U.S. oil company Unocal during its bid to construct a natural gas pipeline from Turkmenistan to Pakistan across Taliban-controlled Afghanistan). The Tajik, Uzbek, and Hazara coalition secured a majority of the cabinet posts, including the powerful ministries of foreign affairs, defense, and interior. After assuming power on December 22, the interim administration spent the next several months preparing for the convocation of a *loya jirga* (a grand council of notables) that would develop procedures for the drafting of a new constitution and the establishment of a permanent government. In the meantime a UN peacekeeping force, dominated by a large British contingent, provided security for the interim government in Kabul as it consolidated its authority and assumed its administrative functions. A group of donor nations pledged about $4.5 billion in aid to finance the reconstruction of the bankrupt, devastated country. The *loya jirga* convened on schedule in June 2002 in Kabul and elected Karzai president of a transitional coalition government that would prepare for a popularly elected government within two years.

While the diplomats planned the political future of the country and Northern Alliance military units liberated one Taliban-held city after another in the winter and early spring of 2002, U.S. marines and special forces had mounted a massive manhunt in the mountain caves of southeast Afghanistan in search of bin Laden, Mullah Omar, and other al-Qaeda and Taliban leaders. Although U.S. soldiers captured some two-hundred fifty militants and transferred them to the U.S. naval base at Cuba's Guantanamo Bay for interrogation, bin Laden, Omar, and most of the other high-level Taliban and al-Qaeda officials apparently escaped across the border into Pakistan. They blended into the large amorphous population of Pashtuns, many of whom retained strong sympathies for the Taliban's radical brand of Islam.

## China after Mao: The Great Awakening

As we have seen, the Nixon-Kissinger administration initiated the rapprochement with the People's Republic of China in 1972 primarily for diplomatic and strategic reasons, namely, to curb what it viewed as the dangerous expansion of Soviet military power and influence throughout the world. But there was also an economic underpinning of the U.S. bid for improved relations with China, based on the unrealistic expectation of American export firms of huge profits from sales to the most world's most populous country. These dreams of penetrating the vast untapped China market were gravely disappointed in the years after the Nixon visit because America's new strategic partner remained closed to foreign trade and investment. After Mao Zedong died on September 9, 1976, at the age of eighty-three, a bitter struggle for the succession brought to power as Communist Party Chairman Hua Guofeng, whom Mao had plucked from obscurity to become premier after the Chinese leader's long-time deputy Zhou Enlai died earlier in the year. Although rhetorically committed to fundamental economic reforms, Hua Guofeng retained the traditional Communist economic practices based on the Soviet model: central economic planning and the promotion of state-run heavy industries such as defense, metallurgy, chemicals, and petroleum; the setting of wages and prices by government fiat rather than by the free market forces of supply and demand; and production for the domestic market rather than for the export trade. The result was stagnant industrial growth and low agricultural productivity, hardly the type of economic performance that would attract the American investment, lending, and trade that the reformers associated with the late Zhou Enlai had deemed critical to China's economic development.

In 1978 Zhou's protégé Deng Xiaoping, who had been purged during the Cultural Revolution for his unorthodox views, regained power as vice premier and promptly displaced his nominal superior Hua Guofeng as the de facto leader of China. In the next three years Deng launched a nationwide campaign to replace the defenders of the old orthodoxy with like-minded reformers who were willing to experiment with new economic policies even if they violated the cherished precepts of Marxist-Leninist doctrine. To achieve the sustained economic growth that Deng Xiaoping and his subordinates envisioned, they instituted a number of radical innovations in the Chinese economic system during the first half of the 1980s: They dismantled the large collective farms and subdivided them into family plots and authorized peasants to sell a portion of their produce on the open market for a profit. They shifted capital investment from heavy to light industry, which put consumer goods in the shops that workers and peasants could purchase with their newly expanded personal incomes. They decentralized industrial production, providing factory managers with greater authority and responsibility for the output of their plants. They encouraged individual entrepreneurs to start small businesses and allowed them to retain the profits they earned. In short, the state gradually loosened its stranglehold over the productive apparatus of the country and permitted the free market to replace central planning as the motive force behind industrial and agricultural production. The result was the most fundamental transformation of the Chinese economy since the establishment of the People's Republic in 1949.

The new reformist leadership around Deng Xiaoping realized that the full-scale economic modernization they had launched at the end of the 1970s could not succeed without the acquisition of two critical factors of production that China sorely lacked: capital and technology. To gain access to these productive factors, China would have to expand its economic contacts with the outside world. That meant that China would have to reorient its production from domestic to foreign markets. Deng Xiaoping had observed the impressive performance of neighboring economic powerhouses like South Korea and Taiwan and was determined to steer China onto the same path of export-oriented growth. It was evident that this new approach required the abandonment of the autarkic economic strategy that China had pursued since the cutoff of Soviet aid in 1960. In short, it meant the integration of China in the international capitalist economic order. In pursuit of this new goal during the 1980s, China eagerly sought loans, investment, trade, and technology from abroad. The government established on the southern coast four special economic zones based on Taiwanese and South Korean models. In these designated areas the subsidiaries of foreign firms were granted special privileges to encourage them to produce goods for export, often through joint ventures with Chinese companies. Foreign investment soon flooded into China from Japan, Taiwan, and Hong Kong, taking advantage of special tax havens that were set up in fourteen designated coastal cities. The results of this remarkable transformation of the Chinese economic system were impressive: The total value of China's two-way foreign trade increased from $4.6 billion in 1970 to about $75 billion in 1988. The Chinese standard of living doubled between 1977 and 1987. Although the interior of the country that was not integrated into the world economy continued to languish behind the booming coastal region, China as a whole was emerging as an important participant in the world capitalist system that Beijing had so vociferously scorned during the Maoist era.

The principal beneficiary of Deng Xiaoping's new "Open Door" policy was Japan, as the complementary character of these two historic adversaries' economic systems brought them into intimate commercial contact with one another. By the mid-1980s Japan had become China's leading trading partner while China had become Japan's second trading partner behind the United States. China supplied Japan with the oil, coal, and strategic raw materials that the resource-poor island nation lacked in exchange for the capital, technology, and high-level manufactured products that China required for its economic takeoff. The United States lagged behind in the global competition for the China market in the 1980s. But by the end of the decade the United States had become China's third source of exports (behind Hong Kong and Japan), keeping alive the old fantasy of the China market as the cure to American economic difficulties. In the early period of the Sino-American commercial relationship the bulk of U.S. exports to China consisted of grain sales from the Midwest. This would change in the early 1980s, when improvements in Chinese agricultural production reduced the country's dependence on food imports and led to more purchases of machinery and technology abroad. In the meantime China had successfully followed in the footsteps of the East Asian Tigers by exploiting its comparative advantage of low labor costs to become a major source of America's clothing and textile imports. Wash-and-wear items with the label "Made in China" undersold and replaced those with "Made in Hong Kong" or "Made in Taiwan," to the benefit of American consumers and the detriment of high-cost American textile firms and their workers.

The major U.S. contribution to China's economic modernization drive during the 1980s was the provision of desperately needed investment capital, technology, and advanced training in management techniques. By the end of the 1980s U.S. firms had placed over $3 billion in joint ventures established in the special economic zones on the southern coast, making the United States the largest foreign direct investor in the country. Second, the U.S. government relaxed the old Cold War restrictions on technology exports to China, enabling American firms to join their Japanese and European counterparts in selling Chinese firms the high technology they would require to fabricate finished products that could compete on the world market. Third, the United States opened its institutions of higher learning to Chinese students eager to obtain the knowledge and training that were unavailable in the primitive educational system at home. By the end of the 1980s more than forty thousand of them were enrolled each year in U.S. universities. Although these students returned with valuable technical and managerial skills that they used to improve the productivity of Chinese industry, they also brought with them the alien customs and ideas to which they had been exposed on American campuses. In the meantime Deng Xiaoping's regime permitted a relaxation of government controls on the flow of information into the country. For the first time Chinese citizens were permitted to purchase foreign books and magazines, listen to foreign radio programs, and watch Western television shows (although access to the Internet would be severely restricted when the rest of the world went "on line" in the 1990s). Millions of Western tourists flocked to China and were allowed to mingle freely with the Chinese people. These foreign influences posed a potential threaten to the rigid control that the Communist Party continued to exercise on Chinese society.

In 1980 China took the decisive step of joining the IMF and the World Bank. Within a few years Beijing was receiving substantial loans from both institutions to correct its balance of payments deficits and finance its long-term development projects. In 1986 China applied for permanent membership in GATT, the organization that set the rules for international trade. By associating with these bulwarks of the Western-dominated world trading and monetary system, this former paragon of Communist orthodoxy had implicitly accepted the rules of market capitalism and repudiated the neo-Marxist dependency theory that had become fashionable in the Third World during the 1970s.

As Deng Xiaoping intensified China's economic links with the developed world, he also avidly pursued a closer diplomatic and military relationship with the United States on the basis of the two countries' shared concerns about Soviet expansion. As we have seen, this reorientation of Beijing's foreign policy toward cooperation with Washington had begun even before Deng's accession: The Chinese government that had once promoted Communist revolutions across the globe aligned with the United States and South Africa in support of an anti-Communist insurgency against the Soviet-backed government in Angola in 1975–1976. It developed cordial relations with the anti-Communist regime of Mobutu Sésé Sékó in Zaire and supported the Western operations to rescue the Central African despot in 1977–1978 (see page 290). It terminated support for Communist-led insurgencies in Burma, Indonesia, Malaysia, the Philippines, and Thailand in order to win favor and promote trade with their anti-Communist governments.

The Carter administration, which was becoming disillusioned with the policy of Soviet-American détente in the late 1970s, greeted this new direction in Chinese foreign policy with undisguised enthusiasm. National Security Adviser Zbigniew Brzezinski persuaded the president that a revival of the Sino-American connection, which had languished since the euphoric aftermath of the Nixon visit in 1972, would send a useful message to Moscow. Brzezinski was dispatched on a highly publicized mission to China in May 1978 with instructions to propose closer Sino-American cooperation against the Soviet Union across the globe. On August 19, 1978, Japan (with strong American encouragement) concluded with the People's Republic a Treaty of Peace and Friendship. This important Sino-Japanese agreement included a provocative clause opposing "hegemony" (a code word that the Chinese customarily applied to the Soviet Union). Following in the wake of the American overtures to Beijing, the Sino-Japanese entente was viewed in the Kremlin as part of an

American-orchestrated campaign of containment of the Soviet Union in Asia. That perception was largely correct: Nixon and Kissinger had pursued a Sino-American rapprochement while simultaneously seeking an improvement of relations with the Soviet Union, a triangular strategy that enabled Washington to manage a delicate balance between the two Communist rivals. By contrast, Carter and Brzezinski envisioned an exclusive Sino-American partnership designed to thwart what they viewed as the USSR's bids for influence in Asia and Africa.

Carter's decision to align with China introduced an element of hypocrisy in the American campaign on behalf of human rights in the Soviet Union and Eastern Europe. The expanding crackdown on Soviet dissidents, which included long jail terms for Alexander Ginsburg and Anatoly Shcharansky in July, elicited sharp protests from the same administration in Washington that was avidly pursuing improved relations with China despite its abominable record on human rights. When the Kremlin reversed its repressive policy in August and began to permit several dissidents to emigrate instead of trying, convicting, and imprisoning them, the contrast with China—where nary of peep of dissidence was permitted—became even more pronounced. Yet Washington's courtship of Beijing proceeded without missing a step, while the drumbeat of criticism of Soviet repression continued.

The intense negotiations between Washington and Beijing reached fruition on December 15, 1978, when President Carter announced that the countries had agreed to recognize each other as of January 1, 1979. While noting that the United States would maintain unofficial relations with Taiwan through private channels, he also gave Taipei the requisite one-year notice that the United States–Taiwan mutual security treaty of 1954 would be abrogated. Washington also suspended all arms sales to Taipei for a year, but reserved the right to furnish purely defensive arms to its old ally thereafter. Although gravely disappointed at this loophole, the Chinese government announced that Deng Xiaoping would become the first Chinese Communist leader to visit the United States to celebrate the historic rapprochement.

What prompted Beijing to tolerate something less than a total U.S. break with Taiwan in order to achieve formal diplomatic ties with Washington was its mounting anxiety about the deterioration of relations between China and its erstwhile ally Vietnam. After its triumph over the U.S-backed client state in the south, North Vietnam had presided over the reunification of the country in April 1976. The government in Beijing had always been wary of a powerful, unified Vietnam that might seek hegemony over all of the former French Indochina. Although Mao had supplied weapons to Ho Chi Minh during the latter's war against the French, the Chinese delegation at the Geneva Conference of 1954 had refrained from supporting the unification of Vietnam under Viet Minh auspices (see page 223). The American military intervention during the 1960s had obliged Beijing to support Hanoi in order to prevent it from falling entirely within the Soviet orbit. Ho and his successors had skillfully played the two Communist behemoths against each other to extract from each the maximum military assistance possible. Then shortly after Hanoi's victory in the spring of 1975, relations between the triumphant, self-confident Vietnam and its former patron China began to sour. Disputes broke out along the border between the two Communist countries. Both Hanoi and Beijing claimed the Spratly and Paracel Islands in the South China Sea, a group of uninhabited reefs believed to possess substantial petroleum reserves. In 1974 China had seized the Paracels from the faltering regime in Saigon; a year later Vietnam occupied six of the Spratlys and then challenged China's claim to the Paracels.

Flush with victory and no longer dependent on China for support against the Americans, Vietnam tightened its links with Moscow. In June 1978 Hanoi joined the Soviet-dominated economic organization Comecon. In November of the same year Vietnam concluded a treaty of friendship with the Soviet Union that authorized the stationing of Soviet troops in the country. China felt increasingly squeezed between the Soviet Union to the north and its Vietnamese ally client to the south. These geopolitical conflicts between Beijing and Hanoi were aggravated by the resurgence of ancient ethnic antagonisms that had been submerged during the long common struggle against the French and then the Americans: The Vietnamese government began to take punitive measures against the large Chinese minority in Vietnam that dominated the merchant class in the cities, confiscating their shops and forcibly relocating many them to rural areas. The harassed Chinese in Vietnam began to leave the country in droves, prompting recriminations and increasingly blunt warnings from Beijing.

Amid these mounting Sino-Vietnamese conflicts, Hanoi decided to confirm its dominance over the two other states of the former French Indochina. Soon after the defeat of the U.S.-backed regime in Saigon in the spring of 1975, North Vietnam easily acquired de facto control of neighboring Laos, whose non-Communist regime had fallen to the Pathet Lao insurgents at the same time. At the end of the 1970s, the deteriorating political situation in Cambodia furnished the opportunity for the recently reunified Vietnam to achieve hegemony over that country as well. In the years after the end of the war in Indochina, the population of Cambodia had undergone one of the most traumatic experiences ever endured. Between 1976 and 1978 a Cambodian Communist ideologue named Pol Pot, leader of the Khmer Rouge movement that had seized power from the American-backed regime in Phnom Penh in the spring of 1975, conducted a ruthless campaign to liquidate all remnants of "bourgeois" influences in the country. Inspired by the Cultural Revolution in China, Khmer Rouge officials concentrated their attention on what they regarded as the principal carriers of this virus that had to be eradicated: the urban educated elite. The cities and towns of Cambodia were emptied of their inhabitants, who were forcibly relocated to the countryside for indoctrination in the principles of revolutionary Marxism. They were the fortunate ones. Pol Pot's regime exterminated over a million Cambodians in the worst case of genocide since Hitler's Holocaust. The campaign of annihilation in Cambodia eventually led to skirmishes between the Khmer Rouge killing squads and Vietnamese military units patrolling the border separating the two Communist countries. These tensions finally erupted into all-out war on December 25, 1978, when Vietnam launched a full-scale invasion of its Communist neighbor to the east. The genocidal policies of the Khmer Rouge had so traumatized the population of Cambodia that many of them welcomed the Vietnamese invaders as liberators. The well trained, battle-seasoned Vietnamese army had little trouble reaching the Cambodian capital of Phnom Penh, where they toppled the Khmer Rouge government and set up a Vietnamese puppet state under a Cambodian opponent of Pol Pot named Heng Samrin.

The People's Republic of China fully supported the Khmer Rouge government and expressed vigorous opposition to Vietnam's acquisition of de facto control of Cambodia. Deng Xiaoping decided that Vietnam could not be allowed to get away with such a blatant invasion of its neighbor without a massive show of Chinese force. But the new post-Mao leadership in Beijing prudently sought prior assurances from its new friends in Washington that the United States would not actively oppose any Chinese military operation against Vietnam. During his American visit in January 1979 to celebrate the establishment of diplomatic relations between the two governments, Deng complained to President Carter about Vietnam's aggression in Cambodia and revealed China's plans to respond to it with military force. The irony of this reversal of roles must have prompted Lyndon Johnson, Mao Zedong, and Ho Chi Minh to spin in their graves. The American president expressed disapproval of the Chinese plan to intervene, but gave no indication that the United States would do anything to interfere with it.

On his return to Beijing, Deng sent two hundred thousand Chinese troops and twelve hundred tanks across China's border with Vietnam on February 17, 1979, to "teach it a lesson" for its belligerent actions. The absence of air or naval support suggests that the Chinese offensive was intended merely as an signal of displeasure with Vietnam's invasion of Cambodia rather than a serious attempt to deal Hanoi a military defeat. Despite the fact that Vietnam's most experienced ground troops were on occupation duty in Cambodia, the Chinese People's Liberation Army (which had had no battle experience since the Korean War and was equipped with antiquated weapons) encountered spirited opposition from the experienced Vietnamese units they encountered. After two weeks of heavy fighting, Vietnam began to mobilize its military manpower and economic resources to fight its third major armed struggle since the end of World War II. The Soviet Union started to airlift arms to Hanoi for use against their common Chinese adversary. Then, without warning or explanation, the Chinese army suddenly withdrew from Vietnam and declared the end of its military operation. In this brief, two-week war with China, Vietnam lost some thirty thousand soldiers—more than half of America's total war dead in its nine-year conflict in the region, while Chinese deaths totaled about twenty-six thousand. China's military intervention failed to compel Vietnam to withdraw from Cambodia, to renounce its claims to the Spratly Islands, or to halt its maltreatment of its ethnic Chinese minority. Instead, the Chinese invasion drove Hanoi even closer to Moscow, as reflected in an agreement granting the Soviet Pacific fleet access to the former American naval base at Cam Ranh Bay.

The Vietnamese occupation of Cambodia led to a sharp split within ASEAN, the regional organization of Southeast Asian nations that had been formed in 1967. In a revised version of Eisenhower's domino theory, the government of Thailand warned that Vietnam's domination of Laos and its military occupation of Cambodia directly threatened the security of the other countries of Southeast Asia. The governments of Indonesia and Malaysia, by contrast, were primarily concerned about the danger from Beijing, which had previously supported Communist opposition movements within their countries (see page 251). They therefore favored a strong, assertive Vietnam as a counterweight to China in the region. In the end both Indonesia and Malaysia, out of deference to Thailand's immediate security concerns and to preserve the unity of the regional organization, endorsed ASEAN's condemnation of the Vietnamese invasion and supported its diplomatic campaign to dislodge the Vietnamese army from Cambodia.

But the ASEAN states were not prepared to back the murderous Khmer Rouge, which had retreated from the Cambodian capital and set up guerrilla bases along the border with Thailand in 1980 to harass the Vietnamese-installed regime in Phnom Penh. Instead, ASEAN threw its support to a rival Cambodian opposition group, the Khmer People's National Liberation Front (KPNLF), which had been formed in March 1979 by a group of Cambodian émigrés in Paris led by a businessman named Son Sann. ASEAN also provided some assistance to a third anti-Vietnamese resistance movement headed by the former Prince Sihanouk, which operated in western Cambodia and received support from China as well. In June 1982 the three rival opposition factions joined forces to form a government-in-exile in Kuala Lumpur, Malaysia. The glue that held together this fragile coalition of pro-Sihanouk royalists, middle-class liberals supporting Son Sann, and the Communist Khmer Rouge was their common commitment to expelling the Vietnamese invaders and evicting their stooges from Phnom Penh. The Vietnamese invasion of Cambodia also served to reinforce the Sino-American entente in the last years of the Carter administration, as the two governments also joined forces in support of the insurgents. China supplied the Khmer Rouge guerrillas through Thailand, while the United States furnished arms to the two non-Communist factions in the anti-Vietnamese coalition. As the Cambodian civil war raged throughout the 1980s, Washington and Beijing developed an exceedingly cooperative relationship in opposition to what both governments viewed as the hegemonic objectives of Hanoi and its patron in Moscow. As we have seen, the two governments also joined forces in support of the resistance movement in Afghanistan after the Soviet invasion of that country at the end of 1979 (see page 362).

But the deepening relationship between Washington and Beijing was continually jeopardized by their lingering dispute over the political status of Taiwan. After Carter established diplomatic relations with China at the beginning of 1979, the U.S. Congress passed the Taiwan Relations Act. This legislation reiterated America's intention to sell defensive weapons to the island, warned that the United States would resist any effort by China to regain its renegade province by force, and set up an informal liaison office on Taiwan that was staffed by foreign service officers on temporary leave and functioned as a de facto embassy. In January 1980 Carter resumed selective arms sales to Taiwan after the expiration of the one-year moratorium. These developments outraged the leadership in Beijing, but the worst was yet to come. In January 1981 Ronald Reagan entered the White House after severely criticizing Carter's "sellout" of "the free Republic of China" and even hinting that the restoration of formal diplomatic ties with Taiwan was in order. After a year in office the Reagan administration adamantly reasserted the right to sell whatever weapons it chose to Taiwan and resumed U.S.-Taiwanese coproduction of fighter aircraft. But Reagan's distaste for the Soviet Union eventually led him to endorse a compromise arrangement with China that allayed Beijing's growing anxieties that the two powers were drifting apart over Taiwan. On August 17, 1982, the two governments issued a joint communiqué in which Washington promised a gradual reduction in arms sales to Taiwan while Beijing pledged to seek reunification with its wayward province by nonviolent means. As an indication of its support for China against the Soviet threat along its northern border, Washington sold Beijing a ground satellite-tracking station in 1983 to enhance its nuclear targeting capabilities, anti-submarine sonars, and anti-tank missiles.

In the meantime political developments on Taiwan gradually paved the way for an improvement in the island's relations with the mainland. After Chiang Kai-shek's death in 1975, his son and successor Chiang Ching-kuo loosened the Kuomintang party's iron grip on Taiwan's political life. Indigenous Taiwanese, who had constituted 85 percent of the population before the influx of mainlanders in 1949, were allowed to participate more fully in the country's burgeoning economy. Small opposition parties were permitted to contest local elections and even to send a few representatives to the national parliament. In 1986 Chiang restored civil liberties by lifting the martial law that had been in force since his father's defeated army had retreated to the island. In the following year families were permitted to visit relatives on the mainland for the first time. In 1989 government officials from what was still officially designated as the "Republic of China" began to attend international meetings held in the People's Republic, while Taipei's ritualistic denunciations of the Communist regime in Beijing faded. This emerging political détente between the long-time adversaries was reinforced by their expanding economic ties. The value of trade between the two countries, which was conducted mainly through Hong Kong, had soared from $466 million in 1981 to $2 billion in 1988 and $5.8 billion in 1991.

Beijing avidly pursued its objective of peaceful reunification with Taiwan for the remainder of the 1980s. The 1984 agreement with Great Britain providing for China's recovery of Hong Kong on July 1, 1997, offered a model that Beijing hoped might prove acceptable to Taipei: China agreed to treat Hong Kong as a special administrative region with full autonomy in all but foreign and defense matters. This meant that the former British crown colony could retain its democratic political system, free market economic practices, and separate cultural identity. Deng Xiaoping's motivation for granting such special prerogatives to the citizens of Hong Kong reflected his appreciation of the enormous economic benefits that China derived from the crown colony's status as a gateway to the developed world, through which China conducted a substantial proportion of its foreign trade. Taiwan's booming economy promised similar advantages to China if a mutually acceptable resolution of their long dispute over the island's political status could be arranged. As it sought to recover by peaceful means the two East Asian Tigers Hong Kong and Taiwan, China also endeavored to intensify its economic links and improve its political relations with the rest of non-Communist Asia. Deng Xiaoping assiduously wooed the member-states of ASEAN, which had been formed in the 1960s in reaction to what was viewed as Chinese aggressiveness. He also expanded friendly political ties with Japan to complement the mutually profitable trade relations between the two countries that had developed since the mid-1980s.

As China's relations with its historic adversaries Taiwan, ASEAN, and Japan improved toward the end of the 1980s, the reform-minded government in Beijing had to confront the implications for its own future of the revolutionary political developments in the Soviet Union. The sweeping economic restructuring that Deng

Xiaoping had initiated in China in the first half of the 1980s bore a striking resemblance to Mikhail Gorbachev's innovations in the last half of the decade. But when Gorbachev sought to win public support for his economic reforms by granting greater political freedoms to the Soviet population, he unleashed a set of popular forces that threatened the stability of the regime (see page 321). Deng Xiaoping and his allies in Beijing observed these events with mounting concern. The Chinese reformers were willing to experiment with a carefully managed Chinese version of *perestroika* because it seemed to be the only effective means of promoting the country's economic development. But they were unwilling to tolerate a Chinese version of *glasnost* because it might to destroy the ruling Communist Party's iron grip on political power.

As in Gorbachev's Soviet Union the sudden advent of entrepreneurship in Deng's China had spawned widespread corruption, which in turn generated mounting discontent among urban intellectuals and professionals. The removal of price controls and the resulting inflation alienated industrial workers, whose real wages declined. These and other sources of domestic unrest gave rise, for the first time in the history of the People's Republic, to overt criticism of government policy by organized groups of dissidents. In the first important test of the Chinese Communist government's willingness to tolerate mass political mobilization outside official channels, a million protesting students assembled on Beijing's Tiananmen Square in the spring of 1989 for a peaceful demonstration in support of greater political liberties. In the full view of Western television crews that had coincidentally arrived to cover a state visit by Gorbachev, the Chinese students staged hunger strikes, chanted democratic slogans, and wheeled around a replica of the Statue of Liberty as the symbol of their cause. Hard-liners in the military, the Communist Party, and the government observed with apprehension the declining fortunes of the Communist parties in Eastern Europe and demanded drastic action to prevent China from suffering a similar fate. Deng thereupon called in the People's Liberation Army to suppress the peaceful protest. On June 4 tanks rumbled into the square with guns blazing, massacring about thirteen hundred unarmed civilians and abruptly terminating China's brief experiment with internal political dissent. The subsequent execution and imprisonment of protest leaders signified that Beijing's commitment to economic reform would not be accompanied by the type of political liberalization that was getting out of hand in Russia.

The carnage in Tiananmen Square elicited sharp protests abroad and prompted the imposition of sanctions by China's major trading partners. The Bush administration immediately suspended all military and most economic assistance to Beijing and used its influence in the IMF and the World Bank to force a postponement of new loans to China from those multilateral agencies. Japan canceled all of the aid projects that had been approved before the blood flowed on the streets of Beijing. But these sanctions had no appreciable effect on the Chinese regime. Deng dismissed party Secretary Zhao Ziyang, who had urged a conciliatory policy on the eve of the Tiananmen military operation. He blamed Gorbachev's timidity for fostering the political unrest that was sweeping across Eastern Europe and the Soviet Union itself. Chinese officials reverted to the rhetoric of orthodox Communism in a determined bid to restore domestic order while other Communist regimes were collapsing across the globe.

In June 1990 the Chinese government did manage to offer a conciliatory gesture to world opinion by permitting Fang Lizhi, an eminent physicist who had sought asylum in the United States embassy in Beijing, to leave the country for exile in Great Britain. But very few other dissidents were released, while the government effectively suppressed the emerging political opposition. One by one foreign states began to lift the sanctions to restore normal commercial and financial relations with the PRC, demonstrating once again that political principle will eventually be trumped by economic interest. By the summer of 1990 Japan had opened new lines of credit for China. Throughout the 1990s the Bush and Clinton administrations in Washington granted China annual renewals of most-favored-nation (MFN) status. They rejected congressional demands, which were reminiscent of the trade and human rights debates concerning the Soviet Union in the mid-1970s, that trade concessions be used as a weapon to punish China for its anti-democratic policies.

Throughout the 1990s coastal China intensified its economic contacts with Japan, Taiwan, South Korea, ASEAN, and other countries in the Pacific Rim while recording impressive economic growth for the rest of the decade, Deng Xiaoping's dream of transforming China into a world economic giant while preserving the Communist Party's monopoly on political power at home seemed on the verge of realization when the great Chinese reformer died in 1997. The Clinton administration had been working diligently to facilitate China's entry into the new World Trade Organization (WTO), which replaced GATT in 1995 as the supervisor of global trading rules, by inducing Beijing to lower its protectionist tariff rates and curb the country's widespread violations of intellectual property rights through pirated computer software and compact disk sales. As the result of an agreement reached in the fall of 1999, China finally acquired full membership in the capitalist international economic order at the end of 2001. The door to the world's most populous country (with 1.3 billion consumers) was finally open to foreign economic competition. Some observers predicted that China would reap substantial benefits from its full participation in the global market, with technological innovation and more efficient production practices ushering in a period of prosperity and plenty.

But other experts foresaw a time of troubles for the new China. With the abandonment of protectionism, the influx of competitively priced products from abroad threatened to force the inefficient state enterprises into bankruptcy and their labor force into unemployment. The prospect of hundreds of millions of laid-off workers streaming into the country's largest cities in search of employment threatened to exacerbate the already serious social problems caused by spreading unemployment and rapid urbanization. Along with the menace of social unrest in the economically advanced coastal cities, occasional outbursts of discontent emanated from religious or ethnic minorities in the isolated rural provinces in the west. Buddhists in Tibet retained contacts with the exiled Dalai Lama, who remained a thorn in Beijing's side by tirelessly publicizing his people's grievances against China throughout the world. The Muslims of Xinjiang drew inspiration from their coreligionists in Afghanistan and in the central Asian republics that broke away from the Soviet Union. Another separatist challenge surfaced on Taiwan, where Lee Teng-hui, a native Taiwanese, succeeded President Chiang Ching-huo on the latter's death in 1988. As the date for China's annexation of Hong Kong on July 1, 1997 approached, Taiwan's indigenous inhabitants began openly to discuss the taboo subject of independence. Beijing responded to this provocation with an intimidating show of force, test-firing missiles off the island's coast in 1995 and conducting military exercises in the Taiwan Strait the following year. The prospect of Taiwan's following in the footsteps of Hong Kong fed secessionist sentiment on the island and complicated the stalled negotiations over its political future.

## The Pacification of Cambodia

Apart from Vietnam, the Asian country that had suffered the most death and destruction during the Cold War era was Cambodia, which had been engulfed in a bloody civil war since Vietnamese forces had occupied it and established a puppet state in Phnom Penh in 1978. But the country's long travail began to come to an end as the Cold War itself drew to a close. The reformist Soviet government of Mikhail Gorbachev was intent on improving relations with the United States and China, both of which had violently objected to the Vietnamese occupation and had actively supported the Cambodian resistance groups that were waging guerrilla warfare against the Vietnamese occupiers and their Cambodian collaborators. In response to persistent prodding from its Soviet patron, Hanoi agreed in May 1988 to cut in half its troop strength in Cambodia by the end of the year. When Gorbachev eagerly sought a summit conference with China's Deng Xiaoping to iron out the remaining Sino-Soviet differences, Deng demanded the evacuation of all Vietnamese forces from Cambodia as a precondition for such a meeting. Moscow thereupon turned up the pressure on Hanoi, which finally agreed in April 1989 to withdraw its troops from Cambodia. Deng rewarded Gorbachev for his timely assistance by inviting him to Beijing for the long deferred summit conference in May. Although the historic meeting was overshadowed by the Chinese domestic crisis that resulted in the massacre at Tiananmen Square, the two reforming Communist leaders managed to work out plans for a full normalization of relations and a substantial increase in Sino-Soviet trade. Gorbachev helped ease tensions along the long Sino-Soviet border by announcing that Soviet forces in the Far East would be cut to 120,000 by the end of 1991. In September 1989 the last Vietnamese units evacuated Cambodia, leaving the government that Hanoi had installed in Phnom Penh to fend for itself against its domestic opponents and their supporters abroad. The United States and China in turn promptly suspended their military assistance and diplomatic support for the anti-government coalition.

Hanoi's ten-year military operation in Cambodia, which lasted longer that its war with the United States, was an unmitigated disaster for the country that had so recently achieved its national unification after thirty years of war. The Vietnamese lost as many soldiers in Cambodia—some fifty-five thousand—as the Americans had lost in their conflict in Indochina. Vietnam was plunged into diplomatic isolation, alienating China, the United States, and ASEAN as it put all its eggs in the Soviet basket. Then Hanoi's only foreign supporter began its steady decline, as its satellite empire in Eastern Europe crumbled and its national minorities agitated for secession. The USSR began to evacuate its naval base at Cam Ranh Bay in December 1989 and in the following year announced a major withdrawal of ground troops and a sharp reduction in economic assistance to its old ally. The total cutoff of the Soviet Union's annual financial subsidy of 2 billion rubles to Vietnam in 1991 aggravated an economic crisis that had gripped the latter country since the mid-1980s. The new generation of political leaders in Hanoi that had replaced the old veterans of the French and American wars in 1986 followed in Gorbachev's footsteps by renouncing the centralized economic planning on the Soviet model in favor of a market-based economy and began to solicit Western investment.

The departure of the Vietnamese military forces from Cambodia in 1989 left the government that Hanoi had installed in Phnom Penh with no alternative but to open peace negotiations in Paris with a coalition of three rebel factions that operated under the titular authority of the country's former monarch, Prince Norodom Sihanouk. On October 23, 1991, these talks produced a peace agreement that terminated the twelve-year civil war and confirmed the end of Vietnam's hegemony in Indochina. The pact established a national council, chaired by Sihanouk and comprising representatives of the government and the three rebel groups, that would cooperate with the newly created United Nations Transitional Authority in Cambodia (UNTAC) to restore peace to the war-torn land. The twenty-two-thousand-man UN peacekeeping force arrived in Cambodia in the spring of 1992, the largest of its kind ever deployed by the world organization. UNTAC enforced the cease-fire, supervised the disarmament of the rival armies, and prepared for the first democratic elections in the country's history.

Although the Communist Khmer Rouge faction refused to disarm and boycotted the elections, Cambodians went to the polls in May 1993 and gave a plurality to the party headed by Sihanouk's eldest son, Prince Norodom Ranariddh. In the following month Prince Ranariddh formed a provisional government in partnership with the former head of the Vietnamese-installed regime, Hun Sen. In the fall of 1993, Sihanouk mounted his former throne as head of a constitutional monarchy as the UN peacekeeping force departed. In the following year the governing coalition responded to the escalation of violence by the Khmer Rouge by expelling its representatives from Phnom Penh. Its forces reassembled in jungle hideouts near the border with Thailand and waged a last-ditch guerrilla campaign against government troops that eventually petered out after the death of its murderous leader, Pol Pot, in April 1998. After enduring genocide, foreign invasion, and civil war since the mid-1970s, Cambodia finally returned to relative calm. Vietnam abandoned its hegemonic ambitions for the rest of Indochina after the decline and eventual disappearance of its Soviet patron. Indochina as a whole, which had served as the focal point of conflict between internal forces as well as foreign powers since the end of World War II, entered the twenty-first century in an unaccustomed state of peace, tranquillity, and stability.

## The Reemergence of the "Hermit Nation"

The isolated, inward-looking country of North Korea virtually vanished from the world scene after the end of the Korean War in 1953. The North Korean Communist dictator, Kim Il Sung, ruled his people with an iron fist and effectively insulated his country from all foreign connections or influences. It took part in no international organizations and attended no international conferences for the remainder of the Cold War. While his long-time Communist allies in Moscow and Beijing underwent sweeping internal changes during the 1980s, Kim Il Sung refrained from offering even the slightest gesture toward political or economic reform. Then North Korea suddenly emerged from its obscurity in the early 1990s to became a source of grave concern to the United States. Western intelligence reports revealed that Kim's regime was engaged in a clandestine campaign to acquire a nuclear capability by extracting enough weapons-grade plutonium from the waste products of commercial nuclear reactors situated north of the capital of Pyongyang to build several atomic bombs. Although a signatory of the Non-Proliferation Treaty (NPT), the North Korean government had denied the International Atomic Energy Agency (IAEA) access to its nuclear facilities to verify its adherence to the treaty's provisions. Kim finally bowed to international pressure in 1991 and allowed the IAEA inspectors into the country. But his agents at the suspected nuclear weapons site interfered so brazenly with the inspection team's work that the IAEA cited North Korea for noncompliance. The Clinton administration in Washington, concerned about the threat that a nuclear North Korea would pose to America's nonnuclear allies in the region such as South Korea and Japan, proposed the imposition of UN trade sanctions against the recalcitrant regime until it opened its nuclear sites to outside inspection.

When the eighty-two-year-old North Korean leader died in 1994, his son and successor Kim Jong Il resumed the deadlocked bilateral negotiations with the United States. In the autumn of that year, North Korea finally agreed to shut down its nuclear plants and permit on-site inspections. In exchange for this concession, it secured a pledge from Washington for the delivery of enough oil to offset the resulting loss of nuclear power to meet the country's short-term energy needs. The government in Pyongyang also received assurances that an international consortium led by Japan and South Korea would be formed to finance the construction of light-water reactors, which produce far less plutonium than the graphite-core reactors slated for demolition, to accommodate North Korea's long-term energy requirements. The international consortium envisioned by the 1994 agreement completed arrangements for financing the construction of the light-water reactors in 1998, by which time the IAEA had verified North Korea's compliance with the denuclearization provisions of the accord. But when evidence of violations at other suspected nuclear sites surfaced, Pyongyang refused Washington's requests for unrestricted inspection of those facilities. North Korea then proceeded to fuel anxieties among its neighbors with an unannounced ballistic missile launch over Japanese territory on August 31, 1998. The country was obviously attempting to develop a delivery system for such nuclear weapons as it might produce in the future.

North Korea's foot-dragging on nuclear matters did not prevent a marked improvement of relations between the two Korean states, which remained technically at war with one another because the armistice of 1953 had never been followed up with a peace treaty. Throughout 1998, quadripartite negotiations in search of a peace settlement were conducted in Geneva among representatives of the two Koreas, the United States, and China. But the Geneva talks foundered on Kim Jong-Il's nonnegotiable demand that all U.S. military forces be withdrawn from South Korea as a precondition to an agreement. In November of the same year Pyongyang managed an uncharacteristic gesture of peace and good will toward Seoul by permitting South Korean tourists to visit a scenic mountain in the north for the first time since the formation of the two separate states in 1948. On taking office in February 1998, South Korean President Kim Dae Jung had announced a new "sunshine policy" toward the north that was designed to warm up the frosty relations between the two Korean states. In June 2000 Kim traveled to Pyongyang for a historic summit conference with North Korean leader Kim Jong II, during which the two heads of state agreed to work for reconciliation on the peninsula. This breakthrough was followed by a flurry of unprecedented cross-border contacts, from high-level meetings of military and diplomatic officials from the two countries to a series of exchange visits of families that had been separated by the 1950–1953 war. But the improvement in bilateral relations between the two Koreas was interrupted by the tough policy toward Pyongyang adopted by the new administration in Washington. President George W. Bush criticized the verification procedures of the 1994 nuclear agreement as insufficient and demanded an end to North Korea's program to develop long-range ballistic missiles, which had been revealed in the 1998 missile test over Japan. When North Korea repeated the demand that all U.S. troops be withdrawn from South Korea as a precondition to any negotiations on the verification of denuclearization or a ban on ballistic missiles, the rhetoric from Washington heated up. South Korean President Kim Dae Jung's "sunshine policy" was dealt a harsh blow during his visit to the White House in March 2001, when President Bush publicly denounced North Korea for blocking effective verification procedures and an enraged Kim Jong II responded by canceling several planned meetings and family exchanges. Bush's inclusion of North Korea with Iran and Iraq in the "axis of evil" during his January 2002 State of the Union address appeared to be the final nail in the coffin of the South Korean president's bid for détente with the north, as he served out his final year in office amid mounting domestic problems and scandals.

## The End of the Japanese Miracle

The phenomenal economic growth of Japan since the end of the U.S. occupation came to a screeching halt during the last decade of the twentieth century, when the country that had surpassed all of its competitors but the United States to become the world's second economic power could barely manage an average annual growth rate of 1 percent. The principal cause of the Japanese economic slowdown was the imprudent policies of the country's cash-laden banks and insurance companies, which squandered the savings of the country's thrifty citizens in risky loans to failing firms at home and abroad. When the rest of Asia was engulfed in a serious financial crisis in 1997–1998 (see page 383), the once reliable Japanese engine of economic growth continued to sputter and proved totally incapable of leading the region out of its malaise. The prolonged Japanese recession also coincided with a period of acute insecurity for the country caused by an increasingly assertive China and the emergence of a possible nuclear threat from North Korea. Japan's mounting security concerns and continuing economic weakness prompted Toyko to settle its long-standing differences with Washington over trade protectionism and military spending. The economic boom in the United States softened the customary American complaints about

Japanese "dumping" in the U.S. market and about Japanese barriers to U.S. exports. The old dispute about "burden sharing" in defense spending was ironed out when Japan pledged to increase its share of the costs of maintaining U.S. military forces on its territory to 70 percent by 1995. Objections in Okinawa to the intrusive U.S. military presence on the small island led to a mutually acceptable agreement to convert the large U.S. air base there to a new joint-use civilian-military airport. After renewing the Japanese-American security treaty in April 1996, the two allies signed a joint agreement the following year providing for enhanced military coordination between their armed forces in the event of conflict in the Far East. The North Korean missile launch over Japanese territory in the summer of 1998 prompted the government in Tokyo to endorse the Clinton administration's proposal for a joint program to construct a theater missile defense system in East Asia composed of submarine-based missiles capable of intercepting incoming ballistic missiles.

As Tokyo began to intensify its military cooperation with Washington in the face of what it viewed as mounting security threats from the Asian mainland, the perennial question of Japan's appropriate contribution to the maintenance of security outside Asia resurfaced. After the end of the Cold War the Japanese government modified its longstanding prohibition against the deployment of military forces abroad. Although parliamentary pressure prevented Tokyo from contributing troops to the multinational UN force in the 1991 Gulf War, Japanese mine-sweepers participated in the postwar mission to secure the sea lanes for oil tankers in the first overseas operation of the Japanese navy since World War II. In 1992 the Japanese parliament passed legislation authorizing the Self-Defense Force (SDF) to participate in UN peacekeeping operations. Japanese military engineers played a noncombatant role in the UN peacekeeping force in Cambodia in 1992–1993, the first foreign assignment of Japanese ground troops since the war. But the 1992 law authorizing peacekeeping operations was so hemmed in with qualifications that it severely restricted the SDF's role abroad. When the UN Security Council authorized an Australian peacekeeping force to operate in East Timor in September 1999 after the former Portuguese colony's vote for independence from Indonesia resulted in widespread violence, Japan stuck to the policy of "yen instead of men" that it had pursued during the Gulf War (see page 401). When a blue-helmeted UN multinational force replaced the Australians in East Timor in February 2000, Japan financed roughly half of the costs of the operation in lieu of sending troops. More than half a century after the end of the World War II, the lingering memory of that conflict in Asia continued to prevent Japan from playing a military role commensurate with its economic power and political influence. But as China expanded its nuclear arsenal and North Korea seemed intent on acquiring one, voices were raised in Japan about the need to rethink the country's longstanding reticence in matters of national defense.

## The Search for a Southeast Asian Security System

When the fault lines of the Cold War in Europe were frozen by the end of the 1940s, Asia became the battleground between the United States and the two principal Communist powers' North Korean and Vietnamese allies during the next two decades. The Sino-American rapprochement in the 1970s set in motion a revolutionary transformation in the balance of power in the region, as these two former adversaries joined forces to contain Moscow and its ally in Hanoi. Then the unexpectedly swift disintegration of the Soviet Union in 1991 removed the last strategic rationale for a major U.S. military presence in Asia. After a lengthy dispute with the government of the Philippines over the cost of maintaining U.S. bases in the country, the United States withdrew in November 1992 from its large naval facility at Subic Bay and from Clark Air Base. The closure of the Philippine facilities did not signify the disappearance of U.S. military and naval power from the region: The Bush administration had negotiated compensatory access agreements with Singapore, Indonesia, Malaysia, and Brunei for the U.S. seventh fleet, which retained its home port of Yokosuka in Japan. Some 37,000 American combat troops remained on duty in South Korea to help protect that country from its northern neighbor. But the end of the Soviet threat and the transformation of China from adversary to trading partner caused strategic planners in Washington to focus on priorities in other parts of the world.

The disappearance of the Soviet Union and the recession of U.S. power in the Western Pacific in the early 1990s left China, with its enormous size, population, economic dynamism, and military potential, as the prime candidate to fill the strategic vacuum in the region. Unlike other parts of the world, Asia had no multilateral security enterprise to manage conflict and promote stability in the region. SEATO, which had been established in February 1955 as part of Dulles's global anti-Communist alliance network, never developed into the "Asian NATO" of its creator's dreams and was officially disbanded in June 1977 after the collapse of South Vietnam. The only remaining multilateral organization in the region at the end of the Cold War was ASEAN. But this organization lacked a security component: Its purpose was exclusively political, originally to promote trust between Indonesia and Malaysia after their bitter conflict in the mid-1960s known as the "Confrontation" (see page 248) and eventually to serve as a convenient forum for consultation and cooperation among its members. What prompted this loose-knit group of states to seek a more formal relationship was the increasingly aggressive behavior of China in the region. In February 1992 Beijing reasserted its territorial claims to the Spratly Islands in the South China Sea, threatening to extend China's jurisdiction into the heart of Southeast Asia.

During the 1980s the ASEAN foreign ministers had begun to hold regular conferences with their counterparts from the industrial world to discuss economic issues of mutual interest. At one of these meetings in Singapore in May 1993, the group decided to expand its membership to include Russia, China, Vietnam, and Laos and to expand its customary agenda of economic issues to include a multilateral security dialogue. In July all eighteen governments sent their foreign ministers back to Singapore, where they laid plans for an inaugural meeting the following year of a new organization known as the ASEAN Regional Forum (ARF). The only significant achievement of its inaugural conference at Bangkok in July 1994 was the decision to convene the ARF on an annual basis. To the relief of its neighbors, China had sent its foreign minister to the new organization's founding meeting and fully supported the decision to expand its activities. But the lingering suspicions of Beijing's aggressive intentions were revived in February 1995 when it was discovered that Chinese naval forces had occupied the aptly named Mischief Reef in the South China Sea near the

Philippines and constructed buildings there that flew the Chinese flag. This incident, followed by China's test-firing of missiles near Taiwan and provocative military exercises in the Taiwan Strait in March 1996, lent an air of urgency to the ARF's ambition to become an instrument of regional security policy in Asia. But by the beginning of the new century this ambitious project fell far short of expectations: Although ASEAN rounded out its membership by admitting Vietnam in 1995, Myanmar (formerly Burma) and Laos in 1997, and Cambodia in 1999, its new Regional Forum proved unsuitable for coping with the three potential trouble spots in the area: the Korean peninsula, the Taiwan Strait, and the South China Sea.

As these three conflicts continued to fester, a financial crisis engulfed East Asia in 1997–1998 that threatened to provoke acute instability in the region that had set the world standard for sustained economic growth for the past two decades. The once booming economy of South Korea suffered the most spectacular meltdown. More than ten thousand South Korean companies (including some of the largest steel and automobile firms) failed. The country's banking system teetered on the verge of collapse. The unemployment rate doubled in a year. When the South Korean currency plunged to record lows, the IMF rushed in with a bailout package of $57 billion (its largest ever to a single country). The value of the currencies of Thailand, Indonesia, and the Philippines also dropped to dangerous levels, requiring additional emergency loans from the international lending institution. In desperate need of this emergency financial aid, those countries readily accepted the stringent conditions attached to the IMF loans: They removed restrictions on foreign trade and investment, scrapped state subsidies for inefficient national firms, and generally endeavored to open their economic systems to competition in the world market.

The financial crisis that gripped Indonesia coincided with a wave of popular discontent with the corrupt, autocratic, thirty-two-year-old regime of President Suharto. Amid the collapse of the currency, food shortages, and mounting unemployment, the increasingly unpopular leader was finally forced to resign in May 1998. His successor and protégé, former Vice President Baharuddin Josuf Habibie, was overwhelmed by the spreading economic crisis as well as by a resurgence of separatist agitation in the predominantly Catholic population of East Timor, which predominantly Muslim Indonesia had annexed in the mid-1970s (see page 250). In January 1999 Habibie surprised everyone by abruptly promising to allow the East Timorese to express at the ballot box their preference for either autonomy within Indonesia or independence. The UN-supervised referendum the following August was marred by widespread intimidation of voters by anti-independence militias, which had been armed and trained by officers of the Indonesian army who had not been consulted about the plan to allow the referendum and were intent on preserving control of the province. When 78 percent of the voters chose independence, the militias and the regular army exploded in an orgy of violence and destruction that forced more than a third of the population into exile across the border to Indonesian West Timor. The UN Security Council hastily took Australia up on its offer to dispatch a peacekeeping force to the eastern half of the island to preserve order. In February 2000 a multinational UN force of eighty-five hundred replaced the Australians and began preparations for supervising the wrecked little country's transition to independence, which was finally achieved in May 2002.

One of the reasons that Indonesia had clung so tenaciously to East Timor was the fear that its secession would set a dangerous precedent that might lead to the disintegration of the multiethnic, multilingual, multireligious collection of over seventeen thousand islands that Sukarno had welded into an artificial country. Long simmering resentments at political domination and economic exploitation by the most populous island of Java had produced armed separatist movements in Irian Jaya (West Papua), the province of Aceh in northern Sumatra (with its huge deposits of liquified natural gas), the oil-rich Riau archipelago between Sumatra and Singapore, and the island of Maluku (with its large Christian population amid a predominantly Muslim nation). By the time East Timor voted for independence, Indonesia itself had held its first free elections since the mid-1950s in June 1999. They brought to the presidency the Muslim civic leader named Abdurrahman Wahid. He faced the dual challenge of keeping the country together through concessions to the separatists and reining in the increasingly discontented army, which chafed from its humiliation in East Timor and remained skeptical about the return of unruly democracy after three decades of authoritarian rule. Wahid also was at pains to ensure Indonesia's continuing recovery from the financial crisis of the late 1990s by continuing the economic reforms that had been implemented at the end of the Suharto regime. But the new president himself succumbed to a domestic scandal that led to his impeachment in 2001 and his replacement by Megawati Sukarnoputri, the daughter of the country's founder.

The only country in Southeast Asia that refused to accept the IMF's prescriptions for liberal economic reforms amid the Asian financial crisis was Malaysia. Its veteran prime minister, Mahathir Mohamad, had long advocated a return to a set of beliefs he celebrated as "Asian values," a slogan originally popularized by former Prime Minister Lee Kuan Yew of Singapore. Designed to provide a distinctive regional identity for the diverse population groups within ASEAN, this ideology defended the Confucian principles of close family ties, social hierarchy, and political authoritarianism against the liberalism, individualism, and political pluralism of the "decadent" West. Mahathir blamed the Asian financial crisis of 1996–1997 on Western foreign exchange speculators, refused to go hat in hand to the IMF and other Western lending agencies for relief, and imposed strict exchange controls to protect the country from the destabilizing flows of international capital and the competitive pressures of the world market. The outspoken Malaysian leader's strident critique of the process of "globalization" was widely ridiculed as an atavistic yearning for a premodern era by the advocates of open markets as the engine of economic growth. But Mahathir's broadsides reflected the growing disenchantment of those nations and groups for whom the costs of globalization seemed to outweigh the benefits.

## Instability and Insecurity on the Indian Subcontinent

As we have seen, the end of the Cold War brought relative peace and stability to the countries of East and Southeast Asia—a part of the world where the two superpowers and China had jockeyed for influence, either directly or through allies and clients, since the beginning of the 1950s. In South Asia, the Soviet withdrawal from Afghanistan in 1990 removed the basis for the tacit alliance among the United States, China, and Pakistan during the 1980s in support of the Afghan resistance to

the Soviet occupation. This new strategic environment led to a major geopolitical re-
alignment on the Indian subcontinent in the early 1990s that left the Islamic Republic of Pakistan in an exceedingly advantageous position: It was relieved of the threat
from its long-standing Soviet adversary. Beyond its previously unstable northern
frontier lay an Afghanistan controlled by Islamic militants it had helped to put in
power and whose fundamentalist faith resembled that of the state that had proudly
named its capital Islamabad and subjected its citizens to Islamic religious law
(Sharia). Further to the north lay the newly independent successor states of Soviet
Central Asia with their predominantly Muslim populations. Pakistan accordingly
began to court favor with its northern neighbors on the basis of a shared devotion
to political Islam. This shift in Pakistani foreign policy alienated Islamabad from
Washington and Beijing, its two traditional allies against Moscow: The doctrines of
Islamic fundamentalism that Pakistan preached threatened to destabilize long-time
U.S. allies in the Middle East as well as China's predominantly Muslim province of
Xinjiang.

   In the meantime it had become increasingly evident that Pakistan was secretly
conducting research on nuclear weapons in an effort to catch up to its regional rival
India, which had tested an atomic bomb in 1974 but claimed ever since to have concentrated on the peaceful uses of nuclear energy. The prospect of Pakistan's acquiring what some observers dubbed the "Islamic bomb" had long been a matter of grave
concern to the United States, even in the heyday of the U.S.-Pakistani partnership
during the Cold War. As the Soviet threat receded and evidence of Pakistan's clandestine nuclear program mounted, Washington abruptly suspended its large military
aid program to Pakistan in 1990. The cutoff of U.S. military supplies and the deterioration of its old Cold War alliance with the United States removed the only remaining restraint on Pakistan's determination to develop a nuclear capability. The fraying
of the privileged link between Washington and Islamabad paved the way for an
improvement in the strained relations between the United States and India. This development was accelerated when the demise of Delhi's Soviet patron caused India to
reevaluate its foreign policy commitments. India's repudiation of its old statist economic policies and the opening of its markets to foreign trade and investment, which
had begun under Prime Minister Rajiv Gandhi before his assassination in 1991, also
facilitated an improvement of relations with the United States. By the end of the
1980s India had become an avid participant in the global economic order with its
newly privatized firms and open markets, developing a particular expertise in information technology that promised the country a bright economic future in the twenty-
first century.

   As India's economy continued to boom for the remainder of the 1990s, the escalating arms race between India and Pakistan was exacerbated by a resurgence of their
long-standing conflict over the predominantly Muslim province Kashmir on India's
northern frontier. India blamed Pakistan for supporting the separatist agitation
against India that had broken out in 1989 in the Kashmiri city of Srinegar and continued for the rest of the decade. The bitter rivalry between these two successor states
of the British Raj was rendered all the more threatening to regional security by India's
possession of a nuclear capability and Pakistan's ambition to acquire one. Both
countries had steadfastly refused to sign the Non-Proliferation Treaty and had begun

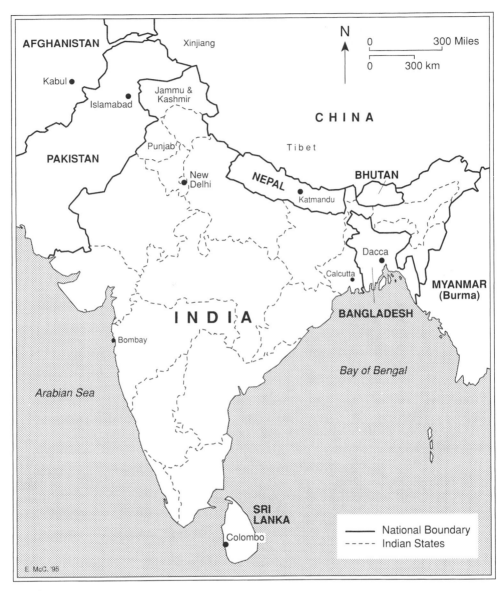

*The Indian Subcontinent*

work on short- and medium-range missiles capable of carrying nuclear warheads. Then in May 1998 India shocked the world by conducting five underground nuclear tests. Although apparently undertaken in reaction to the growing nuclear capability of India's old adversary China, the Indian explosions incited Pakistan to carry out two underground tests of its own later in the month. The United States, which had applied powerful but ineffective pressure on Pakistan to forego a tit-for-tat response to the Indian tests, joined the other major industrial countries in applying economic sanctions on the two new nuclear powers as punishment for their transgressions. But the sanctions had a minimal impact and were eventually removed. The select nuclear club comprising the five permanent members of the UN Security Council had been expanded to seven, with the inclusion of two regional rivals who had fought three conventional wars against each other since their independence in 1947 and whose relations with one another continued to be marked by tension and hostility.

The nuclearization of the Indian subcontinent provided a powerful incentive for the two antagonists in the region to seek an improvement in relations to avert a catastrophe. Hopes for détente soared in February 1999 when Indian Prime Minister Atal Behari Vajpayee, head of the Hindu Nationalist Bharatiya Janata Party that had taken power in 1998 from the Congress Party, met with his Pakistani counterpart Nawaz Sharif in the Pakistani city of Lahore. The resulting Lahore Declaration committed the two countries to noninterference in each other's affairs and proposed future discussions on the two sticky issues of nuclear weapons and Kashmir. But the "spirit of Lahore" evaporated within a few months of that landmark meeting. India test-fired an intermediate-range ballistic missile and Pakistan promptly followed suit. In May the Indian army discovered the presence of some two thousand armed Muslim guerrillas near the village of Kargil on the Indian side of the so-called Line of Control, the cease-fire line in Kashmir that had been established after the first conflict between the two successor states of British India in 1947–1998 and reaffirmed after the Indo-Pakistani war of 1971. Although implausibly denying any connection with the intruders, Pakistan hailed them as Islamic "freedom fighters" like the Mujaheddin that had defeated the Russians in Afghanistan. As India launched air strikes against the invaders, Pakistan was roundly condemned by its former allies in Washington and Beijing for its barely concealed bid to stir up the Kashmir pot. The fighting near Lahore finally wound down in the summer, leaving over 1,000 people dead and several thousand injured. A three-day summit meeting in July 2001 between Indian Prime Minister Vajpayee and General Pervez Musharraf, who had ousted Pakistani Prime Minister Sharif in a bloodless coup in October 1999, failed to prevent the relations between India and Pakistan from reaching their lowest point since the 1971 war.

The September 11, 2001, attacks against the United States had powerful repercussions on the Indian subcontinent. The Bush administration enlisted Pakistan as its principal ally in the region during its military campaign against the al-Qaeda organization and the Taliban regime in Afghanistan that harbored it (see page 366). Washington's need for Islamabad's support in the anti-terrorist campaign in Afghanistan prompted the Bush administration to promote reconciliation between Pakistan and India in order to concentrate on the priority of suppressing al-Qaeda and the Taliban. But the simmering dispute in Kashmir blew up once again to drive the two countries to the brink of war. In December five armed gunmen belonging to Pakistani-based groups active in the Kashmir insurrection attacked the Indian parliament building in New Delhi, killing nine Indian security agents. The Indian government responded by severing all road, railroad, and airline connections to Pakistan, increasing its military forces along the border with Pakistan and along the Line of Control. Attentive to pressure from his own Hindu nationalist party, Vajpayee demanded that Musharraf terminate all support for the insurrection in Kashmir, stem the flow of Muslim extremists into the province, and hand over twenty Pakistanis on India's list of terrorists. Unwilling to antagonize Islamic militants at home (including some within his own military and security forces), the Pakistani leader refused to repudiate the insurgency in Kashmir or to transfer the suspected terrorists. India's indignant denunciation of Pakistan's support for Islamic terrorism in Kashmir proved highly embarrassing to the Bush administration, which conducted its campaign against international terrorism and states that sponsor it with Pakistan as one of its most valued allies. Throughout the spring and summer of 2002, officials in both countries openly discussed the possibility of resorting to nuclear weapons in a military conflict while foreign leaders and diplomats bent their efforts to persuade the two governments to pull back from the brink.

THIRTEEN

# Diplomacy and War
# in the Middle East

## The Unfolding of the Arab-Israeli "Peace Process"

The Yom Kippur War of October 1973 between Israel and the neighboring Arab states precipitated a fundamental transformation of the geopolitical situation in the Middle East: The United States became actively engaged for the first time in the pursuit of a diplomatic settlement of the Arab-Israeli conflict. As we have seen, President Nixon intervened in the 1973 war with the intention of preventing either side from achieving a decisive victory in order to enhance the prospects of a U.S.-sponsored negotiated peace. Since each of the warring parties was beholden to the United States for rescuing it from possible defeat, Secretary of State Kissinger exploited this favorable opportunity for American diplomacy by personally brokering an Egyptian-Israeli disengagement agreement in January 1974 that resulted in a partial Israeli pullback from the Sinai Peninsula. Egyptian president Anwar al-Sadat had come to realize that his alliance with the Soviet Union would not help him achieve his goal of recovering all of the Sinai from Israel, but that cooperation with the United States might. He therefore decided to burn his bridges to Moscow. On March 15, 1976, Sadat abrogated the 1971 Soviet-Egyptian Friendship Treaty and a month later summarily revoked Soviet naval access to Egyptian ports on the Mediterranean and Red Seas. Moscow retaliated by suspending weapons deliveries to Cairo. The United States stepped in to provide Egypt with desperately needed economic assistance, but refused to furnish much military aid to replace the flow of Soviet weapons as long as Egypt maintained its unaccommodating posture toward Israel. In the meantime the prospects for a settlement of the Arab-Israeli conflict had been complicated in 1974 when an Arab summit in Rabat, Morocco, unanimously declared that the PLO was the "sole legitimate representative" of the Palestinian people despite Israel's adamant refusal to negotiate with that organization because of its terrorist attacks.

The Carter administration at first seemed poised to depart both from Kissinger's step-by-step approach to a Middle East peace as well as from his refusal to allow a Soviet role in the peace process. Brezhnev had long insisted that Moscow deserved such a role by virtue of its longstanding support for Egypt, Syria, Iraq, and the PLO.

In a bid to soothe Soviet sensitivities, Secretary of State Vance reversed Kissinger's exclusionary policy by signing a joint agreement with Gromyko in October 1977 endorsing a comprehensive settlement of the Arab-Israeli dispute, which included an eventual Israeli withdrawal to the pre-1967 borders and recognition of the "legitimate rights of the Palestinian people." They agreed to reconvene by the end of the year the Middle East peace conference that had opened briefly to Geneva in December 1973 under joint Soviet-American chairmanship but had been superseded by Kissinger's one-man bid to reach a separate bilateral settlement between Israel and Egypt.

But before the comprehensive talks in Geneva got underway, Sadat decided to take matters into his own hands to secure Egypt's special goals. In a daring improvisation designed to jump-start the stalled peace process, the Egyptian president wangled an invitation to visit Israel from the new right-wing government of Menachem Begin. On November 19, 1977, he flew to Jerusalem and delivered a historic speech to the Israeli parliament in which he declared his willingness to accept the existence of the Jewish state and live in peace with it. Begin promptly returned the visit by meeting with Sadat in Ismailia, Egypt, in December. The hard-line Israeli prime minister indicated that while he would never accept a Palestinian state in the West Bank and Gaza, which Sadat had proposed in order to reassure the other Arab states that he was attentive to Palestinian concerns, he would be willing to discuss the future political status of the Sinai Peninsula. The prospect of ending the humiliating Israeli military occupation of the Egyptian territory was all that Sadat needed to keep the lines of communication to Begin open. The Israeli leader in turn was hopeful of trading land (the Sinai) for peace (with Egypt) without budging an inch on the inadmissible subject of Palestinian sovereignty on the West Bank and Gaza. Although Sadat's dramatic bid for a bilateral deal with Israel was entirely his own idea, Soviet leaders suspected another American plot to exclude them from the region. These suspicions appeared to be confirmed as Sadat openly aligned with the United States.

After witnessing the extraordinary thaw in relations between Israel and Egypt, President Carter abandoned his earlier inclination to cosponsor with the Soviet Union a comprehensive Middle East settlement at Geneva. He decided instead to inject himself directly into the bilateral talks between Cairo and Jerusalem. In September 1978 Sadat and Begin accepted Carter's offer of mediation and his invitation to meet with him at the presidential retreat at Camp David. After thirteen days of hard bargaining in the Maryland mountains the two leaders finally consented, with some firm prodding by their American host, to two framework agreements for future peace treaties. The first was a bilateral understanding between Egypt and Israel, the details of which were to be worked out within three months: Begin reluctantly sacrificed Israel's hard-won strategic depth in the Sinai by agreeing to a phased withdrawal of Israeli military forces from the peninsula over three years. In exchange Sadat promised the restoration of free passage for Israeli ships through the Suez Canal and formal recognition of the Jewish state's right to exist. The second agreement reflected the Egyptian president's desire to allay the suspicions of the Palestinians and their supporters in the other Arab states that Egypt was only looking after its own national interests. It called for negotiations among Egypt, Jordan, Israel, and "representatives of the Palestinian people" (but not the PLO) to establish some form of autonomy for the eight hundred thousand Arabs residing in the West Bank and the five hundred thousand in Gaza. The two most contentious issues in the Arab-Israeli conflict, the political status of Jerusalem and the Golan Heights, were omitted entirely from what came to be known as the Camp David Accords. After six months of negotiations Sadat and Begin finally appeared on the White House lawn and, with President Jimmy Carter serving as official witness, signed an Egyptian-Israeli peace treaty on March 26, 1979.

The Soviet Union's ambitions in the Middle East were temporarily thwarted by the bilateral agreement between Cairo and Jerusalem, the loss of its Egyptian bases, and the emergence of the United States as the broker of peace in the region. Moscow sought to compensate for its eviction from Egypt by expanding military assistance to its other two Mideast clients, Syria and Iraq, both of which took the lead in isolating Egypt within the Arab world. Most of the Arab states denounced Sadat's separate peace with the Jewish state as a selfish betrayal of the Arab cause in general and the Palestinian cause in particular. Shortly after the Egyptian president signed the peace treaty with Begin in Washington, Egypt was expelled from the Arab League and nineteen of the twenty-one Arab states (all save Egypt's friends Sudan and Oman) severed diplomatic relations with Cairo. The Egyptian-Israeli negotiations on autonomy for the West Bank and Gaza got nowhere. They were dismissed as a sham and boycotted by local Palestinian leaders as well as by the government of Jordan (in deference to the sentiments of its majority Palestinian population). The Begin government dashed another Palestinian aspiration in 1980 by formally designating the whole of Jerusalem—including the predominately Arab eastern half of the city that the PLO envisioned as the capital of an independent Palestine—as the capital of the Jewish state.

During the last year of Carter's presidency his preoccupation with the Iran hostage crisis prevented Washington from resuming its energetic role in the Arab-Israeli peace process. Then the Egyptian-Israeli agreement was suddenly brought into question when President Sadat was assassinated on October 6, 1981 by a fanatical Muslim opponent of the Camp David agreement. To the relief of the Israeli government Sadat's successor, Hosni Mubarak, the former commander of the Egyptian air force and vice president since 1975, promptly pledged to honor the peace treaty with Israel. This enabled the Sinai disengagement agreement to proceed according to schedule. While Mubarak continually reaffirmed his predecessor's policy of peaceful relations with Israel, the final Israeli withdrawal from the Sinai took place on April 25, 1982. But progress toward a comprehensive settlement in the Middle East was dead in the water. The Begin government in Jerusalem, which won a resounding victory in the elections of 1981, resumed the tough policy toward Arab states other than Egypt. In June of that year, Israeli bombers destroyed an Iraqi nuclear reactor near Baghdad to prevent Israel's most determined adversary from acquiring a nuclear capability to back up its aggressive rhetoric. In December Begin outraged Syrian president Hafez al-Assad by formally annexing the Golan Heights, which many hoped could serve as a future "land-for-peace" deal with Syria modeled on the Israeli-Egyptian Sinai agreement. These and other actions suggested that Israel's withdrawal from the Sinai was its final concession rather than the first step in a plan to establish peaceful relations with its other Arab neighbors.

Begin was particularly intent on ensuring that the autonomy talks for the West Bank envisioned by the peace treaty would not undermine Israel's control of that territory. The political faction he headed regarded the West Bank (or Judea and Samaria, the biblical name for the area he insisted on using) not as land to be traded for peace like the Sinai but rather as an integral part of historic Israel to be retained at all costs. The West Bank would thereafter become the principal stumbling block to a peace settlement. The conquest of the territory in the 1967 war had provided additional security to Israel, but it also created the excruciating dilemma of how to treat the newly acquired land: Annexation of the West Bank with its eight hundred thousand Arab inhabitants would eventually threaten the Jewish character of Israel in light of the Palestinians' higher birth rate. How could Israel remain a Jewish state once a majority of its citizenry was no longer Jewish? The alternative of annexing the area while denying citizenship to the Palestinians in order to preserve a Jewish political majority would betray the country's democratic traditions.

The Begin government decided to bolster Israel's claim to the West Bank by promoting the expansion of Jewish settlements there (and, to a lesser extent, in Gaza and the Golan Heights). In the decade between the Six Day War of 1967 and the advent of Begin's Likud coalition government in 1977, some eighty-five such settlements had sprouted among Arab towns in the occupied territories. Begin approved twenty-one more settlements in 1980 and 1981, bringing the total number of Jewish inhabitants to about 110,000 in a region in which Jews controlled about a third of the land. As the Jewish settlers established their positions in the West Bank, its Palestinian inhabitants became more and more dependent on the Israeli economy for their livelihood. When large landowners in the area were forced to stop growing crops that competed with Israeli farm products, thousands of unemployed Palestinian agricultural laborers took unskilled jobs in Israel and greatly improved their standard of living. But the economic benefits of incorporation within the Israeli economy were not accompanied by political gains for the Palestinians. When municipal elections held in the West Bank in April 1976 produced mayors sympathetic to the PLO who loudly protested the denial of their people's rights, most were removed or deported by the Israeli authorities. Begin continued this harsh treatment of Palestinian political activism in the early 1980s.

According to the Camp David Accords and the subsequent peace treaty, Israel was committed to negotiating with non-PLO Palestinian representatives over the future of the occupied territories and to grant a measure of autonomy to the region for a five-year interim period pending agreement on the "final status" of the territories. But the continuing construction of the permanent Jewish settlements and the removal of elected Arab mayors in several West Bank cities suggested that the Begin government had no intention of honoring the Camp David pledge to recognize the "legitimate rights of the Palestinian people and their just demands." This was especially true if such a conciliatory policy would in any way enhance the standing of the PLO, which most Israeli leaders regarded as a terrorist organization rather than a legitimate political movement and potential negotiating partner with which one could bargain.

The headquarters of the PLO were located in Beirut, Lebanon, where it had been established in the early 1970s after King Hussein had evicted Arafat and his entourage from their bases in Jordan in 1970–1971 (see page 170). The arrival of the PLO and its fighters brought to an end two unique advantages that Lebanon had enjoyed in the turbulent region within which it was located. The first of those advantages was its relative isolation from the unending cycle of military conflict between its Israeli neighbor and the other Arab states. The second was the relative political harmony that had been preserved between its Muslim and Christian inhabitants, who had figured out how to coexist in a unique power-sharing arrangement for thirty years after World War II (see page 158). But in the spring of 1975 a bloody conflict erupted in Lebanon between the Maronite Christian militias, which resented the arrival of the Palestinians, and a loose-knit collection of Muslims known as the Lebanese National Movement that was soon joined by the PLO. When the official Lebanese army disintegrated and most of its soldiers enlisted in one of the many rival militias that roamed the country, a full-fledged civil war in Lebanon had begun.

As the Christian faction began to falter in the spring of 1976, Syrian President Hafez al-Assad surprised many observers by dispatching his army to rescue the Christian-dominated Lebanese government and its militias from certain defeat at the hands of the Muslim militias and the PLO. Assad apparently intervened to prevent the accession of a coalition of radical Muslims and the PLO that would be independent of Syrian control. After the Muslim League arranged a cease-fire in October 1976, a contingent of some forty thousand Syrian troops remained in northeastern Lebanon to separate the contending factions and preserve order. The Syrians permitted the PLO to train its fighters in southern Lebanon, from where they would occasionally unleash artillery barrages on the Galilee plain of northern Israel and mount raids across the border. After a PLO terrorist attack near the northern Israeli city of Haifa, Begin sent ground forces into southern Lebanon in March 1978 to rout the PLO from its bases there. The Israelis withdrew after three months, leaving behind a narrow buffer zone manned by a Christian militia (called the South Lebanon Army) they had trained and armed as well as a U.N. contingent (the United Nations Interim Forces in Lebanon, or UNIFIL). But neither Israel's Christian allies nor UNIFIL could prevent the PLO from regrouping in southern Lebanon, reorganizing its commando units, and resuming its shelling of Galilee.

These attacks gave the Israeli government the excuse it needed to employ military force against its enemies to the north. Israel had not hesitated to attack the PLO by air, bombarding Arafat's offices in Beirut in July 1980 and Palestinian refugee camps throughout Lebanon. But in the early summer of 1982 the Begin government decided on a full-scale ground invasion of Lebanon that was designed to achieve two critical objectives: The first was to establish once and for all a secure northern border that would prevent Palestinian artillery fire and commando raids; the second was to smash the political and military infrastructure of the PLO in Lebanon, so that Israel could deal with moderate Palestinian rivals to the PLO to reach an acceptable settlement for the West Bank. Apparently believing that he had been given the green light by U.S. Secretary of State Alexander Haig, Begin dispatched about 60,000 Israeli infantry troops accompanied by more than 500 tanks and 90 F-15 and F-16 jet fighters across the Lebanese frontier on June 6, 1982. The Israeli ground forces and tank columns promptly overran the PLO strongholds in southern Lebanon, as the government in Jerusalem announced that the purpose of the invasion was to expel the PLO fighters from the area and create an expanded 25-mile wide security zone to protect Israel's northern frontier.

But Israeli Defense Minister Ariel Sharon had a more ambitious goal in mind. He ordered the invasion force to continue its northward advance toward West Beirut, where PLO headquarters were located. As the Israeli infantry and armored columns approached the Lebanese capital, the Israeli air force took the precaution of removing the threat of Syrian intervention. Its U.S.-built jet fighters armed with air-to-surface missiles wiped out all of the Soviet-built Syrian surface-to-air missile sites that Assad had deployed in the Bekaa Valley of eastern Lebanon; the Israeli planes also used their American Sidewinder air-to-air missiles to destroy almost half of Syria's Soviet-built MiG jet fighters. For the next two months Israeli forces besieged Beirut, bombing and shelling the western part of the city in an effort to destroy the PLO leadership.

The Reagan administration responded with stern disapproval of the Israeli actions in Lebanon. In August the United States organized an American, French, and Italian rescue operation to oversee the evacuation of PLO officials and fighters from Beirut, and later imposed a temporary embargo on future sales of F-16 fighter planes to Israel to signal its displeasure. An additional sign of Washington's irritation with Jerusalem came on September 1, 1982, when President Reagan unveiled a new proposal to resolve the Palestinian-Israeli conflict after it had become evident that the autonomy talks mandated by the Camp David Accord had reached a dead end. The Reagan initiative rejected both extremes of an independent Palestinian state and an Israeli annexation of the West Bank and Gaza in favor of a "Jordanian solution": Palestinian self-rule in association with Hussein's kingdom. The Reagan Plan was doomed from the very beginning. The Israelis rejected it despite private assurances from Washington that existing Israeli settlements in the occupied territories could remain. Arafat and the leaders of other Arab states reiterated their long-standing demand for a fully independent Palestinian state under PLO leadership. When dissident factions within the Palestinian movement drove Arafat from his base in Northern Lebanon in late 1983, the resilient Palestinian leader relocated his headquarters to Tunis.

In the meantime the leader of the Maronite Christian forces in Lebanon, Bashir Gemayel, was elected president of the devastated country. Detested by the Palestinians as an Israeli stooge, Gemayel was assassinated on September 14. Israeli military forces promptly reoccupied West Beirut to preserve order as tensions mounted throughout the country. Three days later Israeli military authorities permitted Maronite Christian gunmen to enter two Palestinian refugee camps, where they avenged Gemayel's murder by massacring about eight hundred unarmed civilians. President Reagan immediately ordered the return of the multinational military contingent to protect the Palestinians from Christian Lebanese wrath. But the reappearance of U.S., French, and Italian peacekeeping forces antagonized the Shiite Muslims located in the southern part of Lebanon, who suspected the Westerners of supporting Christian predominance there. Syrian President Hafez al-Assad, a Shiite of the Alawi sect who maintained some fifty thousand troops in the northeastern part of the country to protect Syrian interests, also resented the Western military presence as a threat to his hegemonic ambitions in the country. On October 23, 1983, a car filled with explosives blew up a U.S. marine barracks outside Beirut, killing 247 men. Unwilling to put further American lives at risk, Reagan withdrew U.S. military forces from Lebanon in March 1984 and abandoned all hope of restoring peace and security in that troubled country.

Israel too had become disillusioned with its military operation in Lebanon, which had succeeded in evicting the PLO but failed to restore order and stability beyond its northern border. From the summer of 1984 to the summer of 1985, a coalition government in Jerusalem led by Labor party leader Shimon Peres removed all Israeli troops from Lebanon (except for the so-called security zone in the south where units remained to support the local Christian militia there). With Syrian forces operating in the northeast, Israeli troops ensconced in the south, and various sectarian militias patrolling other areas, the central Lebanese government headed by Amin Gemayel, brother of the slain Christian leader, had lost effective political control of the country. By the mid-1980s, the optimism engendered by the Camp David Accord gave way to a bleak pessimism about the prospects of reaching a mutually acceptable resolution of the Israeli-Palestinian problem. Not a single other Arab state joined Egypt in acknowledging Israel's right to exist. The negotiations concerning Palestinian autonomy in the occupied territories that had begun in August 1979 remained stalemated, while successive Israeli governments granted tax subsidies and low-interest loans to promote new Jewish settlements on the West Bank. The bilateral agreement between Israel and Egypt, which brought security for the Jewish state along its western border and restored the Sinai to Egyptian control, seemed to be the end rather than the beginning of the "peace process" in the Middle East.

## The Iranian Revolution, the Iran-Iraq War, and the Intifada

As we have seen, the regime of Shah Mohammed Reza Pahlevi in Iran had became a staunch U.S. ally after the failure of a Soviet-backed secessionist in its northernmost province in 1946. In 1953 the CIA helped to restore the shah to power after he had fled into exile amid a bitter political dispute with the nationalist politician Mohammed Mossadegh, who had sought to nationalize the British and American oil companies that exploited the country's abundant petroleum reserves (see page 101). By the mid-1950s American firms had acquired equal control of Iranian oil production with the British-owned Anglo-Iranian Oil Company through an arrangement that brought substantial oil royalties to the shah's treasury. Iran continued to play an active role in the U.S. campaign to contain Soviet expansion in South Asia, joining the Baghdad Pact (later renamed the Central Treaty Organization) in 1955 and providing U.S. intelligence with valuable electronic surveillance bases on the Soviet border.

In the early 1970s the Nixon administration began to equip the shah's military and naval forces with sophisticated weapons to enable Iran to replace Great Britain, which had recently removed its last remaining naval units from the Persian Gulf, as the agent of stability in that economically and strategically important region. Then the phenomenal increase in world oil prices after the 1973 embargo left Iran awash in petrodollars, which the shah used both to build up his army and to sponsor an ambitious program of economic modernization. Within a few years, Iran's newfound wealth from oil exports paradoxically proved to be the shah's undoing: Profligate

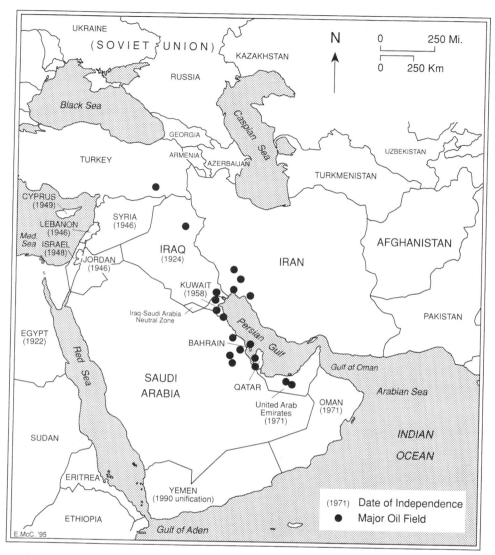

*The Middle East at the Beginning of the Twenty-First Century*

government spending on wasteful public works programs generated a hyperinflation that wiped out the savings of retirees and others living on fixed incomes, turning them into bitter opponents of the regime. The neglect of agriculture in this reckless bid for rapid industrialization wreaked havoc with impoverished small landowners and their farm workers, forcing them to migrate to Teheran and other big cities that lacked adequate social services to accommodate them. The local merchants of the bazaar resented the expanding influence of multinational (but mainly American) corporations on the Iranian economy. The influx of Western technicians, business-people, and advisers with their modern customs and dress offended the conservative

Shiite Muslim clergy. The urban intelligentsia was alienated by the increasingly repressive policies of the regime and its hated secret police, the SAVAK, which had
imprisoned thousands of political dissidents. Everyone was disgusted by the widespread corruption and lavish lifestyle of the shah's entourage.

In January 1979 this mélange of popular grievances erupted in massive street
demonstrations in several Iranian cities, which prompted the shah to leave the country in order to stave off a revolution. But his last-minute attempt to turn over power
to a hand-picked successor failed. The octogenarian Shiite clerical leader Ayatollah
Ruhollah Khomeini, who had been exiled by the shah for his vociferous opposition
to the regime and had become the leading spokesperson for the opposition, returned
to Iran in February and assumed power amid universal acclaim. The revered Ayatollah
proceeded to transform the country from a secular, modernizing monarchy into a fundamentalist Islamic Republic. The new government forbade the "decadent" Western-
style behavior long tolerated by the shah, such as immodest attire for women and
the consumption of alcohol. All of the strands of cooperation that had connected
Iran to the United States were abruptly severed. The extensive American economic
interests in the country were confiscated. U.S. military and intelligence personnel
were expelled and their electronic surveillance facilities on the Soviet border were
closed. All of the pro-American members of the old political and military elite that
had not been able to escape into exile were either jailed or executed. Iran withdrew
from the U.S.-sponsored Central Treaty Organization (CENTO), causing the rapid
demise of that relic of the Eisenhower-Dulles era. Washington was put on notice that
Teheran would no longer play the role of American surrogate in the Persian Gulf that
Nixon had assigned to it, nor even retain a diplomatically correct relationship with
the United States. On the contrary, Iran would take the lead in organizing Islamic
groups throughout the Middle East in opposition to what Khomeini regularly referred
to as "the Great Satan."

The Iranian revolution caught both superpowers completely by surprise. The
Carter administration had been so confident of the shah's continued survival that it
felt free to exert pressure on him to liberalize his autocratic political system as part of
its global campaign for human rights. The anti-American orientation of the new
regime in Teheran may have given the leaders in the Kremlin some satisfaction, but
if so it was short-lived. The Ayatollah Khomeini denounced atheistic Communism
and decadent capitalism with equal vehemence. His campaign to export the principles of Islamic fundamentalism posed a potential threat to Moscow's authority in the
Islamic republics of Soviet Central Asia. Potential victims of "Khomeinism" in the
Middle East included not only pro-Western governments in Saudi Arabia and Egypt
but also such Soviet clients as the secular Baathist regimes of Syria and Iraq. So the
Kremlin was in no position to gloat over or profit from the ejection of its Cold War
adversary from Iran.

Nevertheless, it was the United States that suffered the most devastating consequences of the Iranian revolution during the last year of Jimmy Carter's presidency.
When the ex-shah left his temporary refuge in Mexico to seek medical treatment for
cancer in the United States, Iranian militants suspected a U.S. plot to restore him to
his throne similar to the coup that the CIA had facilitated in 1953. Hundreds of them
stormed the American embassy in Teheran on November 4, 1979, and took sixty-

nine diplomatic and consular personnel hostage in an effort to blackmail the U.S. government into extraditing the deposed monarch to Iran for trial. After releasing sixteen female and African American hostages in December as a gesture of good will, the militants (with the tacit consent of the Iranian government) held the remaining fifty-three even after the shah's death in July 1980. Relations between Washington and Teheran degenerated, while the Iran hostage crisis consumed the Carter administration for the rest of its term. The U.S. government prohibited all American trade with Iran, froze $12 billion worth of Iranian assets in U.S. banks, and mounted an abortive rescue mission in April 1980, all to no avail. The hostages remained in captivity until they were set free on the very day Carter turned the White House over to Ronald Reagan in January 1981. A wave of anti-American sentiment swept across the Muslim world, as sympathizers of the Iranian revolution attacked United States diplomatic missions from Libya to Pakistan.

During his exile in southern Iraq, the Ayatollah Khomeini had forged strong connections with the Shiite Muslims in the southern part of that country. They constituted 55 percent of the Iraqi population but were excluded from power by the Sunni leadership that dominated the secularist Baath ruling party in Baghdad. Saddam Hussein, who had risen through the Baath hierarchy to become president in 1979 after executing his principal rivals, began to worry that Khomeini's fundamentalist brand of Shiite Islam might spread to Iraq and destabilize the country by inciting its Shiite majority to revolt. After arresting Shiite clerics in southern Iraq and then expelling all Shiites of Iranian origin, Hussein revived an old border dispute between the two countries at the head of the Persian Gulf in 1980. In September 1980 Hussein abrogated the Algiers Agreement of 1975, which had settled the border conflict largely in Iran's favor, and sent Iraqi forces across the Iranian frontier along a three-hundred-mile front.

Hussein anticipated a rapid victory because of Iran's internal political instability, the disarray of its army after the wholesale purges of the shah's officer corps, and the international isolation of Khomeini's regime. But after Iraqi troops drove deep into Iranian territory and attained their maximum advance by the spring of 1981, the Iranian forces managed to mount a ferocious counterattack in the air and then on the ground. The result was a long stalemate, punctuated by bloody offensives and counteroffensives as well as devastating attacks on the petroleum production facilities of the two belligerents. Iraq had profited from the dramatic increase of oil revenues during the second half of the 1970s to build up what would soon become the world's fifth largest military force, purchasing state-of-the-art weapons from the Soviet Union and France. When Iraq's oil revenues began to decline in 1982 because of oversupply on the world market and the destruction of its production facilities, Saddam Hussein began to borrow heavily from his Arab supporters in the Persian Gulf (principally Saudi Arabia, Kuwait, and the United Arab Emirates). But Hussein's bid to unite the Arab world behind his country's war against non-Arab Iran was not entirely successful. Syria's President Hafez al-Assad, who also presided over a secular Baath Arab regime, threw its support to the non-Arab, Islamic regime in Iran because Assad considered Saddam Hussein his chief rival for leadership in the Arab world. The radical governments of Algeria, Libya, and South Yemen split with their Arab partners and backed Iran as well.

The Iranian government compensated for the inferiority of its military leadership and weaponry by whipping its troops into a frenzy of patriotic enthusiasm, declaring the conflict with secularist Iraq a *jihad* (Islamic holy war) and hurling young soldiers against entrenched Iraqi positions in "human wave" assaults that reminded some analysts of the suicidal offensives of the Somme and Passchendaele. Another feature of the Iran-Iraq War that was reminiscent of World War I was the Iraqi army's employment of chemical warfare agents such as mustard gas, first against the Kurdish population of the north (which had sided with the Iranians against its own government) and later on Iranian civilians. In the spring of 1985 Iran launched a major offensive toward the border, to which Iraq responded by conducting bombing raids on Teheran and other Iranian cities. When Iran retaliated with missile attacks against Baghdad, the "war of the cities" became a tragic component of the conflict as civilians perished in increasing numbers.

Since Western Europe and Japan had become extremely dependent on Persian Gulf oil, the world's major powers were inevitably drawn into the bloody confrontation between the region's two rival powers. The Soviet Union supported its long-time ally Iraq with weapons, as did France (which had extensive oil interests in the country). The Reagan administration in Washington "tilted" in favor of Iraq during the war because of the multitude of American grievances against Iran it had inherited from the Carter years. But Washington also secretly sold U.S. and Israeli weapons to Teheran, in the hopes of strengthening moderate factions within the Iranian leadership and securing the release of Americans held hostage in Lebanon by Iranian-backed Shiite groups. When Iran began to attack oil tankers in the Gulf as part of its campaign against Iraq, the U.S. navy began to reflag and escort Kuwaiti tankers in 1987 to assert the principle of freedom of navigation. All of these developments demonstrated that the Persian Gulf was too vital a region for the major world powers to remain disengaged from the destructive combat there.

As the threat of foreign involvement in the war increased, the morale of the Iranian army suddenly deteriorated. Although Iran had earlier responded to Iraqi requests for a cease-fire with the patently unacceptable proviso that Saddam Hussein be removed from power, it finally agreed to a truce without conditions in July 1988. As a United Nations observer team arrived the following month to supervise the cease-fire, the two belligerents toted up the costs of the eight-year war: About 300,000 Iranians and 135,000 Iraqis perished, while about 750,000 on both sides sustained serious injuries. The total direct and indirect costs of the conflict were estimated at $600 billion for Iran and $400 billion for Iraq. Despite the horrendous human and material losses on both sides, the war ended essentially in a stalemate, with neither country gaining territory, resources, or population as a reward for its enormous sacrifices.

While the Iran-Iraq War riveted the attention of the Arab governments, the plight of the Palestinians in the occupied territories was largely forgotten. An entire generation of Palestinian youth had grown up in Gaza and the West Bank under the Israeli occupation, bridling under the stringent restrictions on their civil liberties and resentful of their dependence on Israel for jobs. Bitter at the Arab states for ignoring their plight and disillusioned with the PLO for its failure to secure Palestinian self-determination, young Palestinians in the occupied territories began in the mid-1980s to take out their frustrations on the Israeli Defense Force and the Israeli settlers in isolated acts of violence. Then on December 9, 1987, an automobile accident in which four Palestinians were killed by an Israeli vehicle sparked a spontaneous popular uprising that came to be known as the Intifada, or "shaking off." During the next year more than 150 Palestinians were killed and 11,500 were wounded in a series of pitched battles between rock-throwing youths and Israeli military forces.

Caught completely off guard by the insurrection in the occupied territories, Arafat skillfully co-opted the Intifada's disorganized leadership and exploited widespread international revulsion at the harsh Israeli actions in the West Bank and Gaza to revive his organization's flagging fortunes. While the hard-line Likud government of Israeli Prime Minister Yitzhak Shamir defiantly declined to negotiate with what it regarded as a terrorist organization dedicated to the destruction of the Jewish state, the PLO leader mounted a spirited diplomatic initiative on behalf of the Palestinian cause. In the summer of 1988 his spokespersons publicly broached for the first time the idea of a Palestinian state confined to the West Bank and Gaza that would coexist with Israel within its pre-1967 borders. The following November at the Arab League summit meeting in Algiers, the PLO's "parliament-in-exile," the Palestine National Council (PNC), officially endorsed UN Resolution 242 as the basis for a Middle East settlement and proclaimed the establishment of an independent Palestinian state in the West Bank and Gaza. Within three days all of the Arab and Muslim nations of the world extended formal diplomatic recognition to the PLO's "government in exile" in Tunis. Arafat hoped to profit from widespread American criticism of Israel's crackdown in the occupied territories to open a dialogue with Washington, with a view to securing its assistance in pressuring the recalcitrant Shamir into negotiating with the PLO. But the United States had long insisted on avoiding all contact with Arafat's organization as long as it refused to renounce terrorism as a means of achieving its political objectives. So the Palestinian leader was prompted to take a dramatic step at a press conference in Geneva in December 1988, when he explicitly recognized Israel's right to exist in peace and security and formally renounced terrorism as a means of achieving Palestinian statehood. U.S. Secretary of State George Shultz responded to this significant gesture by announcing that his government would open direct negotiations with the PLO in Tunis. The following year the Arab League signaled its de facto acceptance of the prospect of negotiations with Israel by readmitting Egypt despite its 1979 peace treaty with the Jewish state. By the end of the decade the prospects for a peaceful settlement in the Middle East seemed better than at any time since the Israeli invasion of Lebanon in 1982.

## The Context and Consequences of the Gulf War

The one Arab country that refused to participate in this movement in favor of a diplomatic solution to the Israeli-Palestinian conflict was Iraq. After the cease-fire in the Iran-Iraq War in 1988, Iraqi President Saddam Hussein began to build up his battle-seasoned army for what some observers believed would be some kind of provocative military action against Israel. But on August 2, 1990, Iraqi forces unexpectedly invaded the oil-rich emirate of Kuwait at the mouth of the Persian Gulf. When its ruling al-Sabah family fled to Saudi Arabia, Hussein announced the annexation of

Kuwait two days later. Iraq's longstanding territorial claims against Kuwait had been reinforced by new grievances: Saddam Hussein accused the al-Sabahs of devastating Iraq's economy by expanding oil production to depress the world price of his country's only source of export earnings and of secretly diverting oil from Iraq's wells. Most important of all, the Iraqi leader indignantly denounced Kuwait for refusing to forgive the huge debt that Iraq had incurred to finance its costly war with Iran. But whatever the cause of the Iraqi action, its repercussions were far-reaching: Hussein had amassed sufficient military forces and equipment in Kuwait and southern Iraq to invade the conservative oil monarchy of Saudi Arabia. With Iraq in control of Kuwait and Saudi Arabia, Saddam Hussein would possess more than 40 percent of the world's oil reserves.

The Bush administration in Washington took the lead in organizing the international response to the Iraqi invasion and was pleased to receive support from an unexpected source: The Soviet Union, Iraq's longtime ally and supplier during the Cold War, endorsed collective action in response to the invasion of Kuwait because of President Gorbachev's new policy of cooperation with the West. As a result the United Nations Security Council unanimously approved trade sanctions against Iraq on August 9. Within weeks a multinational naval force had entered the Persian Gulf to enforce the sanctions with a de facto blockade. Over fifty thousand U.S. air and ground forces together with their supplies were air- and sea-lifted to Saudi Arabia in operation "Desert Shield" to protect that oil-rich kingdom from an Iraqi attack. When the trade sanctions and intense diplomatic pressure failed to evict the Iraqi units from Kuwait, the Security Council passed a resolution on November 29 setting a January 15, 1991, deadline for Iraq to begin its withdrawal or face a military response by UN forces. Hussein's last-ditch attempt to win Arab sympathy and support by characterizing the impending conflict as a *jihad* against the West and Israel fell on deaf ears in most Arab countries. Saudi Arabia, Egypt, and even Syria (Iraq's traditional rival in the region) joined the motley UN coalition whose forces assembled in Saudi Arabia in preparation for possible military action.

The day after the expiration of the January 15 deadline, Operation Desert Shield gave way to Operation Desert Storm: The U.S.-led coalition, with significant participation by British, French, Italian, and Saudi forces, launched a massive air campaign against Baghdad from bases in Saudi Arabia and Turkey and from aircraft carriers in the Persian Gulf. Within days the entire Iraqi air force was either grounded or dispatched to Iran, which retained the planes as partial payment of its claims for war reparations dating from the Iran-Iraq War. The Iraqi air defense system was rendered inoperative by high-speed missiles. Having thus achieved total air superiority the coalition pounded Iraqi targets for forty-three days with "smart" bombs and cruise missiles, destroying the country's electric power grid, halting weapons production, and obliterating Hussein's own headquarters. In the meantime a formidable allied ground force of almost 540,000 troops from thirty-one countries (including nine U.S., one British, one French, and the equivalent of four Arab/Islamic divisions) had assembled in the coalition's staging area in Saudi Arabia. Equipped with over 3,400 tanks and 1,600 artillery pieces and supported by 1,736 land-based and carrier-based aircraft, this massive military coalition launched a carefully planned ground operation (code-named Operation Desert Sabre) on February 24 to evict the Iraqi army from Kuwait. That objective was achieved within four days, as more than eighty-six thousand Iraqi soldiers surrendered while the rest retreated in total disarray. As allied aircraft decimated Iraqi troops fleeing on the road leading from Kuwait City north toward the Iraqi city of Basra, President Bush ordered a halt to the military advance into Iraq: The objective of liberating Kuwait had been achieved, and the U.S. president was unwilling to become embroiled in a potentially hazardous and costly military operation deep in Iraqi territory.

A number of important consequences flowed from the sweeping victory of the allied coalition in the Gulf War. Above all, it dashed Iraq's hopes of achieving regional dominance in the Persian Gulf by imposing a set of severe restraints on the country's sovereignty in order to prevent Saddam Hussein from rebuilding his military power. When the Iraqi leader used his personal army (the Republican Guard) to brutally suppress Kurdish separatists in the north and Shiite rebels in the south, the UN established "no-fly zones" in the Kurdish and Shiite areas that were declared off limits to Iraqi aircraft and protected by U.S. and British planes. Since Iraq had used chemical weapons against Iran during the Iran-Iraq War and was widely suspected of producing nuclear and biological weapons as well, a team from the United Nations Special Commission on Disarmament (UNSCOM) was dispatched to the country to identify and supervise the destruction of weapons of mass destruction and the plants that produced them. Stringent economic sanctions were imposed on the country until it fully complied with the UN's disarmament and inspection requirements. It was prevented from exporting its oil, except for a limited amount to pay for food, medicines, and other non-military goods. Although about $1 billion worth of Iraqi oil was smuggled through Turkey, Jordan, and Iran every year, the economy was devastated by the sharp drop in export earnings.

For the next several years Saddam Hussein successfully obstructed UNSCOM's efforts to gain access to the suspected weapons sites. His ability to do so was facilitated by the disintegration of the original consensus among the five permanent members of the Security Council concerning an appropriate policy toward Iraq: When UNSCOM complained to the Council about Baghdad's obstructionist tactics in the autumn of 1997, Russia, China, and France began to express misgivings about the devastating effects on the Iraqi civilian populations of the economic sanctions. In 1998 UNSCOM's discovery of evidence of an Iraqi chemical weapons program led to further obstructionism, which in turn prompted a four-day Anglo-American assault against Iraq with bombers and cruise missiles. In the meantime the exasperated U.S. and British governments had mounted a campaign of political warfare to overthrow the recalcitrant government in Baghdad, sponsoring radio propaganda broadcasts within Iraq to incite resistance to the regime and financing Iraqi opposition groups and Kurdish political organizations operating abroad. Hussein responded by expelling the UN inspection team from Iraq, accusing its members of commiting espionage on behalf of the United States. For the remainder of the twentieth century, the campaign to contain Saddam Hussein continued to operate: U.S. and British aircraft patrolled the "no-fly" zones in the north and south, a blatant challenge to Iraq's national sovereignty that its government was powerless to prevent. The economic sanctions imposed during the Gulf War remained in effect, causing widespread distress among the civilian population. But the news was not all bad for the Iraqi leader. He had ended the irritating and intrusive inspections previously mounted by UNSCOM, enabling him to resume the clandestine program of producing weapons of mass destruction that had prompted the inspections in the first place. He and his military and political henchmen lived lives of comfort and luxury amid the deteriorating economic conditions caused by the sanctions. The coalition that had evicted the Iraqi army from Kuwait was in disarray, with some of its members favoring an end to the aerial surveillance and the economic sanctions. In short, at the beginning of the twenty-first century Baghdad's defiant strongman remained firmly in the saddle. Then the new Bush administration in Washington promptly abandoned the Clinton policy of containment in favor of a policy of confrontation. Vice President Dick Cheney and Secretary of Defense Donald Rumsfeld led a faction that openly pressed for military intervention to topple Saddam Hussein before he could acquire weapons of mass destruction and the means to deliver them. Washington was at pains to persuade its allies in Europe and the Arab world to support such an externally engineered "regime change" in Baghdad, without much success.

## The Revival of Hope for Regional Peace and Stability

While the United States–led coalition maintained stringent military and economic sanctions on Iraq in a futile campaign to compel it to renounce weapons of mass destruction, Washington imposed a series of restrictions on Iran as well in what came to be known as a policy of "dual containment" of these two historic adversaries. The United States remained concerned about two aspects of Iranian policy. The first was Iran's financial support to radical Shiite movements abroad. The most prominent of these was Hizbollah (Arabic for "Party of God") in southern Lebanon, which carried out occasional violent acts against Israeli forces there. The second was Iran's suspected campaign to develop nuclear weapons. But while Saddam Hussein remained steadfastly resistant to outside influences and tightened his control of Iraqi society, the death of Ayatollah Ruhollah Khomeini in June 1989 set in motion a remarkable evolution in Iran away from the fanatical, fundamentalist, theocratic policies that he had initiated. In an entirely smooth transition President Ayatollah Ali Khamenei replaced Khomeini as Supreme Leader, while the moderate, pragmatic speaker of the Iranian parliament, Hojatoleslam Hashemi Rafsanjani, succeeded Khamenei as president. Within a year the supporters of the new president had gained control of the parliament. The result was a notable relaxation of the stringent restrictions on civil liberties and cultural expression imposed during Khomeini's rule. Whereas the late Ayatollah had concentrated on purifying Iranian society by eradicating foreign influences and restoring the authority of Islamic teachings, Rafsanjani's priorities were the reconstruction and economic development of the country to rescue it from the devastating effects of the long war with Iraq. By the time of his reelection as president in 1993, the Islamic Revolution had entered into a new phase in which the moderate forces seemed poised to challenge the supreme authority of the clerics. This trend was accelerated in May 1997, when the reformist cleric Mohammed Khatami was unexpectedly elected to succeed Rafsanjani with almost 70 percent of the vote. Khatami went much further than his predecessor in challenging the authority of the ruling clique of clerics headed by Supreme Leader Ayatollah Khamenei, which retained control of foreign and defense policy. Appealing to youth, women, and other groups that were chafing at the remaining restrictions on civil liberties and cultural freedom, the new Iranian head of state relaxed many of those restrictions while calling for improved relations with the Western world. A genuine civil society gradually emerged within Iran in the last decade of the twentieth century without threatening the preeminence of the Shiite clerical traditions that had been at the heart of the 1979 revolution. During the same period Iran began to recover economically from the destructive effects of the 1980s war and strove to regain its former status as a regional power.

With its traditional rival Iraq weakened by Western economic sanctions and aerial supervision, Iran developed an increasingly competitive relationship with Pakistan during the second half of the 1990s. As we have seen, Iran was drawn into the Afghan civil war that erupted after the overthrow of the Soviet-installed government in Kabul in 1992. The Persian-speaking Shiite faction that it supported was decisively defeated by the fundamentalist Sunni Pashtun group known as Taliban that was backed by Pakistan. It appeared to many observers that Islamabad, supported by its Taliban protégés in Kabul, had replaced Teheran as the spearhead of the fundamentalist cause in the Islamic world after the death of Ayatollah Khomeini and the emergence of pragmatist reformers in the Iranian leadership. But despite this turn toward domestic moderation, Iran retained its old Khomeinist commitment to the cause of Shiite fundamentalism abroad: Most notably, it continued to finance the radical Shiite movement Hizbollah's guerrilla campaign against Israel from bases in southern Lebanon.

An unforeseen consequence of the Gulf War of January–February 1991 was the renewal of diplomatic attempts to revive the Arab-Israeli peace negotiations that had stalled since the Israeli invasion of Lebanon in 1982. Bush seemed much more willing than Reagan had been to apply pressure on Israel to compromise on the issue of Palestinian rights in the occupied territories. Shortly before the advent of the allied bombing campaign against Iraq, the American president met with Syrian President Hafez al-Assad in Geneva and pledged to do everything in his power to promote a satisfactory settlement of the Arab-Israeli conflict after the defeat of Iraq. Bush had insisted on excluding Israel from the emerging anti-Iraqi coalition for fear of antagonizing the other Arab members; he then leaned on the Shamir government to refrain from retaliating after Saddam Hussein launched some forty Russian-made SCUD missiles against Israeli cities early in the war in a bid for Arab popular support against the U.S.-led coalition.

After the cease-fire in the Gulf War was signed in April 1991, U.S. Secretary of State James Baker undertook a whirlwind tour of the Middle East in search of a comprehensive settlement to the Arab-Israeli conflict. After an intensive round of talks, he was able to persuade Israel and the Arab states in the region (including, to everyone's surprise, Syria) to attend an international conference cosponsored by the United States and the Soviet Union. The usual obstacle posed by Israel's adamant refusal to attend a conference at which the PLO was present had vanished. Arafat's organization had been dealt a serious setback in the Arab world when it opted to support Iraq during the Gulf War: Saudi Arabia, Kuwait, and the Gulf sheikdoms retaliated by slashing their financial assistance to the PLO from $120 million in 1990 to

$40 million in 1992. In the meantime Arafat lost his most prominent foreign sup-
porter outside the Arab world when the Soviet Union collapsed at the end of 1991.
The diplomatic isolation and financial straits of the PLO enhanced the prestige and
influence of the local Palestinian leadership in the West Bank and Gaza. So Baker
adroitly arranged for the inclusion of a group of Palestinian representatives uncon-
nected to the PLO in the Jordanian delegation to the international conference, which
convened in Madrid on October 30, 1991. The opening session in the royal palace
was followed by bilateral talks between Israel and Syria, Israel and Lebanon, and
Israel and the joint Jordanian-Palestinian delegation. The Camp David "Framework
for Peace in the Middle East" served as the basis for negotiations. The Madrid talks
represented the first face-to-face contacts between Arab and Israeli leaders since the
Camp David conference of 1978 (and the first ever between Palestinians and Israelis).
But they soon reached an impasse over several intractable issues: The hardest nut to
crack was the Shamir government's insistence on continuing the expansion of Jewish
settlements in the West Bank and Gaza, which complicated any future agreement for
Palestinian autonomy in those two territories.

Then the political situation in Israel changed dramatically in June 1992. The right-
wing Likud government that had governed the country (either alone or in coalition
with Labor) for the past fifteen years was defeated in parliamentary elections. The
victorious coalition headed by the Labor party had campaigned on a program of ending the unrest in the occupied territories through diplomacy rather than military
force. The new Labor Prime Minister, Yitzhak Rabin, suspended most construction
projects in the West Bank as a gesture of good will and openly expressed an interest
in exploring ways of promoting Palestinian autonomy in the occupied territories.
This trend toward accommodation in Israel coincided with the growing popularity
within Gaza and the West Bank of a Muslim extremist group called Hamas (an Arabic word meaning "zeal" and also the acronym for the Islamic Resistance Movement), which was funded by Iran and other sympathetic governments such as Sudan.
Hamas profited from Arafat's long absence in distant Tunis and his financial difficulties after the Gulf War to challenge the PLO's authority among Palestinians in the
occupied territories. Hamas won broad support among the Palestinian masses by initiating Islamic social welfare and educational programs and issuing virulent political
attacks on the PLO for its impotence in the face of the Israeli occupation. The new
Labor government in Jerusalem consequently began to regard Arafat's organization,
which the Likud had derided as a nest of terrorists with which it would never negotiate, as a paragon of moderation in comparison to Hamas and other fundamentalist
Muslim groups.

In the meantime the deadlocked Middle East peace talks in Madrid had resumed
in Washington after a four-month hiatus in April 1993. But the discussions got
nowhere because of the absence of the PLO, whose approval would be required for
any agreement that might be reached between the Israelis and the Palestinians in the
Jordanian delegation. While these unwieldy multilateral negotiations droned on
without result in the full glare of publicity, sensational press reports in the summer
revealed that several clandestine meetings between Israeli and PLO representatives
had been held since January in Oslo under the sponsorship of Norwegian Foreign
Minister Johan Jorgan Holst. On August 20, 1993, Israeli and PLO representatives

*Israeli Prime Minister Yitzhak Rabin and PLO chairman Yasser Arafat shake hands on the White House lawn in September 1993 after the signing of the Oslo accord. This was seen as an extraordinary and hopeful development at the time, but hopes of a final peace settlement disintegrated with the assassination of Rabin in 1995 and the escalation of hostilities between Palestinians and Israelis beginning in 2000. (White House Photograph)*

initialed a Declaration of Principles, which is often referred to as the Oslo I accord. A few weeks later Arafat and Rabin sent each other letters confirming the PLO's recognition of Israel and its renunciation of violence in exchange for Israel's recognition of the PLO as the official representative of the Palestinian people. Although the United States had been completely bypassed in this direct negotiation between PLO and Israel officials, President Bill Clinton invited Arafat and Rabin to Washington for the formal signing of the Oslo I accord on September 13. The historic handshake on the White House lawn between the prime minister of Israel and the head of the PLO marked a historic turning point in the long and bloody history of the Arab-Israeli conflict.

In addition to the provisions for reciprocal recognition, the Oslo Declaration of Principles contained a blueprint for future negotiations concerning the political future of the Gaza Strip and the West Bank. It stipulated the Israeli evacuation of all of Gaza and of the West Bank city of Jericho, together with the establishment of a Palestinian administrative organ that would gradually assume control over internal affairs of the liberated areas for an interim period of five years. In the meantime the two parties would negotiate a permanent peace settlement that was tentatively scheduled to take effect by December 1998. After the completion of the Israeli military withdrawal from the two specified areas in May 1994, a triumphant Arafat entered

Gaza in July and then traveled to Jericho to swear in members of the new Palestinian Authority (PA). Whereas the PLO had teetered on the verge of bankruptcy when the Gulf oil monarchies cut off their subsidies in response to Arafat's support of Iraq during the Gulf War, the PA received a pledge from forty donor countries and international lending agencies of $2 billion during the five-year transitional period until sufficient tax revenues from the areas transferred to its control could be raised to finance its administrative operations. From impoverished pariah Arafat had become a respected world statesman in less than five years. The PLO leader, together with Rabin and Israeli Foreign Minister Shimon Peres, shared the 1994 Nobel Peace Prize for their remarkable success in laying the groundwork for a Mideast peace.

In the meantime Jordan's King Hussein, eager for American aid to rebuild his economy that had been devastated by the Gulf War, became the next Arab leader to make peace with the Jewish state. The Jordanian monarch followed in Arafat's footsteps to the White House lawn on July 25, 1994, where he joined Rabin in declaring the end of the state of war that had existed between their two countries for forty-six years. After the U.S. Congress voted to forgive a substantial portion of the Jordanian debt, Clinton traveled to the Jordanian-Israeli border just north of Aqaba to witness the signing of the formal peace treaty between the two long-time antagonists on October 26. Since Jordan had already relinquished its claim to the West Bank territory that it had conquered in 1948 and lost to Israel in 1967, Hussein's conditions for a peace agreement with Israel were easy for Rabin to accept: a water access agreement to the Jordan River and the exclusive right to protect Muslim holy places in Jerusalem.

The breathtaking progress in the Mideast peace process during the first half of the 1990s, which produced historic agreements between Israel and the PLO and between Israel and Jordan, had left Syria in the lurch. Whereas Assad had joined the Madrid talks and permitted his representatives to continue negotiations with Israel after the Oslo accord, the Syrian leader had clearly been outmaneuvered by Arafat and Hussein as they made their own separate peace with the Jewish state. The main bone of contention between the two countries was the barren plateau known as the Golan Heights that Israel had seized from Syria during the 1967 war. Although lacking the West Bank's sentimental significance for Israeli public opinion, the strategic and economic stakes involved in possession of the Golan were high: Before 1967 Syria had been able to use it to shell the Galilee plain in northern Israel. Since 1967 Israel used it as an early warning post to monitor Syrian military activity. As the site of the headwaters of the Jordan River, which produced 40 percent of Israel's water supply, the Golan had an economic importance as well. Assad had suspended bilateral negotiations with Israel in February 1994, when a right-wing Jewish settler massacred twenty-nine Muslim worshipers at a mosque in Hebron (a West Bank city with a five-hundred-person Jewish settlement that was slated for transfer to Palestinian control). Although the Syrian leader permitted the U.S.-sponsored bilateral talks to continue in December 1995–January 1996, the two sides were continually stymied in an irresolvable deadlock: Syria demanded a prior Israeli commitment to a total withdrawal from the Golan, while Israel insisted that Syria issue a prior pledge to make peace and take steps to reduce terrorist attacks against Israel from the areas of Lebanon that it controlled. While Syria dragged its heels in these talks with Israel, it encountered a new threat from the north when its old adversary Turkey concluded a strategic alliance with the Jewish state in 1996 with the encouragement of the two countries' American ally. The new Ankara-Jerusalem axis confronted Assad with the threat of Turkish military intervention should he decide to resort to military force to regain the Golan. In light of Syria's weak position, its negotiations with Israel faded into insignificance and produced no concrete results.

In the meantime Israel and the Palestinian Authority had approved a comprehensive plan for the implementation of the September 1993 interim accord. In an agreement (often referred to as Oslo II) reached in the Red Sea resort town of Taba on September 24, 1995, and signed in Washington four days later, Israel set the stage for the so-called final status talks on the West Bank by transferring more territory there to Palestinian political control. Soon thereafter the Israeli Defense Forces began to redeploy from six West Bank cities and towns (including Jesus's birthplace, Bethlehem), while the PA assumed administrative and security functions there. This step-by-step transfer of land and power infuriated Jewish settlers in the West Bank and their supporters in Israel itself, who denounced Rabin for sacrificing a part of biblical Israel and threatening the security of the Israeli settlements that remained. Amid a wave of protests by opponents of the Oslo process, Rabin was assassinated in Tel Aviv on November 4, 1995, by a Jewish extremist who accused him of betraying the country. In the early spring of 1996 Hamas orchestrated a series of terrorist attacks that killed almost sixty civilians in several Israeli cities. But the Israeli and Palestinian opponents of the peace process did not succeed in derailing it: Rabin's successor Shimon Peres honored the Oslo II agreement and proceeded with the evacuation of the six West Bank towns. The supporters of the peace process won a comfortable majority in the elections for a Palestinian Legislative Council on January 20, 1996, while Arafat was overwhelmingly elected president. Later that spring the new president convened the old Palestinian National Council, which declared its intention to cancel the clauses in the PLO charter calling for the destruction of Israel. The next day the Israeli Labor party formally abandoned its long-time opposition to the creation of a Palestinian state. Palestinian groups opposed to the peace process such as Hamas boycotted the electoral campaign, preferring bombs to ballots as a means of achieving liberation.

The final status talks opened in Taba on May 5, 1996. The Palestinian delegation made its ultimate priority abundantly clear: the establishment of an independent Palestinian state next to Israel in Gaza and the West Bank, with East Jerusalem as its capital. It rapidly became clear that three matters in dispute would prove insoluble. The first was that both sides claimed as their capital the holy city of Jerusalem, which had been partitioned between Israel and Jordan in 1948 and then unified under Israeli control after the Six Day War in 1967. The second was the demand of three million Palestinian refugees from the first Arab-Israeli war of 1948–1949 residing in half a dozen Arab countries to return to their ancestral homes. The third was the question of how Israel could provide adequate security for the 120,000 Jews who were scattered in isolated settlements throughout the predominately Arab territories of the West Bank as more territory was transferred to the Palestinians there and violent clashes between the two antagonistic groups increased.

The hopes of reaching a resolution of these thorny issues were dashed in the Israeli elections of May 1996, when the Labor government of Shimon Peres was ousted by the Likud coalition. Exploiting Israeli anxiety caused by a rash of Hamas suicide bombings, Likud leader Benjamin Netanyahu took office after a campaign in which he denounced the 1993 Oslo accords and the subsequent agreements they had produced, refused to accept a Palestinian state, and defiantly announced that Jerusalem would be the eternal and undivided capital of Israel. Once in power he promptly ended the four-year partial freeze on the expansion of Israeli settlements in the West Bank and provided financial subsidies for several new ones, bringing the Jewish settler population of the region to 150,000 by the end of the year.* The increase in Israeli settlements provoked massive protests and outbreaks of violence among the Palestinians in the West Bank as well as in Israel itself. The new hard-line Israeli government responded to the outbreak of stone-throwing and suicide bombings by sealing Israel's borders with the West Bank and Gaza, causing great economic hardship for the more than 100,000 Palestinian day laborers who worked in Israel. Arafat refrained from explicitly condemning the escalating violence for fear of losing control of his constituency to Hamas, which (along with other more moderate Palestinian critics) had begun to denounce the corruption and dictatorial policies of the PLO. The anomalous status of the city of Hebron was typical of the potentially explosive situation in the West Bank: In January 1997 Netanyahu reluctantly agreed to remove the Israeli army from the city and turn over 80 percent of its territory to Palestinian control, leaving some one thousand Israeli soldiers to protect the enclave of five hundred Jewish settlers who defiantly remained in the city amid its 160,000 Palestinians.

As the bilateral negotiations for a permanent settlement got nowhere throughout the year 1998, Arafat began to make noises about a unilateral declaration of Palestinian statehood in Gaza and the West Bank when the five-year interim period specified by the Oslo II agreement expired on May 4, 1999. The Clinton administration responded to this threat with a preemptive effort to bring the two sides together in October 1998 by inviting Arafat and Netanyahu to a conference at the Wye Plantation in Maryland near Washington, DC. After nine days of hard bargaining, which was joined by King Hussein (who was dying of cancer), the Palestinian and Israeli leaders signed the Wye River Memorandum. It provided for additional Israeli military withdrawals from the West Bank, which would leave the Palestinian Authority in charge of roughly 20 percent of the area, in exchange for Arafat's promise to clamp down on Palestinian violence there. After the first of three designated withdrawals, Netanyahu accused the PA of failing to live up to its commitments in the Wye Memorandum and suspended the procedure in December. But the Israeli-Palestinian peace process was given a powerful shot in the arm in the Israeli elections of May 1999, when the Labor party was swept back into power under the standard of its new leader, former general Ehud Barak. Like Rabin, Barak was a decorated war hero who possessed the requisite patriotic credentials to take daring political risks for peace with his country's Arab antagonists. He immediately attempted to revive not only the suspended negotiations with Arafat but also the talks with Syria that Assad had

---

*The total number of Israeli settlers in the West Bank and Gaya would increase to more than 200,000 by the beginning of the twenty-first century.

broken off in March 1996. The Palestinian track led to a meeting between Barak and Arafat at the Egyptian resort of Sharm-el-Sheik in September 1999, which produced a revision of the Wye River agreement endorsing the immediate resumption of final status talks on all of the issues in dispute—Israeli settlements, Palestinian refugees, water rights, and the status of Jerusalem. In the meantime Barak resumed the military withdrawal from the West Bank that Netanyahu had suspended.

Clinton mounted a heroic effort in the final months of his presidency to broker a deal that both Arafat and Barak could accept. He presided over a marathon fifteen-day negotiating session between the Israeli and Palestinian leaders at the presidential retreat of Camp David in July 2000. In the course of these talks Barak submitted what seemed to be an extraordinarily generous proposal that went a long way toward meeting two important Palestinian demands: First, Israel would withdraw from 90 percent of the West Bank and Gaza, which would be transformed into the Palestinian state that Arafat and his supporters had sought for so long; second, the non-Jewish sections of Jerusalem and the Muslim holy sites in the city would revert to Palestinian control. Only on the Palestinian insistence of the "right of return" for the refugees from the 1948 war did Barak dig in his heels: He was unwilling to allow his country to be flooded with returning Palestinians who, with the existing Arab citizens of Israel, might eventually outnumber the Jews in the Jewish state. Despite intense pressure from Clinton to respond with a creative counter-offer, Arafat rejected Barak's proposal out of hand, reiterating his demand that Israel pull back to its pre-1967 borders (which would have meant the loss of the Jewish quarter of Jerusalem, including the Western or "Wailing" Wall). Subsequent meetings between Israeli and Palestinian negotiators and a last-ditch effort by Clinton to broker a deal in the autumn of 2000 and January 2001 failed to produce an agreement.

In the meantime a seemingly trivial incident ended up destroying all hope of bringing the two sides together and ignited a new explosion of lethal violence: In September 2000 the Israeli right-wing political leader Ariel Sharon, long blamed by Palestinians for the massacre of Palestinian refugees by Christian Phalangists in Lebanon in 1982, decided to enhance his political popularity by paying a well publicized visit to the holy site in Jerusalem that Jews call the Temple Mount, on which Solomon's and later Herod's Temple once stood. But the mount also contains the al-Aqsa Mosque and the Dome of the Rock, a shrine constructed in the seventh century on the spot where Muslims believe Muhammed stood before ascending into heaven. Enraged at what they regarded as the desecration of the third-holiest shrine of Islam (behind Mecca and Medina), Palestinian youths began assaulting Jews near the Wailing Wall. Israeli security forces responded by killing or wounding dozens of the rioters. Soon the West Bank and Gaza were ablaze with such violence that observers began referring to the "second intifada." Palestinian snipers targeted Israeli civilians while Israeli security forces assassinated Palestinian militants and used helicopter gunships and tanks against Palestinian Authority installations to punish Arafat for what Israel saw as his failure to employ his security forces to maintain order.

Israeli public concern about this resurgence of violence and about the concessions Barak had offered Arafat at Camp David led to his decisive defeat at the polls in February 2001 by the right-wing Likud party headed by Ariel Sharon. The old hard-liner grabbed the reins of power intent on crushing the second intifada, while Arafat seemed incapable of or unwilling to rein in the increasingly audacious Palestinian gunmen. The new Bush administration in the United States initially refused to renew its predecessor's aggressive diplomacy in the Palestinian-Israeli conflict for fear of being dragged into a hopelessly messy situation. But Washington's global campaign against Islamic terrorism after September 11, as well as its plan to overthrow Saddam Hussein in Iraq, required the support of allies in the Arab world such as Saudi Arabia, Jordan, and Egypt; and the leaders of those states insisted that the U.S. resume the diplomatic efforts to reach a settlement of the Israeli-Palestinian conflict that had seemed within reach in the final year of the Clinton administration. In the autumn of 2001 President Bush issued an unprecedented public announcement of U.S. support for the creation of a Palestinian state and appointed retired Marine Corps General Anthony Zinni as his special representative to the Middle East with instructions to open discussions with both sides.* In February 2002 Crown Prince Abdullah, the de facto leader of Saudi Arabia, sought to jump-start the stalled peace process with the proposal that Israel withdraw to its pre-1967 borders in exchange for the normalization of relations with all of the Arab states, a bold initiative that was endorsed (with certain qualifications) by all twenty-two members of the League of Arab States at its March 2002 summit in Beirut.

But the Saudi peace plan was buried amid a new wave of killing that engulfed the West Bank in the spring and summer of 2002. Palestinian suicide bombers recruited by Hamas, Islamic Jihad, and a radical faction of Arafat's own al-Fatah movement called the al-Aqsa Martyrs Brigade targeted Israeli civilians in the West Bank and in Israel proper. Sharon responded to the suicide bombings by sending the Israeli Defense Force (IDF) into Palestinian cities such as Ramallah, Bethlehem, and Jenin that had been evacuated under the Oslo agreement. In the course of conducting house-to-house searches for suspected Palestinian terrorists and bulldozing their suspected hideouts, Israeli forces killed and injured several unarmed Palestinian civilians, further stoking the fires of resentment and revenge. By the summer of 2002 the Palestinian Authority's headquarters in Ramallah and its political, economic, and security infrastructure in the occupied territories lay in ruins. The Israeli government had long since broken off all contact with Arafat, whom it accused of tacitly approving the terrorist attacks, holding him as a virtual prisoner amid the rubble of his administrative offices in Ramallah. The man who had shaken hands with Israeli prime ministers and shared the Nobel Peace Prize for facilitating what once seemed to be the beginning of the end of this long and bloody struggle was shunted to the sidelines as U.S., Israeli, and moderate Arab leaders sought alternative Palestinian spokespersons to resuscitate the moribund negotiations over peace and security in the region.

Neither the Barak nor the Sharon government was successful in reviving the negotiations with Syria, one of the two remaining Arab states bordering Israel that had not made peace with the Jewish state. The other was Lebanon, which was occupied militarily and dominated politically by Syria. While Israel and the PLO labored in

---

*General Zinni's mission, followed by one by Secretary of State Colin Powell, failed to record any progress as the violence escalated.

vain to convert the Oslo agreements into a final settlement, the peace process was periodically threatened by sporadic clashes between the Israeli army and Hizbollah in the "security zone" that Israel had established beyond its northern border with Lebanon after withdrawing from that troubled country in 1985. Supported by the Shiite-controlled governments of Iran and Syria*, Hizbollah had continually tried to sabotage the peace process. In the summer of 1993 it shelled Israeli military posts in the Lebanese security zone as well as targets in northern Israel. Israel retaliated with a ferocious assault on Shiite villages in southern Lebanon suspected of harboring Hizbollah guerrillas, causing a mass exodus of almost a tenth of Lebanon's population from their homes. Three years later the resumption of Hizbollah rocket attacks against northern Israel provoked the most intense Israeli air attacks in Lebanon since the 1982 invasion.

By the end of the decade it had became evident that Syrian President Hafez al-Assad, whose forty thousand troops in Lebanon assured him predominance there, was uninterested in reining in Hizbollah as part of a bilateral deal with Israel. Since 1996 Israel had offered to withdraw from the security zone without a formal peace treaty if the Lebanese government would curb Hizbollah, something it had no power to accomplish. Exasperated by its eighteen-year-long travail in southern Lebanon (which had resulted in many Israeli military casualties but did little to secure Israel's security against Hizbollah rocket attacks), the Barak government decided in March 2000 to withdraw by July with or without an agreement. As the Israeli forces moved south according to plan, Hizbollah fighters promptly moved in to fill the vacuum and take their revenge against the South Lebanon Army (the predominately Christian militia that had cooperated with the Israel army in the "security zone"). The beginning of the new century did not bring with it much hope for the long-postponed comprehensive peace settlement in the Middle East. The election of Sharon in early 2001, coupled with increasing violence in the Palestinian occupied territories, suggested that the process begun at Oslo eight years earlier may have reached a dead end.

---

*Syrian President Hafez al-Assad was a member of the Alawite sect, a small offshoot of Shiite Islam.

# EPILOGUE:
# A WORLD OF NATIONS IN THE
# ERA OF GLOBALIZATION

At the end of the Cold War, scholars eagerly searched for a new label to designate the emerging international order that began to take shape in the last decade of the twentieth century. But we had become so accustomed to the charged atmosphere of global conflict and crisis in which the two superpowers competed with one another across the globe that we could not imagine what to call the new era that was upon us. The best we could manage was the unimaginative title "Post–Cold War Order." Unable to define the emerging international system by identifying its own salient features, we were reduced to contrasting it with the tumultuous period that had preceded it.

But in the closing years of the twentieth century, people began to notice a fundamental characteristic about the new world order that had little to do with the Cold War. It reflected a set of important trends that had been sweeping the planet for decades but somehow escaped the notice of all but the most insightful students of the world scene. The term "globalization" rapidly achieved almost universal acceptance as the slogan for the new era that began at the opening of the last decade of the twentieth century and continued well into the century in which we now live. The defining characteristic of this new era was the growing power and importance of a diverse set of nongovernmental international organizations that transcended national boundaries and escaped the supervision of the political entities that had dominated the history of international relations for the past four hundred years, the sovereign national states.

Some observers even went so far as to claim that the nation-state was rapidly receding in significance, while these various nonstate actors acquired powers and assumed responsibilities long monopolized by governments. According to this analysis, the people of the twenty-first century would increasingly conceive of their identity not as citizens of a particular nation but either as members of this or that transnational entity or as citizens of the world community. Either way, the organizing principle that has pervaded this book—a sovereign state acting to promote and protect its own vital interests as its governing elite defines them at a particular time—may seem to some an increasingly irrelevant concept for the history of international relations in the era of globalization. Some have even suggested that the term "international relations" itself has become anachronistic, since interactions between national political units no longer represent the most important part of the story of how the world operates.

Three profound developments in the last decade of the twentieth century were primarily responsible for this trend that we call globalization. The first was the revolution in information technology: Spectacular innovations in fiberoptics and microchip technologies gave rise to a vast interactive communications network that made it at least theoretically possible for every person on earth to have virtually instantaneous access to every other person and for everyone to read messages anywhere they are posted. The media through which such information flowed were the television set (with its efficient infrastructure, the cable and the satellite) and the computer (with its spectacular interactive tool, the Internet, made available to the public in 1990). These new technologies undermined the ability of authoritarian governments to manage the flow of information to their people and therefore posed a formidable threat to the stability of those regimes. They also enhanced the ability of transnational organizations of all kinds to maintain contact with their members across the globe and publicize their grievances and concerns to the entire world.

A second development went hand in hand with this revolution in information technology to accelerate the trend toward globalization: This was the liberalization of trade and capital markets that engulfed the entire world during the 1990s, from the former statist regimes of Latin America to the former Communist systems of Eastern Europe, Russia, and, eventually, China. The Internet together with cable and satellite television accorded advertisers access to consumers on a previously unimaginable scale, creating a genuinely global market for the first time that transcended the authority of governments. Multinational corporations increasingly dominated the supply side of this world market, producing and marketing their products without regard to these firms' country of origin or its particular interests. Companies that faced high labor costs or burdensome environmental regulations in the developed world shifted their factories to countries in the developing world whose destitute citizens were willing to work for much lower wages or whose governments had little interest in enforcing costly environmental standards to combat industrial pollution. In the financial field, currency traders, mutual and pension funds, insurance companies, and individual investors shifted their investments with the click of a mouse from one nation to another in search of higher returns. This unprecedented mobility of capital generated acute financial instability in the countries from which this "hot money" fled, causing wide fluctuations in interest rates (which hurt local businesses and home buyers), currency values (which affected the cost of imports), and employment opportunities (which hurt everybody). In this way, the impersonal operation of the global market directly undermined individual governments' ability to manage their economic affairs.

A third related trend in the closing decade of the twentieth century was what some observers have called the emergence of a "global culture" and others have called "the Americanization of the world." To describe the remarkable spread of American popular culture through film, television, and electronic communications throughout the world, political scientists have devised the concept of "soft power": According to this analysis, the world's only remaining superpower strove to expand its influence in the world not only through the traditional instruments of military force or economic leverage ("hard power"), but also through the use of advertising and publicity to persuade the populations of other countries to embrace its values and institutions as their own. Examples of this phenomenon include the global proliferation of American fashion (sneakers for the feet, blue jeans for the legs, sweatshirts emblazoned with the names of U.S. universities for the chest, the baseball cap worn backward for the head); consumption and leisure activities (Coca Cola, McDonald's, Pizza Hut, Starbucks); and entertainment (Hollywood films, television programs, Blockbuster Video, Disney theme parks, hip hop, and other musical trends). Even the French, traditionally protective of their cultural heritage and resistant to American popular trends, jumped on the bandwagon: At the beginning of the 1990s a Disneyland sprouted outside Paris. By the end of the decade, French merchants were selling jack o'lanterns and witches' costumes to customers celebrating Halloween as though it were an indigenous festival. Students of popular culture have been quick to point out that the societies appropriating such American cultural symbols do not slavishly adopt them but rather transform them beyond recognition in the course of adapting them to local circumstances. But the fact remains that the institutions and customs of a single great power have exerted a powerful attraction on the populations (particularly the youth) of the rest of the world.

The integration of capital, technology, information, and culture across national borders did not transpire without provoking a powerful backlash from those who felt threatened by these new trends. Some of this opposition emanated from political leaders such as Mahathir Mohamad of Malaysia, who denounced multinational corporations, international speculators, and Western values during the Asian financial crisis of 1996–1997 for ruining his country's finances and corrupting its culture (see page 385). But some of the most vocal protests against this new threat to national sovereignty were ironically mounted by international nongovernmental organizations (INGOs) that also operated across national frontiers and employed such high-tech symbols of globalization as the Internet and cell phones to publicize their grievances. INGOs concerned about the danger to labor rights and environmental standards posed by the relocation by multinational corporations to low-wage regions of the developing world orchestrated large-scale protests (such as those in Seattle in 2000 and Genoa in 2001) during meetings of such preeminent agents of globalization as the International Monetary Fund, the World Bank, and the World Trade Organization.

These increasingly vocal and occasionally violent protests by critics of globalization from the industrial world paled beside the acts of massive terrorism mounted by transnational movements in the developing world that were dedicated to a fundamentalist brand of Islam. On February 26, 1993, an Islamic terrorist group headed by Ramzi Yousef masterminded a car bombing of the World Trade Center in New York City that killed six people and injured more than one thousand. The attacks on the World Trade Center and the Pentagon on September 11, 2001, by operatives of Osama bin Laden's al-Qaeda organization based in Afghanistan provoked a worldwide antiterrorist campaign by the Bush administration against al-Qaeda and the Taliban regime in Afghanistan that hosted it (see page 366). In videotaped remarks Bin Laden defended his organization's attacks against American assets as a justifiable response to Washington's support for Israel against the Palestinians and the blasphemous presence of American military forces in Saudi Arabia near the Muslim holy sites of Mecca and Medina. But the Islamic fundamentalists' violent campaign against the United States also represented a much broader protest against the modernizing trends associated with globalization. The secular, libertarian, freewheeling style of Western societies that was portrayed by the world's mass media clashed directly with the strict codes of dress, speech, behavior, and gender relations that operated in many Islamic societies. To the fanatical devotées of this orthodoxy, Muslims had to defend their faith against the decadent ideas and institutions of the West that were spreading throughout the world as part of the process of globalization. The governments of the Islamic world were incapable of leading such a campaign, since most of them were controlled by political elites that were militarily and economically dependent on the West. It therefore fell to transnational organizations such as al-Qaeda to mount the counteroffensive against the corrupting influences of Western ways. Since they lacked the conventional military forces and equipment of a sovereign state, it was argued, they had to rely on terrorism to attain their objectives.

The transnational appeal of a militant political Islam, with 1.3 billion potential believers spread across dozens of countries from Morocco to Indonesia, was strengthened by the desperate economic conditions in most of those societies. The predominantly Muslim countries of North Africa, the Middle East, and South Asia had not benefited from the export-driven economic development that had improved the living standards of many other developing countries in East Asia and Latin America in the last two decades of the twentieth century. This failure to participate in the worldwide trend of economic growth produced a group of alienated, underemployed young men for whom a fundamentalist brand of religious faith provided consolation and for some of whom the promise of martyrdom in the struggle against the infidels in the West meant salvation in the next life. In this way militant Islam became the most formidable obstacle to the process of globalization that many observers had identified as the ineluctable wave of the future after the Cold War came to an end. Time will tell whether the twenty-first century will be dominated by what one political scientist has called "the clash of civilizations" and another has called "McWorld vs. Jihad": a global conflict pitting an American-led group of democratic, secular, capitalist societies committed to modernization against a fundamentalist Islamic world of hierarchical, theocratic societies dedicated to preserving their traditional way of life against the threat of modernity.

There has been much discussion in the course of the last decade about the emergence of a "global community" amid a "world without borders" in which sovereign states and their control of force and economic resources will no longer be important. According to this school of thought, regional economic and political unions; transnational corporations, banks, social, political, and religious movements; drug cartels; organized crime networks; terrorist groups; and nongovernmental organizations are replacing nation-states as the significant actors on the world stage. All of the major issues that confront the world of the twenty-first century, such as arms control, the degradation of the environment, terrorism, narcotics trafficking, war crimes, the spread of infectious diseases such as AIDS, human rights, and so on, have global consequences and therefore require global solutions.

But an enduring challenge to this new vision of globalism and international cooperation has emerged in the foreign policy of the world's only remaining superpower. It has taken the form of an insistent reaffirmation of national sovereignty reinforced by a willingness to act unilaterally when the vital interests of the United States were deemed to be at stake. This vision led the United States to withhold its support for a wide range of international agreements that were accepted by most other nations of the world but considered incompatible with U.S. security or economic objectives: the Comprehensive Test Ban Treaty, the Land Mines Convention, the Biological Weapons Convention, the Kyoto Protocol on global warming, and the Anti-Ballistic Missile Treaty, among others. A particular nation-state enjoying overwhelming superiority in military power, economic leverage, and political influence in the world predictably resisted restrictions on its freedom of action codified in international agreements. The American public's reverence for the U.S. constitution and legal system had long inspired an attitude of American exceptionalism, which rejected the authority of international organizations that lack accountability or trustworthy instruments of enforcement. The attacks on the United States on September 11, 2001, reinforced this preoccupation with the interests of the nation and the security of its citizens. The war on international terrorism would be waged not by the United Nations or some other international entity but rather by the United States, acting on its own. In the early years of the twenty-first century, it seemed likely that the United States would continue to pursue an independent, unilateral course in world affairs in defense of its vital national interests, rather than become the first hegemonic world power in history to subordinate its foreign policy to the requirements of a global community as defined by international organizations and codified by international law.

At the end of World War II, when the period covered by this book begins, the newly established United Nations organization consisted of fifty sovereign states. Shortly before this volume went to press in the summer of 2002, East Timor became the 190th member of the world organization. This quadrupling of the membership of the United Nations since its creation was, as we have seen, largely a result of the decline of the European colonial empires and the disintegration of the Soviet Union. This proliferation of sovereign political entities in the world since 1945 and its consequences for the international order form the underlying theme of this book. It may seem intolerably old-fashioned to the theorists of globalization to focus on nation-states pursuing what their ruling elites deem to be their vital interests as the dominant force in world affairs. It may also seem passé to dwell on the persistence of national identity and national self-consciousness in an era of emerging supranational organizations and institutions. But if the developments of the last half century that are chronicled in this volume yield a lesson worth pondering, it is surely that (to paraphrase Mark Twain) the reports of the demise of the nation state are premature.

# SELECT BIBLIOGRAPHY

**The Early Cold War**

Allison, Graham and Philip Zelikow. *Essence of Decision: Explaining the Cuban Missile Crisis* (1999).

Brands, H. W., Jr. *Cold Warriors: Eisenhower's Generation and American Foreign Policy* (1988).

Brown, Colin, and Peter J. Mooney. *Cold War to Detente, 1945–1980* (1981).

Divine, Robert A. *Eisenhower and the Cold War* (1980).

Eisenberg, Carolyn. *Drawing the Line: The American Decision to Divide Germany, 1944– 1949* (1998).

Gaddis, John Lewis. *The United States and the Origins of the Cold War, 1941–1947* (1972).

Grosser, Alfred. *The Western Alliance* (1980).

Hogan, Michael J. *The Marshall Plan: America, Britain and the Reconstruction of Western Europe, 1947–1952* (1987).

Hoopes, Townsend. *The Devil and John Foster Dulles* (1973).

Iatrides, John O. *Revolt in Athens* (1972).

Judge, Edward H., and John W. Langden. *A Hard and Bitter Peace* (1996).

Kuniholm, Bruce R. *The Origins of the Cold War in the Near East: Great Power Conflict and Diplomacy in Iran, Turkey, and Greece* (1980).

LaFeber, Walter. *America, Russia, and the Cold War* (1996).

Leffler, Melvin P. *A Preponderance of Power: National Security, the Truman Administration, and the Cold War* (1992).

Mastny, Vojtech. *The Cold War and Soviet Insecurity: The Stalin Years* (1996).

———. *Russsia's Road to the Cold War: Diplomacy, Warfare, and the Politics of Communism, 1941–1945* (1979).

McCauley, Martin, ed. *Communist Power in Europe, 1944–1949* (1977).

Paterson, Thomas. *Soviet-American Confrontation, Postwar Reconstruction, and the Origins of the Cold War* (1973).

Pollard, Robert A. *Economic Security and the Origins of the Cold War* (1985).

Powaski, Ronald E. *The Cold War* (1998).

Schick, Jack. *The Berlin Crises, 1958–1962* (1974).

Sherwin, Martin. *A World Destroyed: Hiroshima and the Origins of the Arms Race* (2001).

Wolfe, Thomas. *Soviet Power and Europe, 1945–1970* (1970).

Yergin, Daniel. *Shattered Peace: The Origins of the Cold War and the National Security State* (1977).

Zubok, Vladislav, and Constantine Pleshakov. *Inside the Kremlin's Cold War: From Stalin to Khrushchev* (1996).

## Détente, the Arms Race, and Arms Control

Bailey, Kathleen C. *Doomsday Weapons in the Hands of Many* (1991).

Bell, Coral. *The Diplomacy of Détente: The Kissinger Era* (1977).

Carter, April. *Success and Failure in Arms Control Negotiations* (1989).

Muller, Harald, et al. *Nuclear Non-Proliferation and Global Order* (1994).

Nitze, Paul, et al. *Securing the Seas: The Soviet Naval Challenge and Western Alliance Options* (1979).

Roberts, Brad. *Chemical Disarmament and International Security* (1992).

Rueckert, George L. *Global Double Zero: The INF Treaty from Its Origins to Implementation* (1993).

Sampson, Anthony. *The Arms Bazaar in the Nineties: From Krupp to Saddam* (1991).

Schulzinger, Robert D. *Henry Kissinger: Doctor of Diplomacy* (1989).

Scott, Harriet F., and William F. Scott. *The Armed Forces of the USSR* (1979).

Smith, Gerard C. *Doubletalk. The Story of the First Strategic Arms Limitation Talks* (1980).

Weber, Steve. *Cooperation and Discord in U.S.-Soviet Arms Control* (1991).

Willrich, Mason, and John Rhinelander, eds. *SALT: The Moscow Agreements and Beyond* (1974).

## The Revival of East-West Conflict and the End of the Cold War

Beschloss, Michael, and Strobe Talbot. *At the Highest Level* (1993).

Blacker, Coit D. *Reluctant Warriors: The United States, the Soviet Union, and Arms Control* (1987).

Gaddis, John Lewis. *The United States and the End of the Cold War* (1992).

Gartoff, Raymond L. *Détente and Confrontation* (1985).

———. *The Great Transition: American-Soviet Relations and the End of the Cold War* (1994).

Hogan, Michael J., ed. *The End of the Cold War: Its Meaning and Implications* (1992).

Holm, Hans Henrich, and Nikolaj Peterson. *The European Missiles Crisis* (1984).

Kennedy, Paul. *The Rise and Fall of the Great Powers* (1987).

Mastny, Vojtech. *Helsinki, Human Rights, and European Security* (1986).

Simonian, Haig. *The Privileged Partnership: Franco-German Relations in the European Community, 1969–1984* (1985).

Zelikow, Philip, and Condoleezza Rice. *Germany United and Europe Transformed* (1997).

## The Post–Cold War Era

Allison, Roy. *Military Forces in the Soviet Successor States* (1993).

Baehr, Peter R., and Leon Gordenker. *The United Nations in the 1990s* (1992).

Berdal, Mats R. *Whither UN Peacekeeping?* (1993).

Dannreuther, Roland. *Creating New States in Central Asia* (1994).

Fukuyama, Francis. *The End of History and the Last Man* (1993).

Fromkin, David. *Kosovo Crossing* (1999).

Glenny, Misha. *The Fall of Yugoslavia* (1992).

Goldman, Marshall I. *Lost Opportunity: Why Economic Reforms in Russia Have Not Worked* (1994).

Huntington, Samuel. *The Clash of Civilizations and the Remaking of World Order* (1998).

Nevers, Renée de. *Russia's Strategic Renovation* (1994).

Nye, Joseph. *The Paradox of American Power* (2002).

Roberts, Adam, and Benedict Kingsburg, eds. *United Nations, Divided World: The U.N.'s Role in International Relations* (1993).

Stokes, Gail. *The Walls Came Tumbling Down: The Collapse of Communism in Eastern Europe* (1993).

Taylor, Trevor. *The Collapse of the Soviet Empire: Managing the Regional Fallout* (1992).

Zielonka, Jan. *Security in Central Europe* (1992).


## The International Economic Order

Ahrari, Mohammed E. *OPEC: The Failing Giant* (1986).

Belassa, Bela. *Change and Challenge in the World Economy* (1985).

Bhagwati, Jagdish. *The World Trading System at Risk* (1991).

Garten, Jeffrey E. *A Cold Peace: America, Japan, Germany, and the Struggle for Supremacy* (1992).

Geiger, Theodore. *The Future of the International System: The United States and the World Political Economy* (1988).

Gowa, Joanne. *Closing the Gold Window: Domestic Politics and the End of Bretton Woods* (1983).

Hart, Jeffrey A., and Joan E. Spero. *The Politics of International Economic Relations* (2001).

Homouda, Omar F., et al., eds. *The Future of the International Monetary System* (1989).

Keohane, Robert. *After Hegemony: Cooperation and Discord in the World Political Economy* (1984).

Lairson, Thomas, and David Skidmore. *International Political Economy: The Struggle for Power and Wealth* (1997).

Mason, E. S., and R. E. Asher. *The World Bank since Bretton Woods* (1973).

Oppenheim, Philip. *Trade Wars: Japan versus the West* (1992).

Putnam, Robert D., and Nicholas Bayne. *Hanging Together: Cooperation and Conflict in the Seven-Power Summits* (1987).

Solomon, Robert. *The International Monetary System, 1945–1976* (1977).

Wee, Herman van der. *Prosperity and Upheaval: The World Economy, 1945–1980* (1987).

**Europe East and West**

Garton Ash, Timothy. *In Europe's Name: Germany and the Divided Continent* (1993).

Ginsburgs, George B., and Alvin Z. Rubenstein, eds. *Soviet Foreign Policy toward Western Europe* (1978).

Griffith, William E. *The Ostpolitik of the Federal Republic of Germany* (1978).

Harrison, Michael. *Reluctant Ally: France and Atlantic Security* (1981).

Jarausch, Konrad H. *The Rush to German Unity* (1994).

Jopp, Mathias. *The Strategic Implications of European Integration* (1994).

Marsh, David. *The Bundesbank: The Bank That Rules Europe* (1994).

Mayne, Richard. *The Recovery of Europe, 1945–1973* (1973).

McGeehan, Robert. *The German Rearmament Question: American Diplomacy and European Defense after World War II* (1971).

Morgan, Roger. *The United States and West Germany* (1974).

Mortimer, Edward. *European Security after the Cold War* (1992).

Pierre, Andrew. *Nuclear Politics: The British Experience with an Independent Strategic Force, 1939–1970* (1972).

Remington, Robin A. *The Warsaw Pact* (1971).

Schaefer, Henry W. *COMECON and the Politics of Integration* (1972).

Sugar, Peter F., and Ivo J. Lederer, eds. *Nationalism in Eastern Europe* (1969).

Urwin, D. W. *The Community of Europe: A History of Integration since 1945* (1991).

Valenta, Jiri. *Soviet Intervention in Czechoslovakia, 1968* (1979).

Wallace, William. *The Transformation of Western Europe* (1990).

Walsh, A. E., and J. Paxton. *Into Europe: The Structure and Development of the Common Market* (1972).

Wettig, Gerhard. *Community and Conflict in the Socialist Camp: The Soviet Union, East Germany, and the German Problem, 1965–1972* (1975).

Wood, David M. and Birol A. Yeşilada. *The Emerging European Union* (1996).

Young, John W. *Cold War Europe, 1945–1989: A Political History* (1991).

Zinner, Paul E. *Revolution in Hungary* (1964).


**Latin America**

Allison, Graham, and Philip Zelikow. *Essence of Decision: Explaining the Cuban Missile Crisis* (1999).

Ashby, Timothy. *The Bear in the Backyard: Moscow's Caribbean Strategy* (1987).

Bethell, Leslie, and Ian Roxborough, eds. *Latin America between the Second World War and the Cold War, 1944–1948* (1992).

Biles, Robert E. *Inter-American Relations: The Latin American Perspective* (1988).

Brock, Philip, M. B. Connoly, and C. Gonzalez-Vega, eds. *Latin American Debt and Readjustment* (1989).

Carothers, Tom H. *In the Name of Democracy: U.S. Policy toward Latin America in the Reagan Years* (1991).

Child, Jack. *Geopolitics and Conflict in South America: Quarrels among Neighbors* (1985).

Coatsworth, John H. *Central America and the United States: The Clients and the Colossus* (1994).

Desch, Michael C. *When the Third World Matters: Latin America and United States Grand Strategy* (1993).

Dietz, James L., and J. L. Street. *Latin America's Economic Development* (1987).

Dominguez, Jorge I. *To Make the World Safe for Revolution: Cuba's Foreign Policy* (1989).

Falcoff, Mark. *Modern Chile, 1970–1989* (1989).

Farer, Tom J. *The Grand Strategy of the United States in Latin America* (1988).

Findling, John E. *Close Neighbors, Distant Friends: United States-Central American Relations* (1987).

Higgins, Trumbull. *The Perfect Failure: Kennedy, Eisenhower, and the Bay of Pigs* (1987).

Kagan, Robert. *A Twilight Struggle: American Power and Nicaragua, 1977–1990* (1996).

Kjonnerod, L. Erik, ed. *Evolving U.S. Strategy for Latin America and the Caribbean* (1992).

LeFeber, Walter. *Inevitable Revolutions: The United States in Central America* (1983).

Levinson, J., and Juan de Onis. *The Alliance That Lost Its Way: A Critical Report on the Alliance for Progress* (1970).

McDonald, Scott B. *Mountain High, White Avalanche: Cocaine and Power in the Andes States and Panama* (1989).

Miller, Nicola. *Soviet Relations with Latin America, 1959–1987* (1989).

Pastor, Robert. *Whirlpool: U.S. Foreign Policy toward Latin American and the Caribbean* (1992).

Paterson, Thomas G. *Contesting Castro: The United States and the Triumph of the Cuban Revolution* (1994).

Rabe, Stephen. *Eisenhower and Latin America: The Foreign Policy of Anticommunism* (1988).

Ramirez, Miguel D., Antonio Jorge, and Jorge Salazar-Carrillo, eds. *The Latin American Debt* (1992).

Roette, Riordan, ed. *Political and Economic Liberalization in Mexico* (1993).

Sigmund, Paul E. *The United States and Democracy in Chile* (1993).

Smith, Peter H. *Talons of the Eagle: Dynamics of U.S.-Latin American Relations* (1996).

Tussie, Diana, ed. *Latin America in the World Economy* (1983).

**Asia and the Pacific**

Acharya, Amitav. *A New Regional Order in South-East Asia: ASEAN in the Post-Cold War Era* (1991).

Boyd, Gavin. *Pacific Trade, Investment, and Politics* (1989).

Buckley, Roger. *U.S.-Japan Alliance Diplomacy, 1945–1990* (1992).

Chang, Gordon H. *Friends and Enemies: The United States, China, and the Soviet Union, 1948–1972* (1990).

Chiang, Hsiang-tse. *The United States and China* (1988).

Cohen, Warren I., and Akira Iriye, eds. *The Great Powers in East Asia, 1953–1960* (1990).

Cumings, Bruce. *The Origins of the Korean War* (1981).

Dickson, Bruce, and Harry Harding, eds. *Economic Relations in the Asian-Pacific Region* (1987).

Dower, John W. *Embracing Defeat: Japan in the Wake of World War II* (1999).

Ellison, Herbert J. *Japan and the Pacific Quadrille: The Major Powers in East Asia* (1987).

Foot, Rosemary. *The Wrong War: American Policy and the Dimensions of the Korean Conflict, 1950–1953* (1985).

Hardt, John P., and Young C. Kim, eds. *Economic Cooperation in the Asia-Pacific Region* (1990).

Heering, George C. *America's Longest War: The United States and Vietnam, 1950–1975* (1986).

Howell, Jude. *China Opens Its Doors: The Politics of Economic Transition* (1993).

Isserman, Maurice. *The Korean War* (1992).

Irving, R. E. M. *The First Indochina War: French and American Policy, 1945–1954* (1975).

Kerkvliet, Benedict J. *The Huk Rebellion* (1977).

Kim, Ilpyong J. *The Strategic Triangle: China, the United States, and the Soviet Union* (1987).

Kim, Samuel S. *China and the World* (1989).

Kleinberg, Robert. *China's "Opening" to the Outside World: The Experiment with Foreign Capitalism* (1990).

Klenner, Wolfgang, ed. *Trends of Economic Development in East Asia* (1989).

Lee, William T. *The Korean War Was Stalin's Show* (1999).

Leifer, Michael. *ASEAN and the Security of South-East Asia* (1989).

Linder, Steffan B. *The Pacific Century: Economic and Political Consequences of Asian-Pacific Dynamism* (1986).

Low, Alfred D. *The Sino-Soviet Dispute* (1978).

Nagai, Yonasuke, and Akira Iriye, eds. *The Origins of the Cold War in Asia* (1977).

Nakamure, Takafusa. *The Postwar Japanese Economy: Its Development and Structure* (1981).

Nelsen, Harvey W. *Power and Insecurity: Beijing, Moscow, and Washington, 1949–1988* (1989).

Olson, James S., and Randy Roberts. *Where the Domino Fell: America and Vietnam, 1945–1995* (1996).

Schaller, Michael. *The American Occupation of Japan* (1985).

Searingen, Robert. *The Soviet Union and Postwar Japan: Escalating Challenge and Response* (1978).

Thompson, Roger C. *The Pacific Basin since 1945* (1994).

Weathersby, Kathryn. *Soviet Aims in Korea and the Origins of the Korean War, 1945–1950: Evidence from Russian Archives* (1993).

Wolferen, Karel G. von. *The Enigma of Japanese Power* (1989).

Woronoff, Jon. *Asia's "Miracle" Economies* (1991).

Wurfel, David, and Bruce Burton, eds. *The Political Economy of Foreign Policy in Southeast Asia* (1990).

Yahuda, Michael. *The International Politics of the Asia-Pacific, 1945–1995* (1996).

## The Middle East and North Africa

Aronson, Geoffrey. *Creating Facts: Israel, Palestinians, and the West Bank* (1987).

Bain, Kenneth Ray. *The March to Zion: United States Policy and the Founding of Israel* (1979).

Battah, Abdalla M., and Yehuda Lukacs, eds. *The Arab-Israeli Conflict: Two Decades of Change* (1988).

Bickerton, Ian J., and Carla L. Klausner. *A Concise History of the Arab-Israeli Conflict* (1998).

Freedman, Laurence, and Efraim Karsh. *The Gulf Conflict, 1990–1991* (1993).

Friedman, Thomas. *From Beirut to Jerusalem* (1989).

Gilmour, David. *Lebanon: The Fractured Country* (1983).

Hiro, Dilip. *Holy Wars: The Rise of Islamic Fundamentalism* (1989).

Holden, David, and Richard Johns. *The House of Saud* (1981).

Horne, Alistair. *A Savage War of Peace: Algeria 1954–1962* (1987).

Hurewitz, J. C. *Soviet-American Rivalry in the Middle East* (1969).

Karsh, Ephraim, ed. *The Iran-Iraq War: Impact and Implications* (1989).

Klass, Rosanne, ed. *Afghanistan: The Great Game Revisited* (1988).

Kyle, Keith. *Suez* (1991).

Louis, William Roger, and Roger Owen, eds. *Suez, 1956: The Crisis and Its Consequences* (1989).

Lustik, Ian S., ed. *Arab-Israeli Relations in World Politics* (1994).

McCausland, Jeffrey. *The Gulf Conflict: A Military Analysis* (1993).

Melman, Yossi, and Dan Raviv. *Behind the Uprising: Israelis, Jordanians, and Palestinians* (1989).

Munson, Henry Jr. *Islam and Revolution in the Middle East* (1988).

Organsky, F. K. *The $36 Billion Bargain: Strategy and Politics in U.S. Assistance to Israel* (1990).

Polk, W. R. *The United States and the Arab World* (1965).

Quandt, William B. *Camp David: Peacemaking and Politics* (1986).

———. *Decade of Decision: American Policy toward the Arab-Israeli Conflict, 1967–1976* (1977).

———. *The Middle East: Ten Years after Camp David* (1988).

Rashid, Ahmed. *Taliban: Militant Islam, Oil, and Fundamentalism in Central Asia* (2000).

Rubin, Barry. *Paved with Good Intentions: The American Experience and Iran* (1980).

Salibi, Karnal S. *Crossroads to Civil War: Lebanon, 1958–1976* (1976).

Schoenbaum, David. *The United States and the State of Israel* (1993).

Seale, Patrick. *The Struggle for Syria: A Study in Post-War Arab Politics, 1945–1958* (1986).

Smolansky, Oles. *The Soviet Union and the Arab World under Khrushchev* (1974).

———. *The USSR and Iraq: The Soviet Quest for Influence* (1991).

Urban, Mark L. *War in Afghanistan* (1988).

## Sub-Saharan Africa

Albright, David E. *The USSR and Sub-Saharan Africa in the 1980s* (1983).

Aluko, Olajide. *Africa and the Great Powers in the 1980s* (1987).

Bala, Mohammed. *Africa and Non-Alignment: A Study in the Foreign Relations of New Nations* (1982).

Barber, James, and John Barratt. *South Africa's Foreign Policy: The Search for Status and Security, 1945–1988* (1990).

Calvocoressi, Peter. *Independent Africa and the World* (1985).

Chamberlain, M. E. *Decolonization: The Fall of European Empires* (1985).

Davidson, Basil. *The Black Man's Burden: Africa and the Curse of the Nation-State* (1992).

Dickson, David. *United States Foreign Policy towards Sub-Saharan Africa* (1985).

Farer, Tom J. *Clouds on the Horn of Africa: The Widening Storm* (1979).

Fieldhouse, D. K. *Black Africa, 1945–1980: Economic Decolonization and Arrested Development* (1986).

Gavshon, Arthur. *Crisis in Africa: Battleground of East and West* (1984).

Hargreaves, John D. *The End of Colonial Rule in West Africa: Essays in Contemporary History* (1979).

Havnevik, Kjell, ed. *The IMF and the World Bank in Africa* (1987).

Holland, R. F. *European Decolonization, 1918–1981: An Introductory Survey* (1985).

Lapping, Brian. *The End of Empire* (1989).

Noer, Thomas J. *Cold War and Black Liberation: The United States and White Rule in Africa, 1948–1968* (1985).

Onimode, Bade, ed. *The IMF, the World Bank, and African Debt* (1989).

Onwuka, Ralph I., and Timothy M. Shaw. *Africa and World Politics* (1989).

Parfitt, Trevor. *The African Debt Crisis* (1989).

Riley, Stephen A. *African Debt and Western Interests* (1989).

Sandbrook, Richard. *The Politics of Africa's Economic Recovery* (1993).

Shaw, Timothy. *Reformism and Revisionism in Africa's Political Economy in the 1990s* (1993).

Somerville, Keith. *Foreign Military Intervention in Africa* (1990).

Wright, Stephen, and Janice N. Brownfoot. *Africa and World Politics* (1987).

# INDEX